W9-DJJ-888

DISCARDED

Converging Operations
in the Study of
Visual Selective Attention

Converging Operations in the Study of Visual Selective Attention

Edited by Arthur F. Kramer,
Michael G. H. Coles,
and Gordon D. Logan

AMERICAN PSYCHOLOGICAL ASSOCIATION
WASHINGTON, DC

Copyright © 1996 by the American Psychological Association. All rights reserved. Except as permitted under the United States Copyright Act of 1976, no part of this publication may be reproduced or distributed in any form or by any means, or stored in a database or retrieval system, without the prior written permission of the publisher.

Published by
American Psychological Association
750 First Street, NE
Washington, DC 20002

Copies may be ordered from
APA Order Department
P.O. Box 2710
Hyattsville, MD 20784

In the UK and Europe, copies may be ordered from
American Psychological Association
3 Henrietta Street
Covent Garden, London
WC2E 8LU England

Typeset in Minion by University Graphics, Inc., York, PA

Printer: Data Reproductions Corp., Rochester Hills, MI
Cover Designer: Berg Design, Albany, NY
Technical/Production Editor: Molly R. Flickinger

Library of Congress Cataloging-in-Publication Data
Converging operations in the study of visual selective attention/edited by Arthur F. Kramer, Michael G. H. Coles, and Gordon D. Logan.
　　p.　cm.
Includes bibliographical references and index.
ISBN 1-55798-329-1 (acid-free paper)
1. Visual perception. 2. Selectivity (Psychology) 3. Visual discrimination. I. Kramer, Arthur F. II. Coles, Michael G. H. III. Logan, Gordon D.
BF241.C65　1995
152.14—dc20　　　　　　　　　　　　　　　　　　　　　　　95-32418
　　　　　　　　　　　　　　　　　　　　　　　　　　　　　　CIP

British Library Cataloguing-in-Publication Data
A CIP record is available from the British Library

Printed in the United States of America
First edition

APA Science Volumes

Taste, Experience, and Feeding: Development and Learning
Temperament: Individual Differences at the Interface of Biology and Behavior
Through the Looking Glass: Issues of Psychological Well-Being in Captive Nonhuman Primates

APA expects to publish volumes on the following conference topics:

Attribution Processes, Person Perception, and Social Interaction: The Legacy of Ned Jones

Changing Ecological Approaches to Development: Organism–Environment Mutualities

Children Exposed to Family Violence

Conceptual Structure and Processes: Emergence, Discovery, and Change

Genetic, Ethological, and Evolutionary Perspectives on Human Development

Global Prospects for Education: Development, Culture, and Schooling

Maintaining and Promoting Integrity in Behavioral Science Research

Marital and Family Therapy Outcome and Process Research

Measuring Changes in Patients Following Psychological and Pharmacological Interventions

Psychophysiological Study of Attention

Stereotypes: Brain–Behavior Relationships

Work Team Dynamics and Productivity in the Context of Diversity

As part of its continuing and expanding commitment to enhance the dissemination of scientific psychological knowledge, the Science Directorate of the APA established a Scientific Conferences Program. A series of volumes resulting from these conferences is produced jointly by the Science Directorate and the Office of Communications. A call for proposals is issued twice annually by the Scientific Directorate, which, collaboratively with the APA Board of Scientific Affairs, evaluates the proposals and selects several conferences for funding. This important effort has resulted in an exceptional series of meetings and scholarly volumes, each of which has contributed to the dissemination of research and dialogue in these topical areas.

The APA Science Directorate's conferences funding program has supported 39 conferences since its inception in 1988. To date, 27 volumes resulting from conferences have been published.

WILLIAM C. HOWELL, PHD
Executive Director

VIRGINIA E. HOLT
Assistant Executive Director

Contents

Contributors

Lourdes Anllo-Vento, University of California, San Diego

Juan Botella, Independent University of Madrid, Spain

Claus Bundesen, University of Copenhagen, Denmark

Vincent P. Clark, National Institute of Mental Health, Bethesda, Maryland

Asher Cohen, Hebrew University, Jerusalem, Israel

Michael G. H. Coles, University of Illinois at Urbana–Champaign

David Diller, Indiana University

Jon Driver, University of Cambridge, Cambridge, England

Charles L. Folk, Villanova University

*Kevin J. Hawley, University of Utah

Hans-Jochen Heinze, Otto V. Guericke University, Magdeburg, Germany

Steven A. Hillyard, University of California, San Diego

Glyn W. Humphreys, University of Birmingham, Edgbaston, Birmingham, England

James C. Johnston, National Aeronautics and Space Administration, Ames Research Center

William A. Johnston, University of Utah

Arthur F. Kramer, University of Illinois at Urbana–Champaign

Gordon D. Logan, University of Illinois at Urbana–Champaign

Steven J. Luck, University of Iowa

G. Ron Mangun, University of California, Davis

Robert S. McCann, National Aeronautics and Space Administration, Ames Research Center

Bruce Milliken, McMaster University

J. Toby Mordkoff, Bryn Mawr College

---

*Deceased

W. Trammell Neill, Adelphi University

Andrew Olson, University of Birmingham, Edgbaston, Birmingham, England

Robert Rafal, Veterans Administration Medical Center, Martinez, California

Roger W. Remington, National Aeronautics and Space Administration, Ames Research Center

M. Jane Riddoch, University of Birmingham, Edgbaston, Birmingham, England

Cristina Romani, University of Birmingham, Edgbaston, Birmingham, England

Irene S. Schwarting, University of Utah

Richard M. Shiffrin, Indiana University

Jan Theeuwes, TNO Human Factors Research Institute, Soesterberg, The Netherlands

Steven P. Tipper, University of North Wales, Bangor

Leslie A. Valdes, St. Cloud State University

A. H. C. van der Heijden, Leiden University, Leiden, The Netherlands

Stephen E. Watson, Brooks Air Force Base, San Antonio, Texas

Jeremy M. Wolfe, Harvard Medical School

Steven Yantis, Johns Hopkins University

Preface

In the last 15 years, research on attention has flourished. Efforts have been focused more sharply in those years than in the decade preceding them on addressing visual selective attention. The effort has also been more diverse than it was previously, incorporating a wider variety of paradigms and methodologies. New methods have proliferated almost as soon as they were developed. Brain processes have become as important as cognition, and methodologies for localizing brain functions have been adapted quickly to the study of visual attention. Many researchers have studied patients with brain damage, testing hypotheses about the localization of attention systems and the representations on which they operate. Brain-imaging techniques have had a large impact on the field. First, structural imaging provided converging evidence on the nature, locus, and size of lesions in brain-damaged patients. Then, functional imaging provided a window onto brain activity in attentional tasks in "normal" subjects, converging with evidence from event-related potentials recorded from the scalp, which provided better temporal but poorer spatial resolution.

Behavioral work on attention took great strides during the same period. Cuing methodologies were developed and exploited for a variety of purposes. Positive and negative priming techniques developed and proliferated. Theoretical developments have kept pace with empirical advances, with formal mathematical theories, on the one hand, and connectionist modeling on the other. It was a great time to be studying visual spatial attention.

The purpose of this book is to capture the present state of the art in research on visual selective attention, focusing on the broad theme of converging operations. To that end, we asked for contributions that reflected four converging approaches: behavioral studies, computational modeling, patient research, and various neural-imaging techniques. We were interested in cutting-edge research from current and future leaders of the field, hoping that the book would help set the agenda for future research as well as document accomplishments from the recent and not-so-recent past.

Another purpose of the book was to honor Charles W. Eriksen on the occasion of his retirement from the Department of Psychology at the University of Illinois. Eriksen's research career has been an inspiration for much of the current work, ranging from his seminal 1956 article with Garner and Hake on the theory of converging operations to his contributions in the 1970s, 1980s, and 1990s to basic research on visual selective attention. Many of the contributors to this book came to Illinois for a 3-day conference in May 1994 to pay tribute to Eriksen and report the work described in their chapters. We hope that the book conveys the excitement and vigorous interchange that the presentations generated.

This book and the conference have been supported by the American Psychological Association and by the Department of Psychology, the College of Liberal Arts and Sciences, and the Beckman Institute for Advanced Science and Technology at the University of Illinois.

GORDON D. LOGAN
MICHAEL G. H. COLES
ARTHUR F. KRAMER

Introduction

Gordon D. Logan, Michael G. H. Coles, and Arthur F. Kramer

In 1956, Garner, Hake, and Eriksen published the article "Operationism and the Concept of Perception," which introduced the idea of converging operations to the budding field of cognitive psychology. Their aim was to change the focus of psychological research from overt behavior to the processes that underlie overt behavior, without abandoning experimental methods that were based on the measurement of overt behavior. Behaviorists before them had (rightly) eschewed interpretations based on internal processes in favor of interpretations of behavior because there was usually a one-to-one correspondence between behavior and internal processes (i.e., there was only one measure of behavior to identify with the internal process). Garner et al. suggested measuring different behavioral manifestations of the same underlying process and looking for agreement, or convergence, among them. Rather than defining a process by a single experimental operation, they suggested defining it with several operations that converged on a single construct.

Garner et al.'s (1956) article was one of the flagship publications that led the cognitive revolution. Classic articles by G. A. Miller (1956), by Broadbent (1957), and by Newell, Shaw, and Simon (1958) provided many of the phenomena that changed the dominant paradigm from animal learning to human cognition, and Chomsky's (1959) article provided an incisive theoretical analysis that undercut the behaviorist doctrine; but the Garner et al. (1956) article provided the methodological basis on which the new cognitive psychology would stand. The idea of converging operations had a tremendous impact in its time, and that impact continues today. Much of modern research on cognition is carried out, knowingly or unknowingly, within the paradigm of converging operations that was introduced in the 1956 article. Research on attention, from 1956 to the pres-

We are grateful to Don Dulany for his help in interpreting the historical context of Garner et al.'s (1956) converging operations article.

ent, is an excellent example of the application of the paradigm, as the chapters in this book attest.

OPERATIONISM AND MENTAL PROCESSES

Modern students of psychology are aware of the behaviorist years, from 1913 to the 1950s, and of the cognitive revolution that ended that era. To many, the central assumption of cognitive psychology—that behavior is produced by the action of underlying mental processes—seems so obvious that they cannot see how anyone could ever have thought differently. Behaviorism seems to have been a bad idea that is best forgotten. However, the same students must acknowledge that behaviorism got us out of the armchairs and into the laboratories, making psychology a science. For this reason, it is important to understand the behaviorist doctrine that produced that movement.

The key concept in the behaviorist doctrine was the idea of operationism, introduced to psychology by the physicist Bridgman (1927, 1945). Operationism, stated baldly, is the idea that scientific concepts are defined in terms of the experimental operations that are used to produce or assess them. Hunger is what is produced by food deprivation, perception is the ability to discriminate between stimuli, and so on. To many, this will seem like the familiar concept of operational definition, which is commonplace in modern psychology—cognitive and otherwise. However, the operationist doctrine went beyond simple operational definition: According to Bridgman (1927), "the concept is synonymous with the corresponding set of operations" (p. 5). There was nothing more to concepts like hunger and perception than food deprivation and discriminatory ability. In a book that was popular at the time that Garner et al. wrote their article, Allport (1955) claimed that "a perception can be regarded as nothing more nor less than a discriminatory response" (p. 53). This strict operationist view of psychological concepts left no room for internal processes and no role for internal mechanisms. The subject matter of psychology consisted of the operations performed by the experimenter and the behavior exhibited by the subject. Imagine no cognition.

SEPARATING PERCEPTION FROM RESPONSE

Garner, Hake, and Eriksen, individually and in all possible pairwise collaborations, were interested in perception and took exception to defining perception in terms of responses. It seemed to them, collectively and individually, that perceptual processes and response processes made separate and possibly independent contributions to the behaviors they were interested in. The idea of converging operations was developed to provide a basis for achieving this separation empirically. According to Garner et al. (1956), "converging operations may be thought of as any set of two or more experimental operations which allow the selection or elimination of alternative hypotheses or concepts which could explain an experimental result" (pp. 150–151).

Charles Eriksen (1955), in particular, was interested in perceptual defense, an early precursor to modern work on subliminal perception proposing that perceptual thresholds were higher for vulgar words such as *fuck* and *shit* than for neutral words such as *fudge* and *shut*. It seemed clear to him that the effect could reflect response processes instead of (or as well as) perceptual processes. Subjects may be reluctant to say *fuck*, even though they saw it clearly. However, the operationist doctrine denied the distinction between perception and response, arguing that the discriminatory response was the perception—in effect, taking what subjects said for what they saw. Garner et al. (1956) proposed a clever experiment to separate perceptual processes from response processes. They thought that, if subjects were instructed to say vulgar words when they saw neutral ones and say neutral words when they saw vulgar ones, then the thresholds should remain high for vulgar words if perceptual defense was a perceptual phenomenon, but the thresholds should be higher for neutral words (which required a vulgar response) if perceptual defense was a response phenomenon. The experiment, conducted later by Zajonc (1962), supported the response hypothesis.

SELECTIVE INFLUENCE

The perceptual defense experiment illustrates one of the key premises of the idea of converging operations: selective influence. An experimental manipulation may affect one process and no others. Some manipulations, such as exposure duration and stimulus intensity, should affect perception but not response. Other manipulations, such as response competition and social acceptability, should affect response but not perception. An experimental design including both types of manipulations should allow one to localize phenomena in one process or the other. The Zajonc (1962) version of the experiment that Garner et al. (1956) proposed separated perception of vulgar and neutral words from report of vulgar and neutral words and localized the phenomenon of perceptual defense in the response system.

The idea of selective influence remains important today. It is the cornerstone of most modern investigations. Sternberg's (1969) additive factors logic, developed to discover the mental processes underlying reaction times, relies on the assumption of selective influence to isolate processing stages. Variables that affect the same stage interact, and variables that affect different stages have additive effects. There have been many criticisms of Sternberg's logic (see e.g., Coles, 1989; C. W. Eriksen & Schultz, 1979; McClelland, 1979; J. Miller, 1993), but the criticisms focus mainly on Sternberg's ideas about how information is transmitted from one stage to another. The idea of selective influence is essential and accepted by almost everyone.[1]

CONVERGENCE

The other key premise of the idea of converging operations is *convergence:* Different manipulations can affect the same process. Thus, exposure duration and stimulus intensity both affect perception. Response competition and response criteria both affect response processes. The idea that the effects of two different manipulations converge on a single process was important for three reasons. First, it challenged the strict operationist doctrine that the concept was the operation. This doctrine asserted that different manipulations meant different concepts, so that the perception that was identified with manipulations of exposure duration was not the same perception that was identified with manipulations of stimulus intensity. The idea that different operations could converge on the same concept suggested that there was more to the concept than the operations that defined it.

Second, the idea of convergence broke the circularity inherent in operational definitions. The strict operationist doctrine of one-to-one correspondence between operations and concepts made it impossible to dis-

---

[1]The idea that selective influence is possible is generally accepted. However, there is some debate about whether selective influence is a valid assumption for particular variables. For example, as Garner et al. (1956) anticipated, many people believe that varying the number of stimulus–response alternatives affects more than one stage of processing.

tinguish between the operations and the concepts. They were one and the same. The idea of convergence identified different operations with the same concept, and that allowed investigators to test the validity of their assumptions about relations between operations and concepts. If exposure duration and stimulus intensity both affected perception, then they should interact when manipulated jointly (and they do).

Third, the idea of converging operations moved psychology from the operationist theory of the meaning of psychological concepts to the modern idea of "network" specification of meaning (Hempel, 1965; Quine, 1961). According to the network view, the meaning of a concept stems from its relations to the other concepts with which it interacts in a larger theory. Thus, concepts of perception and response make sense in a larger theory in which a perceptual system translates stimulus energy to internal representations and a response system translates internal representations into action. The concept is defined in terms of its relation to other concepts, not just in terms of its empirical manifestations or the operations that affect it. Put differently, the idea of converging operations introduced to the field the modern idea of identifying processes with computational functions. Specifying a concept computationally (a) makes clear its relations to other concepts that participate in related computations and (b) allows the theorist to deduce the operations that affect the concept (selectively) from the input and output of the computation and the algorithm that implements it (Marr, 1982).

Garner et al. (1956) brought us to the brink but did not make the leap themselves from operationism to computational or network specification of meaning. While they said that "the value of a set of converging operations depends less on the nature of the operations themselves than on the alternative hypotheses or properties which are being considered" (pp. 151–152)—apparently endorsing the network theory of specification of meaning—they ultimately backed off, arguing that "a concept has no meaning other than that derived from the operations on which it is based, and unless those operations are known, the concept cannot be known either" (p. 152). Nevertheless, their work gave subsequent generations courage and reasoning with which to take the leap, and the network theory (and modern computational approaches) replaced strict operationism. Internal processes became the proper domain of scientific psychology.

WHAT CONVERGING OPERATIONS ARE AND ARE NOT

"Converging operations . . . [are a] set of two or more experimental operations which allow the selection or elimination of alternative hypotheses or concepts" (Garner et al., 1956, p. 150). "They are called converging operations because they are not perfectly correlated and thus can converge on a single concept. . . . Ideally, converging operations would be orthogonal (completely independent) since such operations are the most efficient, . . . [but] a sufficient number of partially converging operations can still provide a precise delimitation of alternative concepts" (Garner et al., 1956, p. 151).

Garner et al. (1956) distinguished between converging operations and parallel operations, which included repeat operations (replications) and transformation operations (replication with different materials). They argued that parallel operations could not distinguish between alternative concepts because they merely repeat the initial observation, perhaps in different clothing. Thus, none of the alternative interpretations that could have accounted for the first result have been ruled out. Repeat and transformation operations may be useful in many respects. For example, they may demonstrate that a phenomenon generalizes across materials or to different ranges of an independent variable. However, they do not rule out alternative hypotheses (unless the hypotheses are that the phenomenon depends on certain materials or on a certain range of the independent variable). Truly different operations are required to rule out alternative interpretations.

Garner et al. (1956) said that "it is quite legitimate to use assumed converging operations in place of operations actually carried out" (p. 152), arguing that it was not logically necessary to replicate an operation whose effect was well established. In their view, assumptions could take the place of actual experimental manipulations. Thus, experiments that explore new operations that should affect a process in the same way as a well-known operation need not replicate the original one. On the one hand, this is reasonable, because no experiment can recapitulate the entire literature. On the other hand, if one has a particular operation in mind to be compared with the new one, then the experiment is more convincing if the two are manipulated together.

In suggesting assumed converging operations, Garner et al. (1956) appeared to be endorsing network specification, in which the meaning of a concept depends on its assumed or postulated relations to other concepts. Under this premise, one need not actually replicate an operation to relate it to the operation that one is currently interested in. One need only specify the logical and theoretical connections between that operation and the one of interest. Again, Garner et al. (1956) backed off from an outright endorsement of the network view, arguing that "the validity of our concepts rests entirely on the validity of the operations, whether carried out or assumed" (p. 152). Nevertheless, they laid the groundwork for much of the practice in modern research. We use the introduction and discussion sections of our articles to describe the assumed converging operations that link the concepts we study to the broader network of concepts that form the global theories we test, and we use the method and results sections to describe the converging operations we implement. In many cases, assumed converging operations outnumber the implemented ones, but we should not lose sight of the idea, promulgated by Garner et al. (1956), that the principle is the same.

CONVERGING OPERATIONS AND ATTENTION

About a decade after the seminal article by Garner and Hake, Eriksen began applying the idea of converging operations to attention. Attention was a prime candidate for converging operations research because it was clearly an internal process, the kind that had been eschewed because of behaviorist operationism (but see Lovie, 1983). Eriksen began by focusing on the bar probe task, which Averbach and Coriell (1961) developed as an alternative (a converging operation) to Sperling's (1960) partial report paradigm. In the bar probe task, subjects are presented with a multielement display, usually containing letters, and one of the elements is cued by a bar marker presented next to it. The task is to report the cued item. Reaction time and accuracy are the major dependent variables. Averbach and Coriell were primarily interested in the decay of visual information after the display was turned off, so they delayed the probe, presenting it after the display. Eriksen, by contrast, was interested in selective attention and the role that the probe played in directing attention to regions of the display. He presented the bar probe at the same time as the display, and sometimes before it.

Eriksen proposed a spotlight metaphor for selective attention in the bar probe task and used converging operations to study the properties of the spotlight. There were two main variables that should have converging influences on the spotlight process: time and distance. Eriksen studied both of them. In studies with his students, he found that time was important: Reaction time was faster and accuracy was higher if the bar marker preceded the display. The effect reached asymptote at delays of 100 ms–150 ms, which Eriksen interpreted as the time required to move the spotlight and focus it on the cued item (C. W. Eriksen & Collins, 1969; C. W. Eriksen & Hoffman, 1972). To rule out the alternative hypothesis that the effect depended on eye movements, he replicated the experiments while monitoring eye position; he found the same results with the eyes held steady (Colegate, Hoffman, & Eriksen, 1973). Thus, the effect was due to an internal attentional process, not external movements of the eyes.

Space was important as well. Reaction time was faster and accuracy was higher if the other items in the display were distant from the target. The effect was greater if the neighboring items were potential targets (e.g., other letters) than if they were simply irrelevant (e.g., dots; C. W. Eriksen & Hoffman, 1972, 1973; C. W. Eriksen & Rohrbaugh, 1970). Eriksen interpreted these effects as evidence that the attentional spotlight had limited spatial extent—less than 1° of visual angle.

The principle of converging operations led Eriksen away from the bar probe task. Together with Barbara Eriksen (B. A. Eriksen & Eriksen, 1974), he developed the flanker task for studying the spatial extent of the spotlight without the requirement to search for a bar probe or a target. The target was always located in the same central position, flanked by distractors at various distances. Consistent with the work from the bar probe task, interference was greatest if the distractors fell within 1° of visual angle of the target.

The flanker task allowed Eriksen to address another issue that initiated the idea of converging operations: the separation of perception and response in the interference observed from flanking distractors. Distractors close to the target produced interference, but the interference was greater if the distractors were response incompatible (i.e., led to the opposite response to the target) than if they were neutral (i.e., led to neither of the alternative responses), and the interference was less if the distractors were response compatible (i.e., led to the same response as the target) than if they were neutral. The response-compatibility effects were separable from the distance effects, and Eriksen interpreted them in terms of response competition, an idea with much currency today.

The body of Eriksen's work is a convincing demonstration of the utility of converging operations. He used different paradigms, manipulations, and dependent measures to converge on theories of attention. And much of the field followed his lead. The principle of converging operations is used routinely in attention research and more generally in research on perception and cognition.

In the past 15 years, visual spatial attention has become the dominant paradigm of attention research, and the principle of converging operations has been a central, unifying theme. Attention is currently studied from a variety of perspectives, including behavioral research; computational modeling; investigations of neurologically challenged patients; analysis of event-related brain potentials (ERPs); and neural-imaging techniques, such as positron emission tomography (PET) and functional magnetic resonance imaging (fMRI). A significant aspect of this work is that most researchers are aware of the different approaches, and many make serious attempts to integrate them. The different operations appear to be truly converging on common processes of attention.

CONVERGING OPERATIONS: THE BOOK

This book is intended to represent the cutting edge of research that applies the converging operations approach to the study of visual selective attention. It begins with five tutorial reviews. Three of the reviews address converging approaches to the study of attention. First, Bundesen presents the history of formal models of attention, from the early 1960s to the present. Hillyard et al. review modern neuroimaging techniques, including PET, fMRI, and ERP, as they are applied to the study of attention. And Rafal reviews recent neurological work on the effects of brain damage on attentional abilities. Two other reviews present state-of-the-art analyses of current topics in attention that were motivated by Eriksen's research. Neill and Valdes review facilitatory and inhibitory effects of attention, which can be traced back to Eriksen's work with the flanker task, and Yantis reviews the phenomenon of attentional capture, which is related to Eriksen's work with the bar probe task.

Subsequent chapters present reports of empirical research and theoretical analyses of attention, with an eye to converging operations. Some continue the themes of the tutorial reviews: Chapters by Folk and Remington, by Theeuwes, and by W. A. Johnston, Schwarting, and Hawley address attentional capture. Those by Tipper and Milliken, by Mordkoff, and by Botella address facilitatory and inhibitory effects. And Driver as well as Humphreys, Olson, Romani, and Riddoch report research with patients. Other chapters address current themes not covered by the tutorials. Shiffrin, Diller, and Cohen; Wolfe; J. C. Johnston, McCann, and Remington; and Van der Heijden all report research on the architecture of the attentional system. Chapters by Kramer and Watson and by Logan report research on the representations underlying attentional selection.

Converging operations is a dominant theme in all of the chapters. Most of the empirical chapters include two or more converging operations in the experiments they report. Every chapter assumes converging operations, making sense of the theory and data that apply to the specific topic in terms of a broader network of theory that has accrued since the beginning of scientific research on attention.

REFERENCES

Allport, F. H. (1955). *Theories of perception and the concept of structure.* New York: Wiley.

Averbach, E., & Coriell, A. S. (1961). Short-term memory in vision. *Bell System Technical Journal, 40,* 309–328.

Bridgman, P. W. (1927). *The logic of modern physics.* New York: Macmillan.

Bridgman, P. W. (1945). Some general principles of operational analysis. *Psychological Review, 52,* 246–249.

Broadbent, D. E. (1957). A mechanical model of human attention and immediate memory. *Psychological Review, 64,* 205–215.

Chomsky, N. (1959). Review of B. F. Skinner's *Verbal Behavior* [Book review]. *Language, 35,* 26–58.

Colegate, R. L., Hoffman, J. E., & Eriksen, C. W. (1973). Selective encoding from multielement visual displays. *Perception and Psychophysics, 14,* 217–224.

Coles, M. G. H. (1989). Modern mind-brain reading: Psychophysiology, physiology, and cognition. *Psychophysiology, 26,* 251–269.

Eriksen, B. A., & Eriksen, C. W. (1974). Effects of noise letters upon identification of a target letter in a nonsearch task. *Perception and Psychophysics, 16,* 143–149.

Eriksen, C. W. (1955). Subception: Fact or artifact. *Psychological Review, 63*, 74–80.

Eriksen, C. W., & Collins, J. F. (1969). Temporal course of selective attention. *Journal of Experimental Psychology, 80*, 254–261.

Eriksen, C. W., & Hoffman, J. E. (1972). Temporal and spatial characteristics of selective encoding from visual displays. *Perception and Psychophysics, 12*, 201–204.

Eriksen, C. W., & Hoffman, J. E. (1973). The extent of processing of noise elements during selective encoding. *Perception and Psychophysics, 14*, 115–160.

Eriksen, C. W., & Rohrbaugh, J. (1970). Visual masking in multielement displays. *Journal of Experimental Psychology, 83*, 147–154.

Eriksen, C. W., & Schultz, D. W. (1979). Information processing in visual search: A continuous flow conception and experimental results. *Perception and Psychophysics, 25*, 249–263.

Garner, W. R., Hake, H. W., & Eriksen, C. W. (1956). Operationism and the concept of perception. *Psychological Review, 63*, 149–159.

Hempel, C. G. (1965). Aspects of scientific explanation. In C. G. Hempel (Ed.), *Aspects of scientific explanation and other essays in the philosophy of science* (pp. 331–496). New York: Macmillan.

Lovie, A. D. (1983). Attention and behaviourism: Fact and fiction. *British Journal of Psychology, 74*, 301–310.

Marr, D. (1982). *Vision.* New York: Freeman.

McClelland, J. L. (1979). On the time relations of mental processes: An examination of systems of processes in cascade. *Psychological Review, 86*, 287–330.

Miller, G. A. (1956). The magical number seven plus or minus two: Some limits on our capacity for processing information. *Psychological Review, 63*, 81–97.

Miller, J. (1993). A queue-series model for reaction time, with discrete-stage and continuous-flow models as special cases. *Psychological Review, 100*, 702–715.

Newell, A., Shaw, J. C., & Simon, H. A. (1958). Elements of a theory of human problem solving. *Psychological Review, 65*, 151–166.

Sperling, G. (1960). The information available in brief visual presentations. *Psychological Monographs, 74*(11, Whole No. 498), 1–29.

Sternberg, S. (1969). The discovery of processing stages: Extensions of Donders' methods. In W. G. Koster (Ed.), *Attention and performance II* (pp. 276–315). Amsterdam: North-Holland.

Quine, W. V. O. (1961). Two dogmas of empiricism. In W. V. O. Quine (Ed.), *From a logical point* of view (2nd ed., pp. 20–46). New York: Harper & Row.

Zajonc, R. B. (1962). Response suppression in perceptual defense. *Journal of Experimental Psychology, 64*, 206–214.

Formal Models of Visual Attention: A Tutorial Review

Claus Bundesen

This chapter presents a selective review of formal models of visual attention. It focuses on models that provide quantitative accounts of human performance in divided- or focused-attention tasks such as visual whole report, partial report, search, and detection.

The review is organized into four sections. The first section treats serial processing models. It traces the development from simple serial scanning models to selective serial models. Related choice models are also considered. The second section treats parallel processing models, covering independent channels models, limited-capacity models, and race-based models of selection. The third section reviews a unified theory of visual recognition and attentional selection, and the final section considers connectionist models.

SERIAL MODELS
Simple Serial Models
Whole Report

Much work on formal models of visual attention was stimulated by modern investigations of the span of apprehension (Averbach & Coriell, 1961;

Thanks are due to Gordon Logan, reviewers John Duncan and Jeremy Wolfe, my colleagues Axel Larsen and Hitomi Shibuya, and my students Kristján Jul Houmann, Søren Kyllingsbaek, and Rune Møller Jensen for valuable comments on a draft of this chapter. Preparation of the chapter was supported by a grant from the International Human Frontier Science Program Organization.

Sperling, 1960, 1963). For example, in so-called whole-report experiments, Sperling (1963) instructed subjects to report as many letters as possible from a briefly exposed array of unrelated letters (randomly selected consonants) that was followed by a pattern mask. The number of correctly reported letters (the score) depended on the stimulus-onset asynchrony (SOA) between the letter array and the mask. Corrected for guessing, the score appeared to be zero when the SOA was smaller than some threshold t_0. As the SOA exceeded t_0, the mean score initially increased at a high rate (about one letter per 10–15 ms) and then leveled off as it approached a value of about four letters or the number of letters in the stimulus, whichever was smaller.

Sperling (1963) proposed a simple serial model to account for the initial strong and approximately linear increase in mean score as SOA exceeded t_0. By this model, the subject encodes (*scans*) one letter at a time, requiring 10–15 ms to encode a letter. The serial encoding is interrupted when the stimulus is terminated by the mask or when the number of encoded letters reaches the immediate memory span of the subject.

The simple serial model for whole-report behavior was later rejected by Sperling (1967). The rejection was based on the observation that as exposure duration increases, all items in a display are reported with above-chance accuracy before any one item can be reported with perfect accuracy. Data for a typical subject are illustrated in Figure 1, which shows the accuracy of report as a function of exposure duration for each location in a horizontal array of five letters terminated by a pattern mask. For this subject, the order of the successive locations reported correctly was generally left-to-right (1 to 5), except that Location 5 was reported correctly at shorter exposures than Location 4. The observation that all locations begin to be reported at better than chance levels even at the briefest exposures could be accommodated by a simple serial model if the order of scanning was supposed to vary from trial to trial (Sperling, 1967, Footnote 1), but Sperling preferred a parallel-processing interpretation.

Detection

Estes and Taylor (1964) developed a detection task and proposed a stochastic serial model for analyzing the results. Subjects were presented with brief displays of randomly selected consonants. Two letters were predesignated as targets, and the rest as distractors. Each display contained just one of the two targets, and the subject was required to state the identity

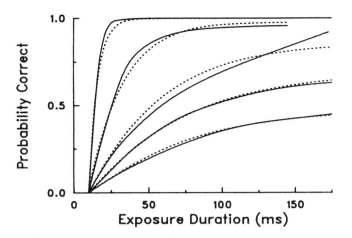

Figure 1

Probability correct in whole report as a function of exposure duration for each display location in a horizontal array of five letters (Sperling, 1967). Observed data for one typical subject are represented by five solid curves. A theoretical fit by a parallel processing model is indicated by dotted curves. If display locations are numbered from left to right and observed curves or theoretical curves are numbered from top to bottom, Curve 1 = Location 1, Curve 2 = Location 2, Curve 3 = Location 3, Curve 4 = Location 5, and Curve 5 = Location 4. Reprinted from " A Theory of Visual Attention," by C. Bundesen, 1990, *Psychological Review*, *97*, p. 531. Copyright by the American Psychological Association. Solid curves are from "Successive Approximations to a Model for Short-Term Memory," by G. Sperling, 1967, *Acta Psychologica*, *27*, p. 289. Copyright 1967 by Elsevier. Adapted with permission.

of this target, guessing whenever unsure. Pre- and postexposure fields were dark.

The stochastic serial model for the task assumes that during and following the display, until the sensory trace of the stimulus has faded away, the stimulus letters are scanned one at a time. As each letter is scanned, it is classified either as a target or as a distractor, and if it is classified as a target, its identity is reported. If the stimulus trace fades away before the target is scanned, the subject gives a report at random. Thus, if a total of S letters are scanned from a display of N letters, the probability of a correct report is given by

$$p_c = S/N + (1 - S/N) \times 0.5, \qquad (1)$$

namely, the probability that the target is among the S letters that are scanned plus the complement of this probability times the probability of a correct guess.

The number of scanned letters, S, is limited by the display size N (clearly, $S \leq N$). It is also limited by the time available for scanning. Scanning of a single letter takes a fixed time (Δt), so the number of letters that can be scanned during stimulus exposure increases approximately linearly with the exposure time. At any time t after stimulus offset, the conditional probability that the stimulus trace fades away before time $t + \Delta t$, provided that the trace is intact at time t, is assumed to be a constant independent of t. Thus, the time available for scanning varies so that the number of letters that can be scanned after stimulus offset is geometrically distributed.

Estes and Taylor (1964, 1965) estimated the number of scanned letters, S, from the observed probability of correct report, p_c, by use of Equation 1. S was an increasing function of display size, and the shape of the function agreed well with predictions by the stochastic serial model. In other respects, however, the model seemed to fail. Specifically, Estes and Taylor (1965) and Wolford, Wessel, and Estes (1968) investigated effects of multiple, redundant targets in the detection task. In one experiment, for example, each stimulus display consisted of 16 letters, which included 1, 2, or 4 identical targets (Bs or Fs). The task was to report the type of target (B vs. F) that appeared in the display. The observed probabilities of correct report varied with the number of targets, and the size of this effect accorded with the assumption that detections of multiple targets are independent events. Also, the probability of correct report depended little on the distance between two targets in the display, which goes against the idea that the processed items are adjacent along a scanning path. Finally, response latencies varied little with the number of targets in a display. These findings led Wolford et al. (1968) to conclude that letters in their displays were sampled in parallel and independently.

Search

Following Nickerson (1966), Sternberg (1967), and Atkinson, Holmgren, and Juola (1969), simple serial models have been used extensively in analyzing reaction time data from visual search experiments. In most experiments on visual search, the subject is instructed to decide "as quickly as possible" whether a predesignated target is present in a display that contains one or no occurrences of the target. Positive (*present*) and negative (*absent*) reaction times are analyzed as functions of display size. The method of analysis was spelled out by Sternberg (1966, 1969a, 1969b) and further developed by Schneider and Shiffrin (1977). The basics are as follows.

By a simple serial model, items are scanned one by one. As each item is scanned, it is classified as a target or as a distractor. A negative reaction is initiated if and when all items have been scanned and classified as distractors, so the number of items processed before a negative reaction is initiated equals the display size, N. In a *self-terminating search process*, a positive reaction is initiated if and when a target is found. Because the order in which items are scanned is independent of their status as targets versus distractors, the mean number of items processed before a positive reaction is initiated equals $(1 + 2 + \ldots + N)/N = (1 + N)/2$. In an *exhaustive search process*, a positive reaction is made if a target is found, but the reaction is not initiated until all N items have been processed. Thus, the rate of increase in mean negative reaction time as a function of display size equals the mean time taken to process one item, Δt. The rate of increase in mean positive reaction time equals $\Delta t/2$ if the search process is self-terminating, but Δt if the search process is exhaustive. (For more general analyses, see Townsend & van Zandt, 1990; van Zandt & Townsend, 1993.)

Treisman, Sykes, and Gelade (1977) introduced a widespread distinction between feature and conjunction search. In *feature search,* the target differs from the distractors by possessing a simple physical feature (e.g., a particular color, size, or curvature) not shared by any of the distractors. In *conjunction search,* the target differs from the distractors by showing a predefined conjunction of physical features (say, both a particular color and a particular shape), but the target is not unique in any of the component features of the conjunction (i.e., in color or in shape). For example, in a study by Treisman and Gelade (1980, Experiment 1, conjunction condition), the task was to search for a green *T* among distractors that were brown *T*s and green *X*s in nearly equal numbers.

Many experiments on conjunction search or feature search with low target–distractor discriminability have yielded positive and negative mean reaction times that are approximately linear functions of display size, with fairly steep slopes and a positive-to-negative slope ratio of about 1:2. For example, in the conjunction condition of Experiment 1 of Treisman and Gelade (1980), the positive reaction time function was approximately linear with a slope of 29 ms per item, the negative reaction time function was approximately linear with a slope of 67 ms per item, and the positive-to-negative slope ratio was 0.43. In Experiment 2 of Treisman and Gelade (1980), search for a red *O* among green *O*s and red *N*s yielded a positive reaction time function with a slope constant of 21 ms per item, a negative function with a slope constant of 40 ms per item, and a slope ratio of 0.52. Nearly the same slope constants and a slope ratio of 0.53 were found by Treisman and Gormican (1988) as overall means across 37 conditions of feature search with low target–distractor discriminability.

The pattern of approximately linear reaction time functions with positive-to-negative slope ratios of about 1:2 conforms to predictions from simple self-terminating serial models, and Treisman and her colleagues (e.g., Treisman, 1988; Treisman & Gelade, 1980; Treisman et al., 1977) have concluded that conjunction search is performed by scanning items one at a time. However, rather similar predictions hold if attention is shifted among small nonoverlapping groups of items so that processing is parallel within groups but serial between groups, and shifting is random with respect to the distinction between target and distractors. In this case, the total processing time should be approximately a linear function of the number of groups processed, and the mean number of groups processed should be approximately linearly related to display size for both positive and negative displays, with a positive-to-negative slope ratio of 1:2. Pashler (1987) proposed this sort of explanation for conjunction search, and Treisman and Gormican (1988) proposed the same sort of explanation for feature search with low target–distractor discriminability.

Selective Serial Models

In selective serial models, items in the stimulus display are attended (scanned) one at a time, but the serial order in which items are attended depends on their status as targets versus distractors: When a target and a distractor compete for attention, the target is more likely to win.

The first selective serial model of visual search was developed by Hoffman (1978, 1979). It built on findings on the temporal course of selective attention made in Eriksen's laboratory (Colegate, Hoffman, & Eriksen, 1973; Eriksen & Collins, 1969). As argued by Hoffman, the findings cast doubt on the notion that attention can be shifted from item to item at the high rates presumed in simple (nonselective) serial models of processing.

Consider the study of Colegate et al. (1973). Subjects were presented with circular arrays of 8 or 12 letters. Each array was centered on fixation and about 2° of visual angle in diameter. The array was preceded by a bar designating one of the letters for report. (The bar was positioned on an imaginary radius from the center of the display through the indicated position; it fell outside the circular array, but its near end was close to the indicated letter.) As the SOA between the bar and the letter array was increased from zero up to about 250 ms, mean reaction time to voice the indicated letter decreased, but with further increase in SOA, the mean reaction time was essentially constant. Apparently, the time taken to prepare for the target by covertly shifting attention to the indicated position never exceeded 250 ms. Thus, the mean time taken to shift attention to the target location in response to the bar should be at most 250 ms.

On the other hand, the reduction in mean reaction time obtained by increasing the SOA between the bar and the letter array from zero up to 250 ms was about 80 ms (estimated from Figures 1 and 2 of Colegate et al., 1973). Control trials with a neutral warning signal indicated that when SOA was 250 ms, nonselective "alerting" effects (cf. Posner & Boies, 1971) of the presentation of the bar had vanished at the time the letter array was presented. Apparently, the saving in mean reaction time by having attention shifted to the target location before the presentation of the letter array was 80 ms. If so, then the mean time taken to shift attention to the target location in response to the bar should be at least 80 ms.

According to this analysis of the data of Colegate et al. (1973), the mean latency of first selecting an item (the bar) and then shifting attention to a spatial location near that item (the target location) was somewhere between 80 ms and 250 ms. From partly the same data, Hoffman (1978, 1979) suggested a mean value of 100 ms. The data cast doubt on simple serial models of visual search, according to which a process involving selection of an item and a subsequent shift of attention to another item should occur at rates as high as once every 40 ms (Treisman & Gelade, 1980, Experiment 2) or once every 10 ms (see Sperling, Budiansky, Spivak, & Johnson, 1971).

Two-Stage Model Of Visual Search

In the selective serial model developed by Hoffman (1978, 1979), visual search is a two-stage process in which a parallel evaluation of the entire stimulus display guides a slow serial processor (cf. Neisser, 1967). The parallel evaluation is preattentive and quick, but error prone. For each item in the display, the outcome is an overall measure of the similarity between this item and the prespecified targets. If the similarity value exceeds a certain criterion, the item is placed on a candidate list. Items not placed on the candidate list receive no further processing.

Items on the candidate list are serially transferred to the second stage of processing (which consists of exhaustive serial comparison against members of the prespecified set of targets). The serial transfer mechanism is the same as the spatial selective attention mechanism studied by Colegate et al. (1973). This mechanism is slow (about one item per 100 ms), but it makes search efficient by transferring items in order of decreasing overall similarity to the prespecified targets. Thus, if there is a target in the display, the target is likely to be among the first items that are transferred to the second stage of processing.

Hoffman (1978) described a computer simulation of the model. The simulation provided fits to reaction times and error rates from two experiments on search through sequentially presented displays.

Guided Search Model

Wolfe, Cave, and Franzel (1989) and Cave and Wolfe (1990) developed a selective serial model, which they called Guided Search. The model combines elements of the two-stage model of Hoffman (1978, 1979) with elements of the feature integration theory of Treisman and her associates (Treisman, 1988; Treisman & Gelade, 1980; Treisman et al., 1977). As in feature integration theory, simple stimulus features such as color, size, and orientation are registered automatically, without attention, and in parallel across the visual field. Registration of objects (items that are defined by conjunctions of features) requires a further stage of processing during which attention is directed serially to each object. As in Hoffman's model, the outcome of the first, parallel stage of processing guides the serial processing at the second stage. The guidance works as follows.

For each feature dimension (e.g., color, size, or orientation), the parallel stage generates an array of activation values (attention values). The array forms a map of the visual field. Each activation value is a sum of a bottom-up and a top-down component. For a particular location within a map for a given feature dimension, the bottom-up component is a measure of differences between the value of the feature at that location and values of the same feature at other locations. In computer simulations of the model, the set of locations considered corresponds to the set of items in the stimulus display. If f_i is the feature value for item i, and display items are numbered $1, 2, \ldots, N$, then the bottom-up component of the activation for item i is given by

$$\exp\left[\sum_{\substack{j=1 \\ j\neq i}}^{N} | f_i - f_j |/(N - 1)\right].$$

The top-down component for a feature dimension at a particular location is a measure of the difference between the value of the feature at that location and the target value for the feature dimension. In simulations, the top-down component of the activation for item i is given by

$$-d\,| f_i - t |,$$

where $d \geq 0$, f_i is the feature value for item i, t is the target value for the feature dimension, and coefficient d is a measure of effectiveness, which varies with the feature dimension.

After activations (attention values) have been calculated in separate maps for each feature dimension, they are summed across feature dimensions to produce a single overall activation map (cf. the saliency map of Koch & Ullman, 1985). In simulations, a certain level of Gaussian noise is also added at each location. The final overall activation values represent the evaluation given by the parallel stage of how likely the stimulus at each location is to be the target.

Whereas the parallel stage suggests probable targets, the serial stage classifies each item it processes as a target or as a distractor. Items are processed one by one in order of decreasing activation in the overall activation map. The serial processing stops when a target is found or when all items with activations above a certain value have been processed. Thus, as in Hoffman's (1978, 1979) model, the serial stage selects items by working its way down a candidate list provided by the parallel stage.

Consider how the model works when a target is present and the level of Gaussian noise is zero. In feature search, say, for a red target among black distractors, the target differs from every other item in color, so the positive, bottom-up component of its activation in the color map is high. As the target item has the prespecified target color, the nonpositive, top-down component of its activation in the color map is zero. Hence, the total color activation for the target is high. Each distractor gets a small amount of positive, bottom-up color activation, because it differs from the target item in color, and a certain amount of negative, top-down color activation because its color differs from the prespecified target color. Thus, the total color activation of a distractor is low. In feature dimensions other than color, there should be no differences between target and distractors. Therefore, in the overall activation map, the activation for the target should be considerably higher than the activations for the distractors.

In conjunction search, say, for a red vertical target among black vertical and red horizontal distractors in nearly equal numbers, each item differs from approximately half the other items in color, and the same is true with respect to orientation. Bottom-up components of activation are therefore about the same for all items in the display. Because of the top-down component, the color activations for all the red items are higher than the color activations for the black items. Similarly, the orientation activations for vertical items are higher than the orientation activations for horizontal items. The target is the only item with high activations in both feature dimensions. Thus, in the overall activation map, the activation for the target should be higher than activations for distractors, but the difference between target and distractor activations should be smaller in the conjunction search than it was in the feature search.

In both feature and conjunction search, the activation for the target should be higher than activations for distractors, provided that the level of Gaussian noise is zero. Accordingly, when a target is present and the noise level is zero, the target should be the first item processed at the serial stage, regardless of the number of distractors in the display. Positive (present) reaction times should therefore be independent of display size. Negative (absent) reaction times depend on the amount of activation an item must have in order to be processed at the serial stage. With an appropriately high activation threshold, the negative reaction time function should also be flat.

The pattern of predicted search times changes if a high level of Gaussian noise is assumed. At the limit, as the variance of the noise distribution tends toward infinity, guidance from the parallel stage vanishes, and the model becomes indistinguishable from a simple serial model. Thus, with a high level of noise, the model predicts approximately linear reaction time functions with a positive-to-negative slope ratio of 1:2.

With intermediate levels of noise, the model makes differential predictions for feature versus conjunction search. Because the difference between target and distractor activations is smaller in conjunction than feature search, the signal-to-noise ratio in the overall activation map is smaller in conjunction search, so guidance from the parallel stage is less effective. For this reason, effects of display size are greater in conjunction than feature search.

The guided search model accounts for many findings from experiments on visual search. It was motivated, in particular, by demonstrations of fast conjunction search (Nakayama & Silverman, 1986; Wolfe et al., 1989) that seemed to undermine the basis of feature integration theory (see Duncan & Humphreys, 1989; also see Treisman, 1988, 1993, and Treisman & Sato, 1990, for modifications of feature integration theory that are closely related to those made in the guided search model). Some demonstrations of fast conjunction search (Nakayama & Silverman, 1986) are accommodated by assuming that for some feature dimensions, top-down control is very effective. Other demonstrations (Wolfe et al., 1989) are accommodated by assuming that in some subjects, the level of Gaussian noise is very low. Further applications and developments of the model are found in Wolfe (1994, and chap. 8 in this volume).

Related Choice Models

The selective serial models for visual search are paralleled by choice models developed for partial report (Bundesen, Pedersen, & Larsen, 1984; Bundesen, Shibuya, & Larsen, 1985). In a sense, choice models are neutral on the issue of parallel versus serial processing, but the first formulation of a choice model for partial report was serial in spirit. The formulation was inspired by Duncan's (1980, 1981, 1983, 1984, 1985) theory of visual attention.

In a *partial-report experiment,* the subject is instructed to respond to a briefly exposed display showing a mixture of targets (e.g., red letters) and distractors (e.g., black letters) by reporting as many targets as possible while ignoring the distractors (cf. Sperling, 1960). Scores for displays without distractors provide a whole-report baseline. The choice model (Bundesen et al., 1984, 1985) assumes that whether partial or whole report is required, performance reflects the number of targets that enter a limited-capacity, short-term memory store (cf. Sperling, 1967). Any target that enters the store is correctly reported with probability θ, regardless of the fate of other items. Items entering the store may be targets, distractors, or extraneous noise, but the total number of items entering the store is limited by the storage capacity (K items).

Read-in to the short-term store is viewed as selective sampling of items without replacement. The selective sampling continues until K items have been sampled. The selection occurs in accordance with a Luce (1959) ratio rule. Specifically, for a given selection criterion, there is a scale v with the following property: If U is the set of all items remaining after selection of $k - 1$ items ($1 \leq k \leq K$), and i is a member of U, then the probability that item i is the kth to be selected equals

$$v(i)/ \sum_{j \in U} v(j). \tag{2}$$

In words, items are assigned weights or impacts in such a way that the probability that any not-yet-selected item will be the next one to be selected equals the impact of that item divided by the sum of impacts for all items not yet selected.

Four-Parameter Model

A four-parameter version of the choice model for partial report is obtained by adding two simplifying assumptions. First, all targets have identical impacts and all distractors have identical impacts, so no generality is lost by setting the impact of a target to 1 and the impact of a distractor to α, where α is a constant. Second, the number of extraneous noise items (in the experimental situation or in long-term memory) is large in relation to K, and each one has a small probability of being sampled on a given trial, so the total impact of the not-yet-selected extraneous noise items, ϵ, is essentially constant during a trial.

The two simplifying assumptions leave the following parameters: the capacity of the short-term store, K; the impact of a distractor, α; the total impact of extraneous noise items, ϵ; and the probability that a target that has entered the short-term store will be reported, θ. Parameter α is a measure for efficiency of selection (the efficiency of selecting targets rather than distractors). If α is zero, selection is perfect. If α equals one, sampling is nonselective.

To see how the model works, consider a subject trying to select as many targets as possible from a display containing T targets and D distractors. Let K equal 4. Regardless of T and D, a total of four items is transferred to the short-term store. If both T and D are greater than one, the probability that, for instance, the first item selected is a target, the second a distractor, the third an extraneous noise item, and the fourth a target is given by the product of $T/[T + \alpha D + \epsilon]$, $\alpha D/[(T - 1) + \alpha D + \epsilon]$, $\epsilon/[(T - 1) + \alpha (D - 1) + \epsilon]$, and $(T - 1)/[(T - 1) + \alpha (D - 1) + \epsilon]$. In the case where two targets enter the short-term store, the expected probability distribution for the number of targets correctly reported is the binomial distribution for two Bernoulli trials with probability θ for success.

Three-Parameter Model

A further simplification can be made when T and D are large in relation to K and the analysis is based on observed mean scores (rather than the underlying frequency distributions of scores). When T and D are large, the predicted mean score (the mean number of targets reported) is closely proportional to the product of parameters K and θ (given that parameters α and ϵ are kept constant). Accordingly, when the analysis is based on observed mean scores, the four-parameter model effectively reduces to a three-parameter model with a single parameter K' representing the product of K and θ. Computationally, the three-parameter model is identical to the four-parameter model with parameter θ kept constant at a value of 1 and $K = K'$.

Goodness of Fit

The choice model has accounted very well for partial report performance as a function of number of targets, number of distractors, and selection criterion (Bundesen, 1987; Bundesen et al., 1984, 1985). Bundesen et al. (1984) fitted the three-parameter version of the model to mean scores observed in a variety of conditions with partial reports based on brightness, color, shape, and alphanumeric class. In all conditions, exposure time was kept constant, pre- and postexposure fields were dark, and the subject was informed about the selection criterion before the stimulus display was presented. Estimates for parameter K' (the product of K and θ, where K is the capacity of the short-term store, and θ is the probability that a target that has entered the store will be reported) showed little variation across conditions, and estimates for parameter ϵ (total impact of extraneous noise with impact per target as the unit) were small. Estimates for parameter α (impact per distractor with impact per target as the unit) varied widely across conditions, and the variation in this one parameter accounted for changes in performance with different selection criteria. In data obtained by averaging across conditions, the model accounted for 99% of the variance with the numbers of targets and distractors.

Bundesen et al. (1985) fitted the four-parameter version of the model to individual frequency distributions of the number of correctly reported targets as functions of number of targets and number of distractors for selection by color and selection by alphanumeric class. Excellent fits were obtained with parameter ϵ kept constant near zero. Estimates for K, θ, and α were plausible and consistent with previous findings. To illustrate, estimates for K averaged 3.57 for the color conditions and 3.52 for the alphanumeric conditions.[1] Estimates for θ averaged 0.92 for color conditions and exactly the same for alphanumeric conditions. Estimates for α varied widely with the selection criterion, averaging 0.05 for color and 0.36 for alphanumeric conditions.

Comment

As pointed out by Hoffman (1978), findings from Eriksen's laboratory on the time taken to shift attention in response to a visual cue (Colegate et al., 1973; Eriksen & Collins, 1969) cast doubt on the notion that attention can be shifted between stimulus items at the high rates presumed in simple (nonselective) serial models. Hoffman (1978, 1979) showed that a selective serial model can resolve the conflict between data suggesting that attention shifting is slow (e.g., Colegate et al., 1973) and data showing only slight effects of display size in visual search (e.g., 10 ms per item; Sperling

---

[1] All parameters were treated as continuous. For nonintegral values of K, predicted values were calculated as weighted averages so that, for instance, a value of 3.57 for K was treated as a mixture of values of 3 and 4, with a probability of .57 for sampling four items on a trial.

et al., 1971). The conflict can be resolved by assuming that the serial processing is limited to targets and targetlike items. This assumption, however, provides no resolution of a related problem for serial models: the conflict between data suggesting that attention shifting is slow and data suggesting processing rates of up to one item per 10–15 ms in whole report (e.g., Sperling, 1963), that is, in a task in which all items are targets.

Additional evidence that attention shifting is slow has been provided by Reeves and Sperling (1986), Remington and Pierce (1984), Sperling and Reeves (1980), Tsal (1983), and Weichselgartner and Sperling (1987). Pashler and Badgio (1987, Experiments 2 and 3) made a more direct test of the feasibility of rapid serial scanning. Subjects were instructed to report the highest digit in a linear array of four digits. Reactions were nonspeeded, but reaction time versions of the task had shown clear effects of display size (20–40 ms per item; Pashler & Badgio, 1985). Each digit was presented for about 67 ms and was preceded and followed by masks. The probability of a correct report was found to be the same regardless of whether the four digits were presented simultaneously or in two successive pairs from left to right (Experiment 2). Probability correct was also the same in blocks in which the four digits were presented successively, one at a time, from left to right, as in blocks in which the order of presentation was irregular and unpredictable (Experiment 3). The results suggest that subjects were unable to shift attention as rapidly as once every 67 ms. (For further results and discussion, see Duncan, Ward, & Shapiro, 1994; Mackeben & Nakayama, 1993.)

PARALLEL MODELS

Independent Channels Models

The first thoroughgoing parallel models of visual processing of multielement displays were the independent channels models developed by Eriksen and his colleagues (Eriksen, 1966; Eriksen & Lappin, 1965, 1967; Eriksen & Spencer, 1969). They were based on a hypothesis of perceptual independence. The hypothesis is that display items presented to separated foveal areas are processed in parallel and independently up to and including the level of form identification. The hypothesized independence implies that the way a display item is processed is independent of random variations in the way in which other display items are processed. It also implies that the way an item is processed is independent of display size.

Whole Report

Eriksen and Lappin (1967; also see Eriksen, 1966, Experiment 3) tested an independent channels model for whole report. Their stimulus displays contained 1, 2, 3, or 4 letters, which were randomly drawn from the set {A, O, U}. The letters appeared at one or more corners of an imaginary square centered on the fixation point. The probability that a particular letter would occur at a particular corner was independent of whatever other letters appeared in the display.

By the independent channels model, the probability of correct report of any given letter should be independent of display size and independent of random variations in accuracy of report for other letters in the display. Thus, under a given set of viewing conditions, the number of correctly reported letters obtained with display size N should follow a binomial distribution for N Bernoulli trials with a certain probability p for success, where p is a constant independent of N. Equivalently, the number of errors should be binomially distributed with parameters N and $1 - p$.

Figure 2 shows a fit of the independent channels model to the proportion of trials having 0, 1, and 2 or more errors as a function of display size with level of exposure duration as the parameter. As can be seen, the fit is very close for all display sizes and all three exposure-duration conditions.

Detection

Eriksen and Lappin (1965; also see Eriksen, 1966, Experiment 1) developed an independent channels model for a detection task. Subjects were presented with brief displays of 1, 2, 4, or 6 occurrences of the same stimulus letter. The letter was either A, T, or U, and the task was to make a forced choice among the three possibilities and to give a confidence rating on a 3-point scale (*certain*, *think so*, and *guess*).

The model assumes that each occurrence of a letter in a stimulus display results in one of three possible perceptual states (s_1, s_2, or s_3), one for each of the three possible confidence ratings. The probability $p(s_i)$ of state s_i is a constant independent of display size and independent of random variations in the processing of other display items. Each state s_i is associated with a hit rate h_i. On trials in which only one occurrence of a letter is presented, the probability that the letter is correctly identified equals $p(s_1)\ h_1 + p(s_2)\ h_2 + p(s_3)\ h_3$. When multiple occurrences of a letter are

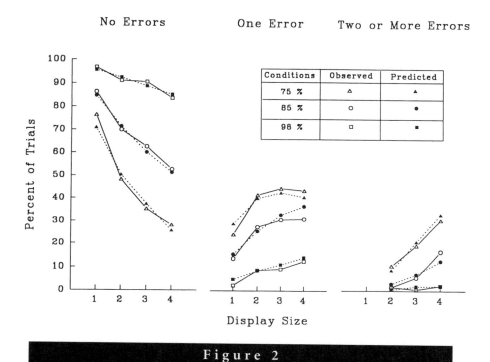

No Errors　　　**One Error**　　**Two or More Errors**

Conditions	Observed	Predicted
75 %	△	▲
85 %	○	●
98 %	□	■

Display Size

Figure 2

Mean proportion of trials having 0, 1, and 2 or more errors as a function of display size and level of exposure duration in the whole-report experiment by Eriksen and Lappin (1967). Group data for 4 subjects. Exposure duration conditions were determined for each subject so as to yield about 75%, 85%, and 98% correct reports, respectively, at a display size of 1. From "Independence in the Perception of Simultaneously Presented Forms at Brief Durations," by C. W. Eriksen and J. S. Lappin, 1967, *Journal of Experimental Psychology, 73*, p. 470. Copyright 1967 by the American Psychological Association. Adapted with permission of the author.

presented, different states may be generated by different occurrences. In such conditions, probability correct equals the highest hit rate associated with any of the generated states. This model provided a fair account of performance in the detection task.

Search

Eriksen and Spencer (1969) advanced an independent channels model for visual search in a study that pioneered the use of sequential presentation techniques. Subjects were required to decide whether an *A* (target) had occurred in a sequence of letters presented on a trial. The sequence contained at most one occurrence of *A* and a varying number of *T*s and *U*s. The letters appeared around the perimeter of an imaginary circle centered on fixation. Each letter was presented for a few milliseconds with the interval between letters varying from 5 ms up to several seconds. Pre- and postexposure fields were dark.

The rate of presentation had little or no effect on accuracy as measured by a variant of the index d'. However, display size (the number of letters in the sequence) was important. With increase in display size, accuracy decreased, because the false-alarm rate increased disproportionately relative to the hit rate.

A fair description of the results was obtained by the following model. The probability that a target letter would be correctly detected was a constant p independent of display size and rate of presentation. Similarly, the probability that a particular distractor would be correctly rejected (i.e., not seen as a target) was a constant q independent of display size and rate of presentation. A false alarm was made on a target-absent trial if not all distractors were rejected. Thus, the probability of a false alarm on a trial with a display consisting of N distractors was $1 - q^N$. A hit was made on a target-present trial if the target was detected or not all distractors were rejected. Accordingly, the probability of a hit on a trial with a target and $N - 1$ distractors was $p + (1 - p)(1 - q^{N-1})$.

Further Developments

Further support for the notion of independent channels was provided by Egeth, Jonides, and Wall (1972), Gardner (1973), Shiffrin and Gardner (1972), and Shiffrin and Geisler (1973). Kinchla (1974) developed an elegant formalization of independent channels models based on signal-detection theory (cf. Swets, 1984). He found excellent fits to Eriksen and Spencer's (1969) data on effects of display size and data by Kinchla and Collyer (1974) on effects of redundant targets.

More recently, the notion of independent channels (unlimited-capacity parallel processing) has been used very widely to account for cases in which visual search is highly efficient (small effects of display size). As pointed out by Treisman and her associates (e.g., Treisman & Gelade, 1980; Treisman et al., 1977), this includes cases of feature search with high target–distractor discriminability. As argued by Schneider and Shiffrin (1977) and Shiffrin and Schneider (1977), it also seems to include cases of search for more complex targets such as particular alphanumeric characters when subjects have been trained consistently in detecting those particular targets (but see Czerwinski, Lightfoot, & Shiffrin, 1992; Logan, 1992).

Limited-Capacity Models

The linear relations between mean reaction time and display size predicted by simple serial models cannot be explained by parallel models with independent channels (unlimited-capacity parallel models; cf. Sternberg, 1966, 1967). To be specific, consider a display of N items that are processed in parallel. Suppose processing time distributions for individual items are independent of N, mutually independent, and identical, with nonzero variance. Then the mean time taken to complete processing of the N items is an increasing, negatively accelerated function of N, no matter what the shape of the processing time distributions (see Townsend & Ashby, 1983, p. 92, for a proof).

Atkinson et al. (1969) and Townsend (1969) showed that linearly increasing mean reaction time functions of display size can be explained by parallel models with limited processing capacity. As an example, consider again a display of N items that are processed in parallel. Let $v_i(t)$ be the hazard function for the processing time of item i (i.e., $v_i[t]$ is the conditional probability density that item i completes processing at time t, given that item i has not completed processing before time t). Regard $v_i(t)$ as the amount of processing capacity devoted to item i at time t, and suppose the total processing capacity spread across items in the display is a constant C, that is,

$$\sum_{i=1}^{N} v_i(t) = C. \tag{3}$$

Then the time to the first completion is exponentially distributed with rate parameter C. When the first completion occurs, the processing capacity is supposed to be redistributed among the remaining $N - 1$ items, so the time from the first to the second completion is exponentially distributed with the same rate parameter C. The process repeats until all N items have been completed. As a result, the time taken to complete processing of the N items is gamma distributed with parameters N and C. Hence, the mean time increases linearly with display size N.

Multicomponent Model

Rumelhart (1970) proposed a multicomponent model with limited processing capacity for perception of briefly exposed visual displays. The model assumes that items (alphanumeric characters) in the stimulus display are processed in parallel and independently in the sense that the way an item is processed is independent of random variations in the ways other items are processed. Each item consists of multiple components (features), and recognition requires that k features of the item are extracted.

Extractions of features from items in the display are assumed to be events of the Poisson type. They happen at a mean rate of C features per second, where C is the overall processing capacity. Processing capacity C is independent of display size, but C depends on stimulus contrast, and C is fixed until the offset of the display. The processing capacity is distributed among the items in the display in accordance with attentional weights. Let w_i be the attentional weight of item i in a display of N items. Then features are extracted from item i at a Poisson rate of

$$C \, w_i / \sum_{j=1}^{N} w_j$$

per second. Following stimulus offset, processing capacity C decays with time constant μ, but C is reduced by presentation of a mask. For briefly exposed displays, the number of correctly reported items is bounded by the limited rate of feature extraction (parameter C) but not by limitations in storage capacity.

Rumelhart (1970) showed the multicomponent model to fit a wide range of data on whole and partial report (Sperling, 1960), detection (e.g., Estes & Taylor, 1964, 1965), and backward masking (e.g., Eriksen & Collins, 1964, 1965). However, two types of evidence go against the model. First, predictions by the model of effects of exposure duration in whole report have been grossly in error (see Shibuya & Bundesen, 1988, Figure 5; Townsend & Ashby, 1983, Figure 11.10). The error seems related to the fact that limitations in short-term storage capacity are ignored (cf. Shibuya & Bundesen, 1988).

Second, much evidence suggesting unlimited-capacity parallel processing goes against the multicomponent model. For example, demonstrations of feature search with little effect of display size (e.g., Treisman & Gelade, 1980) go against the assumption that main limitations on processing capacity are found at the stage of feature extraction.

Optimal Capacity-Allocation Model

Shaw (1978; Shaw & Shaw, 1977) developed an optimal capacity allocation model, which is neutral on the stage of processing at which capacity limitations are found. It generalizes the limited-capacity model of Atkinson et al. (1969) and Townsend (1969) to situations in which the probability that a target occurs at a given location varies across display locations.

Consider processing of a display with N possible target locations, only one of which contains a target. Let $v_i(t)$ be the value at time t of the hazard function for recognition of the target, given that the target occurs at location i. Parameter $v_i(t)$ is regarded as the amount of processing capacity allocated to location i at time t, and the total processing capacity C spread across the possible target locations is assumed to be fixed (cf. Equation 3).

An *allocation policy* (cf. Kahneman, 1973) is a way of allocating and reallocating the total processing capacity C among the display locations. For any distribution of the probability of target occurrence across the display locations, there is an *optimal allocation policy*—an allocation policy that, for any time t, maximizes the probability that the target has been recognized by time t (cf. M. L. Shaw, 1978; also see Townsend & Ashby, 1983, pp. 139–145). After considerable experience with a given probability distribution, the subject is assumed to adopt the optimal allocation policy.

The optimal allocation policy requires that if all N locations are equally likely to contain the target, each location is allocated a capacity of C/N. Suppose the display locations are at different levels of prior probability of containing the target, and let Level 1 be the highest level, Level 2 the second highest, and so on. The optimal policy then requires that, at first, all processing capacity is evenly distributed across the locations at Level 1. As time passes without the targets being found, the posterior probability that the target is present at a given location at Level 1 approaches the posterior probability that the target is present at a given location at Level 2. If and when the two probabilities become equally great before the target has been found, processing capacity is reallocated and evenly distributed across all locations at Levels 1 and 2. If needed, the process repeats so that, at last, the capacity is evenly distributed across all of the possible target locations.

By the definition of the hazard function $v_i(t)$, the probability $p_i(t)$ that the target is recognized by time t, given that the target occurs at location i, is given by

$$p_i(t) = 1 - \exp[-V_i(t)], \qquad (4)$$

where

$$V_i(t) = \int_0^t v_i(x)\ dx \qquad (5)$$

(cf., e.g., Luce, 1986, p. 15). Parameter $V_i(t)$ is called the *cumulated processing capacity* at location i. By Equations 3 and 5,

$$\sum_{i=1}^{N} V_i(t) = Ct,$$

which implies that, summed across display locations, the cumulated processing capacity is independent of the allocation policy.

Shaw and Shaw (1977) compared performance between two different distributions of the probability of target occurrence across display locations. The subjects' task was to report a single letter that appeared at one of eight possible locations, which were equally spaced along the circumference of an imaginary circle centered on fixation. Exposures were brief (about 25 ms) and postmasked. In one condition, the eight location probabilities were all equal. In the other condition, the location probabilities reached a maximum value of .25 at the top and the bottom of the display. By use of Equation 4, the cumulated processing capacity $V_i(t)$ was estimated at each location i in either condition. For each of the 4 subjects, estimates of the cumulated processing capacity, summed across display locations, were virtually constant across conditions. For 3 out of the 4 subjects, the way in which the cumulated capacity was distributed across display locations closely approximated the optimal allocation.

Shaw (1978) fitted the optimal capacity-allocation model to differences in mean reaction time between high- and low-probability locations in a reaction time version of the detection task introduced by Estes and

Taylor (1964). The model provided reasonable fits for 10 out of 14 subjects. This empirical support is not overwhelming, but the principle of optimization seems important (cf. Sperling, 1984), and goodness of fit might be improved by including time costs of reallocations of processing capacity (shifts of attention; cf. Bundesen, 1990, p. 537).

Zoom Lens Model

According to the optimal capacity-allocation model of Shaw (1978), attention can be split among noncontiguous locations in the visual field: Processing capacity can be allocated to several separated locations at the same time. Eriksen and Yeh (1985) and Eriksen and St. James (1986) proposed an alternative conception, a zoom lens model of the visual attentional field. In this conception, the attentional field can vary in size from an area subtending less than 1° of visual angle to the full size of the visual field. Because total processing capacity is limited, the amount of processing capacity allocated to a given attended location decreases as the size of the attentional field increases. However, the attentional field cannot be split among noncontiguous locations. Direct tests of this hypothesis have been attempted, but the issue is still open (cf. Eriksen & Webb, 1989).

Race Models of Selection

In race models of selection from multielement displays, display items are processed in parallel, and attentional selection is made of those items that first finish processing (the winners of the race). Thus, selection of targets rather than distractors is based on processing of targets being faster than processing of distractors (Bundesen, 1987; Bundesen et al., 1985; for related work, see Meijers & Eijkman, 1977; Miller, 1982; Mordkoff & Egeth, 1993; Mordkoff & Yantis, 1991; Van der Heijden, La Heij, & Boer, 1983; also see Logan, 1988; Logan & Cowan, 1984; Logan, Cowan, & Davis, 1984; Meyer, Irwin, Osman, & Kounios, 1988).

Bundesen et al. (1985) showed that the choice rule expressed in Equation 2 is implied by race models in which items are processed independently and processing times are exponentially distributed (see Bundesen, 1993b, for a thorough analysis). Thus, the good fits of the choice model for partial report to the data of Bundesen et al. (1984, 1985) may be interpreted as fits by exponential independent race models with unlimited processing capacity or, alternatively, with limited processing capacity and constant attentional weights. In the unlimited-capacity interpretation, the impact of an item is proportional to the exponential rate parameter of the distribution function for the processing time of the item. Setting the rate at which a target is processed at 1 per unit of time, parameter α is the rate at which a distractor is processed, and parameter ϵ is the overall rate of noise processing (the sum of all rate parameters for extraneous noise items).

In the simplest limited-capacity interpretation, parameter α is the ratio of the attentional weight of a distractor to the attentional weight of a target, and parameter ϵ is the ratio of the sum of the attentional weights of all noise items to the attentional weight of a target. This interpretation assumes that processing rates for targets and distractors would be identical if α equaled 1 so that the amount of processing capacity captured by a distractor was the same as the amount of processing capacity devoted to a target.

A Fixed-Capacity Independent Race Model (FIRM)

Independent race models with unlimited processing capacity and models with limited processing capacity and constant attentional weights are differentiated by temporal characteristics of processing. Shibuya and Bundesen (1988) investigated partial report performance as a function of exposure duration by using stimulus displays terminated by pattern masks. Each display was a circular array of letters and digits, centered on fixation, and the task was to report the digits. Exposure duration ranged from 10 to 200 ms. Nonparametric analyses of the results strongly suggested that performance was constrained by limitations in both processing capacity and storage capacity (cf. Sperling, 1963, 1967), and a four-parameter exponential independent race model that assumes fixed processing capacity, fixed storage capacity, and time-invariant selectivity fitted the data very well. The assumptions may be spelled out as follows.

At a first stage of processing, sensory evidence is collected for each item (letter or digit) in the stimulus display that the item is a target (digit). The strength of this evidence is (a) approximately the same, w_1, for any target in the display as for any other target in the display and (b) approximately the same, w_0, for any distractor in the display as for any other distractor in the display.

At the next stage of processing, items are sampled into a short-term memory store. The capacity of the sampling process is fixed at C items/s, and this processing capacity is distributed over the items in the stimulus display so that the capacity allocated to an individual item is directly proportional to the strength of the evidence (w_1 or w_0) that the item is a target. Thus, w_1 and w_0 serve as attentional weights. For a display with T targets and D distractors, the capacity allocated to each target equals $Cw_1/(Tw_1 + Dw_0)$, which reduces to $C/(T + \alpha D)$, where $\alpha = w_0/w_1$. Similarly, the capacity allocated to each distractor equals $Cw_0/(Tw_1 + Dw_0)$, which reduces to $\alpha C/(T + \alpha D)$. Once distributed over a given display, processing capacity is not redistributed over that display.

The sampling process is activated t_1 ms after the onset of the stimulus display. During the period in which the sampling process is active, the conditional probability density that an individual item will be sampled at a given moment of time, provided that the item has not been sampled before this moment, is a constant equal to the amount of processing capacity allocated to the item. Thus, as long as the sampling process is active, the unconditional probability density that the item will be sampled t ms ($t > 0$) from the beginning of the sampling period equals $\mu \exp(-\mu t)$, where $\mu = C/(T + \alpha D)$ if the item is a target, but $\mu = \alpha C/(T + \alpha D)$ if the item is a distractor.

The sampling process continues until either (a) the number of items sampled equals K, where K is the storage capacity of the short-term memory store, or (b) t_2 ms have elapsed after onset of the mask. The difference between delays t_1 and t_2 (i.e., $t_1 - t_2$) is denoted t_0, and t_0 is a constant.

Finally, overt responses are based on the contents of the short-term store: The number of targets correctly reported from a given display (the score) is approximately the same as the number of targets sampled from the display.

With these assumptions the model predicts the entire probability distribution of the score as a function of number of targets, number of distractors, and exposure duration for any values of parameters C (processing capacity), α (ratio of the attentional weight of a distractor to the attentional weight of a target), K (short-term storage capacity), and t_0 (longest effective exposure duration).[2]

---

[2]Parameters ϵ (ratio of the sum of the attentional weights of all extraneous noise items to the attentional weight of a target) and θ (probability that a target that has entered the short-term store will be reported) were not included in the model. Omitting the parameters from the model corresponds to setting $\epsilon = 0$ and $\theta = 1$ under the conditions of the experiment.

As illustrated in Figure 3, maximum-likelihood fits to the data were remarkably good. The figure is a cumulative frequency diagram for an individual subject showing the relative frequency of scores of j or more (correctly reported targets) as a function of exposure duration, with j, number of targets T, and number of distractors D as the parameters. The theoretical fit is represented by smooth curves. The fit was obtained with parameter C at about 49 items/s, α at 0.40, K at 3.74 items, and t_0 at 19 ms. (See Shibuya, 1991, for comparison of the fit provided by FIRM with fits by other serial and parallel models. Also see Shibuya, 1993, for further elaboration and testing of FIRM.)

UNIFIED THEORY OF VISUAL RECOGNITION AND ATTENTIONAL SELECTION

Bundesen (1990) attempted to integrate findings on single-stimulus recognition, whole report, partial report, detection, and search in a general theory of visual attention (TVA). In TVA, both visual recognition and selection of elements in the visual field consist in making perceptual categorizations. A perceptual categorization has the form "x belongs to i," where x is an element in the visual field and i is a perceptual category. Examples of perceptual categories are the class of red elements (a color category), the class of letters of type A (a shape category), and the class of elements in the right visual field (a location category).

That a perceptual categorization is made means that the categorization is encoded into a limited-capacity short-term memory store. If and when one makes the perceptual categorization that x belongs to i (i.e., if and when the perceptual categorization is encoded into the short-term store), element x is said both to be selected and to be recognized as a member of category i. Thus, an element is said to be selected if, and only if, it is recognized as a member of one or another category. Similarly, an element is said to be represented in the short-term store if, and only if, some categorization of the element is represented in the store.

Whether an element in the visual field gets selected depends on temporal factors. At the moment a perceptual categorization of the element completes processing, the categorization enters the short-term store, provided that memory space for the categorization is available in the store. The capacity of the store is limited to K different elements, and space is available for a new categorization of element x if element x is already represented in the store or if less than K elements are represented in the store. There is no room for a categorization of element x if the short-term store has been filled up with other elements. If a categorization that completes processing fails to enter the short-term store, the categorization is lost.

When a subject prepares for sampling information from a new stimulus field, the short-term store is supposed to be cleared so that memory space will be available for encoding K elements from the stimulus field. The elements that become encoded into the store are those elements that first complete processing with respect to some categorization. In this way, the selection process becomes a race between perceptual categorization processes.

Let processing of a stimulus display begin at Time 0 and consider the event that a particular perceptual categorization, "x belongs to i," completes processing at time t. The hazard function of this event is denoted $v(x, i)$. It is assumed that

$$v(x, i) = \eta(x, i)\beta_i \frac{w_x}{\sum\limits_{z \in S} w_z}, \qquad (6)$$

where $\eta(x, i)$ is the instantaneous strength of the sensory evidence that element x belongs to category i, β_i is a perceptual bias associated with category i, S is the set of all elements in the visual field, and w_x and w_z are attentional weights of elements x and z, respectively.

Attentional weights are derived from pertinence values. Every perceptual category is associated with a pertinence value, which is a measure of the current importance of attending to elements that belong to the category. The attentional weight of an element x in the visual field is given by

$$w_x = \sum\limits_{j \in R} \eta(x, j)\pi_j, \qquad (7)$$

where R is the set of all perceptual categories, $\eta(x, j)$ is the instantaneous strength of the sensory evidence that element x belongs to category j, and π_j is the pertinence value of category j.

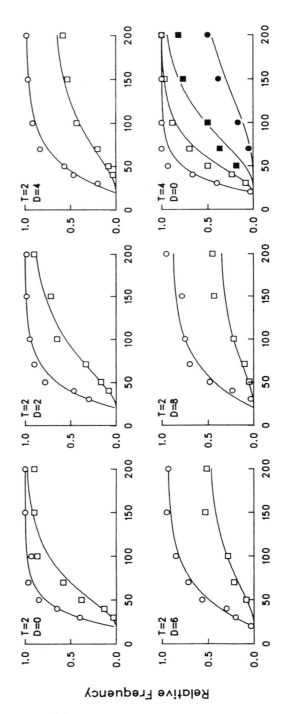

Relative Frequency

28

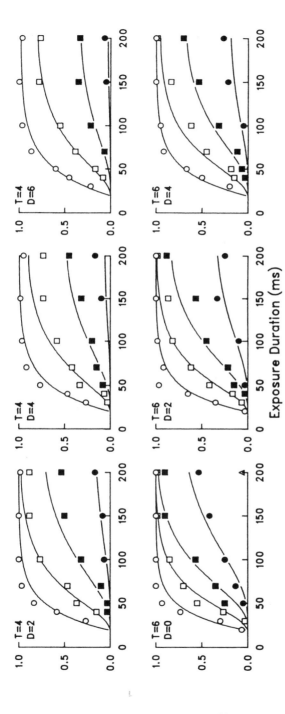

Figure 3

Relative frequency of scores of j or more (correctly reported targets) as a function of exposure duration with j, number of targets T, and number of distractors D as parameters in the experiment of Shibuya and Bundesen (1988). Data are shown for Subject MP. Parameter j varies within panels; j is 1 (open circles), 2 (open squares), 3 (solid squares), 4 (solid circles), or 5 (triangle). T and D vary among panels. Smooth curves represent a theoretical fit to the data by the fixed-capacity independent race model. For clarity, observed frequencies less than .02 were omitted from the figure. Reprinted from "Visual Selection From Multielement Displays: Measuring and Modeling Effects of Exposure Duration," by H. Shibuya and C. Bundesen, 1988, *Journal of Experimental Psychology: Human Perception and Performance*, p. 595. Copyright 1988 by the American Psychological Association.

By Equation 6, v values are functions of eta values, beta values, and attentional weights. By Equation 7, attentional weights are functions of eta and pi values. Therefore, by substituting from Equation 7 into Equation 6, v values can be expressed as functions of eta, beta, and pi values. When eta, beta, and pi values are given, processing times for different perceptual categorizations are supposed to be stochastically independent.

In most applications of the theory to analysis of experimental data, eta, beta, and pi values are assumed to be constant during the presentation of a stimulus display. When eta, beta, and pi values are constant, v values are also constant. The v values were defined as hazard functions, and when v values are kept constant, processing times become exponentially distributed. The v value of the perceptual categorization that element x belongs to category i becomes the exponential rate parameter for the processing time of this perceptual categorization.

Mechanisms of Selection

Equations 6 and 7 describe two mechanisms of selection: a mechanism for selection of elements (filtering) and a mechanism for selection of categories (pigeonholing; cf. Broadbent, 1970). The filtering mechanism is represented by pertinence values and attentional weights. As an example, if selection of red elements is wanted, the pertinence of red should be high. Equation 7 implies that when red has a high pertinence, red elements get high attentional weights. Accordingly, by Equation 6, processing of red elements is fast, so (categorizations of) red elements are likely to win the processing race and be encoded into the short-term memory store.

The pigeonholing mechanism is represented by perceptual bias parameters. Whereas pertinence values determine which elements are selected, perceptual bias parameters determine how the elements are categorized. If particular types of categorizations (e.g., categorizations with respect to alphanumeric identity) are desired, bias parameters of the relevant categories should be high. By Equation 6, then, the desired types of categorizations are likely to be made.

Applications

TVA has been applied to findings from a broad range of paradigms concerned with single-stimulus recognition and selection from multielement displays (see Bundesen, 1990, 1991, 1993a; also see critical discussions by Van der Heijden, 1993, and Van der Velde & Van der Heijden, 1993). For single-stimulus recognition, the theory provides a simple derivation of a successful model of effects of visual discriminability and bias: the biased-choice model of Luce (1963).

Limited-Capacity Parallel Processing

For selection from multielement displays, the fixed-capacity independent race model of Shibuya and Bundesen (1988), FIRM, can be derived as a special case of TVA. FIRM describes the selection process as a race between the elements in the visual field. TVA describes the selection process as a race between perceptual categorizations of elements in the visual field. The correspondence between FIRM and TVA is established by identifying the encoding of an element in the short-term store with the encoding of a perceptual categorization of the element. The K parameter of FIRM corresponds to the K parameter of TVA, and the attentional weights of FIRM correspond to the attentional weights of TVA, the w parameters.

Finally consider the C parameter of FIRM and the associated assumption that the total processing capacity is fixed. In TVA, the total processing capacity C can be defined as the sum of v values across all perceptual categorizations of all elements in the visual field,

$$C = \sum_{x \in S} \sum_{i \in R} v(x, i). \tag{8}$$

By Equation 6 of TVA, C can often be treated as a constant. For example, let the stimulus material consist of elements that are equal in discriminability and the like. Specifically, suppose there is a constant k such that

$$\sum_{i \in R} \eta(x, i)\beta_i = k$$

for every element x. By Equations 6 and 8,

$$C = \sum_{x \in S} \sum_{i \in R} \eta(x, i)\beta_i w_x / \sum_{z \in S} w_z = k.$$

Thus, for the given stimulus material, the processing capacity C is fixed at k.

Independent Channels Behavior

By Equation 6, interference prevails in the perception of simultaneous elements in the visual field. For any element with a positive attentional weight, the rate of processing decreases by increase in the number of simultaneous elements with positive weights. In most experimental conditions, the set of elements that compete for attention (the set of elements with positive attentional weights) consists of the experimenter-defined targets and distractors in the stimulus display. Attention is captured by the targets and distractors when the display is presented, and performance agrees with expectations from a limited-capacity parallel model.

In other conditions, the set of elements that compete for attention is a fixed set of information sources (channels), which are monitored for appearance of the targets defined by the experimenter. Attention is allocated to the information sources (e.g., particular parts of the surface of a display screen) before the targets are presented. If the allocation of attention remains stable, the rate at which a target is processed is independent of the number of simultaneous targets in the channels. Thus, performance conforms to predictions from an unlimited-capacity parallel model (an independent channels model). The strategy of monitoring a fixed set of information sources should be most efficient when the set is small. This was the case, for example, in the whole-report experiment of Eriksen and Lappin (1967).

Approximations to independent channels behavior should also be observed in search for a single target among distractors, when the attentional weights of the distractors are small in relation to the weight of the target. This applies to search with high target–distractor discriminability (e.g., Egeth et al., 1972; Eriksen & Spencer, 1969; Treisman & Gelade, 1980). It also applies to search with moderate target–distractor discriminability after extended consistent practice (e.g., Schneider & Fisk, 1982; Schneider & Shiffrin, 1977; Shiffrin & Schneider, 1977; see Bundesen, 1990, pp. 540–542, for a model of development of pertinence with practice).

Serial Processing

Reallocation of attention is supposed to be slow. However, serial processing is assumed to occur when the time cost of shifting (reallocating) attention is outweighed by gain in speed of processing once attention has been shifted. To illustrate, suppose targets and distractors are equal in attentional weights, and consider search through a set of two display items. If the items are processed in parallel with a total capacity of C, the mean time to the first completion of an item is C^{-1}, and the mean time from the first to the second completion is $(C/2)^{-1} = 2\ C^{-1}$. If processing is serial with a capacity of C, the mean time to the first completion is again C^{-1}. The mean time from the first to the second completion is $s + C^{-1}$, where s is the time taken to shift attention between items. Therefore, to optimize performance, processing should be serial if, and only if, $s < C^{-1}$. For example, if C^{-1} is 100 ms per item, processing should be serial if a shift of attention takes less than 100 ms.

Bundesen (1990) extended this line of reasoning and considered the time cost of shifting attention to a group of n items and then processing the n items in parallel. The time cost per member of the group was found to be least if group size n equals $C \times s$ or the smallest integer greater than $C \times s$. Numerical calculations suggested that typical data on slow feature (Treisman & Gormican, 1988) and conjunction (Treisman & Gelade, 1980) search can be explained by attention shifting among groups of display items so that processing is parallel within groups but serial between groups.

CONNECTIONIST MODELS

Formal theories like TVA are highly abstract. Connectionist models are attempts to theorize at a level that is closer to neurobiology. In connectionist models, processing is viewed as a flow of activation through a network of neuronlike units, which are linked together by facilitatory and inhibitory connections (cf. McClelland & Rumelhart, 1986; Rumelhart & McClelland, 1986). A good example of a connectionist model of visual attention is the search via recursive rejection (SERR) model of Humphreys and Müller (1993), which is described below. Other important examples are the neural network model for selective attention and pattern recognition by Fukushima (1986), the multiple object recognition and attentional selection (MORSEL) model of Mozer (1991), and the selective attention model (SLAM) of Phaf, Van der Heijden, and Hudson (1990; see also Van der Heijden, 1992).

Search via Recursive Rejection Model

The search via recursive rejection (SERR) model of Humphreys and Müller (1993) is a connectionist implementation of aspects of the theory of visual search proposed by Duncan and Humphreys (1989). According to Duncan and Humphreys, both features and conjunctions are encoded in parallel across the visual field, and both feature and conjunction search show continuous variations in efficiency depending on similarity relations between display items. Search efficiency increases with decreased similarity of target to distractors and increased similarity between distractors. In SERR, the effects are produced by grouping processes. Similar items tend to group, and members of a group are selected together. In search for a target, the groups are selected and rejected one by one (recursive rejection) until the target is found (respond present) or no items are left (respond absent; for related proposals, see Bundesen & Pedersen, 1983; Treisman, 1982).

Architecture

SERR comprises six levels of representations: retinal array, single-feature maps, combined-feature maps, map of locations, matching maps, and template (decision) units. Each map consists of units that can be in one of two states, on (1) or off (0). Stimulus displays are represented as patterns of on and off states of the units in the retinal array. Permissible stimuli are vertical or horizontal lines of a certain width and length. Units at the single-feature level are detectors for such lines at particular locations. They receive input from the retinal array through linear filters. Here, and elsewhere, the probability that a unit is on increases with its net input in accordance with a Boltzmann machine activation function (cf. Hinton & Sejnowski, 1986). The output from units at the single-feature level goes to units at the combined-feature level. These are detectors for simple conjunctions of line segments (L junctions or line terminators) at particular locations.

Location units receive input from all combined-feature units within a particular spatial area. They code whether conjunctions are present at particular spatial locations, but they do not code the identity of the conjunctions. The location units gate transfer of activation from combined-feature units to units in the match maps.

For each type of target or distractor in the stimulus, there is a match map and a template unit. Each unit in the match map samples a particular location on the combined-feature maps for evidence for or against its particular type of target or distractor. It is turned on only when it is supported by appropriate input from both the combined-feature units and its corresponding unit in the location map. Grouping is implemented in the match maps by within-map facilitatory connections and between-map inhibitory connections. Thus, coding of a particular type of target or distractor at a given location facilitates coding of the same type of item at other locations and inhibits coding of any other type of item.

The template unit for a given type of target or distractor receives a net input equal to the number of units that are on in its corresponding match map minus the number of units that are on in the other match maps. On each iteration of the network, only one of the templates is incremented, and the probability that a particular template gets the increment increases with its net input. If and when a target template reaches threshold, a positive (target-present) response is made. If a template for a type of distractors reaches threshold, the group of distractors of this type is rejected and excluded from further search. This is done by inhibiting all units in the match map corresponding to the distractor template and by disabling the location gating units at positions supported only by the inhibited match map. A negative (target-absent) response is made if and when no items are left for search and no target has been found.

Simulations

Reaction times are measured in terms of network iterations (i.e., the time it takes to update all units in the network). Simulations have been run with displays consisting of four types of items: Ts rotated either 0°, 90°, 180°, or 270° from upright. Search for an inverted T among identical Ts of one of the other three types (homogeneous displays) produces faster negative than positive responses and reaction times that are nearly independent of display size. This agrees with human performance. It comes about because the distractors form a single group, which is rapidly selected and rejected.

Search for an inverted T in displays containing all of the three remaining types of Ts (heterogeneous displays) produces another pattern of results. In this case, miss rates are very high at large display sizes. The miss rates can be reduced by including a process of error checking in the model so that negative responses require that a number of independent runs of the network have yielded negative decisions. When error checking is included, SERR simulates human performance with heterogeneous displays by generating approximately linear reaction time functions of display size with positive-to-negative slope ratios of about 1:2.

Humphreys and Müller (1993) and Müller, Humphreys, and Donnelly (1994) tested SERR's behavior with several variations of the basic task, including search for one or both of two identical targets (inverted *T*s). At a qualitative level, the results showed fair agreement with data from human subjects. It remains to be seen how robust these findings are under variations of model parameters (e.g., weights on connections) and changes in details of the architecture.

CONCLUSION

The first formal models of visual attention were the serial scanning models of Sperling, Estes, and others and the independent channels models developed by Eriksen and his colleagues. Empirical tests of the models brought important discoveries, but no simple resolution of the serial versus parallel processing issue. Some experiments provided evidence of serial or limited-capacity parallel processing, and others showed independent channels behavior. Attempts to integrate the empirical findings led to selective serial models, parallel models with differential attentional weighting (including race models of selection), and a unified theory of visual recognition and attentional selection. Attempts to theorize at a level closer to neurobiology resulted in connectionist formulations. No extant model has accounted for the full range of empirical findings, but remarkable progress has been made.

REFERENCES

Atkinson, R. C., Holmgren, J. E., & Juola, J. F. (1969). Processing time as influenced by the number of elements in a visual display. *Perception and Psychophysics, 6,* 321–326.

Averbach, E., & Coriell, A. S. (1961). Short-term memory in vision. *Bell System Technical Journal, 40,* 309–328.

Broadbent, D. E. (1970). Stimulus set and response set: Two kinds of selective attention. In D. I. Mostofsky (Ed.), *Attention: Contemporary theory and analysis* (pp. 51–60). New York: Appleton-Century-Crofts.

Bundesen, C. (1987). Visual attention: Race models for selection from multielement displays. *Psychological Research, 49,* 113–121.

Bundesen, C. (1990). A theory of visual attention. *Psychological Review, 97,* 523–547.

Bundesen, C. (1991). Visual selection of features and objects: Is location special? A reinterpretation of Nissen's (1985) findings. *Perception and Psychophysics, 50,* 87–89.

Bundesen, C. (1993a). The notion of elements in the visual field in a theory of visual attention: A reply to Van der Velde and Van der Heijden (1993). *Perception and Psychophysics, 53,* 350–352.

Bundesen, C. (1993b). The relationship between independent race models and Luce's choice axiom. *Journal of Mathematical Psychology, 37,* 446–471.

Bundesen, C., & Pedersen, L. F. (1983). Color segregation and visual search. *Perception and Psychophysics, 33,* 487–493.

Bundesen, C., Pedersen, L. F., & Larsen, A. (1984). Measuring efficiency of selection from briefly exposed visual displays: A model for partial report. *Journal of Experimental Psychology: Human Perception and Performance, 10,* 329–339.

Bundesen, C., Shibuya, H., & Larsen, A. (1985). Visual selection from multielement displays: A model for partial report. In M. I. Posner & O. S. M. Marin (Eds.), *Attention and performance XI* (pp. 631–649). Hillsdale, NJ: Erlbaum.

Cave, K. R., & Wolfe, J. M. (1990). Modeling the role of parallel processing in visual search. *Cognitive Psychology, 22,* 225–271.

Colegate, R. L., Hoffman, J. E., & Eriksen, C. W. (1973). Selective encoding from multielement visual displays. *Perception and Psychophysics, 14,* 217–224.

Czerwinski, M., Lightfoot, N., & Shiffrin, R. M. (1992). Automatization and training in visual search. *American Journal of Psychology, 105,* 271–315.

Duncan, J. (1980). The locus of interference in the perception of simultaneous stimuli. *Psychological Review, 87,* 272–300.

Duncan, J. (1981). Directing attention in the visual field. *Perception and Psychophysics, 30,* 90–93.

Duncan, J. (1983). Perceptual selection based on alphanumeric class: Evidence from partial reports. *Perception and Psychophysics, 33,* 533–547.

Duncan, J. (1984). Selective attention and the organization of visual information. *Journal of Experimental Psychology: General, 113,* 501–517.

Duncan, J. (1985). Visual search and visual attention. In M. I. Posner & O. S. M. Marin (Eds.), *Attention and performance XI* (pp. 85–105). Hillsdale, NJ: Erlbaum.

Duncan, J., & Humphreys, G. W. (1989). Visual search and stimulus similarity. *Psychological Review, 96*, 433–458.

Duncan, J., Ward, R., & Shapiro, K. (1994). Direct measurement of attentional dwell time in human vision. *Nature, 369*, 313–315.

Egeth, H., Jonides, J., & Wall, S. (1972). Parallel processing of multielement displays. *Cognitive Psychology, 3*, 674–698.

Eriksen, C. W. (1966). Independence of successive inputs and uncorrelated error in visual form perception. *Journal of Experimental Psychology, 72*, 26–35.

Eriksen, C. W., & Collins, J. F. (1964). Backward masking in vision. *Psychonomic Science, 1*, 101–102.

Eriksen, C. W., & Collins, J. F. (1965). A reinterpretation of one form of backward and forward masking in visual perception. *Journal of Experimental Psychology, 70*, 343–351.

Eriksen, C. W., & Collins, J. F. (1969). Temporal course of selective attention. *Journal of Experimental Psychology, 80*, 254–261.

Eriksen, C. W., & Lappin, J. S. (1965). Internal perceptual system noise and redundancy in simultaneous inputs in form identification. *Psychonomic Science, 2*, 351–352.

Eriksen, C. W., & Lappin, J. S. (1967). Independence in the perception of simultaneously presented forms at brief durations. *Journal of Experimental Psychology, 73*, 468–472.

Eriksen, C. W., & Spencer, T. (1969). Rate of information processing in visual perception: Some results and methodological considerations. *Journal of Experimental Psychology Monograph, 79*(2, Pt. 2).

Eriksen, C. W., & St. James, J. D. (1986). Visual attention within and around the field of focal attention: A zoom lens model. *Perception and Psychophysics, 40*, 225–240.

Eriksen, C. W., & Webb, J. M. (1989). Shifting of attentional focus within and about a visual display. *Perception and Psychophysics, 45*, 175–183.

Eriksen, C. W., & Yeh, Y. (1985). Allocation of attention in the visual field. *Journal of Experimental Psychology: Human Perception and Performance, 11*, 583–597.

Estes, W. K., & Taylor, H. A. (1964). A detection method and probabilistic models for assessing information processing from brief visual displays. *Proceedings of the National Academy of Sciences, USA, 52*, 446–454.

Estes, W. K., & Taylor, H. A. (1965). Visual detection in relation to display size and redundancy of critical elements. *Perception and Psychophysics, 1*, 9–16.

Fukushima, K. (1986). A neural network model for selective attention in visual pattern recognition. *Biological Cybernetics, 55*, 5–15.

Gardner, G. T. (1973). Evidence for independent parallel channels in tachistoscopic perception. *Cognitive Psychology, 4*, 130–155.

Hinton, G. E., & Sejnowski, T. J. (1986). Learning and relearning in Boltzmann machines. In D. E. Rumelhart & J. L. McClelland (Eds.), *Parallel distributed processing* (Vol. 1, pp. 282–317). Cambridge, MA: MIT Press.

Hoffman, J. E. (1978). Search through a sequentially presented visual display. *Perception and Psychophysics, 23*, 1–11.

Hoffman, J. E. (1979). A two-stage model of visual search. *Perception and Psychophysics, 25*, 319–327.

Humphreys, G. W., & Müller, H. J. (1993). Search via recursive rejection (SERR): A connectionist model of visual search. *Cognitive Psychology, 25*, 43–110.

Kahneman, D. (1973). *Attention and effort.* Englewood Cliffs, NJ: Prentice Hall.

Kinchla, R. A. (1974). Detecting target elements in multielement arrays: A confusability model. *Perception and Psychophysics, 15*, 149–158.

Kinchla, R. A., & Collyer, C. E. (1974). Detecting a target letter in briefly presented arrays: A confidence rating analysis in terms of a weighted additive effects model. *Perception and Psychophysics, 16*, 117–122.

Koch, C., & Ullman, S. (1985). Shifts in selective visual attention: Towards the underlying neural circuitry. *Human Neurobiology, 4*, 219–227.

Logan, G. D. (1988). Toward an instance theory of automatization. *Psychological Review, 95*, 492–527.

Logan, G. D. (1992). Attention and preattention in theories of automaticity. *American Journal of Psychology, 105*, 317–339.

Logan, G. D., & Cowan, W. B. (1984). On the ability to inhibit thought and action: A theory of an act of control. *Psychological Review, 91*, 295–327.

Logan, G. D., Cowan, W. B., & Davis, K. A. (1984). On the ability to inhibit simple and choice reaction time responses: A model and a method. *Journal of Experimental Psychology: Human Perception and Performance, 10*, 276–291.

Luce, R. D. (1959). *Individual choice behavior.* New York: Wiley.

Luce, R. D. (1963). Detection and recognition. In R. D. Luce, R. R. Bush, & E. Galanter (Eds.), *Handbook of mathematical psychology* (Vol. 1, pp. 103–189). New York: Wiley.

Luce, R. D. (1986). *Response times: Their role in inferring elementary mental organization.* New York: Oxford University Press.

Mackeben, M., & Nakayama, K. (1993). Express attentional shifts. *Vision Research, 33*, 85–90.

McClelland, J. L., & Rumelhart, D. E. (Eds.). (1986). *Parallel distributed processing* (Vol. 2). Cambridge, MA: MIT Press.

Meijers, L. M. M., & Eijkman, E. G. J. (1977). Distributions of simple RT with single and double stimuli. *Perception and Psychophysics, 22,* 41–48.

Meyer, D. E., Irwin, D. E., Osman, A. M., & Kounios, J. (1988). The dynamics of cognition and action: Mental processes inferred from speed–accuracy decomposition. *Psychological Review, 95,* 183–237.

Miller, J. (1982). Divided attention: Evidence for coactivation with redundant signals. *Cognitive Psychology, 14,* 247–279.

Mordkoff, J. T., & Egeth, H. E. (1993). Response time and accuracy revisited: Converging support for the interactive race model. *Journal of Experimental Psychology: Human Perception and Performance, 19,* 981–991.

Mordkoff, J. T., & Yantis, S. (1991). An interactive race model of divided attention. *Journal of Experimental Psychology: Human Perception and Performance, 17,* 520–538.

Mozer, M. C. (1991). *The perception of multiple objects: A connectionist approach.* Cambridge, MA: MIT Press.

Müller, H. J., Humphreys, G. W., & Donnelly, N. (1994). Search via recursive rejection (SERR): Visual search for single and dual form-conjunction targets. *Journal of Experimental Psychology: Human Perception and Performance, 20,* 235–258.

Nakayama, K., & Silverman, G. H. (1986). Serial and parallel processing of visual feature conjunctions. *Nature, 320,* 264–265.

Neisser, U. (1967). *Cognitive psychology.* New York: Appleton-Century-Crofts.

Nickerson, R. S. (1966). Response times with a memory-dependent decision task. *Journal of Experimental Psychology, 72,* 761–769.

Pashler, H. (1987). Detecting conjunctions of color and form: Reassessing the serial search hypothesis. *Perception and Psychophysics, 41,* 191–201.

Pashler, H., & Badgio, P. C. (1985). Visual attention and stimulus identification. *Journal of Experimental Psychology: Human Perception and Performance, 11,* 105–121.

Pashler, H., & Badgio, P. C. (1987). Attentional issues in the identification of alphanumeric characters. In M. Coltheart (Ed.), *Attention and performance XII: The psychology of reading* (pp. 63–81). Hillsdale, NJ: Erlbaum.

Phaf, R. H., Van der Heijden, A. H. C., & Hudson, P. T. W. (1990). SLAM: A connectionist model for attention in visual selection tasks. *Cognitive Psychology, 22,* 273–341.

Posner, M. I., & Boies, S. J. (1971). Components of attention. *Psychological Review, 78,* 391–408.

Reeves, A., & Sperling, G. (1986). Attention gating in short-term visual memory. *Psychological Review, 93*, 180–206.

Remington, R., & Pierce, L. (1984). Moving attention: Evidence for time-invariant shifts of visual selective attention. *Perception and Psychophysics, 35*, 393–399.

Rumelhart, D. E. (1970). A multicomponent theory of the perception of briefly exposed visual displays. *Journal of Mathematical Psychology, 7*, 191–218.

Rumelhart, D. E., & McClelland, J. L. (Eds.). (1986). *Parallel distributed processing* (Vol. 1). Cambridge, MA: MIT Press.

Schneider, W., & Fisk, A. D. (1982). Degree of consistent training: Improvements in search performance and automatic process development. *Perception and Psychophysics, 31*, 160–168.

Schneider, W., & Shiffrin, R. M. (1977). Controlled and automatic human information processing: I. Detection, search, and attention. *Psychological Review, 84*, 1–66.

Shaw, M. L. (1978). A capacity allocation model for reaction time. *Journal of Experimental Psychology: Human Perception and Performance, 4*, 586–598.

Shaw, M. L., & Shaw, P. (1977). Optimal allocation of cognitive resources to spatial locations. *Journal of Experimental Psychology: Human Perception and Performance, 3*, 201–211.

Shibuya, H. (1991). Comparison between stochastic models for visual selection. In J.-P. Doignon & J.-C. Falmagne (Eds.), *Mathematical psychology: Current developments* (pp. 337–356). New York: Springer-Verlag.

Shibuya, H. (1993). Efficiency of visual selection in duplex and conjunction conditions in partial report. *Perception and Psychophysics, 54*, 716–732.

Shibuya, H., & Bundesen, C. (1988). Visual selection from multielement displays: Measuring and modeling effects of exposure duration. *Journal of Experimental Psychology: Human Perception and Performance, 14*, 591–600.

Shiffrin, R. M., & Gardner, G. T. (1972). Visual processing capacity and attentional control. *Journal of Experimental Psychology, 93*, 72–82.

Shiffrin, R. M., & Geisler, W. S. (1973). Visual recognition in a theory of information processing. In R. L. Solso (Ed.), *Contemporary issues in cognitive psychology: The Loyola Symposium* (pp. 53–101). New York: Halsted Press.

Shiffrin, R. M., & Schneider, W. (1977). Controlled and automatic human information processing: II. Perceptual learning, automatic attending, and a general theory. *Psychological Review, 84*, 127–190.

Sperling, G. (1960). The information available in brief visual presentations. *Psychological Monographs, 74*(11, Whole No. 498).

41

Sperling, G. (1963). A model for visual memory tasks. *Human Factors, 5,* 19–31.

Sperling, G. (1967). Successive approximations to a model for short-term memory. *Acta Psychologica, 27,* 285–292.

Sperling, G. (1984). A unified theory of attention and signal detection. In R. Parasuraman & D. R. Davies (Eds.), *Varieties of attention* (pp. 103–181). San Diego, CA: Academic Press.

Sperling, G., Budiansky, J., Spivak, J. G., & Johnson, M. C. (1971). Extremely rapid visual search: The maximum rate of scanning letters for the presence of a numeral. *Science, 174,* 307–311.

Sperling, G., & Reeves, A. (1980). Measuring the reaction time of a shift of visual attention. In R. S. Nickerson (Ed.), *Attention and performance VIII* (pp. 347–360). Hillsdale, NJ: Erlbaum.

Sternberg, S. (1966). High-speed scanning in human memory. *Science, 153,* 652–654.

Sternberg, S. (1967, April). *Scanning a persisting visual image versus a memorized list.* Paper presented at the annual meeting of the Eastern Psychological Association, Boston.

Sternberg, S. (1969a). The discovery of processing stages: Extensions of Donders' method. *Acta Psychologica, 30,* 276–315.

Sternberg, S. (1969b). Memory-scanning: Mental processes revealed by reaction-time experiments. *American Scientist, 57,* 421–457.

Swets, J. A. (1984). Mathematical models of attention. In R. Parasuraman & D. R. Davies (Eds.), *Varieties of attention* (pp. 183–242). San Diego, CA: Academic Press.

Townsend, J. T. (1969). Mock parallel and serial models and experimental detection of these. In *Purdue Centennial Symposium on Information Processing* (pp. 617–628). Purdue University.

Townsend, J. T., & Ashby, F. G. (1983). *The stochastic modeling of elementary psychological processes.* Cambridge, England: Cambridge University Press.

Townsend, J. T., & van Zandt, T. (1990). New theoretical results on testing self-terminating vs. exhaustive processing in rapid search experiments. In H.-G. Geissler (Ed.), *Psychological explorations of mental structures* (pp. 469–489). Toronto: Hogrefe & Huber.

Treisman, A. M. (1982). Perceptual grouping and attention in visual search for features and for objects. *Journal of Experimental Psychology: Human Perception and Performance, 8,* 194–214.

Treisman, A. M. (1988). Features and objects: The fourteenth Bartlett memorial lecture. *Quarterly Journal of Experimental Psychology, 40A,* 201–237.

Treisman, A. M. (1993). The perception of features and objects. In A. Baddeley & L. Weiskrantz (Eds.), *Attention: Selection, awareness, and control* (pp. 5–35). New York: Oxford University Press.

Treisman, A. M., & Gelade, G. (1980). A feature-integration theory of attention. *Cognitive Psychology, 12,* 97–136.

Treisman, A. M., & Gormican, S. (1988). Feature analysis in early vision: Evidence from search asymmetries. *Psychological Review, 95,* 15–48.

Treisman, A. M., & Sato, S. (1990). Conjunction search revisited. *Journal of Experimental Psychology: Human Perception and Performance, 16,* 459–478.

Treisman, A. M., Sykes, M., & Gelade, G. (1977). Selective attention and stimulus integration. In S. Dornic (Ed.), *Attention and performance VI* (pp. 333–361). Hillsdale, NJ: Erlbaum.

Tsal, Y. (1983). Movements of attention across the visual field. *Journal of Experimental Psychology: Human Perception and Performance, 9,* 523–530.

Van der Heijden, A. H. C. (1992). *Selective attention in vision.* London: Routledge.

Van der Heijden, A. H. C. (1993). The role of position in object selection in vision. *Psychological Research, 56,* 44–58.

Van der Heijden, A. H. C., La Heij, W., & Boer, J. P. A. (1983). Parallel processing of redundant targets in simple visual search tasks. *Psychological Research, 45,* 235–254.

Van der Velde, F., & Van der Heijden, A. H. C. (1993). An element in the visual field is just a conjunction of attributes: A critique of Bundesen (1991). *Perception and Psychophysics, 53,* 345–349.

van Zandt, T., & Townsend, J. T. (1993). Self-terminating versus exhaustive processes in rapid visual and memory search: An evaluative review. *Perception and Psychophysics, 53,* 563–580.

Weichselgartner, E., & Sperling, G. (1987). Dynamics of automatic and controlled visual attention. *Science, 238,* 778–780.

Wolfe, J. M. (1994). Guided search 2.0: A revised model of visual search. *Psychonomic Bulletin & Review, 1,* 202–238.

Wolfe, J. M., Cave, K. R., & Franzel, S. L. (1989). Guided search: An alternative to the feature integration model for visual search. *Journal of Experimental Psychology: Human Perception and Performance, 15,* 419–433.

Wolford, G. L., Wessel, D. L., & Estes, W. K. (1968). Further evidence concerning scanning and sampling assumptions of visual detection models. *Perception and Psychophysics, 3,* 439–444.

2

Attentional Capture in Vision

Steven Yantis

Vision provides organisms with information about what is where in their environment. *Visual attention* refers to the process of selecting a portion of the available sensory information for object identification and localization. Just what is selected in any given instance depends on two major factors: (a) the properties of the scene and (b) the expectations, beliefs, and goals of the observer. Attention may be captured by an unexpected or salient visual event (a stimulus-driven or bottom-up influence), or attention may be voluntarily directed toward an object that is relevant to the observer's current goals (a goal-directed or top-down influence). In most instances, some combination of these two influences determines how attention is distributed. In this chapter, I review some current approaches to the study of visual attention, with special emphasis on the claims made about stimulus-driven and goal-directed mechanisms. Two key questions are whether attention can ever be captured in a completely stimulus-driven fashion and whether it can ever be directed in a completely goal-directed fashion. Significant theoretical disagreement surrounds these and related questions.

Preparation of this chapter was supported by Grant 92-0186 from the Air Force Office of Scientific Research and Grant R01-MH43924 from the National Institute of Mental Health. I am grateful to A. Kramer, J. Theeuwes, and especially to J. Johnston, whose comments greatly improved the chapter.

Much of the evidence concerning attentional capture was anticipated a century ago by William James (1890) in his chapter on attention in *The Principles of Psychology:*

> In *passive immediate sensorial attention* the stimulus is a sense-impression, either very intense, voluminous, or sudden,—in which case it makes no difference what its nature may be, whether sight, sound, smell, blow, or inner pain,—or else it is an *instinctive* stimulus, a perception which, by reason of its nature rather than its mere force, appears to some one of our normal congenital impulses and has a directly exciting quality. . . . [Examples include] strange things, moving things, wild animals, bright things, pretty things, metallic things, words, blows, blood, etc., etc., etc. (pp. 416–417)

Here I take James to mean that certain stimuli are salient by default, either because the brain is hardwired to attend to them or because of extensive but incidental perceptual learning during a normal observer's lifetime. James's examples of stimuli that engaged passive immediate sensorial attention were apparently based on his own intuition rather than experimental evidence. Current evidence suggests that some of these examples should be deleted from his list (e.g., motion: see Hillstrom & Yantis, 1994). One goal of this chapter is to examine the implications of recent experimental evidence for everyday conceptions of attentional capture.

ON THE AMBIGUITY OF *POP-OUT* IN VISUAL ATTENTION

Almost everyone has a strong intuition about what sorts of events capture attention. Most people would agree that salient stimuli such as a sudden movement or a bright color against a drab background tend to draw attention naturally, perhaps even involuntarily. Experimental psychologists attempt to operationalize the salience of an attribute by assessing how efficiently an object with that attribute can be detected or identified in a standard laboratory task such as visual search. It is well known, for example, that a target stimulus that differs substantially from nontargets in a dimension such as color or orientation can be found rapidly and accurately in visual search. It is implicitly but widely assumed that visual salience defined this way entails attentional capture.

One embodiment of this implicit assumption is the term *pop-out*. The origins of this term are shrouded in the mists of the 1960s and 1970s, and the meanings conveyed by it are just as vague. At least two distinct readings of the term can be discerned: According to one meaning, perceptual *pop-out* refers to any stimulus that can be detected efficiently in visual search tasks. Efficient detection is often indexed by the relative independence of response time (RT) and the number of elements to be searched in multielement visual search tasks (or by minimal effects of perceptual load on accuracy).[1] This is a straightforward, empirical definition of the term, corresponding to what might be called *conspicuity*.

A second meaning is often conflated with the first: According to this meaning, *pop-out* refers to stimuli that capture attention automatically, without intention, in a purely bottom-up fashion (e.g., Bravo & Nakayama, 1992; Koch & Ullman, 1985; Nothdurft, 1993). The subjective impression one has in searching for stimuli that satisfy the first definition of pop-out is that the stimulus is immediately and effortlessly manifest, and this subjective impression is at least in part responsible for the implicit second meaning of the term.

However, these two meanings of *pop-out* are different, even though authors sometimes write as if they are the same. Most experiments establishing that an element can be efficiently selected in visual search do not provide any evidence one way or the other about whether it captures attention in a bottom-up fashion. This is because in most such experiments, the salient element is explicitly the target of search.

In this chapter, a stimulus is said to be "salient" if it can be detected efficiently in visual search (e.g., as indexed by a display-size function with a near-zero slope) and also creates a subjective sense of conspicuity (see footnote 1). Salience so defined does not imply automaticity or lack of intention. The expression "stimulus-driven attentional capture" is reserved for events in which attention is drawn to a perceptual object that is not explicitly related to the observer's perceptual goals or intentions. In my view, an event cannot be said to capture attention in this sense if that event was part of the observer's deliberate state of attentional readiness.[2] For ex-

---

[1]Certain stimuli satisfy this criterion (e.g., triple conjunction targets as studied by Wolfe, Cave, and Franzel, 1989) but would not be said to "pop out" in standard usage. The term *pop-out* seems to require a subjective sense of effortless detection that goes beyond objective measurements such as shallow search slope.

[2]There is not universal agreement concerning this point. For a discussion, see the exchange between Yantis (1993b) and Folk, Remington, and Johnston (1993).

ample, a target element that is merely salient (e.g., a vertical red target appearing among tilted blue nontargets) cannot be said to capture attention because the vertical red bar, as target, was central to the observer's deliberate attentional set. Further experimentation (in which red is an irrelevant stimulus attribute) would be required before it could be determined whether the vertical red bar did in fact *capture* attention. Yantis and Egeth (1994) have carried out this experiment and found that when a highly salient attribute like a red element in a background of blue elements is known to be task irrelevant, it does not draw attention (this and related results are discussed in more detail later).

The term *pop-out*, then, has two different meanings—salience and capture—that should remain separate. Given this ambiguity, authors would do well to avoid it and instead use terms that more clearly convey their intended meaning.

ATTENTION ALLOCATION THROUGH SPATIAL CUES

In the late 1960s, C. W. Eriksen and his students began a seminal series of studies concerned with subjects' abilities to direct attention to locations in space (e.g., Colegate, Hoffman, & Eriksen, 1973; Eriksen & Collins, 1969; Eriksen & Hoffman, 1972a, 1972b, 1973). In the experiments, subjects were required to identify a letter that had been spatially cued by a bar marker presented in advance of or simultaneously with an array of several letters. The experiments had several goals, including elucidation of the time course of attention allocation, examination of the extent to which to-be-ignored stimuli could in fact be ignored, and assessment of the spatial extent of the attentional window. These studies led to an explosion of research in spatial attention both because of the experimental paradigms that Eriksen and colleagues introduced and because of the questions that they posed.

Among the issues that aroused the greatest interest was the extent to which the cue itself could be said to capture attention automatically. A natural distinction arose between indirect cues (often called central or symbolic cues) and direct cues (often called peripheral cues).[3] Indirect cues require some kind of interpretation (e.g., assess the orientation of an arrowhead and then direct attention to the indicated location), which is by definition top-down and controlled, whereas direct cues call attention to themselves or their local neighborhood without the need for additional interpretation.

One of the earliest studies to compare the effects of the two cue types was reported by Jonides (1981). Observers were required to identify a letter (press the left button if an *L* was present in the display and the right button if an *R* was present) that appeared in one of eight locations defined on the circumference of an imaginary circle several degrees of visual angle in radius. In advance of the letter display, an arrowhead appeared indicating a location within the array. When the cue indicated the location of the target (*L* or *R*), it was said to be *valid;* when it indicated a location occupied by a nontarget, it was said to be *invalid.* Two types of cues were used: an (indirect) central cue that appeared at fixation (and therefore appeared more than 3° of visual angle away from the indicated location), and a (direct) peripheral cue that appeared immediately adjacent to the indicated location. Jonides argued that the two cues had qualitatively different effects on attention: The central cue required a voluntary and effortful redistribution of attention to the indicated location, whereas the peripheral cue automatically captured attention, and this capture was resistant to suppression.

Experiment 2 of Jonides (1981) illustrated the resistance to suppression. In this experiment, the cues were valid on just 12.5% of the trials (i.e., with 8 display locations, the cue position was random and therefore had no predictive value). Subjects were divided into two groups: The "attend" group was instructed to use the cue to deliberately direct attention to the cued location on each trial; the "ignore" group was told that the cue validity was at chance and that they should therefore ignore the cue if possible. The results were clear: There was a substantial effect of cue validity for both indirect and direct cues in the attend group (i.e., responses were faster and more accurate for valid-cue than for invalid-cue trials); in contrast, although subjects in the ignore group produced no effect of cue va-

---

[3]The distinction between *central* and *peripheral* cues has been confusing. Some authors use these terms to refer to the locations in the visual display occupied by the cue; other authors use them to refer to the presumed attentional locus at which the two types of cues have their effects. In the latter usage, a central (symbolic) cue is used to direct attention to a location other than that occupied by the cue itself, whereas a peripheral cue attracts attention to itself. Of course, it could easily be the case that a cue appearing in the visual periphery directs attention elsewhere. To avoid confusion, the terms *central* and *peripheral* are used only to refer to the spatial location of a cue; the terms *indirect* and *direct* are used to refer to the functional properties of the cue, as described in the text.

lidity at all for indirect (central) cues, valid direct (peripheral) cues still produced faster RTs than invalid direct cues did. These results strongly suggest that direct cues cannot easily be ignored even when they are known to be irrelevant to the task. This represents a strong form of attentional capture.

Remington, Johnston, and Yantis (1992) extended this result in experiments designed to maximize subjects' incentive to ignore a peripheral cue. Subjects were required to identify a target character appearing in one of four boxes surrounding fixation. A salient peripheral cue surrounded one of the boxes on each trial. In some trial blocks, the cue always appeared at the target's location (*SAME* blocks); in other blocks, the cue always appeared at a different location (*DIF* blocks). Subjects were strongly encouraged to ignore the cue in DIF blocks if possible, because it would never coincide with the target location. This manipulation was stronger than that used by Jonides (1981): In his Experiment 2, the cue did occasionally indicate the target location, and so there was no incentive for subjects to actively ignore the cue. In the experiments of Remington et al. (1992), the incentive to ignore the cue was strong and explicit. Nevertheless, subjects were clearly unable to ignore the cue: RT in DIF blocks was always slower than in SAME blocks.

Many additional experiments have been carried out to assess the relative effectiveness of direct and indirect cues in the allocation of attention. Müller and Rabbitt (1989) measured identification and localization accuracy for a briefly flashed rotated *T* as a function of its position relative to a central arrow cue and a peripheral box brightening. The indirect central cue provided useful information about the location of the upcoming target and presumably elicited a deliberate shift of attention to the indicated location. Like Jonides (1981), Müller and Rabbitt found that the indirect peripheral cue was resistant to suppression when it was known to be irrelevant. In addition, they found that the time courses of the facilitation and inhibition produced by the two types of cue were different: Direct cues produced effects that occurred earlier and dissipated with time, whereas indirect cues produced effects that peaked later and remained strong for a fairly long time. On the basis of these and other results, Müller and Rabbitt (1989) concluded that there are two separate attentional mechanisms: a reflexive mechanism that is triggered by a peripheral display change (although it is not clear that the display change must be peripheral to have this effect), and a voluntary mechanism that requires a deliberate effort on the part of the observer and that can be voluntarily halted or involuntarily interrupted by an automatic attention response.

This conclusion was echoed by Nakayama and Mackeben (1989). In their experiments, observers searched for a conjunctively defined target (vertical and horizontal black and white bars) appearing in an array of up to 64 elements presented briefly and then masked. A small square surrounded the location that would eventually contain the target at various moments in time before the test array appeared (this duration was called the cue-lead time). Accuracy was measured as a function of cue-lead time: It increased to a maximum at a cue-lead time of about 150–200 ms and then declined to an asymptotic but above-chance level. Nakayama and Mackeben argued that this pattern reflected the operation of two distinct attentional mechanisms. One is a sustained component that depends on a deliberate intent on the part of the subject to direct attention to the cued location; this component increases monotonically with time to a moderate level and remains there. The second is a transient component that is automatically summoned[4] to the cued location when the cue has an abrupt onset; facilitation due to this component increases rapidly and then dissipates completely within a few hundred ms. When the two components are superimposed, the obtained pattern of performance emerges. Using a somewhat different task, Cheal and Lyon (1991) came to a similar conclusion.

These studies suggest that there may be two separable mechanisms that control the locus of attention. That they are separate is suggested by the fact that they exhibit different time courses (the bottom-up or transient component has a fast rise and fall, and the top-down or sustained component has a slower rise followed by a steady state) and one appears to require intention and effort but the other does not.

In an effort to determine the relative effectiveness of attentional capture by a direct cue and deliberate attention allocation via an indirect cue, Yantis and Jonides (1990) placed the two types of stimuli into competition. In their Experiment 2, for example, an array of four letters appeared

---

[4]Nakayama and Mackeben (1989) assumed that the transient component is not subject to voluntary control, although their experiments did not test this assumption directly, because the cue was always known to indicate a task-relevant location, and so subjects were always motivated to deliberately attend to the cue.

on each trial, and observers were to determine whether an *E* or an *H* was present and press a corresponding key. Within each array, one letter appeared with an abrupt visual onset in a previously blank location, and the remaining letters appeared in previously occupied locations, and so did not exhibit an abrupt onset (I say more about this procedure in a later section). The onset letters served the role in this experiment of a direct cue. The position of the target was uncorrelated with the position of the onset letter; even so, previous experiments had shown that such onset stimuli capture visual attention. Added to this procedure was a central arrowhead cue, which always correctly indicated the position that was to be occupied by the target letter. Subjects were informed of this contingency and encouraged to focus attention on the indicated location if possible. The indirect central cue appeared either 200 ms before the letters, simultaneously with them, or 200 ms after the letters appeared. The first of these three conditions provided enough time to focus attention on the cued location in advance, but the second and third did not.

Two possible outcomes were of particular interest. First, if onset stimuli capture attention in a purely bottom-up fashion regardless of the subject's state of attentional readiness, then RT to identify the target should be faster when the cued target happens to be the onset letter than when the onset letter appears elsewhere in the array, even when attention has been focused in advance on the target. However, if focusing attention can prevent capture by abrupt onset, then RTs should not be influenced by the location of the onset stimulus when attention has been effectively focused in advance. The results were consistent with the latter possibility: RT when the target happened to be an onset letter was the same as when the target was a no-onset letter (and the onset was elsewhere), but only when attention was focused in advance. In contrast, when attention could not be focused in advance, there was a substantial RT advantage for onset targets. This result reveals that when attention is focused in advance, an abrupt visual onset does not capture attention in a strongly stimulus-driven fashion. Koshino, Warner, and Juola (1992) and Theeuwes (1991b, 1995) have replicated and extended this finding.

The experiments reviewed in this section suggest that cues requiring some form of interpretation to direct attention have effects that are clearly distinct from cues that attract attention directly. They differ in their time course (slow and monotonically increasing effects vs. rapid and single peaked effects) and in their relative effectiveness (cues that are used to deliberately guide focused attention apparently can override attentional capture by stimuli that would otherwise capture attention).

SINGLETONS, PARALLEL SEARCH, AND ATTENTIONAL CAPTURE

In the last section, I reviewed evidence concerning the attentional consequences of a spatial cue. A cue, by definition, is not itself a to-be-reported stimulus but an indicator the only purpose of which is to direct attention (intentionally or not). In this section, I review studies that examine the attentional effects of various stimulus attributes that are not distinct visual events but features of the to-be-reported stimuli themselves. The focus will be on stimuli with salient visual features that can efficiently guide attention. I use Pashler's (1988) term "feature singleton" to refer to a stimulus that differs substantially from nearby stimuli along one or more feature dimensions.[5] For example, in an array of vertical blue bars, a single vertical red bar would be a singleton (as would a horizontal blue bar, a horizontal red bar, or a blue circle).

Visual Search for Features

It has been known for a long time that feature singletons are easy to find in visual search. Neisser (1967) found that targets were rapidly and accurately detected in visual search when they were dissimilar to nontargets in shape (e.g., locating Cs and Os among Es and Hs). Egeth, Jonides, and Wall (1972) showed that detecting the presence of a 4 among Cs or vice versa was very efficient: RTs to detect a shape singleton did not increase

---

[5]A featural singleton is an element that has a feature value within a perceptual dimension that is locally unique (e.g., a red element in a background of blue elements, or a vertical bar in a field of tilted bars). The extent to which an element can be considered a singleton in some dimension is an increasing function of the difference between the singleton feature value and the neighboring values in that dimension (contributing to local feature contrast; Nothdurft, 1993), and of the similarity between the nonsingleton feature values in the relevant dimension (contributing to perceptual grouping of the background elements; Duncan & Humphreys, 1989). A singleton need not be the only element with the property in question within the entire visual field (although in many studies it is unique); it is only necessary that it be sufficiently different from its neighbors to be locally disparate.

with display size, as they would in a search for, say, a rotated *T* among rotated *Ls*. Egeth et al. (1972) characterized such searches as reflecting the operation of an array of independent parallel channels, each of which is capable of yielding a "target-present" response.

Later, Treisman and Gelade (1980) incorporated the finding that unique visual features can be detected without display size effects into their feature integration theory of visual attention. According to the theory, multidimensional stimuli are initially represented within a set of independent feature maps, each coding the locations of objects that contain a given feature (e.g., there might be a set of color maps each representing a different hue, and a set of orientation maps each representing a different orientation, etc.). According to the theory, subjects determine whether a feature singleton is present by monitoring the relevant feature map for any activation. Because a singleton target is present if and only if there is any activation in the relevant feature map, this strategy can be carried out "in parallel" and therefore very efficiently. (Note that Treisman and Gelade did not suggest that feature singletons *capture* attention; the mechanism by which efficient search was carried out required a deliberate strategy to monitor a map.) This strategy stands in contrast to that required when the target is defined as a conjunction of two or more features; in this case, it is necessary to attend serially to locations in the display to ensure that the relevant features are present within the same visual object.

Thus, there is good evidence that targets differing from their background according to a simple feature are efficiently detected in visual search. However, as I stated earlier, this fact is not sufficient to conclude that such targets capture attention. Nevertheless, it has become increasingly common for authors to implicitly assume that feature singletons do capture attention in a purely bottom-up way. The term *pop-out* itself has promoted this assumption by implying animation on the part of the object independent of any intent on the part of the observer.

Do Feature Singletons Capture Attention?

To determine whether feature singletons do indeed capture attention, Jonides and Yantis (1988) carried out an experiment in which the effect of salient singletons that were not part of the observer's attentional set was measured. Three groups of subjects carried out slightly different versions of the experiment. In all three cases, the primary task was the same: to search for a target letter in an array of distractor letters. In each trial of the experiment, one of the letters in the stimulus array was different from all the others in one of three ways. For one group of subjects, the singleton was red and the nonsingletons were green (or vice versa for half the subjects); in a second group, the singleton was bright and the nonsingletons were dim; and in the third group, the singleton had an abrupt onset and the nonsingletons did not have an abrupt onset. In all cases, the position of the singleton was uncorrelated with the position of the target and therefore contained no useful information about where the target would be.

If feature singletons capture attention, then we would expect RTs on trials in which the target coincided with the singleton to be faster than those in which it did not. However, in the color and brightness groups there was no difference between these two types of trials, suggesting that those singletons did not capture attention when they were known to be irrelevant. In contrast, the onset singletons did capture attention; among other things, this result ensured that the experiment was sensitive enough to detect capture had it occurred. Recently, Hillstrom and Yantis (1994) and Yantis and Egeth (1994) have replicated and extended this finding using highly salient motion and color singletons and using simpler oriented bar stimuli. Folk and Annett (1994) asked whether capture would occur if the feature gradient was steeper (they increased local color contrast), and came to the same conclusion: In general, a salient singleton does not capture attention when it is irrelevant to the subject's task.

Attentional Control in Singleton Detection

There have been several recent studies suggesting that under certain conditions feature singletons do appear to capture attention. For example, Theeuwes (1992) carried out several experiments in which observers were required to determine the orientation of a line segment (horizontal or vertical) appearing inside one of several colored forms (diamonds or circles) arranged on the circumference of an imaginary circle centered at fixation. On each trial, the target line was enclosed within a form that differed from all the others in shape or color. For example, the top of Figure 1 depicts a condition in which the target always appeared inside a circle, and diagonal nontarget line segments appeared inside diamonds. On half the trials (the no-distractor condition), all the shapes in the array were green;

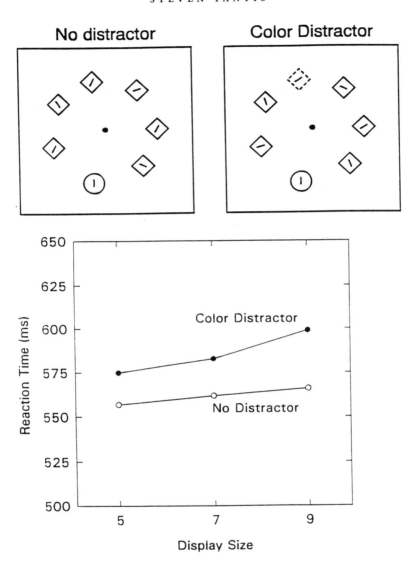

Figure 1

Experiment 1A in Theeuwes (1992). Top: A vertical or horizontal bar always appeared within a green circle (shape singleton). On the left, all the diamonds are green (solid lines); on the right, one of the diamonds is red (dashed lines). Subjects were to press one key if the bar was vertical and another if it was horizontal. Bottom: The presence of the color distractor slowed discrimination times even when it was known to be irrelevant. From "Perceptual Selectivity for Color and Form," by J. Theeuwes, 1992, *Perception and Psychophysics*, *51*, p. 601. Copyright 1992 by the Psychonomic Society, Inc. Adapted with permission.

on the remaining trials (the color-distractor condition), a known, irrelevant color singleton (a red diamond, depicted with dashed lines) was present. The task therefore required subjects to detect the form singleton and judge the orientation of the line segment it contained and to ignore the color singleton when it was present.

Theeuwes (1992) found that the presence of the to-be-ignored color singleton increased RT significantly (Figure 1, bottom). He interpreted this finding as follows: When observers engage in parallel visual search, attention is initially distributed over the visual field; regions of the display containing large local feature differences will then capture attention without regard for the dimension in which the feature contrast occurs. According to this view, a global feature-contrast detector guides attention, and the salience of the singleton, but not its identity, determines the feature to which attention is drawn. It is important to keep in mind that this is not strictly a case of stimulus-driven attentional capture, because the observer has adopted a specific strategy to direct attention according to the output of the feature-contrast detector.

Pashler (1988, Experiment 6) reported very similar results. Subjects looked for a circle target among tilted bars or vice versa. All the elements in the display were the same color (either red or green on any given trial) with the following exception: Within some blocks of trials, two elements in known, fixed positions were rendered in the other color. The target was therefore defined as a form singleton, and on each trial in the critical blocks, there were two irrelevant color singletons. When the identity of the target was not known before the trial, the presence of an irrelevant color singleton reduced the accuracy with which subjects could report the location of the form singleton. These and other experiments strongly suggest that when the target in visual search is defined as a feature singleton, then even singletons known to be irrelevant may draw attention (Folk, Remington, & Johnston, 1992, Experiment 4; Theeuwes, 1991a).

Bacon and Egeth (1994) have recently argued that the critical feature of experiments demonstrating that to-be-ignored singletons can capture attention is that the subject adopt a strategy that they call *singleton-detection mode*. Bacon and Egeth speculated that an irrelevant singleton might not capture attention when the task leads the observer to adopt a different strategy. To test this idea, Bacon and Egeth carried out several experiments modeled after those of Theeuwes (1992). In their Experiment

2, for example, several instances of the target feature were present in the display, rather than just one; in this version of the task, subjects could not enter singleton-detection mode to find the target, because the relevant attribute (e.g., red) was no longer a singleton. In this case, the presence of an irrelevant singleton (e.g., a circle among diamonds) did not disrupt performance, and therefore Bacon and Egeth concluded that it did not capture attention. In Experiment 3, there was always one instance of the target shape, but now the nontargets were heterogeneous, and so the target shape was no longer a singleton. Again, the presence of a color singleton distractor did not slow search, showing that such singletons do not capture attention unless subjects enter singleton-detection mode.

Folk et al. (1992) have set out a general framework for characterizing the interaction between what they call the observer's attentional control setting and the properties of the stimuli in the display. Their main point is that whether a given stimulus attribute will capture attention depends on what the observer is set to perceive in a given situation. To illustrate this idea, consider their Experiment 3 (Figure 2). Observers saw a fixation display, followed by a cue display and then a target display. They were required to decide whether the target on each trial was an *x* or an equal sign (=). Targets were defined in one of two ways: a *color target* was defined as the single red element in the display (the nontargets were white); an *onset target* was the only stimulus in the display (and therefore was uniquely characterized by abrupt onset). A cue display appeared 150 ms before the onset of the target display. Two types of cues were used: A *color cue* consisted of an array of four red dots surrounding one of the four potential target locations (all other locations were surrounded by white dots); an *onset cue* consisted of four white dots surrounding a potential target location, and the remaining locations remained bare. The two cue types were factorially combined with the two target types. Furthermore, within any given block of trials, the cues either corresponded on every trial to the location of the upcoming target (valid blocks) or corresponded on every trial to a nontarget location (invalid blocks). The question, then, was the extent to which subjects were able to suppress attentional capture by the cue in the invalid blocks as a function of the type of target (which defined the attentional control setting) and the type of cue.

The results (illustrated in Figure 3) were quite clear. When the cue and target were of the same type, then cue validity had a substantial effect on

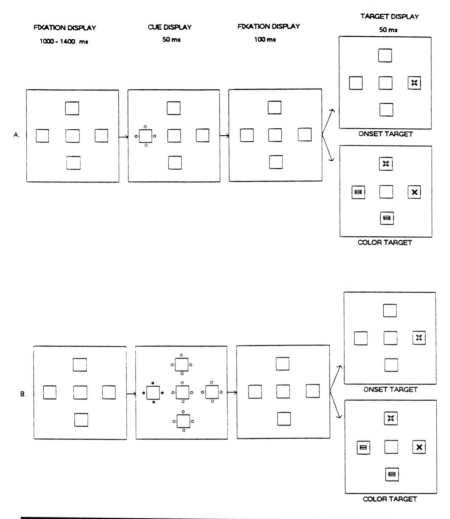

Figure 2

Procedure used by Folk, Remington, and Johnston (1992). On each trial subjects were to press one key if the target was an equal sign (=) and another key if it was an *x*. The target was defined as the only stimulus in the display (onset target) or as the uniquely colored element in the display (color target). Top: Onset cue condition. Bottom: Color cue condition. See text for details. From "Involuntary Covert Orienting Is Contingent on Attentional Control Settings," by C. L. Folk, R. W. Remington, and J. C. Johnston, 1992, *Journal of Experimental Psychology: Human Perception and Performance, 18*, p. 1033. Copyright 1992 by the American Psychological Association. Reprinted with permission of the author.

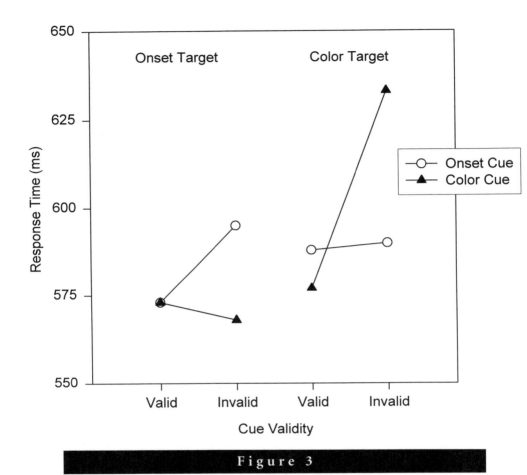

Figure 3

Results from Experiment 3 of Folk, Remington, and Johnston (1992). From "Involuntary Covert Orienting Is Contingent on Attentional Control Settings," by C. L. Folk, R. W. Remington, and J. C. Johnston, 1992, *Journal of Experimental Psychology: Human Perception and Performance, 18*, p. 1038. Copyright 1992 by the American Psychological Association. Reprinted with permission of the author.

RT, but when the cue and target were of different types, then cue validity had virtually no effect. This result suggests that when observers adopt an attentional control setting for a particular color singleton, then any color, even ones that are known to be irrelevant (i.e., the invalid color cues) capture attention. However, if the attentional control setting is for color, then noncolor events such as abrupt visual onsets do not draw attention. Experiment 4 of Folk et al. (1992) revealed that a green cue (i.e., one whose color did not match that of the red target) captured attention as well as the red cue had in their previous experiments. This corroborates the findings of Theeuwes (1992) that an irrelevant singleton that is not identical to the target's defining attribute can draw attention.

Folk et al. (1992) found that performance was not disrupted when color targets were preceded by irrelevant onset cues and vice versa, but they also found that green cues disrupt red targets, and Theeuwes (1992) reported that color singletons capture attention when form singletons are the targets of search. These findings led Folk et al. to speculate that there might be a basic distinction between static and dynamic discontinuities such that if one enters singleton-detection mode for a static discontinuity (e.g., a shape or color singleton), then any static singleton will capture attention but that if one is searching for a dynamic discontinuity (e.g., an abrupt onset singleton), then any dynamic discontinuity will capture attention. To test this hypothesis, Folk, Remington, and Wright (1994) performed several experiments modeled after those of Folk et al. (1992) using onset, color, and motion discontinuities. They found that when observers were set for motion or onset targets, then onset and motion cues interfered, but color cues did not; the reverse was also true. This result is consistent with the hypothesis they proposed.[6]

Theeuwes (1994) has contested the claim that static and dynamic discontinuities are handled separately by the attentional mechanism. Using a standard visual search task without cues, he found that when the target was defined by onset, then the presence of a to-be-ignored color singleton disrupted performance, and when the target was defined as a color singleton, then a to-be-ignored onset singleton disrupted performance. Theeuwes concluded that capture by any singleton is possible given that one is in singleton-detection mode. According to this view, there is no fundamental difference between static and dynamic discontinuities; the key determinant is the relative salience of the singleton elements. Additional work is currently under way in several laboratories to clarify these apparently conflicting outcomes.

---

[6]The position advocated by Folk, Remington, and Johnston (1992) was somewhat stronger than suggested in the text. They asserted that attentional capture is *always* contingent on the deliberate adoption of an appropriate attentional set. Yantis (1993b) argued that this is not the case for abrupt onsets. See Folk, Remington, and Johnston (1993) for a reply.

Summary of Singleton Studies

Together, these studies suggest that irrelevant singletons, although easy to detect (Egeth et al., 1972; Neisser, 1967; Treisman & Gelade, 1980), do not generally capture attention (Folk & Annett, 1994; Hillstrom & Yantis, 1994; Jonides & Yantis, 1988; Yantis & Egeth, 1994). An important exception arises when the target of search is itself a feature singleton, in which case subjects apparently enter singleton-detection mode (Bacon & Egeth, 1994). In that case, irrelevant singletons may capture attention. Folk et al. (1992, 1994) claimed that the specific nature of the attentional control setting one adopts determines what kinds of singletons will involuntarily draw attention: If the target is a static singleton (e.g., a color or form singleton), then any static singleton will capture attention; If the target is a dynamic singleton (e.g., a motion or onset singleton), then any dynamic singleton will capture attention. Theeuwes (1992, 1994) claimed instead that when searching for a singleton, the most salient singleton in the display (static or dynamic) will capture attention. In either case, however, the evidence suggests that an attentional set for a feature singleton can cause even an irrelevant singleton to be attended.

ABRUPT VISUAL ONSETS, NEW PERCEPTUAL OBJECTS, AND ATTENTIONAL CAPTURE

The studies reviewed in the last section led to the conclusion that attention is not captured by even highly salient feature singletons unless observers have adopted an appropriate state of attentional readiness (i.e., singleton-detection mode). One might ask whether any stimulus attribute can be said to capture attention in the strict sense that I outlined at the beginning of the chapter. In other words, are there stimuli that will draw attention even when they are not part of the observer's explicit state of attentional readiness?

A series of experiments carried out in my laboratory has explored the hypothesis that the abrupt appearance of a new perceptual object may capture attention under these conditions. These studies were initially motivated by speculation that abrupt visual onsets may subserve bottom-up visual orienting (e.g., Breitmeyer & Ganz, 1976; Todd & Van Gelder, 1979). Later studies led us to the conclusion that abrupt onsets capture attention by virtue of their status as new perceptual objects, and not merely because they coincide with localized luminance increments. In this section, I review the evidence for these conclusions.

Abrupt Visual Onsets and Attentional Capture

Yantis and Jonides (1984) adopted a technique introduced by Todd and Van Gelder (1979) to examine the attentional effects of abrupt onsets compared with stimuli that do not have abrupt onsets (see Figure 4, top). Each trial began with a display of figure-eight placeholders like those seen on a digital clock. After 1 s, some of the line segments in each figure eight were removed to reveal a letter. Letters so revealed are called no-onset stimuli because they are present but camouflaged long before they are available for identification. Thus, no abrupt onset accompanies their appearance. These are contrasted with onset stimuli, letters that appear in previously blank locations. In Yantis and Jonides (1984), subjects engaged in visual search with display sizes of 2 and 4; the target letter was specified before each trial, and subjects were to press one key as quickly as possible if the target was present and another key if it was absent (the probability that the target was present was fixed at .5). On each trial, one of the stimuli was an onset letter, and the rest were no-onset letters. The position of the target was always completely uncorrelated with the position of the onset, so there was no incentive to deliberately attend to the onset stimulus.

Results from a version of this experiment carried out by Jonides and Yantis (1988) are shown at the bottom of Figure 4. RTs when the target happened to be the onset stimulus were uniformly fast and unaffected by display size. In contrast, when the target was one of the no-onset stimuli, RT increased with display size, and the target-absent slope was about twice the target-present slope. These results suggest that the onset element was identified first during search, and the number of no-onset elements that were present in these conditions was irrelevant.

Because the no-onset letters appeared in locations previously occupied by the figure-eight placeholders, it was possible that the effects observed in Figure 4 were caused by nonattentional factors. For example, the placeholders might have masked the letters and thereby slowed their identification. To ensure that the outcome of this experiment could be attributed to attentional factors, Yantis and Jonides (1984) carried out a control experiment in which observers were shown only one letter and were

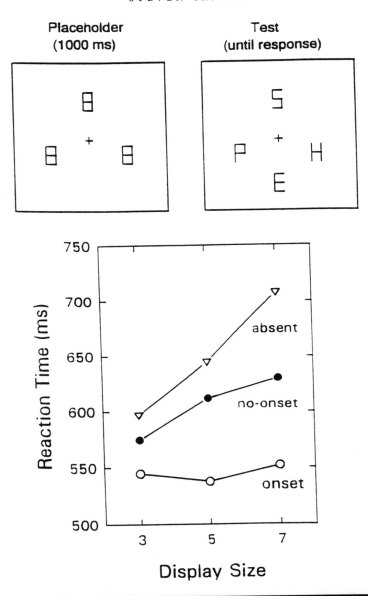

Figure 4

Top: Procedure used by Yantis and Jonides (1984; Jonides & Yantis, 1988). A placeholder array of 7-segment figure eights was displayed for 1 s, followed by a test display of letters. One letter appeared in a previously blank location (the onset letter is an *E* in this example); the remaining letters were revealed by removing a subset of the line segments in the figure eights (the no-onset letters are H, P, and S in this example). Subjects were to deter-

asked to press one of two buttons according to its identity. The letter was shown in the periphery while subjects remained centrally fixated. On each trial, the subject knew precisely where the letter was going to appear: On no-onset trials, the position of the upcoming letter was indicated by the position of the figure-eight placeholder; onset trials began with an array of six dots placed at the vertices of an imaginary figure eight located where the letter would appear. In both cases, observers were instructed to direct their attention to the indicated location in advance of the letter's appearance while remaining fixated. This experiment thus eliminated any difference between onset and no-onset letters that could be attributed to attention; any remaining difference in identification time would then have to be attributed to nonattentional factors. No such difference was observed: Identification of no-onset letters was 10 ms *faster* than identification of onset letters.

The experiments of Yantis and Jonides (1984) involved the appearance of just one abrupt onset in a visual scene; Yantis and Johnson (1990) asked what the attentional consequences were of several simultaneous abrupt onsets. Consider an experiment in which half the elements had abrupt onsets and the remaining elements did not. Several possible outcomes could occur: (a) The presence of more than one onset element might serve to "cancel out" the priority enjoyed by a unique onset element, under the assumption that attention could not be split among more than one element. (b) One of the onset elements might capture attention, with all the remaining onset and no-onset elements receiving equivalent (secondary) priority. (c) All the onset elements might have absolute priority over all the no-onset elements.

To test these various outcomes, subjects engaged in a visual search task with display sizes of 4, 6, 8, and 12 (Experiment 2) and 6, 8, 12, and 16 (Experiment 3). On each trial, half the elements were onsets and half were no-onsets. The target was equally likely to be an onset or a no-onset element. RTs were recorded as a function of display size and whether the target was an onset or a no-onset element.

---

mine whether a prespecified letter was present in the array by pressing one key if it was present and another if it was absent. Bottom: Results from the onset condition in Experiment 1 of Jonides and Yantis (1988). Data are from "Uniqueness of Abrupt Visual Onset in Capturing Attention," by J. Jonides and S. Yantis, 1988, *Perception and Psychophysics, 43,* p. 350. Copyright 1988 by the Psychonomic Society, Inc. Adapted with permission.

Yantis and Johnson (1990) found that responses to onset targets were faster than those to no-onset targets, which rules out Alternative A above: Onsets exhibited higher priority than no-onset letters. Alternative B predicts that the onset and no-onset functions will be parallel to one another, with the intercept difference due to the fact that one of the onset elements is always identified first during search, and sometimes that element is the target. The data also ruled out this possibility, because the onset and no-onset functions significantly deviated from parallelism. According to Alternative C, all the onset elements are identified first, followed by all the no-onset elements; this predicts that the onset and no-onset functions should diverge monotonically for all display sizes. The results also ruled out this possibility: There was divergence for display sizes up to eight, and then the two functions were parallel. Yantis and Johnson (1990, Appendix A) derived predictions for a fourth alternative, according to which a limited number of onset elements are identified first in search, followed by the remaining onset and no-onset elements in random order. According to this alternative, the onset and no-onset functions should diverge up to some critical display size, and then they should be parallel. The critical display size provides an estimate of twice the number of onset elements that exhibited attentional priority. The data from all the experiments reported by Yantis and Johnson (1990) were consistent with this account, and the estimated number of onset elements with priority was four.

Two possible mechanisms can be considered for this prioritization process. According to one mechanism, there exists a queue of limited size into which elements that have tentatively been accorded attentional priority are placed. In the Yantis and Johnson (1990) experiments, a random subset of the onset elements (as many as four of them) would be placed in the priority queue and identified before any other element was. According to a second alternative, all high-priority elements are tagged as such, but the priority tags decay with time. Yantis and Jones (1991) performed several experiments to assess these possibilities. The logic of their experiments was to prolong the time required to identify each element; this manipulation would have no effect on the pattern of RTs according to the structural queue account, but it should reduce the estimated number of onset elements that were processed with priority according to the decaying tag account. To illustrate this approach, consider Experiment 2 of Yantis and Jones (1991). The experiment was very similar to those of

Yantis and Johnson (1990), except that all the elements in each display were visually degraded by superimposing random dots over each element.

As expected, the degradation manipulation slowed RTs overall. More important for discriminating the two accounts of attentional priority, Yantis and Jones (1991) found that the estimated number of onset elements that exhibited attentional priority was smaller in the degraded condition than in the undegraded condition. This finding held not only for the overall mean RTs but for almost every individual subject for whom the estimate changed at all. Yantis and Jones concluded that an attentional priority tag is assigned to onset elements at the start of each trial and that the strength of the tag decays with time until the strengths reach some baseline value, equivalent to the priority of all the no-onset elements in the array.

New Perceptual Objects and Attentional Capture

Why do abrupt visual onsets capture attention? Yantis and Jonides (1984) noted that transient channels in the visual system (which are now associated with the magnocellular pathway in the primate brain; cf. Lennie, Trevarthan, Van Essen, & Wässle, 1990) are highly sensitive to onset and motion; Breitmeyer and Ganz (1977) and others had speculated that this system may somehow mediate attentional capture. This account of attentional capture by abrupt visual onsets was termed the *luminance-increment explanation* by Yantis and Hillstrom (1994). However, there is another property of abrupt onset elements that could provide an explanation for attentional capture. By definition, abrupt onsets accompany the appearance of new perceptual objects in the visual field. It is possible that whenever the visual system has to establish a new visual object representation, a redistribution of attention to the new object is automatically triggered. This makes adaptive sense: Old objects have already been at least partially identified and categorized, but a new object may require an immediate assessment of the danger or food value it represents. Yantis and Hillstrom (1994) called this second account the *new-object explanation.* It was motivated in part by recent object-based theories of visual attention (e.g., Duncan, 1984; Kahneman, Treisman, & Gibbs, 1992; Kanwisher & Driver, 1992). According to these theories, attention is allocated in a visual scene not just to locations, but to perceptual object representations created preattentively by early perceptual organization mechanisms. It is plausible to believe that the creation of a new object representation typically has significant consequences for the organism, and this made the new-object explanation appear to be worth exploring.

All of the onset experiments described so far completely confound these two accounts for why onsets capture attention: The onset elements include a luminance increment and create a new perceptual object. Yantis and Hillstrom (1994) carried out a series of experiments designed to remove this confounding and determine which explanation can better account for the results. Their experiments were virtually identical to those reported by Yantis and Jonides (1984), except that the letter stimuli were defined by equiluminant discontinuities in texture, motion, or binocular disparity. For example, the disparity-defined stimuli consisted of a field of random dots viewed through a pair of goggles configured with liquid crystal shutters over each eye. The shutters were synchronized with the frames of the computer monitor so that the right and left eyes viewed alternate frames of the display. These frames contained elements (figure eights and letters) that differed from the background only in binocular disparity (the elements appeared to float in front of the background texture). This procedure eliminated the luminance-increment difference between onset and no-onset elements and allowed an assessment of whether a new object, even when not accompanied by a luminance increment, captures attention.

Yantis and Hillstrom (1994) found that RTs to new-object targets were significantly faster and increased significantly less with display size than did RTs to old-object targets. They concluded that the appearance of a new perceptual object is sufficient to capture visual attention even without a luminance increment, which is consistent with the new-object explanation for attentional capture by abrupt onsets.

A final experiment provides corroboration for the new-object explanation. Earlier in this chapter, I alluded to experiments carried out by Hillstrom and Yantis (1994) revealing that when an observer engages in visual search for a difficult-to-find form (a rotated *T* among rotated *L*s), then the presence of irrelevant motion at one stimulus location does not interfere with performance. In fact, subjects appeared to be able to ignore motion completely in this situation. This result was surprising: Intuitively, motion is among the most salient stimulus attributes we encounter. Indeed, we often use motion (e.g., wave our arms) to draw attention, and

William James included it on his list of stimuli that engage immediate passive sensorial attention. How can this very strong intuition be reconciled with the experimental result that motion does not seem to capture attention?

Hillstrom and Yantis (1994), following their experiments supporting the new-object explanation for attentional capture, proposed that motion might capture attention *when it causes the creation of a new perceptual object.* Consider the perceptual consequences of motion in the natural environment. Many animals have camouflaging coloration that renders them almost invisible when they are motionless (e.g., certain moths have lichen-like patterns on their wings that blend in with the native tree bark). However, as soon as such an animal begins to move, it segregates instantly from its surroundings and a new perceptual object is created. Hillstrom and Yantis speculated that it is this event, and not motion itself, that captures visual attention.

Hillstrom and Yantis (1994, Experiment 2) tested this idea experimentally by carrying out an experiment in which observers were required to identify a global letter made up of several local letters (Figure 5, left). The global letter was always an *H* or an *S*. The local letters were always the same and not associated with a response within the experiment (*E* or *U*), with one exception: One of the local letters was unique, and it was either compatible (i.e., the same as the global letter), incompatible (i.e., either *H* or *S*, whichever was not the global letter), or neutral (i.e., either *E* or *U*, whichever was not the common neutral letter) with respect to the global letter. Our measure of attentional capture was the extent to which the unique local letter slowed or speeded RT to the global letter.

There were three main conditions in the experiment: the baseline, onset, and motion conditions, respectively (see Figure 5). In the baseline condition, a global figure eight, made up of numerous densely packed local figure eights, was presented for 1 s. The global figure eight was then replaced by a global *H* or *S* made up of local neutral letters plus one unique letter. In the baseline condition, we expected the identity of the unique local letter to have little impact on the time required to identify the global letter for two reasons: First, there was only one relevant local letter embedded among multiple neutral letters; second, the local letter was strongly grouped with its neighbors and so did not stand out as a separate perceptual object and therefore did not afford separate identification.

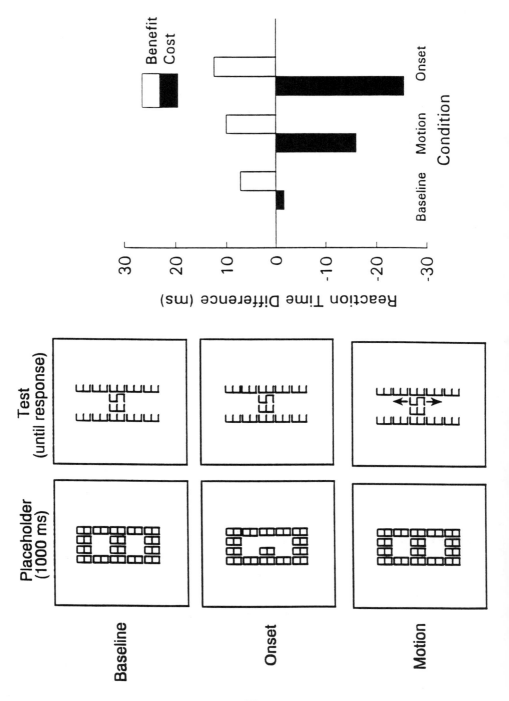

In the onset condition, the unique local letter appeared in a previously blank location. Our previous results with abrupt visual onsets suggested that the appearance of the critical onset letter in this condition should capture attention; we expected this to speed responses to the global letter when the local letter was response compatible and slow responses when the local letter was response incompatible (where speeding and slowing is measured relative to the baseline condition).

In the motion condition, the unique local element started oscillating at the moment the global and local figure eights were replaced by letters. The display was designed so that the local figure eights formed a strong perceptual group at the start of each trial. When the motion began, the moving element segregated immediately from its background and formed a new perceptual object much as a camouflaged animal stands out from its background as soon as it begins to move. According to our hypothesis, motion in this experiment should capture attention because it causes a new perceptual object representation to be created, and this should yield significant facilitation and inhibition, respectively, for compatible and incompatible critical letters.

The RT costs and benefits for each of the three conditions are shown on the right side of Figure 5. The magnitude of the costs and benefits reflects the extent to which the unique local element captured attention. As predicted, the costs and benefits in the baseline condition were minimal, but those in both the onset and the motion conditions were significant. Hillstrom and Yantis (1994) concluded that although motion as such does not capture attention in a stimulus-driven fashion, when motion causes an object to segregate from its background, a new perceptual object representation is created, and this event captures visual attention.

Summary of Abrupt-Onset Studies

Together, the experiments reviewed in this section provide converging evidence that the appearance of a new perceptual object captures attention,

Figure 5

Left: Procedure used in Experiment 2 of Hillstrom and Yantis (1994). See text for details. Right: Results from Experiment 2 of Hillstrom and Yantis (1994). From "Visual Motion And Attentional Capture," by A. P. Hillstrom and S. Yantis, 1994, *Perception and Psychophysics, 55*, p. 406. Copyright 1994 by the Psychonomic Society, Inc. Adapted with permission.

even when there is no incentive for observers to explicitly attend to such events (Hillstrom & Yantis, 1994; Yantis & Hillstrom, 1994; Yantis & Jonides, 1984). This conclusion stands in contrast to the absence of attentional capture by other stimulus attributes such as color, motion, shape, and brightness. It therefore appears to represent a case of pure attentional capture as defined at the beginning of the chapter. Recall, however, that capture by the appearance of a new object is not absolute: Yantis and Jonides (1990) showed that when observers attend to a cued location, an onset elsewhere does not capture attention.

CONCLUDING REMARKS

In this chapter I have reviewed a range of studies that exhibit various forms of attentional capture in vision. At this point it may be helpful to attempt a taxonomy of several different types of attentional capture that have appeared in these studies. I can discern at least three degrees of attentional capture. I do not intend these to be discrete categories, nor should they be considered exhaustive.

The first type of attentional capture is sometimes called "strongly involuntary." It occurs when a perceptual event draws attention even when the observer is actively attempting to ignore it (of course, it is assumed that the retinal location of the object yields equivalent sensory effects in all cases). The basic startle response (e.g., Sokolov, 1958/1963) and certain types of peripheral display change (e.g., Jonides, 1981) may fall into this category.

A second type, termed "weakly involuntary" attentional capture, occurs when an irrelevant attribute (i.e., one that is not part of the observer's deliberate state of attentional readiness) draws attention as long as the observer is not actively attempting to ignore it. The appearance of a new perceptual object apparently yields weakly involuntary (cf. Yantis, 1993a) but not strongly involuntary (cf. Yantis & Jonides, 1990) attentional capture.

A third important category of attentional capture arises when observers adopt a deliberate state of attentional readiness for a feature singleton that is known to define the target of search (what Folk et al., 1992, referred to as an attentional control setting for a singleton, or what Bacon & Egeth, 1994, called "singleton-detection mode"). In this case, attention may be drawn by other more salient singletons, even ones that are known to be irrelevant (e.g., Folk et al., 1992, 1994; Theeuwes, 1992, 1994, 1995). This is a weaker form of capture because it depends at least in part on the observer's state of attentional readiness and reflects an inability to perfectly modulate top-down control.

There exist many varieties of attentional capture, and some of these have been touched on in this chapter. One must be mindful that there are different degrees of capture, ranging from a completely obligatory orienting response to the very mild and nonobligatory form of conspicuity associated with a feature singleton. The most important lesson from this literature is that with few exceptions, these forms of attentional capture do not operate autonomously: There is almost always some interaction between top-down control and stimulus-driven capture.

At the present time, this constellation of results is best characterized by the idea that one's current attentional set plays a modulating role in determining what sorts of stimulus attributes are likely to control the distribution attention in a given task (Folk et al., 1992). An attentional control setting is established based on current perceptual goals. Once the setting is established, however, its influence on the distribution of attention is under stimulus control. Thus, attention may be directed to an element that, although not the target of search, provides a partial match to the current control settings. This idea can account for a number of results described earlier. The evidence for weakly involuntary attentional capture by new perceptual objects suggests that there may exist a "default" or "hardwired" setting that ensures the observer is always prepared to attend to new perceptual objects even without an explicit intent to do so. This framework provides a useful heuristic for characterizing the inescapable interaction between goal-directed and stimulus-driven distribution of attention.

REFERENCES

Bacon, W. F., & Egeth, H. E. (1994). Overriding stimulus-driven attentional capture. *Perception and Psychophysics, 55*, 485–496.

Bravo, M. J., & Nakayama, K. (1992). The role of attention in different visual-search tasks. *Perception and Psychophysics, 51*, 465–472.

Breitmeyer, B. G., & Ganz, L. (1976). Implications of sustained and transient channels for theories of visual pattern masking, saccadic suppression, and information processing. *Psychological Review, 83*, 1–36.

Cheal, M. L., & Lyon, R. D. (1991). Central and peripheral precuing of forced-choice discrimination. *Quarterly Journal of Experimental Psychology, 43A*, 859–880.

Colegate, R. L., Hoffman, J. E., & Eriksen, C. W. (1973). Selective encoding from multielement visual displays. *Perception and Psychophysics, 14*, 217–224.

Duncan, J. (1984). Selective attention and the organization of visual information. *Journal of Experimental Psychology: General, 113*, 501–517.

Duncan, J., & Humphreys, G. W. (1989). Visual search and stimulus similarity. *Psychological Review, 96*, 433–458.

Egeth, H., Jonides, J., & Wall, S. (1972). Parallel processing of multielement displays. *Cognitive Psychology, 3*, 674–698.

Eriksen, C. W., & Collins, J. F. (1969). Temporal course of selective attention. *Journal of Experimental Psychology, 80*, 254–261.

Eriksen, C. W., & Hoffman, J. E. (1972a). Some characteristics of selective attention in visual perception determined by vocal reaction time. *Perception and Psychophysics, 11*, 169–171.

Eriksen, C. W., & Hoffman, J. E. (1972b). Temporal and spatial characteristics of selective encoding from visual displays. *Perception and Psychophysics, 12*, 201–204.

Eriksen, C. W., & Hoffman, J. E. (1973). The extent of processing noise elements during selective encoding from visual displays. *Perception and Psychophysics, 14*, 155–160.

Folk, C. L., & Annett, S. (1994). Do locally defined feature discontinuities capture attention? *Perception and Psychophysics, 56*, 277–287.

Folk, C. L., Remington, R. W., & Johnston, J. C. (1992). Involuntary covert orienting is contingent on attentional control settings. *Journal of Experimental Psychology: Human Perception and Performance, 18*, 1030–1044.

Folk, C. L., Remington, R. W., & Johnston, J. C. (1993). Contingent attentional capture: A reply to Yantis (1993). *Journal of Experimental Psychology: Human Perception and Performance, 19*, 682–685.

Folk, C. L., Remington, R. W., & Wright, J. H. (1994). The structure of attentional control: Contingent attentional capture by apparent motion, abrupt onset, and color. *Journal of Experimental Psychology: Human Perception and Performance, 20*, 317–329.

Hillstrom, A. P., & Yantis, S. (1994). Visual motion and attentional capture. *Perception and Psychophysics, 55*, 399–411.

James, W. (1890). *The principles of psychology* (Vol. 1). New York: Holt.

Jonides, J. (1981). Voluntary versus automatic control over the mind's eye's movement. In J. B. Long & A. D. Baddeley (Eds.), *Attention and performance IX* (pp. 187–203). Hillsdale, NJ: Erlbaum.

Jonides, J., & Yantis, S. (1988). Uniqueness of abrupt visual onset in capturing attention. *Perception and Psychophysics, 43,* 346–354.

Kahneman, D., Treisman, A., & Gibbs, B. J. (1992). The reviewing of object files: Object-specific integration of information. *Cognitive Psychology, 24,* 175–219.

Kanwisher, N., & Driver, J. (1992). Objects, attributes, and visual attention: Which, what and where. *Current Directions in Psychological Science, 1,* 26–31.

Koch, C., & Ullman, S. (1985). Shifts in selective visual attention: Towards the underlying neural circuitry. *Human Neurobiology, 4,* 219–227.

Koshino, H., Warner, C. B., & Juola, J. F. (1992). Relative effectiveness of central, peripheral, and abrupt-onset cues in visual. *Quarterly Journal of Experimental Psychology, 45A,* 609–631.

Lennie, P., Trevarthan, C., Van Essen, D., & Wässle, H. (1990). Parallel processing of visual information. In L. Spillman & J. S. Werner (Eds.), *Visual perception: The neurophysiological foundations* (pp. 103–128). San Diego, CA: Academic Press.

Müller, H. J., & Rabbitt, P. M. A. (1989). Reflexive and voluntary orienting of visual attention: Time course of activation and resistance to interruption. *Journal of Experimental Psychology: Human Perception and Performance, 15,* 315–330.

Nakayama, K., & Mackeben, M. (1989). Sustained and transient components of focal visual attention. *Vision Research, 29,* 1631–1647.

Neisser, U. (1967). *Cognitive psychology.* New York: Appleton-Century-Crofts.

Nothdurft, H. C. (1993). Saliency effects across dimensions in visual search. *Vision Research, 33,* 839–844.

Pashler, H. (1988). Cross-dimensional interaction and texture segregation. *Perception and Psychophysics, 43,* 307–318.

Remington, R. W., Johnston, J. C., & Yantis, S. (1992). Involuntary attentional capture by abrupt onsets. *Perception and Psychophysics, 51,* 279–290.

Sokolov, E. N. (1963). *Perception and the conditioned reflex.* (S. W. Waydenfeld, Trans.). New York: MacMillan. (Original work published 1958)

Theeuwes, J. (1991a). Cross-dimensional perceptual selectivity. *Perception and Psychophysics, 50,* 184–193.

Theeuwes, J. (1991b). Exogenous and endogenous control of attention: The effect of visual onsets and offsets. *Perception and Psychophysics, 49,* 83–90.

Theeuwes, J. (1992). Perceptual selectivity for color and form. *Perception and Psychophysics, 51,* 599–606.

Theeuwes, J. (1994). Stimulus-driven capture and attentional set: Selective search for color and visual abrupt onsets. *Journal of Experimental Psychology: Human Perception and Performance, 20,* 799–806.

Theeuwes, J. (1995). Temporal and spatial characteristics of preattentive and attentive processing. *Visual Cognition, 2,* 221–233.

Todd, J. T., & Van Gelder, P. (1979). Implications of a transient-sustained dichotomy for the measurement of human performance. *Journal of Experimental Psychology: Human Perception and Performance, 5,* 625–636.

Treisman, A., & Gelade, G. (1980). A feature-integration theory of attention. *Cognitive Psychology, 12,* 97–136.

Wolfe, J. M., Cave, K. R., & Franzel, S. L. (1989). Guided search: An alternative to the feature integration model for visual search. *Journal of Experimental Psychology: Human Perception and Performance, 15,* 419–433.

Yantis, S. (1993a). Stimulus-driven attentional capture. *Current Directions in Psychological Science, 2,* 156–161.

Yantis, S. (1993b). Stimulus-driven attentional capture and attentional control settings. *Journal of Experimental Psychology: Human Perception and Performance, 19,* 676–681.

Yantis, S., & Egeth, H. E. (1994). Visual salience and stimulus-driven attentional capture [Abstract]. *Investigative Ophthalmology and Visual Science, 35,* 1619.

Yantis, S., & Hillstrom, A. P. (1994). Stimulus-driven attentional capture: Evidence from equiluminant visual objects. *Journal of Experimental Psychology: Human Perception and Performance, 20,* 95–107.

Yantis, S., & Johnson, D. N. (1990). Mechanisms of attentional priority. *Journal of Experimental Psychology: Human Perception and Performance, 16,* 812–825.

Yantis, S., & Jones, E. (1991). Mechanisms of attentional selection: Temporally-modulated priority tags. *Perception and Psychophysics, 50,* 166–178.

Yantis, S., & Jonides, J. (1984). Abrupt visual onsets and selective attention: Evidence from visual search. *Journal of Experimental Psychology: Human Perception and Performance, 10,* 601–621.

Yantis, S., & Jonides, J. (1990). Abrupt visual onsets and selective attention: Voluntary versus automatic allocation. *Journal of Experimental Psychology: Human Perception and Performance, 16,* 121–134.

3

Facilitatory and Inhibitory Aspects of Attention

W. Trammell Neill and Leslie A. Valdes

I s selective attention accomplished through direct facilitation of relevant processing or through inhibition of irrelevant processing? A phenomenon called *negative priming* is often cited as evidence for the latter alternative. The present chapter first describes the negative priming phenomenon. It then reviews research on the relation of negative priming to interference caused by distracting information. In this chapter, we consider six theories of negative priming and conclude that no current theory provides a completely satisfactory account of the phenomenon. The question of whether selective attention is accomplished through facilitation or inhibition therefore remains unresolved. However, ecological considerations suggest that inhibitory mechanisms may be particularly important for sustained attention to continuous sources of information.

In a natural environment, humans may be confronted with literally hundreds of simultaneous objects and events to which we might respond. We usually manage, somehow, to restrict our thoughts and actions to those objects and events that are relevant to our immediate goals. We call the hypothetical mental process that enables this restriction *selective attention*. Accordingly, some objects and events are selectively "attended," whereas the rest are "ignored."

Attention is usually conceptualized as a process of *facilitation:* It is assumed that some brain mechanism is brought to bear on the attended information, with the consequence that the processing of such information is selectively enhanced. Theories of attention in the 1950s and 1960s postulated a limited-capacity channel, or "bottleneck," in a sequence of processing stages (e.g., Broadbent, 1958; Deutsch & Deutsch, 1963; Treisman, 1964; Welford, 1952). Information that accessed this channel would receive further cognitive processing; information that did not access the channel would simply dissipate at whatever levels to which it had been processed. Research then focused on whether attention was an "early" stage, prior to categorization, or "late," subsequent to categorization.

In the 1970s and 1980s, attention was reconceptualized as a divisible processing capacity, flexibly allocated to different processes as needed. Theorists invoked metaphors such as "mental effort" (Johnston & Heinz, 1979; Kahneman, 1973), a "pool of resources" (Norman & Bobrow, 1975), a "spotlight" (Posner, Snyder, & Davidson, 1980), or a "zoom lens" (C. W. Eriksen & Yeh, 1985). Although Navon (1984) and Allport (1989, 1993) cogently criticized the conception of an undifferentiated, unitary processing capacity, it nonetheless remains a popular view.

Bottleneck and capacity theories make some common assumptions about attention, illustrated in Figure 1a: First, it is generally accepted that information can be processed to some degree without attention. Such processing is often called *preattentive,* in anticipation that something called *attention* will intervene at some point in processing. Second, the mechanism of attention operates directly on attended information (Stimulus 1 [S1] in Figure 1a). Third, attention is necessary for further cognitive processing; without it, further processing (e.g., of S2) cannot occur. In this sense, attention is assumed to *cause* further cognitive processing.

There is, however, a logical alternative, illustrated in Figure 1b: Attention may instead operate on the ignored information. In particular, further processing of irrelevant information (S2) may be directly inhibited, so that processing of relevant information (S1) can proceed without interference. From this point of view, attention does not *cause* further processing, any more than removal of a fallen tree causes an unimpeded flow of traffic or removal of a blood clot causes the flow of blood in an artery or vein.

A further implication of the inhibitory view is that attention is context specific. That is, processing of S1 may require attention when S2 is

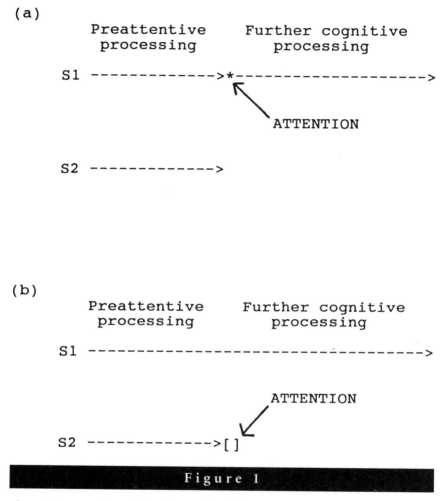

Figure 1

Theoretical conceptions of selective attention: (a) attention as facilitation; (b) attention as inhibition.

present, because the latter interferes with the processing of S1. In the absence of S2, however, processing of S1 may not require any attention at all. To use a familiar example, imagine that you are sitting in your living room, absorbed in reading a book. Because you have habituated to your surroundings, there is little other than the book itself to drive your cognitive activity. Even though the cognitive processing may be quite complex, it may not require attention. To risk a trite 1970s metaphor, you simply "go with the flow."

A natural objection to the inhibitory view is that people ignore much more than we attend. Would it not be more economical to facilitate relevant processing, rather than to inhibit the processing of everything that is irrelevant? This objection overlooks the fact that most of what we ignore does not affect our behavior anyway. It may only be necessary to inhibit processing that would otherwise interfere with goals and intentions. Most of us can chew gum and walk at the same time, not because these are automatic activities, but because the pavement does not affect how we chew, and the taste and feel of gum do not affect how we walk. On the other hand, if you want to *whistle* with gum in your mouth, you may have to inhibit chewing.

NEGATIVE PRIMING

How can researchers distinguish, empirically, between facilitation of relevant processing and inhibition of irrelevant processing? Consider the fate of the ignored information, S2, in Figure 1. According to the facilitatory view (Figure 1a), attention operated only on the attended information, S1. Suppose that after responding to S1, either S2 or a new stimulus became relevant for response: To the extent that there is any trace of past processing, processing of S2 should be facilitated; that is, it should yield a *priming* effect (e.g., Neely, 1976; Posner & Snyder, 1975). At worst, if there is no trace of S2, processing should not be any more difficult than for a new object.

In contrast, according to the inhibitory view (Figure 1b), attention operates on ignored information. If S2 should unexpectedly become relevant for response, its processing would have to overcome any residual effects of the inhibition. If this inhibition outweighs the benefits of the recent preattentive processing, then S2 should be more difficult to process relative to a new object.

By now, many studies have confirmed this latter prediction. Responses to recently ignored objects are often slower and less accurate than to new objects. Tipper (1985; Tipper & Cranston, 1985) popularized the term *negative priming* to describe the inhibitory consequences of ignoring an object.

Negative priming was first demonstrated by Dalrymple-Alford and Budayr (1966) in a version of the Stroop Color and Word Test (Stroop, 1935). The Stroop test requires subjects to quickly name the ink colors in which words are written. The well-known *Stroop effect* is that a word that denotes an incongruent color (e.g., *GREEN* in red ink) interferes with naming the ink color. Dalrymple-Alford and Budayr found that color naming was especially slow if each distractor word in a list named the *next* color—for example, if *GREEN* in red ink was followed by *BLUE* in green ink. They reasoned that naming each color required suppressing the response to the distractor word; if each color name had just been suppressed, responding was slowed by the need to overcome that suppression.

Neill (1977) replicated this effect in reaction times to individual, randomized Stroop stimuli: The response on a given trial n was slower, on average, if the target color happened to match the distractor word presented on trial $n - 1$. Similar effects have since been demonstrated for a wide variety of tasks and materials, including picture naming, letter naming, word naming, lexical decision, semantic categorization, letter matching, abstract shape matching, counting, and localization (see the review by Neill, Valdes, & Terry, 1995).

The basic "negative priming paradigm" consists of a sequence of two trials, which we call the *prime* and the *probe*. On a prime trial, the subject must respond, overtly or covertly, to some designated object or attribute, the *prime target*. The prime target is accompanied by some other object attribute, the *prime distractor*, to which the subject must avoid responding. On the probe trial, the subject responds to a new target, which is either related to the prime distractor or unrelated. Negative priming is defined as slower or less accurate responding to related probe targets as compared with unrelated probe targets.

Negative priming is not easily explained by bottleneck and capacity theories, even though such theories have sometimes incorporated conceptions of inhibition. For example, Treisman (1964) suggested that ignored information is not completely excluded from access to a limited capacity channel but is "attenuated," or weakened. However, attenuation was presumed to apply to sensory channels, such as spatial location, prior to object identification. Hence, identification of an object appearing in an attended channel would not be affected by its previous appearance in an unattended channel. In other words, negative priming implies a postcat-egorical form of selection (Treisman, 1992).

Walley and Weiden (1973) proposed a lateral-inhibition model of attention, analogous to the center-surround mechanism that sharpens contrast in sensory systems (see also Brown, 1979; Carr & Dagenbach, 1990). According to this model, processing channels are mutually inhibitory, in such a way that increasing activation of an attended channel inhibits activation of neighboring channels. However, lateral inhibition would depend on similarity to the attended object, rather than to the ignored object. If a recently ignored object and a new object were equated for similarity to the recently attended object, lateral inhibition would apply equally to both objects. Furthermore, any summation of inhibition with prior activation would result in *positive* priming by the ignored object relative to the new object.

Inhibition is often used to describe the processing cost that occurs for an unexpected stimulus when another stimulus is expected (Neely, 1976; Posner & Snyder, 1975). Theoretically, allocating attention to an expected stimulus makes attention less available for other stimuli. Inhibition in this sense is nonspecific and de facto; it does not reflect an operation on the unattended information (Posner, 1982). Ignored information and new information would therefore be equally deprived of attention. Again, any persisting activation by an ignored object would yield a net facilitation relative to a new object. In contrast, negative priming implies some form of inhibition that is specific to information about the ignored object.

INTERFERENCE AND INHIBITION

Interest in negative priming has grown in recent years, not only because of its theoretical importance, but also because it appears relevant to more global cognitive functioning. Many studies have found that certain groups of people, characterized by cognitive deficits, also exhibit diminished negative priming effects. A number of studies have reported negative priming to be diminished in elderly subjects, relative to young adults (e.g., Hasher, Stolzfus, Zacks, & Rypma, 1991; McDowd & Oseas-Kreger, 1991; Stoltzfus, Hasher, Zacks, Ulivi, & Goldstein, 1993; Tipper, 1991). Tipper, Bourque, Anderson, and Brehaut (1989) also reported diminished negative priming in children. Beech and colleagues have repeatedly found reduced, and even reversed, negative priming in individuals with schizophrenia and "schizotypal" illness (e.g., Beech, Baylis, Smithson, & Claridge, 1989; Beech & Claridge, 1987; Beech, Powell, McWilliam, & Claridge, 1989).

Reliable correlations also occur among college-age subjects. Tipper and Baylis (1987) found that those who scored high on the Cognitive Failures Questionnaire (Broadbent, Cooper, FitzGerald, & Parkes, 1982) showed less negative priming than those with low scores. Gernsbacher and Faust (1991) concluded that subjects who are poor at paragraph comprehension do not effectively inhibit irrelevant information. Westberry (1984) found very large negative priming for subjects who scored high on the Tellegen Absorption Scale, but negligible effects for those who scored low (see also Neill et al., 1995).

These groups do not seem to effectively suppress distracting information, at least in certain laboratory tasks. They often suffer more interference by irrelevant distractors, as well as less negative priming. It is tempting, therefore, to attribute their more general cognitive deficits to inadequate inhibition of irrelevant or distracting information. It should be noted, however, that there are contradictory findings: Some studies have recently reported equivalent negative priming in young and old subjects (Kramer, Humphrey, Larish, & Logan, 1994; Sullivan & Faust, 1993).

It seems plausible that an inhibitory mechanism would function to protect ongoing cognitive processes from interference by irrelevant, distracting information. Hence, individual differences in effective inhibition would predict an inverse correlation between negative priming and interference effects. On the other hand, it is less clear how negative priming should be related to interference within an individual.

If an irrelevant object causes minimal interference, then there would seem to be little need to inhibit its processing. Thus, if inhibition is *reactive* to the degree of experienced interference, then interference and negative priming should be directly correlated. Alternatively, if inhibition occurs independently of interference, then a strong distracting stimulus should be harder to inhibit than a weak one. Thus, if inhibition is *anticipatory*, rather than reactive, negative priming should vary inversely with interference.

Some studies have found negative priming in the absence of any measurable interference (Allport, Tipper, & Chmiel, 1985; Driver & Tipper, 1989; see also Tipper, Weaver, Kirkpatrick, & Lewis, 1991). Such results are important, because presence or absence of interference has often been used to infer whether stimuli are identified without attention. It is now clear that absence of interference cannot be used to infer absence of identification. That is, if a distractor has not been identified, then it could not cause negative priming for another stimulus sharing the same identity. Allport (1989, 1993) argued that interference depends on whether the relevant information can be easily distinguished from the irrelevant—not on whether the irrelevant information has been processed.

Although negative priming can occur without measurable interference, we have generally found that variables that increase interference also increase negative priming. For example, Valdes (1993; Valdes & Neill, 1993) varied target–flanker separation in a variation of the flanker-compatibility paradigm devised by C. W. Eriksen (B. A. Eriksen & Eriksen, 1974; C. W. Eriksen & Hoffman, 1973). Subjects were shown triplets of letters (e.g., *BAB*) and were instructed to press a key corresponding to the central letter (*A, B, C,* or *D*), ignoring the flanking letters.

On prime trials, the flankers could be compatible or incompatible with the target. A number of past studies have demonstrated that flanker compatibility effects decrease as the spatial separation between flankers and target is increased (C. W. Eriksen & Hoffman, 1973; C. W. Eriksen & St. James, 1986; Murphy & Eriksen, 1987). As shown in Table 1, a similar effect was obtained in the present experiment.

Probe trials in this experiment were always incompatible. On one third of probe trials following incompatible prime trials, the target was identical to the prime trial flanker. On the remaining two thirds of the trials, the probe target and flanker were unrelated to the prime trial. As shown in Table 1, a significant 31-ms negative priming effect was obtained when prime trial flankers had been near to the target. Negative priming was reduced to a nonsignificant 7 ms if prime flankers had been far.

In this initial experiment, target–flanker separation was confounded with retinal eccentricity of the flanker. Hence, greater separation might have reduced both interference and negative priming simply because the flanker was harder to see. However, we have since replicated this effect in other experiments, in which retinal eccentricity was controlled.

In one recent experiment, we presented all targets and distractors at clock positions approximately 2° from fixation. The target letter was distinguished by an adjacent bar marker. The distractor appeared in the im-

Table 1

Mean Prime and Probe Trial Reaction Times (in ms), as a Function of
Target–Flanker Proximity and Compatibility on Prime Trials, and
Prime–Probe Relatedness

	Prime–flanker proximity	
Trial type	Near	Far
Prime trials		
Incompatible	686	677
Compatible	642	653
Interference	44	24
Probe trials		
Related	687	673
Unrelated	656	666
Negative priming	31	7

NOTE: Data are from Valdes (1993).

mediately adjacent clock position, or three or five positions away. Both
stimuli appeared for only 150 ms in order to preclude any effect of eye
movements. As expected, reaction time on prime trials was slower when
the distractor was adjacent to the target than when it was separated. Because reaction time did not differ for three- and five-position separations,
we refer to them together as *far*.

In this experiment, negative priming interacted significantly with
target–flanker proximity on the probe trial, as well on the prime trial. As
shown in Table 2, significant negative priming occurred when flanker proximity was near on both prime and probe trials. Interestingly, this effect was
reversed when the separations mismatched. There is some suggestion of a
recovery of negative priming when separation was far on both prime and
probe trials, although this effect was not significant. As we discuss later in
this chapter, other experiments have found negative priming to depend on
the similarity between prime and probe trials. Such results suggest that negative priming is not explained by a simple persistence of inhibition.

We have found positive associations between negative priming and interference in other types of task. For example, Neill and Lissner (1988)

Table 2

**Mean Prime and Probe Trial Reaction Times (in ms) as a Function of
Target–Flanker Proximity and Prime–Probe Relatedness**

	Prime–flanker proximity	
Trial type	Near	Far
Prime trials	892	865
Probe trials (near flankers)		
Related	934	885
Unrelated	891	911
Negative priming	43	−26
Probe trials (far flankers)		
Related	855	886
Unrelated	879	875
Negative priming	−23	12

found both negative priming and interference in a letter-matching task to increase when incompatible distractors were relatively infrequent. Valdes (1993; Neill, Valdes, & Terry, 1992) found more negative priming and more interference in a localization task, when subjects were required to make spatially incompatible responses.

One exception to this pattern was recently reported by Fox (1994). She presented a target and distractor letter to the left and right of fixation, cuing the target with a bar marker. On some trials, the location of the target was precued 150 ms in advance by an asterisk in the target location. As previously found by C. W. Eriksen (C. W. Eriksen & Hoffman, 1973; Murphy & Eriksen, 1987), precuing decreased interference; however, it *increased* negative priming. It appears that precuing might help the subject to discriminate more quickly between the target and distractor, in turn allowing more efficient inhibition of the distractor.

Unfortunately, we were unable to replicate this result in a somewhat similar experiment. We reasoned that with two possible locations, precuing the target location also effectively precues the distractor location. However, with more possible locations, precuing the target location would leave the distractor location uncertain. If negative priming depends on knowing the distractor location, then the effect of precuing should be reduced with more locations.

We manipulated the number of possible locations, two or four, in separate blocks. In half of the two-location blocks, the target and distractor appeared to the left and right of fixation; in the other half, they appeared above and below. In the four-location blocks, targets and distractors could appear in any of these locations. At the beginning of a prime trial, asterisks appeared in the possible locations for 500 ms. In the precued condition, a bar marker appeared 150 ms prior to the letter stimuli; in the unprecued condition, the bar marker appeared only simultaneously with the target. As shown in Table 3, prime trial responses were faster when precued than when not precued and also faster in the two-location condition than in the four-location condition.

On probe trials, asterisks again appeared in the possible locations, followed by a target and simultaneous bar marker; no distractor letter was used. We expected to find increased negative priming when one of two locations had been precued, but not when one of four locations had been precued—that is, a Precuing × Uncertainty interaction. Although we ob-

Table 3

Mean Prime and Probe Trial Reaction Times (in ms) as a Function of Possible Locations (2 or 4), Prime Trial Cuing Condition, and Prime–Probe Relatedness

| | Cuing condition | | | |
| | Precued | | Not precued | |
Trial type	2	4	2	4
Prime trials	697	742	743	776
Probe trials				
Related	524	614	573	569
Unrelated	551	583	530	532
Negative priming	−27	31	43	37

NOTE: Data shown for two-location conditions are collapsed over blocks in which stimuli were displayed on the vertical axis or horizontal axis through fixation. Data shown for four-location conditions do not include those trials in which the target and distractor appeared on different axes.

tained a significant interaction, the pattern was not at all consistent with that reported by Fox (1994): Instead of enhanced negative priming in the precued, two-location condition, we found significant positive priming (or, as indicated, "negative" negative priming). (Kramer et al., 1994, reported a similar result.)

The result of this experiment is interpretable: There may be little interference when precuing makes target selection very easy; it is therefore unnecessary to inhibit the distractor. The distractor might then remain highly available, producing positive priming rather than negative. However, it is not clear why we obtained results opposite to those of Fox (1994). There were a number of procedural differences between the studies, and we hope further research will uncover the reason for the discrepancy. Until then, the effect of spatial precuing on negative priming remains ambiguous.

Pan and Eriksen (1993) recently suggested that the appropriate metaphor for spatial attention is not a spotlight or zoom lens, but an "aperture" or window:

> We suggest that the attentional field effects that we have found . . . may represent inhibition or attenuation of irrelevant stimuli rather than a positive selection mechanism. In other words, with our response-competition paradigm, we have been measuring the inner limits of an inhibitory field around the attended or selected stimuli, rather than the outer limits of an activated field surrounding the attended stimulus location. (p. 142)

Pan and Eriksen explored response-competition effects in two letter-matching experiments, in which they varied separation of the target letters as well as the distance of a distractor. They found that interference from a distractor letter at a *fixed* distance from fixation increased as the separation between targets was increased. Presumably, when the target letters are close, relative to the distractor, the window of attention can be constricted so as to prevent interference by the distractor (Figure 2). When the target letters are separated, the window is necessarily expanded in all directions, which increases the likelihood of encompassing the distractor as well.

Inhibition of the region outside the window seems to suggest that negative priming would increase with distance from a target, rather than decrease, as we have found. However, the area of inhibition is here deter-

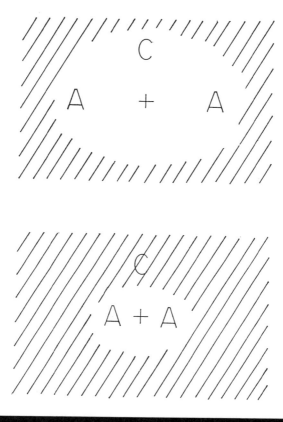

Figure 2

Spatial attention as a function of target separation. Top: When targets are far apart, distractor is included in attentional "window." Bottom: when targets are close together, distractor is excluded from attentional window.

mined by spatial locations, rather than object identity. It may be necessary to inhibit distractor identity only when the distractor falls inside the attended area. Hence, negative priming of distractor identity should increase with proximity to a target.

Pan and Eriksen did not argue that distractors outside the window are not identified. Rather, consistent with late-selection theories, they suggested that distractors are identified irrespective of their distance from targets. Whether the distractor falls inside or outside the window instead determines whether response selection is affected. Just as outside sunlight extends beyond the small area admitted by a window, distractor identity may remain activated behind the inhibitory wall. Such persisting activation would conveniently account for findings of positive priming by distant distractors, as in Table 2.

The Pan and Eriksen (1993) model also accounts for our results with precuing: In the two-location condition, the precue may have allowed subjects to sufficiently constrict the window around the target location, so that the distractor was excluded from the response decision. Because the distractor was excluded by location, rather than identity, persisting activation could facilitate identification when that letter then appeared as a target. In the four-location condition, however, precuing may not have allowed enough time to completely constrict the window around the target location. In this case, distractors might still fall within the window, interfering with the response decision. Identity-based inhibition would then be necessary, resulting in a negative priming effect.

CAUSES OF NEGATIVE PRIMING

What actually causes negative priming? Between the initial presentation of prime trial stimuli and the ultimate probe trial response, there are many cognitive processes that conceivably could be affected by ignoring an object. We review here six very different explanations that have been proposed for negative priming.

Response Suppression

Dalrymple-Alford and Budayr (1966), in their seminal Stroop-task experiment, attributed their effects to suppression of the overt response. Thus, withholding the response "green" to the printed word *GREEN* made that response less available to a subsequent green ink color.

However, simple response suppression does not seem to explain negative priming. This is most evident in experiments in which related and unrelated probes require exactly the same response. For example, subjects in a letter-matching experiment by Neill, Lissner, and Beck (1990) were shown strings of five letters. The subjects judged the second and fourth letters as same or different, ignoring the other letters. Negative priming occurred if an ignored flanker letter on the prime trial appeared as a probe trial target. Most important, this effect occurred regardless of the particular response sequence (Table 4).

Cognitive Deactivation

We think of interference as being caused by the activation of irrelevant cognitive representations. If inhibition serves to ameliorate the effects of interference, a natural hypothesis is that it reverses the activation of those same representations (e.g., Neill, 1979). The deactivation hypothesis, however, sometimes runs into trouble when nonconflicting stimuli are presented on probe trials.

If a cognitive representation is deactivated on a prime trial, that same representation should be harder to reactivate on a probe trial regardless of whether a distractor is also present on the probe trial. The results of some experiments are consistent with this prediction. For example, Neill and Westberry (1987) found negative priming in the Stroop color-naming task for neutral probes consisting of colored zeroes. However,

Table 4

Mean Probe Trial Reaction Times (in ms), as a Function of Prime and Probe Trial Type, and Prime–Probe Relatedness

	Prime trial type	
	Same	Different
Probe trial type	(ABABA)	(ABAEA)
Same trials		
Related (DADAD)	779	819
Unrelated (DCDCD)	766	803
Negative priming	13	16
Different trials		
Related (DADCD)	864	861
Unrelated (DFDCD)	842	849
Negative priming	22	12

NOTE: Examples of stimuli are shown in parentheses. Data are from Neill, Lissner, and Beck (1990).

Lowe (1979) found *positive* priming for colored-dot probes, even though randomly intermixed conflict words still exhibited negative priming.

A series of experiments by Moore (1994) suggests that negative priming depends, in part, on whether the subject expects to encounter interference on the probe trial. If neutral probe stimuli are easily discriminable from conflict stimuli, subjects may in some sense "drop their guard" and disinhibit the recently ignored distractor. There is still disagreement about the conditions under which negative priming does or does not occur (Neill et al., 1995), but it is nonetheless clear that probe conditions can sometimes reverse negative priming to positive, as illustrated in Table 2. Such results indicate that activation by a distractor persists at some level of processing before the locus of inhibition.

Code Coordination

Lowe (1979) suggested that negative priming occurs because the subject gets confused on the probe trial as to whether the target really is the target. For example, if the subject sees the color green but remembers the distractor word *GREEN*, he or she may be uncertain as to whether "green" is really the appropriate response.

Tipper and Cranston (1985) tested this hypothesis in a letter-naming experiment: On prime trials, subjects named a green letter, ignoring a simultaneous red letter. On the probe trial, subjects had to name the red letter. According to the code coordination hypothesis, performance should here be facilitated if the current target corresponded to the recently ignored distractor. For example, if the subject had just ignored a red *A* and now had to respond to a red *A*, he or she should be doubly certain that *A* has the appropriate attribute for selection. However, negative priming, rather than facilitation, still occurred. Thus, something about *A* really was inhibited. Further experiments by Lowe (1985) also refuted the code coordination hypothesis.

Using the same logic as Tipper and Cranston (1985), Park and Kanwisher (1994) found the opposite result in a target localization task. Tipper, Brehaut, and Driver (1990) had demonstrated that locating a target (@) was slowed if it appeared in the same location as a recently ignored distractor (+). Hence, it appeared that an ignored location was inhibited in much the same way as an ignored distractor identity. In one experiment by Park and Kanwisher, subjects responded to the location of an *X* on the prime trial, ignoring a distractor *O*. On the probe trial, subjects then had to respond to the location of an *O*, ignoring an *X*. If the probe target (*O*) appeared in the same location as the prime distractor (also *O*), facilitation occurred. In contrast, if the probe target (*O*) appeared in the same location as the prime target (*X*), inhibition occurred.

Park and Kanwisher (1994) argued that negative priming in the localization task does not really reflect inhibition of location information per se. Rather, an "object file" mismatch at a particular location causes delayed identification of the target (cf. Kahneman, Treisman, & Gibbs, 1992; Treisman, 1992). As we discuss below, this explanation does not account for other aspects of negative priming in the localization task. However, it does raise the possibility that negative priming in the localization task is mediated by different mechanisms than in identification tasks such as that of Tipper (1985).

Cognitive Blocking

Tipper and Cranston (1985) proposed that the representations of ignored stimuli are not deactivated per se, but are blocked from access to response mechanisms. Under certain conditions, the block may be lifted, allowing facilitatory effects to emerge from persisting activation at lower levels. The previously discussed window metaphor for spatial attention, proposed by Pan and Eriksen (1993), is a variation on this hypothesis.

The *cognitive blocking* hypothesis provides a particularly attractive explanation for the effects of backward masking on negative priming (Neill, 1989). When prime trial stimuli are rendered unreportable by a pattern mask, distractors produce positive priming rather than negative (Allport et al., 1985; Marcel, 1980; Neill et al., 1995). Marcel (1980, 1983a, 1983b) has argued that the masking pattern does not prevent perceptual processing per se, but blocks the conscious awareness of such processing. To the extent that the mask itself suffices to block distractors from awareness (or "working memory"; see Neill, 1989, 1993), there is no need to engage any inhibitory mechanism.

A recent set of experiments by Neill and Terry (1993), however, pose problems for a simple interpretation of masking effects on negative priming. In one experiment, prime trial flanking letters were either blanked or replaced by a pattern mask after the subject responded to the target. The masking pattern still eliminated the negative priming effect. Hence, disinhibition of distractors is not easily attributed to the mask blocking them from awareness or working memory. Indeed, the effect of the mask suggests an interaction with processes occurring much later than the initial selective attention to the prime target.

A general blocking of access to response mechanisms also fails to account for interactions of negative priming with stimulus–response (S-R) compatibility, as discussed below.

S-R Mapping

Negative priming interacts strongly with S-R compatibility in localization tasks (Neill, Valdes, & Kennedy, 1994; Neill, Valdes, & Terry, 1992). In one experiment, we required subjects to press a key corresponding to the location of a target letter, S or O, ignoring the location of a distractor X. Subjects were instructed to make the spatially compatible response if the target was an S and to make the spatially reversed response if the target was an O. Hence, S-R compatibility could be manipulated independently and randomly on prime and probe trials. As shown in Figure 3, negative priming occurred only when prime and probe trials required the same mapping rules.

As discussed earlier, Park and Kanwisher (1994) argued that negative priming in the localization task is caused by the perceptual mismatch of the probe to the "object file" previously established for that location. A perceptual mismatch should impair performance to the same degree, regardless of what response is subsequently required to the probe target. However, no such impairment seems to occur if the prime and probe require different mapping rules.

Similarly, the cognitive blocking hypothesis proposed by Tipper and Cranston (1985) and Neill (1989) also does not easily account for the results. That is, the ignored distractor does not appear to be blocked from response mechanisms in general. Rather, it is only the particular response that would have been relevant on the prime trial that seems to have been inhibited.

The results of these experiments suggest that negative priming is caused by the inhibition of a specific S-R mapping. Recent "connectionist" or "parallel distributed processing" models (e.g., McClelland & Rumel-

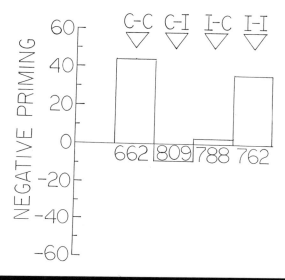

Figure 3

Baseline reaction times and negative priming effects for target localization (in ms), as a function of stimulus–response compatibility on prime and probe trials: Compatible–compatible (C-C), compatible–incompatible (C-I), incompatible–compatible (I-C), and incompatible–incompatible (I-I) prime–probe sequences. (Data are from Neill, Valdes, & Kennedy, 1994.)

hart, 1986; Rumelhart & McClelland, 1986) might account for negative priming in just this fashion. Learning in such models is usually accomplished by a "back-propagation" algorithm that strengthens connections to a correct response and weakens connections to incorrect responses (e.g., Rumelhart, Hinton, & Williams, 1986).

Back-propagation could cause negative priming in either of two ways: First, reinforcement of a correct response would strengthen the connection of that response not only to the prime trial target, but also (inappropriately) to the simultaneously present prime distractor. At the same time, the connection between the prime distractor and other responses (including the appropriate response) would be weakened. Second, the system might detect that the response implicitly activated by the distractor was incompatible with the reinforced correct response, and therefore "punish" that connection.

A recent experiment by Neill and Terry (1995) indicated, however, that negative priming is not merely a result of delayed response retrieval. All previous published experiments on negative priming used reaction time tasks. We investigated whether negative priming would affect identification accuracy for briefly displayed letters, without any pressure to respond quickly. If negative priming simply delays the retrieval of an appropriate response, then there should be no effect when subjects are allowed unlimited time to respond.

In yet another variation of the Eriksen flanking-letter procedure, we presented incompatible letter triplets on prime trials for 100 or 300 ms, followed by a pattern mask. Probe trial triplets were presented for 33, 100, or 300 ms, again followed by a pattern mask. In addition, one quarter of the probe trials were *catch* trials, in which the selected stimuli were not displayed, and only the pattern mask was presented. As shown in Table 5, significant negative priming occurred for the 33- and 100-ms probes, and a marginally significant effect ($p < .10$) also occurred for the 300-ms probes. Catch trials, on the other hand, showed no bias against guessing the ignored prime distractor.

Episodic Retrieval

The discussion so far has assumed that negative priming occurs because something is inhibited on the prime trial, or shortly thereafter, and this

Table 5

Mean Error Percentages on Prime and Probe Trials as a Function of Target Duration (in ms) and Prime–Probe Relatedness

	Target duration			
Trial type	0	33	100	300
Prime trials	—	—	14.38	2.97
Probe trials				
Related	69.09	63.00	13.86	2.86
Unrelated	72.22	54.12	8.07	1.12
Negative priming	−3.13	8.88	5.79	1.74

NOTE: Probe trial data are shown collapsed over prime trial stimulus duration. Data are from Neill and Terry (1995).

inhibition carries over to affect processing on the probe trial. However, it is necessary to consider an alternative possibility: Negative priming is caused specifically by processes occurring on the *probe* trial.

Logan (1988) proposed that automaticity of task performance develops through the accumulation of instances. When a target stimulus appears, it cues the retrieval of past episodes from memory that involve the same stimulus. These episodes are presumed to contain information about the response that was executed. If the response information is appropriate, subjects can respond quickly; they do not have to engage in slow, algorithmic computation of the response.

Adopting Logan's (1988) assumptions, we have suggested that negative priming occurs when the retrieved episode contains inappropriate, rather than appropriate, response information (Neill & Valdes, 1992; Neill, Valdes, Terry, & Gorfein, 1992). As posited by Logan, a probe target may cue the retrieval of recent episodes involving the same stimulus. If the retrieved episode contains information that the stimulus was ignored, the subject may be forced to rely on the slower, algorithmic computation. Negative priming therefore results.

We were led to this explanation by an experiment investigating the persistence of negative priming effects. We found that negative priming depended not only on the delay between the prime and probe, but also on the delay before the prime (Figure 4). That is, negative priming was greatest when the prime trial was temporally distinct from the previous processing episodes. When the prime trial was not temporally distinct, previous episodes may have interfered with retrieval of the prime trial, or the probe target may have cued the retrieval of other episodes prior to the prime.

An episodic retrieval theory would predict that negative priming should be influenced by the retrieval context. We have found in several experiments that negative priming depends on contextual similarity, including previously discussed experiments on target–flanker separation (Table 2) and S-R compatibility (Figure 3). As one more example, we ran an experiment in which we manipulated the onset of flanking letters in both prime and probe trials. On some trials, the flankers were not presented until 400 ms after the target onset; on other trials, the flanker onset coincided with the target.

As shown in Table 6, late-onset flankers produced as much interfer-

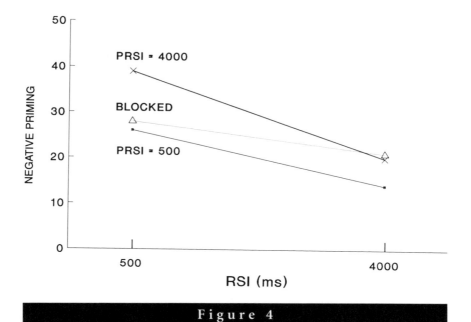

Figure 4

Negative priming effects (in ms) as a function of response–stimulus interval (RSI) between prime and probe, and preceding response–stimulus interval (PRSI) between prime and previous probe. (Data are from Neill, Valdes, Terry, & Gorfein, 1992.)

ence, or compatibility effect, as the early-onset flankers on prime trials. On probe trials, the triple interaction of relatedness, prime distractor onset, and probe distractor onset was highly significant: Robust negative priming occurred only when the prime and probe shared the same distractor onset conditions.

Other researchers have also reported effects of prime–probe similarity. For example, Stolz and Neely (1993) varied the brightness of prime and probe stimuli in a letter-matching task similar to that used by Neill et al. (1990). Again, negative priming depended on similarity: Negative priming was greatest for dim probes following dim primes and for bright probes following bright primes.

Unfortunately, the episodic retrieval theory also does not, by itself, account for all the data on negative priming. In particular, it fails to explain why negative priming sometimes reverses to positive priming, as when nonconflicting probe stimuli are easily distinguished from conflicting stimuli (e.g., Lowe, 1979). Several studies have also found that negative priming is reversed to positive if subjects are encouraged to sacrifice accuracy for speed (Neill, 1979; Neill & Westberry, 1987; Neumann & De-Schepper, 1992). In order to account for such effects, the episodic retrieval theory must be supplemented by some other mechanism that produces positive priming—perhaps persisting activation in a semantic memory system.

CONCLUSION

Six very different, and plausible, explanations have been proposed for negative priming. Simple response suppression and cognitive deactivation do not currently have much support. Code coordination does not appear to account for negative priming in identification tasks, although the results of Park and Kanwisher (1994) suggest that it might apply to localization tasks. Cognitive blocking and S-R disconnection both have points in their

Table 6

Mean Prime and Probe Trial Reaction Times (in ms) as a Function of Flanker Onset, Flanker Compatibility (Prime Trials), and Prime–Probe Relatedness

	Prime flanker onset	
Trial type	Early	Late
Prime trials		
Incompatible	818	826
Compatible	806	805
Interference	12	21
Probe trials (early onset)		
Related	856	812
Unrelated	824	803
Negative priming	32	9
Probe trials (late onset)		
Related	844	833
Unrelated	843	798
Negative priming	1	35

favor, but also points against. The episodic retrieval theory accommodates much of the published data (see discussion by Neill et al., 1995; Neill, Valdes, Terry, & Gorfein, 1992), but even that theory fails to explain all relevant findings.

In other words, we do not really know what causes negative priming. No single explanation seems wholly adequate. Negative priming may reflect more than one of the proposed mechanisms, or it may reflect none of them. In regard to the questions raised in the introduction to this chapter, the important observation is that some evidence implicates the involvement of processes subsequent to the selective attention and response to a prime target. Therefore, we cannot assume that negative priming directly indexes inhibition during the selection of relevant versus irrelevant information.

Does this mean that we should dismiss negative priming as unimportant? To do so would be to disregard the strong evidence that negative priming is associated with individual differences in effective cognitive functioning. If negative priming is not an index of initial selection, why is it important?

We may have erred in thinking of negative priming as merely an accidental by-product of selective attention. Rather, it may itself be an adaptive mechanism for *sustaining* selective attention. As noted by Tipper, Weaver, Cameron, Brehaut, and Bastedo (1991), objects that are irrelevant in a natural context will probably remain irrelevant over some time. Any mechanism that prevents such objects from affecting behavior is likely to be adaptive, even if that mechanism operates after the initial act of selective attention.

Interference from distracting stimuli diminishes if the same distracting stimuli are repeated across trials (e.g., Greenwald, 1972). Even in the Stroop color-word task, responses are relatively fast if the same distractor word appears on both prime and probe trials (Neill, 1978; Neumann & DeSchepper, 1991). In retrospect, such sequences are probably more ecologically relevant than sequences in which an ignored object unexpectedly becomes relevant.

An understanding of sustained selective attention may ultimately prove to be more important than an understanding of the initial selection processes. After all, initial selection occurs in a fraction of a second; sustained selective attention may be required over seconds, minutes, and sometimes hours. An individual who is delayed for a few milliseconds in selecting relevant information should probably not pilot a jet airplane. Otherwise, he or she would probably get along just fine in life. However, an individual who is continuously distracted by the same irrelevant information would probably be severely impaired.

Whether the initial allocation of "further cognitive processes" (Figure 1) to relevant information is accomplished through facilitation or inhibition remains an open question. However, selective attention clearly does have inhibitory consequences, and it is likely that such inhibition functions to facilitate adaptive cognitive functioning over time.

REFERENCES

Allport, A. (1989). Visual attention. In M. I. Posner (Ed.), *Foundations of cognitive science* (pp. 631–682). Cambridge, MA: MIT Press.

Allport, A. (1993). Attention and control: Have we been asking the wrong questions? A critical review of twenty-five years. In D. E. Meyer & S. Kornblum (Eds.), *Attention and performance XIV* (pp. 183–218). Cambridge, MA: MIT Press.

Allport, D. A., Tipper, S. P., & Chmiel, N. R. J. (1985). Perceptual integration and postcategorical filtering. In M. I. Posner (Ed.), *Attention and performance XI* (pp. 107–132). Hillsdale, NJ: Erlbaum.

Beech, A., Baylis, G. C., Smithson, P., & Claridge, G. (1989). Individual differences in schizotypy as reflected in measures of cognitive inhibition. *British Journal of Clinical Psychology, 28,* 117–129.

Beech, A., & Claridge, G. (1987). Individual differences in negative priming: Relations with schizotypal personality traits. *British Journal of Psychology, 78,* 349–356.

Beech, A., Powell, T., McWilliam, J., & Claridge, G. (1989). Evidence of reduced "cognitive inhibition" in schizophrenia. *British Journal of Clinical Psychology, 28,* 110–116.

Broadbent, D. E. (1958). *Perception and communication.* Elmsford, NY: Pergamon Press.

Broadbent, D. E., Cooper, P. F., FitzGerald, P., & Parkes, K. R. (1982). The Cognitive Failures Questionnaire (CFQ) and its correlates. *British Journal of Clinical Psychology, 21,* 1–16.

Brown, A. S. (1979). Priming effects in semantic memory retrieval processes. *Journal of Experimental Psychology: Human Learning and Memory, 5,* 65–77.

Carr, T. H., & Dagenbach, D. (1990). Semantic priming and repetition priming from masked words: Evidence from a center-surround attentional mechanism in perceptual recognition. *Journal of Experimental Psychology: Learning, Memory, and Cognition, 16,* 341–350.

Dalrymple-Alford, E. C., & Budayr, B. (1966). Examination of some aspects of the Stroop color-word test. *Perceptual and Motor Skills, 23,* 1211–1214.

Deutsch, J. A., & Deutsch, D. (1963). Attention: Some theoretical considerations. *Psychological Review, 70,* 80–90.

Driver, J., & Tipper, S. P. (1989). On the nonselectivity of "selective" seeing: Contrasts between interference and priming in selective attention. *Journal of Experimental Psychology: Human Perception and Performance, 15,* 304–314.

Eriksen, B. A., & Eriksen, C. W. (1974). Effects of noise letters upon the identification of a target letter in a nonsearch task. *Perception and Psychophysics, 16,* 143–149.

Eriksen, C. W., & Hoffman, J. E. (1973). The extent of processing noise elements during selective encoding from visual displays. *Perception and Psychophysics, 14,* 155–160.

Eriksen, C. W., & St. James, J. D. (1986). Visual attention within and around the field of focal attention: A zoom lens model. *Perception and Psychophysics, 40,* 225–240.

Eriksen, C. W., & Yeh, Y. (1985). Allocation of attention in the visual field. *Journal of Experimental Psychology: Human Perception and Performance, 11,* 583–597.

Fox, E. (1994). Interference and negative priming from ignored distractors: The role of selection difficulty. *Perception and Psychophysics, 56,* 565–574.

Gernsbacher, M. A., & Faust, M. E. (1991). The mechanism of suppression: A component of general comprehension skill. *Journal of Experimental Psychology: Learning, Memory, and Cognition, 17,* 245–262.

Greenwald, A. G. (1972). Evidence of both perceptual filtering and response suppression for rejected messages in selective attention. *Journal of Experimental Psychology, 94,* 58–67.

Hasher, L., Stoltzfus, E. R., Zacks, L. T., & Rypma, B. (1991). Age and inhibition. *Journal of Experimental Psychology, 17,* 163–169.

Johnston, W. A., & Heinz, S. P. (1979). Flexibility and capacity demands of attention. *Journal of Experimental Psychology: General, 107,* 420–435.

Kahneman, D. (1973). *Attention and effort.* Englewood Cliffs, NJ: Prentice Hall.

Kahneman, D., Treisman, A., & Gibbs, B. J. (1992). The reviewing of object files: Object-specific integration of information. *Cognitive Psychology, 24,* 175–219.

Kramer, A. F., Humphrey, D. G., Larish, J. F., & Logan, G. D. (1994). Aging and inhibition: Beyond a unitary view of inhibitory processing in attention. *Psychology and Aging, 9,* 491–512.

Logan, G. D. (1988). Toward an instance theory of automatization. *Psychological Review, 95,* 492–527.

Lowe, D. G. (1979). Strategies, context, and the mechanism of response inhibition. *Memory and Cognition, 7,* 382–389.

Lowe, D. G. (1985). Further investigations of inhibitory mechanisms in attention. *Memory and Cognition, 13,* 74–80.

Marcel, A. J. (1980). Conscious and preconscious recognition of polysemous words: Locating the selective effects of prior verbal context. In R. S. Nickerson (Ed.), *Attention and performance VIII* (pp. 435–437). Hillsdale, NJ: Erlbaum.

Marcel, A. J. (1983a). Conscious and unconscious perception: An approach to the relations between phenomenal experience and perceptual processes. *Cognitive Psychology, 15,* 238–300.

Marcel, A. J. (1983b). Conscious and unconscious perception: Experiments on visual masking and word recognition. *Cognitive Psychology, 15,* 197–237.

McClelland, J. L., & Rumelhart, D. E. (Eds.). (1986). *Parallel distributed processing: Explorations in the microstructure of cognition. Vol. 2: Psychological and biological models.* Cambridge, MA: MIT Press.

McDowd, J. M., & Oseas-Kreger, D. M. (1991). Aging, inhibitory processes, and negative priming. *Journal of Gerontology: Psychological Sciences, 46,* 340–345.

Moore, C. M. (1994). Negative priming depends on probe-trial conflict: Where has all the inhibition gone? *Perception and Psychophysics, 56,* 133–147.

Murphy, T. D., & Eriksen, C. W. (1987). Temporal changes in the distribution of attention in the visual field in response to precues. *Perception and Psychophysics, 42,* 576–586.

Navon, D. (1984). Resources: A theoretical soupstone? *Psychological Review, 91,* 216–234.

Neely, J. H. (1976). Semantic priming and retrieval from lexical memory: Evidence for facilitatory and inhibitory processes. *Memory and Cognition, 4,* 648–654.

Neill, W. T. (1977). Inhibitory and facilitatory processes in selective attention. *Journal of Experimental Psychology: Human Perception and Performance, 3,* 444–450.

Neill, W. T. (1978). Attention: The coordination of internal codes (Doctoral dissertation, University of Oregon, 1977). *Dissertation Abstracts International, 38,* 5067B. (University Microfilms No. 78–2551)

Neill, W. T. (1979). Switching attention within and between categories: Evidence for intracategory inhibition. *Memory and Cognition, 7,* 283–290.

Neill, W. T. (1989). Ambiguity and context: An activation–suppression model. In D. S. Gorfein (Ed.), *Resolving semantic ambiguity* (pp. 63–83). New York: Springer-Verlag.

Neill, W. T. (1993). Consciousness, not focal attention, is causally effective in human information processing: Commentary on Velmans (1991). *Behavioral and Brain Sciences, 16,* 406–407.

Neill, W. T., & Lissner, L. S. (1988, April). *Attention and selective inhibition in alphanumeric character matching.* Paper presented at the meeting of the Eastern Psychological Association, Buffalo, NY.

Neill, W. T., Lissner, L. S., & Beck, J. L. (1990). Negative priming in *same–different* matching: Further evidence for a central locus of inhibition. *Perception and Psychophysics, 48,* 398–400.

Neill, W. T., & Terry, K. M. (1993, November). *Negative priming: Effects of pattern masking.* Paper presented at the meeting of the Psychonomic Society, Washington, DC.

Neill, W. T., & Terry, K. M. (1995). Negative priming without reaction time: Effects on identification of masked letters. *Psychonomic Bulletin and Review, 2,* 121–123.

Neill, W. T., & Valdes, L. A. (1992). The persistence of negative priming: Steady-state or decay? *Journal of Experimental Psychology: Learning, Memory, and Cognition, 18,* 565–576.

Neill, W. T., Valdes, L. A., & Kennedy, C. E. (1994, April). *Negative priming: Effects of S-R compatibility.* Paper presented at the meeting of the Eastern Psychological Association, Providence, RI.

Neill, W. T., Valdes, L. A., & Terry, K. M. (1992, November). *Negative priming in target localization.* Paper presented at the meeting of the Psychonomic Society, St. Louis, MO.

Neill, W. T., Valdes, L. A., & Terry, K. M. (1995). Selective attention and the inhibitory control of cognition. In F. N. Dempster & C. J. Brainerd (Eds.), *Interference and inhibition in cognition* (pp. 207–261). San Diego, CA: Academic Press.

Neill, W. T., Valdes, L. A., Terry, K. M., & Gorfein, D. S. (1992). Persistence of negative priming: II. Evidence for episodic trace retrieval. *Journal of Experimental Psychology: Learning, Memory, and Cognition, 18,* 993–1000.

Neill, W. T., & Westberry, R. L. (1987). Selective attention and the suppression of cognitive noise. *Journal of Experimental Psychology: Learning, Memory, and Cognition, 13,* 327–334.

Neumann, E., & DeSchepper, B. G. (1991). Costs and benefits of target activation and distractor inhibition in selective attention. *Journal of Experimental Psychology: Learning, Memory, and Cognition, 17,* 1136–1145.

Neumann, E., & DeSchepper, B. G. (1992). An inhibition based fan effect: Evidence for an active suppression mechanism in selective attention. *Canadian Journal of Psychology, 46,* 1–40.

Norman, D. A., & Bobrow, D. G. (1975). On data-limited and resource-limited processes. *Cognitive Psychology, 7,* 44–64.

Pan, K., & Eriksen, C. W. (1993). Attentional distribution in the visual field during *same-different* judgments as assessed by response competition. *Perception and Psychophysics, 53,* 134–144.

Park, J., & Kanwisher, N. (1994). Negative priming for spatial locations: Identity mismatching, not distractor inhibition. *Journal of Experimental Psychology: Human Perception and Performance, 20,* 613–623.

Posner, M. I. (1992). Cumulative development of attention theory. *American Psychologist, 37,* 168–179.

Posner, M. I., & Snyder, C. R. R. (1975). Facilitation and inhibition in the processing of signals. In P. M. A. Rabbitt & S. Dornic (Eds.), *Attention and performance V* (pp. 669–682). San Diego, CA: Academic Press.

Posner, M. I., Snyder, C. R. R., & Davidson, B. J. (1980). Attention and the detection of signals. *Journal of Experimental Psychology: General, 109,* 160–174.

Rumelhart, D. E., Hinton, G. E., & Williams, R. L. (1986). Learning internal representations by error propagation. In D. E. Rumelhart & J. L. McClelland (Eds.), *Parallel distributed processing: Explorations in the microstructure of cognition. Vol. 1: Foundations* (pp. 318–362). Cambridge, MA: MIT Press.

Rumelhart, D. E., & McClelland, J. L. (Eds.). (1986). *Parallel distributed processing: Explorations in the microstructure of cognition. Vol. 1: Foundations.* Cambridge, MA: MIT Press.

Stolz, J. A., & Neely, J. H. (1993). *Stimulus intensity and negative priming: Processing difficulty or memory confusion effects?* Unpublished manuscript.

Stoltzfus, E. R., Hasher, L., Zacks, R. T., Ulivi, M. S., & Goldstein, D. (1993). Investigations of inhibition and interference in younger and older adults. *Journal of Gerontology: Psychological Sciences, 48,* 179–188.

Stroop, J. R. (1935). Studies of interference in serial verbal reactions. *Journal of Experimental Psychology, 18,* 643–662.

Sullivan, M. P., & Faust, M. E. (1993). Evidence for identity inhibition during selective attention in old adults. *Psychology and Aging, 13,* 51–65.

Tipper, S. P. (1985). The negative priming effect: Inhibitory priming by ignored objects. *Quarterly Journal of Experimental Psychology, 37A,* 571–590.

Tipper, S. P. (1991). Less attentional selectivity as a result of declining inhibition in older adults. *Bulletin of the Psychonomic Society, 29*, 45–47.

Tipper, S. P., & Baylis, G. C. (1987). Individual differences in selective attention: The relation of priming and interference to cognitive failure. *Personality and Individual Differences, 8*, 667–675.

Tipper, S. P., Bourque, T., Anderson, S., & Brehaut, J. (1989). Mechanisms of attention: A developmental study. *Journal of Experimental Child Psychology, 48*, 353–378.

Tipper, S. P., Brehaut, J. C., & Driver, J. (1990). Selection of moving and static objects for the control of spatially directed action. *Journal of Experimental Psychology: Human Perception and Performance, 16*, 492–504.

Tipper, S. P., & Cranston, M. (1985). Selective attention and priming: Inhibitory and facilitatory effects of ignored primes. *Quarterly Journal of Experimental Psychology, 37A*, 591–611.

Tipper, S. P., Weaver, B., Cameron, S., Brehaut, J. C., & Bastedo, J. (1991). Inhibitory mechanisms of attention in identification tasks: Time-course and disruption. *Journal of Experimental Psychology: Learning, Memory, and Cognition, 17*, 681–692.

Tipper, S. P., Weaver, B., Kirkpatrick, J., & Lewis, S. (1991). Inhibitory mechanisms of attention: Locus, stability, and relationship with distractor interference effects. *British Journal of Psychology, 82*, 507–520.

Treisman, A. M. (1964). Monitoring and storage of irrelevant messages in selective attention. *Journal of Verbal Learning and Verbal Behavior, 3*, 449–459.

Treisman, A. M. (1992). Perceiving and re-perceiving objects. *American Psychologist, 47*, 862–875.

Valdes, L. A. (1993). *The relation of negative priming to interference.* Unpublished doctoral dissertation, Adelphi University, Garden City, NY.

Valdes, L. A., & Neill, W. T. (1993, April). *Does negative priming depend on interference?* Paper presented at the meeting of the Eastern Psychological Association, Arlington, VA.

Walley, R. E., & Weiden, T. D. (1973). Lateral inhibition and cognitive masking: A neuropsychological theory of attention. *Psychological Review, 80*, 284–302.

Welford, A. T. (1952). The "psychological refractory period" and the timing of high-speed performance: A review and a theory. *British Journal of Psychology, 43*, 2–19.

Westberry, R. L. (1984). The nature of attentional control as a personality dimension (Doctoral dissertation, University of South Florida, 1983). *Dissertation Abstracts International, 45*, 1034B.

4

Neuroimaging Approaches to the Study of Visual Attention: A Tutorial

Steven A. Hillyard, Lourdes Anllo-Vento, Vincent P. Clark, Hans-Jochen Heinze, Steven J. Luck, and G. Ron Mangun

C urrent neuroimaging techniques are providing increasingly detailed information about the spatiotemporal patterns of brain activity associated with sensory, perceptual, and cognitive processes. In particular, much has been learned about the anatomy and physiology of the human visual system and the brain systems that mediate selective visual attention (Hillyard, 1993; Petersen, Fiez, & Corbetta, 1992). In their groundbreaking article, Garner, Hake, and Eriksen (1956) pointed out that physiological as well as behavioral measures may be used as converging operations to define and differentiate stages of information processing. In this chapter we consider how evidence from neuroimaging studies can serve as converging operations with behavioral data to advance the development of psychological theories of visual attention.

NEUROIMAGING TECHNIQUES

Two complementary classes of neuroimaging techniques are presently in widespread use. The first includes positron emission tomography (PET)

Invaluable contributions to the work reported here were made by J. Hansen, T. Rubin, H. Hinrichs, and M. Scholz. Support was provided by grants from the National Institute of Mental Health (MH-25594 and MH-00930), the Office of Naval Research (N00014-89-J-0806), the National Institutes of Health (NS17778), the McDonnell Pew Foundation, and the Deutsche Forschungsgemeinschaft.

and functional magnetic resonance imaging (fMRI), which register changes in the metabolic activity of nerve cell populations or, more commonly, changes in regional cerebral blood flow associated with neural activity. These measurements of blood flow or metabolism have a relatively low time resolution, on the order of seconds to minutes, which is limited ultimately by the slow response time of the physiological processes themselves. However, both PET and the less invasive fMRI can yield three-dimensional images of the multiple brain regions that may be activated in a given task situation, which have an anatomical resolution of the order of 1 cm or better (Fox & Woldorff, 1994; Petersen et al., 1992).

The second class of neuroimaging techniques includes recordings of the electric and magnetic fields that are generated by the ionic currents associated with synchronous synaptic activity and cell firing patterns in neural populations. When triggered by an external stimulus or otherwise time-locked to a sensory, motor, or cognitive event, these fields are termed *event-related potentials* (ERPs) and *event-related magnetic fields* (ERFs), respectively (Hillyard, 1993; Hillyard & Picton, 1987). Both ERP and ERF recordings consist of a time series of waves of varying field strength and polarity (Figure 1), which reflect the patterns of activation within nerve cell populations with a high degree of temporal precision (in the range of milliseconds). These precisely timed wave sequences are usually described in terms of *components*—the various peaks and troughs in the waveform or their underlying neural generators. When these recordings are made noninvasively from scalp or surface sites, as is generally the case, the component amplitudes are so small that they require computer averaging across multiple events to be resolved. However, unlike the PET and fMRI techniques, ERP averaging typically retains the temporal microstructure of the neural activation sequences.

With surface-recorded ERPs or ERFs, the locations of the active neural populations can only be estimated indirectly rather than seen directly as is the case with PET and fMRI. This indirect calculation of neural generator locations from surface field distributions is known as the *inverse problem*. The validity of these source localizations has been improved considerably by recent approaches to solving the inverse problem that take into account the anatomical organization of the cortex and the electrical conductances of the brain (Dale & Sereno, 1993). An important direction for future research will be to combine the high temporal resolution of elec-

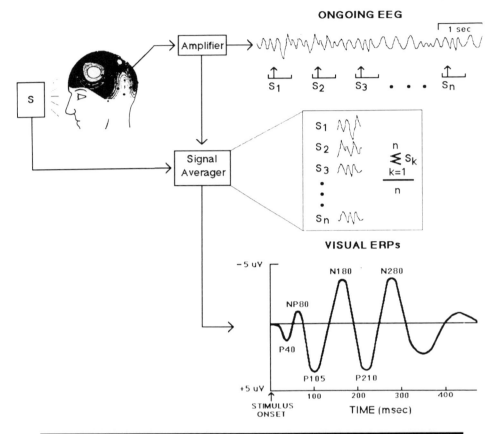

ONGOING EEG

VISUAL ERPs

Figure 1

General methods for recording visual event-related potentials (ERPs). Scalp-recorded ERPs triggered by stimulus (S) presentations are first amplified and then signal averaged to obtain an adequate signal to noise ratio. Signal averaging usually involves summation of the raw electroencephalogram (EEG) from each electrode site during time epochs following presentation of successive stimuli (S1, S2, . . .). Components of the visual ERP time-locked to stimulus onset are revealed in the averaged waveform below. Components recorded over the occipital lobe are shown, labeled according to their polarity, positive (P) or negative (N), and peak latency in ms. The P40 is generally too small to observe except in response to very bright flashes. The polarity-reversing NP80 is also known as C1, and the P105 and N180 are also labeled P1 and N1, respectively. The voltage distribution of each component may be mapped across the scalp to gain insight into its anatomical origin.

trical or magnetic recordings with the high spatial resolution of PET or fMRI in common experiments in order to characterize fully the event-related patterns of neural activity (Fox & Woldorff, 1994; Heinze et al., 1994b). Also of importance in this endeavor are intracranial recordings of ERPs directly from brain tissue in neurosurgical patients (e.g., Allison et al., 1993).

ATTENTIONAL NETWORKS IN THE BRAIN

When describing the attentional systems of the brain, it is important to distinguish between the sensory projection pathways that encode incoming information and the control circuitry that determines which stimuli entering the sensory pathways are to be selectively enhanced or suppressed. In the case of visual attention, several interconnected brain areas have been identified both by neuroimaging and neuropsychological studies as playing a key role in the control of attention. These areas include the dorsolateral prefrontal cortex, the anterior cingulate gyrus, the posterior parietal lobe, and the pulvinar nucleus of the thalamus (Posner & Dehaene, 1994). Current evidence indicates that the dorsolateral prefrontal cortex initiates and maintains the selective sensory bias in working memory, whereas the posterior parietal cortex is responsible for monitoring the locations of stimuli with respect to the body and in shifting attention from one location to another in the visual field (e.g., Corbetta, Miezin, Shulman, & Petersen, 1993). It has been postulated that these areas constitute an executive network for attentional control that selectively modulates sensory processing via anatomical projections to the visual cortical areas of the *ventral stream*, in which stimulus features and objects are encoded (Corbetta, Miezin, Dobmeyer, Shulman, & Petersen, 1991; Desimone, Wessinger, Thomas, & Schneider, 1990; LaBerge, 1995).

Neuroimaging studies have revealed a good deal about the mechanisms by which attentional control is exerted over the sensory projection areas. Studies using PET have shown that attending to a particular stimulus feature such as color produces enhanced neural activity in the cortical zones that are specialized for the sensory processing of that feature (Corbetta et al., 1991; Haxby et al., 1993). This suggests that attention acts by amplifying sensory signals within the cortical areas that encode the attended feature (Posner & Dehaene, 1994). Studies of ERP changes have also indicated that attention may sometimes act by selectively amplifying or suppressing sensory evoked activity in modality-specific cortical areas.

ERPS AND VISUAL ATTENTION

The analysis of ERPs and visual selective attention was pioneered by Robert Eason and Russell Harter and their associates in a series of studies beginning more than 25 years ago (Eason, 1981; Eason, Harter, & White, 1969; Harter & Aine, 1984; Harter, Aine, & Schroeder, 1982). In these experiments, attended and unattended stimuli were presented in randomized order, and the attended stimuli were found to elicit enlarged ERP components over the time range 100–400 ms. Prominent among these components was a broad negative wave that Harter and associates (1982) termed the "selection negativity" (SN). They found that the onset latency of the SN varied with the stimulus feature being attended and was earliest for selection based on stimulus location, with successively longer latencies for selection by contour, color, spatial frequency, orientation, and feature conjunctions.

Harter and Aine (1984) proposed that the SN represents evoked neural activity in feature-selective "channels," which is enhanced when attention is directed toward that sensory channel. This proposal accords well with the aforementioned PET evidence for amplification of neural activity in feature-specific cortical areas. There has been some controversy, however, concerning the mechanism of these ERP attention effects—whether they in fact represent an amplification of evoked feature-specific neural activity or whether they represent the engagement of specialized neural systems for processing the attended stimuli (Hillyard & Mangun, 1987). Subsequent research has shown that both types of attention effects can be identified and that attention to location is characterized by its own unique ERP signature.

The main focus of this chapter is to demonstrate how ERP recordings can help to reveal the timing and organization of stimulus selection processes in the brain's attentional networks. This physiological evidence is evaluated from two interrelated perspectives: first, how ERP data can serve as converging operations to help resolve key theoretical issues in visual attention research and, second, how the underlying attention mechanisms are implemented in the brain.

ISSUES IN THE STUDY OF VISUAL ATTENTION

Is Spatial Attention Special?

It is well known that human observers can shift their attention rapidly across a visual scene, even in the absence of eye movements, and that stimuli presented to an attended location are detected and discriminated more accurately than are stimuli falling outside the attended zone (Van der Heijden, 1992). The mechanism of this spatial attention effect has been vigorously debated—in particular the question of whether it is mediated at an early or late stage of visual processing. On the one hand, it has been proposed that visuospatial attention facilitates early visual encoding and perceptual representations of stimuli occurring within the "spotlight" of attention (e.g., Reinitz, 1990). On the other hand, it has been argued that attentional control is exerted at late, postperceptual levels and acts by biasing decision or response processes to favor inputs at attended locations (e.g., Sperling & Dosher, 1986). A further point of debate is whether attention to location plays a special role in perception relative to selection of other stimulus features; for example, Treisman and Gelade (1980) have proposed that in order to properly integrate the constituent features of an object, focal attention must be directed toward the object's location.

Recordings of ERPs in visuospatial attention tasks provide converging evidence with respect to these theoretical questions. Studies in several different paradigms have shown that spatial attention is associated with a characteristic pattern of ERP changes. This attention effect was illustrated in an experiment by Mangun, Hillyard, and Luck (1993), in which stimuli were flashed rapidly and in random order to four locations in the visual field (Figure 2). When subjects focused attention on the flashes at one location (ignoring the other three), the visual ERP elicited by those attended flashes showed marked amplitude increases in the early evoked positive (P) and negative (N) waves, termed *P1* (80–110 ms) and *N1* (140–190 ms) components, as well as in a subsequent N2 (220–280 ms) wave. The P1 and N1 waves were largest in amplitude over narrow zones of the extrastriate visual cortex of the occipital lobe, consistent with neural generators in those regions. The attention effect took the form of an amplitude enhancement of the P1 and N1 waves, with little change in their timing or scalp distribution. This suggests that spatial attention acts as a gain control mechanism that modulates sensory evoked activity in the pos-

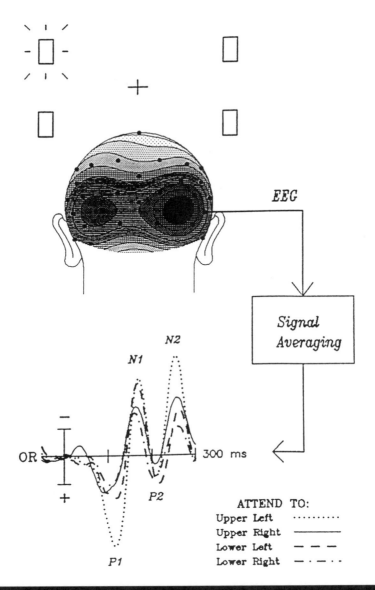

Figure 2

Visual event-related potentials (ERPs) show enhanced P1, N1, and N2 components when spatial attention is focused on the stimulus location. Grand averaged ERPs from a contralateral occipital scalp site are shown in response to upper left field flashes under each of the four attention conditions. The shading on the head represents the scalp topography of the P1 component to attended upper left flashes measured at 108 ms, with darker areas representing greater positive voltages. EEG = electroencephalogram. From *Attention and Performance, XIV: Synergies in Experimental Psychology, Artificial Intelligence, and Cognitive Neuroscience* (p. 224), edited by D. Meyer and S. Kornblaum, 1993, Cambridge, MA: MIT Press. Copyright 1993 by MIT Press. Reprinted with permission.

terior extrastriate visual cortex, producing a relative amplification of inputs arising from attended locations.

This P1–N1 amplitude modulation appears to be a unique signature of attention to location and has been observed in several different types of spatial attention tasks, including (a) sustained focal attention to stimulus sequences, (b) cued orienting to likely target locations, and (c) visual search for feature conjunction targets in multielement displays (reviewed in Hillyard, Mangun, Woldorff, & Luck, 1995; Luck, Fan, & Hillyard, 1993). In contrast, paying attention to nonspatial features is characterized by very different ERP configurations, typically dominated by a broad SN that has its onset at around 150–200 ms. Figure 3 shows the SN elicited by stimuli of an attended color presented within a randomized sequence of colored check patterns; the SN is distributed over the contralateral occipital scalp and is accompanied by an anterior positivity that peaks at around 200 ms. This prolonged SN is elicited when attention is directed to any of a variety of nonspatial cues (Harter & Aine, 1984; Kenemans, Kok, & Smulders, 1993) and clearly reflects a qualitatively different selection mechanism from the phasic P1–N1 amplitude modulation produced by attention to location.

Evidence for Early Selection

In studies where relevant stimuli were designated by both spatial and non-spatial features, selection for location was found to have primacy over selection for other features such as color. In an experiment by Hillyard and Münte (1984), for example, red and blue bars were flashed equiprobably and in random order to the left and right visual fields, and subjects had to attend to one of the four color–location combinations at a time. As shown in Figure 4 (upper row), all stimuli at the attended location, regardless of color, elicited enlarged P1, N1, and N2 waves compared with stimuli at unattended locations. In contrast, stimuli of the attended color elicited a broad SN over the interval 150–300 ms (middle row). The timing and waveform of these attention effects can be seen in the difference ERPs formed by subtracting the unattended ERPs from the attended ERPs of each type. Significantly, the differential SN to attended-color stimuli was greatly attenuated for stimuli in the unattended half field. This implies that selection for color is hierarchically contingent on the earlier selection for location; in other words, only stimuli at the attended locations

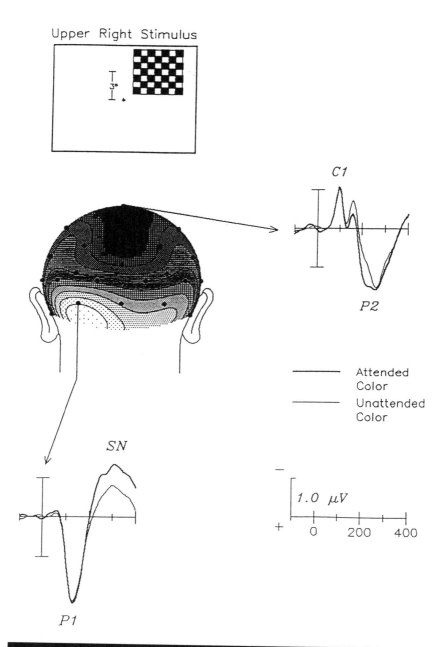

Figure 3

Event-related potential (ERP) changes during attention to color. Anterior recording sites show a parallel positive shift to attended stimuli. Topographic map is based on 30-channel recording of the SN in the attended minus unattended difference wave over the time window 150–300 ms. (Data are from Rubin, Luck, Anllo-Vento, Hansen, & Hillyard, 1993.)

ERPS INDEX HIERARCHY OF SELECTION

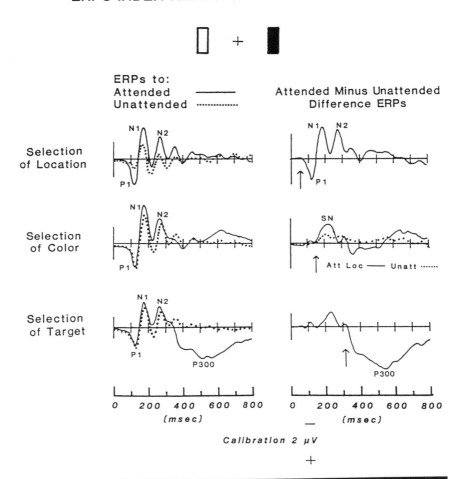

Figure 4

Event-related potentials (ERPs) index hierarchical feature selection in a multidimensional attention task (Hillyard & Münte, 1984). Grand averaged ERPs to the attended location (Att Loc; regardless of color) show enhanced P1, N1, and N2 components (top waveforms). ERPs to attended-color flashes elicited a broad selection negativity (SN) that was greatly reduced for flashes at the unattended (Unatt) location (middle waveforms). The ERPs to targets of the attended color and location show an additional P300 component, preceded by a smaller N2 wave (lower tracings). From *Neurobiology of Higher Cognitive Function* (p. 290), edited by A. B. Scheibel and A. F. Wechsler, 1990, New York: Guilford Press. Copyright 1990 by Guilford Press. Reprinted with permission.

that elicit large P1–N1 components are processed further for their color attributes. These results are in agreement with proposals that early selection by location can gate the registration of simple feature information (Kahneman & Treisman, 1984). Other ERP studies of attention to multifeature stimuli have demonstrated that both contingent and parallel independent cue selections may be reflected in the SN component (Kenemans et al., 1993; Previc & Harter, 1982; Wijers, Mulder, Okita, & Mulder, 1989).

These findings from ERP studies converge with early selection theories of attention in several respects. First, the short latency of the P1 effect (onset at 70–80 ms) and its origin in posterior extrastriate cortex imply that stimulus selection is occurring at a level in which only elementary visual features and patterns are represented, prior to the more anterior areas of the inferior temporal lobe where fully analyzed objects are encoded (Ungerleider & Haxby, 1994). Second, the above-mentioned ERP studies of attention to multifeature stimuli suggest that the extent of processing of one stimulus feature (e.g., color) can be contingent on selection for another feature (e.g., location); such a hierarchical contingency conflicts with one of the basic tenets of late selection theory, namely, that stimulus features are all processed automatically and in parallel up to the level of object recognition. Third, selection for location is manifested by enhanced early ERP amplitudes not only for task-relevant stimuli, but also for irrelevant and physically distinctive probe stimuli presented to attended and unattended locations (Heinze, Luck, Mangun, & Hillyard, 1990; Luck et al., 1993; Mangun & Hillyard, 1990). This modulation of probe-evoked ERPs implies an early selection mechanism that is based solely on location and does not take into account higher order features of the stimuli.

Neural Systems Mediating Spatial Attention

In the study of Mangun et al. (1993), it was concluded that the earliest attention-sensitive component (the P1) was generated in extrastriate cortex of the ventral-lateral occipital lobe rather than in the primary visual (striate) cortex. This conclusion was based on analysis of the scalp distribution of the P1 attention effect and on its failure to invert in polarity for upper versus lower field stimulation; such an inversion would be expected for a neural generator in the striate cortex because of its anatomical and retinotopic organization. An earlier evoked component having an onset latency of 50–60 ms (the C1 wave) did show such a polarity reversal over the midline occipital lobe and thus appeared to originate from the striate cortex. Significantly, this component did not vary as a function of attention.

Further ERP studies have confirmed that spatial attention first affects visual processing at the level of extrastriate rather than striate cortex (Clark, 1993; Gomez, Clark, Luck, Fan, & Hillyard, 1994). Clark, Fan, and Hillyard (1995) verified that the C1 component showed a polarity inversion as a function of stimulus elevation and, using inverse source modeling techniques, concluded that the neural generator of the C1 was localized in the mesial occipital lobe, in which lies the striate cortex. In a spatial attention task using stimuli positioned to produce maximal C1 amplitudes, the C1 was found to be unchanged by shifts of attention between the left and right visual fields (Clark, 1993; Figure 5). The subsequent P1 and N1 components, however, were substantially enlarged for attended-field stimuli as in previous studies. Both the P1 and N1 attention effects were found to consist of multiple subcomponents that shifted in scalp topography throughout their time course. Although inverse source analysis has limitations in resolving the locations of concurrently active neural generators, it was found that the P1 and N1 attention effects could be largely accounted for by generators in ventral and lateral extrastriate cortical areas within the occipital lobe.

A recent study that combined ERP analysis with PET (Heinze et al., 1994b) has verified that spatial attention acts to modulate visual inputs in the ventral extrastriate cortex. In this study, subjects attended to either the left or right halves of bilateral arrays of symbols that were flashed at a rapid rate. In one experimental session, subjects participated in separate attend-left, attend-right, and passive control trials after receiving intravenous injections of a positron-emitting tracer (H_2O_{15}). The patterns of increased cerebral blood flow revealed by PET scanning during task performance are shown in Figure 6. Significant blood flow increases (reflecting increased neuronal activity) were observed in the ventral extrastriate cortex of the hemisphere contralateral to the attended visual field. Additional regions showing PET activation included the anterior cingulate gyrus and the posterior thalamus (region of the pulvinar).

In a separate session, ERPs were recorded from 30 scalp sites while the same subjects performed the same task. As in previous studies (Heinze et

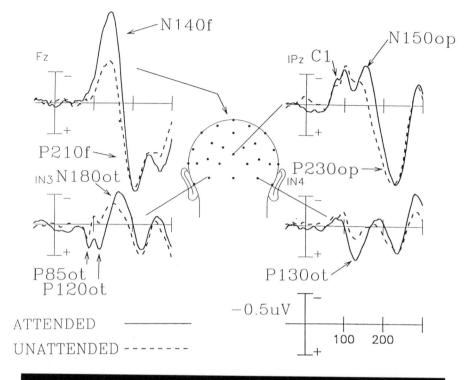

Figure 5

Event-related potentials (ERPs) recorded from four different scalp sites in a spatial attention task (Clark, 1993). Grand averaged ERPs shown are in response to right field flashes.
Note that paying attention to the flashes enhanced subcomponents of the P1 wave over the
occipitotemporal scalp (P85ot, P120ot, P130ot) and subcomponents of the N1 wave over
frontal (N140f), occipitoparietal (N150op), and occipitotemporal scalp (N180ot). The C1
component, however, which was localized to generators in primary visual (striate) cortex,
did not change significantly as a function of attention. Small circular check patterns (2.3°
in diameter) were flashed in random order to upper left and right visual field positions 8°
lateral to fixation and 12° above the horizontal meridian. Intervals between successive stimulus onsets varied between 150 and 450 ms. Subjects attended to either the left or right field
flashes on each run and detected targets (10%) having a slightly smaller check size.

al., 1990), an increased P1 component (80–140 ms) was observed over the
hemisphere contralateral to the attended visual field. Inverse source modeling showed that the neural generator of this enlarged P1 wave could be
accurately represented by a dipolar source in ventral extrastriate visual cor-

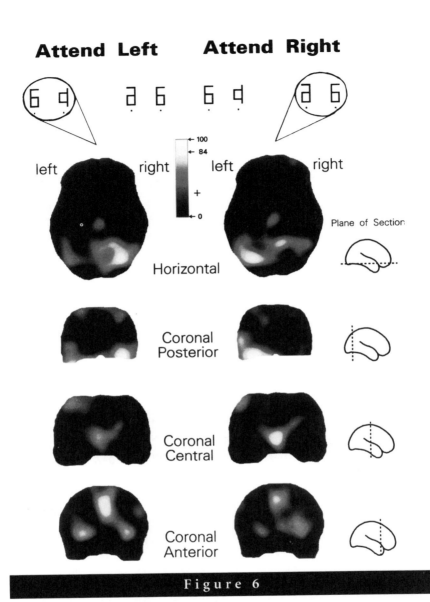

Figure 6

Cortical and subcortical brain areas activated during focused spatial attention. One of the stimulus arrays is shown at the top, with the direction of attention indicated by the spotlight. Further arrays are shown in Figure 8. The task was to attend to the pair of symbols in either the left or right visual field on a given trial, and to press a button when the attended symbols matched (25% of trials). Symbol arrays were flashed briefly at intervals of 250–550 ms between onsets. The PET images shown were formed by subtracting the activation patterns of a passive condition from those of the attend-left (left column) and attend-right (right column) conditions. Upper two rows of images show significant activation in the ventral extrastriate visual cortex of the hemisphere contralateral to the direction of attention. Further activations were seen in the thalamus (third row of images) and in the anterior cingulate gyrus (bottom row of images).

tex, at virtually the same location as the focus of PET activation (see Figure 7). Thus, the combined use of ERP and PET revealed both the timing (80–140 ms poststimulus onset) and the cortical localization (fusiform gyrus of the ventral occipital lobe) of the stimulus selection process during spatial attention.

These ERP and PET studies provide strong support for the hypothesis that a major mechanism of spatial attention is the selective amplitude modulation of visual information in multiple extrastriate cortical areas. This proposal is consistent with the results of neurophysiological studies in attentive monkeys (Desimone et al., 1990) and other PET studies in humans (Corbetta et al., 1991; Haxby et al., 1991), which have identified multiple extrastriate regions as the site of attentional control over visual information processing.

LaBerge (1995) has proposed an anatomical model for visuospatial attention that incorporates evidence from neurophysiological, neuropsychological, PET, and ERP studies. In this model, the flow of information through extrastriate visual areas is modulated by means of bias signals arising from the pulvinar nucleus of the thalamus; the preferential bias for attended-location stimuli arises from an attentional control network that includes the prefrontal and posterior parietal cortices and is relayed to the cortical sensory areas via the pulvinar. In this framework, we propose that the increased P1 and N1 amplitude modulation during spatial attention reflects a gain control over visual information flow in extrastriate cortex, primarily in those areas of the ventral stream that encode stimulus features and objects (Ungerleider & Haxby, 1994). This mechanism appears to produce a relative amplification of stimulus information within the spotlight of attention and a relative suppression of spatially disparate inputs, so that the latter are not processed in detail for either their secondary features or their higher object or semantic properties (McCarthy & Nobre, 1993).

The Spotlight of Attention: Unitary or Divisible?

There is general agreement that attention may be allocated to selected regions of the visual fields in a rapid and flexible manner to optimize the intake of relevant information. Different proposals have been advanced, however, concerning the spatial properties of this attentional allocation. On the basis of reaction time evidence from spatial cuing experiments,

Subtracted Attend Left Minus Right

A.

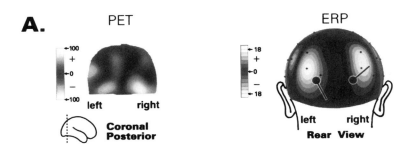

PET

+100
+
0
−
−100

left   right

**Coronal
Posterior**

ERP

18
+
0
−
18

left   right

Rear View

B. PET-ERP CO-Localization

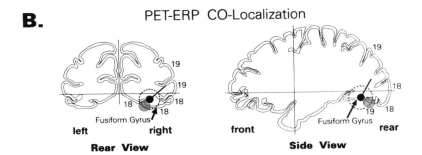

19
19
18   18
18
Fusiform Gyrus

left   right

Rear View

19
18
19   18
Fusiform Gyrus   rear

front

Side View

Figure 7

Comparison of positron emission tomography (PET) and event-related potential (ERP) attention effects. In order to control for effects of general arousal, patterns of brain activity were examined in difference images formed by subtracting the attend-right from the attend-left conditions. A: The difference image for the PET activation in the fusiform gyrus (left) is compared with the difference image for the topographic distribution of the attention-sensitive P1 component (80–140 ms; right). The surface P1 distribution could be modeled accurately (accounting for 97.8% of the variance in the scalp voltage) by a pair of dipoles in the ventral occipital cortex. The dipoles in left and right hemispheres have opposed polarities due to their being calculated from the difference image. B: Inverse dipole models of the ERP attention effect and PET activations mapped onto coronal (left) and sagittal (right) sections of the brain from the Talairach and Tournoux (1988) atlas. The dashed line surrounding the dipole indicates the region over which changes in dipole position affected the residual variance of the model by 2% or less. Note that the zone of the PET activation in the posterior fusiform gyrus (shaded outlined circle) overlaps the zone of the dipole error range. The dipole orientation was consistent with a maximum current source on the scalp over the lateral occipital region, as shown in Panel A.

Posner, Snyder, and Davidson (1980) concluded that attention is deployed in the form of a unitary spotlight that cannot be divided between non-contiguous zones of the visual field. This idea was extended by Eriksen and colleagues (Eriksen & St. James, 1986; Eriksen & Yeh, 1985), who proposed that the unitary attentional focus could expand or contract to match the size of the region being attended in the manner of a zoom lens; the rate of information intake within this attended zone would then vary inversely with its size. In contrast, other investigators have concluded that attention may be allocated to separated zones of the visual field and thus does not invariably take the form of a unified spotlight (Castiello & Umilta, 1992; LaBerge & Brown, 1989; Shaw & Shaw, 1977).

The question of whether the focus of attention can be split into spatially separated beams was investigated in an ERP study by Heinze et al. (1994a). The general approach required subjects either to focus attention on two adjacent items in a horizontal array or to divide attention between two spatially separated items within the array. The allocation of attention to the relevant items and to intervening and surrounding items was assessed by examining the ERP amplitudes elicited by irrelevant probe stimuli that were flashed unpredictably at all locations. Previous work (Heinze et al., 1990) has shown that the amplitude of the P1 component (80–140 ms) to irrelevant probes varied systematically as a function of attentional allocation within multi-item displays such as those used here.

In this study, the stimuli consisted of four-item arrays of symbols flashed in rapid sequence (Figure 8). The task was to attend (on different runs) either to an adjacent pair of symbols (Positions 1–2 or 3–4) or to a separated pair (Positions 1–3 or 2–4) and to press a button whenever the pair of attended symbols matched; these matches (targets) occurred on a random 25% of the trials. Randomly interspersed among the symbol arrays were irrelevant flashed rectangles (probes) that could occur at any of the four stimulus positions.

The behavioral results were in accord with Eriksen and St. James's (1986) zoom lens model: subjects were faster and more accurate at detecting the matching targets when attending to adjacent rather than separated locations in the display. Moreover, the probe-evoked ERPs indicated that subjects maintained a single, expanded focus of attention when attending to separated items and did not divide their focus into two beams that excluded the intervening item. In particular, the P1 amplitude was

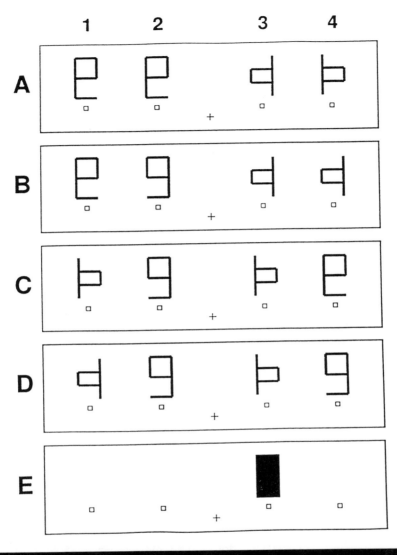

Figure 8

Examples of successive stimulus arrays (A–D) that were flashed at intervals of 250–350 ms (between onsets) in the studies of Heinze et al. (1994a, 1994b). The arrays shown contain matching symbols at positions 1–2 (A), 3–4 (B), 1–3 (C), and 2–4 (D); these matches were targets under each of the respective attention conditions. Panel E shows the task-irrelevant probe stimulus that was flashed at random at the various stimulus positions. Over a block of stimuli, 60% of the arrays were task relevant and 40% were probes. The fixation cross and dots marking the four locations were displayed continuously. From "Attention to Adjacent and Separate Positions in Space: An Electrophysiological Analysis," by H.-J. Heinze et al., 1994, *Perception and Psychophysics, 56*, p. 45. Copyright 1994 by The Psychonomic Society. Reprinted with permission.

equally enlarged in response to probes at the intermediate, irrelevant location as to probes at the relevant locations themselves (Figure 9). Only the probes to the irrelevant locations surrounding the attended pair of items showed a reduced P1 amplitude. Thus, the behavioral and ERP results were both in line with the zoom lens hypothesis that subjects use a unitary attentional focus that encompasses intervening locations, even when those locations hold irrelevant and potentially conflicting information.

In a study of commissurotomized (split-brain) patients, Luck, Hillyard, Mangun, and Gazzaniga (1994) obtained evidence that the corpus callosum was responsible for maintaining this unity of attentional focus during visual search. In a task that required scanning a visual display to detect a feature conjunction target, it was shown that split-brain patients could search bilaterally symmetrical displays approximately twice as fast as they could search a lateralized display having the same number of items. In contrast, neurologically normal control subjects searched unilateral and bilateral displays with equal speed. This finding indicates that surgical transection of the corpus callosum allows each of the separated hemispheres to scan its respective hemifield independently, with its own attentional spotlight. Evidently, the intact corpus callosum unifies the attentional systems of the two cerebral hemispheres.

Cued Orienting of Spatial Attention

The spatial allocation of attention has been studied most extensively in tasks that involve the trial-by-trial cuing of the location where relevant information is most likely to be presented (e.g., Eriksen & Yeh, 1985; Luck, Hillyard, Mouloua, et al., 1994; Posner, 1980). Typically, it is found that stimuli presented at precued locations are detected more rapidly and accurately than are stimuli at uncued locations. The nature of this cuing effect has been vigorously debated, with some authors proposing a mechanism of facilitated sensory processing (Posner et al., 1980) and others favoring postperceptual factors such as decision bias or statistical noise reduction (Shiu & Pashler, 1994; Sperling & Dosher, 1986).

Several ERP studies of spatial cuing tasks have found that the speeding of reaction times to stimuli at precued locations is associated with enhanced early P1 or N1 components or both in the visual ERP to those stimuli (Anllo-Vento, 1995; Eimer, 1994; Harter, Miller, Price, LaLonde, &

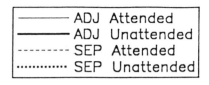

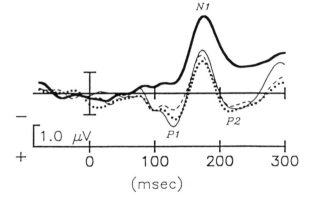

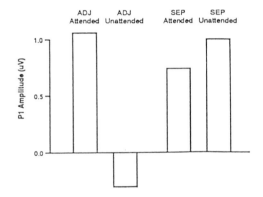

Figure 9

Grand-averaged event-related potentials (ERPs) to probes flashed to the inner stimulus positions (2 and 3 combined) under different attention conditions. On ADJ-attended trials, subjects were attending to an adjacent pair of locations (1–2 or 3–4), and the probe was flashed at the inner attended location; on ADJ-unattended trials, the probe was flashed at the inner unattended location. On SEP-attended trials subjects were attending to separated positions 1–3 or 2–4, and the probe was flashed at the inner attended positions; on SEP-unattended trials, the probe was flashed to the intervening unattended location. Note that the ERP to the latter probe exhibits as large a P1 wave as do the probes to the attended locations. ERPs were recorded from an occipitotemporal electrode site contralateral to the visual field of the probe; the mean P1 amplitudes measured over 90–150 ms are graphed below. From "Attention to Adjacent and Separate Positions in Space: An Electrophysiological Analysis," by H.-J. Heinze et al., 1994, *Perception and Psychophysics, 56*, p. 48. Copyright 1994 by The Psychonomic Society. Reprinted with permission.

Keyes, 1989; Hillyard, Luck, & Mangun, 1994; Mangun & Hillyard, 1991). These ERP results provide strong support for a mechanism of early sensory facilitation—again at the level of the extrastriate visual cortex—during the spatial cuing of attention. It has also been found that spatial precuing enhances the detectability of masked threshold-level flashes (Hawkins et al., 1990; Luck, Hillyard, Mouloua, et al., 1994). This behavioral finding provides further support for the view that advance cuing of a relevant location activates an attentional mechanism that improves the quality (i.e., signal-to-noise ratio) of sensory information taken in from that location.

Recordings of ERPs in the aforementioned threshold detection task (Luck, Hillyard, Mouloua, et al., 1994) provided further insight into the attentional mechanisms involved. Subjects were cued by a control arrow (or arrows) as to the most likely of four locations where a near-threshold target might occur. It was found that the ERP evoked by valid (precued) stimuli showed an enhanced N1 component relative to a neutral cue condition (all locations precued), whereas the invalid (uncued) stimulus elicited a reduced P1 amplitude relative to the neutral condition (Figure 10). In other words, the benefits of spatial precuing involved an enhancement of sensory evoked activity to valid cues, whereas the costs were associated with a suppression of evoked activity to invalid cues. Because costs and benefits were associated with separate ERP components, however, it appears that they were produced by qualitatively different attentional mechanisms that exert control over the flow of visual information in the cortex at different stages of processing. Thus, the answer to the traditional question of whether attention produces enhancement of attended information or suppression of unattended information appears to be that both mechanisms may operate (at least in the case of cued spatial attention), but at different stages. Although it remains to be seen whether this qualitative difference between mechanisms of costs and benefits extends to other task situations, it seems reasonable to consider that some instances of asymmetric costs and benefits in cuing studies (e.g., Hawkins et al., 1990) may result from such a difference.

Visual Search

Visual search experiments have suggested that detection of a multifeature conjunction target in an array of confusable items requires the serial ap-

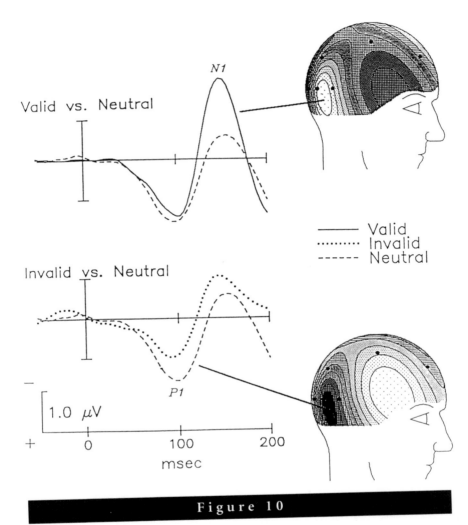

Figure 10

Event-related potentials (ERPs) in a spatial cuing experiment (Luck, Hillyard, Mouloua, et al., 1994), in which an arrow precue indicated the most likely location of a near-threshold target that was followed immediately by a diffuse mask stimulus. The ERPs at left were elicited by the target–mask complex and were recorded from an occipital scalp site contralateral to the position of the eliciting target–mask stimulus. Head maps show the approximate scalp current density distributions of the N1 benefits effect (top) and the P1 costs effect (bottom), which are spline-interpolated over 12 electrode sites. Darker shading indicates positive values of current density emerging from the scalp; lighter shading represents increasingly negative values. From *The Cognitive Neurosciences* (p. 678), edited by M. S. Gazzaniga, 1995, Cambridge, MA: MIT Press. Copyright 1995 by MIT Press. Reprinted with permission.

plication of "focal attention" (Treisman & Gormican, 1988) to the array items. A basic theoretical question is whether the same attentional processes are engaged during both visual search and spatial cuing tasks. We addressed this question by recording ERPs to irrelevant probe stimuli that were flashed at either target or nontarget locations in a search array (Luck et al., 1993; Luck & Hillyard, 1995). When subjects searched for a conjunction target, the probe-evoked P1 and N1 components were enhanced for probes flashed at the target location relative to nontarget locations. Our interpretation was that the focusing of attention within a search array engages attentional mechanisms in common with the spatial cuing of attention, because very similar patterns of ERP changes were produced in the two situations.

Further insight into how attention operates during visual search was obtained by recording ERPs to the search arrays themselves. In tasks where subjects were required to detect target stimuli in the presence of competing distractor items, a negative component appeared in the ERP elicited by the entire array (Luck & Hillyard, 1990). This component had a latency in the N2 range (200–300 ms) and was largest over the posterior (p) scalp contralateral (c) to the visual field of the target item; hence, this component was labeled the *N2pc*. Because the N2pc was not elicited by targets presented in the absence of distractors, it was hypothesized that this ERP reflects an attentional process that suppresses or filters the competing information from surrounding distractors (Luck & Hillyard, 1994a, 1994b).

Figure 11 summarizes the results of several experiments that were undertaken to test this hypothesis. In these experiments, arrays of one or eight items were presented and subjects indicated whether a predefined target stimulus was present within each array. In most cases, one item within each array contained a simple feature that was absent from the remaining items and thus appeared to pop out from the background (e.g., a single horizontal bar in an array of vertical bars). The ERP waveforms elicited by target-present and target-absent arrays were then compared. As shown at the top of Figure 11, target-present arrays elicited a negative-going N2pc component at electrode sites overlying the visual cortex contralateral to the position of the target item. Arrays containing a nontarget item that was very similar to the target item also elicited an N2pc component (Figure 11, second row), but arrays containing a dissimilar nontarget item did not (Figure 11, third row). The absence of the N2pc com-

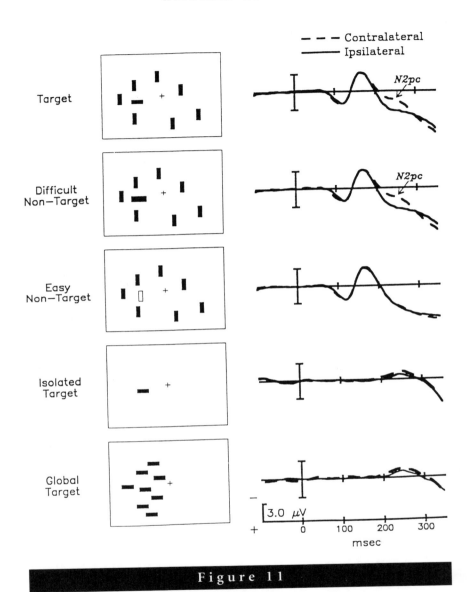

Figure 11

Event-related potentials (ERPs) elicited by different types of stimulus arrays in visual search tasks. ERPs are grand averaged over 12 subjects. The ERPs shown for isolated targets and global targets are difference waves formed by subtracting the ERP to nontargets from the ERP to targets. See text for detailed description. (Data are from Luck & Hillyard, 1994a.)

ponent for easily distinguishable nontargets indicates that the N2pc is contingent on a preliminary stimulus analysis, whereas the presence of the N2pc for difficult nontargets indicates that it is triggered prior to the final identification of a stimulus as a target. This suggests that the process reflected by the N2pc component is interposed between an initial feature analysis stage and the completion of stimulus identification. The N2pc component elicited by targets was virtually eliminated when the distractor items were removed from the search arrays (Figure 11, fourth row) or when all of the search items were identical (Figure 11, bottom row), supporting the proposal that the N2pc reflects the suppression of information arising from competing distractor items.

The scalp topography of the N2pc indicates that its neural generator source is highly posterior, within the visual areas of the occipital lobe (Figure 12). In fact, the topographic focus of the N2pc component was situated at least as posteriorly as the focus of the P1 component, even though the N2pc has its onset approximately 100 ms after the P1 component (Luck & Hillyard, 1994b). This suggests that the N2pc component reflects feedback from higher areas—in other words, re-entrant processing. Thus, the N2pc component appears to index an attentional process that suppresses conflicting information arising from distractor items in occipital visual cortex after a preliminary feature analysis has indicated that a target item is likely to be present in the array (Luck, 1994). A similar filtering of distractors was observed in recordings of single neurons in visual areas V4 and IT of the macaque (Chelazzi, Miller, Duncan, & Desimone, 1993). Such a mechanism is consistent with guided search models (Wolfe, Cave, & Franzel, 1989), which propose that preattentive processes can be used to guide attentional filtering during visual search.

CONCLUSION

Evidence from neuroimaging studies is being used increasingly to evaluate alternative psychological models of attentional processes, following the logic of converging operations developed by C.W. Eriksen and associates. The ERP studies reviewed in this chapter provide converging data that bear on a number of specific questions that are under active investigation by cognitive researchers. In particular, these ERP findings lend support the following conclusions: (a) Visuospatial attention is special and uses mech-

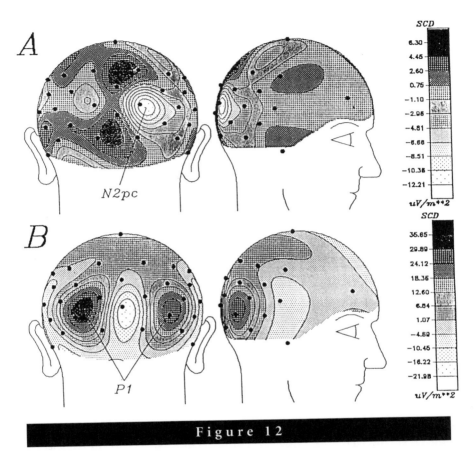

Figure 12

A: Isocontour map of the scalp current density (SCD) of the N2pc component (at 200–250 ms) elicited by target search arrays containing color pop-out items. Map is arranged so that the left and right sides of the outline head represent electrode sites ipsilateral and contralateral to the pop-out item, respectively. B: Scalp current density map of the P1 component (80–120 ms) elicited by homogeneous (nontarget) search arrays. Dark shading represents current sources and light shading represents current sinks associated with the event-related potential (ERP) components. Reprinted from "Spatial Filtering During Visual Search: Evidence From Human Electrophysiology," by S. J. Luck and S. A. Hillyard, 1994b, *Journal of Experimental Psychology: Human Perception and Performance, 20,* p. 1011. Copyright 1994 by the American Psychological Association.

anisms that differ from those used when selection is based on nonspatial features; (b) these spatial attention mechanisms are engaged in several types of task situations, including sustained attention, cued attention, and visual search; (c) spatial attention involves an amplitude modulation (gain control) of sensory processing and constitutes an early selection mechanism that acts prior to selection of other stimulus features and before the completion of object identification; (d) the spotlight of spatial attention is not readily divisible into separate beams; (e) cuing of probable stimulus location results in improved perceptual processing associated with early modulation of sensory input; (f) this early input modulation appears to act at different levels of processing for validly and invalidly cued stimuli—costs are associated with a suppression of cortical inputs at a latency of 80–130 ms and benefits with enhanced inputs at 140–180 ms; (g) visual search mechanisms include both an early suppression of irrelevant (distractor) locations at 80–130 ms and a later filtering of distractors at 200–250 ms on the basis of a preliminary, feature-based analysis of the stimulus array. Future studies that combine ERP (or ERF) recordings with other neuroimaging methods should further illuminate cognitive theories of attention as well as the underlying neural mechanisms.

REFERENCES

Allison, T., Begleiter, A., McCarthy, G., Roessler, E., Nobre, A. C., & Spencer, D. D. (1993). Electrophysiological studies of color processing in human visual cortex. *Electroencephalography of Clinical Neurophysiology, 88,* 343–355.

Anllo-Vento, L. (1995). Shifting attention in visual space: The effects of peripheral cuing on brain cortical potentials. *International Journal of Neuroscience, 80,* 353–370.

Castiello, U., & Umilta, C. (1992). Splitting focal attention. *Journal of Experimental Psychology: Human Perception and Performance, 18,* 837–848.

Chelazzi, L., Miller, E. K., Duncan, J., & Desimone, R. (1993). A neural basis for visual search in inferior temporal cortex. *Nature, 363,* 345–347.

Clark, V. P. (1993). *Localization and identification of functional regions within the human visual system.* Unpublished doctoral dissertation, University of California, San Diego.

Clark, V. P., Fan, S., & Hillyard, S. A. (1995). Identification of early visually evoked potential generators by retinotopic and topographic analyses. *Human Brain Mapping, 2,* 170–187.

Corbetta, M., Miezin, F. M., Dobmeyer, S., Shulman, G. L., & Petersen, S. E. (1991). Selective and divided attention during visual discriminations of shape, color, and speed: Functional anatomy by positron emission tomography. *Journal of Neuroscience, 11,* 2383–2402.

Corbetta, M., Miezin, F. M., Shulman, G.L., & Petersen, S. E. (1993). A PET study of visuospatial attention. *Journal of Neuroscience, 13,* 1202–1226.

Dale, A. M., & Sereno, M. I. (1993). Improved localization of cortical activity by combining EEG and MEG with MRI cortical surface reconstruction: A linear approach. *Journal of Cognitive Neuroscience, 5,* 162–176.

Desimone, R., Wessinger, M., Thomas, L., & Schneider, W. (1990). Attentional control of visual perception: Cortical and subcortical mechanisms. *Cold Spring Harbor Symposium on Quantitative Biology, 55,* 963–971.

Eason, R. G. (1981). Visual evoked potential correlates of early neural filtering during selective attention. *Bulletin of the Psychonomic Society, 18,* 203–206.

Eason, R., Harter, M., & White, C. (1969). Effects of attention and arousal on visually evoked cortical potentials and reaction time in man. *Physiology and Behavior, 4,* 283–289.

Eimer, M. (1994). Sensory gating as a mechanism for visual spatial orienting: Electrophysiological evidence from trial-by-trial cuing experiments. *Perception and Psychophysics, 55,* 667–675.

Eriksen, C. W., & St. James, J. D. (1986). Visual attention within and around the field of focal attention: A zoom lens model. *Perception and Psychophysics, 40,* 225–240.

Eriksen, C. W., & Yeh, Y. Y. (1985). Allocation of attention in the visual field. *Journal of Experimental Psychology: Human Perception and Performance, 11,* 583–597.

Fox, P. T., & Woldorff, M. G. (1994). Integrating human brain maps. *Current Opinion in Neurobiology, 4,* 151–156.

Garner, W. R., Hake, H. W., & Eriksen, C. W. (1956). Operationism and the concept of perception. *Psychology Review, 63,* 149–159.

Gomez, C. M., Clark, V. P., Luck, S. J., Fan, S., & Hillyard, S. A. (1994). Sources of attention-sensitive visual event-related potentials. *Brain Topography, 7,* 41–51.

Harter, M. R., & Aine, C. J. (1984). Brain mechanisms of visual selective attention. In R. Parasuraman & D. R. Davies (Eds.), *Varieties of attention* (pp. 293–321). San Diego, CA: Academic Press.

Harter, M. R., Aine, C., & Schroeder, C. (1982). Hemispheric differences in the neural processing of stimulus location and type: Effects of selective attention on visual evoked potentials. *Neuropsychologia, 20,* 421–438.

Harter, M. R., Miller, S. L., Price, N. J., LaLonde, M. E., & Keyes, A. L. (1989). Neural processes involved in directing attention. *Journal of Cognitive Neuroscience, 1,* 223–237.

Hawkins, H. L., Hillyard, S. A., Luck, S. J., Mouloua, M., Downing, C. J., & Woodward, D. P. (1990). Visual attention modulates signal detectability. *Journal of Experimental Psychology: Human Perception and Performance, 16*, 802–811.

Haxby, J. V., Grady, C. L., Horwitz, B., Salerno, J., Ungerleider, L. G., Mishkin, M., & Schapiro, M. B. (1993). Dissociation of object and spatial visual processing pathways in human extrastriate cortex. In B. Gulyas, D. Ottoson, & P. E. Roland (Eds.), *Functional organisation of human visual cortex* (pp. 329–340). Elmsford, NY: Pergamon Press.

Haxby, J. V., Grady, C. L., Horwitz, B., Ungerleider, L. G., Mishikin, M., Carson, R. E., Herscovitch, P., Schapiro, M. B., & Rapoport, S. I. (1991). Dissociation of object and spatial visual processing pathways in human extrastriate cortex. *Proceedings of the National Academy of Sciences, 88*, 1621–1625.

Heinze, H. J., Luck, S. J., Mangun, G. R., & Hillyard, S. A. (1990). Visual event-related potentials index focused attention within bilateral stimulus arrays: I. Evidence for early selection. *Electroencephalography and Clinical Neurophysiology, 75*, 511–527.

Heinze, H. J., Luck, S. J., Munte, T. F., Goes, A., Mangun, G. R., & Hillyard, S. A. (1994a). Attention to adjacent and separate positions in space: An electrophysiological analysis. *Perception and Psychophysics, 56*, 42–52.

Heinze, H. J., Mangun, G. R., Burchert, W., Hinrichs, H., Scholz, M., Münte, T. F., Gös, A., Scherg, M., Johannes, S., Hundeshagen, H., Gazzaniga, M. S., & Hillyard, S. A. (1994b). Combined spatial and temporal imaging of brain activity during visual selective attention in humans. *Nature, 372*, 543–546.

Hillyard, S. A. (1993). Electrical and magnetic brain recordings: Contributions to cognitive neuroscience. *Current Opinion in Neurobiology, 3*, 217–224.

Hillyard, S. A., Luck, S. J., & Mangun, G. R. (1994). The cuing of attention to visual field locations: Analysis with ERP recordings. In H. J. Heinze, T. F. Munte, & G. R. Mangun (Eds.), *Cognitive electrophysiology: Event-related brain potentials in basic and clinical research* (pp. 1–25). Boston: Birkhausen.

Hillyard, S. A., & Mangun, G. R. (1987). Commentary: Sensory gating as a physiological mechanism for visual selective attention. In R. Johnson, Jr., J. W. Rohrbaugh, & R. Parasuraman (Eds.), *Current trends in event-related potential research* (pp. 61–67). Amsterdam: Elsevier.

Hillyard, S. A., Mangun, G. R., Woldorff, M. G., & Luck, S. J. (1995). Neural systems mediating selective attention. In M. S. Gazzaniga (Ed.), *The cognitive neurosciences* (pp. 665–681). Cambridge, MA: MIT Press.

Hillyard, S. A., & Münte, T. F. (1984). Selective attention to color and locational cues:

An analysis with event-related brain potentials. *Perception and Psychophysics,* *36,* 185–198.

Hillyard, S. A., & Picton, T. W. (1987). Electrophysiology of cognition. In F. Plum (Ed.), *Handbook of physiology higher functions of the nervous system, section 1: The nervous system: Vol. V. Higher functions of the brain, Part 2* (pp. 519–584). Baltimore: Waverly Press.

Kahneman, D., & Treisman, A. (1984). Changing views of attention and automaticity. In R. Parasurman & R. Davies (Eds.), *Varieties of attention* (pp. 29–61). San Diego, CA: Academic Press.

Kenemans, J. L., Kok, A., & Smulders, F. T. Y. (1993). Event-related potentials to conjunctions of spatial frequency and orientation as a function of stimulus parameters and response requirements. *Electroencephalography and Clinical Neurophysiology, 88,* 51–63.

LaBerge, D. (1995). Computational and anatomical models of selective attention in object identification. In M. S. Gazzaniga (Ed.), *The cognitive neurosciences* (pp. 649–664). Cambridge, MA: MIT Press.

LaBerge, D., & Brown, V. (1989). Theory of attentional operations in shape identification. *Psychological Review, 96,* 101–124.

Luck, S. J. (1994). Cognitive and neural mechanisms of visual search. *Current Opinion in Neurobiology, 4,* 183–188.

Luck, S. J., Fan, S., & Hillyard, S. A. (1993). Attention-related modulation of sensory-evoked brain activity in a visual search task. *Journal of Cognitive Neuroscience, 5,* 188–195.

Luck, S. J., & Hillyard, S. A. (1990). Electrophysiological evidence for parallel and serial processing during visual search. *Perception and Psychophysics, 48,* 603–617.

Luck, S. J., & Hillyard, S. A. (1994a). Electrophysiological correlates of feature analysis during visual search. *Psychophysiology, 31,* 291–308.

Luck, S. J., & Hillyard, S. A. (1994b). Spatial filtering during visual search: Evidence from human electrophysiology. *Journal of Experimental Psychology: Human Perception and Performance, 20,* 1000–1014.

Luck, S. J., & Hillyard, S. A. (1995). The role of attention in feature detection and conjunction discrimination: An electrophysiological analysis. *International Journal of Neuroscience, 80,* 281–297.

Luck, S. J., Hillyard, S. A., Mangun, G. R., & Gazzaniga, M. S. (1994). Independent attentional scanning in the separated hemispheres of split-brain patients. *Journal of Cognitive Neuroscience, 6,* 84–91.

Luck, S. J., Hillyard, S. A., Mouloua, M., Woldorff, M. G., Clark, V. P., & Hawkins,

H. L. (1994). Effects of spatial cuing on luminance detectability: Psychophysical and electrophysiological evidence for early selection. *Journal of Experimental Psychology: Human Perception and Performance, 20,* 887–904.

Mangun, G. R., & Hillyard, S. A. (1990). Electrophysiological studies of visual selective attention in humans. In A. B. Scheibel & A. F. Wechsler (Eds.), *Neurobiology of higher cognitive function* (pp. 271–295). New York: Guilford Press.

Mangun, G. R., & Hillyard, S. A. (1991). Modulations of sensory-evoked brain potentials indicate changes in perceptual processing during visual-spatial priming. *Journal of Experimental Psychology: Human Perception and Performance, 17,* 1057–1074.

Mangun, G. R., Hillyard, S. A., & Luck, S. J. (1993). Electrocortical substrates of visual selective attention. In D. Meyer & S. Kornblum (Eds.), *Attention and performance XIV* (pp. 219–243). Cambridge, MA: MIT Press.

McCarthy, G., & Nobre, A. C. (1993). Modulation of semantic processing by spatial selective attention. *Electroencephalography and Clinical Neurophysiology, 88,* 210–219.

Petersen, S. E., Fiez, J. A., & Corbetta, M. (1992). Neuroimaging. *Current Opinion in Neurobiology, 2,* 217–222.

Posner, M. I. (1980). Orienting of attention. *Quarterly Journal of Experimental Psychology, 32,* 3–25.

Posner, M. I., & Dehaene, S. (1994). Attentional networks. *Trends in Neurosciences, 17,* 75–79.

Posner, M. I., Snyder, C. R. R., & Davidson, B. J. (1980). Attention and the detection of signals. *Journal of Experimental Psychology: General, 109,* 160–174.

Previc, F. H., & Harter, M. R. (1982). Electrophysiological and behavioral indicants of selective attention to multifeature gratings. *Perception & Psychophysics, 32,* 465–472.

Reinitz, M. T. (1990). Effects of spatially directed attention on visual encoding. *Perception & Psychophysics, 47,* 497–505.

Rubin, T. C., Luck, S. J., Anllo-Vento, L., Hansen, J. C., & Hillyard, S. A. (1993). Attention to color: Evidence from multichannel human electrophysiology. *Abstracts of the Society for Neuroscience, 19,* 563.

Shaw, M. L., & Shaw, P. (1977). Optimal allocation of cognitive resources to spatial locations. *Journal of Experimental Psychology: Human Perception and Performance, 3,* 201–211.

Shiu, L., & Pashler, H. (1994). Negligible effect of spatial precuing on identification of single digits. *Journal of Experimental Psychology: Human Perception and Performance, 20,* 1037–1054.

Sperling, G., & Dosher, B. A. (1986). Strategy and optimization in human information processing. In K. R. Boff, L. Kaufman, & J. P. Thomas (Eds.), *Handbook of perception and human performance* (Vol. 1, pp. 2–65). New York: Wiley.

Talairach, J., & Tournoux, P. (1988). *Co-planar stereotaxic atlas of the human brain: 3-Dimensional proportional system: An approach to cerebral imaging.* New York: Thieme Medical Publishing.

Treisman, A. M., & Gelade, G. (1980). A feature-integration theory of attention. *Cognitive Psychology, 12,* 97–136.

Treisman, A., & Gormican, S. (1988). Feature analysis in early vision: Evidence from search asymmetries. *Psychological Review, 95,* 15–48.

Ungerleider, L. G., & Haxby, J. V. (1994). What and where in the human brain. *Current Opinion in Neurobiology, 4,* 157–165.

Van der Heijden, A. H. C. (1992). *Selective attention in vision.* London: Routledge & Kegan Paul.

Wijers, A. A., Mulder, G., Okita, T., & Mulder, L. J. M. (1989). Event-related potentials during memory search and selective attention to letter size and conjunctions of letter size and color. *Psychophysiology, 26,* 529–547.

Wolfe, J. M., Cave, K. R., & Franzel, S. L. (1989). Guided search: An alternative to the feature integration model for visual search. *Journal of Experimental Psychology: Human Perception and Performance, 15,* 419–433.

5

Visual Attention: Converging Operations From Neurology and Psychology

Robert Rafal

H uman infants, even newborns, are attracted to orient to the human face (Johnson & Morton, 1991). The reader with any military training will know from harsh experience that this social orienting is a very powerful reflex. Troops being inspected on parade are required to stand to attention with the eyes fixed straight ahead. They are not permitted to turn toward the inspector when approached, and even when directly confronted and interrogated, they are expected to "look through" the drill instructor. It is very hard not to orient to someone who approaches you, looks you in the eye, and yells at you. To inhibit this social orienting reflex takes great discipline (which is, for military purposes, the point of the exercise). Nevertheless, after being punished with enough pushups, the recruit can learn to inhibit the powerful impulse to orient.

In everyday life there are constantly competing demands on attention from the outside world as well as from internally generated goals. The need for mechanisms to arbitrate between these competing demands is obvious, so that they can be integrated to provide coherent and adaptive be-

I thank Marie Banich, Michael Coles, Gordon Logan, and Lynn Robertson for their suggestions. Parts of this work were supported by Public Health Service Grants MH41544 and MH51400.

havior. This point is well illustrated by the hapless soldier who has not yet learned to use voluntary systems for allocating attention to inhibit reflexive orienting. In this chapter I review the neurobiology of these neural mechanisms for orienting attention from a neurological perspective. The content of the chapter draws on knowledge from cognitive science, neural science, and clinical neurology. It focuses on spatial orienting as a model system for understanding mind–brain relationships and for appreciating the biological basis of a basic mental process in health and disease. The themes of this chapter seem especially appropriate to honor Charles Eriksen. He pioneered research on visual attention and established it as a valid issue for scientific inquiry and a major concern of psychological science. The framework and approach followed here, moreover, pays tribute to his emphasis on the importance of converging operations in the study of the mind.

SYNDROMES AND METHOD

Given the power of reflexive orienting in everyday life, it is striking that people who have suffered injuries to specific brain regions may not orient spontaneously even to some compelling stimuli. Patients with unilateral lesions destroying all of the primary visual (striate) cortex of the occipital lobe have a visual sensory defect obliterating the entire contralesional visual field: a *hemianopia*. When presented with objects or light flashes anywhere in the visual field opposite the lesion (often right up to the midline) they will be unaware of them and deny seeing them. This is so even when there is no other stimulus present in a darkened room, and even when they are told to expect signals there.

Nevertheless, these patients can learn to compensate quite well for their restricted visual field. For example, some hemianopic individuals continue to drive and compensate for their field defect by learning to make frequent eye movements to the affected side (Lovsund, Hedin, & Tornros, 1991). Driving with a hemianopia is not safe—and it is against medical advice—but the amazing thing is that that these individuals do not have more accidents than they do. In isolation, a hemianopia, especially if it spares the most central, parafoveal region (macular sparing), is typically not experienced as a severe impairment by the patient.

In contrast, patients with a lesion of the temperoparietal cortex, although they have no primary deficit of sensation, are often severely handicapped by the syndrome of neglect. When the syndrome is severe, the patient will not even turn to a visitor speaking from the contralesional side. Instead, the patient may turn to the good (or ipsilesional) side and look for the person addressing him or her. If there happens to be another person on the good side, the patient may reply to that person and carry on the conversation with the wrong individual. Patients with neglect may fail to eat food from one side of their plate or fail to shave or to apply makeup to one side of their face.

The clinician distinguishes neglect from hemianopia by testing for a sign called *extinction*. The patient is asked to keep the eyes fixed on the examiner's face and to report objects (or a wiggling finger) presented in one or both visual fields. Unlike the patient with hemianopia, who will not see an object presented in the blind field, a patient with neglect will often report the presence of an object presented by itself in the field opposite the lesion (contralesional). When another object is presented simultaneously in the other (ipsilesional) field, however, the patient usually will not see the contralesional stimulus and will insist that there is nothing there.

In the acute stage of severe neglect, the patient is often unaware of the fact that he or she has had a stroke or that there is anything wrong—even if one side of the body is totally paralyzed, a condition referred to as *anosognosia*. This can result in behavior that is not only disorganized and poorly integrated, but at times bizarre. Perhaps the most striking example of this is the "misoplegia" described by Critchley (1979). The neglected limb is treated as a hostile intruder and at times even damaged by the patient. When shown his or her own hand and asked to identify it, the patient may reply that "it's your hand." Occasionally, on happening to touch the neglected arm with the good hand, the patient may complain about it; one of my patients even called to insist that someone "get this nurse out of my bed."

Fortunately it is rare for such severe neglect to persist. After a time the attention defect may not be obvious at all and may only be elicited by testing for extinction. Eventually, clinical extinction (as tested at the bedside) may become inconsistent, and the problem may only be manifest with experimental testing in which brief stimuli are presented simultaneously. However, a patient with even mild extinction is more likely to have practical problems in everyday life than does a patient with hemianopia. Such a patient is much more at risk of an accident if he or she drives. Less serious, but still embarrassing, is the situation where a man walks into the ladies' room because he misses the first two letters in the sign *WOMEN.*

In this chapter I review some of what is known about the psychobiology of the clinical disorders neglect and hemianopia, and of some other more rare syndromes. The goals of the current analysis are twofold: to understand how attentional processes operate in regulating normal perception and action and to identify the neural basis of visual attention. The methodological approaches to these two issues may be quite different. Each focuses on different questions and requires investigation at a different level of analysis.

By studying patients with certain syndromes, researchers can learn much about how visual attention operates and for which kinds of processing and actions it is required. For example, the study of patients with visual neglect can tell us much about early vision: what kind of visual processing occurs at a preattentive level, how this information can influence behavior outside of conscious awareness, and what role attention plays in integrating perceptual features and selecting objects and actions for awareness in guiding goal-directed behavior. It can be informative to ask, for an individual patient, what information is processed in the neglected field? Is it a region of space that is being neglected? Or does neglect operate on a viewer-centered, object-centered, environment-centered, or action-centered frame of reference?

However, the study of patients with clinical syndromes such as neglect may not be very helpful when the goal is to identify the neural substrates and the circuitry of visual attention. Patients with such striking clinical syndromes as neglect typically have large lesions that affect several brain areas. Moreover, neglect can occur with lesions in very different brain regions: parietal lobe, frontal eye fields, cingulate cortex, basal ganglia, thalamus, or midbrain. The pathophysiologic basis of neglect after such diverse lesions may be quite different from patient to patient. The reason for defective orienting may be quite different in each case. The neglect syndrome, for example, constitutes a heterogeneous group of disorders consisting of one or more component deficits in any given patient. Its manifestations depend on the extent and chronicity of the lesion, as well as on the patient's individual brain architecture and personal history.

For these reasons, although single-case studies can reveal much about the architecture of normal cognition, a very different approach is necessary to investigate the specific contributions of the parietal lobe, midbrain, pulvinar, or prefrontal cortex or their dynamic interaction. These anatomical questions require the study of groups of patients with well-circumscribed lesions affecting one of the structures in the network but sparing others. This approach generally requires the selection of patients with relatively small lesions who may not manifest, in the chronic stage of illness when the remote (diaschesis) effects on other parts of the network have resolved, any clinically obvious attentional disorder.

This kind of analysis has become possible only in the past decade or so with the development of neuroimaging techniques with high resolution, such as computerized axial tomography (CT) and magnetic resonance imaging (MRI). During this same period that the lesion method has matured in the study of human cognition, other methods of dynamic brain imaging such as event-related potential recordings (from scalp or implanted electrodes), positron emission tomography, magnetoencephalography, and functional MRI have provided converging findings in both brain-injured and normal human subjects. Investigators are now beginning to put together these various strands of research.

In this chapter I first review what has been learned about the role of specific brain structures in orienting attention to locations in the visual field. I then consider what attention does in regulating perception and action; that is, what attention does in integrating features into objects and in selecting objects or parts of objects for further processing, conscious awareness, or goal-directed action. I conclude the chapter by coming back to the problem of visual neglect and attempting a synthesis of knowledge about this syndrome that explains its component symptoms, their pathophysiological bases, and how one might understand the interactions of the component symptoms in the daily lives of individuals who have it. Both syndrome-based observations and anatomy-based studies are considered (Robertson, Knight, Rafal, & Shimamura, 1993) in order to illustrate how each approach contributes to the understanding of the mechanisms and functions of visual attention.

NEURAL MECHANISMS FOR ORIENTING ATTENTION TO LOCATIONS IN THE VISUAL FIELD

Measuring Shifts of Covert Attention

I begin by introducing an experimental paradigm used for measuring the orienting of attention to a location in the visual field to detect a luminance change there. When Posner first began to examine this problem in humans in the mid-1970s, he selected it because it fostered an active contact with a converging strand of research in neuroscience. Because this is a simple cognitive act that humans share with other animals, there is a growing literature in neurophysiology that begins to link this behavior to its neural substrates. The paradigm Posner developed for measuring covert shifts of visual attention (Posner, 1980) was designed to be simple enough to relate to studies done in animals. This simplicity also made it possible to examine brain mechanisms for orienting attention in humans through the study of brain-injured individuals and more recently to trace the development of these mechanisms in infants (Clohessy, Posner, & Rothbart, 1991; Johnson, 1990; Rothbart, Posner, & Boylan, 1991). The past decade has revealed quite a bit about the neural basis for visual orienting in humans.

The purpose of the paradigm is to permit the measurement of covert shifts of attention. *Covert orienting* refers to the allocating of attention to a point in space independent of eye position (overt orienting). Although people usually move attention and the eyes in concert, it is possible to show that overt and covert orienting can occur separately. Take the example of the quarterback who looks at one potential receiver downfield while selecting the intended receiver "out of the corner of the eye."

In a typical spatial attention experiment using the precuing method, the subject is asked to respond, by pressing a key, to the appearance of a target at a peripheral location. The target is preceded by a precue that may summon attention to the target location (valid cue) or to the wrong location (invalid cue) or may have only an alerting value and provide no spatial information (neutral cue). The cue may be a flash of light at one of the possible target locations (see Figure 1, left panel) or an arrow in the center of the display instructing the subject where to expect the forthcoming target signal (see Figure 1, right panel). As I show later, these two

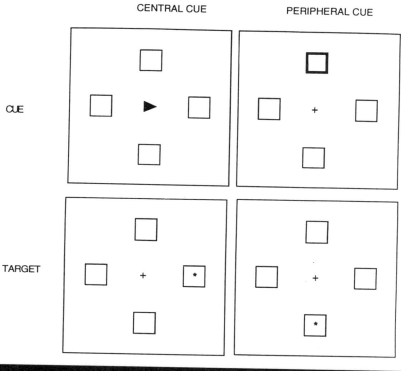

Figure 1

The left panel shows the display used in measuring endogenous attention movements, and the right panel shows the display used for measuring reflexive orienting to exogenous cues. The subjects' task was to press a response key as soon as they detect a target (the large asterisk) in any of the four boxes (bottom). Each trial begins (top) with the presentation of a precue, which summons attention to one of the possible target locations. The effectiveness of the cue in summoning attention is inferred from the difference in reaction time when the target appears at the cued location (valid cue condition) in comparison with an uncued location (invalid cue condition). Two examples of the possible conditions are shown. The left panel shows a valid endogenous cue in the horizontal plane. The right panel shows an invalid exogenous cue in the vertical plane. Endogenous cues and exogenous cues were studies in different blocks of trials. The experiment depicted here was used to study patients with progressive supranuclear palsy; vertical and horizontal shifts of attention were compared. In the comparable experiment used to study patients with unilateral cortical lesions, only left and right cues and targets were used; contralesional shifts of attention were compared with shifts toward the ipsilesional field.

types of cues may be used to examine whether a given lesion has different effects on reflexive orienting (peripheral cue) or voluntary orienting (central cue). In most of the studies that have been done in neurologic patients, the task is simply to detect the appearance of a large, bright visual signal and make a simple reaction time (RT) keypress response. Other dependent variables may be used, however, including saccade latency to make an eye movement to the target, or discrimination efficiency (as measure by either choice RT or discrimination accuracy).

Orienting of attention results in increased efficiency of target processing at cued locations (valid cue) relative to uncued locations (a neutral or an invalid cue). Experiments of this kind have indicated that orienting to a spatial location has both facilitatory and inhibitory components (Posner, 1980). Compared with a neutral cue condition, performance at the attended location is facilitated, whereas processing and responding to signals at other locations are less efficient. These effects have been demonstrated in a variety of situations including detecting suprathreshold luminance changes (brightening or dimming; Posner & Cohen, 1984), signal-detection studies of near-threshold stimuli (Bashinski & Bacharach, 1980; Downing, 1988), discrimination tasks (Egly & Homa, 1991; Henderson, 1991), and using event-related potentials recorded from the scalp (Hillyard, 1993; Rugg, Milner, Lines, & Phalp, 1987).

The experimental paradigm shown in Figure 1 has the virtue of revealing several putative components of visual orienting. When an individual is attending to an object of interest, attention is engaged at the location of that object. If attention is to be deployed elsewhere, it must first be disengaged from its current focus and then be moved to the new location. In this paradigm, normal detection when the cue is valid implies that the individual is able to move attention in response to the cue. If a valid cue affords no benefit in performance and no difference in detection is observed between valid and invalid cue conditions, it could be inferred that the individual is unable to move attention. If, on the other hand, the individual is able to move attention in response to a valid cue, but is selectively impaired in detection when the cue is invalid, then there will be a large difference in detection performance in valid and invalid cue conditions and a deficit in disengaging attention can be inferred. The reader may recognize this last case as familiar. As described earlier, a patient with a parietal lobe lesion causing extinction is relatively unimpaired in detecting a signal presented alone in the contralesional field and therefore is manifestly competent to move attention toward that field. When a competing stimulus is presented simultaneously in the ipsilesional field, however, attention becomes stuck there and the patient is unable to disengage attention to detect the contralesional stimulus.

Posner and Petersen (1990) have argued that these three elementary operations—disengage, move, and engage—are mediated by different anatomic structures within a distributed posterior brain system. The primary evidence for this account derives from observations that lesions in different brain regions can selectively impair each of these operations, as revealed by the location-precuing paradigm. The following sections summarize some of that evidence.

The Mechanism of Extinction: Disengaging Attention After Parietal Lesions

In our initial study of covert orienting in patients with parietal lesions (Posner, Walker, Friedrich, & Rafal, 1984), patients were selected solely on the basis of having a lesion involving the parietal lobe. Some had acute lesions and some chronic, some had strokes, and some had tumors or other etiologies. In many the lesion also extended beyond the parietal lobe to involve the frontal lobe as well. Some patients had obvious neglect, some had extinction without more evident neglect symptoms, and some had no clinically detectable attention defect. The experiment showed that all patients, even those patients who did not have neglect or show clinical extinction on conventional examination, demonstrated an "extinction-like-reaction-time pattern" (Posner, Inhoff, Friedrich, & Cohen, 1987; Posner et al., 1984; Posner, Walker, Friedrich, & Rafal, 1987). Detection RT in the field opposite to the lesion (contralesional field) was not slowed much (and in some patients not slowed at all compared with the ipsilesional field) if a valid cue was given. So, the patients were able to use the precue to move their attention to the contralesional field, and when they did so their performance for contralesional targets was relatively unimpaired. When, however, a cue summoned attention toward the ipsilesional field and the target subsequently occurred in the opposite, contralesional field (invalid cue), detection RT slowed dramatically.

In a more recent study conducted by Senechal in my laboratory, designed to extend the findings of Posner et al. (1984), the purpose was twofold. First she sought to compare exogenously triggered orienting (toward peripheral cues) and endogenously generated orienting (from central cues). Each patient was tested with nonpredictive peripheral cues and predictive (80% valid) central arrows cues as shown in Figure 1. Additionally, this investigation was intended to specify the anatomic basis of the disengage deficit. It examined only patients who had chronic lesions (at least 2 years after the stroke) restricted to the posterior association cortex in one hemisphere and sparing the frontal lobes. None of these patients had any residual clinical neglect or extinction. That is, subjects were recruited on the basis of anatomic criteria, not syndromic.

This investigation also sought to identify which areas of posterior association cortex were most critical for producing a disengage deficit; to this end, subgroups of patients with posterior association cortex lesions were compared with one another. The greatest deficits were found in those patients in whom the lesion involved the temporoparietal junction (TPJ; see Figure 2). Those whose lesions were restricted to inferior parietal lobule or superior parietal lobule showed less abnormality. Similarly, neurologic control patients with chronic unilateral lesions re-

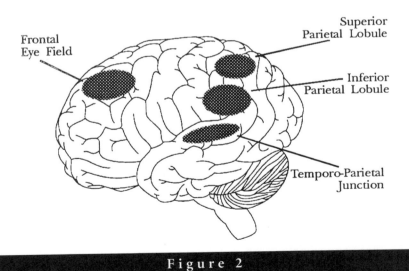

Figure 2

The neuroanatomy of spatial attention. Lateral view of the human brain showing the visual areas of the occipital lobe, inferior and superior parietal lobes, temporoparietal junction, and dorsolateral prefrontal cortex including the frontal eye fields.

stricted to dorsolateral prefrontal cortex were also relatively unimpaired in covert orienting.

The data for the patients with TPJ lesions are shown in Figure 3. This figure shows a comparison of the effects of lesions of the TPJ with those of the midbrain (to be discussed later) on orienting attention to peripheral and central cues. The figure depicts the severity of the deficit in orienting attention toward the affected field by showing the difference in detection RT between the affected and unaffected field for valid and invalid cues. For the TPJ lesion patients, two points are noteworthy. First, contralesional orienting was most severely impaired in the invalid cue condition, again confirming the role of posterior association cortex in disengaging attention. Second, this deficit was greater for central cues than for uninformative peripheral cues. This result suggests that the TPJ plays an important role in controlling the voluntary allocation of covert attention. I later contrast this pattern with that found in patients with lesions of the midbrain.

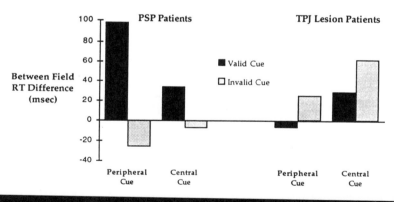

Figure 3

Covert orienting in patients with progressive supranuclear palsy (PSP) and temporoparietal junction lesions (TPJ). The results are depicted as the difference in detection reaction time (RT) between the more affected and the more normal visual fields. A greater difference in a given condition thus indicates a greater impairment in orienting in that condition. For the PSP patients (left) and the TPJ lesion patients (right), the between-fields detection RT differences are shown (in ms) for valid and invalid peripheral and central cues. The PSP patients were more impaired in the valid cue condition, especially with peripheral cues, whereas the TPJ lesion patients were more impaired in the invalid cue condition, especially for central cues.

The covert orienting studies considered above examined the effect of lesions on detection of a luminance change in a relatively uncluttered field. They show that the extinction phenomenon is caused by a deficit in attention. Yet extinction is just one component of the neglect symptom complex. Other symptoms of neglect include defective exploratory behavior as revealed by tasks such as line bisection, drawing, and cancellation. To understand how the deficit in disengaging attention can contribute to deficient exploration researchers must examine attentional search in a cluttered field in which many objects are competing for attention. This is a more typical situation in the world.

Eglin, Robertson, and Knight (1989) used a visual search task of the type developed by Treisman. They varied the side of a predesignated conjunction target (one defined by a specific color and shape, requiring the conjunction of more than one feature to identify) among a variable number of distractors and measured the time to find the target. When distractors were present, they could occur in either the ipsilesional field or the contralesional field. As long as no distractors appeared on the ipsilesional side of the display, no differences were found in locating a target on the neglected and intact sides. In other words, in displays that were limited to the ipsilesional side of a page, there were no objects to attract attention to the intact side and so nothing from which to disengage attention. Under these circumstances, the patients searched the display on the left as readily as they searched displays on the right. In contrast, for bilateral displays, in which distractors were present in both fields, search times increased as a function of the number of distractors or objects in the ipsilesional field. Each distractor on the intact side tripled the search time to locate the contralesional target. That is, the difficulty in disengaging attention from the ipsilesional field of distractors to move attention to the contralesional field depended on the number of items in the display.

Mark, Kooistra, and Heilman (1988) described an elegantly simple demonstration that patients with neglect have difficulty in disengaging attention when ipsilesional items are present. They used a line cancellation task, a conventional bedside method for demonstrating and measuring neglect. The patient is shown a page filled with lines and is asked to "cross them all out." Typically a patient with left hemineglect fails to cross out many of the items on the left side of the page. Mark et al. (1988) compared this conventional cancellation task with another condition in which they asked the patient to erase all the lines. As each line was erased, and thus no longer present, the patient no longer had to disengage from it before moving on. Performance was strikingly better in this erasure task than in the conventional line cancellation task.

Unlike in hemianopia, which affects a visual field or part of a field, in patients with neglect the difficulty in disengaging attention is found even when the cue and target are both presented in the ipsilesional (or good) field (Posner et al., 1987). That is, extinction is contingent on the direction in which attention must move, not only the visual field being tested. Although the direction of attention movement is an important factor, the visual field (i.e., ipsilateral or contralateral to the lesion) is as well. Disengaging attention to move vertically up or down is more impaired for attention movements in the contralesional field than the ipsilesional field (Baynes, Holtzman, & Volpe, 1986; Egly, Driver, & Rafal, 1994). Moreover, extinction does not necessarily operate in retinotopic coordinates. Ladavas (1987) and Farah, Brunn, Wong, Wallace, and Carpenter (1990) showed, by having patients turn their head so that left or right became up or down, that neglect or extinction can be relative to environmental coordinates. Again, this contrasts sharply with hemianopia in which the defect is decisively retinotopic. Evidence presented below indicates that neglect also occurs for an object-based frame of reference.

Midbrain Mechanisms for Reflexive Orienting to Exogenous Signals

The encephalization of visual function in cerebral cortex is a relatively new development in phylogeny. The geniculostriate pathway is fully developed only in mammals. The demands of increasingly complex visual cognition presumably generated the evolutionary pressures leading to the development of a completely new, parallel visual pathway in mammals. In lower vertebrates vision is mediated by input through the retinotectal pathway to the superior colliculus of the midbrain. What function does the phylogenetically older midbrain pathway serve in humans?

My laboratory has addressed this question by seeking converging evidence from three sources: (a) Patients with lesions of the midbrain have been examined to define what visually guided behaviors were impaired; (b) patients with hemianopia due to lesions of the visual cortex were examined to determine what visually guided behaviors were preserved when only the midbrain visual pathway was available; and (c) extrageniculate vision has been studied in normal subjects by comparing the orienting of attention into the temporal and nasal hemifields. As discussed later, this last approach exploits a difference in the normal anatomy of cortical and subcortical visual systems: The phylogenetically older midbrain pathway is asymmetrically represented, with the temporal hemifield receiving more visual information.

Orienting of Visual Attention in Progressive Supranuclear Palsy

Progressive supranuclear palsy (PSP) is a progressive degenerative disorder affecting subcortical nucleii of the diencephalon, midbrain, cerebellum, and brain stem. Because the basal ganglia and the substantia nigra are involved, the clinical picture shares many features with Parkinson's disease. In addition, however, there is degeneration, unique to this disease, involving the superior colliculus and adjacent peritectal region. This pathology results in the distinctive paralysis of voluntary eye movements especially in the vertical plane. The study of these patients affords a special opportunity to understand the function of the midbrain extrageniculate pathways in regulating human visually guided behavior.

The midbrain pathology of this disease not only produces a compromise of eye movements but also results in a striking and distinctive global derangement of visually guided behavior (Rafal, 1992). Although visual acuity is not affected, patients with PSP behave as if they are blind, even at a stage in the disease when their eyes are not totally paralyzed. They do not orient to establish eye contact with persons who approach them or engage them in conversation, nor do they look down at their plate while eating.

Using the same paradigm described earlier for studying covert orienting (see Figure 1) Rafal, Posner, Friedman, Inhoff, and Bernstein (1988) showed that PSP patients are slow not only in moving their eyes but also in moving covert visual attention. Because PSP causes greater impairment in vertical than in horizontal saccades, the speeds of orienting covert attention in the vertical and horizontal planes were compared. Patients with Parkinson's disease served as control subjects. It was predicted that vertical attention movements would be impaired in PSP patients but not in the control subjects. The experiment depicted in Figure 1 was used to compare reflexive covert orienting to exogenous signals (peripheral cue condition) with endogenously allocated covert attention (central cues).

In this experiment patients with Parkinson's disease showed comparable attention shifts in the vertical and horizontal plane for both endogenous and exogenous cues. The results for the PSP patients are shown in Figure 3 on the left and show a striking contrast with the deficit seen in patients with temperoparietal lesions (shown on the right side of the figure). The PSP patients were not impaired in orienting in the vertical as compared with the horizontal plane in the invalid cue condition. Only in the valid cue condition were the PSP patients more impaired in the vertical plane. Moreover, this impairment was chiefly for peripheral cues. Whereas valid peripheral cues produced a large benefit in detection RT within 50 ms of cue onset in the horizontal plane (compared with the invalid cue RTs), these patients showed no benefit for valid cues in the vertical plane until after 150 ms.

These results indicate that the midbrain lesions in PSP that impair vertical eye movements also impair the movement of covert attention in the vertical plane. Moreover, they show that the midbrain and temperoparietal regions have different functions in the orienting of covert attention. The midbrain seems to be involved in the movement of attention, especially for reflexive attention shifts. In contrast the temperoparietal region appears to have a more selective role in disengaging attention. As shown in Figure 3, however, patients with TPJ lesions also appear to be impaired in contralesional orienting in the valid cue condition with central cues, suggesting that this region may also play a role in moving covert attention endogenously.

Reflexive Orienting to Temporal and Nasal Hemifields in Normal Subjects

Converging evidence that the retinotectal pathway normally contributes to reflexive orienting was obtained from a study of normal adults (Rafal, Henik, & Smith, 1991). This study exploited a lateralized neuroanatomic arrangement of retinotectal pathways that distinguishes them from those of the geniculostriate system; namely, more direct projections to the colliculus from the temporal hemifield. As shown in Figure 4, the geniculostriate pathway, which is the dominant pathway to the visual cortex in the

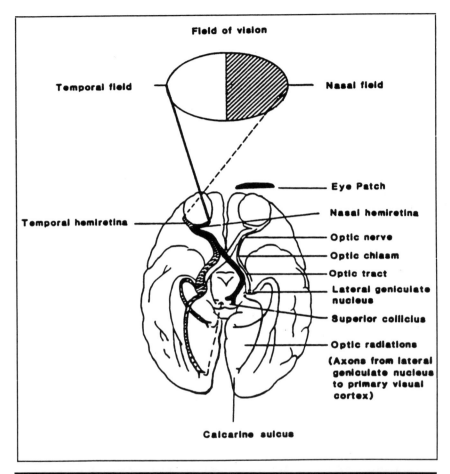

Figure 4

Visual pathways in the phylogenetically older subcortical retina–midbrain (retinotectal) pathway and the dominant geniculostriate pathway to visual cortex in the occipital lobe. In contrast to the geniculostriate pathway, which has binocular afferents, the retinotectal pathway is dominantly monocular and has a greater representation from the temporal hemifield. From *An Introduction to Neurophysiology* (p. 95), by J. F. Stein, 1982, Oxford, England: Blackwell Scientific. Copyright 1982 by Blackwell Scientific. Adapted with permission.

occipital lobe, carries both crossed and uncrossed fibers, so that the visual cortex of each hemisphere receives binocular projections representing the contralateral visual field from both eyes. In contrast, the more primitive midbrain pathways are dominantly monocular: Each colliculus receives mainly crossed fibers from the contralateral eye. Moreover, these projections are asymmetrically represented so that each eye receives visual information mainly from the temporal hemifield. Thus, a functional asymmetry between temporal and nasal hemifield activation can serve as a marker for collicular function.

In our study neurologically normal adults were tested under monocular viewing conditions and responded to the detection of a peripheral signal by making either a saccade to it or a choice RT manual keypress. Attention was summoned by noninformative peripheral precues, and the benefits and costs of attention were calculated relative to a central precue condition. Both the benefits and costs of orienting attention were greater when attention was summoned by signals in the temporal hemifield, and this temporal hemifield advantage was present for both saccade and manual responses.

Blindsight: Saccade Inhibition by Signals in the Hemianopic Field

In PSP patients it is possible to learn how spatial orienting is impaired when midbrain function is impaired. The study of hemianopic patients provides converging evidence for midbrain function by allowing investigators to examine the converse situation. Examining the effects on orienting behavior from unseen signals in the blind field of hemianopic patients can reveal what visuomotor function is preserved when only the retinotectal pathway is competent to process visual input.

The dominance of the geniculostriate pathway in human vision over the phylogenetically older retinotectal pathways is obvious in hemianopic patients who have suffered complete unilateral destruction of the striate cortex or its geniculostriate afferents. They are blind in the entire hemifield contralateral to the lesion and cannot see even salient signals, such as a waving hand, within the scotoma (the blind area). They are unable to report such events and deny any awareness of them.

As mentioned earlier, it is quite striking how well these patients compensate for their visual loss. With time their visual behavior and function in everyday life gives only an occasional hint that they have lost half their visual field. There is some evidence that this remarkable compensation may be mediated, in part, by preserved retinotectal visual pathways. These pathways process information that, although not accessible to conscious awareness, can nevertheless trigger orienting responses toward the hemianopic field. This "blindsight" has been demonstrated by requiring hemianopic subjects to move their eyes or reach toward signals they cannot "see" and by using forced-choice discrimination tasks (Weiskrantz, 1986). The physiologic mechanisms mediating blindsight remain uncertain, and the role of the retinotectal pathway is controversial. In some patients there is "residual vision," which could be mediated by spared geniculostriate fibers and which could reflect degraded cortical vision near the perceptual threshold. Other investigators propose that some blindsight phenomena reflect processing of visual input from retinotectal afferents to the superior colliculus.

Figure 5 (top) shows an experiment used to demonstrate that blindsight can be mediated by extrageniculate visual pathways to the midbrain (Rafal, Smith, Krantz, Cohen, & Brennan, 1990). Rafal et al. studied patients who had suffered an occipital stroke destroying the geniculostriate pathway; they were blind in the visual field opposite the lesion and could not report the presence or absence of stimuli presented there. They maintained fixation on the middle of a video display and on each trial made an eye movement to the appearance of a target in the intact hemifield. Blindsight was inferred from the effect of simultaneous or immediately preceding presentation, in the blind hemifield, of an unseen visual distractor (which had the same eccentricity and luminance change as the saccade target.)

The results (see Figure 5, bottom) showed that unseen distractor signals presented to the blind, temporal (but not nasal) hemifield of hemianopic patients increased the latency of saccades directed to targets presented in the intact visual field. These results provide direct evidence that there is a reflexive activation of retinotectal pathways to prime the oculomotor system and that this activation inhibits saccades to the opposite field. These observations provide further converging evidence implicating the midbrain in reflexive orienting. This inhibitory effect on eye movements was clearly reflexive and occurred without any awareness of the sig-

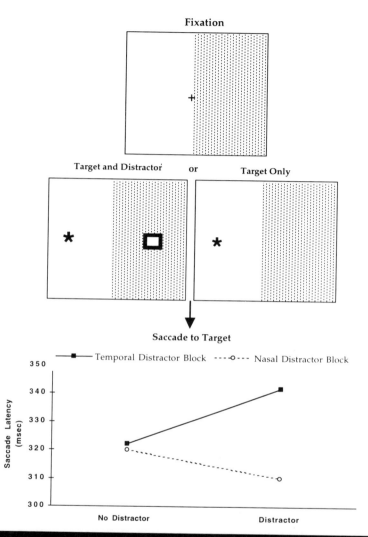

Figure 5

Saccade inhibition by signals in the hemianopic field. Top: The experimental display and task for a patient with right hemianopia. The hemianopic field is depicted by stippling. The task was to make a saccadic eye movement to a target appearing on the left (in the intact field). On some trials the box on the right brightened (the distractor). The patient did not see the distractor. On blocks in which the right eye was patched the distractor was in the nasal hemifield; on blocks in which the left eye was patched the distractor was in the temporal hemifield. In this experiment the effect of the unseen distractor on saccade latency was measured compared with the no-distractor condition. Bottom: Results of the experiment for 5 hemianopic patients. Means of the median saccade latency (in ms) in the distractor and no-distractor conditions are shown for blocks in which the distractor in the blind field was temporal and nasal.

nal activating it. Moreover, the observation that this reflex occurred in the temporal hemifield of hemianopic patients lacking a visual cortex provides strong evidence for mediation of this reflex by subcortical midbrain pathways.

A Midbrain Mechanism for Inhibiting Reorienting

We have seen that there is converging evidence from PSP patients, hemianopic patients, and normal individuals that the midbrain retinotectal pathway is important in reflexive orienting to exogenous visual signals. This visual grasp reflex is obviously an important primitive function that is useful and necessary for survival. However, people do have voluntary control over their ability to deploy attention in the visual field. This ability presumably developed as cortical mechanisms evolved to permit a greater flexibility of behavior, and higher centers elaborated inhibitory mechanisms for regulating these primitive reflexes. One such mechanism turns out to be mediated by the midbrain itself. Posner and Cohen (1984) showed that a peripheral luminance change does not only automatically summon attention. They showed that this initial orienting is superseded, after a few hundred milliseconds, by an "inhibition of return" that slows detection of signals at the stimulated location. With others, I have found converging evidence from PSP patients and from normal subjects that this inhibition of return is generated through the midbrain retinotectal pathway. Inhibition of return was measured in PSP patients (Posner, Rafal, Choate, & Vaughn, 1985) and in the temporal and nasal hemifields of normal subjects (Rafal et al., 1991). In these experiments subjects first saw a peripheral box flash, and then a box in the center was brightened to summon attention back to the middle of the display. The target then appeared, with equal probability, either at the location of the first cue or at the uncued location in the opposite visual field.

Figure 6 (top) shows the results of this experiment in 6 PSP patients in whom inhibition of return was compared in the vertical and horizontal plane. Detection RT was slower at the cued location—an inhibition resulting from the cue—in the horizontal plane. However, no inhibition of return was activated by signals above or below fixation. In control subjects with Parkinson's disease, inhibition of return was present in both the vertical and the horizontal planes. The same experiment was done in normal adults to compare the activation of inhibition of return by cues pre-

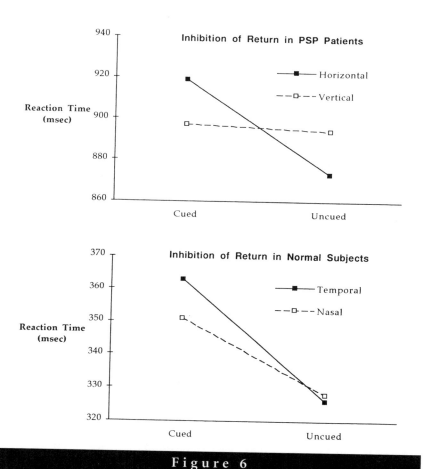

Figure 6

Midbrain involvement in generating inhibition of return. Top: Mean reaction time (RT) in the experiment comparing inhibition of return in the vertical and horizontal plane in six patients with progressive supranuclear palsy (PSP). Inhibition of return is manifest as slower detection RTs for targets appearing at the recently cued location and is not activated by cues in the vertical plane. Bottom: Mean RT in the experiment comparing inhibition of return in temporal and nasal hemifields on normal subjects. Inhibition of return is manifest as slower detection RTs for targets appearing at the recently cued location and is larger when the cue is presented to the temporal hemifield.

sented in the temporal and nasal hemifields. Figure 6 (bottom) shows that RTs were slower for targets appearing at the first cued location and that this inhibition of return effect was greater when the cue was presented in the temporal hemifield.

This converging evidence indicates that activation of the retinotectal system by a signal in the visual periphery causes both a reflexive orienting of attention to the signal and a subsequent inhibition that biases against reorienting to the same location, and thereby favors novelty in sampling the visual environment. Rafal, Calabresi, Brennan, and Sciolto (1989) proposed that inhibition of return also functions to coordinate the oculomotor system's responses to exogenous and endogenous information. In everyday life, exogenous sensory signals are constantly competing with endogenous control for access to the oculomotor apparatus. An inhibitory mechanism for mediating between them is required. There are adaptive advantages to orienting automatically to new sensory signals occurring in the visual periphery. However, it is also necessary to be able to control visual attention and eye movements endogenously under voluntary guidance. Although automatic orienting in response to new and salient events occurring in our visual periphery serves an important defensive and social function, its tight linkage with the generation of inhibition of return may permit us to search our environment strategically, under voluntary control, without continual distraction by repeated extraneous stimulation.

Effect of Prefrontal Cortex Lesions on Reflexive and Voluntary Orienting

In a recent study, Henik, Rafal, and Rhodes (1994) showed that lesions of one specific area of the frontal lobes, the frontal eye fields in the superior dorsolateral prefrontal cortex, affect eye movement latency and that these lesions have opposite effects on endogenously activated and visually guided saccades to external signals. In this experiment exogenously triggered saccades were made to peripheral targets appearing either contralateral or ipsilateral to the lesion. Endogenously generated saccades were made in response to an arrow in the center of the display that pointed toward the field either contralateral or ipsilateral to the lesion. The patients tested in this study all had a single, chronic unilateral lesion restricted to the dorsolateral prefrontal cortex. In 9 patients the lesion extended into the frontal eye field; 7 patients in whom the lesion spared the frontal eye fields served as neurological control patients (see Figure 2).

As shown in Figure 7, endogenous saccades were slower to the con-

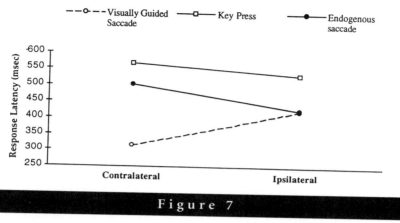

Figure 7

Mean of the median latencies for visually guided and voluntary saccades, and keypress response times for 9 patients with lesions of frontal eye field lesions.

tralesional field, whereas exogenously triggered saccades were faster to the contralesional field. These results indicate that frontal eye field lesions have two separate effects on eye movement: (a) The frontal eye fields are involved in generating endogenous saccades and lesions in this region therefore increase their latency and (b) the frontal eye fields have inhibitory connections to the midbrain, and lesions in this area result in disinhibition of midbrain oculomotor centers and a consequent decrease in latency for reflexive saccades to exogenous signals. Does this result reflect a more efficient detection due to the work of an uninhibited colliculus or does it reflect an uninhibited oculomotor reaction? When the same patients were asked to make keypress responses to peripheral targets, they had slower RTs for targets appearing in the contralesional field. That is, with the same display opposite effects were found for saccade and keypress responses. Responses were faster to contralesional signals only when the response was a saccade.

Pashler and O'Brien (1993) found converging evidence in normal subjects that exogenously triggered saccades are automatic and do not tap resources requiring cortical involvement, whereas endogenously generated saccades do. Endogenous saccades result in a psychological refractory period for other tasks, whereas exogenously triggered saccades do not.

VISUAL ATTENTION AND OBJECT RECOGNITION

Here I return to the problem of visual neglect to see what can be learned from it about the role of attention in object recognition. Having considered earlier that extinction reflects a pathologic inhibitory consequence of allocating attention to one location at the expense of others, the question becomes, What is inhibited in "extinguished" stimuli? Certainly detection is impaired in patients with extinction; that is, the ability to report awareness of the signal—defined, operationally, as the ability to make an arbitrary response to it (Posner, Snyder, & Davidson, 1980). Is it the case that all perceptual processing of the extinguished object is inhibited? If not, to what level is information about the extinguished object processed? Is neglect a deficit in attending to a location in the visual field, or is it manifest in an object-based frame of reference?

In this section I examine what is neglected in visual neglect. First, I review a growing body of evidence that neglected objects undergo extensive perceptual processing and that neglect occurs at a late stage of selection for action. I then review another growing body of evidence from neuropsychology that attention operates on both location-based and object-based frames of reference.

Information Processing at Unattended Locations

In a seminal study, Volpe, Ledoux, and Gazzaniga (1979) showed that some patients with neglect were able to tell whether an object in the contralesional field was the same or different from one in the ipsilesional field—even though they could not tell what the object was. So some information is available from the extinguished object. It has recently been shown that perceptual degradation of stimuli in normal subjects also causes a loss of the ability to identify objects before the ability to make same–different judgments is lost (Farah, Monheit, & Wallace, 1991). So the findings of Volpe et al. do not in themselves indicate that perceptual processing is fully preserved in extinguished stimuli.

A modification of the simple clinical test for extinction provides evidence for processing of information in the neglected field. I have found that when some patients with relatively mild neglect are simultaneously presented with two different objects, they can be much less likely to show extinction than when two identical objects are shown. Information in the unattended field is clearly processed sufficiently to provide the visual system the information that it is different from its counterpart in the ipsilesional field. This difference signal triggers an orienting response leading to detection and ultimately discrimination. But do the stimuli need to be identical or just similar for extinction to occur? I became intrigued by this question by accident one day when I showed a patient two different types of fork (a white plastic picnic fork in one field and a silver metal dinner fork in the other). He reported only seeing one fork in his right field (see Rafal, 1994, Figure 2). Even though these objects differed visually, the fact that they were classified the same seemed to determine whether the patient oriented to one or to both.

Baylis, Rafal, and Driver (1993) extended this clinical observation in 5 patients with extinction. Colored letters were presented either unilaterally or bilaterally, and the patients were asked to report what they saw on each side. The critical trials were those in which bilateral targets were presented and in which the patient reported seeing nothing in the contralesional field. In one condition they were asked to name only the letter or letters (X or E) and in another to report only the color or colors (red or green). This study confirmed that extinction occurred much more frequently when the bilateral stimuli were identical in the attribute to be reported. On blocks in which the task was to report the name of the letter, extinction was not ameliorated if the stimuli were of different colors and vice versa for the color-report blocks. This pattern of extinction seems likely to be related to repetition blindness seen in normal individuals under rapid, serial visual presentation.

Berti and Rizzolatti (1992) provided evidence from neglect patients that extinguished objects are processed to a categorical level of representation. Their subjects categorized line drawings presented in their ipsilesional field. Their performance was better not only when the same drawing was presented simultaneously in the contralesional, extinguished visual field, but also when the drawing in the contralesional field was a different object in the same category as the target object in the ipsilesional field. Ladavas has recently confirmed these findings and documented that the patients showed chance performance on explicit report of the stimuli in the neglected field (Ladavas, Paladini, & Cubelli, 1993). McGlinchey-Berroth, Milberg, Verfaellie, Alexander, and Kilduff (1993) gave a lexical decision task to 4 patients with left hemineglect. A letter string was presented in the center of the display and the patients' RT was measured to respond whether it constituted an English word. Each trial began with a picture presented briefly in either the ipsilesional or contralesional field, and this prime could either be semantically related to the target word or unrelated. This kind of priming generally facilitates RT responses in the lexical decision task when the target word is semantically related to the prime stimulus. In the patients, primes presented in the contralesional field produced just as much priming as did those in the ipsilesional field, even though they were not able to identify the contralesional primes.

The emerging evidence suggests that clinical extinction involves an inhibitory process that operates at a late level of selection. It is not perceptual or categorical processing that is inhibited, but access to awareness. If this is the case, then unattended information may influence behavior without the usual advantages afforded by endogenous control. A dramatic example of this was shown by a patient reported by Marshall and Halligan (1988). Their patient with left neglect was shown a picture with two houses, one on the right and the other on the left. The picture depicted the house on the left as being on fire. The patient did not notice this and reported that the two houses looked just alike. Nevertheless, when asked to choose which house she would prefer to live in, she chose the house on the right—although she could not offer any explanation of this preference. Although such dramatic findings have not been ubiquitous in studies of neglect patients, this kind of observation in patients with neglect is consistent with experimental findings that information that is extinguished can influence feelings and behavior even though the patient is not consciously aware of it.

There is accumulating evidence from the study of neglect patients that a great deal of visual information is processed without visual attention. This preattentive visual processing, based on elementary visual features and gestalt grouping principles, parses the visual scene into candidate objects that, in turn, may summon spatial attention to facilitate recognition of the objects. Symmetry is a good example of the kind of feature that serves to parse the visual field into candidate objects. Observations in a patient with visual neglect (Driver, Baylis, & Rafal, 1993) demonstrate that symmetry is processed at a preattentive level as part of this parsing process. This patient experienced the same effect of symmetry as do normal subjects in distinguishing figure from ground, even though he performed at chance when asked to determine whether the shapes were symmetric or not. That is, even though his attentional deficit prevented him from telling whether shapes were symmetrical or not, he nevertheless perceived symmetric shapes as being candidate objects in the visual scene.

These examples show that neglected information is processed to an advanced stage in which the meanings of the neglected objects are, in fact, encoded. Yet this information is somehow prevented from making contact with neural systems that permit access to awareness. Does this neglected information have direct contact with systems controlling motor activity? In a situation where a given stimulus is tightly associated with a specific motor act (moving the foot to the brake pedal when the light turns red), does neglected information activate response channels with which it has become associated?

The flanker interference task introduced by Eriksen is a useful tool for investigating not only the extent of perceptual processing outside the focus of visual attention (Eriksen & St. James, 1986; Eriksen & Yeh, 1985) but also the effectiveness of this information in activating response channels for motor responses (Coles, Gratton, Bashore, Eriksen, & Donchin, 1985; Gratton, Coles, Sirevaag, Eriksen, & Donchin, 1988). Cohen, Ivry, Rafal, and Kohn (1995) recently examined flanker interference in patients with visual neglect. The patients were asked to respond to color patches (red or green) presented in the center of a display screen. On each trial a flanking color patch was presented simultaneously with this visual target either in the neglected visual field contralateral to the lesion or in the ipsilesional field. The flanker, which the patients were instructed to ignore, could be the same as the target and therefore congruent with the required response; or it could code the opposite, incongruent response; or it could be blue (a neutral color). The results indicated comparable flanker interference effects from the neglected flankers as from the flankers in the intact visual field. These findings indicate not only that perceptual processing of the flankers is preserved in the neglected visual field but also that the flankers are effective in activating response channels with which they have been associated. Moreover, these findings indicate that the anatomic pathways involved in transducing a stimulus to response code activation do not require intact parietal lobe function or the conscious awareness of the stimulus.

Researchers in my laboratory recently investigated brain regions that are critical for response channel activation in the flanker paradigm and found that unilateral lesions of the dorsolateral prefrontal cortex resulted in reduced flanker interference by stimuli in the contralesional field (Rafal et al., 1995). This is really quite a striking dissociation between two types of brain injury. Lesions of the posterior association cortex that impair attention and prevent awareness of the flanker stimuli still preserve the activation of response channels that lead to flanker interference; lesions of the prefrontal cortex, which do not affect awareness of the flanker stimuli or the ability of the patients to respond to them, do abolish or reduce flanker interference by contralesional stimuli.

These two contrasting findings tell us several things about attention, perception, and selection for action as revealed by the Eriksen flanker paradigm. First, these observations provide further evidence for preattentive visual processing and response code activation. They shed further light on the neural circuitry implicated in transducing visual stimuli into motor responses. They are also important because they indicate that a reduction of flanker interference need not necessarily reflect early selection that prevents perceptual processing of the stimuli. It is possible that increased perceptual load, for example, may not reduce flanker interference because it reduces attentional resources and compromises perception at an early stage of processing (Lavie & Tsal, 1994), but because it encumbers resources needed later in processing at a level for transducing percept into action.

Attention to Objects and Locations

Because parietal lobe lesions clearly affect perception more at some locations (i.e., contralesionally) than others, it seems understandable that the effect should have been construed as a deficit in attending to locations. Nevertheless, there has been some controversy within psychology concerning whether spatial attention acts to select spatial locations or whether it is allocated to objects. Neuropsychological investigations have played a critical role in resolving this controversy. There is now evidence for both location-based and object-based attentional mechanisms with different neural substrates. In this section I review evidence for object-based attentional selection in patients with visual neglect and in patients with simultaneous agnosia from Bálint's syndrome due to biparietal lesions. I then consider recent evidence for a hemispheric asymmetry in shifting attention between objects and locations in patients with parietal lesions and in split-brain patients.

Object-Based Neglect

Extinction due to parietal lesions is manifest with respect to the reference frame being viewed by the patient. Robertson has shown this in a variant of the usual bedside test for extinction (see Rafal, 1994, Figure 1). The examiner tests for extinction by wiggling a finger on each of his or her hands. In one condition the examiner's body and face are rotated to the left (i.e., the reference frame is rotated counterclockwise). In this condition the patient detects the upper finger wiggle and extinguishes the lower; that is, there is extinction of the left side of the reference frame. In contrast, when the examiner's body and face are rotated to the right (i.e., the reference frame is rotated clockwise), the patient detects the lower finger wiggle and extinguishes the upper; that is, there is now extinction of the opposite spatial location, but this again is on the left side of the reference frame, in this case the object (the examiner) being attended.

Behrmann and Tipper (1994) recently reported object-based neglect that could move to the ipsilesional side of the object after it rotated. RT was measured to targets appearing in either the left (contralesional) or right (ipsilesional) side of a dumbbell. Patients were slower to respond to targets on the left. If the dumbbell rotated, however, such that the two sides of the dumbbell reversed field, RTs were prolonged for targets on the right.

Driver and Halligan (1991) asked a patient with left hemineglect to examine two nonsense shapes, one above the other, and to determine whether the shapes were the same or different. When the shapes were different, they could differ in a feature on the right or left side. As expected, more errors occurred (i.e., the patient judged them to be identical when they were in fact different) when the distinguishing feature was on the left side. On some trials, the shapes were rotated 45° clockwise or counterclockwise. This manipulation was contrived to generate conditions where the distinguishing feature was on the left side of the object, but in the right visual field. The critical question was whether neglect errors were more determined by the visual field of the distinguishing feature, relative to the patient's viewer-centered coordinates, or by the reference frame of the objects. The results showed that the patients' errors in this task were determined by the location of the distinguishing feature on the object rather than by its position in the visual field.

Not all attempts to identify object-based neglect have been successful; a contrast of studies that demonstrated object-based neglect and those that did not is instructive. Farah et al. (1990) asked patients to name colors surrounding pictures of common objects. When the pictures were rotated, the colors neglected did not rotate with the object; that is, neglect remained location based rather than object based. Behrman and Moscovitch (in press) used the same paradigm and confirmed the lack of object-based neglect with object drawings. However, object-based neglect was manifest in the special case where the objects were asymmetric letters. That is, object-based neglect was manifest when the object's identity was uniquely defined by its principal axis.

Figure 8 shows a task used to demonstrate that visual neglect is determined based on the principal axis of objects (Driver, Baylis, Goodrich, & Rafal, 1994). The patients' task was simply to determine whether there was a gap in the top of the middle triangle. The principal axis of the triangle (i.e., which way it appeared to point) was manipulated by the way in which the central triangle was grouped with the others. In the figure

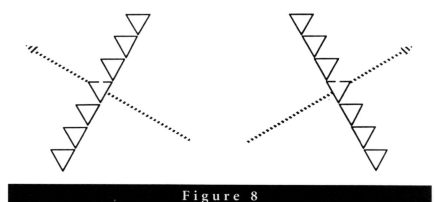

Figure 8

Figures used by Driver, Baylis, Goodrich, and Rafal (1994) to study axis-based visual neglect. From "Axis-Based Neglect of Visual Shapes," by J. Driver, G. C. Baylis, S. J. Goodrich, and R. D. Rafal, 1994, *Neuropsychologia, 32*, p. 1359. Copyright 1994 by Elsevier Science. Reprinted with permission.

on the right the alignment of the triangles (from southwest to northeast) causes them to appear to be pointing toward the northwest, and the gap in the top of the central triangle is perceived to appear on the right side of its perceived principal axis. In the figure on the left the alignment of the triangles (from southeast to northwest) causes them to appear pointing toward the northeast; and the gap in the top of the central triangle is perceived to appear on the left side of its perceived principal axis. Results in 3 patients with left hemineglect showed that all missed more of the gaps in the condition on the right in which the gap was on the perceived left of the triangle.

Object-centered visual attention has also been inferred from the reading errors of neglect patients. In a striking demonstration of neglect dyslexia reported by Hillis and Caramazza (1991), a patient with right hemineglect made more errors at the end of the word regardless of the orientation of the word on the page; that is, even when the word was upside down such that the right end of the word was in the left visual field. Patients with neglect make fewer reading errors when they read pronounceable nonwords than when they read words (Brunn & Farah, 1991; Sieroff, Pollatsek, & Posner, 1988). The study by Brunn and Farah incorporated cancellation or line bisection tasks along with the reading task. Less neglect was found on these secondary tasks when the primary task required reading a word than a nonword. This suggests that word processing causes an automatic deployment of attention to encompass the word and, in patients with left neglect, this draws their attention to the left. Friedrich, Walker, and Posner (1985) showed patients two letter strings presented one above the other in a matching task. Patients made fewer errors in reporting that different letter strings were the same when the letter strings formed words than when they consisted of nonwords.

Bálint's Syndrome

Perhaps the most dramatic evidence for object-based attentional selection is seen in patients with bilateral lesions of posterior parietal lobes or parieto-occipital junction who manifest simultaneous agnosia. In this classical syndrome of Bálint the patient can only see one object at a time. In a case report in 1919 of a 30-year-old Great War veteran who had a gunshot wound through the parieto-occipital regions, Holmes and Horax (1919) detailed this syndrome and provided an analysis that stands as definitive: "The essential feature was his inability to direct attention to, and to take cognizance of, two or more objects" (p. 402). Because of this constriction of visual attention (what Bálint referred to as the psychic field of gaze), the patient can attend to only one object at a time regardless of the size of the object.

Patients with Bálint's syndrome have great difficulty in making judgments comparing two objects or parts of objects. They cannot say which of two objects is smaller or closer, nor can they say which of two lines is longer or whether two angles are same or different. Nevertheless, as Holmes and Horax (1919) noted in their patient,

> though he failed to distinguish any difference in the length of lines, even if it was as great as 50 per cent, he could always recognize whether a quadrilateral rectangular figure was a square or not. . . . He explained that in order to decide whether a figure was or was not a square, he did not compare the length of its sides but, "on a first glance I see the whole figure and know whether it is a square or not." (p. 394)
>
> His power of recognizing promptly the shape of a simple geometrical figure demonstrates that in this we do not naturally depend on the comparison of lines and angles, but that we apprehend shapes as a whole and accept them as unities. (p. 402)

Bálint first observed the dramatic constriction of visual attention in a patient whom he examined in 1903 (Husain & Stein, 1988). His patient did "not take notice of things lying to either side of the object" (p. 90). One way of looking at the syndrome is to view these patients as having difficulty in disengaging to move in any direction—essentially a bilateral disengage deficit (Farah, 1990). This cannot be the whole story, though, because the distinctive feature of this syndrome is simultaneous agnosia: That is, the patient cannot attend to more than one object even if the objects spatially overlap. This cardinal feature of this syndrome shows that the restriction is object based rather than space based. For example, one of my patients was unable to look at my face and tell me whether I was wearing glasses (although she reported that she could clearly seem my face or my glasses at different times). Shown a cross filling a circle, the patient with Bálint's syndrome may report one or the other. Shown a six-pointed star constructed of two triangles of a different color, the patient may see only one triangle (Luria, 1964). No strictly space-based model of attention can accommodate such a striking phenomenon: These patients are unable to disengage from one object to attend to another at the same location.

Luria (1964) emphasized that the defect in these patients was in attending to objects. He showed that a patient who, when shown two adjacent circles, only saw one of them; when the two circles were connected by a line, the patient saw a single object (a dumbbell or spectacles.) Applying a similar approach, Humphreys and Riddoch (1993) have provided elegant experimental evidence that formally confirms the object-based restriction in Bálint's syndrome. Two Bálint's patients were shown 32 circles that were all red, all green, or half red and half green. The task was to report whether each display contained one or two colors. The critical test was when the display contained two colors. In one condition, the spaces between the circles contained randomly placed black lines. In two further conditions the lines connected either pairs of same-colored circles or pairs of different-colored circles. Both patients were better at correctly reporting the presence of two colors when the lines connected different-colored pairs of circles. Circles connected by a line are perceived as a single object (e.g., as a dumbbell). When each object contained both red and green, the patients could report the presence of the two colors. If each object contained only a single color, the patients had great difficulty as their attention tended to lock onto a single object.

I have been amazed by the degree to which small and at times barely perceptible features in the visual scene can grab the attention of patients and blind them to other salient features. One of my patients was being shown some simple shapes drawn on a sheet of stationery. After looking for several seconds, she shook her head and, in great frustration, reported, "I'm sorry doctor, but I can't make it out. The watermark on the paper is so distracting."

Some recent observations in a patient with Bálint's syndrome, being studied in conjunction with Lynn Robertson and Anne Treisman and their associates, have shed some new light on this syndrome. This 56-year-old man had suffered a right parieto-occipital stroke 2 years earlier that had left him with only mild disabilities. Six months before testing he had a second stroke (due to cardiac embolus) in the left parieto-occipital area. After this stroke he remained lucid with intact language and memory, independent in daily activities, ambulatory, and able to manage his own affairs. Yet although his visual acuity was good and his visual field intact, he was functionally blind.

He exhibited the classical symptom complex of Bálint's syndrome. He had spatial disorientation and had to be escorted in the hospital (although by this time he was able to get about in his home all right). Although eye movements to command were intact and optokinetic nystagmus preserved, he had great difficulty following moving objects with his eyes. He had great difficulty in seeing more than one object at a time and could not tell which of two objects was closer to him. Unlike some patients with Bálint's syndrome, however, he could judge whether objects were moving toward or away from him. He did not blink to a visual threat and could not reach accurately toward objects. Given a pencil and asked to place a dot in the center of a circle drawn on a piece of paper, he usually did not even get the point in the circle. When the examiner moved the pencil, however, and he was asked to report when the point reached the center, he did much better: He always got the point within the circle and often accurately in the middle.

He had no difficulty recognizing faces, objects, shapes, words, or colors. Visual acuity was 20/15 with both eyes, and visual fields were intact with dynamic perimetry. Visual contrast sensitivity was intact. Examination by V. Ramachandran revealed that he was able to perceive apparent motion, see at least some illusory contours, and experience illusory motion and that he could perceive shape from shading and shape from motion. Three-dimensional experience of shapes in random-dot stereograms was preserved and he experienced depth from shading. He also could parse figure from ground based, for example, on symmetry, even though he could not reliably tell if one object was in front of or behind another using depth or occlusion cues.

Over a period of several months he was shown hierarchical figures, of the type shown in Figure 9, on numerous occasions. Most of these were large letters constructed out of smaller letters, and he was simply asked to report what he saw. In every instance he reported the local element first; on only two occasions during this entire period did he also report the global element. His attention was consistently captured by the local element. When the global letter was made up of several different letters, he reported seeing "the alphabet."

Figure 9

Drawing of hierarchical stimuli by two patients. Left: The figure the patients were asked to copy is a hierarchical pattern in which the large letter at the global level is an M constructed from small Zs at the local level. Middle: Global organization is lost in this drawing by a patient with a right hemisphere lesion. Right: Only the global organization of the figure is preserved while the local details are lost in this copy by a patient with a left hemisphere lesion. From "Hemispheric Specialization of Memory for Visual Hierarchical Stimuli," by D. C. Delis, L. C. Robertson, and R. Efron, 1986, *Neuropsychologia, 24,* p. 206. Copyright 1986 by Elsevier Science. Reprinted with permission.

Although his performance was, in this regard, reminiscent of that seen in patients with lesions of the right temperoparietal junction (Robertson, Lamb, & Knight, 1988), this area was spared in this man. It was also clear that, unlike those patients, his local bias was not due to a failure to process information at the global level. Preattentive processing of the global form was found to be preserved. This was made apparent through reaction time studies with figures in which the global and local levels could be either incongruent or congruent. He always reported the local level but, unlike patients with TPJ lesions who exhibit no interference from incongruent information, he showed a large interfering effect of the global letter if it was incongruent. Thus, his failure to identify the global element was clearly not due to a failure to process global information but to an inability to attend to it.

As with patients with unilateral extinction, this patient also showed large interference effects from spatially separated stimuli of which he was not aware. In one experiment using a flanker task (Eriksen & Yeh, 1985), he was shown colored squares in the center of the display that could be either red or green, and his RT to name the color was measured. The target color square in the center remained visible until he responded. On each trial another colored square was briefly flashed (for 16 ms) 8° above, below, or to the right of the color patch. This distractor was either the same color as the target or incongruent. When it was shown alone without the center target he had no difficulty discriminating this distractor. Yet when it was presented with the target, he was unable to report it, even when encouraged to try to ignore the color in the center; nor could he report, above chance performance, whether there were one or two stimuli or one or two colors present. Although he could not demonstrate any awareness of the distractor patch when it was presented with the center target, it nevertheless strongly affected his RT to name the center target color. The large interference effect in this patient is remarkable not only because it was activated by information processed outside of the patient's awareness, but because of the eccentricities—the distance of 8° between targets and flanker. At these eccentricities, normal subjects show small interference effects at best.

A recent study by Friedman-Hill, Robertson, and Treisman (1995) may help explain the robust flanker interference in this patient. They observed that he experienced an extraordinary degree of illusory conjunction. He could not distinguish the location of objects across a wide area of the visual field and almost randomly combined the component features of these objects. Cohen and Rafal (1991) described a patient with a left temporoparietal lesion who made an exceptional number of illusory conjunctions in the field contralateral to her lesion. She had no neglect, extinction, or other clinical deficit of visual attention, but when tested on the covert orienting task (Posner et al., 1984), she showed the extinction-like reaction time pattern with difficulty in disengaging her attention. Unlike the patient with Bálint's syndrome described by Friedman-Hill et al. (1995), who had severe disability and made illusory conjunction miscombinations between objects widely separated in the visual field, the patient reported by Cohen and Rafal (1991) made only illusory conjunctions between objects adjacent to one another.

The differences in the illusory conjunction errors made by these two patients indicate that they made illusory conjunctions for quite different reasons. The patient of Cohen and Rafal (1991) made illusory conjunctions due to a deficit in attention and made them only under circumstances where attention was necessary for accurate binding of features.

When objects were farther apart, there was sufficient spatial information available in feature maps to prevent miscombinations. Our patient with Bálint's syndrome (Friedman-Hill et al., 1995), in contrast, made illusory conjunctions between widely separated objects in the visual field because he lacked a representation of space necessary to assign a given feature to a given object.

In this patient we observed that the objects he locked onto were not randomly selected. A distinctive feature in his visual field captured his attention and strongly biased what he was likely to see. For instance, he was more likely to report the *Q* in a background of *O*s than an *O* in a background of *Q*s . He was also able to more accurately report a red *O* among green *X*s in a visual display than a red *O* among red *X*s and green *O*s. When the task required serial attentional search for a conjunction target, he found it impossible, and performance was at chance (Rafal & Robertson, 1995).

Coslett and Saffran (1991) showed, in a different patient with Bálint's syndrome, that unattended information can be processed to a semantic level. With brief, simultaneous presentation of two words or drawings, their patient identified both stimuli significantly more frequently when the stimuli were semantically related than when they were unrelated.

Study of patients with neglect or extinction and of those with simultaneous agnosia in Bálint's syndrome can tell researchers what features of objects and properties of displays of objects are preattentively processed and require attention. Once attention is deployed it is captured by objects, and it is the object—not only the location—from which attention must be disengaged in order to move elsewhere. While attention is allocated to an object, preattentive processes continue to operate outside the ken of the individual, and these guide ongoing orienting behavior.

Hemispheric Asymmetry for Disengaging From Locations and Objects

The plight of the patient with Bálint's syndrome suggests that bilateral parietal lobe lesions disrupt attending to both location and object-based representations. A recent study in patients with chronic, unilateral parietal lesions suggests that the right and left parietal lobes may make different contributions to location and object-based processing. Egly, Driver, and Rafal (1994) used a modification of the covert orienting paradigm to measure both space- and object-based attention shifts in normal subjects and patients with chronic lesions of the posterior association cortex. They used a detection task similar to that shown in Figure 1, except that the display used two elongated rectangles instead of the two square boxes shown in Figure 1. On each trial part of an object was cued by flashing the end of one of the rectangles, and then the target was presented either at the location of the cue or at an uncued location. The critical manipulation in this experiment occurred on those trials in which the target appeared at an uncued location. On these invalid cue trials, the target could either occur within the same rectangle that had been cued (at the other end of it), or an equal distance away from the cue at one end of the other rectangle, which had not been cued. Thus, it was possible to measure the costs of reorienting on invalid trials for within-object attention shifts in comparison to between-objects attention shifts. In normal subjects cuing effects (or costs) were greater for shifting attention between than within objects. So the effects of moving between locations in space and the additional effect of shifting attention between objects were identified. Similar effects were found in an experiment in which the objects were defined by circles grouped in rows and columns rather than rectangles.

Several findings in the patient groups were noteworthy. First, both patient groups (left- or right-hemisphere lesion) evidenced larger costs to respond to targets in their contralesional than ipsilesional fields, again replicating the deficit in disengaging attention. The important new finding was a difference between the two patient groups in shifting attention between objects. Although both patient groups showed problems in disengaging attention from their intact field, the disengage deficit in patients with left-hemisphere lesions occurred only for between-objects shifts of attention. This finding suggests that the right parietal lobe may be involved in shifting attention between locations, whereas the left parietal lobe plays a specific role in shifting attention between objects. We have recently confirmed this conclusion in a commissurotomized patent with disconnected neocortices (Egly, Rafal, Driver, & Starreveld, 1994). In his right visual field, normal costs for shifting between objects were observed; no object-based costs were observed for attention shifts in the left visual field.

THE SYMPTOM COMPLEX OF THE NEGLECT SYNDROME: A SYNTHESIS

This chapter began with and introduction of the syndrome of hemineglect and a consideration of the phenomenon of extinction. In this section I try to integrate much of what has been learned about the neural mechanisms for orienting spatial attention to better appreciate the neglect syndrome. I end, then, with an attempted synthesis of the neglect symptom complex.

Extinction is one component of the neglect syndrome—a defect in orienting to an exogenous signal when attention is engaged ipsilateral to it. Other components of the neglect syndrome can be related to deficits in endogenously generated exploration and manipulation of contralesional space (as demonstrated clinically by line bisection, cancellation, or drawing tasks). Patients with lesions in different regions may manifest different aspects of the neglect syndrome. The common denominator of the neglect syndrome, asymmetric spatial orienting, may occur in different patients for different reasons (Kinsbourne, 1987). The symptoms of neglect may reflect an abnormality of reflexive orienting or of voluntary orienting or a failure of integration of these two modes of orienting (Butter, 1987).

A number of pathophysiological mechanisms have been advanced to account for these difficulties (Table 1). I review some of them here and consider which might contribute to another salient characteristic of the clinical syndrome of neglect; namely, that it tends to be more severe and more persistent after lesions of the right hemisphere.

Intention Disorders

Some patients can show neglect in cancellation or line bisection tasks but not show extinction. So neglect behavior can result from a motor bias (directional hypokinesia), which is separable from defects in spatial attention. There have been several clever demonstrations of this dissociation between defects of spatial attention and those of motor bias or intention. By using pulleys or mirrors (Coslett, Bowers, Fitzpatrick, Haws, & Heilman, 1990; Mijovic, 1991; Tegner & Levander, 1991) in cancellation tasks, it has been possible to dissociate perceptual (attentional)

Table 1

Pathophysiologic Mechanisms Contributing to the Neglect Syndrome

Pathophysiological mechanism causing deficit	Putative neural substrate
Disengaging covert attention	Temporoparietal junction (TPJ)
Voluntary shifts of attention	Superior parietal lobule/TPJ
Hyperengaging to local elements	Right temporoparietal junction
Directional orienting bias	Hemispheric rivalry
Hyperreflexive orienting to ipsilesional field	Superior colliculus
Arousal	Right-hemisphere dominance for arousal
Representation of space	Parietal or dorsolateral prefrontal cortex
Generating voluntary saccades	Frontal eye fields
Motor intention	Dorsolateral prefrontal cortex, basal ganglia
Motivation for strategic orienting and sustained attention	Cingulate gyrus
Spatial working memory	Dorsolateral prefrontal cortex

and motor (intentional) components of neglect behavior. With these manipulations ipsilesional hand movements can be made to produce perceptual orienting in the contralesional direction. In patients whose sole problem is a contralesional motor bias (an intention disorder), this manipulation facilitates task performance. In patients whose sole problem is attentional, the same manipulation will not help. These studies have demonstrated that one or both kinds of deficit can contribute to neglect behavior. The degree to which each contributes varies from patient to patient. As might be expected, the more frontal lesions produce more problems with intention, whereas the more posterior lesions cause a deficit in attention. Many patients with the full-blown, severe neglect syndrome have large lesions affecting the posterior and frontal association cortices.

Deficits of Endogenous or Voluntary Orienting

As discussed earlier, lesions of the frontal eye fields produce an impairment in generating contralesional voluntary saccadic eye movements. Patients with lesions of the parietal lobe that cause extinction may be able to compensate by making voluntary eye movements toward the contralesional field. If the lesion extends rostrally into the frontal eye fields, however, this compensatory mechanism will become unavailable to the patient, thereby aggravating neglect. Lesions of the TPJ (see Figure 3) appear also to produce a deficit in endogenously moving covert visual attention.

The degree to which a given patient with neglect has a defect in voluntary orienting of attention or motivation may have a lot to do with his or her rehabilitation potential. Patients whose voluntary orienting mechanisms are preserved may have a better chance of compensating for extinction by being trained to "remember to look to your left." This may account for why the literature indicates such variability in the efficacy of such approaches to rehabilitation (Heilman & Valenstein, 1979; Riddoch & Humphreys, 1983). As investigators learn more about the precise morbid anatomy of the component mechanisms contributing to neglect, it should be possible to consider the degree and location of damage in each individual patient to make a more rational assessment of rehabilitation potential and the best approach to take in retraining.

Deficits in the Representation of Space: Representation Theories of Neglect

Neglect can result not only in the failure to perceive or to respond to contralesional signals or objects, but also in a lack of conscious access to the contralesional side of visual images stored in memory (Bisiach, 1993). Bisiach and Luzzatti (1978) asked a patients with left hemineglect to imagine themselves in the Piazza del Duomo in Milan. In one condition they asked the patients to imagine themselves at one end of the square, looking toward the cathedral dominating the other end of the square, and to describe what they would be able to see. In another condition the patients were asked to imagine themselves standing on the cathedral steps facing the opposite way. In both circumstances the patients reported fewer landmarks on the contralesional side of the mental image. That is, in one condition they failed to report landmarks on one side of the square; in the other they reported the landmarks that they had failed to report and instead omitted the landmarks that they had mention when imagining themselves to look in the opposite direction. (For non-Milanese patients a base-ball imagery task may be substituted. In one condition the patient is asked to imagine him or herself as the catcher and to name the positions of all the players that he would be able to see. Then the patient is told to imag-ine being in center field and is asked the same question.)

These kinds of observations have engendered an account of neglect in which the parietal lobes are assumed to maintain a representation of space in viewer-centered coordinates and in which parietal lesions pro-duce a degradation of the contralesional representation. An elegant ex-perimental test of this account (Bisiach, Luzzatti, & Perani, 1979) had pa-tients view cloudlike shapes that were passed slowly behind a slit (so that only part of the shape could be seen at any moment). On each trial they were shown two shapes that could be either the same or different, and they were asked to respond whether the shapes were the same or not. On the trials in which the shapes were different, they could be different on their left or right side. The patients made more errors on this task when shapes were different from each other on the contralesional end than on the ip-silesional end.

The neuroanatomical and pathophysiological basis for the deficit of spatial representation in neglect requires further study (Kinsella, Oliver, Ng, Packer, & Stark, 1993). Some authors have considered spatial repre-sentation in terms of oculomotor coding (Duhamel, Goldberg, Fitzgib-bon, Sirigu, & Grafman, 1992; Gianotti, 1993), whereas others have em-phasized spatial working memory (Funahashi, Bruce, & Goldman, 1993). Recent reports show that perceptual neglect and neglect of internal im-agery may be dissociated. Two patients with perceptual neglect and mainly parietal lesions did not evidence neglect in visual imagery (Anderson, 1993), whereas a patient with a frontal lesion causing neglect of imagined scenes did not have perceptual neglect (Guariglia, Padovani, Pantano, & Pizzamiglio, 1993).

Hemispheric Asymmetry for the Control of Attention

One of the explanations that has been advanced to account for the fact that neglect is more common, more severe, and more protracted after right-hemisphere lesions assumes that the right hemisphere is dominant for spatial attention or for the maintenance of spatial representations. These accounts propose that the right hemisphere has neural mechanisms for attending to both visual fields, whereas the left hemisphere attends predominantly to the right visual field (Heilman, Bowers, Valenstein, & Watson, 1987; Heilman, Valenstein, & Watson, 1985; Weintraub & Mesulam, 1987). Recent positron emissions tomography work has revealed an asymmetric right-hemisphere activation during visual attention particularly in the right superior parietal lobule (Corbetta, Miezin, Shulman, & Petersen, 1993).

Hemispheric Asymmetry for the Control of Arousal

Selective orienting within the visual field may also be affected by the level of arousal, and hypoarousal is one putative mechanism contributing to clinical neglect. Unilateral lesions of ascending activating pathways, especially those originating in the mesencephalic reticular formation, can produce neglect (Heilman et al., 1985). The greater prevalence of neglect after right-hemisphere lesions has also been ascribed to a right-hemisphere dominance for arousal (Heilman & Van den Abell, 1979, 1980; Posner et al., 1987).

Aggravation of Neglect by the Local Bias Caused by Right TPJ Lesions

Figure 9 (Delis, Robertson, & Efron, 1986) shows the copying of a patient with a large stroke of the right hemisphere and that of a patient with a large stroke involving the left hemisphere. The right-hemisphere lesion causes almost the complete exclusion of the global organization of the figure, whereas the left-hemisphere lesion causes the exclusion of local detail. Studies of patients with chronic, focal lesions involving the TPJ have revealed that this brain area is asymmetrically organized: The right TPJ is critical for global processing and the left for local processing (Robertson et al., 1988).

This perceptual local bias after right-TPJ lesions is one reason why lesions in this area are the most common to cause clinical neglect (Vallar, 1993). Certainly the interaction of the local bias with a difficulty in disengaging attention is an important factor in producing the classic constructional signs of neglect in paper-and-pencil tasks. A patient writing a number on a clock face will have far more difficulty in disengaging from that number to fill in the rest of the clock if he or she loses sight of the whole clock. If the lesion involves the inferior parietal lobule on the right but spares the TPJ, the patient may have extinction. He or she may also, when constructing a clock, work slowly from right to left; however, if he or she is able to maintain a global view of the task at hand and to perceive the clock face while working on individual numbers, he or she will eventually be successful in completing the clock drawing. Halligan and Marshall (1994) have shown the importance of the local bias as a contributor to neglect. They demonstrated that cuing neglect patients to attend more globally (to "expand the attentional spotlight") ameliorates neglect.

Lezak (1994) has emphasized the importance of this aspect of right-hemisphere damage in causing serious characterologic disturbances. Patients can get locked on to local details or parts of objects and fail entirely to perceive the critical big picture. This "piecemeal perception" carries over into everyday life in failures to adequately interpret social situations or critical elements necessary for everyday problem solving. As a result they may not be aware of the circumstances of their disability, its implications for future planning, or the effects of their behavior on other people. They become less capable of empathy, of motivation to improve their circumstances, or of realistically planning for the future. Although patients with right-hemisphere lesions tend to be spared the depressive reactions of their counterparts with left-hemisphere lesions (as well, of course, as aphasia) they nevertheless tend to have greater disability and social morbidity. They can simply be harder to live with, and it is a sad but salient fact that patients with right-hemisphere lesions are less likely to return home to live with their families and are more likely to spend the rest of their days in nursing care facilities.

Hyperorienting to the Ipsilesional Field

One model of the neurobiologic basis of spatial attention postulates that each hemisphere, when activated, mediates an orienting response in the contralateral direction (Kinsbourne, 1977, 1993). According to this account, neglect results from a unilateral lesion because of a breakdown in the balance of hemispheric rivalry so that the nonlesioned hemisphere generates an unopposed orienting response to the side of the lesion. Experimental observations in patients with hemineglect provide some support for this view (Ladavas, Del Pesce, & Provinciali, 1989).

This account is consistent with reports that production of a countervailing orienting bias by vestibular stimulation can transiently alleviate not only symptoms of visual (Cappa, Sterzi, Vallar, & Bisiach, 1987; Rubens, 1985) and somatosensory (Vallar, Bottini, Rusconi, & Sterzi, 1993) neglect, but also the lack of awareness of the deficit (anosognosia; Bisiach, Rusconi, & Vallar, 1991). A shift in spatial representation by vibration of neck muscles (Karnath, Christ, & Hartje, 1993) or by optokinetic stimulation (Pizzamiglio, Frasca, Guariglia, Inaccia, & Antonucci, 1990) can also decrease neglect.

Part of this ipsilesional orienting bias may be due to hyperreflexive exogenous orienting. One variant of the hemispheric rivalry account emphasizes putative mutually inhibitory callosal connections between the hemispheres. According to this account, when one hemisphere is lesioned, homologous regions of the opposite hemisphere, which normally receive inhibitory projections from the damaged region, become disinhibited and hyperorient attention to the ipsilesional side.

Seyal, Ro, and Rafal (in press) have recently obtained some support for this hypothesis from a study measuring the effects transcranial magnetic stimulation (TMS) on thresholds for tactile perception in the thumb in normal subjects. A suprathreshold (i.e., sufficiently strong to activate a twitch in the contralateral thumb when applied over motor cortex) TMS stimulus transiently inactivates the subjacent cortex. The Seyal et al. study examined whether the hemisphere opposite the TMS stimulus would show signs of disinhibition manifested as a reduced threshold to detect a tactile stimulus in the thumb ipsilateral to the TMS lesion. Results supported the attentional disinhibition account by showing a reduced ipsilateral tactile threshold after parietal (3 or 5 cm posterior to motor cortex) TMS, but not when TMS was applied at control locations over the motor cortex or 5 cm anterior to it.

Another mechanism that has been suggested for this hyperreflexive orienting further postulates a cortical–subcortical interaction. According to this account, the unlesioned parietal lobe that becomes disinhibited tonically increases activity in the superior colliculus ipsilateral to it, whereas the colliculus on the side of the lesion loses some normally present tonic activation. As a result, parietal lesions also produce an imbalance in the activity of subcortical structures involved in orienting such as the superior colliculus. The contralesional superior colliculus becomes disinhibited, and this results in exaggerated reflexive orienting to signals in the ipsilesional field. This hyperorienting may, in turn, account for the difficulties in disengaging attention to move in a contralesional direction.

Sprague's experiments in the cat confirmed that this kind of cortical–subcortical interaction is important in regulating visually guided orienting behavior (Sprague, 1966). He rendered cats blind in one visual field by removing occipital and parietal cortex, then showed that vision in this field improved if the opposite superior colliculus was removed or if the inhibitory connections were severed between the contralesional substantia nigra pars reticulata and the ipsilesional colliculus (Wallace, Rosenquist, & Sprague, 1989, 1990). This Sprague effect is thought to work in the following way. Parieto-occipital projections to the ipsilateral superior colliculus normally exert a tonic facilitation. After parietal lesions the colliculus loses this tonic activation. Because there are inhibitory connections between the two colliculi, the opposite superior colliculus becomes disinhibited, and this in turn produces disinhibited reflexive orienting to ipsilesional signals.

The Sprague effect demonstrates (at least in cats) that neglect is aggravated by disinhibition of subcortical visual pathways on the side opposite the cortical lesions and that prevention of visual input to this colliculus can alleviate neglect. Now it is obviously not an option to surgically remove the contralesional superior colliculus in humans who have suffered parietal lobe strokes. Nevertheless, we have seen that it is possible to decrease collicular activation, and reflexive orienting, by occluding one eye with a patch. Posner and Rafal (1987) suggested that patching the eye on the side of the lesion might help reduce symptoms of neglect. Studies in both monkeys and in patients with neglect indicate that this maneuver may have some benefit (Butter, Kirsch, & Reeves, 1990; Duel, 1987).

CONCLUDING REMARKS

In everyday life there are constant competing demands on attention by the outside world as well as from internally generated goals. A distributed network of neural structures orchestrates the orienting of attention and reconciles these competing demands. When these neural processes are working as they should, people seem to handle the competing demands of the outside world and those needed for planned activity so seamlessly that these subsystems seem to be one. Damage to the brain reveals how dependent humans are on the efficient coordination of attention for coherent perception, thought, and action. Advances in cognitive science and anatomic and functional neuroimaging have helped researchers to begin to understand the specific contributions of each of these brain areas. At the same time, the study of neurologic patients provides some very direct approaches to some of the central questions in the science of mind.

REFERENCES

Anderson, B. (1993). Spared awareness for the left side of internal visual images in patients with left-sided extrapersonal neglect. *Neurology, 43*, 213–216.

Bashinski, H. S., & Bacharach, V. R. (1980). Enhancement of perceptual sensitivity as the result of selectively attending to spatial locations. *Perception and Psychophysics, 28*, 241–248.

Baylis, G., Rafal, R., & Driver, J. (1993). Attentional set determines extinction following parietal lesions. *Journal of Cognitive Neuroscience, 5*, 453–466.

Baynes, K., Holtzman, H. D., & Volpe, B. T. (1986). Components of visual attention: Alterations in response pattern to visual stimuli following parietal lobe infarction. *Brain, 109*, 99–114.

Behrman, M., & Moscovitch, M. (in press). Object-centered neglect in patients with unilateral neglect: Effects of left-right coordinates of objects. *Journal of Cognitive Neuroscience.*

Behrmann, M., & Tipper, S. P. (1994). Object-based visual attention: Evidence from unilateral neglect. In C. Umilta & M. Moscovitch (Eds.), *Attention and performance 15. Conscious and nonconscious processing and cognitive functioning* (pp. 351–375). Cambridge, MA: MIT Press.

Berti, A., & Rizzolatti, G. (1992). Visual processing without awareness: Evidence from unilateral neglect. *Journal of Cognitive Neuroscience, 4*, 345–351.

Bisiach, E. (1993). Mental representation in unilateral neglect and related disorders: The Twentieth Bartlett Memorial Lecture. *Quarterly Journal of Experimental Psychology, 46A*, 435–462.

Bisiach, E., & Luzzatti, C. (1978). Unilateral neglect of representational space. *Cortex, 14*, 129–133.

Bisiach, E., Luzzatti, C., & Perani, D. (1979). Unilateral neglect, representational schema and consciousness. *Brain, 102*, 609–618.

Bisiach, E., Rusconi, M. L., & Vallar, G. (1991). Remission of somatoparaphrenic delusion through vestibular stimulation. *Neuropsychologia, 29*, 1029–1031.

Brunn, J. L., & Farah, M. J. (1991). The relationship between spatial attention and reading: Evidence from the neglect syndrome. *Cognitive Neuropsychology, 8,* 59–75.

Butter, C. M. (1987). Varieties of attention and disturbances of attention: A neuropsychological analysis. In M. Jeannerod (Ed.), *Neurophysiological and neuropsychological aspects of spatial neglect* (pp. 1–24). Amsterdam: North-Holland.

Butter, C. M., Kirsch, N. L., & Reeves, G. (1990). The effect of lateralized dynamic stimuli on unilateral spatial neglect following right hemisphere lesions. *Restorative Neurology and Neuroscience, 2,* 39–46.

Cappa, S. F., Sterzi, R., Vallar, G., & Bisiach, E. (1987). Remission of hemineglect and anosognosia after vestibular stimulation. *Neuropsychologia, 25,* 775–782.

Clohessy, A., Posner, M. I., & Rothbart, M. K. (1991). The development of inhibition of return in early infancy. *Journal of Cognitive Neuroscience, 3,* 346–357.

Cohen, A., Ivry, R., Rafal, R., & Kohn, C. (1995). Response code activation by stimuli in the neglected visual field. *Neuropsychology, 9,* 165–173.

Cohen, A., & Rafal, R. (1991). Attention and feature integration: Illusory conjunctions in a patient with a parietal lobe lesion. *Psychological Science, 2,* 106–110.

Coles, M. G., Gratton, G., Bashore, T. R., Eriksen, C. W., & Donchin, E. (1985). A psychophysiological investigation of the continuous flow model of human information processing. *Journal of Experimental Psychology: Human Perception and Performance, 11,* 529–553.

Corbetta, M., Miezin, F. M., Shulman, G. L., & Petersen, S. E. (1993). A PET study of visuospatial attention. *Journal of Neuroscience, 13,* 1202–1226.

Coslett, H. B., Bowers, D., Fitzpatrick, E., Haws, B., & Heilman, K. M. (1990). Directional hypokinesia and hemispatial inattention in neglect. *Brain, 113,* 475–486.

Coslett, H. B., & Saffran, E. (1991). Simultanagnosia: To see but not two see. *Brain, 113,* 1523–1545.

Critchley, M. (1979). *The divine banquet of the brain.* New York: Raven Press.

Delis, D. C., Robertson, L. C., & Efron, R. (1986). Hemispheric specialization of memory for visual hierarchical stimuli. *Neuropsychologia, 24,* 205–214.

Downing, C. J. (1988). Expectancy and visual–spatial attention: Effects on perceptual quality. *Journal of Experimental Psychology: Human Perception and Performance, 14,* 188–202.

Driver, J., Baylis, G. C., Goodrich, S. J., & Rafal, R. D. (1994). Axis-based neglect of visual shapes. *Neuropsychologia, 32,* 1353–1365.

Driver, J., Baylis, G., & Rafal, R. (1993). Preserved figure-ground segmentation and symmetry perception in a patient with neglect. *Nature, 360,* 73–75.

Driver, J., & Halligan, P. W. (1991). Can visual neglect operate in object-centered coordinates? An affirmative single case study. *Cognitive Neuropsychology, 8,* 475–494.

Duel, R. K. (1987). Neural dysfunction during hemineglect after cortical damage in two monkey models. In M. Jeannerod (Ed.), *Neurophysiological and neuropsychological aspects of spatial neglect* (pp. 315–334). Amsterdam: North-Holland.

Duhamel, J., Goldberg, M., Fitzgibbon, E. J., Sirigu, A., & Grafman, J. (1992). Saccadic dysmetria in a patient with a right frontoparietal lesion. *Brain, 115,* 1387–1402.

Eglin, M., Robertson, L. C., & Knight, R. T. (1989). Visual search performance in the neglect syndrome. *Journal of Cognitive Neuroscience, 1,* 372–385.

Egly, R., Driver, J., & Rafal, R. (1994). Shifting visual attention between objects and locations: Evidence from normal and parietal lesion subjects. *Journal of Experimental Psychology: General, 123, 161–172.*

Egly, R., & Homa, D. (1991). Reallocation of visual attention. *Journal of Experimental Psychology: Human Perception and Performance, 17,* 142–159.

Egly, R., Rafal, R., Driver, J., & Starreveld, Y. (1994). Hemispheric specialization for object-based attention in a split-brain patient. *Psychological Science, 5,* 380–383.

Eriksen, C. W., & St. James, J. D. (1986). Visual attention within and around the field of focal attention: A zoom lens model. *Perception & Psychophysics, 40,* 225–240.

Eriksen, C. W., & Yeh, Y. (1985). Allocation of attention in the visual field. *Journal of Experimental Psychology: Human Perception and Performance, 11,* 583–597.

Farah, M. J. (1990). *Visual agnosia.* Cambridge, MA: MIT Press.

Farah, M. J., Brunn, J. L., Wong, A. B., Wallace, M. A., & Carpenter, P. A. (1990). Frames of reference for allocating attention to space: Evidence from the neglect syndrome. *Neuropsychologia, 28,* 335–347.

Farah, M. J., Monheit, M. A., & Wallace, M. A. (1991). Unconscious perception of "extinguished" visual stimuli: Reassessing the evidence. *Neuropsychologia, 49,* 105–116.

Friedman-Hill, S. R., Robertson, L.C., & Treisman, A. (1995). Parietal contributions to visual feature binding: Evidence from a patient with bilateral lesions. *Science, 269,* 853–855.

Friedrich, F. J., Walker, J. A., & Posner, M. I. (1985). Effects of parietal lesions on visual matching: Implications for reading errors. *Cognitive Neuropsychology, 2,* 253–264.

Funahashi, S., Bruce, C. J., & Goldman, R. P. (1993). Dorsolateral prefrontal lesions and oculomotor delayed-response performance: Evidence for mnemonic "scotomas." *Journal of Neuroscience, 13,* 1479–1497.

Gianotti, G. (1993). The role of spontaneous eye movements in orienting attention and in unilateral neglect. In I. H. Robertson & J. C. Marshall (Eds.), *Unilateral neglect: Clinical and experimental studies* (pp. 107–122). Hillsdale, NJ: Erlbaum.

Gratton, G., Coles, M. G., Sirevaag, E. J., Eriksen, C. W., & Donchin, E. (1988). Pre- and poststimulus activation of response channels: A psychophysiological analysis. *Journal of Experimental Psychology: Human Perception and Performance, 14,* 331–344.

Guariglia, C., Padovani, A., Pantano, P., & Pizzamiglio, L. (1993). Unilateral neglect restricted to visual imagery. *Nature, 364,* 235–237.

Halligan, P. W., & Marshall, J. C. (1994). Right-sided cueing can ameliorate left neglect. *Neuropsychological Rehabilitation, 4,* 463–473.

Heilman, K. M., Bowers, D., Valenstein, E., & Watson, R. (1987). Hemispace and hemispatial neglect. In M. Jeannerod (Eds.), *Neurophysiological and neuropsychological aspects of spatial neglect* (pp. 115–150). Amsterdam: North-Holland.

Heilman, K. M., & Valenstein, E. (1979). Mechanisms underlying hemispatial neglect. *Annals of Neurology, 5,* 166–170.

Heilman, K. M., Valenstein, E., & Watson, R. T. (1985). The neglect syndrome. In J. A. M. Fredricks (Ed.), *Clinical neuropsychology* (pp. 153–183). New York: Elsevier Science.

Heilman, K. M., & Van den Abell, T. (1979). Right hemisphere dominance for mediating cerebral activation. *Neuropsychologia, 17,* 315–321.

Heilman, K. M., & Van den Abell, T. (1980). Right hemisphere dominance for attention: The mechanisms underlying hemispheric asymmetries of inattention (neglect). *Neurology, 30,* 327–330.

Henderson, J. M. (1991). Stimulus discrimination following covert attentional orienting to an exogenous cue. *Journal of Experimental Psychology: Human Perception and Performance, 17,* 91–106.

Henik, A., Rafal, R., & Rhodes, D. (1994). Endogenously generated and visually guided saccades after lesions of the human frontal eye fields. *Journal of Cognitive Neuroscience, 6,* 400–411.

Hillis, A. E., & Caramazza, A. (1991). Deficit to stimulus-centered, letter shape representations in a case of "unilateral neglect." *Neuropsychologia, 29,* 1223–1240.

Hillyard, S. A. (1993). Electrical and magnetic brain recordings: Contributions to cognitive neuroscience. *Current Opinion in Neurobiology, 3,* 217–224.

Holmes, G., & Horax, G. (1919). Disturbances of spatial orientation and visual attention, with loss of stereoscopic vision. *Archives of Neurology and Psychiatry, 1,* 385–407.

Humphreys, G. W., & Riddoch, M. J. (1993). Interactive attentional systems in unilateral visual neglect. In I. H. Robertson & J. C. Marshall (Eds.), *Unilateral neglect: Clinical and experimental studies* (pp. 139–168). Hillsdale, NJ: Erlbaum.

Husain, M., & Stein, J. (1988). Rezso Bálint and his most celebrated case. *Archives of Neurology, 45,* 89–93.

Johnson, M. H. (1990). Cortical maturation and the development of visual attention in early infancy. *Journal of Cognitive Neuroscience, 2,* 81–95.

Johnson, M. H., & Morton, J. (1991). *Biology and cognitive development: The case of face recognition.* New York: Basil Blackwell.

Karnath, H. O., Christ, K., & Hartje, W. (1993). Decrease of contralateral neglect by neck muscle vibration and spatial orientation of trunk midline. *Brain, 116,* 383–396.

Kinsbourne, M. (1977). Hemi-neglect and hemisphere rivalry. In E. A. Weinstein & R. P. Friedland (Eds.), *Advances in neurology* (pp. 41–49). New York: Raven Press.

Kinsbourne, M. (1987). Mechanisms of unilateral neglect. In M. Jeannerod (Eds.), *Neurophysiological and neuropsychological aspects of spatial neglect* (pp. 235–258). Amsterdam: North-Holland.

Kinsbourne, M. (1993). Orientational bias model of unilateral neglect: Evidence from attentional gradients within hemispace. In I. H. Robertson & J. C. Marshall (Eds.), *Unilateral neglect: Clinical and experimental studies* (pp. 63–86). Hillsdale, NJ: Erlbaum.

Kinsella, G., Oliver, J., Ng, K., Packer, S., & Stark, R. (1993). Analysis of the syndrome of unilateral neglect. *Cortex, 29,* 135–140.

Ladavas, E. (1987). Is the hemispatial deficit produced by right parietal damage associated with retinal or gravitational coordinates? *Brain, 110,* 167–180.

Ladavas, E., Del Pesce, M., & Provinciali, L. (1989). Unilateral attention deficits and hemispheric asymmetries in the control of visual attention. *Neuropsychologia, 27,* 353–366.

Ladavas, E., Paladini, R., & Cubelli, R. (1993). Implicit associative priming in a patient with left visual neglect. *Neuropsychologia, 31,* 1307–1320.

Lavie, N., & Tsal, Y. (1994). Perceptual load as a major determinant of the locus of selection in visual attention. *Perception and Psychophysics, 56,* 183–197.

Lezak, M. D. (1994). Domains of behavior from a neuropsychological perspective:

The whole story. In W. D. Spaulding (Ed.), *Integrative views of motivation, cognition, and emotion: Nebraska Symposium on Motivation* (pp. 23–55). Lincoln: University of Nebraska Press.

Lovsund, P., Hedin, A., & Tornros, J. (1991). Effects on driving performance of visual field defects: A driving simulator study. *Accident Analysis and Prevention, 23*, 331–342.

Luria, A. R. (1964). Disorders of "simultaneous perception" in a case of bilateral occipito-parietal brain injury. *Brain, 82*, 437–449.

Mark, V. W., Kooistra, C. A., & Heilman, K. M. (1988). Hemispatial neglect affected by non-neglected stimuli. *Neurology, 38*, 1207–1211.

Marshall, J. C., & Halligan, P. W. (1988). Blindsight and insight in visuo-spatial neglect. *Nature, 336*, 766–767.

McGlinchey-Berroth, R., Milberg, W. P., Verfaellie, M., Alexander, M., & Kilduff, P. T. (1993). Semantic processing in the neglected visual field: Evidence from a lexical decision task. *Cognitive Neuropsychology, 10*, 79–108.

Mijovic, D. (1991). Mechanisms of visual–spatial neglect: Absence of directional hypokinesia in spatial exploration. *Brain, 114*, 1575–1593.

Pashler, H., & O'Brien, S. (1993). Dual-task interference and the cerebral hemispheres. *Journal of Experimental Psychology: Human Perception and Performance, 19*, 315–330.

Pizzamiglio, L., Frasca, R., Guariglia, C., Inaccia, R., & Antonucci, G. (1990). Effect of optokinetic stimulation in patients with visual neglect. *Cortex, 26*, 535–540.

Posner, M. I. (1980). Orienting of attention. *Quarterly Journal of Experimental Psychology, 32*, 3–25.

Posner, M. I., & Cohen, Y. (1984). Components of visual orienting. In H. Bouma & D. Bouwhuis (Eds.), *Attention and performance X* (pp. 531–556). Hillsdale, NJ: Erlbaum.

Posner, M. I., Inhoff, A. W., Friedrich, F. J., & Cohen, A. (1987). Isolating attentional systems: A cognitive-anatomical analysis. *Psychobiology, 15*, 107–121.

Posner, M. I., & Petersen, S. (1990). The attention system of the human brain. *Annual Reviews of Neuroscience, 13*, 25–42.

Posner, M. I., & Rafal, R. D. (1987). Cognitive theories of attention and the rehabilitation of attentional deficits. In R. J. Meir, L. Diller, & A. L. Benton (Eds.), *Neuropsychological rehabilitation* (pp. 182–201). London: Churchill Livingston.

Posner, M. I., Rafal, R. D., Choate, L., & Vaughn, J. (1985). Inhibition of return: Neural basis and function. *Cognitive Neuropsychology, 2*, 211–228.

Posner, M. I., Snyder, C. R. R., & Davidson, B. (1980). Attention and the detection of signals. *Journal of Experimental Psychology: General, 109,* 160–174.

Posner, M. I., Walker, J. A., Friedrich, F. J., & Rafal, R. (1984). Effects of parietal injury on covert orienting of visual attention. *Journal of Neuroscience, 4,* 1863–1874.

Posner, M. I., Walker, J. A., Friedrich, F. J., & Rafal, R. D. (1987). How do the parietal lobes direct covert attention? *Neuropsychologia, 25,* 135–146.

Rafal, R. D. (1992). Visually guided behavior in progressive supranuclear palsy. In I. Litvan & Y. Agid (Eds.), *Progressive supranuclear palsy: Clinical and research approaches.* Oxford, England: Oxford University Press.

Rafal, R. D. (1994). Neglect. *Current Opinion in Neurobiology, 4,* 2312–2316.

Rafal, R. D., Calabresi, P., Brennan, C., & Sciolto, T. (1989). Saccade preparation inhibits reorienting to recently attended locations. *Journal of Experimental Psychology: Human Perception and Performance, 15,* 673–685.

Rafal, R. D., Gershberg, F., Egly, R., Ivry, R., Kingstone, A., & Ro, T. (1995). *Response channel activation and the lateral prefrontal cortex.* Manuscript submitted for publication.

Rafal, R., Henik, A., & Smith, J. (1991). Extrageniculate contributions to reflexive visual orienting in normal humans: A temporal hemifield advantage. *Journal of Cognitive Neuroscience, 3,* 323–329.

Rafal, R. D., Posner, M. I., Friedman, J. H., Inhoff, A. W., & Bernstein, E. (1988). Orienting of visual attention in progressive supranuclear palsy. *Brain, 111,* 267–280.

Rafal, R., & Robertson, L. (1995). The neurology of visual attention. In M. S. Gazzaniga (Ed.), *The cognitive neurosciences* (pp. 625–648). Cambridge, MA: MIT Press.

Rafal, R., Smith, J., Krantz, J., Cohen, A., & Brennan, C. (1990). Extrageniculate vision in hemianopic humans: Saccade inhibition by signals in the blind field. *Science, 250,* 118–121.

Riddoch, M. J., & Humphreys, G. W. (1983). The effect of cueing on unilateral neglect. *Neuropsychologia, 21,* 589–599.

Robertson, L. C., Knight, R. T., Rafal, R. D., & Shimamura, A. (1993). Cognitive neuropyschology is more than single case studies. *Journal of Experimental Psychology: Learning, Memory, and Cognition, 17,* 710–717.

Robertson, L. C., Lamb, M. R., & Knight, R. T. (1988). Effects of lesions of the temporal-parietal junction on perceptual and attentional processing in humans. *Journal of Neuroscience, 8,* 3757–3769.

Rothbart, M. K., Posner, M. I., & Boylan, A. (1991). Regulatory mechanisms in infant development. In J. Enns (Ed.), *The development of attention: Research and theory*. Amsterdam: North-Holland.

Rubens, A. B. (1985). Caloric stimulation and unilateral visual neglect. *Neurology, 35*, 1019–1024.

Rugg, M. D., Milner, A. D., Lines, C. R., & Phalp, R. (1987). Modulation of visual event-related potentials by spatial and non-spatial visual selective attention. *Neuropsychologia, 15*, 85–96.

Seyal, M., Ro, T., & Rafal, R. (in press). Perception of subthreshold cutaneous stimuli following transcranial magnetic stimulation of ipsilateral parietal cortex. *Annals of Neurology*.

Sieroff, E., Pollatsek, A., & Posner, M. I. (1988). Recognition of visual letter strings following injury to the posterior visual spatial attention system. *Cognitive Neuropsychology, 5*, 427–449.

Sprague, J. M. (1966). Interaction of cortex and superior colliculus in mediation of peripherally summoned behavior in the cat. *Science, 153*, 1544–1547.

Tegner, R., & Levander, M. (1991). Through a looking glass: A new technique to demonstrate directional hypokinesia in unilateral neglect. *Brain, 113*, 1943–1951.

Vallar, G. (1993). The anatomical basis of spatial neglect in humans. In I. H. Robertson & J. C. Marshall (Eds.), *Unilateral neglect: Clinical and experimental studies* (pp. 27–62). Hillsdale, NJ: Erlbaum.

Vallar, G., Bottini, G., Rusconi, M. L., & Sterzi, R. (1993). Exploring somatosensory hemineglect by vestibular stimulation. *Brain, 116*, 71–86.

Volpe, B. T., Ledoux, J. E., & Gazzaniga, M. S. (1979). Information processing in an "extinguished" visual field. *Nature, 282*, 722–724.

Wallace, S. F., Rosenquist, A. C., & Sprague, J. M. (1989). Recovery from cortical blindness mediated by destruction of nontectotectal fibers in the commissure of the superior colliculus in the cat. *Journal of Comparative Neurology, 284*, 429–450.

Wallace, S. F., Rosenquist, A. C., & Sprague, J. M. (1990). Ibotenic acid lesions of the lateral substantia nigra restore visual orientation behavior in the hemianopic cat. *Journal of Comparative Neurology, 296*, 222–252.

Weintraub, S., & Mesulam, M. M. (1987). Right cerebral hemisphere dominance in spatial attention. *Archives of Neurology, 44*, 621–625.

Weiskrantz, L. (1986). *Blindsight: A case study and implications*. Oxford, England: Oxford University Press.

6

What Can Visual Neglect and Extinction Reveal About the Extent of "Preattentive" Processing?

Jon Driver

T he theme of this book is the importance of convergent operations. The convergent approach seeks an overarching theory for very diverse sources of evidence, each of which has its own advantages and disadvantages, but all of which should constrain each other in a mutual fashion. Of course, this admirable goal can be much easier to eulogize than to realize in practice. The present chapter critically examines just one convergent method for studying human attention, namely, the attempt to relate normal findings on attention to neuropsychological findings from brain-injured individuals. Although this approach has quite a history for other mental faculties (see McCarthy & Warrington, 1990), it is relatively novel in the study of attention and has only just begun to address one issue that has long been prominent in the literature on individuals with normal brain functioning. This issue is the early- versus late-selection debate over the extent of processing for unattended stimuli. Below I review recent findings from brain-injury patients that may illuminate this issue and also

My research was supported by the Medical Research Council (United Kingdom) and the Science and Engineering Research Council (United Kingdom). I thank Henry Howlett, Glyn Humphreys, Art Kramer, Toby Mordkoff, and, especially Nilli Lavie for helpful comments.

consider how previous work with individuals with normal brain functioning might be brought to bear on subsequent patient studies.

Focusing the chapter on an issue from the literature on normal subjects might be taken to imply that the grand theories will always derive from the study of individuals with normal brain functioning and can simply be tested against the deficits of patients in addition. However, the influence can operate equally well in the reverse direction, with neurological observations from patients suggesting new theoretical approaches, which can then be tested in nonpatient populations. For example, Rizzolatti's premotor theory of attention (e.g., Rizzolatti & Gallese, 1988) was derived primarily from studying the effects of lesions. According to this theory, attentional modulation of sensory processing derives from the preparation of selective actions within various distinct sensorimotor systems (e.g., preparing a saccade to a particular location). This lesion-based theory has led to reconsideration of the role that sensorimotor integration may play in normal attention (see Allport, 1993). As a second illustration that patient studies might usefully influence normal research, numerous dissociations within neuropsychology suggest the existence of multiple attentional systems (see Posner & Petersen, 1990; Robertson & Marshall, 1993), each subserving different functions, different sectors of space, or different classes of stimuli and actions. The challenge of testing these new ideas against normal functioning largely remains to be taken up.

ATTENTIONAL DEFICITS AFTER BRAIN INJURY

The textbook neurological syndromes currently thought of as attentional deficits (namely, unilateral neglect, extinction, and Bálint's syndrome) are described in full elsewhere (Rafal, chap. 5 in this volume), together with suitable warnings that labeling each of these as a syndrome is primarily convenient. Such labeling is almost certainly an oversimplification, as each syndrome can fractionate into different subtypes on closer inspection (see reviews in Robertson & Marshall, 1993), just as for other neurological syndromes such as aphasia. For purposes of exposition, I indulge here briefly in an oversimplified depiction of neglect and extinction that ignores such complexities.

Unilateral neglect is a relatively common disorder associated particularly, but not exclusively, with lesions of the right parietal lobe (Vallar, 1993). Its hallmark is that the patient fails to acknowledge or respond appropriately toward stimuli falling toward the contralesional side (see Bisiach & Vallar, 1988, for review). *Extinction* refers to an ostensibly similar impairment (Bender, 1952), albeit with a tighter operational definition, which again follows unilateral injury. The patient fails to detect a contralesional stimulus (as in neglect), but only when another stimulus is presented concurrently at a more ipsilesional location (Anton, 1899; Kinsbourne, 1977). Given an isolated contralesional stimulus, detection appears to be normal in extinction patients (in fact, it is usually at ceiling, which may obscure a subtle deficit). Clinicians usually test for extinction with the informal but effective procedure of *confrontation*, in which the patient has to report finger movements on either or both of the clinician's outstretched hands while fixating on the clinician's nose. It can be readily detected in more formal procedures by simply presenting one or two brief stimuli on computer screens and requiring that every stimulus be named or detected (e.g., Baylis, Driver, & Rafal, 1993; Karnath, 1988; Volpe, Le Doux, & Gazzaniga, 1979; Ward, Goodrich, & Driver, 1994). Like neglect, extinction is traditionally associated with the right parietal lobe, although it can certainly be found after other unilateral lesions, such as occipitotemporal, in both monkeys (Desimone & Duncan, 1995) and people (Berti et al., 1992; Vallar, Rusconi, Bignamini, Geminiani, & Perani, 1994).

Why are neglect and extinction increasingly considered to be attentional impairments? Several reasons for such a characterization are considered below (and also by Rafal and by Humphreys, in chaps. 5 and 13, respectively, in this volume). However, it must be conceded that none of the arguments are logically watertight. Rather, the suggestion that these deficits are attentional should be regarded as a plausible working hypothesis, useful to the extent that studies of patients with these deficits inform the study of normal attention, and vice versa. As investigators devise satisfactory operational definitions of attention, or of various kinds of attention, these can be applied in analyzing patients' performance. Conversely, observations on the patients themselves may lead to new operational definitions that can be applied to normal individuals. There is clearly a risk of circularity in all this. On the other hand, as Weiskrantz (1986) once remarked to philosophers pushing him for a definition of consciousness, if we knew exactly what the thing was, we would not be studying normal humans, patients, and a variety of animals in an effort to find out. Researchers may be in a similar situation within the general area of studying attention, which is perhaps best regarded as an umbrella term for a host of issues concerning selective perception and action (Driver, 1994). Various specific processes under this general heading can be defined more precisely, as the present volume attests.

The fundamental reason that neglect and extinction are often considered attentional disorders is that the patient seems in principle capable of perceiving or responding to a particular stimulus in a given location, and yet does not. In other words, peripheral sensory or motor losses can be ruled out as a complete explanation of the failure to acknowledge or respond to a contralesional stimulus. Thus, the severity of visual neglect does not correlate with the extent of any visual field cuts (Halligan, Marshall, & Wade 1990), although the two can be hard to distinguish without detailed testing (Walker, Findlay, Young, & Welch, 1991). Nor does neglect seem readily explained by a motoric deficit alone, because many patients (though not all; Tegner & Levander, 1991) will fail to acknowledge contralesional information even when required to do so with ipsilesional responses.

Similarly, in extinction the preserved detection of isolated contralesional events is usually taken to indicate that basic sensory function is intact, so that peripheral sensory loss cannot explain the contralesional misses on double-stimulation trials. A purely motoric deficit also seems inappropriate as an explanation. Why, for instance, should a verbal detection response fail for contralesional stimuli only under double stimulation? In sum, basic sensory or motor impairments alone do not provide a compelling explanation for the ostensive deficits in neglect and extinction[1]. One is therefore tempted to invoke an impairment in some intervening selective process between initial perceptual processing and peripheral responding, and this seems tantamount to many textbook definitions

---

[1] These arguments about extinction can be challenged. As noted earlier, performance is usually at ceiling for isolated contralesional stimuli. This could mask a subtle sensory impairment relative to isolated ipsilesional stimuli, which might be exacerbated by competition with the ipsilesional item on double-stimulation trials. The argument against a motoric explanation seems stronger. However, Kinsbourne (1993) provides a possible hemipheric-competition account for why verbal responses (presumably involving the left hemisphere in most subjects) would be more fragile for stimuli in the left visual field when presented along with stimuli in the right visual field that would also activate the left hemisphere and thus lead to a rightward bias.

of attention (though a cynic might remark that this is precisely because such definitions are so imprecise).

Another reason the deficits are often considered attentional is that they can be modulated by ostensibly attentive manipulations. Thus, in some cases at least, a patient may acknowledge an otherwise neglected stimulus once his or her attention is drawn to it (e.g., by a visual cue, a verbal hint, or an instruction to name some additional stimulus on the contralesional side; Butter, Kirsch, & Reeves, 1990; Riddoch & Humphreys, 1983). Likewise, extinction can be overcome by an attentional manipulation in at least some cases. Instructing the patient to report only contralesional events and to ignore any ipsilesional events can reduce contralesional misses on double-stimulation trials (Karnath, 1988). Although such studies are important (e.g., in establishing that some forms of extinction are not purely stimulus driven), it is doubtful whether they entail that the underlying deficit must be attentional. On the positive side, one might try to argue that if attention can make up for the deficit, inadequate attention must have been the problem in the first place. On the negative side, one might equally well argue that intact attentional mechanisms are modulating disrupted perceptual mechanisms in these studies and, indeed, cite the very effect of the attentional instruction as evidence that attention can still operate effectively.

The final and perhaps most persuasive argument is that patients suffering from these clinical deficits demonstrate abnormal attention as defined operationally, for instance in terms of the costs and benefits of covert orienting in Posner's (1980) well-known cuing paradigm. This approach has led to celebrated successes in fractionating covert orienting into distinct hypothetical subprocesses (e.g., disengaging or moving vs. reengaging attention). These can in turn be related to distinct neural subsystems (Posner, 1988; Posner, Walker, Friedrich, & Rafal, 1984) by studying the particular patterns of impairment after different lesions or diseases (see Rafal, chap. 5 in this volume). One can really only question this approach by questioning the operational definitions of attention themselves (Cohen & Farah, 1991).

For these reasons, among others, I cautiously adopt the working hypothesis that it may at least be useful to consider neglect and extinction as primarily attentional. I can then examine whether the details of these deficits square with recent studies and theories of normal attentional function. Should neglected or extinguished stimuli in patients be equated with unattended stimuli in normal individuals? In considering such issues, the reader should bear in mind the particular way in which a stimulus is deemed unattended, extinguished, or neglected for each of the examples described below.

EARLY VERSUS LATE SELECTION IN NORMAL INDIVIDUALS

The classic theoretical issues in the study of normal selective attention, since Cherry (1953) and Broadbent (1958) first galvanized the field, are the extent of processing prior to attentional selection and how such processing constrains the ease of selecting target information on the basis of various attributes. The initial shadowing studies in audition suggested an early-selection model on which processing of various supposedly low-level attributes (e.g., pitch or location) takes place *without* attention. Because these attributes are coded for all stimuli, one can use these attributes to select particular stimuli for further "semantic" perceptual processing (e.g., identifying words or their meaning), which only takes place *with* attention. This account was soon challenged by late-selection proposals that attention selects among fully completed percepts for the control of action and for entry into long-term memory (e.g., Deutsch & Deutsch, 1964). As most textbooks describe, many subsequent studies found that although processing for the nonshadowed message in dichotic listening seems incomplete when addressed with *direct* measures such as later recall (Cherry, 1953; Moray, 1959), or even with on-line monitoring of the nonshadowed ear (Treisman & Geffen, 1967), such processing seems considerably fuller when assessed with *indirect* on-line measures. These include reaction times to a related shadowed word (Lewis, 1970), disambiguation of the shadowed message (Lackner & Garret, 1972; MacKay, 1973), galvanic skin responses to nonshadowed words that were previously conditioned (Corteen & Dunn, 1974), and so on. A possibly critical factor that all these indirect measures share is that they do not require any deliberate responses to the unattended (i.e., nonshadowed) stimuli. Explicit responses are made to just the relevant stimuli, and processing of irrelevant stimuli is examined indirectly without asking the subject to make any explicit judgment for them.

The early- versus late-selection debate was soon extended to include the visual modality, and continues largely unabated in the literature on normal populations to this day (e.g., Driver & Tipper, 1989; Fox, 1995; Yantis & Johnston, 1990), although some real progress has been made (see Lavie, in press). Charles Eriksen (e.g., B. A. Eriksen & Eriksen, 1974; C. W. Eriksen & Hoffman, 1973) introduced one of the most widely used techniques for examining the extent of distractor processing in normal vision, namely, the response–competition method, which is considered in full elsewhere (Mordkoff, chap. 18 in this volume). As described below, this method can be adapted to study the deficits of neuropsychological patients.

In recent years, some authors (e.g., Allport, 1989, 1993) have questioned whether the early- versus late-selection debate has proved to be something of a red herring. As Allport argued, it is perhaps too narrowly focused, with too many implicit assumptions. For example, the debate assumes that physical processing of attributes such as color or location is trivial and that only abstract categorization (for the meaning of a stimulus) provides a real challenge to the nervous system. This assumption now seems naive, because color does not correspond simply to wavelength, and location does not correspond simply to retinal position, so even these so-called "physical" attributes provide a considerable processing challenge. The traditional debate also assumes that the putative physical processing precedes the more abstract processing in a strictly serial fashion, whereas there is now evidence for extensively parallel processing in vision, together with abundant feedback from higher to lower levels. Nonetheless, despite these shortcomings in the conventional formulation of the question, the extent of processing for unattended stimuli does remain a fundamental issue.

Until quite recently, the neuropsychological literature seems to have lagged somewhat behind such issues in regard to neglected or extinguished stimuli, and certainly behind the indirect methods that have been developed to assess these issues for unattended stimuli in individuals with normal brain functioning. On the other hand, neuropsychology has arguably been in the vanguard on related issues in other areas (say, blindsight; Weiskrantz, 1986), producing innumerable demonstrations that stimuli can be "implicitly" processed to a greater extent than the ostensive behavior of the patient would immediately suggest (e.g., Bauer, 1984; Milner, 1962; Warrington & Shallice, 1979). Below I review recent studies that have examined the extent of implicit processing in neglect and extinction. My intention is to highlight whether there is any useful analogy to the extent of processing for unattended stimuli in normals. Two processing issues are addressed, and these should be kept distinct. First, what is the extent of processing for neglected, extinguished, or unattended stimuli in various situations? Second, to what extent is this processing implicit rather than explicit?

DIRECT MEASURES OF THE PROCESSING FOR EXTINGUISHED OR NEGLECTED STIMULI

In the studies under this heading, the patient has to respond explicitly concerning some aspect of the contralesional stimuli. Volpe et al. (1979) provided one of the first studies of the extent of processing for extinguished stimuli with such a method (but see Anton, 1899, p. 105, for a related clinical anecdote). Volpe et al. reported four unilateral parietal patients who could name line drawings or words presented singly to either visual field, but who failed to name contralesional stimuli on double stimulation. Despite this extinction for naming, the patients were able to judge whether two simultaneous stimuli were the same or different, even though they reportedly denied any experience of a contralesional event on such trials. This paradoxical result seems to imply substantial processing for the extinguished stimulus, in apparent agreement with late-selection results for unattended visual stimuli in non-brain-injured individuals (e.g., Driver & Tipper, 1989; Tipper & Driver, 1988). Moreover, because the contralesional stimulus was apparently not detected on double trials, with patients feeling that their same–different judgments were mere guesses, the residual processing might be considered "implicit" (although this would be a somewhat unorthodox use of the term, because an explicit same–different judgment was in fact required for the contralesional stimulus).

The Volpe et al. (1979) study has been criticized on several grounds. Berti et al. (1992) pointed out that because the *same* pairs were *physically* identical, the same–different judgment under double stimulation might be made on the basis of low-level contralesional information. Although this point does not explain why such information would be available for a matching judgment, yet not for phenomenal detection, it does undermine the conclusion of full semantic processing for the extinguished item.

Berti et al. themselves reported a patient who showed extinction after unilateral temporal (rather than parietal) injury, although this extinction only applied to naming, not to detection (cf. Volpe et al.'s parietal patients). The patient with temporal injury could make accurate same–different judgments even when the *same* pairs were visually dissimilar (e.g., two different types of corkscrew) and the *different* pairs were visually similar (e.g., a rolled-up umbrella and a pen). In this case, the same–different judgments could apparently be based on quite abstract information.

However, Berti et al.'s (1992) temporal patient was able to identify contralesional objects explicitly under double stimulation on *same* trials, failing to do so only on *different* trials. Accordingly, as the authors acknowledged, their results do not entail full but implicit semantic processing of an extinguished object. Instead, the results may arise simply because initial explicit processing of an ipsilesional object can prime processing of related contralesional objects, which would otherwise suffer as a result of the lesion. This priming would take place only on *same* trials, hence producing contralesional identification on these trials alone, and thus providing an explicit basis for the correct same–different judgments. Such an explanation is reminiscent of attenuation theory (Treisman, 1969), which posits that semantic effects in normal individuals from primed unattended stimuli may be based only on partial information (see Miller, 1987).

Farah, Monheit, and Wallace (1991) criticized the Volpe et al. (1979) study on different methodological grounds, and their objections apply equally to Berti et al.'s (1992) work. They pointed out that forced-choice same–different responses require less perceptual information about the contralesional stimulus (and have vastly different chance rates) than explicit naming responses. They were able to mimic the phenomenon reported by Volpe et al. (i.e., impaired naming on one side during double stimulation, yet with preserved interfield comparisons) in normal subjects, simply by degrading the stimulus on one side. This demonstration shows that the neuropsychological results are in principle consistent with degraded explicit perceptions for contralesional stimuli, rather than entailing full but implicit perceptions for the affected side.

In a further study on the extent of processing for extinguished information, Baylis et al. (1993) made the clinical observation that parietal extinction (as opposed to the temporal extinction studied by Berti et al., 1992) can be more severe when two identical objects are held up for the patient to report rather than when two different objects are presented. They followed up this clinical observation with a computerized task in which five parietal-extinction patients were briefly presented with colored letters in either or both visual fields. In some blocks of trials they had to report the color (red, green, or nothing) on each side, while in other blocks they reported the shape (*O*, *E*, or nothing). On double-stimulation trials, the patients made more erroneous *nothing* responses for the contralesional side when the two concurrent stimuli were identical on the reported dimension. Their relation on the currently irrelevant dimension had no such effect. Because the extent of extinction depended on the relation between the two stimuli, one might argue that this relation (for color in the color blocks and for shape in the shape blocks) must have been coded even for the stimulus that went unreported.

The difficulty with identical stimuli in Baylis et al.'s (1993) parietal study may seem paradoxical in the light of the priming argument offered above for Berti et al.'s (1992) temporal data, where it was suggested that initial processing of the ipsilesional item should *benefit* processing of a related contralesional item. In the Baylis et al. study, such a relation is clearly detrimental rather than beneficial (see also Humphreys, chap. 13 in this volume, for further discussion of the beneficial versus detrimental effects from similarity in extinction). Fortunately, this apparent paradox finds a possible resolution by reference to the literature on normal subjects. On the one hand, there are many cases in which repeating a stimulus or presenting two related stimuli leads to facilitatory priming in normal individuals (e.g., Monsell, 1985). On the other hand, when identical stimuli are briefly presented concurrently or at short lags, normal people often fail to detect both, reporting only one of the two occurrences ("repetition blindness"; Kanwisher, 1987). For instance, Kanwisher, Driver, and Machado (in press) have recently observed directly analogous data to those found by Baylis et al. (i.e., detrimental effects of repetition in color or shape, provided that the repeated dimension is relevant) but in normal subjects, using brief masked displays.

The apparent conflict between facilitatory priming and repetition blindness (i.e., benefits vs. costs from repetition, respectively) has been resolved by proposing two distinct forms of visual representation (Kanwisher, 1987; Kanwisher & Driver, 1992). *Type* recognition (the triggering of a representation in long-term memory for the category of a stimulus) is distinguished from *token* individuation of the current instances of the category (thus, a display such as *AA* would comprise two tokens but one type). Repetition is held to facilitate type recognition (producing conventional facilitatory priming effects) but to impair token individuation (because multiple tokens have to be formed for the same type). In line with such an account, Baylis et al. (1993) suggested that the deficit in parietal-lobe extinction may primarily apply to processes of token individuation, with type recognition proceeding normally for contralesional stimuli, even when these are extinguished because no token is formed. Indeed, Baylis et al.'s data imply that such preserved contralesional type recognition can itself contribute to parietal extinction, which is exacerbated when the same type is coded for the two sides. In contrast to their patients, Berti et al.'s (1992) patient had extinction after temporal-lobe injury, and this applied only to concurrent identification and not to concurrent detection. As we have seen, this individual apparently had impaired type recognition for contralesional stimuli (which would be facilitated by a relation with the ipsilesional stimulus, as observed) rather than any particular difficulty in token individuation (which would be exacerbated by any repetition, which was not found). Indeed, she could always detect when two stimuli were simultaneously present; her only difficulty was in identifying what they both were.

I return to the type–token account later, and to the possibility of parietal versus temporal substrates, respectively, for the two forms of representation. Note, however, that even with the type–token interpretation of Baylis et al.'s (1993) data, their results would demonstrate only that colors and simple aspects of shape (sufficient to distinguish an *E* from an *O*) can be coded implicitly for an extinguished item. This would fall short of establishing the semantic processing that is disputed for unattended stimuli in individuals with normal functioning within the traditional early-versus late-selection debate.

INDIRECT MEASURES OF THE PROCESSING OF EXTINGUISHED OR NEGLECTED STIMULI

Studies under this heading have also sought evidence that extinguished or neglected stimuli may be extensively processed. The difference is that their measure of contralesional processing does not rely on any deliberate response to the contralesional stimuli. Vallar, Sandroni, Rusconi, and Barbieri (1991) found preserved visual evoked potentials for contralesional stimuli that two patients with left neglect failed to detect. This pioneering study does not address the semantic processing disputed in the early- versus late-selection debate, but the method could presumably be adapted to do so (e.g., by looking for evoked responses to neglected stimuli that indicate face or word recognition).

In a well-known clinical observation, Marshall and Halligan (1988) claimed to find implicit semantic processing of neglected contralesional information by asking an indirect question. They presented their patient, who had right-parietal left neglect, with two line drawings of a house, one above the other. The drawings were identical except for the depiction of flames on the contralesional side of one house. When asked whether the two drawings differed (identity question), the patient insisted that they could not be distinguished. However, when subsequently asked a curious and repeated question about which of these apparently identical houses she would prefer to live in (dwelling question), she showed a statistical preference for the house without the flames, apparently demonstrating implicit semantic processing of the neglected information.

Although provocative, this observation cannot be taken as conclusive. First, as the subliminal perception literature documents, there is the potential problem of unintended experimenter effects in such informal over-the-table methods, which may have influenced the patient's dwelling decisions. Second, it is difficult to assess the extent to which the patient was aware of contralesional information at the point of answering the dwelling questions (and the extent to which eye-movement patterns may have differed during the identity questions versus the dwelling questions). Finally, even if one accepts the result as watertight, could full *semantic* processing (rather than just partial physical processing) be inferred from the statistical dwelling preference? Perhaps the patient took the flames to be flowers instead of a fire, and decided she would prefer the house with less gardening required. The point behind this flippant remark is that although the dwelling preference might be taken to imply some degree of implicit processing for neglected information, it does not establish the full extent of this processing.

Marshall and Halligan's (1988) provocative article has stimulated further work on this very issue, such as a study that I suggested to Berti and

Rizzolatti (1992). They required 7 patients with left neglect to make a speeded animal–vegetable decision for target line drawings presented in the ipsilesional visual field, and preceded 400 ms earlier by a prime line drawing in the contralesional field. The drawings were presented briefly to preclude any role for overt eye movements during presentation. The contralesional prime could be identical to the ipsilesional target, or from the same category, or from the opposite category. Categorizations of the ipsilesional target were slower in the latter case. Thus, the category of the contralesional prime had a clear effect (even though it was presented in a reportedly hemianopic field for 5 of the 7 patients), implying some degree of type recognition. This study provides more convincing support for the full but implicit semantic processing of neglected stimuli that Marshall and Halligan (1988) proposed. However, as with any single study, several objections and further questions can be raised.

A critical issue in such studies is to establish that the effective stimulus was indeed neglected or extinguished. Berti and Rizzolatti (1992) addressed this simply by requiring their patients to describe in full what they saw after each of 24 practice trials that preceded the 72 experimental trials. Two patients (those without hemianopia) spontaneously reported seeing objects on the right and on the left, whereas the remainder described only the right stimuli spontaneously. However, can one really conclude that the latter subjects absolutely never experienced any left stimulus in the subsequent 72 trials, when they were both more practiced and possibly primed to seek further stimuli by the preliminary questioning? The methodological problem here is somewhat reminiscent of the controversy over subliminal perception in the literature on normal subjects (e.g., Marcel, 1983), where one has to convince the skeptics (e.g., Holender, 1986) that an effect is truly implicit by applying very stringent criteria for explicit knowledge (e.g., by assessing this knowledge on every priming trial rather than just during practice; by establishing that d' is indistinguishable from zero for these trials with a forced-choice response, and so on; see Kemp-Wheeler & Hill, 1988; Cheeseman & Merikle, 1984; and the commentaries on Holender, 1986). On the other hand, in the literature on normal subjects the operational criteria for "subliminal" and "unattended" are usually very different, with the latter much less stringent. The subject is certainly aware, for example, that sounds are entering the nonshadowed ear during dichotic listening.

A further possible objection to Berti and Rizzolatti's (1992) study concerns whether it establishes truly semantic processing. Their experiment sought to go beyond physical processing by using congruent pairs of different stimuli from within the same category, as well as identical pairs. However, it is well known that items within categories such as animals or vegetables have substantial visual similarity (e.g., Damasio, Tranel, & Damasio, 1993). A control for such factors was attempted by using nonsense primes derived from the outline shapes of target objects. However, this condition was applied for only 2 of the 7 patients, and, although performance was numerically intermediate between the congruent and incongruent primes, it did not differ significantly from either. In any case, it is unclear that outline information is the only source of within-category similarity (e.g., all the animals had eyes, the vegetables leaves and textures, which were never present in the nonsense controls).

A final methodological objection (for true aficionados of the early-versus late-selection debate) is that the contralesional stimuli may have been effective only because they themselves were already highly primed, an objection that also applies to many studies of unattended processing in normal subjects (see Johnston & Dark, 1986; Miller, 1987). There were only eight animal pictures and six fruit pictures in Berti and Rizzolatti's (1992) entire experiment, so each presumably appeared several times as the target during the 96 trials. Attenuation versions of early selection (e.g., Treisman, 1969) have long argued that unattended stimuli are categorized as a particular type only when that classification is already highly primed and can therefore be triggered on the basis of very little information. The same might be suggested for neglected stimuli. Taking all these potential criticisms together, it is clear that the verdict must remain open on the precise level of representation at which the effects took place in Berti and Rizzolatti's provocative study.

A similar uncertainty applies to a pioneering study by Audet, Bub, and Lecours (1991), who adapted the response–competition paradigm of B. A. Eriksen and Eriksen (1974) to study the extent of processing for neglected stimuli. They required two left-neglect patients, one of whom had hemianopia, to name a target letter (*T* or *K*) presented at fixation. A distractor letter was presented 2° to its left or 2° above it and could be congruent, incongruent, or neutral (an *O*). The vertical distractors were intended to provide a baseline measure of distractor processing within an unimpaired region, for comparison with the horizontal distractors on the neglected side. Somewhat surprisingly, neither horizontal nor vertical distractors produced any effect when presented simultaneously with the target. However, vertical distractors produced the expected effects for both patients (i.e., facilitation when congruent, interference when incongruent) when preceding the target by 250 ms and remaining visible for 650 ms. For one patient, horizontal distractors to the left of the target had no effect under these timing conditions. For the other patient, they now produced a reliable facilitation effect when congruent. Curiously, this effect was found in the patient with hemianopia, although the left distractor was perhaps sufficiently near fixation to fall in macular vision.

Audet et al. (1991) followed up the result for the latter patient with two further studies. Increasing the proportion of congruent trials without informing the patient increased the facilitation effect from vertical congruent distractors but not from horizontal congruent distractors, suggesting that only the former could be used strategically (this conclusion follows the logic of studies of normal subjects by Taylor, 1977; but see Mordkoff, chap. 18 in this volume, for a nonstrategic perspective on probability effects). On the other hand, in a final study the patient was explicitly instructed that horizontal distractors tended to predict the target, and this led to an interference effect from them when incongruent for the first time.

The Audet et al. (1991) study was groundbreaking in several respects: for instance, in its comparison of vertical versus horizontal distractors, in the examination of strategic factors, and in underlining the possible differences between neglect patients. It does have two main weaknesses, however. As with Berti and Rizzolatti's (1992) experiment, the evidence that the effective distractors were actually neglected is circumstantial. Both patients were simply asked at the end of each block of 32 trials whether they saw one or two items when responding, and both volunteered that they did see two in the blocks with vertical distractors, but not in those blocks with a left distractor (except in one block for the patient who showed effects from horizontal distractors). Doubts about the adequacy of such an informal and retrospective measure of awareness can be raised, especially when one considers that each distractor was presented in isolation for 250 ms and for 650 ms in total. Moreover, the patient who showed the distractor effects had previously been found to detect the presence of both right and left stimuli with 87% accuracy under simultaneous double stimulation, using briefer displays of a mere 150 ms. Finally, because the three letters (*T*, *K*, and *O*) might be distinguished on the basis of low-level visual features (e.g., horizontal, tilted, and curved lines, respectively), the distractor effects cannot in any case be taken as unequivocal evidence for the semantic processing disputed in the traditional early- versus late-selection debate.

The latter objection does not apply to a recent study by McGlinchey-Berroth, Milberg, Verfaellie, Alexander, and Kilduff (1993). They required 4 patients with left neglect (but no hemianopia) and 1 patient with left hemianopia (but no neglect) to make a lexical decision to a letter string at fixation. This was preceded 600 ms earlier by two concurrent drawings on either side of fixation, one depicting a common object, while the other was just scrambled lines (which probably had a different spatial-frequency composition to the meaningful drawing). These drawings were presented briefly to preclude eye movements during them. The main findings for neglect patients was that lexical decision to the target word was faster when the preceding meaningful drawing was of a semantically related object (e.g., a pictured baseball bat followed by the letter string *ball*), regardless of whether the meaningful drawing had appeared in the left or right visual field. Indeed, this priming effect was very large (mean advantage of 1,032 ms for related words) compared with that found for age-matched controls (mean advantage of 46 ms). No priming effect was found for the hemianopic patient (cf. Audet et al., 1991; Berti & Rizzolatti, 1992).

It is unclear why the priming effect was so much larger (in both absolute and proportional terms) for the neglect patients than for the normal controls. Nonetheless, McGlinchey-Berroth et al. (1993) took the equivalent priming from the two visual fields within the patients as evidence that implicit perceptual processing was quite normal in their contralesional field. The normal subjects similarly showed no significant effect for the visual field of prime. On the other hand, they did show a numerical trend for greater priming from a related object on the left (mean of 70 ms) versus right (22 ms). If further normal subjects were to render this trend significant, it would shed a somewhat different light on the equivalent priming from both visual fields in the patients. Against a normal baseline of larger effects from left objects than from right, equivalent effects for the two sides in neglect patients would no longer imply that processing was completely unimpaired on the left side.

Nevertheless, McGlinchey-Berroth et al.'s (1993) results clearly demonstrate a semantic effect from a contralesional object in neglect patients. There are no physical similarities between a pictured object and the name of a related object (as previously pointed out by Tipper & Driver, 1988, in a priming study of unattended processing for normal subjects). Moreover, each stimulus appeared only once, ruling out any explanation in terms of a small and repeated stimulus-set that allowed categorization on the basis of restricted input. Thus, there can be little dispute over the abstract level of representation at which the priming effects took place in McGlinchey-Berroth et al.'s study.

What about the other methodological concern I have discussed, namely, whether the effective contralesional stimuli were truly neglected or extinguished? This was addressed with a follow-up experiment. The same patients were again presented with prime displays comprising a drawing of a common object on one side and scrambled lines on the other side, just as before. However, they now had to make an explicit judgment about the meaningful object in this prime display, whereas previously no response had been required to it. The task was to judge which of two subsequent pictures the meaningful prime matched, either the one above fixation or the one below.

Three of the 4 neglect patients were at chance in this matching task when the meaningful prime was on the left (although one of these patients was also at chance for objects on the right, raising the concern that some difficulty in the matching task may underestimate the patients' explicit perceptual abilities). Taking the neglect patients together, the group was above chance for right objects, and at chance for left objects, leading to a significant difference between the visual fields for this explicit matching task, which contrasts with the null effect of visual field in the previous implicit priming task.

My only methodological concern about this admirably thorough study is as follows. The inference that the effective contralesional primes were truly neglected depends on extrapolation across two separate experiments. Perhaps the patients actually had more explicit information about contralesional objects in the first priming study than they did in the second matching study. This might seem unlikely given that the prime display was relevant to their explicit task in the matching task but not in the priming task. On the other hand, suppose that for this very reason the patients tried to concentrate on the prime objects in the matching task, but simply adopted a passive (or more global) strategy for the prime display during the lexical decision task. If they began by concentrating on the ipsilesional prime in the matching task (as a result of the lateral bias produced by their brain damage), they might then have difficulty disengaging from this stimulus (Posner et al., 1984) to deal with the contralesional prime. This disengage difficulty would be circumvented in the priming task by means of the passive global strategy I have suggested.

As a final methodological concern, note that the matching task does not test whether the neglect patients were aware of the contralesional drawings in the sense of merely detecting them. Instead, it measures their ability to match their identity, a less stringent criterion than that required in the normal subliminal perception literature (e.g., Cheeseman & Merikle, 1984). On the other hand, as noted earlier, a strict detection criterion is rarely demanded in the study of unattended processing for normal subjects.

Ladavas, Paladini, and Cubelli (1993) recently reported a single patient with left neglect but no hemianopia following a right-hemisphere stroke and claimed to observe semantic priming from contralesional stimuli that were neglected even by the detection criterion. A prime word was presented briefly in the left visual field, followed at a variable delay by a target letter string in the right visual field that required a speeded lexical decision. A conventional semantic priming effect was found (correct responses to word targets were on average 84 ms faster when preceded by a related word; e.g., *sangue–rosso*, or blood–red in English). As with the McGlinchey-Berroth et al. (1993) study, this demonstrates that contralesional stimuli can achieve an abstract level of representation in at least some neglect patients, because the semantically related word pairs had no physical similarity and were not presented repeatedly. But once again, the question arises as to whether the effective contralesional primes were truly neglected (especially as these were now presented in isolation, with no concurrent ipsilesional stimulus to extinguish them).

Ladavas et al. (1993) addressed this issue with four follow-up studies. They found that the patient could not correctly read aloud the briefly presented words in the contralesional field, although 24% of his responses were visually or semantically related to the target. Although this demonstrates a contralesional impairment relative to controls, the related responses seem inconsistent with the complete absence of any explicit awareness for contralesional words, suggesting instead partial explicit knowledge (both visual and semantic), which might be sufficient to yield a semantic priming effect on subsequent ipsilesional words. On the other hand, one could perhaps argue that this partial knowledge was actually implicit, simply biasing the patient's guesses. Further studies found the patient unable to make correct lexical decisions for brief contralesional strings, unable to classify contralesional words as living or nonliving, and importantly, unable even to detect the presence or absence of a brief contralesional word in a forced choice. The latter result seems paradoxical, given the partial visual and semantic partial knowledge apparent in the reading task. On the other hand, it would accord with one of the most controversial results in the normal literature on subliminal perception. Marcel (1983) reported that as the duration of a masked letter-string was reduced in normal subjects, detection judgments fell off *before* graphemic similarity forced-choice judgments, which in turn fell off before semantic similarity judgments.

Ladavas et al.'s (1993) study does suffer from the problem that the forced-choice judgments about the contralesional stimulus, including detection, were implemented in separate studies from the priming measure. Indeed, the sequence and temporal separation of the studies is not specified, let alone the levels of fatigue, practice, dark adaptation, or response bias (e.g., if the patient always responded *no* in the detection task, which is unreported, any residual sensitivity would be masked by a high criterion). Such methodological shortcomings would certainly concern skeptics in the subliminal-perception literature (see Holender, 1986). Nevertheless, as noted earlier, the operational criterion for a subliminal stimulus is usually more severe than that for an unattended stimulus in the normal literature. On the face of it, the contralesional words seem to have passed even the former criterion in Ladavas et al.'s patient, at least at the time of the detection task. The only refuge for a skeptic is to demand that forced-choice detection be implemented on every single priming trial, with present and absent response categories used equally often across trials.

SUMMARY OF PREVIOUS
NEUROPSYCHOLOGICAL RESEARCH

Recent studies of neglect and extinction have established that considerably more processing takes pace for stimuli toward the affected side than might be expected given the ostensive behavior of the patients toward those stimuli. It is still (just) possible to remain skeptical about whether these effects are truly implicit or subconscious, and future patient studies might do well to follow the methodological procedures introduced by Jacoby and associates (e.g., Jacoby & Kelley, 1992) for studying this issue in normal subjects. Nevertheless, there are now conclusive demonstrations that processing can proceed to an abstract level of representation for stimuli in the contralesional visual field of a neglect patient (e.g., Ladavas et al., 1993). This can apparently take place even in the presence of a concurrent ipsilesional stimulus, although to date this has been shown conclusively only when the ipsilesional item is meaningless (McGlinchey-Berroth et al., 1993). Successive studies have used increasingly sophisticated methods to rule out skeptical accounts of previous data, largely drawing on techniques already established by the normal literature on early versus late selection, or on subliminal perception.

The recent priming results have been used (e.g., by Ladavas et al., 1993) to advance a more precise version of an argument we encountered and questioned earlier. This is the proposal that neglect and extinction must be attentional deficits, because perceptual processing of contralesional stimuli can apparently be preserved to quite high levels; witness the semantic priming and interference effects they produce. On the other hand, the normal literature continues to debate whether attention affects perceptual processing (e.g., Driver & Tipper, 1989; Fox, 1995; Yantis & Johnston, 1990). If it does, then surely attentional deficits actually should lead to severe perceptual deficits. From this perspective, it may seem natural to interpret the neglect and extinction findings I have reviewed as supporting an extreme late-selection model of attention. However, I think they fall short of entailing such a drastic conclusion. Indeed, these pioneering studies on neglect and extinction raise almost as many questions as they answer. Below I discuss these remaining questions, first from the conventional perspective of the early- versus-late selection debate and then from a perspective that attempts to broaden this debate.

QUESTIONS FOR FUTURE RESEARCH

The neuropsychological literature on the extent of residual processing in neglect currently finds itself in an analogous situation to the early- versus late-selection debate in the literature of the 1970s. Initial observations with explicit response measures (analogous to the ostensive behavior of a neglect patient toward contralesional stimuli) suggest very restricted perceptual processing for unattended stimuli. However, by the time Keele and Neill (1978) reviewed the normal literature, this hypothesis of restricted processing had apparently been overturned by numerous demonstrations that irrelevant stimuli can produce semantic effects when measured with indirect or implicit measures (analogously to the recent priming findings for neglect and extinction).

On the basis of these semantic effects found in normal subjects, researchers were leaping to the conclusion that preattentive perceptual processing was automatic and quite unlimited in capacity (e.g., Keele & Neill, 1978). However, this hardly follows from observations of semantic priming or interference from a single stimulus, deemed irrelevant by the experimenter but perhaps hard to ignore. First, there may be substantial differences between the processing of one irrelevant stimulus in a sparse display, versus all of the many objects in a cluttered scene (see Lavie, in press; Lavie & Tsal, 1994). Second, a semantic effect on reaction time entails only a certain degree of semantic activation. Perhaps the activation for unattended or neglected stimuli is less extensive, precise, or durable than that for attended or ipsilesional stimuli. McGlinchey-Berroth et al. (1993) and Audet et al. (1991) have provided a useful empirical start here, with their comparison of priming from ipsilesional versus contralesional visual fields, and of interference from vertical vesus horizontal distractors.

A third reason for caution about the extent of residual processing in neglect stems from the history of similar issues for unattended processing in normal people. A wide range of normal studies have found that semantic interference effects from incongruent distractors can dissipate when distractors are made more physically distinct from targets (as originally found by B. A. Eriksen & Eriksen, 1974) or when the processing demands for targets are increased (Lavie, in press; Lavie & Tsal, 1994). Although negative priming effects on a subsequent target can be found even from distractors that do not interfere with a concurrent target (Driver &

Tipper, 1989; Fox, 1995), these priming effects apparently also decline when the number of items in a scene is increased (Neumann & DeSchepper, 1992). Thus, although there is abundant evidence that irrelevant stimuli can be processed to high levels in normal subjects under some circumstances (e.g., B. A. Eriksen & Eriksen, 1974; Tipper & Driver, 1988), it seems clear that neither extreme early- nor late-selection views do justice to the full complexity of the data. Some compromise view, or some more sophisticated approach, is obviously required for normal performance.

A strict late-selection approach to residual processing in neglect seems likely to prove similarly inadequate. The pioneering studies reviewed above have played an important role in establishing that contralesional stimuli can have semantic effects, but this simply leads to further questions. Because such effects are not always present for unattended stimuli in normal subjects (e.g., B. A. Eriksen & Eriksen, 1974; Lavie, in press; Neumann & DeSchepper, 1992; Yantis & Johnston, 1990), one would not expect to find them ubiquitously for neglect patients, even if attention were indeed their sole deficit. Future research must determine whether the boundary conditions for observing semantic effects from neglected and extinguished stimuli mirror those already found for unattended stimuli in individuals with normal functioning.

Thus, several questions about residual processing in neglect remain, even from the perspective of the early- versus late-selection debate. I turn now to the many additional questions that this normal debate overlooks. As discussed earlier, the traditional scope of this debate has been rather narrow, focusing exclusively on semantic processing (i.e., the process of type recognition discussed earlier). This is unfortunate, because it is abundantly clear that vision does much more than just categorize stimuli as members of a familiar type. For instance, it can provide the three-dimensional layout of entirely unfamiliar objects and surfaces in order to control our actions (Gibson, 1979). People do not need to recognize an object in order to pick it up, for example.

As discussed earlier, vision can also distinguish between multiple instances of the same type (e.g., representing all three As and both Ns in the word banana), which I have attributed to the formation of distinct episodic tokens for the various instances of a semantic type (Kanwisher, 1987; Kanwisher & Driver, 1992). Kahneman and Treisman (1984; Kahneman, Treisman, & Gibbs, 1992) have recently argued that vision can similarly segment scenes into distinct "things" (or episodic tokens) even when these do not conform to any familiar type, or when their ascribed type changes over time. For instance, when an initial misidentification of an approaching object is corrected, the phenomenal unity of the approaching thing is still maintained.

Thus, in addition to categorizing stimuli as instances of familiar types that are coded in long-term semantic memory, vision distinguishes between current instances of these types in terms of episodic information (e.g., their particular position, orientation, or movement relative to the observer at this very moment). The latter episodic information can be as important in controlling our ongoing behavior as information about the semantic type; for instance, when we pick up an object.

The studies of neglect and extinction described above have been concerned solely with the derivation of abstract semantic information, rather than with these more episodic visual characteristics. The studies suggest that residual type recognition can proceed for contralesional stimuli, but they have not investigated whether more episodic attributes (such as the current location, orientation, size, movement, continuity, or number of stimulus types) can also be coded contralesionally. Future studies of this issue could well turn the early- versus late-selection debate on its head. For instance, they might find that although abstract semantic information is still coded for neglected stimuli, many of the more concrete or physical stimulus attributes (e.g., location, size, orientation relative to the viewer, etc.) are no longer represented contralesionally, even though these attributes are held to be processed without attention by all the rival theories.

A TENTATIVE HYPOTHESIS BASED ON ANATOMY

This paradoxical result (i.e., preserved semantic coding but impaired physical coding in neglect) might be predicted on the basis of recent distinctions between dorsal and ventral streams in the primate visual system. For some time, this anatomical distinction has been associated with a functional division between the processing of *what* (i.e., identity information) and *where* (i.e., location information), ascribed to the temporal–ventral pathway and the parietal–dorsal pathways, respectively (e.g. Mishkin, Ungerleider, & Macko, 1983). Recent accounts (e.g., Goodale & Milner, 1993; McCarthy, 1993) suggest that a more appropriate functional division may be between the recognition of familiar categories (within the ventral stream) and the control of ongoing action by episodic aspects of the visual scene such as the current layout of objects relative to the actor (coded within the dorsal stream). Speculatively, one might identify this ventral function with the process of type recognition discussed above and the dorsal function with the process of token individuation via episodic information. Given that most neglect or extinction patients have unilateral damage to just the dorsal pathway, one would then predict disrupted coding of episodic or token information for contralesional stimuli, as in Baylis et al.'s (1993) account of their extinction data. On the other hand, type recognition should be preserved for neglected or extinguished stimuli within the intact ventral pathway, as suggested by the many patient studies reviewed above.

CONCLUSION

My original aim in reviewing these studies was to determine whether there is any useful analogy to be drawn between unattended processing in normal subjects and residual processing in neglect or extinction. The studies considered above certainly illustrate that at the very least, there is much common theoretical and methodological ground. Similar questions can be asked about the processing of unattended and neglected information, and similar methodological problems and solutions arise. Equally, similar questions remain to be asked in the two areas (e.g., about the many perceptual processes beyond type recognition). The parallels are thus highly suggestive at present. The neuropsychological literature currently finds itself in a similar state to early- versus late-selection research on normal subjects, with a few clear demonstrations that semantic effects are possible from neglected stimuli, but rather less evidence on the boundary conditions for this.

A few differences between neglected and unattended stimuli are worth noting, nonetheless. First, it is now clear that there is more than one form of neglect (see Robertson & Marshall, 1993) and that the fate of neglected information may accordingly differ between patients (e.g., Audet et al., 1991). This suggests either that neglected stimuli should not be directly equated with unattended stimuli or that there may be correspondingly numerous ways for a stimulus to be "unattended" in normal subjects.

A second difference is that priming effects for irrelevant distractors on response to subsequent related targets are usually negative in normal subjects (e.g., Fox, 1995; Tipper, 1985; Tipper & Driver, 1988). That is, response is delayed rather than facilitated by a previous related distractor. By contrast, the priming effects from contralesional stimuli in the patient studies reviewed above were invariably facilitatory (Berti & Rizzolatti, 1992; Ladavas et al., 1993; McGlinchey-Berroth et al., 1993). Either type of priming reveals a degree of semantic processing, but why should the valency be opposed in non-brain-injured individuals and brain-injured individuals? Two alternative accounts have been suggested for the valency of negative priming in normal subjects. Tipper (1985) argued that active inhibition may operate as a mechanism to prevent identified distractors from controlling overt responses. Neill, Valdes, Terry, and Gorfein (1992) suggested that episodic memory for the preceding trial, where the current target (or a related item) appeared as a distractor, leads to confusion over the target's current role.

Both these accounts might be extended to explain why the priming from contralesional items in neglect patients has a positive rather than negative valency. Active inhibition may no longer be necessary for irrelevant contralesional items, because these rarely capture control of the patients' behavior and thus may no longer compete for response. Alternatively, it may be that episodic traces are no longer formed for contralesional stimuli. This has not been tested, to my knowledge, even though exclusion from episodic memory is perhaps the best documented effect of inattention in normal individuals.

The episodic account for the positive valency of priming in neglect would be consistent with the tentative anatomical hypothesis developed above. According to this hypothesis, contralesional items undergo only type recognition, which takes place within the relatively unimpaired ventral pathway, where the long-term intrinsic properties of stimuli are represented. More episodic information, which codes the incidental properties that a stimulus currently has from the perceiver's viewpoint, and which thus distinguishes the stimulus as a unique token, is thought to rely on the dorsal pathway. Because this pathway is damaged unilaterally in the vast majority of neglect and extinction patients, such episodic information may no longer be derived or stored appropriately for contralesional stimuli.

REFERENCES

Allport, A. (1989). Visual attention. In M. I. Posner (Ed.), *Foundations of cognitive science* (pp. 631–682). Cambridge, MA: MIT Press.

Allport, A. (1993). Attention and control: Have we been asking the wrong questions? A critical review of twenty-five years. In D. E. Meyer & S. Kornblum (Eds.), *Attention and performance XIV* (pp. 183–218). Cambridge, MA: MIT Press.

Anton, G. (1899). Über die Selbstwahrnehmung der Herderkrankungen des Gehirns durch den Kranken bei Rindenblindheit und Rindentaubheit [On the self-awareness of neurological deficits in patients with cortical blindness and deafness]. *Archives of Psychiatric Nervous Disorders, 32*, 86–111.

Audet, T., Bub, D., & Lecours, A. R. (1991). Visual neglect and left-sided context effects. *Brain & Cognition, 16*, 11–28.

Bauer, R. M. (1984). Autonomic recognition of names and faces in propsopagnosia: A neuropsychological application of the Guilty Knowledge Test. *Neuropsychologia, 22*, 457–469.

Baylis, G. C., Driver, J., & Rafal, R. D. (1993). Visual extinction and stimulus repetition. *Journal of Cognitive Neuroscience, 5*, 453–466.

Bender, M. B. (1952). *Disorders in perception.* Springfield, IL: Charles C Thomas.

Berti, A., Allport, A., Driver, J., Dienes, Z., Oxbury, J., & Oxbury, S. (1992). Levels of processing for stimuli in an "extinguished" visual field. *Neuropsychologia, 30*, 403–415.

Berti, A., & Rizzolatti, G. (1992). Visual processing without awareness: Evidence from unilateral neglect. *Journal of Cognitive Neuroscience, 4*, 345–351.

Bisiach, E., & Vallar, G. (1988). Hemineglect in humans. In F. Boller & J. Grafman (Eds.), *Handbook of neuropsychology* (Vol. 1, pp. 95–232). Amsterdam: Elsevier.

Broadbent, D. E. (1958). *Perception and communication.* Elmsford, NY: Pergamon Press.

Butter, C. M., Kirsch, N. L., & Reeves, G. (1990). The effect of lateralised dynamic stimuli on unilateral neglect after right hemisphere lesions. *Restorative Neurology and Neuroscience, 2*, 39–46.

Cheeseman, J., & Merikle, P. M. (1984). Priming with and without awareness. *Perception & Psychophysics, 36*, 387–395.

Cherry, E. C. (1953). Some experiments on the recognition of speech with one and with two ears. *Journal of the Acoustical Society of America, 25*, 975–979.

Cohen, J., & Farah, M. (1991, November). *Disengaging from the disengage operation.* Paper presented at the 32nd meeting of the Psychonomic Society, San Francisco.

Corteen, R. S., & Dunn, D. (1974). Shock-associated words in a nonattended message: A test for momentary awareness. *Journal of Experimental Psychology, 102,* 1143–1144.

Damasio, A., Tranel, A., & Damasio, H. (1993). Similarity of structure and the profile of visual recognition deficits. *Journal of Cognitive Neuroscience, 5,* 371–372.

Desimone, R., & Duncan, J. (1995). Neural mechanisms of selective visual attention. *Annual Review of Neuroscience, 18,* 193–222.

Deutsch, J. A., & Deutsch, D. (1964). Attention: Some theoretical considerations. *Psychological Review, 87,* 272–300.

Driver, J. (1994). Unilateral neglect and normal attention. *Neuropsychological Rehabilitation, 4,* 123–126.

Driver, J., & Tipper, S. P. (1989). On the nonselectivity of "selective" seeing: Contrasts between interference and priming in selective attention. *Journal of Experimental Psychology: Human Perception and Performance, 15,* 304–314.

Eriksen, B. A., & Eriksen, C. W. (1974). Effects of noise-letters on identification of a target letter in a nonsearch task. *Perception & Psychophysics, 16,* 143–149.

Eriksen, C. W., & Hoffman, J. E. (1973). The extent of processing of noise elements during selective encoding from visual displays. *Perception & Psychophysics, 14,* 155–160.

Farah, M. J., Monheit, M. A., & Wallace, M. A. (1991). Unconscious perception of "extinguished" visual stimuli: Reassessing the evidence. *Neuropsychologia, 29,* 949–958.

Fox, E. (1995). Precuing target location reduces interference but not negative priming from visual distractors. *Quarterly Journal of Experimental Psychology, 48A,* 26–40.

Goodale, M. A., & Milner, A. D. (1993). Separate visual pathways for perception and action. *Trends in Neuroscience, 15,* 20–25.

Gibson, J. J. (1979). *The ecological approach to visual perception.* Boston: Houghton Mifflin.

Halligan, P. W., Marshall, J. C., & Wade, D. T. (1990). Do visual field deficits exacerbate visuo-spatial neglect? *Journal of Neurology, Neurosurgery and Psychiatry, 53,* 487–491.

Holender, D. (1986). Semantic activation without conscious identification in dichotic listening, parafoveal vision and visual masking: A survey and appraisal. *Behavioural and Brain Sciences, 9,* 1–23.

Jacoby, L. L., & Kelley, C. M. (1992). A process-dissociation framework for investigating unconscious influences: Freudian slips, projective tests, subliminal perception, and signal detection theory. *Current Directions in Psychological Science,* *1,* 174–179.

Johnston, W. A., & Dark, V. J. (1986). Selective attention. *Annual Review of Psychology, 37,* 43–75.

Kahneman, D., & Treisman, A. (1984). Changing views of attention and automaticity. In R. Parasuraman & D. R. Davies (Eds.), *Varieties of attention* (pp. 29–61). San Diego, CA: Academic Press.

Kahneman, D., Treisman, A., & Gibbs, B. J. (1992). The reviewing of object-files: Object-specific integration of information. *Cognitive Psychology, 24,* 175–219.

Kanwisher, N. G. (1987). Repetition blindness: Type recognition without token individuation. *Cognition, 27,* 117–143.

Kanwisher, N. G., & Driver, J. (1992). Objects, attributes and visual attention: Which, what and where. *Current Directions in Psychological Science, 1,* 26–31.

Kanwisher, N. G., Driver, J., & Machado, L. (in press). Spatial repetition blindness is modulated by selective attention to color or shape. *Cognitive Psychology.*

Karnath, H. (1988). Deficits of attention in acute and recovered visual hemineglect. *Neuropsychologia, 26,* 27–43.

Keele, S. W., & Neill, W. T. (1978). Mechanisms of attention. In E. C. Carterette & M. P. Friedman (Eds.), *Handbook of perception* (Vol. 9, pp. 3–47). San Diego, CA: Academic Press.

Kemp-Wheeler, S. M., & Hill, A. B. (1988). Semantic priming without awareness: Some methodological considerations and replications. *Quarterly Journal of Experimental Psychology, 40A,* 671–692.

Kinsbourne, M. (1977). Hemineglect and hemispheric rivalry. *Advances in Neurology, 18,* 41–49.

Kinsbourne, M. (1993). Orientational bias model of unilateral neglect. In I. H. Robertson & J. C. Marshall (Eds.), *Unilateral neglect: Clinical and experimental findings* (pp. 63–86). Hillsdale, NJ: Erlbaum.

Lackner, J. R., & Garret, M. F. (1972). Resolving ambiguity: Effects of biasing context in the unattended ear. *Cognition, 1,* 359–372.

Ladavas, E., Paladini, R., & Cubelli, R. (1993). Implicit associative priming in a patient with left visual neglect. *Neuropsychologia, 31,* 1307–1320.

Lavie, N. (in press). Perceptual load as a necessary condition for selective attention. *Journal of Experimental Psychology: Human Perception and Performance.*

Lavie, N., & Tsal, Y. (1994). Perceptual load as a major determinant of the locus of selection in visual attention. *Perception & Psychophysics, 56,* 183–197.

Lewis, J. (1970). Semantic processing of unattended messages using dichotic listening. *Journal of Experimental Psychology, 85,* 225–228.

MacKay, D. (1973). Aspects of the theory of comprehension, memory, and attention. *Quarterly Journal of Psychology, 25,* 22–40.

Marcel, A. J. (1983). Conscious and unconscious perception: Experiments on visual masking. *Cognitive Psychology, 15,* 197–237.

Marshall, J. C., & Halligan, P. W. (1988). Blindsight and insight into visuo-spatial neglect. *Nature, 336,* 766–767.

McCarthy, R. A. (1993). Assembling routines and addressing representations: An alternative conceptualization of "what" and "where" in the human brain. In N. Eilan, E. McCarthy, & W. Brewer (Eds.), *Spatial representation: Problems in philosophy and psychology* (pp. 373–399). Oxford, England: Basil Blackwell.

McCarthy, R. A., & Warrington, E. K. (1990). *Cognitive neuropsychology: A clinical introduction.* San Diego, CA: Academic Press.

McGlinchey-Berroth, R., Milberg, W. P., Verfaellie, M., Alexander, M., & Kilduff, P. T. (1993). Semantic processing in the neglected visual field: Evidence from a lexical decision task. *Cognitive Neuropsychology, 10,* 79–108.

Miller, J. (1987). Priming is not necessary for selective attention failures: Semantic effects of unattended, unprimed letters. *Perception & Psychophysics, 41,* 419–434.

Milner, B. (1962). *Les troubles de memoire accompagnant des lesions hippocampiques bilaterales: Physiologie de l'hippocampe* [Memory deficits after bilateral hippocampal lesions: The physiology of the hippocampus]. Paris: CNRS.

Mishkin, M., Ungerleider, L. G., & Macko, K. A. (1983). Object vision and spatial vision: Two cortical pathways. *Trends in Neuroscience, 6,* 414–417.

Monsell, S. (1985). Repetition and the lexicon. In A. W. Ellis (Ed.), *Progress in the psychology of language* (pp. 72–86). Hillsdale, NJ: Erlbaum.

Moray, N. (1959). Attention in dichotic listening: affective cues and the influence of instructions. *Quarterly Journal of Experimental Psychology, 11,* 56–60.

Neill, W. T., Valdes, L. A., Terry, K. M., & Gorfein, D. S. (1992). Persistence of negative priming: II. Evidence for episodic trace retrieval. *Journal of Experimental Psychology: Learning, Memory, and Cognition, 18,* 993–1000.

Neumann, E., & DeSchepper, B. G. (1992). An inhibition-based fan effect: Evidence for an active suppression mechanism in selective attention. *Canadian Journal of Psychology, 46,* 1–40.

Posner, M. I. (1980). Orienting of attention. *Quarterly Journal of Experimental Psychology, 32,* 3–25.

Posner, M. I. (1988). Structures and functions of selective attention. In T. Boll & B. Bryant (Eds.), *Master lectures in clinical neuropsychology and brain function: Research, measurement and practice* (pp. 169–202). Washington, DC: American Psychological Association.

Posner, M. I., & Petersen, S. E. (1990). The attention system of the human brain. *Annual Review of Neuroscience, 13,* 25–42.

Posner, M. I., Walker, J. A., Friedrich, F. J., & Rafal, R. D. (1984). Effects of parietal injury on covert orienting of attention. *Journal of Neuroscience, 4,* 1863–1874.

Riddoch, M. J., & Humphreys, G. W. (1983). The effect of cuing on unilateral neglect. *Neuropsychologia, 21,* 589–599.

Rizzolatti, G., & Gallese, V. (1988). Mechanisms and theories of spatial neglect. In F. Boller & J. Grafman (Eds.), *Handbook of neuropsychology* (Vol. 1, pp. 233–246). Amsterdam: Elsevier.

Robertson, I. H., & Marshall, J. C. (1993). *Unilateral neglect: Clinical and experimental findings.* Hillsdale, NJ: Erlbaum.

Taylor, D. A. (1977). Time course of context effects. *Journal of Experimental Psychology: General, 106,* 404–426.

Tegner, R., & Levander, M. (1991). Through a looking glass: A new technique to demonstrate directional hypokinesia in unilateral neglect. *Brain, 114,* 1943–1951.

Tipper, S. P. (1985). The negative priming effect: Inhibitory effects of ignored primes. *Quarterly Journal of Experimental Psychology, 37A,* 571–590.

Tipper, S. P., & Driver, J. (1988). Negative priming between pictures and words in a selective attention task: Evidence for semantic processing of ignored stimuli. *Memory and Cognition, 16,* 64–70.

Treisman, A. M. (1969). Strategies and models of selective attention. *Psychological Review, 76,* 282–299.

Treisman, A. M., & Geffen, G. (1967). Selective attention: Perception or response? *Quarterly Journal of Experimental Psychology, 19,* 1–17.

Vallar, G. (1993). The anatomical basis of spatial hemineglect in humans. In I. H. Robertson & J. C. Marshall (Eds.), *Unilateral neglect: Clinical and experimental findings* (pp. 27–59). Hillsdale, NJ: Erlbaum.

Vallar, G., Sandroni, P., Rusconi, M. L., & Barbieri, S. (1991). Hemianopia, hemianethesia, and spatial neglect. *Neurology, 41,* 1918–1922.

Vallar, G., Rusconi, M. L., Bignamini, L., Geminiani, G., & Perani, D. (1994). Anatomical correlates of visual and tactile extinction in humans: A clinical CT scan study. *Journal of Neurology, Neurosurgery and Psychiatry, 57,* 464–470.

Volpe, B. T., LeDoux, J. E., & Gazzaniga, M. S. (1979). Information processing of stimuli in an "extinguished" visual field. *Nature, 282,* 722–724.

Walker, R., Findlay, J. M., Young, A. W., & Welch, J. (1991). Disentangling neglect and hemianopia. *Neuropsychologia, 29,* 1019–1027.

Ward, R., Goodrich, S., & Driver, J. (1994). Grouping reduces visual extinction: Neuropsychological evidence for weight-linkage in visual selection. *Visual Cognition, 1,* 101–129.

Warrington, E. K., & Shallice, T. (1979). Semantic access dyslexia. *Brain, 102,* 43–63.

Weiskrantz, L. (1986). *Blindsight: A case study and implications.* Oxford, England: Oxford University Press.

Yantis, S., & Johnston, J. C. (1990). On the locus of visual selective attention: Evidence from focused attention tasks. *Journal of Experimental Psychology: Human Perception and Performance, 16,* 135–149.

7

Processing Visual Information in an Unattended Location

Richard M. Shiffrin, David Diller, and Asher Cohen

Charles Eriksen has a lengthy and rich record of fundamental contributions to the study of visual attention. Many of his findings (e.g., see C. W. Eriksen, 1990) bear on the following question: What is the nature of processing of information from one visual location when attention is directed to some other visual location? Perhaps the best known of these results is the so-called flanker effect: The subject is asked to judge whether a centrally presented character is in one of two classes. Irrelevant, to-be-ignored characters are presented to the sides of the central character; on the average these flankers are not diagnostic of the correct response. Nonetheless, the flankers produce a response-compatibility effect: They speed responding when the response to which they have been assigned matches that assigned to the central character and slow responding when the responses mismatch (e.g., B. A. Eriksen & C. W. Eriksen, 1974). Also, the compatibility of the response assignment generally outweighs similarity of visual form between flankers and target, demonstrating fairly deep analysis of the flankers. The flanker studies (and related studies in which the target is in a cued position in a circle

This research was supported by National Institute of Mental Health Grant 12717.

of letters, flanked by letters varying in compatibility, as discussed by C. W. Eriksen, 1990) provide perhaps the major line of evidence for mandatory, automatic processing of information from locations other than those to which attention is directed.

Generally, the size of the flanker compatibility effect drops off as the distance of the flankers from the attended, relevant position increases (see Miller, 1991, for a summary). It seems likely, therefore, that attention is involved in the processing of the flankers, probably due to a spread of attention to regions near the target character. Infinitely precise spatial focusing of attention is, of course, an impossibility, but it is nonetheless interesting that attention spreads beyond the target character location (especially given the recent emphasis on object-based perception and attention; e.g., Kahneman & Treisman, 1984, 1992). For present purposes, however, the question remains open: Are characters in unattended locations processed?

There are two main lines of evidence for the view that attention is needed to process information from a visual location. The first is found in Yantis and Johnston (1990). In one paradigm a target character was presented in advance of a trial. A trial began with presentation of a location cue without any letters, followed after 200 ms by a circle of eight letters. If a target was present it was in the cued location. The subjects indicated whether the cued position did or did not contain a target. In these studies there occasionally was a redundant target character in one of the other locations. Except for adjacent locations, the presence of a redundant target did not speed response time. In another paradigm, the subject indicated which of two critical characters was present in the cued location; a single additional character that was response compatible or response incompatible sometimes appeared elsewhere in the display. This extra character did not affect response time unless it was adjacent to the cued location. Yantis and Johnston (1990) noted that these results demonstrate selection to be quite effective. How early in the stages of processing is this selection is a more subtle question. Their results seem to argue against even minimal processing of information in locations distant from the current attentional focus, assuming that such processing would have produced redundancy gains. In light of many extant demonstrations of processing effects caused by visual information in widespread locations in the visual field (albeit in situations where attention is also widespread), Yantis and Johnston proposed a model in which subjects can select the level or depth of processing at which strict selection is introduced. However, it is possible that processing did occur but did not affect the response at the attended location. This alternative was noted and not preferred by Yantis and Johnston, but it requires reconsideration in light of the findings reported in this chapter.

The second line of evidence is found in C. W. Eriksen, Webb, and Fournier (1990). To ease exposition, we describe their results using our terminology. The subject had to identify an *N* or *H* that was presented in one location of a ring of eight letters (the other presented characters being selected from *M*, *W*, and *A*). A location cue was presented 50 ms before any letters appeared. The cued location deserved attention because it was likely to contain a target (with probability 1/2). Then two displays of letters were presented in succession: a prime display presented for 50 ms followed by a target display presented for another 50 ms. Simultaneously with the advent of the target display, a second location cue was presented, indicating a position that would contain a target if the first cued location did not.

When the first cued location contained a target it was present there in both the prime and target displays. On the other 50% of the trials, during the prime display, a noise letter appeared in the first cued location, and one of three kinds of letters, termed a *prime*, appeared in the second cued location: an *N*, *H*, or noise character. Then the target display appeared, with an *N* or *H* in the second cued location. The relationship of the prime to the target could be compatible (e.g., *N-N*), neutral (e.g., *A-N*) or incompatible (e.g., *H-N*). The idea was to see whether the prime–target compatibility affected response times. Because processing of the prime in Cued Location 2 took place while attention was at Cued Location 1, a compatibility effect would suggest processing in the absence of attention.

These compatibility effects were not seen by C. W. Eriksen et al. (1990). They did find compatibility effects in other conditions in which attention could have reached Location 2 in time to have been applied to the prime. They discussed two explanations. First, like Yantis and Johnston (1990), they noted the simplest conclusion: that unattended locations do not receive processing. However, also like Yantis and Johnston, they noted the considerable literature suggesting processing from distributed locations in the visual field. They therefore suggested a model in which attentive and automatic processing take place independently, with automatic processing not a first stage that feeds into the attentive processes, and with the attentive system overwriting and suppressing the automatic system.

We also note some recent findings based on the C. W. Eriksen et al. (1990) paradigm by Goolkasian and Garver (in press). They used a paradigm similar to that of the second of the C. W. Eriksen et al. (1990) studies, with the cue to the second location occurring while the prime was still present (albeit for only 25 ms). In these studies, compatibility effects were observed (though some were quite small), and in one study the sizes of the effects were increased when the nontarget items in the display were visually dissimilar from the target items. For present purposes it is hard to interpret these findings because it is difficult to know how much attention the prime received, if any.

Although the C. W. Eriksen et al. (1990) and Yantis and Johnston (1990) studies seemed to provide evidence against processing from unattended locations, the conclusions may have been premature. First, we felt that the difficulty of the required discrimination may have worked against finding an effect. We therefore used a paradigm in which a discrimination of X from O was required (with distractors E, F, and H). The simplicity of the required X-O discrimination prevents the drawing of conclusions about the depth of any processing that is found, but that is an orthogonal question (currently under investigation) that we do not try to answer in this chapter. Additionally, we worried that Eriksen et al. may not have allowed sufficient time for attention to be moved and for processing of the prime to take place. We therefore carried out a number of variants of their paradigm in which the first cue occurred 185 ms in advance of the prime display, the prime display was presented for 150 ms, and the second cue occurred immediately thereafter, with the onset of the target display. Space constraints and the fact that the series of studies is not quite complete preclude reporting the results in this chapter. Instead, we report results from related studies, with the same stimuli and timing, but using only one cue. These were originally designed as control conditions for the two-cue paradigm, but they lead to important conclusions in their own right.

EXPERIMENT 1: PRIMING FROM INFORMATION PRESENTED TO AN UNATTENDED LOCATION— RESPONSE TIME MEASURES

The basic idea was to cue one of the eight locations in a spatial array (in advance of any letter presentations), allowing attention to be focused on this location. Then two successive displays of letters were presented. First a display termed a *prime display* was presented for 150 ms. Among the eight letters in the prime display was an *O*, an *X*, or neither; the *O* or *X* was called the *prime* and its location was independent of the cue (one eighth of the time the prime was in the cued location). Then the prime display was replaced by a target display. The target display always had an *O* or *X* in the cued location, plus seven neutral characters in the other locations. The subject's task was the identification of the *X* or *O* in the target display. We were interested in any speeding or slowing of target responses caused by the prime. In particular, we wanted to see if the compatibility and distance between the prime and target affected response time (our main concern) and accuracy (our secondary concern).

The sequence of events on a typical trial of Experiment 1a is illustrated in Figure 1. A central fixation point appeared for 1,000 ms. Then a cue appeared as an underline below one of the eight locations and remained present throughout the trial. After 185 ms, a circle of eight letters (the prime display) appeared and remained for 150 ms. The circle subtended about 2.1° of visual angle, with each letter about 0.26° high and 0.17° wide. When the 150-ms period was over, this circle was replaced by a new circle of eight letters (the target display) in the same locations, which remained present until the response. This new circle contained an *X* or *O* in the cued location, and the subject indicated which was the case. Thus, the total time from the cue to the onset of the target display was 335 ms. The only letters that could change between the prime and target displays were those in the cued position and in the noncued position that contained an *X* or *O* prime; thus, attraction of attention by change itself would tend to produce compatibility effects when the prime was distant from the target.

On one third of the trials the prime display contained neither an *X* or *O*, and such trials were termed *neutral primes* (neutral–target [N-T]).

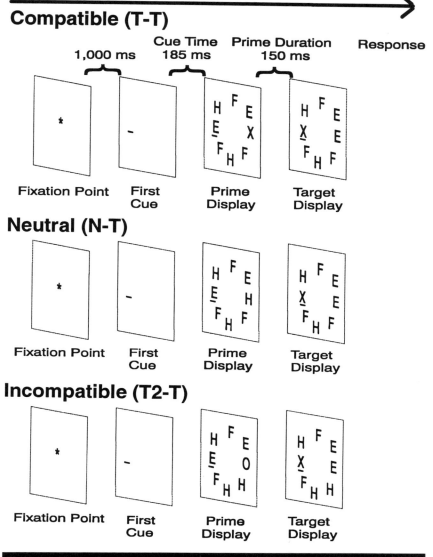

Timing

Compatible (T-T)

Figure 1

Sequence of events and a sample trial for the three compatibility conditions of Experiment 1a. In this example the location cue was provided 185 ms before any letters appeared (termed C335). The sample trials depict the situation when the prime was opposite the display from the cued location (at a distance of 4). The prime was presented for 150 ms and then disappeared; the target then appeared in the cued location and remained until the response was made. T-T = target–target; N-T = neutral–target; T2-T = target 2–target.

On one third of the trials the prime display contained (somewhere) the same letter as the target; such trials were termed *compatible primes* (target–target, or T-T). On one third of the trials the prime display contained an *O* if the target was *X* and an *X* if the target was *O;* such trials were termed *incompatible primes* (target 2–target, or T2-T). The distance (clockwise or counterclockwise around the circle of letters) from the prime to target was of interest in our studies; it was termed the *prime-to-target distance* and had the values 0, 1, 2, 3, and 4.

Experiments 1b and 1c were identical to Experiment 1a, except that the point in time at which the cue was first presented was varied. In Experiment 1b the cue appeared 50 ms before the prime display (200 ms before the onset of the target display). In Experiment 1c the time of occurrence of the cue was varied randomly across blocks: In one block the cue appeared simultaneously with the start of the prime display (150 ms before the onset of the target display); in a second block the cue appeared 75 ms after the start of the prime display (75 ms before the onset of the target display); in a third block the cue appeared 150 ms after the prime display (i.e., when the prime display disappeared, concurrently with the start of the target display). Over the three studies the five conditions are denoted by the number of milliseconds the cue preceded the start of the target display: C335, C200, C150, C75, and C0.

The first block of trials on each day of Experiments 1a, 1b, and 1c served as practice; the other trials were experimental trials. (Each day's practice lessened the size of compatibility effects at locations immediately adjacent to the target, but the patterns of the data were otherwise similar, so we report data averaged across days.) In Experiment 1a, 7 subjects participated for 2 days; there were 490 experimental trials for each combination of positive or negative compatibility and prime–target distance, and 2,450 experimental neutral trials. In Experiment 1b, 6 subjects participated for 2 days; there were 432 experimental trials for each combination of compatibility and prime–target distance, and 2,160 neutral trials. In Experiment 1c, 7 subjects participated for 3 days; in this study each location rather than each prime–target distance was given an equal number of trials, so for each type of positive and negative compatibility there were 240 experimental trials at prime–target distances of 0 and 4, and 480 experimental trials at the other prime–target distances. There were 1,920 neutral trials.

RESULTS AND DISCUSSION

The response times were first truncated by eliminating for each condition the slowest and fastest 1% of the responses. The times were then analyzed in terms of means and medians, with the pattern of results being the same visually and statistically for the two methods. Because we are fitting the results with a quantitative model, we present the means in this chapter.

The results of Experiment 1a, Condition C335, are shown in Figure 2, in the top two panels (row 1). The mean response times for the correct

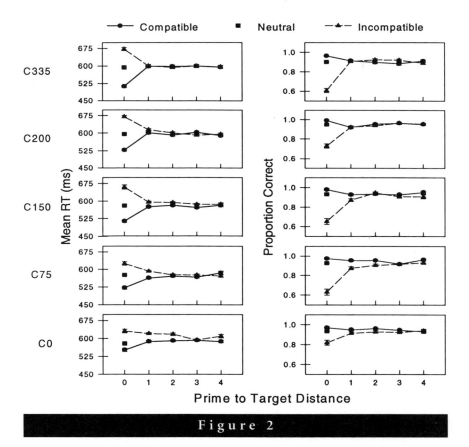

Figure 2

Mean response time (RT; left columns) and accuracy (right columns) for Experiments 1a, 1b, and 1c. The rows give the results for the different cue delays. Row 1 = C335; row 2 = C200; row 3 = C150; row 4 = C75; row 5 = C0. Each panel gives results for the three compatibility conditions as a function of prime–target distance.

responses are graphed in the left-hand panel for each priming condition, for each distance of the prime from the target location. The corresponding accuracy of response is given in the right-hand panel. A strong compatibility effect is seen at the cued location. This is not surprising because this is where attention was placed. In addition, there were many errors in the incompatible case. These were undoubtedly anticipation errors, because their average speed is much faster than that for correct responses (the average error times and correct response times across all five cuing conditions, for T2-T when the prime and target were in the same location, were 461 ms and 651 ms, respectively). These anticipation errors were largely restricted to the cued location, implicating a strong role of attention: If the subjects were simply responding to any X or O seen, then such errors would be associated with incompatible primes in all locations. Thus, subjects clearly used the cue to direct attention to the cued location.

A most important result is the lack of any compatibility effect when the prime was anywhere other than the cued location. On first inspection, these results are similar to those of Yantis and Johnston (1990) and those of C. W. Eriksen et al. (1990) and seem to argue against processing at unattended locations. However, our delayed cuing conditions may require modification of this interpretation.

The remaining cuing conditions are graphed in Figure 2, in the panels in rows 2 through 5. One might expect that increasing the delay of cue would increasingly cause all locations to be attended, or perhaps cause none to be attended. If so, the compatibility effects would both be reduced greatly in size and be distributed evenly across prime–target distances. The actual findings were quite different: In each cue condition a large compatibility effect was found at the cued location, with very little effect at other locations (except for the nearby locations for the most delayed cue). This pattern held true even when the cue was delayed until after the prime disappeared, making a strong case that the prime had been processed even when presented in an unattended, or little attended, location.

When comparing these results with those in the literature, the important point is that the failure with observe an effect on response time is not necessarily indicative of a lack of processing. Thus, our results are similar to those of Yantis and Johnston (1990), but the interpretation is different: We argue that concurrently presented, distant, redundant targets in the Yantis and Johnston paradigm might well be processed, but even if they are, they are not entered into a response-producing mechanism, because attention is never directed toward their location. In our paradigm, attention directed to a location after the fact (e.g., Experiment 1c) demonstrates processing that has taken place in that location.

One might try to account for the delayed cuing results by suggesting that attention is widely distributed across locations until the cue arrives. However, it is difficult to use a unitary attention hypothesis to explain simultaneously two effects: why the compatibility effect remains so large in the cued location when the cue is delayed and why primes in a distant noncued location produce no compatibility effect. In addition, a strategy of diffuse attention given to all eight locations (prior to the arrival of the cue) would seem to imply a much larger compatibility effect when there are fewer locations to be given attention. In another study, with the cue given 50 ms prior to the prime display, there were only two characters in each display, one at the cued location and one in a random one of the other seven locations (and no masks at the other locations). The results from this study are indistinguishable from those for the corresponding eight-character study (see Figure 2, row 2).

We believe our results suggest one of two interpretations: In Model 1, each location is processed regardless of attention, and the information stored in a form that retains a position code. This information does not get entered into the system that produces responses until attention is directed to its location. Model 2 is very similar but for the interpretation of Stage 1. In Model 2, attention has two quite different and more or less independent roles. In this model, attention is required to process information from a location. Attention is first used to cause processing from locations where it is applied (and in the present studies it would be applied at all locations), but the results of such processing do not enter into processes used to produce a response. Instead, the results of this Stage 1 processing are stored with a location code. A second type of attention is used to select certain locations (the cued location in the present study) and transfer the results of Stage 1 processing from those locations to a response-producing mechanism.

Although slight evidence against Model 2 is provided by the control study with only two characters per display (because Stage 1 attention would be distributed to fewer locations, presumably improving performance and increasing compatibility effects), Models 1 and 2 are difficult to distinguish on the basis of the present studies (the studies with two cues are better suited to distinguish these two models). At the end of this chapter we demonstrate the feasibility of a model with Stage 1 processing without attention by fitting a quantitative version of Model 1 to the data.

EXPERIMENT 2: PRIMING FROM INFORMATION PRESENTED TO AN UNATTENDED LOCATION— ACCURACY MEASURES

The subjects in Experiment 1 were asked to respond as quickly and accurately as possible, but they could have responded perfectly if they had abandoned any attempt to respond quickly, because the target displays remained until a response was made. In Experiment 2 we presented the target display briefly and followed it with a mask. The display time for the target display was adjusted for each subject, and for each set of blocks, which included one block of each condition, to produce an average accuracy level of about 70%.

The design for Experiment 2a is illustrated in Figure 3. It was similar to that for Experiment 1a, but had a mask that followed the target display. There were two conditions, one in which the mask was presented only at the cued position (and hence always covered the target) and one in which all locations were masked. The subjects' task was the identification of the target, defined as the character in the cued location that occurred just prior to the mask. (Subjects generally said they adopted a strategy of reporting the first, or only, X or O seen, a subjective observation in line with the large number of anticipation errors when the prime and the target lead to opposite responses.)

Experiments 2b and 2c varied from 2a only in the time at which the cue was presented. In Experiment 2a, the cue was presented 185 ms before the prime display or 335 ms before the target display. In Experiment 2b, the cue occurred at the start of the prime display or 150 ms before the target display. In Experiment 2c the cue occurred at the start of the target display (after the prime had disappeared).

There were 11 subjects in Experiment 2, who participated for 3 days, with the first block of each day serving as practice. For each cuing delay and positive and negative compatibility there were 262 experimental tri-

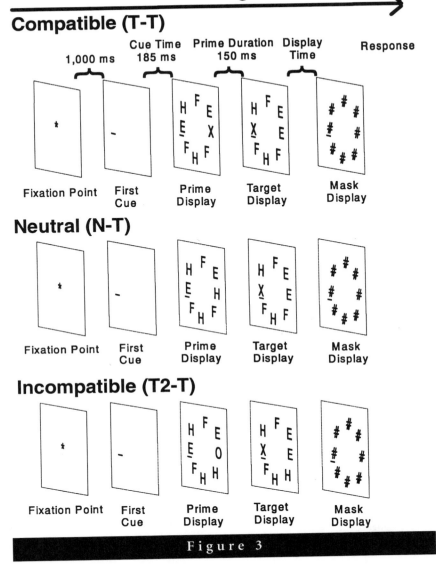

Figure 3

Sequence of events and a sample trial for the three compatibility conditions of Experiment 2a. In this example the location cue was provided 185 ms before any letters appeared (termed C335). The sample trials depict the situation when the prime was opposite the display from the cued location (at a distance of 4). The prime was presented for 150 ms and then disappeared; the target then appeared in the cued location for a short period of time (adjusted to produce an accuracy level of about 70%) and was masked. The figure shows the condition in which all locations are masked. In the other condition, only the location containing the target is masked. T-T = target–target; N-T = neutral–target; T2-T = target 2–target.

als at prime–target distances of 0 and 4, and 524 trials at the other prime–target distances. There were 2,096 neutral trials.

RESULTS AND DISCUSSION

The two masking conditions (all letters masked, or just the target masked) did not produce different results and are combined in the following analyses.

The accuracy results are shown as a function of compatibility and the prime–target distance, in Figure 4, in panels corresponding to the three cue delays. These results closely match those found in Experiment 1. There was a large effect of compatibility when the prime occurred in the cued location, and little if any effect of compatibility when the prime was elsewhere (except for primes adjacent to the target when the cue was delayed). The compatibility effect in the cued location was large at all cue delays, but did lessen somewhat as the delay increased.

The interpretation of these findings is identical to that for Experiment 1: Information is processed at all locations (either automatically or due to a particular type of attention process) and stored with a location code. When attention is allocated to a location, the information from Stage 1 is transferred to a response-producing mechanism.

A MODEL FOR SPATIAL PROCESSING

We present a somewhat simplified model designed to illustrate the major components necessary to predict the accuracy and mean response time results from Experiments 1 and 2. We doubt that our present data allow us to choose between appropriate versions of Model 1 and Model 2. Here we present a version of Model 1. We have decided not to incorporate in the model (as yet) the idea that the attention window might sometimes enclose locations adjacent to the cued location. Figure 5 illustrates the components of the model.

1. There are two stages of information accumulation, the first operating on the input signal automatically and independently of attention, and the second opened and closed by attention and accumulating information used to produce a response.

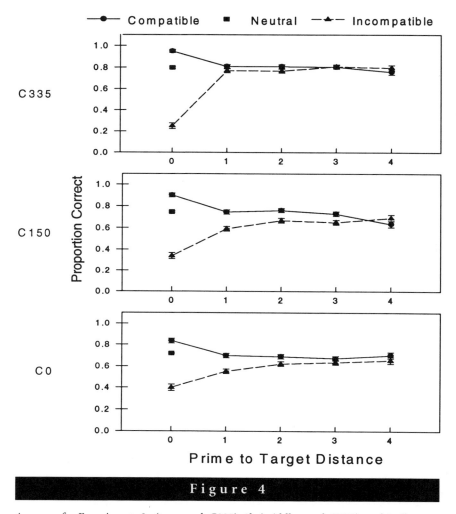

Figure 4

Accuracy for Experiments 2a (top panel, C335), 2b (middle panel, C150), and 2c (bottom panel, C0), summed across the two masking conditions for the three compatibility conditions, as a function of prime–target distance.

2. Stage 1 has input buffers accumulating information for the three classes of stimuli we used (rounds, slants, and horizontals or verticals) at each location (eight in our studies); thus, there are 24 input buffers.

   a. When input first arrives at a location, there is a period of time, δ, when general information is accumulated that does not distinguish one character from another, followed by accumulation of distinguishing information. If one input immediately follows another in a location, distinguishing information about the new input begins to be extracted at once, without the imposition of a new period of time, δ. The period δ corresponds to what C. W. Eriksen et al. (1990) referred to as perceptual inertia. It is needed to account for the fact that the T-T condition is much less than 150 ms faster than the N-T condition.[1]

b. Distinguishing information is accumulated as a function of time, t:

$$I(C, L, t + 1) = I(C, L, t) + \alpha[1 - I(C, L, t)]. \qquad (1)$$

Equation 1 states that once distinguishing information starts to accumulate, information about character type C in location L accumulates at a decreasing rate (scaled by α, $0 < \alpha < 1.0$) toward an asymptotic value of 1.0, so long as character type C remains present in location L. (The asymptotic value is an arbitrary scaling constant that we have set for convenience to 1.0.)

c. When the character type in a location is changed, information in the buffer for that character type and location begins to decay:

$$I(C, L, t + 1) = \beta I(C, L, t). \qquad (2)$$

Equation 2 states that at each time step when a character type is no longer present in a location, the information in the corresponding buffer decays by a factor β, $0 < \beta < 1.0$.

d. Information accumulation and decay in the input buffers are not affected by attention.

---

[1]Because incompatible primes are present in our study, subjects may have delayed responding to the first character seen in order to reduce errors when such trials occurred (although enormous numbers of errors were nonetheless made in this case). This might provide an alternative to the account adopted in the body of this chapter. We also note an interesting finding from an earlier study carried out by the first and third authors and Mike Fragassi. We compared a condition with a duration of 100 ms for the prime display with another of 150-ms duration for the prime display. In each of these the advantage of T-T over N-T was much less than the prime display duration. However, one can compare these two conditions with each other for the N-T and T2-T cases, because in each case the response is initiated after the prime display and hence ought to be slowed by any difference in its duration. In fact, the response time to N-T was 45 ms slower in the 150-ms condition than in the 100-ms condition, and the response time to T2-T was 51 ms slower in the 150-ms condition than in the 100-ms condition. This additivity lends further credence to the idea that there is some dead time when a stimulus first appears in a location. Whatever the account of the reaction time differences across compatibility conditions, this additivity suggests that times are tightly controlled by onsets and offsets of the presented characters.

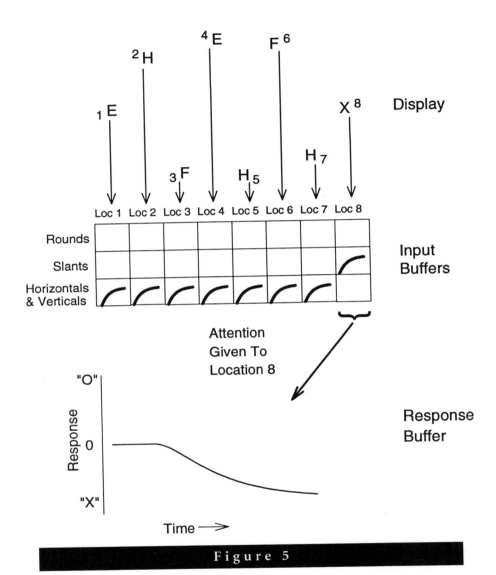

Figure 5

A depiction of Model 1, involving automatic processing of input information in each location (Loc), followed by attentionally driven readout of selected location buffers into a response buffer.

3. When attention is allocated to a location, or split between several locations, the information concerning targets in the buffers at those locations is read out into a response buffer.

a. The response buffer starts at zero and accumulates information, R. We arbitrarily let net evidence for O be positive and net evidence for X be negative.

b. When attention is directed toward location i, there is a period of time, τ, until the movement of attention is accomplished. Then information is read from the location i into the response buffer as follows:

$$R(t + 1) = R(t) + I(O, i, t) - I(X, i, t). \qquad (3)$$

Equation 3 states that the change in the amount of O versus X information in the response buffer in a unit of time is just the current value of the input buffer for O in the attended location minus the current value of the input buffer for X in the attended location.

4. The probability of deciding to emit a response at a given unit of time, given a response has not yet been emitted (i.e., the hazard function for response emission), depends primarily on the absolute value of the amount of information accumulated in the response buffer, R:

$$P(D, t) = 1 - \exp(-\gamma |R(t)|^\epsilon + \lambda). \qquad (4)$$

The term λ reflects a certain base level of response tendency, even when R is zero. Thus this equation states that the hazard function for response emission starts at a low base level and climbs exponentially toward 1.0 as R increases.

5. The probability of emitting an O response, given a decision to emit a response, depends on the value of R:

$$P(O|D) = GAU(R/\theta \,|\, 0, 1). \qquad (5)$$

In Equation 5, $GAU(\text{---} \,|\, 0, 1)$ refers to the cumulative standard normal distribution. This equation treats O and X symmetrically and states that the probability of responding O grows from 0.0 to 1.0, in the shape of a cumulative normal distribution, as the value of R ranges from highly negative to highly positive.

6. When a decision to emit a response is made, the response occurs an average of θ ms later.

The model was fit only to the data for prime–target distance of zero. It was applied to the accuracy and mean response time data, as a function of prime compatibility, for the five cue-delay conditions of Experiment 1. The best fitting parameter values are given in Table 1. Predictions based on these parameters are given as dashed lines in Figures 6 (response time) and 7 (accuracy). Because the model in its present simplified form predicts no priming effect at prime–target distances greater than zero, the figures graph the predictions for the neutral condition for each other distance and give the data for those distances for reference (but the data for these distances were not part of the parameter estimation process).

This model is clearly capable of predicting the primary patterns of findings from our studies (with the exception of adjacency effects, which would require an extension of the model). As such it demonstrates the sufficiency of a model in which processing in Stage 1 occurs at all locations independent of attention. We regard this model as a first step, a model that can serve as a base for the modeling of the more complex data patterns from the two-cue versions of the present studies. The quantitative details are left for future refinement. For present purposes, note only the

Table 1

Best Fitting Parameter Values for Model 1 Applied to the Data From Experiment 1

Parameter name	Parameter value
δ	70
α	0.0126
β	0.989
τ	0
γ	0.0000746
ϵ	1.0
λ	0.000802
θ	268
σ	6.6

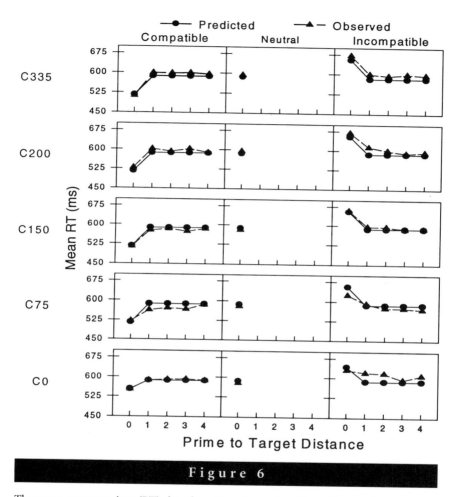

Figure 6

The mean response time (RT) data from Experiment 1, with predictions from Model 1 (based on the best fitting parameter values given in Table 1).

following: Although the exponent in the hazard function (ϵ) and the decay rate (β) were estimated to be about 1.0, and the time to start reading information into the response buffer after cue presentation (τ) was estimated to be 0.0, one should not jump to the conclusion that these parameters are unnecessary: Each will almost certainly be needed for future applications. The only puzzling estimate is that for τ, because it surely takes some time greater than zero to focus attention on the cued location.

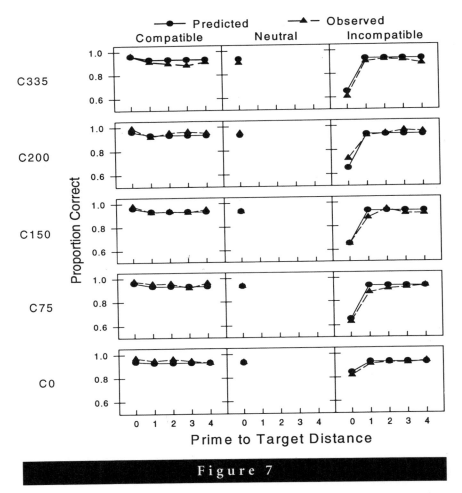

Figure 7

The accuracy data from Experiment 1, with predictions from Model 1 (based on the best fitting parameter values given in Table 1).

However, our power to estimate this parameter may not be high—setting τ to 50 ms also gave an excellent fit.

An extended version of this model may also be applied to the accuracy studies (Experiment 2) by using the actual target times and assuming decay from the input buffers when the mask occurs. A free fit of such a model did a good job of fitting the accuracy data, but space limitations prevent our discussing this application and the degree to which the same parameter values can be carried over from Experiment 1 to Experiment 2.

The data collected in these studies, and the modeling exercise, provide a demonstration of the viability of a model in which information is processed and stored from a visual location during a period of time when attention is directed to a distant visual location. However, an alternative model, in which attention plays two somewhat independent roles, one of which is to enable Stage 1 processing from a location, may also be consistent with our findings. We have been carrying out, and are continuing to carry out, research based on the paradigm of C. W. Eriksen et al. (1990) in an attempt to distinguish these two models.

REFERENCES

Eriksen, B. A., & Eriksen, C. W. (1974). Effects of noise letters upon the identification of a target letter in a nonsearch task. *Perception and Psychophysics, 16,* 143–149.

Eriksen, C. W. (1990). Attentional search of the visual field. In D. Brogan (Ed.), *Visual search* (pp. 3–19). New York: Taylor & Francis.

Eriksen, C. W., Webb, J. W., & Fournier, L. R. (1990). How much processing do nonattended stimuli receive? Apparently very little, but.... *Perception and Psychophysics, 47,* 477–488.

Goolkasian, P., & Garver, D. K. (in press). Evidence for processing letters at uncued locations. *American Journal of Psychology.*

Kahneman, D., & Treisman, A. (1984). Changing views of attention and automaticity. In R. Parasuraman & D. A. Davies (Eds.), *Varieties of attention* (pp. 29–61). San Diego, CA: Academic Press.

Kahneman, D., & Treisman, A. (1992). The reviewing of object files: Object-specific integration of information. *Cognitive Psychology, 24,* 175–219.

Miller, J. (1991). The flanker compatibility effect as a function of visual angle, attentional focus, visual transients, and perceptual load: A search for boundary conditions. *Perception and Psychophysics, 49,* 270–288.

Yantis, S., & Johnston, J. C. (1990). On the locus of visual selection: Evidence from focused attention tasks. *Journal of Experimental Psychology: Human Perception and Performance, 16,* 135–149.

8

Extending Guided Search: Why Guided Search Needs a Preattentive "Item Map"

Jeremy M. Wolfe

*G*uided Search is a model that seeks to explain how humans find one visual stimulus in a world filled with other, distracting stimuli. Complex stimuli like faces and words can only be identified one at a time. Attention must be deployed to an item before it can be fully identified. The heart of Guided Search is the idea that relatively simple processes can be used to guide attention intelligently so that, for example, in a search for a round skin-colored face one does not waste time examining an elongated green tree. Attention could be guided from location to location or from item to item in the visual field. The experiments discussed in this chapter argue for item-by-item guidance.

There is wide agreement on the existence of bottlenecks in human information processing (Kahneman, 1973; Neisser, 1967).[1] Humans cannot handle all of the demands placed on them at the same time. This is not a new observation. For example, in Shakespeare's *As You Like It*, Celia meets Orlando in the woods. When Rosalind, who loves Orlando, asks Celia for

I thank Gordon Logan, Lex Van der Heijden, Claus Bundesen, Patricia O'Neill, Greg Gancarz, and Sara Bennett for comments on a draft of this chapter and Alex Bilsky, Stacia Friedman-Hill, and Charles Pokorny for help collecting data. This work was supported by grants from the National Institutes of Health, National Eye Institute (EY05087), and the Air Force Office of Scientific Research (93NL105).

[1]Wide, but not universal, agreement (see Van der Heijden, chap. 17, this volume).

247

information about this meeting, she gives instructions for response comparable to the most arduous laboratory attention tasks:

> What did he when thou saw'st him? What said he? How looked he? Wherein went he? What makes he here? Where remains he? How parted he with thee? And when shalt thou see him again? Answer me in one word. (*As You Like It* 3.2.218–222)

Celia, a paleocognitive scientist, recognizes a bottleneck and responds

> you must borrow me Gargantua's mouth first; "tis a word too great for any mouth of this age's size." (*As You Like It* 3.2.223–224)

The play, having other business at hand, does not pursue the locus of this bottleneck. Celia seems to propose a motor or final common path limit. But the task could be limited at the level of response selection (Pashler, 1992, 1994) or memory scanning (Sternberg, 1969). Bottlenecks limit the flow of information at multiple loci in processing. The study of visual processing has provided one of the clearest examples of a processing bottleneck. There is fairly wide agreement that the initial stages of visual processing are spatially parallel, with all loci in the visual field processed at once and with no cost at Locus 1 for concurrent processing at Locus 2. At some point in the journey from image to perception and action, however, there is a bottleneck. Attention selects some stimuli for more processing than others. One can debate whether this attentional selection is early (e.g., Mack, Tang, Tuma, & Kahn, 1992) or late (e.g., Johnston, Hawley, & Farnham, 1993). One can also ask whether the selection implies serial processing of single locations or items (Treisman & Gelade, 1980), or whether selection implies differential allocation or processing resources to multiple loci in parallel (e.g., Kinchla, 1977). There seems little point, however, in arguing about the existence of some attentional selection.

The constriction in processing is quite severe. Consider a search for an *S* among mirror-reversed *S*s as shown in Figure 1. This is most likely a serial self-terminating search (Kwak, Dagenbach, & Egeth, 1991). Whether it is serial or limited capacity parallel, the search proceeds at a rate equivalent to the serial processing of one item every 40–60 ms. Looking out at any visually rich scene, it is clear that this is a potentially crippling limit. At 25 items per second, it could take many seconds to process a complex scene when the demands for action might require a much shorter response time.

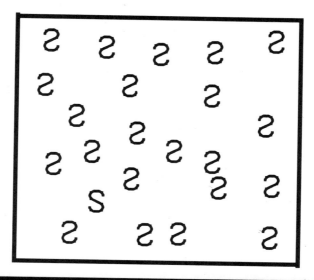

Figure 1

Search for an *S* among mirror-reversed *S*s is serial and self-terminating.

Obviously, the search in Figure 1 is an unusual case. Most searches, in the world or in the laboratory, do not require serial examination of all items. Some items and loci are removed from consideration prior to the bottleneck. Put another way, the parallel processes lying before the bottleneck guide the deployment of attention. The rules of that guidance are the subject of the Guided Search model developed in our laboratory (Cave & Wolfe, 1990; Wolfe, 1992b, 1994a; Wolfe, Cave, & Franzel, 1989). This chapter briefly reviews Guided Search 2.0 (GS2), the most recently published version of the model, and discusses data that illustrate some of the shortcomings of the model and one direction for its future development.

GUIDED SEARCH 2.0

Basic Features

A full account of GS2 is found in Wolfe (1994a). Figure 2 shows the basic architecture of the model. The input stimulus is filtered through broadly tuned channels for a limited set of basic features. This occurs in parallel across the visual field. There are perhaps a dozen basic features

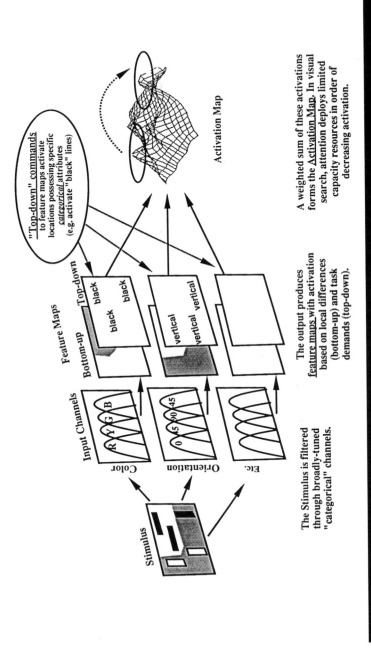

"Top-down" commands to feature maps activate locations possessing specific *categorical* attributes (e.g. activate "black" lines)

Activation Map

A weighted sum of these activations forms the Activation Map. In visual search, attention deploys limited capacity resources in order of decreasing activation.

Feature Maps

Bottom-up   Top-down

black

black   black

vertical

vertical   vertical

The output produces feature maps with activation based on local differences (bottom-up) and task demands (top-down).

Input Channels

R Y G B

Color

0 45 90 45

Orientation

Etc.

The Stimulus is filtered through broadly-tuned "categorical" channels.

Stimulus

Figure 2

The architecture for Guided Search 2.0. From "Guided Search 2.0: A Revised Model of Visual Search," by J. M. Wolfe, 1994, *Psychonomic Bulletin and Review, 1,* p. 205. Copyright 1994 by the Psychonomic Society. Reprinted with permission.

(see Wolfe, 1994a, for a review), including such obvious candidates as color, orientation, and motion and some less obvious properties such as "lustre" (Wolfe & Franzel, 1988) and pictorial depth cues (Enns & Rensink, 1990). These less basic "basic features" make an important point. Parallel processing of visual information extends beyond early vision to a level that handles more complex properties of surfaces (e.g., He & Nakayama, 1992, 1994) and their relationship to one another (e.g., occlusion; Enns & Rensink, 1992). Further evidence that visual search uses relatively "late" parallel representations comes from experiments that show that "basic features" in visual search can be built up of primitives from other feature spaces (e.g., oriented items defined by color, texture, motion, and so on; Bravo & Blake, 1990; Cavanagh, Arguin, & Treisman, 1990).

Bottom-Up Activation

For purposes of the guidance of attention, there are two consequences of the parallel processing of basic features: *bottom-up*, stimulus-driven activation and *top-down*, user-driven activation. Bottom-up activation is based on local differences. A locus where color is changing will receive bottom-up activation in a color processor. An item of unique orientation will receive a large amount of bottom-up activation in an orientation processor because it will be different from all of its neighbors (see Figure 3a). The strength of bottom-up activation is a function of the magnitude of the difference between an item and its neighbors (see Figure 3b). The

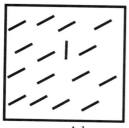

a: A large
orientation difference

b: A small
orientation difference

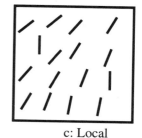

c: Local
differences are critical

Figure 3

Illustrations of bottom-up activation.

identity of more remote items is less important (see Figure 3c; Nothdurft, 1991, 1993a, 1993c). If the difference is large enough, attention will be guided to the target immediately on every trial and reaction time (RT) will be independent of set size. Bottom-up activation does not specify the source of the activation. A red item surrounded by green items produces a peak of activation that in principle could be identical to a peak produced by vertical surrounded by horizontal items.

The magnitude of the difference required to produce parallel search for target amidst homogeneous distractors can be called a "preattentive just noticeable difference" (pJND). Interestingly, the pJNDs are much larger than classical JNDs and are not related to those JNDs by a simple scale factor (Nagy & Sanchez, 1990). This local differencing aspect of parallel processing is what Julesz referred to as the calculation of "texton gradients" (Julesz, 1986). Different features appear to have different abilities to attract attention bottom-up, with abrupt onset and/or the creation of new objects being, perhaps, the most forceful (Jonides & Yantis, 1988; Yantis, 1993; Yantis & Jones, 1991).

Top-Down Activation

Guidance of attention that was entirely stimulus driven would not be particularly useful. It is important to be able to guide attention toward currently relevant features in the visual input. Otherwise, a search for a coin dropped on the sidewalk might be continuously disrupted by a more salient, flashing neon sign. It is obvious that people can bring search under volitional control. It is less obvious, but nevertheless true, that our ability to command parallel processing is limited in interesting ways. For instance, in Figure 4a, it is hard to search for the vertical item among distractors tilted 20° to either side. It is hard, not because subjects cannot discriminate 0° from ±20°, but because top-down control is limited to a very small set of apparently categorical items. In orientation, these appear to correspond roughly to the terms *steep, shallow, left, right,* and *tilted* (Wolfe, Friedman-Hill, Stewart, & O'Connell, 1992). It may be that the limit reflects an ability to select only a single, broadly tuned input channel in top-down processing (Foster & Ward, 1991).

To give an example, in Figure 4a, all of the items are steep. In Figure

a: It is hard to find "vertical" among other "steep" items.

b: It is quite easy to find "steep" among "shallow" items.

c: It is hard to find the "steepest" item.

Figure 4

Illustrations of top-down processing of orientation.

4b, search is easier because the target is the only steep item (10° among ±50°). In Figure 4c, search is hard again even though the angular distance from target to distractors is the same as in Figure 4b (10° among −30° and +70°). The search in Figure 4c is hard because the target is not categorically unique. It possesses steep and right properties but is presented among shallow right and steep left distractors.

Another important limitation on top-down processing is an inability to search efficiently for an item defined by a conjunction of two instances of a single type of feature. Thus, it is possible to search for a red or a green item among items of various colors, but search for a conjunctively defined item that is red *and* green among items that contain red *or* green, but not both, is very inefficient (Wolfe et al., 1990). This is different from the case of across-feature conjunctions (e.g., Color × Orientation—find the item that is red and vertical among items that are either red or vertical but not both.) Across-feature conjunctions can be very efficient (see Wolfe et al., 1989, and discussion below). This is not just a problem with color processing. Size × Size and Orientation × Orientation conjunctions are also very inefficient (Bilsky & Wolfe, 1994; and see Logan, 1994, for a class of difficult Shape × Shape conjunctions). There is one situation in which search for within-feature conjunctions is also efficient. This important exception is discussed below.

The Activation Map and the Mechanics of Search

In GS2, top-down and bottom-up activation build up in each feature processor independently. These independent activations are then combined into a general *activation map*. In visual search, attention is then deployed to the most active locus. If that does not contain a target, attention is redeployed to the next most active locus, until the target is found or the search is terminated. The activity in the activation map cannot be a simple sum (or average) or all the independent activations. It must be weighted to emphasize useful information and limit the impact of useless activation. For example, consider a search for a red line among orange lines of various orientations. There will be substantial bottom-up activity in the orientation processor that is irrelevant to the task. Efficient search, which is possible in such cases, requires that the orientation activation not mask the color activation. The weighting of color information would be high in this case and the weighting of orientation information would be low.

Pokorny and I used a different task to test the ability to ignore irrelevant activations. In this case, the activation came from abrupt onsets of the sort that Yantis and his colleagues have found can attract attention even when they are irrelevant to the task (Yantis & Jones, 1991; Yantis & Jonides, 1990). We asked if such onsets *must* attract attention. In the baseline condition, our subjects searched for a *T* among *L*s. The *T* and *L*s could be in any of four 90° rotations from upright. This is a standard serial search task yielding RT × Set Size slopes of about 20 ms/item on target trials and 40 ms/item on blank trials. In the abrupt-onset condition, white spots appeared on the screen in the regions between the *T*s and *L*s at a rate of one every 40 ms. If subjects had been unable to keep the activations due to these highly salient abrupt onsets out of the activation map that guides attention, search would have been massively impaired. As can be seen in Figure 5, there is a 50-ms increase in RT across set sizes, but the slopes remain the same in the two conditions, strongly suggesting that the abrupt onsets were not allowed to interfere with search. (Note that Yantis has also reported that abrupt onsets do not capture attention if they are known not to mark the target; Yantis & Jonides, 1990.)

In the current simulation of Guided Search, the weights that modulate the input from the feature processors to the activation map are set at

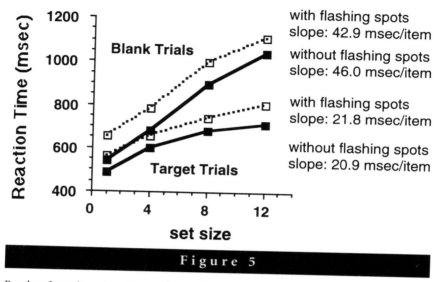

Figure 5

Results of searching for a *T* among *L*s with and without flashing spots. Flashing spots, appearing at a rate of one every 40 ms, do not produce an increase in the slope of Reaction Time × Set Size functions for a serial search for a *T* among *L*s.

the beginning of an "experiment" by instruction. That is, if the simulation is given a search for a red line target among orange lines of random orientation, it determines at the outset to largely ignore orientation information. This is not terribly realistic. It is more reasonable to imagine that the subject implicitly learns which preattentive processes contain signal and which, for all their activation, contain merely noise. Recently, Gancarz and I have given the simulation this learning ability. After each target-present trial, the simulation receives feedback that allows it to compare the activation of the target item with the average activation of other items. In this manner, it creates a signal-to-noise ratio for each parallel processor. The contribution of a processor to the overall activation map is increased if the ratio is greater than one and decreased otherwise. With appropriate limits to prevent the contributions from getting too large or too small, this simple learning mechanism produces a good approximation of the desired results. Processes that contain noise make little contribution. Processes that contain usable signals make stronger contributions.

This does assume feedback after each trial. It would be interesting to see if the performance of our subjects changed if we eliminated the feedback.

The architecture of feature processes feeding an activation map makes it possible to guide attention to likely loci for targets defined by conjunctions of two or more features even though no parallel process, by itself, is sensitive to conjunctive properties. Take a search for a red vertical line among 50% red horizontal and 50% green vertical distractors. Top-down activation in a color processor can activate all red items. Top-down processing in an orientation processor can activate all vertical (steep) items. The combination of these two sources of information will produce greater activation of an item that is both red and vertical. Indeed, if the system were noise free, this guidance of attention would be perfect and search for conjunctions should be no harder than search for salient single features. Search for conjunction can be highly efficient, with slopes near 0 ms/item (e.g., Wolfe, 1992a), but, in general, conjunction searches are somewhat less efficient than feature searches with slopes in the vicinity of 5–12 ms/item (Alkhateeb, Morland, Ruddock, & Savage, 1990; Cohen & Ivry, 1991; Dehaene, 1989; Egeth, Virzi, & Garbart, 1984; McLeod, Driver, Dienes, & Crisp, 1991; Quinlan & Humphreys, 1987; Treisman & Sato, 1990; Wolfe et al., 1989). Apparently, there is noise that will produce peaks of activation in the activation map that do not correspond to a target location. Search for a conjunction therefore becomes a serial search through a subset of the items. When differences between targets and distractors are large, that subset is quite small. The signal is almost always larger than the noise. As a result, slopes of RT $\times$ Set Size functions are near zero. In more demanding conjunction tasks, attention is incorrectly deployed to a greater number of distractors. The number of incorrect deployments, averaged across many trials, is proportional to set size, and so the RT $\times$ Set Size functions rise more steeply, approaching the slopes of serial search in the limit.

In Guided Search, parallel, serial, and guided searches are not qualitatively different. They lie on a continuum defined by the signal-to-noise ratio in the activation map. Thus, a *parallel* search is a search where the activation signal is so much larger than the background noise that attention is deployed first to the target location on all target-present trials. The subset in which attention is deployed contains only a single item: the target. The resulting RT $\times$ Set Size function is independent of set size. A fully serial search is a search with no parallel guidance. If preattentive processes cannot differentiate between targets and distractors (e.g., the searches in Figure 1 or Figure 5), search will be random over the entire set of items. If serial examination of items proceeds at a rate of one item every 40–60 ms, this will produce slopes of 20–30 ms/item on target trials and 40–60 ms/item on blank trials. In a guided search, the activation signal from the preattentive processes biases deployment of attention toward the target item but some distractor locations develop comparable levels of activation. The result is a serial search through a subset of the items.

Search Termination

Serial self-terminating searches produce 2:1 slope ratios. In a retrospective analysis of a large body of search data, Chun and I found that the average slope ratio between blank and target trials was about 2:1 across a wide range of tasks including conjunction searches (Chun & Wolfe, in press). Understanding search termination is easy enough in true serial searches. Target trial searches end when the target is found and blank trials end when all items have been examined and rejected. Serial search through a subset is more problematic. What should happen in guided searches (or, for that matter, parallel searches)? When should the subject abandon an unsuccessful search? Within the framework of the Guided Search model, there are at least two plausible mechanisms for quitting. As attention is deployed from peak to peak in the activation map, subjects could quit when none of the remaining peaks are high enough to warrant examination. That is, if the subject learns (implicitly, it is assumed) that virtually no target in the present task ever has an activation below some value, then search can be abandoned when no peaks remain above that value. Of course, the few targets with these low activations will not be found, generating miss errors. Alternatively, subjects could give up and guess when a search has gone on too long. That is, if the subject knows (again, implicitly) that almost any target should have been found within N ms, then search can be terminated if it goes on longer than N ms. If the probability of guessing increases with time, and most of the guesses are *no*s, the result will be error rates that increase somewhat with set size and a few false-alarm errors. There is evidence for activation and timing thresholds in search termination (Chun & Wolfe, in press). These timing and activation thresholds are fixed but change with feedback, becoming more conservative when errors are made and more liberal if correct responses are made. The GS2 simulation (Chun & Wolfe, in press; Wolfe, 1994a) incorporates both rules and does a reasonable job of reproducing the error rates, blank trial RTs, and 2:1 slope ratios seen in the human data.[2]

A PREATTENTIVE ITEM MAP

The GS2 model can simulate a wide range of tasks from feature searches to conjunction searches to serial searches. It yields results that are very similar to the results obtained in experiments on groups of human subjects. Much more detail about the GS2 model and simulation can be found elsewhere (Wolfe, 1994a). GS2, however, has its limitations. Specifically, for this chapter the focus on preattentive processing of features has obscured the need for preattentive processing of items to which to attach those disembodied features. In Triesman's original feature integration theory (Treisman & Gelade, 1980), features are processed preattentively. "Items" in the form of "object files" await the application of attention (Kahneman & Treisman, 1984). Most other work on visual search is similar in that it treats the preattentive feature as channels or filters for relatively primitive properties of the input. In the remainder of this chapter I argue for the need for a preattentive representation of items.

Top and Bottom

One place to begin is with a problem with the analysis of orientation reviewed above. As noted for purposes of the guidance of attention, orientation seems to be specified in terms of simple categories such as *steep* and *shallow*. This poses a problem as illustrated in Figure 6.

A line rotated through 180° is indistinguishable from an unrotated version. This is not true for most objects rotated through 180°. Both arrows in Figure 6b are steep, but to state the obvious, they are not the same.

In Figure 7, the search for an up arrow appears to be quite easy, and, indeed, informal experiments on two well-practiced subjects yielded target trial slopes under 5 ms/item.[3] Of course, this and other related exper-

---

[2]To get the slope ratios to work, Guided Search assumes that the variability of an activation signal decreases as the activation level rises. Details can be found in Chun and Wolfe (in press) and Wolfe (1994a).

[3]For a similar example with somewhat different purpose, see Enns and Rensink (1993).

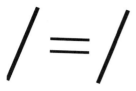

Here, 20° = 200°.

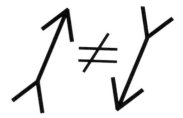

Here, it does not.

Figure 6

Visual search results, based on search for line segments, ignore the possibility that top and bottom are features.

iments need to be run on more subjects, and there are a host of control experiments that one would want to do before making any definitive statement about the status of preattentive processing of top and bottom. However, for the sake of argument, suppose that these results are confirmed. How should they be understood? It could be that the standard work on orientation has been done with impoverished stimuli and that the orientation is better represented over 360° than over 180°. The alternative is that top and bottom are separable from orientation. After all, all of the

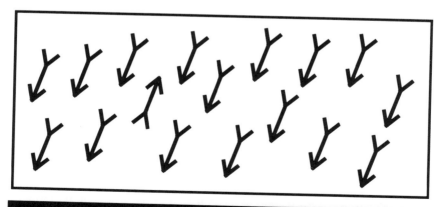

Figure 7

In this search, it appears that the up arrow pops out of a field of down arrows.

items in Figure 7 are "steep" in some meaningful sense. If top and bottom are represented in a different preattentive process, what is that process? Unlike other basic features, top and bottom must be the top and bottom *of something*. Color, orientation, motion, and so forth can all be surface properties that may or may not describe a whole item. Top and bottom are qualitatively different. Imagine a swirling amorphous cloud of features filling the visual field. Imagine that no definable items or objects can be seen. You could still see red. You could still see a vertical. However, you could not see top without also seeing an item that could have a top.

Parts and Wholes

Top and bottom are properties of items. There is other evidence that the structure of items is available preattentively. The inefficiency of Color × Color Conjunctions was described above (Wolfe et al., 1990). To reiterate with a different example of that class of search, it is hard to find a house painted half red and half yellow among houses painted red and blue and houses painted blue and yellow ($M = 38.9$ ms/item for target trials; Wolfe Friedman-Hill, & Bilsky, 1994). As promised earlier, there is a case where search for Color × Color conjunctions is efficient. If subjects search for a red house with yellow windows among red houses with blue windows and blue houses with yellow windows, slopes of RT × Set Size functions are comparable to those seen in standard across-feature conjunctions ($M = 13.1$ ms/item for target trials; Wolfe et al., 1994). It is the structure of the items that appears to be critical. Color × Color conjunctions are efficient when the color of the whole item is conjoined with the color of a part of that item. Conjunctions of the colors of two parts are inefficient.

Part and *whole* are terms of convenience here. Subjects and experimenters tend to spontaneously describe the stimuli in these experiments in part–whole terms, but we are not in a position to say with assurance that the preattentive representation is in terms of parts and whole items. It seems clear that something about the structure of the items is critical here, but we do not fully understand the details. In one series of experiments we found that *surroundedness* is a relevant aspect of the structure (Wolfe et al., 1994). The more one area surrounds another, the more the former acts as a whole and the later as a part. Stimuli for an experiment illustrating this point are shown in Figure 8 with the slopes from the resulting searches given below each type of item.

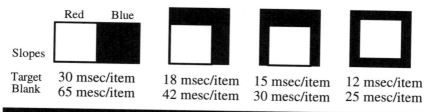

	Red	Blue			
Slopes					
Target	30 msec/item		18 msec/item	15 msec/item	12 msec/item
Blank	65 mesc/item		42 mesc/item	30 mesc/item	25 mesc/item

Figure 8

The more that a region of one color surrounds a region of another color, the easier it is to search for a target defined by a Color × Color conjunction.

In all cases, subjects searched for the red–blue target among red–yellow and yellow–blue distractors. The different-colored regions were of identical area and the colors were equiluminous. Other experiments have shown that the division of items into parts and wholes is under some degree of volitional control. Part and whole labels cannot be assigned at random, but using stimuli like the one shown in Figure 9, we (Wolfe et al., 1994) were able to assign a *part* label to the large circle in one condition (search for the green box with the red circle) and assign a *whole* label to the same large circle in another condition (search for the red circle with the yellow spot).

Like Color × Color conjunctions, Size × Size conjunctions are influenced by the structure of the items. It is hard to find the item with big and small parts but relatively easy to find a big item with small parts (Bilsky, Wolfe, & Friedman-Hill, 1994). Interestingly, Orientation × Orienta-

One can search for the whole green cube with the red circle part.

A green cube with a red circle and a yellow dot.

One can search for the whole red circle with the yellow dot part.

Figure 9

Stimulus used to show that a stimulus component that is a part in one visual search can be the whole item in another.

tion conjunctions do not show a similar sensitivity to part–whole structure. Every one of the large number of Orientation × Orientation conjunctions that we have tried have proven to be highly inefficient (Bilsky et al., 1994). Perhaps absolute orientations of parts and wholes are not coded because they do not stay invariant in the environment. A red item with yellow parts will be red with yellow if it falls over. The same cannot be said of a vertical item with a horizontal part. The relative angular relationship between parts or between parts and wholes may be more robust, and there is evidence for preattentive coding of angular relations (Wolfe & Friedman-Hill, 1992).

Continuous Stimuli and the Ownership of Borders

In most visual search experiments, preattentive processing could be by items, locations, or patches of disembodied features. When the display consists of stimuli presented in isolation on a homogeneous background, division into items is easy and not particularly useful. Attention can be guided to a red vertical item in isolation by finding redness and verticalness in the same place. Real-world stimuli, however, do not offer items in neat isolation on blank backgrounds. Real-world stimuli are continuous. They are also difficult to use in controlled visual search experiments. We (Wolfe et al., 1994) have devised a class of stimuli that are more continuous and naturalistic than standard laboratory stimuli. At the same time, they preserve our ability to place targets and distractors at arbitrary locations from trial to trial. The stimuli are created out of a set of square "tiles." The tiles are drawn so that any regular packing of them will produce a continuous image. Using a set that looked something like aerial views of terrain, I demonstrated that the basic findings of laboratory search studies could be replicated with stimuli of this sort (Wolfe, 1994b).

A different example is shown in Figure 10. Efficient search (~6 ms/item) for conjunctions of color and orientation can be done with stimuli of this sort and it makes little difference if the leaves are in front of or behind the lattice. As illustrated on the right of the figure, this raises a problem for Guided Search and other models. The figure on the right is merely a blowup of a piece of the stimulus on the left. It points out that because the green leaf is occluded ∪y a vertical segment of the lattice, there is a green vertical contour in the image. If the target is green vertical, why is there no evidence that this spurious green vertical acts as a distractor?

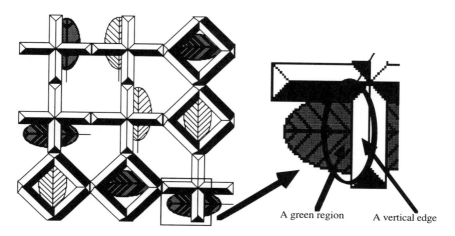

Search for the green (gray) vertical leaf.   Why isn't this "green vertical"?

Figure 10

Continuous stimuli create spurious conjunctions. Here the occlusion of a green leaf produces a green vertical contour in the image. However, these spurious conjunctions do not seriously interfere with search for targets defined by the true conjunctions of these features.

Naive observers have trouble seeing that this is a potential problem. The introspective answer is clear (and probably correct). This green vertical is not a problem because, in a real sense, it does not exist. The greenness and the verticalness are parts of two different items. They seem to lie in two different depth planes. Featural attributes are not disembodied in perception, they are "owned" by objects or items (Nakayama & Shimojo, 1990; Nakayama, Shimojo, & Silverman, 1989). The vertical feature is owned by the lattice. The green feature is owned by the leaf. Obviously, for this to work in an account of guided visual search, these owners must exist preattentively. They do not need to exist in their final form as *lattice* or *leaf,* but they do need to exist as items that can have featural labels attached to them.

The Item Map: Proposal and Implications

To summarize, preattentive processing of top and bottom, if it exists, implies preattentive processing of items that can have tops and bottoms.

Preattentive sensitivity to the part–whole structure of items, which certainly does exist, implies preattentive processing of items that can have parts and wholes. The failure of spurious conjunctions of features to interfere with visual search for items defined by the same conjunction of features implies that basic features can be preattentively assigned to items. My proposal, therefore, is that preattentive processing is not limited to parallel extraction of energy in different sets of feature-tuned channels. Preattentive processing appears to include an initial division of the stimulus into items for subsequent attentive examination.

At this stage, it is hard to be very specific about the nature of the preattentive item representation. Many experiments are needed before it is clear how, for example, parts and wholes are represented. Whether there is a limit on the number of preattentively available items is also got to be determined. Perhaps only a few items can be parsed at a time. A version of this idea can be found in Pylyshyn's finger of instantiation (FINST) model. Specifically, in discussing subitizing, Trick and Pylyshyn suggested that a limited-capacity, preattentive process can handle around five items at once (Trick & Pylyshyn, 1994). Their model does not address the specific search issues discussed here, but in effect, they are proposing that about five of Treisman's "object files" (Kahneman & Triesman, 1984) can be set up at once.

The notion of a fixed or nearly fixed number of items (or FINSTs, if they are the same thing) seems problematic here. Evidence for preattentive item processing (e.g., the part–whole experiments described above) comes from displays with many more than five items. Perhaps the critical idea to borrow from the FINST model is that the item map may be parallel but of limited capacity. Faced with the need to process a host of items in a search for a green leaf, that capacity is spread thin, creating a crude division of the field into items. Different tasks would change the deployment of this limited resource. Faced with the demand to keep track of the movements of a subset of moving items, perhaps the limit is reduced to about five (Yantis, 1992). Faced with a very small number of items, perhaps the capacity is adequate to allow all of the items to be represented in a manner that allows them to make contact with stored representations in memory. For instance, three letters might all activate their respective representations in memory and activations of flanking items might interfere with response to a target letter (Eriksen & Hoffman, 1973).[4] Negative priming might be a similar example where two items are so fully processed that the distractor representation must be inhibited in order to respond to the target (Tipper, 1985, 1992).

The idea of a resource that can be applied broadly with weak effect or narrowly with strong effect is not new. See Nakayama (1990) or Treisman (1993) for a couple of recent examples. It must also be stressed that the connection between preattentive processing of items in visual search and effects like the flanker effect, subitizing, and negative priming is highly speculative.

Is This Just "Late Selection" Revisited?

The proposal that people preattentively parse the visual scene into items has an air of "late selection" about it. However, preattentive items are not merely late selection with another name. It may be that items are found preattentively but, in visual search experiments, there appear to be profound limits on available information about those items. Classic late selection has items reaching their representations in memory in parallel. However, it is clear that the preattentive representation of items is not this elaborate. For example, there is no parallel processing of faces (Nothdurft, 1993b), let alone of face recognition. At an even more basic level, there may be no preattentive representation of spatial relationships such as up, down, left, and right. The orientation of a single element may be known, but subjects show no sign of parallel processing of relationships such as "Is the '+' above the '−'?" (Logan, 1994). This may explain why preattentive processes seem unable to distinguish between Ts and Ls (Bergen & Julesz, 1983).

It may be that this view of preattentive processing provides a link between early and late selection models. If, as discussed above, the preattentive item map is a limited capacity parallel processor, perhaps it can fully process a small number of items, allowing for the late selection results that are seen in flanker tasks, negative priming, and, perhaps, novel pop-out (Hawley, Johnston, & Farnham, 1994; Johnston et al., 1993). A

---

[4] I recognize that it is quite a reach from visual search for red houses with yellow windows to the flanker effect, but it seemed appropriate in light of the occasion.

proposal of this sort has recently been put forward by Lavie and Tsal (1994), but the matter remains open.

SUMMARY

Guided Search 2.0 gives an account of a wide range of visual search tasks. However, it is not a complete theory of visual search. On the basis of the issues and data presented here, I argue that this model or, indeed, any model of visual search, will need to include some ability to parse the visual scene into searchable items in parallel.

REFERENCES

Alkhateeb, W. F., Morland, A. B., Ruddock, K. H. & Savage, C. J. (1990). Spatial, colour, and contrast response characteristics of mechanisms which mediate discrimination of pattern orientation and magnification. *Spatial Vision, 5*(2), 143–157.

Bergen, J. R., & Julesz, B. (1983). Rapid discrimination of visual patterns. *IEEE Transaction on Systems, Man, and Cybernetics, SMC-13,* 857–863.

Bilsky, A. A., & Wolfe, J. M. (1994). Part–whole information is useful in Size × Size but not in Orientation × Orientation conjunction searches. *Perception and Psychophysics, 57,* 749–761.

Bilsky, A. A., Wolfe, J. M., & Friedman-Hill, S. R. (1994). Part–whole information is useful in Size × Size but not in Orientation × Orientation conjunction searches. *Investigative Ophthalmology and Visual Science, 35,* 1622.

Bravo, M., & Blake, R. (1990). Preattentive vision and perceptual groups. *Perception, 19,* 515–522.

Cavanagh, P., Arguin, M., & Treisman, A. (1990). Effect of surface medium on visual search for orientation and size features. *Journal of Experimental Psychology: Human Perception and Performance, 16,* 479–492.

Cave, K. R., & Wolfe, J. M. (1990). Modeling the role of parallel processing in visual search. *Cognitive Psychology, 22,* 225–271.

Chun, M. M., & Wolfe, J. M. (in press). Just say no: How are visual searches terminated when there is no target present? *Cognitive Psychology.*

Cohen, A., & Ivry, R. B. (1991). Density effects in conjunction search: Evidence for coarse location mechanisms of feature integration. *Journal of Experimental Psychology: Human Perception and Performance, 17,* 891–901.

Dehaene, S. (1989). Discriminability and dimensionality effects in visual search for featural conjunctions: A functional pop-out. *Perception and Psychophysics, 46,* 72–80.

Egeth, H. E., Virzi, R. A., & Garbart, H. (1984). Searching for conjunctively defined targets. *Journal of Experimental Psychology: Human Perception and Performance, 10,* 32–39.

Enns, J. T., & Rensink, R. A. (1990). Scene based properties influence visual search. *Science, 247,* 721–723.

Enns, J. T., & Rensink, R. A. (1992). An object completion process in early vision. *Investigative Ophthalmology and Visual Science, 33,* 1263.

Enns, J. T., & Rensink, R. A. (1993). A model for the rapid discrimination of line drawing in early vision. In D. Brogan, A. Gale, & K. Carr (Eds.), *Visual search* (Vol. 2, pp. 73–89). London: Taylor & Francis.

Eriksen, C. W., & Hoffman, J. E. (1973). The extent of processing of noise elements during selective encoding from visual displays. *Perception and Psychophysics, 14,* 155–160.

Foster, D. H., & Ward, P. A. (1991). Horizontal-vertical filters in early vision predict anomalous line-orientation frequencies. *Proceedings of the Royal Society (London B), 243,* 83–86.

Hawley, K. J., Johnston, W. A., & Farnham, J. M. (1994). Novel popout with non-sense string: Effects of predictability of string length and spatial location. *Perception and Psychophysics, 55,* 261–268.

He, J. J., & Nakayama, K. (1992). Surfaces vs. features in visual search. *Nature, 359,* 231–233.

He, J. J., & Nakayama, K. (1994). Perceiving textures: Beyond filtering. *Vision Research, 34,* 151–162.

Johnston, W. A., Hawley, K. J., & Farnham, J. M. (1993). Novel popout: Empirical boundaries and tentative theory. *Journal of Experimental Psychology: Human Perception and Performance, 19,* 140–153.

Jonides, J., & Yantis, S. (1988). Uniqueness of abrupt visual onset in capturing attention. *Perception & Psychophysics, 43,* 346–354.

Julesz, B. (1986). Texton gradients: The texton theory revisited. *Biological Cybernetics, 54,* 245–251.

Kahneman, D. (1973). *Attention and effort.* Englewood Cliffs, NJ: Prentice Hall.

Kahneman, D., & Treisman, A. (1984). Changing views of attention and automaticity. In R. Parasuraman & D. R. Davies (Eds.), *Varieties of attention* (pp. 29–61). San Diego, CA: Academic Press.

Kinchla, R. A. (1977). The role of structural redundancy in the perception of targets. *Perception and Psychophysics, 22,* 19–30.

Kwak, H., Dagenbach, D., & Egeth, H. (1991). Further evidence for a time-independent shift of the focus of attention. *Perception and Psychophysics, 49,* 473–480.

Lavie, N., & Tsal, Y. (1994). Perceptual load as a major determinant of the locus of selection in visual attention. *Perception and Psychophysics, 56,* 183–197.

Logan, G. D. (1994). Spatial attention and the apprehension of spatial relations. *Journal of Experimental Psychology: Human Perception and Performance, 20,* 1015–1036.

Mack, A., Tang, B., Tuma, R., & Kahn, S. (1992). Perceptual organization and attention. *Cognitive Psychology, 24,* 475–501.

McLeod, P., Driver, J., Dienes, Z., & Crisp, J. (1991). Filtering by movement in visual search. *Journal of Experimental Psychology: Human Perception and Performance, 17,* 55–64.

Nagy, A. L., & Sanchez, R. R. (1990). Critical color differences determined with a visual search task. *Journal of the Optical Society of America A, 7,* 1209–1217.

Nakayama, K. I. (1990). The iconic bottleneck and the tenuous link between early visual processing and perception. In C. Blakemore (Ed.), *Vision: Coding and efficiency* (pp. 411–422). Cambridge, England: Cambridge University Press.

Nakayama, K., & Shimojo, S. (1990). Towards a neural understanding of visual surface representation. In T. Sejnowski, E. R. Kandel, C. F. Stevens, & J. D. Watson (Eds.), *The brain* (pp. 911–924). New York: Cold Spring Harbor Laboratory.

Nakayama, K., Shimojo, S., & Silverman, G. H. (1989). Stereoscopic depth: Its relation to image segmentation, grouping and the recognition of occluded objects. *Perception, 18,* 55–68.

Neisser, U. (1967). *Cognitive psychology.* New York: Appleton-Century-Crofts.

Nothdurft, H.-C. (1991). Texture segmentation and pop-out from orientation contrast. *Vision Research, 31,* 1073–1078.

Nothdurft, H.-C. (1993a). The conspicuousness of orientation and visual motion. *Spatial Vision, 7,* 341–366.

Nothdurft, H.-C. (1993b). Faces and facial expression do not pop-out. *Perception, 22,* 1287–1298.

Nothdurft, H.-C. (1993c). The role of features in preattentive vision: Comparison of orientation, motion and color cues. *Vision Research, 33,* 1937–1958.

Pashler, H. (1992). Attentional limitations in doing two things at the same time. *Current Directions in Psychological Science, 1*(2), 44–48.

Pashler, H. (1994). Dual task interference in simple tasks: Data and theory. *Psychological Bulletin, 116,* 220–244.

Quinlan, P. T., & Humphreys, G. W. (1987). Visual search for targets defined by combinations of color, shape, and size: An examination of the task constraints on feature and conjunction searches. *Perception and Psychophysics, 41,* 455–472.

Sternberg, S. (1969). High-speed scanning in human memory. *Science, 153,* 652–654.

Tipper, S. P. (1985). The negative priming effect: Inhibitory priming by ignored objects. *Quarterly Journal of Experimental Psychology, 37A,* 571–590.

Tipper, S. P. (1992). Selection for action: The role of inhibitory mechanisms. *Current Directions in Psychological Research, 1,* 105–108.

Treisman, A. (1993). The perception of features and objects. In A. Baddeley & L. Weiskrantz (Eds.), *Attention: Selection, awareness, and control* (pp. 5–35). Oxford, England: Clarendon Press.

Treisman, A., & Gelade, G. (1980). A feature-integration theory of attention. *Cognitive Psychology, 12,* 97–136.

Treisman, A., & Sato, S. (1990). Conjunction search revisited. *Journal of Experimental Psychology: Human Perception and Performance, 16,* 459–478.

Trick, L. M., & Pylyshyn, Z. W. (1994). Why are small and large numbers enumerated differently? A limited-capacity preattentive stage in vision. *Psychological Review, 101,* 80–102.

Wolfe, J. M. (1992a). "Effortless" texture segmentation and "parallel" visual search are not the same thing. *Vision Research, 32,* 757–763.

Wolfe, J. M. (1992b). The parallel guidance of visual attention. *Current Directions in Psychological Science, 1*(4), 125–128.

Wolfe, J. M. (1994a). Guided Search 2.0: A revised model of visual search. *Psychonomic Bulletin and Review, 1,* 202–238.

Wolfe, J. M. (1994b). Visual search in continuous, naturalistic stimuli. *Vision Research, 34,* 1187–1195.

Wolfe, J. M., Cave, K. R., & Franzel, S. L. (1989). Guided search: An alternative to the feature integration model for visual search. *Journal of Experimental Psychology: Human Perception and Performance, 15,* 419–433.

Wolfe, J. M., & Franzel, S. L. (1988). Binocularity and visual search. *Perception and Psychophysics, 44,* 81–93.

Wolfe, J. M., & Friedman-Hill, S. R. (1992). Visual search for orientation: The role of angular relations between targets and distractors. *Spatial Vision, 6,* 199–208.

Wolfe, J. M., Friedman-Hill, S. R., & Bilsky, A. B. (1994). Parallel processing of part/whole information in visual search tasks. *Perception and Psychophysics, 55,* 537–550.

Wolfe, J. M., Friedman-Hill, S. R., Stewart, M. I., & O'Connell, K. M. (1992). The role of categorization in visual search for orientation. *Journal of Experimental Psychology: Human Perception and Performance, 18,* 34–49.

Wolfe, J. M., Yu, K. P., Stewart, M. I., Shorter, A. D., Friedman-Hill, S. R., & Cave, K. R. (1990). Limitations on the parallel guidance of visual search: Color × Color and Orientation × Orientation conjunctions. *Journal of Experimental Psychology: Human Perception and Performance, 16,* 879–892.

Yantis, S. (1992). Multielement visual tracking: Attention and perceptual organization. *Cognitive Psychology, 24,* 295–340.

Yantis, S. (1993). Stimulus-driven attentional capture. *Current Directions in Psychological Science, 2*(5), 156–161.

Yantis, S., & Jones, E. (1991). Mechanisms of attentional priority: Temporally modulated priority tags. *Perception and Psychophysics, 50,* 166–178.

Yantis, S., & Jonides, J. (1990). Abrupt visual onsets and selective attention: Voluntary versus automatic allocation. *Journal of Experimental Psychology: Human Perception and Performance, 16,* 121–134.

9

When Knowledge Does Not Help: Limitations on the Flexibility of Attentional Control

Charles L. Folk and Roger W. Remington

M echanisms for allocating spatial attention must satisfy to two competing goals. On the one hand, efficiency requires the selective allocation of limited resources only to those objects or events important to the current goals of the organism. On the other hand, adaptability requires the allocation of resources to new objects or events that, although potentially irrelevant to current behavioral goals, may nonetheless hold important ecological information requiring the establishment of a new goal. Historically, these two goals have been mapped on to two distinct modes of attentional control, referred to as *endogenous* (goal-directed) and *exogenous* (stimulus-driven) control, respectively (Eriksen & Hoffman, 1972; Jonides, 1981; Posner, 1980). The latter has also been referred to as "attentional capture" (Yantis & Jonides, 1984).

Recent evidence suggests that these two modes of control can more appropriately be considered endpoints on a continuum, occurring in their pure form only under very limited conditions, if at all (e.g., Bacon & Egeth, 1994; Folk, Remington, & Johnston, 1992; Folk, Remington, &

This research was supported by funds provided by National Aeronautics and Space Administration—Ames Research Center, Moffett Field, California, under Interchange NCA2-797. We thank Jim Johnston and Gordon Logan for helpful comments regarding this work.

Wright, 1994; Yantis, 1993; Yantis & Jonides, 1990). This implies that attentional deployment is normally the result of an interaction between endogenous and exogenous factors. Indeed, the notion of such an interaction is a dominant aspect of many current models of attention allocation (Bundesen, 1990; Cave & Wolfe, 1990; Duncan & Humphreys, 1989; Folk, Remington, & Johnston, 1993; Koch & Ullman, 1985; Treisman & Sato, 1990).

One clear example of the interplay between goal-directed and stimulus-driven attention allocation is the effect of advance knowledge on the ability of certain stimulus events, such as abrupt visual onsets, to produce attentional capture. Abrupt onsets have been shown to be particularly effective in producing stimulus-driven shifts of attention when no obvious attentional set is in effect (e.g., Jonides & Yantis, 1988; Remington, Johnston, & Yantis, 1992). In fact, it has been argued that only abrupt onsets (or, more specifically, the abrupt appearance of a new object) can produce attentional capture under such conditions (Jonides & Yantis, 1988; Yantis & Hillstrom, 1994). Given specific foreknowledge of the defining characteristics of a target stimulus, however, an irrelevant, abrupt-onset distractor has been shown to have virtually no effect on performance. For example, Yantis and Jonides (1990) found that when subjects were given a 200-ms precue indicating the subsequent location of a target stimulus, an irrelevant abrupt-onset character no longer produced evidence of attentional capture. Similarly, Folk et al. (1992) found that when given advance information about a defining feature of the relevant target (e.g., color), the effects of an irrelevant, abrupt-onset distractor were eliminated.

Folk et al. (1992) also found that when targets were defined by a feature other than abrupt onset, such as a discontinuity or being a "singleton" in color, irrelevant singletons sharing the same dimension did produce evidence of attentional capture (see also Bacon & Egeth, 1994; Pashler, 1988; Theeuwes, 1992). In short, irrelevant events that shared the defining feature of the target produced attentional capture and events that did not produced no evidence of capture. These results suggest that attentional capture is dependent not on the occurrence of specific stimulus properties, as proposed by Jonides and Yantis (1988), but on the relationship between the properties of the irrelevant event and the current goals of the observer.

CONTINGENT ATTENTIONAL CAPTURE

On the basis of these and other results, Folk et al. (1993) have argued that the existing data on attentional capture can be parsimoniously accommodated by assuming that capture is ultimately contingent on variable, endogenous "attentional control settings." These control settings are assumed to reflect high-level behavioral goals and to be instantiated "off-line." Stimulus events that match the current control setting will produce an involuntary shift of attention, even if the events are known to be irrelevant. Events that do not match the current control setting will not produce a shift of attention. Thus, attentional capture is not a purely stimulus-driven phenomenon specific to certain stimulus events, but instead reflects conditions in which a conflict exists between high-level behavioral goals and specific, "on-line" goals to withhold an attentional response to a particular stimulus. Under this framework, the apparent unique ability of abrupt onsets to produce attentional capture reflects either subtle task characteristics that encourage a control setting for onsets or perhaps an enduring predisposition to set the allocation system for onsets.

The notion that involuntary shifts of spatial attention are contingent on an endogenous attentional set is consistent with a growing number of studies showing that otherwise involuntary or "automatic" attentional effects can be modulated by strategic factors. For example, there is evidence that the magnitude of classic Stroop effects is dependent on whether the irrelevant color words are members of the response set or not (Proctor, 1978; Tzelgov, Henik, & Berger, 1992). In addition, the magnitudes of semantic priming effects have been shown to depend on the nature of the task performed on the prime stimulus (Friedrich, Henik, & Tzelgov, 1991; Henik, Friedrich, & Kellogg, 1983; Henik, Friedrich, Tzelgov, & Tramer, 1994; Smith, 1979; Smith, Theodor, & Franklin, 1983). Specifically, semantic priming is eliminated when set to search for a specific letter in the prime rather than reading the prime. Similarly, Keren, O'Hara, and Skelton (1977) have shown that compatibility effects associated with irrelevant flankers in an Eriksen-type task depend on the level of processing required for targets. For example, the effects of irrelevant flanking noise letters that were physically similar or dissimilar to two central targets depended on whether the targets were judged on physical, categorical, or name similarity. In all of these studies, the effect of unattended, irrelevant information was dependent on whether the information was part of a task set or not. This is consistent with Logan's (1978) proposal that reaction time tasks can be considered "prepared reflexes" in which a sequence of processing operations, or attentional control settings (Folk et al., 1992), are "programmed" or established "off-line" and then run off automatically on stimulus presentation. Thus, the nature of "on-line" processing of a given stimulus on a given trial is contingent on the relationship between the stimulus and the task set for that trial.

FLEXIBILITY OF ATTENTIONAL CONTROL

Given that advance knowledge of the task characteristics can lead to the establishment of attentional control settings or a "task set," an important issue concerns the flexibility with which control settings can be established. How sensitive are control settings to variations in task constraints? Are there limits to the specificity of attentional control settings? Investigating such issues can lead to a more complete understanding of the underlying functional architecture of attentional control (Folk et al., 1993), as well as the mechanisms by which attentional control settings are instantiated. For example, finding that only certain types of advance task information affect attention allocation might suggest that attentional control settings are limited to certain classes of stimulus properties or that control settings involve the selective activation of task-relevant stimulus properties rather than the suppression of irrelevant properties.

It has recently been argued that the flexibility of top-down attentional control over attentional capture is actually quite limited (Theeuwes, 1991, 1992). In a visual search task, Theeuwes (1992) found that an irrelevant discontinuity in color (i.e., a "color singleton") produced a significant distraction effect (i.e., attentional capture) when searching for a discontinuity in shape (i.e., a "form singleton"), even when the exact shape of the target was known in advance. Theeuwes argued that subjects were unable to establish a top-down set for a specific form feature and that attentional allocation was driven entirely by the relative bottom-up salience of the singletons, independent of the features by which they were defined. Bacon and Egeth (1994), however, recently showed that including multiple shape discontinuities in Theeuwes' displays completely eliminated the distracting effects of irrelevant color singletons. Bacon and Egeth argued that their manipulation forced subjects from a "singleton search mode" with the original Theeuwes displays into a "feature search mode" with the modified displays. In other words, with slight variations in the nature of the task, subjects were able to adopt attentional control settings for specific shape values. Similar results have been reported by Folk and Remington (1993), who found evidence for control settings for specific color values.

FOCUS OF THESE EXPERIMENTS

In the present studies, we further explored the flexibility of attentional control by investigating the nature of attentional control settings for locations in space. As discussed above, Yantis and Jonides (1990) have shown that the ability of an irrelevant abrupt onset to capture attention is completely eliminated if subjects are given valid advance information about the location of the target. One interpretation of these results is that knowing the target location allows subjects to establish a control setting for a particular location in space, thereby rendering stimuli occurring at nontarget locations (i.e., stimuli inconsistent with the attentional control setting) incapable of capturing attention. In the present studies we investigated whether similar effects would be observed when subjects were provided with advance knowledge of the distractor, rather than the target, location. Our goal was to determine if the attentional control system is flexible enough to use such information to eliminate capture by an irrelevant abrupt onset. A related goal was to begin to address the underlying mechanisms through which control settings are instantiated. For example, if control settings involve the suppression of irrelevant information, then we might expect that providing advance knowledge of the location of an abrupt-onset distractor should eliminate its ability to capture attention. If, however, control settings involve only the activation or facilitation of relevant information, then knowledge of the distractor location (with no information about target location) might prove relatively useless, and abrupt-onset distractors should still produce attentional capture.

EXPERIMENT 1

Method

Subjects

Sixteen Villanova University students, ranging in age from 18 to 20 years, participated to partially fulfill a course requirement. All reported normal or corrected-to-normal visual acuity.

Apparatus

Stimuli were presented on a Princeton (Princeton, NJ) SR-12 color monitor driven by a Zenith (St. Joseph, MI) 286 microcomputer equipped with a Sigma (Fremont, CA) C400 high-resolution color graphics card.

Task

The general task involved the speeded, forced-choice identification of a target character (i.e., an X or an =) appearing in one of four peripheral boxes centered on fixation. Four blocked, within-subjects conditions were created by factorially combining the presence or absence of a peripheral, abrupt-onset distractor with the presence or absence of a central, symbolic cue. Distractors always occurred at a location where the subsequent target would not appear. Thus, any cost in response time for trials containing a distractor relative to trials containing no distractor was assumed to reflect attentional capture. When a central cue was present, it always indicated the location of the subsequent distractor (in distractor conditions) or a location where the target would not appear (in no-distractor conditions). The stimulus onset asynchrony (SOA) between presentation of the central cue and peripheral distractor was varied from 100 to 400 ms in an effort to explore the time course for the establishment of any observed attentional set for location.

Stimuli

Subjects were presented with a sequence of four basic displays consisting of a fixation display, a cue display, a distractor display, and a target display. Examples of each of these displays along with their sequence of presentation are shown in Figure 1. The fixation display consisted of four peripheral boxes and one central box, each measuring 1.15° of visual angle from a viewing distance of approximately 40 cm. The four outer boxes were located at the vertices of an imaginary diamond centered on the fifth box, with a center-to-vertex distance of 4.7° of visual angle. The inside of the center box contained eight additional line segments arranged as a diamond surrounding a plus sign (+). All boxes were light gray (IBM color designation 8) against the black CRT screen.

The cue display consisted of the fixation display with a subset of the lines forming the central box removed. When a cue appeared, lines were removed to form a *T* oriented toward one of the peripheral boxes. When a cue did not appear, lines were removed to form a plus sign.

The distractor displays consisted of the cue display with the addition of four small circles, each subtending 0.36° of visual angle, around the four sides of one of the five boxes. The circles were placed so that each was centered approximately 0.3° peripheral to its respective side of the box. The circles were high-contrast white (IBM color designation 15) against the black CRT screen. In conditions where distractors did not appear, the cue display simply remained on the screen during the distractor display interval.

Target displays consisted of the cue display with the addition of a single character appearing in one of the four peripheral boxes. This target character was either an *X* or an =, subtended 0.57° of visual angle, and appeared as high-contrast white (IBM color designation 15) against the black monitor screen.

Design

The four within-subjects conditions (i.e., no cue–no distractor, no cue–distractor, cue–no distractor, cue–distractor) were run in separate blocks of 144 trials. Condition order was varied across subjects according to a Latin square. Within each block, the SOA between the cue display and the distractor display varied randomly across six values (100, 150, 200, 250, 300, and 400 ms). Each target (i.e., *X* or =) appeared equally often in each of the four outer boxes, as did distractors when they appeared. Distractors and targets, however, never appeared at the same location on any given trial. Each combination of target type, target location, and distractor location occurred equally often at each of the six SOAs.

Ten practice trials were presented at the beginning of each block. In addition, after any trial on which an error was made, a "buffer" trial, chosen randomly from the set of possible trial parameters for that condition, was inserted.

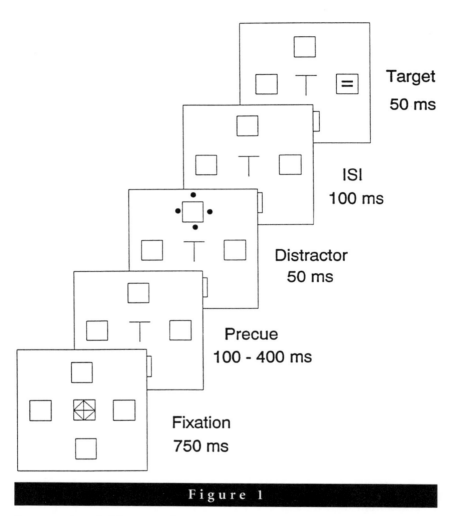

Target
50 ms

ISI
100 ms

Distractor
50 ms

Precue
100 - 400 ms

Fixation
750 ms

Figure 1

Representation of trial events and stimuli in Experiment 1. ISI = interstimulus interval.

Procedure

Subjects were fully informed of the fact that targets would never appear at the distractor location. In addition, they were encouraged to take advantage of the information provided by the cue if possible. Subjects were instructed to respond "as quickly as you can while making as few errors as possible." Maintaining fixation on the center box in the display was heavily stressed. The subject was seated at a distance of approximately 40 cm from the computer CRT screen.

Each condition began with the presentation of a screen indicating which of the four conditions would follow. Subjects then pressed a key to begin the sequence of trials in that condition. A message appeared at the end of each condition instructing the subject to rest before beginning the next block. Subjects then pressed a key when they were ready to continue.

The sequence of events on a given trial began with a 250-ms offset of the center box, followed by a 750-ms presentation of the fixation display. The cue display was then presented for one of the six SOAs, followed by a 50-ms presentation of the distractor display. The cue display then appeared again for 100 ms, followed by a 50-ms presentation of the target display, which was then replaced by the original fixation display. The next trial began 1,000 ms after the subject's response.

Subjects were instructed to press the "Ins" ("0") key on the bottom of the keyboard's numeric keypad with their left index finger if an equal sign was presented, and the "Del" (".") key with their right index finger if an X was presented. A 500-ms, 1000-Hz tone was sounded by the computer for an incorrect response. If a response was not made within 1,500 ms, an error was scored and the trial sequence continued.

Response time and error status for each trial were measured and recorded by the computer. Response time was measured from the onset of the target display until a response was made. Practice trials, error trials, buffer trials, and trials on which response time was less than 200 ms were excluded from the data analysis.

Results

Mean response times and error rates as a function of condition and SOA are shown in Figure 2. An analysis of variance (ANOVA) was conducted on the mean response times with distractor status (no distractor, distractor), cue status (no cue, cue), and SOA as within-subject factors. Distractor status produced a significant main effect, with longer response times associated with trials on which a distractor appeared, $F(1, 15) = 8.49, p < .01$. Overall, response times also decreased with SOA, $F(5, 75) = 3.68, p < .01$. The effect of SOA was only marginally dependent on cue status, $F(5, 75) = 2.46, p = .04$. In contrast, the effect of SOA was heavily influenced

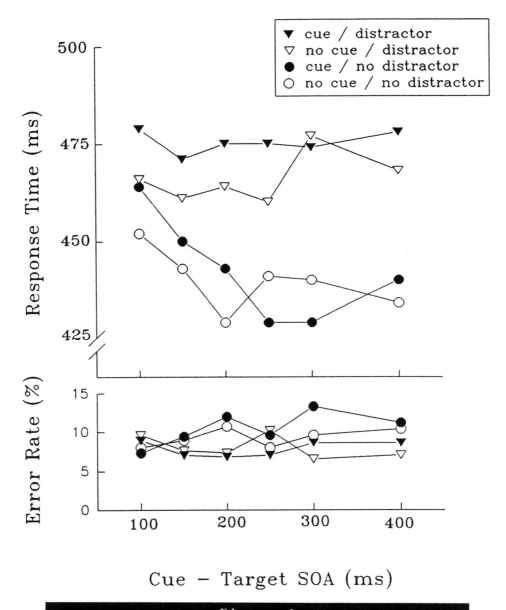

Cue − Target SOA (ms)

Figure 2

Average mean response times and error rates as a function of cue-distractor SOA, cue status, and distractor status in Experiment 1. SOA = stimulus onset asynchrony.

by distractor status, $F(5, 75) = 3.95$, $p < .01$, for the Distractor Status × SOA interaction. Specifically, response times remained relatively constant across SOAs on distractor trials and decreased with SOA on no-distractor trials.

Error rates averaged just under 9%. An ANOVA on the error rates revealed no significant main effects or interaction.

Discussion

The results of this experiment are relatively straightforward. The presence of an abrupt-onset distractor produced evidence of attentional capture even when subjects knew where the distractor would appear. Specifically, the presence of a distractor produced a cost in response time regardless of the presence or absence of a precue identifying the impending location of the distractor. Moreover, this effect was present even when the precue preceded the distractor by nearly 500 ms.

Given the length of each condition (i.e., 144 trials), it is possible that overall means may have obscured cue effects that emerge with practice. To check this possibility, an additional analysis was conducted comparing performance in the first half of each condition to performance in the second half. Response times were significantly faster overall in the second half of each condition, $F(1, 15) = 20.49$, $p < .001$. There was a trend toward a reduction in the magnitude of the distractor effect in the second block, but this effect was not reliable, $F(1, 15) = 4.15$, $p > .05$.

In summary, the results of this experiment suggest that subjects were unable to use advance information about the location of the abrupt-onset distractor to eliminate its ability to capture attention, at least within the time parameters explored. These results also suggest that the findings of Yantis and Jonides (1990), in which a 200-ms precue for the target location eliminated attentional capture by an irrelevant abrupt onset, probably reflect a facilitative effect for target location, rather than suppression of nontarget locations.

EXPERIMENT 2

The inability of subjects to use distractor location information in Experiment 1 does not necessarily imply that such information could never be used to establish a spatial control setting that would eliminate capture by the distractor. It is possible, for example, that a control setting based on distractor location requires longer than 500 ms to establish. In the second experiment, we attempted to eliminate the requirement to rapidly establish an attentional set from trial to trial. Instead of providing an advance precue on each trial, distractor location was held constant throughout each block of trials. Thus, subjects knew with absolute certainty that the distractor would appear at a particular location on every trial in a given block. A control condition was also included in which distractor location varied randomly from trial to trial.

An additional modification to the task was included. It has recently been pointed out that response time differences between distractor and no-distractor conditions can reflect nonspatial distraction effects that are independent of shifts of spatial attention (Folk & Remington, 1993). To be certain that the costs produced by the distractor in Experiment 1 reflect shifts of spatial attention, an irrelevant distractor appeared on every trial, but the location of the distractor was completely uncorrelated with the location of the subsequent target. Because the distractor provided no information regarding the location of the target, subjects had no incentive to voluntarily shift attention to the distractor. Consequently, any difference in response times for trials on which the distractor appeared at the same location as the target and those on which the distractor appeared at a different location than the target must reflect an involuntary shift of spatial attention.

Method

Subjects

Twenty-five paid volunteers, recruited from the National Aeronautics and Space Administration—Ames subject pool participated. All reported normal or corrected-to-normal visual acuity. Eleven subjects participated in the fixed-distractor condition and 13 in the random-distractor condition (see below).

Apparatus

Stimuli were presented on a NEC (Boxborough, MA) 4-D display driven by a Compaq (Houston, TX) 486 computer equipped with an Orchid (Fremont, CA) Wondercard VGA color graphics board.

Stimuli

The stimuli were identical to those used in the first experiment, with a few exceptions. First, on all displays, the central box was replaced by a small fixation cross measuring approximately 0.2° of visual angle. Second, in experimental blocks, a distractor appeared on every distractor display (i.e., no-distractor displays were eliminated). Finally, cue displays were eliminated from the design.

Design

Two between-subjects distractor conditions, consisting of 10 blocks of 32 trials each, were created by varying the certainty of the distractor location. In the fixed condition, the distractor appeared around the same box on every trial in a block, with the particular box varying across blocks. The order in which distractor locations were presented was varied across subjects. In the random condition, the location of the distractor varied randomly from trial to trial within a block. Each of these two conditions was preceded by 96 practice trials on which no distractor occurred.

Within a block of trials, each of the two possible targets appeared equally often in each of the four boxes. In the random condition, the distractor also appeared equally often at each location. For every block in both conditions, the target appeared at the distractor location on one-quarter of the trials and at a nondistractor location on three quarters of the trials. Thus, given four possible locations, the distractor provided no information about the target location.

Procedure

Subjects were fully informed of the relationship between distractor location and target location and were encouraged to ignore the distractor if possible. They were also fully informed of whether the distractor location was fixed or whether it would vary randomly.

The trial sequence began with a 250 blink of the fixation cross, followed by a random period defined by the hazard function of an exponential distribution with a mean of 450 ms. The distractor display then appeared for 60 ms, after which the fixation display reappeared for 60 ms. The target display then appeared for 60 ms, followed once again by the fixation display. If subjects committed an error, the word *ERROR* appeared in the middle of the screen for 500 ms, followed by the fixation display for 500 ms. In all other respects, the procedure was identical to that used in Experiment 1.

Results

Mean response times and error rates as a function of distractor condition (fixed vs. random) and distractor location (same vs. different from target location) are shown in Figure 3. A 2 × 2 mixed ANOVA on the mean response times yielded a highly significant main effect of distractor location, $F(1, 23) = 34.73, p < .0001$. Specifically, response times were, on average, 23 ms higher when the target and distractor appeared at different locations than when they appeared at the same location. This effect was evident for both the random and fixed-distractor conditions, as the interaction failed to even approach significance $(F < 1)$. Surprisingly, the between-subjects main effect of distractor condition also failed to reach significance $(F < 1)$.

Error rates averaged 6.7% and followed the same pattern as response times. Although there was a slight trend toward higher error rates in the random condition, a mixed ANOVA yielded no significant effects.

Discussion

There are two central conclusions to be drawn from this study. First, the fact that performance varied as a function of the spatial relationship between distractor location and target location suggests that abrupt-onset distractors produced shifts in the distribution of spatial attention rather than producing some nonspatial distraction effect. Second, consistent with the results of Experiment 1, the significant effect of distractor location in the fixed-distractor condition suggests that even with "chronic" knowledge of the distractor location, subjects were unable to suppress capture by the distractor appearing at that location.

As with Experiment 1, however, it is possible that mean response times for a block may obscure intrablock phenomena such as habituation to the distractor. To test this possibility, an additional analysis was conducted in which performance on the first half of the trials in each block was compared with performance on the last half of trials in each block. The main effect of distractor location was once again significant, $F(1, 23) = 53.22$, $p < .0001$, and there was no interaction of distractor location with block

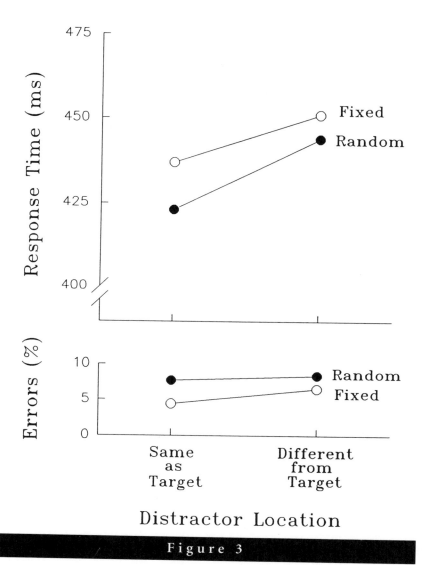

Figure 3

Average mean response times and error rates as a function of distractor location and distractor condition in Experiment 2.

half, nor any three-way interaction of distractor location, block half, and distractor condition (for both, $F < 1$). This indicates that for both random and fixed-distractor conditions, there was no evidence of any habituation of attentional capture as a block progressed.

Attentional capture by a distractor appearing at the same location trial after trial is clearly consistent with the notion that the attentional control system is incapable of establishing a spatial attentional set that suppresses capture by a stimulus at a known location. One could argue, however, that subjects may not be incapable of using knowledge of the distractor location to eliminate capture, but they may simply be unwilling to do so, given the constraints of the task. Recall that in an effort to be certain any effects of cue location reflect true shifts of spatial attention, the target appeared at the distractor location on 25% of the trials. If the distractor location is suppressed, then rapid target processing might be compromised on 25% of the trials. The overall cost associated target processing on those 25% of trials may have been greater than the cost of attentional capture by the distractor. Thus, the apparent inability to use information about distractor location may simply reflect a conflict between two behavioral goals that are mutually exclusive—rapid target acquisition and suppression of distractors.

EXPERIMENT 3

In the third experiment, we attempted to remove any potential conflict between the goals of distractor suppression and target acquisition. Specifically, distractors always appeared at locations in between the potential target locations, never at a target location. Given that Experiment 2 established that the distractors were indeed producing shifts of spatial attention, in the present experiment we returned to measuring capture in terms of performance differences between distractor and no-distractor trials. As in Experiment 2, in one condition distractor location was fixed throughout a block of trials, and in another condition distractor location varied randomly from trial to trial.

With the present design, suppressing attentional capture at distractor locations should have no effect at all on the efficiency of target acquisition because distractors, when present, never appeared at a potential target location. Thus, if subjects are capable of establishing a spatial control setting based on knowledge of the distractor location, then attentional capture should be eliminated in the fixed location condition, but not the random location condition. If subjects are simply unable to use knowledge of the distractor location to establish a control setting, then capture should be apparent in both conditions.

Method

Subjects

Forty-two student volunteers from Villanova University participated in this study. Of these, 20 took part in the fixed-distractor condition and 22 in the random-distractor condition. All subjects received either $5 or extra credit in an undergraduate course. All had near visual acuity of 20/30 or better as measured by a Titmus II (Petersburg, VA) Vision Tester.

Apparatus

The apparatus was identical to that used in Experiment 1.

Stimuli

Stimuli were identical to those used in Experiment 2 with two exceptions. First, on half of the distractor displays, no distractor appeared. Second, when a distractor did appear, it was located 4.7° of visual angle from fixation at one of four corners of an imaginary square centered on fixation. In other words, it appeared at one of the four blank locations in between the four outer boxes.

Design

In both fixed and random location conditions, subjects received four blocks of no-distractor trials and four blocks of distractor trials. A no-distractor block was always presented first and subsequent blocks alternated between the two conditions. Each block consisted of 32 trials, with each target (X vs. $=$) appearing equally often in each of the four outer boxes. In the fixed-distractor condition, the distractor appeared at the same location on every trial in a block. The particular location varied across blocks, and the order of location was balanced across subjects using a Latin square. In the random-distractor condition, the distractor location varied randomly from trial to trial within a block but appeared equally often at each possible distractor location.

Procedure

Subjects were informed of the difference between distractor and no-distractor blocks. In addition, they were fully informed with respect to whether the distraction location was random or fixed. The sequence of events on a given trial began with a 250-ms blink of the fixation cross followed by an interval randomly chosen from the set 1,000, 1,100, 1,200,

1,300, or 1,400 ms. The cue display was then presented for 50 ms followed by the fixation display for 100 ms and then the target display for 50 ms. The fixation display then reappeared until the next trial began.

Results

Mean response times and error rates as a function of distractor condition (fixed vs. random) and distractor status (no distractor vs. distractor) are shown in Figure 4. A 2 × 2 mixed ANOVA on the mean response times yielded a significant 11-ms main effect of distractor status, $F(1, 23) = 7.76$, $p < .01$. The presence of a distractor had an influence in both random and fixed-distractor conditions, because the interaction between distractor condition and distractor status failed to even approach significance ($F < 1$). As in Experiment 2, the between-subjects main effect of distractor condition also failed to reach significance, $F(1, 40) = 1.38$, $p > .05$.

Error rates were quite low, averaging only 2.1%. Error rates were slightly higher in the no-distractor condition (2.3%) than in the distractor condition (1.8%). A mixed ANOVA showed that this trend was marginally significant, $F(1, 40) = 4.35$, $p = .04$. Although suggestive of a speed–accuracy trade-off, this small effect on errors was confounded with practice; the no-distractor condition was always the first condition presented to subjects. Consistent with this interpretation is the fact that error rates for no-distractor and distractor conditions differed by no more than 0.5% ($M = 0.2$%) in all but the first block of trials. In the first block, error rates differed by nearly 2%. Given this pattern, and the low error rates overall, it is unlikely that the response times were contaminated by a speed–accuracy trade-off.

Discussion

The pattern of overall means in the present experiment is identical to that found in Experiment 2. Irrelevant abrupt-onset distractors produced evidence of attentional capture regardless of whether subjects had advance knowledge of the exact location of the distractor. Moreover, this effect was evident even when distractors never occurred at potential target locations.

One obvious difference between the results of Experiment 2 and the present experiment, however, is the magnitude of the distractor effect. In Experiment 2 the distractor location effect was more than twice as large

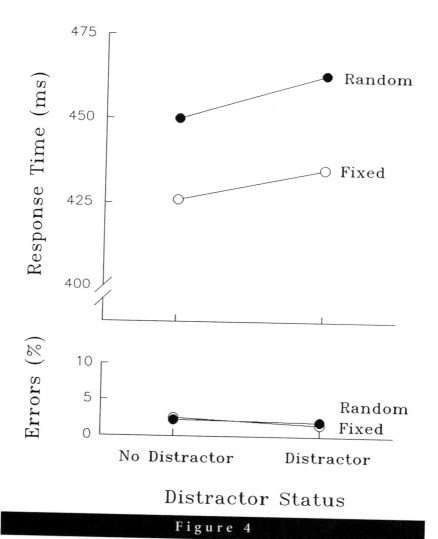

Figure 4

Average mean response times and error rates as a function of distractor location and distractor condition in Experiment 3.

(23 ms) as the distractor effect in the present experiment (11 ms). There are several potential accounts of this difference. First, given that the no-distractor condition always came first in the present experiment, practice effects may have mitigated the true magnitude of the distractor effect. Second, the distractor location effect in Experiment 2 measures the combined

effect of costs produced by the distractor on different-location trials and benefits on same-location trials. Assuming the no-distractor condition in the present experiment represents a conservative baseline, the distractor effect is a conservative estimate of only costs associated with shifts of attention to nontarget locations.

One final possibility is that the distraction effect may vary within a block, producing mean response times that are a mixture of early trials on which the distractor captured attention and late trials on which it did not. To assess this possibility, a half-block analysis was conducted as in the first two experiments. This time the analysis revealed a significant interaction between block half and distractor status, $F(1, 40) = 10.76$, $p < .01$. Specifically, the presence of a distractor produced a 20-ms cost relative to no-distractor trials for the first half block and a 2-ms effect in the second half block. This pattern was evident for both the fixed- and random-distractor conditions, because the three-way interaction was not significant, $F(1, 40) = 1.07$, $p > .05$. Thus, this analysis suggests that the distraction effect in the present experiment is just as large as in Experiment 2 for the first half of each block, but is virtually eliminated by the end of each block.

How are we to account for the reduction in the distraction effect as a block progresses? One possibility is that with practice, subjects are indeed able to actively establish an attentional control setting that suppresses the effect of distractors at nontarget locations. There are several reasons to suspect, however, that the reduction in distraction reflects a form of passive habituation rather than active suppression. First, if the effect were due to the active application of strategic control settings, then one might reasonably expect that the ability to strategically control the effect of distractors would vary depending on whether the distractor position was fixed or random. There was, however, no evidence of any difference in the nature of the half block effect as a function of distractor condition. Of course, it is possible that the same control setting might, in fact, be able to handle both fixed and random distractors. For example, subjects may learn to adopt a suppressive set for all distractor locations, rendering any distractor location, be it fixed or random, incapable of producing capture. However, if subjects learn to adopt a single control strategy, then we might expect distraction effects to show up only in the first half of the first block. That is, having learned how to establish the effective control setting in the first block, we might expect that setting to remain in effect throughout the experiment. In fact, in additional analyses, we found that the half block effect was present in each block of the experiment. Thus, we tentatively conclude that the present data are more consistent with a passive habituation process rather than the active establishment of an attentional control setting. Given little evidence of habituation in the previous experiments, however, we suspect that the conditions under which habituation occurs are directly related to what control settings are in effect, a point discussed in more detail below.

GENERAL DISCUSSION

This series of experiments was conducted to explore the flexibility of attentional control settings for spatial location and to begin to address the underlying mechanisms by which attentional control settings are instantiated. Subjects were provided with advance information about the location of an irrelevant abruptly onset distractor through the use of trial-by-trial spatial cuing (Experiment 1) or by holding the distractor location constant throughout a block of trials (Experiments 2 and 3). The only condition in which attentional capture was eliminated was after repeated presentations of distractors that could never appear at potential target locations (Experiment 3).

How can the we account for the pattern of results across the three experiments? We propose that the results are consistent with the general notion that task characteristics determine and constrain the nature of attentional control settings in any given situation and that attentional capture reflects conflicting behavioral goals. The primary task goal in all three experiments was to locate an abrupt-onset target that could occur at one of four potential locations. To accomplish this goal, we assume that two concurrent control settings are established, one for abrupt onset and one for potential target locations. Thus, when an abrupt-onset distractor appears at a potential target location, it satisfies both control settings and therefore captures attention, even though subjects "know" where the distractor will appear. (Note that when target location is cued or known, as in Yantis & Jonides, 1990, there is no need to establish a control setting for onset, because a set for the target location eliminates the need to find the target. Thus, a single control setting *for* the target location satisfies the simultaneous goals of target acquisition and distractor suppression.) When the abrupt-onset distractor always appears at nontarget locations, as in Experiment 3, it still satisfies the abrupt-onset control setting, but not the target locations setting. We propose that when the distractor does not satisfy both control settings, the attentional response to abrupt onset eventually habituates. By this logic, the lack of habituation or half-block effects in Experiments 1 and 2 reflects the fact that the distractor satisfied both settings.[1]

One underlying assumption of this model is that with respect to spatial locations, attentional control settings are instantiated through the facilitation of relevant locations rather than the suppression of attentional responses to information at irrelevant locations. The design of these experiments allowed subjects every possible opportunity to suppress shifts of attention to information at known irrelevant locations, and there was no evidence that they were able, or at the very least, willing, to do so. Thus, on the basis of the current experiments, as discussed above, we propose that the elimination of capture by distractors at irrelevant locations when relevant locations are known in advance, such as found by Yantis and Jonides (1990), reflects a control setting *for* the relevant location rather than a setting *against* irrelevant locations.

The present studies represent an exploration of the limitations on the flexibility of attentional control. The specific model outlined above is obviously tentative, and it may be specific to attentional control settings for location. Clearly, further research is needed to determine if the effects observed here generalize to other forms of attentional control. For example, an obvious follow-up to the present experiments would be to determine whether similar effects would be observed with stimulus properties such as discontinuities in color (Folk et al., 1992; Folk & Remington, 1993). Nonetheless, the present studies provide converging evidence that the phenomenon of attentional capture is contingent on endogenous attentional control settings that are determined by task constraints.

---

[1]One might argue that because targets never appeared at the cued location in Experiment 1, a distractor appearing at that location does not satisfy the "potential target location setting." Although on any given trial the target did not appear at the distractor location, the target and distractor locations varied across trials. Thus, a distractor location on one trial might become the target location on the next trial. We assume that given the relatively short precue duration, subjects were simply unable to alter the potential target location set on-line.

REFERENCES

Bacon, W. F., & Egeth, H. (1994). Overriding stimulus-driven attentional capture. *Perception and Psychophysics, 55*, 485–496.

Bundesen, C. (1990). A theory of visual attention. *Psychological Review, 97*, 523–547.

Cave, K. R., & Wolfe, J. M. (1990). Modelling the role of parallel processing in visual search. *Cognitive Psychology, 22*, 225–271.

Duncan, J., & Humphreys, G. W. (1989). Visual search and stimulus similarity. *Psychological Review, 96*, 433–458.

Eriksen, C. W., & Hoffman, J. E. (1972). Temporal and spatial characteristics of selective encoding from visual displays. *Perception and Psychophysics, 12*, 201–204.

Folk, C. L., & Remington, R. W. (1993, November). *Selectivity in attentional capture by featural singletons.* Paper presented at the annual meeting of the Psychonomic Society, Washington, DC.

Folk, C. L., Remington, R. W., & Johnston, J. C. (1992). Involuntary covert orienting is contingent on attentional control settings. *Journal of Experimental Psychology: Human Perception and Performance, 18*, 1030–1044.

Folk, C. L., Remington, R. W., & Johnston, J. C. (1993). Contingent attentional capture: A reply to Yantis (1993). *Journal of Experimental Psychology: Human Perception and Performance, 19*, 682–685.

Folk, C. L., Remington, R. W., & Wright, J. H. (1994). The structure of attentional control: Contingent attentional capture by apparent motion, abrupt onset, and color. *Journal of Experimental Psychology: Human Perception and Performance, 20*, 317–329.

Friedrich, F. J., Henik, A., Tzelgov, J. (1991). Automatic processes in lexical access and spreading activation. *Journal of Experimental Psychology: Human Perception and Performance, 17*, 792–806.

Henik, A., Friedrich, F. J., & Kellogg, W. A. (1983). The dependence of semantic relatedness effects upon prime processing. *Memory and Cognition, 11*, 366–373.

Henik, A., Friedrich, F. J., Tzelgov, & Tramer, S. (1994). Capacity demands of automatic processes in semantic priming. *Memory and Cognition, 22*, 157–168.

Jonides, J. (1981). Voluntary vs. automatic control over the mind's eye's movement. In J. B. Long & A. D. Baddeley (Eds.), *Attention and performance, IX* (pp. 187–203). Hillsdale, NJ: Erlbaum.

Jonides, J., & Yantis, S. (1988). Uniqueness of abrupt visual onset in capturing attention. *Perception and Psychophysics, 43*, 346–354.

Keren, G., O'Hara, W., & Skelton, J. (1977). Levels of noise processing and attentional control. *Journal of Experimental Psychology: Human Perception and Performance, 3,* 653–664.

Koch, C., & Ullman, S. (1985). Shifts in selective visual attention: Toward the underlying neural circuitry. *Human Neurobiology, 4,* 219–227.

Logan, G. (1978). Attention in character-classification tasks: Evidence for the automaticity of component stages. *Journal of Experimental Psychology: General, 107,* 32–63.

Pashler, H. (1988). Cross-dimensional interaction and texture segregation. *Perception and Psychophysics, 43,* 307–318.

Posner, M. I. (1980). Orienting of attention. *Quarterly Journal of Experimental Psychology, 32,* 3–25.

Proctor, R. W. (1978). Sources of color-word interference in the Stroop color-naming task. *Perception and Psychophysics, 23,* 413–419.

Remington, R. W., Johnston, J. C., & Yantis, S. (1992). Involuntary attentional capture by abrupt onsets. *Perception and Psychophysics, 51,* 279–290.

Smith, M. C. (1979). Contextual facilitation in a letter search task depends on how the prime is processed. *Journal of Experimental Psychology: Human Perception and Performance, 5,* 239–251.

Smith, M. C., Theodor, L., & Franklin, P. E. (1983). The relationship between contextual facilitation and depth of processing. *Journal of Experimental Psychology: Learning, Memory, and Cognition, 9,* 697–712.

Theeuwes, J. (1991). Cross-dimensional perceptual selectivity. *Perception and Psychophysics, 50,* 184–193.

Theeuwes, J. (1992). Perceptual selectivity for color and form. *Perception and Psychophysics, 51,* 599–606.

Treisman, A., & Sato, S. (1990). Conjunction search revisited. *Journal of Experimental Psychology: Human Perception and Performance, 16,* 459–478.

Tzelgov, J., Henik, A., & Berger, J. (1992). Controlling Stroop effects by manipulating expectations for color words. *Memory and Cognition, 20,* 727–735.

Yantis, S. (1993). Stimulus-driven attentional capture and attentional control settings. *Journal of Experimental Psychology: Human Perception and Performance, 19,* 676–681.

Yantis, S., & Hillstrom, A. P. (1994). Stimulus-driven attentional capture: Evidence from equiluminant visual objects. *Journal of Experimental Psychology: Human Perception and Performance, 20,* 95–107.

Yantis, S., & Jonides, J. (1984). Abrupt visual onsets and selective attention: Evidence from visual search. *Journal of Experimental Psychology: Human Perception and Performance, 10,* 601–621.

Yantis, S., & Jonides, J. (1990). Abrupt visual onsets and selective attention: Voluntary versus automatic allocation. *Journal of Experimental Psychology: Human Perception and Performance, 16,* 121–134.

10

Perceptual Selectivity for Color and Form: On the Nature of the Interference Effect

Jan Theeuwes

Among the most fundamental issues of visual attention research is the extent to which visual selection is controlled by properties of the stimulus or by the intentions, goals, and beliefs of the observer (see e.g., Theeuwes, 1994a; Yantis, 1993). Before selective attention operates, preattentive processes perform some basic analyses segmenting the visual field into functional perceptual units. The crucial question is the extent to which the allocation of attention to these perceptual units is under the goal-directed control of the observer (intentions, goals, beliefs) or under stimulus-driven control. Goal-directed control is referred to as top-down selection and is said to occur when the observer intentionally selects only those objects required to perform the task at hand. Stimulus-driven control is referred to as bottom-up selection and is said to occur when attention is captured by the properties of the stimulus, irrespective of the intentions or goals of the observer.

Clear evidence for top-down control is provided by Posner (1980; Posner, Snyder, & Davidson, 1980) in tasks in which a central cue (e.g., an arrowhead) indicates the likely target location. Spatially valid cues typically

I thank Chip Folk, Tram Neill, and Art Kramer for their helpful comments on a draft of this chapter.

result in benefits (shorter latencies) and spatially invalid cues result in costs (longer latencies), indicating that subjects are capable of endogenously directing spatial attention to a limited spatial location. These findings led to the conceptualization of visual attention as something like a spotlight (e.g., C. W. Eriksen & Yeh, 1985; Posner, 1980) that can move serially through visual space encompassing a small limited region at a time. The notion that attention can be endogenously directed to a spatial location is relatively undisputed and confirmed by various studies using various paradigms (e.g., Bashinski & Bacharach, 1980; Jonides, 1981; Theeuwes, 1989, 1991b; Van der Heijden, Wolters, Groep, & Hagenaar, 1987; Yantis & Jonides, 1990).

In all studies showing top-down control of attention, in anticipation of the target event, subjects focus their attention on a particular limited spatial region. Because spatial attention is directed to the location of the impending target, it has been claimed that visual selection—controlling which object embedded in an array of other objects is selected for further processing—takes place before the search display comes on (e.g., Theeuwes, 1994a, 1994b). Because the cuing procedure eliminates spatial uncertainty and therefore search, it is not necessary to select a target object among other objects. Consequently, it is not necessary to divide attention over the visual field, which might imply that preattentive parallel segmentation that breaks up the visual field into functional units does not occur. Note that focusing of attention before display onset results in a serial attentional deployment of the visual field (i.e., serial search).

Recently, a considerable debate has erupted regarding the extent to which attention can be endogenously directed to nonspatial stimulus features such as color, shape, brightness, size, and so forth that are available at the early preattentive level (e.g., Bacon & Egeth, 1994; Duncan & Humphreys, 1989; Folk, Remington, & Johnston, 1992, 1993; Theeuwes, 1991a, 1992, 1993, 1994a, 1994b; Wolfe, Cave, & Franzel, 1989; Yantis, 1993). The crucial question is whether it is possible to exert top-down control over the preattentive stage so that only those objects having task-relevant stimulus features are selected.

In a series of studies, I have pitted goal-directed selection against stimulus-driven selection in a search task in which a singleton target could appear at any location in the visual field (Theevwes, 1991a, 1992, 1994b, in press).Rather than focusing attention onto a restricted area, subjects were required to divide attention over the visual field and select only the object necessary to perform the task. Typically, in singleton search tasks (i.e., the defining attribute of the target is a featural singleton), time to detect the target is independent of the number of elements in the display (e.g., Egeth, Jonides, & Wall, 1972; Treisman & Gelade, 1980), suggesting that the complete display is encoded in parallel along a set of primitive features at the early preattentive stage of processing. The singleton target is said to "pop-out" of the display without effort on part of the observer.

In these types of singleton search tasks, I showed that even when observers adopted a clear top-down attentional set to search for a singleton, performance was disrupted by an irrelevant featural singleton in a different dimension from the relevant singleton (Theevwes, 1991a, 1992). These experiments showed that top-down selection of a particular known-to-be-relevant singleton cannot override bottom-up interference from a known-to-be-irrelevant distractor singleton. For example, in one study (Theeuwes, 1992), observers had an attentional set for a shape singleton because they searched for a green circle among green diamonds. When on some trials an irrelevant color singleton was present (i.e., one of the diamonds was red) response latencies to find the target singleton increased. Even though observers had a clear attentional set to attend to a particular shape singleton (a green circle), the presence of an irrelevant singleton caused interference. It was shown that selectivity depended solely on the relative saliency of the stimulus attributes: When the shape singleton was more salient than the color singleton (yellowish red vs. yellowish green), the shape singleton interfered with search for the color singleton, and vice versa. It was concluded that in singleton search tasks in which a preattentive segmentation process is used to detect the target, top-down control cannot override the stimulus-driven capture that arises due to the appearance of a more salient stimulus attribute. I have claimed that in visual tasks in which the defining attribute is a singleton, selection occurs in a purely stimulus-driven fashion (Theevwes, 1991a, 1992).

Recently, Bacon and Egeth (1994) showed that this type of stimulus-driven selection only occurs in singleton search in which subjects have the opportunity to look for the odd man out (referred to as the "singleton search mode"). When subjects have to search for a specific shape (e.g., search for a green circle between green diamonds and green triangles) the distracting effect of the singleton disappeared, suggesting that when a so-called "feature search mode" is applied, top-down control at the early preattentive stage seems possible. It should be noted, however, that in two other studies (Theeuwes, 1992, 1994b) subjects had the opportunity to apply this "feature search mode" because they knew the exact shape and color of the singleton they were looking for. If the "feature search mode" as suggested by Bacon and Egeth (1994) is viable, then for some reason subjects did not apply this strategy in my (Theevwes, 1992, 1994b, and in Bacon & Egeth, 1994, Experiment 1) studies even though it would have been beneficial, possibly attenuating the distraction caused by the irrelevant singleton.

Although alternative hypotheses are viable in conditions in which the target is not a singleton, as in the Bacon and Egeth (1994) study, the basic finding that goal-directed selection toward a particular known singleton cannot override the stimulus-driven attraction caused by an irrelevant singleton has been confirmed by various studies (Bacon & Egeth, 1994, Experiment 1; Pashler, 1988, Experiment 6; Theeuwes, 1991a, 1992, 1994b). In order to understand the mechanisms underlying goal-directed versus stimulus-driven selection, it is important to consider the basis for this interference.

On the one hand, I (Theeuwes, 1991a, 1992, 1993, 1994b) have claimed that the interference effect in singleton search is due to involuntary capture of attention by the irrelevant singleton. Because several studies (Theeuwes, 1991a, 1992, 1994b) showed that in singleton search selectivity completely depended on the relative saliency of the target and distractor singletons, I suggested that attention is always captured first by the most salient singleton irrespective of whether the "popping-out" singleton is a target or a distractor. According to this notion, in singleton search the presence of the irrelevant singleton causes spatial distraction, in the sense that irrespective of what subjects are looking for (i.e., irrespective of any top-down control), spatial attention is automatically and involuntarily captured by the most salient singleton. If this singleton is the target, a response is given. If it is not the target, attention is automatically switched to the next salient singleton. It has been suggested that the preattentive process simply calculates differences in features within dimensions and the most salient singleton gets focal attention first. The source of the preattentively calculated difference signal (whether it is caused by a color singleton or a form singleton) can be recognized only after attention has moved to the location of the difference signal. In other words, the subject knows only whether the singleton was the target after selecting the location having the large difference signal. Obviously, given this account, the interference effect is due to the stimulus-driven capture of attention.

The alternative view is that there is top-down control at the preattentive level, suggesting that observers intentionally select only the task-relevant singleton. Irrespective of the saliency of the singletons present in the visual field, attention is immediately directed toward the singleton relevant for the task at hand. In this view, the increase in reaction time in trials in which an irrelevant singleton is present is due to nonspatial distraction (e.g., Folk & Remington, 1993). For example, the preattentive processing of the target singleton may take somewhat longer because of the noise produced by the irrelevant singleton. Because in distractor trials the target singleton pops out somewhat later, reaction time in these trials is increased relative to trails in which there is no distractor (see, e.g., Theeuwes, 1992). Alternatively, it is possible that the preattentive stage segments the visual field into two possible objects, the target singleton and the distractor singleton, and the mere presence of another perceptual object slows down shifting of attention to the relevant object. According to this idea, when two distinct perceptual objects compete for attention, "filtering costs" in the sense described, for example, by Treisman, Kahneman, and Burkell (1983) may cause an increase in the time to find the target singleton. Note that a nonspatial distraction explanation is compatible with the notion that top-down control at the preattentive level can selectively guide spatial focal attention to the target singleton (e.g., Bacon & Egeth, 1994; Hoffman, 1978, 1979; Treisman & Sato, 1990; Wolfe et al., 1989).

The present study was designed to test whether the distraction effect in singleton search is due to spatial distraction (i.e., attention is exogenously captured by the irrelevant singleton) or due to nonspatial distraction (i.e., attention is endogenously shifted to the location of the target singleton, yet due to the irrelevant singleton this shifting takes longer). The task used in the present study was similar to that of an earlier study (Theeuwes, 1992) in which subjects always searched for a green diamond among green circles. In one condition, a colored distractor singleton was present (i.e., one of the circles was red). The earlier study (Theeuwes, 1992) showed that in this type of task, the red distractor singleton is so salient that it slows down search for the target shape singleton (see also Bacon &

Egeth, 1994, Experiment 1). Instead of discriminating a line inside the target shape as in other studies (Bacon & Egeth, 1994; Theeuwes, 1991a, 1992, 1994b), in the present study, subjects responded to a letter centered in the target shape. When the letter was an *R* they responded with their right hand, when it was an *L* they responded with their left hand, response assignments that can be considered highly compatible. The letters in all other nontarget shapes were randomly *R*s and *L*s. There was a clear separation between the defining (the diamond) and reporting (the letter inside the diamond) attributes of the target (Duncan, 1985). This guarantees that the stimulus information available at the preattentive level separating target from nontarget elements (the singleton diamond among circles) tells nothing about which response to choose (*R* or *L*). Such a separation enables the decoupling of perceptual and response selection factors (see Theeuwes, 1992, 1994b, for a discussion).

In order to test the hypotheses described above, the letter inside the distracting singleton was systematically manipulated. On half of the trials the letter inside the distractor and target singleton were identical ("compatible" condition; e.g., in both shapes an *L* or in both shapes an *R*), in the other half of the trials they were different ("incompatible" condition; e.g., in the target singleton an *R* and in the distractor singleton an *L*, and vice versa). If the distracting effect is spatial in the sense that attention is always first captured by the (more salient) irrelevant singleton, then incompatible letters centered inside the irrelevant singleton should cause longer response latencies than compatible letters. Because attention is captured by the irrelevant singleton, the singleton receives focal attention first, resulting in the mandatory processing of all attributes of that object (e.g., Kramer & Jacobson, 1991). In line with the work of C. W. Eriksen and colleagues (B. A. Eriksen & Eriksen, 1974; C. W. Eriksen & Hoffman, 1972, 1973), it is expected that the processing of response-incompatible letters produces performance costs relative to response-compatible letters.

Alternatively, if the distracting effect of the irrelevant singleton is nonspatial in the sense that attention is not shifted to the distractor but instead is more slowly allocated to the location of the target singleton, then the compatibility manipulation should not have an effect. Because focal attention is not shifted to the location of the irrelevant singleton, the letter inside the irrelevant singleton should have no effect on the response to the letter appearing in the target singleton.

EXPERIMENT 1

Subjects viewed equispaced multielement displays (7 or 9) in which they responded to the letter inside the diamond. Display size was manipulated in order to check whether search was performed in parallel, ensuring that the preattentive parallel stage was involved in detecting the shape singleton. Variation in display size (7 or 9) was relatively small to ensure that the saliency of the target and distractor singletons was about the same in the two display size conditions. As suggested earlier (Theeuwes, 1994a), the saliency of the singleton possibly depends on the density (distance between the elements) and the number of nonunique elements present in the display (see also Green, 1991; Todd & Kramer, 1994). Very large display sizes were not included because closely spaced elements would result in typical flanker compatibility effects as defined by Eriksen, lateral masking effects, or both.

Method

Subjects

Eight right-handed subjects, ranging in age from 18 to 26 years, participated as paid volunteers. All had normal or corrected-to-normal vision and reported having no color vision defects.

Apparatus

An SX-386 personal computer (G2) with a NEC Multisync 3D VGA color screen (resolution=640 × 350), using a Micro Experimental Laboratory software package (Schneider, 1988) to control the timing of the events, generated pictures and recorded reaction times. The [/]-key and the [z]-key of the computer keyboard were used as response buttons. Each subject was tested in a sound-attenuated, dimly lit room, with his or her head resting on a chin rest. The CRT was located at eye level, 100 cm from the chin rest.

Stimuli

The stimulus display consisted of seven or nine colored shapes equally spaced around the fixation point on an imaginary circle whose radius was 3.6° of visual angle. The target shape was a diamond (45° rotated square) 1.37° on a side presented in green (Commission Internationale de l'Eclairage x, y chromaticity coordinates of .309, .597). The nontarget shapes were circles 1.26° in size presented in the same color. In the distractor condition, one of the circles was presented in red (coordinates of .572, .399). The colors were matched for luminance (16.0 cd/m²). Centered inside each shape was a white capital Roman letter *L* or *R* (0.57° × 0.29°) having a luminance of 45.0 cd/m². In the compatible distractor condition, the letter inside the target shape (the diamond) matched the letter inside the red circle distractor (e.g., an *R* in the green diamond and an *R* in the red circle or an *L* in the green diamond and an *L* in the red circle). In the incompatible distractor condition, the letter inside the diamond was different from the letter inside the red circle distractor (e.g., an *L* in the green diamond and *R* in the red circle or an *R* in the green diamond and *L* in the green circle).

The closest separation between the letters was 2.5° center to center at display size nine. The closest separation of the nearest contours of the outline shapes was 1.2° at display size 9.

The fixation cross was presented in white (45.0 cd/m²) on a gray background (2.5 cd/m²). The colorimetric and photometric measurements were carried out by means of a spectroradiometer (Photo Research, Type PR-703A/M [Chatsworth, CA]). The detector head of this device was directed toward patches of the colors used in this experiment. The patches were displayed at the center of the computer screen. Figure 1 shows examples of the displays with display size seven both for the no-distractor, compatible distractor, and incompatible distractor conditions.

Procedure

Subjects were instructed to report the letter (*R* or *L*) inside the green diamond and to press with their left index finger the [z]-key for *L* and with their right index finger the [/]-key for *R*.

Each subject performed 208 trials in each of the two conditions. Half of the subjects started with the no-distractor, the other half with the distractor condition. Subjects first received a practice half-block of 104 trials in each condition. In the distractor condition, in half of the trials, the letter inside the green diamond target matched the letter inside the red circle distractor (compatible condition). In the other half of the distractor trials, the letter inside the green diamond target was different from the letter inside the red circle distractor (incompatible condition). Target and distractor were positioned at random locations within the display. There

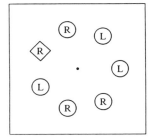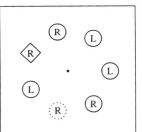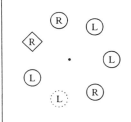

Figure 1

Sample stimulus displays (with display size seven). In the no-distractor condition (left panel) the green diamond target shape appears among green circles. In the compatible distractor condition (middle), the letter inside the green diamond target shape (in this case the letter *R*) is identical to the letter inside the red circle distractor. In the incompatible distractor condition (right), the letter inside the green diamond target shape is different from the letter inside the red circle distractor. Solid lines indicate targets that are green, and dotted lines indicate targets that are red.

were equal numbers of *R* and *L* targets. The *R*s and *L*s inside nontarget circles were randomly distributed within a display. Display size (7 or 9) was randomized within blocks.

Within each session there were short breaks after every 52 trials, during which subjects received feedback about their performance (percentage errors and mean reaction time) on the preceding block of trials. It was emphasized that subjects should fixate the central dot and not move their eyes during the course of any trial. It was stressed that a steady fixation would reduce response time (RT) and make the task easier. Both speed and accuracy were emphasized. A warning beep informed subjects that an error had been committed. If no response was made after 2 s, the trial was counted as an error.

Results

Response times longer than 1 s were counted as errors, which led to a loss of 0.82% of the trials. Figure 2 presents the subjects' mean RTs and error percentages. The individual mean correct RTs were submitted to an analysis of variance (ANOVA) with distractor (no-distractor vs. distractor) and display size (7 or 9) as factors. There was a main effect on RT of distrac-

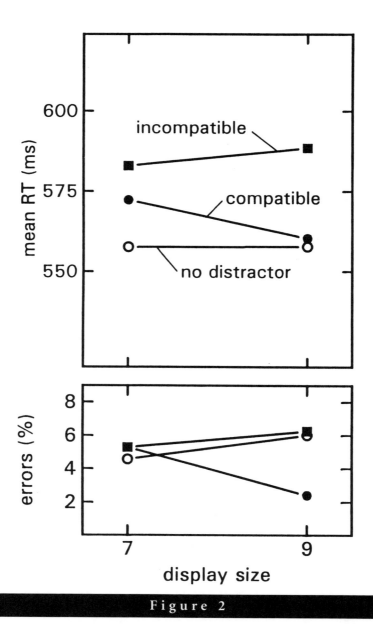

Figure 2

Mean response times (RTs) and error percentages as a function of display size for search without a distractor and search with a compatible or incompatible distractor.

tor, $F(1, 7) = 6.6$, $p < .05$, indicating that RTs in the no-distractor condition were reliably faster than in the distractor condition, a result that confirms earlier findings (Theeuwes, 1992).

The individual mean correct RTs for the distractor condition were entered into an ANOVA with compatibility (compatible, incompatible) and display size (7 or 9) as factors. There was only a main effect on RT of compatibility, $F(1, 7) = 5.9$, $p < .05$. The factor display size and the Display Size × Compatibility interaction failed to reach significance. This analysis shows, as is clear from Figure 2, that the RTs in the incompatible condition were significantly slower than in the compatible condition.

Planned comparisons showed that the mean RT of the incompatible condition was reliably slower than the mean RT of the no-distractor condition ($p < .05$). There was no difference between the compatible and the no-distractor condition.

The mean slopes for the no-distractor, compatible, and incompatible conditions were 0.0, −5.9, and 2.8 ms, respectively. None of the slopes were significantly different from zero, $t(7) < 0.33$, indicating preattentive parallel search across all items in the display (e.g., Treisman & Gormican, 1988).

In order to achieve homogeneity of the error rate variance, the mean error rates per cell were transformed by means of an arcsine transformation. Individual mean arcsine transformed error rates were entered into the same ANOVAs as performed on the response latencies. None of the effects were significant, indicating that differences in response latencies were not due to a speed–accuracy trade-off.

Discussion

The results of this experiment are fairly clear: The identity of the letter inside the distractor singleton does have an effect on responding to the letter appearing inside the target singleton. When the letter inside the distractor is identical to the letter inside the target singleton, it is compatible with the response, giving relatively fast RTs. When the letter inside the distractor is different from the letter inside the target singleton, it is incompatible with the response, causing slower response times. The present findings are entirely consistent with the hypothesis that the distracting effect is spatial in the sense that attention is exogenously captured by the more salient, yet irrelevant singleton.

EXPERIMENT 2

Although the results of the previous experiment clearly support the hypothesis that attention is captured by the most salient singleton, other support for the hypothesis is desirable. To test whether the present findings are robust, Experiment 2 used a different display layout, a different procedure, and a limited exposure duration. The display consisted of a 4×4 rectangular stimulus array containing 16 shapes. In Experiment 2 the distraction condition was mixed within blocks, instead of being presented in separate blocks. Unlike in Experiment 1, this does not allow subjects to adopt a different strategy on different blocks. This manipulation makes it possible to ensure that the compatibility effect as found in Experiment 1 is not due to subjects' adapting a different strategy on distraction blocks. Finally, exposure duration of the display was limited to 200 ms, a duration too short to make directed eye movements. This manipulation ensures that the effects reported are due to attention capture, not confounded by directed eye movements toward the target or distractor location.

Method

Subjects

Eight subjects ranging in age between 17 and 25 years participated in the experiment.

Stimuli and Procedure

The task was identical to Experiment 1, except that the stimulus display always consisted of 16 colored shapes (same dimensions and colorimetric values as in Experiment 1) presented on 4×4 rectangular stimulus array ($8.2° \times 8.2°$) spaced around the fixation point. The center-to-center separation between the letters located inside the shapes was 2.3° of visual angle. The closest separation between the outline shapes was 1.1°.

There was one block of 120 trials. In half of the trials there was no distractor, in the other half there was a red circle distractor. In half of the distractor trials, the letter inside the distractor was identical to the letter in the target singleton, in the other half it was different. Target and distractor were positioned at random locations within the 4 × 4 grid. Subjects received one practice block of 120 trials. There was feedback every 60 trials.

Results and Discussion

Response times longer than 1,200 ms were counted as errors, which led to a loss of 1.0% of the trials. The means of response latencies and error rates are shown in Table 1. The difference of 38 ms between the compatible and incompatible conditions, $t(7) = 5.26, p < .01$, replicates the findings of Experiment 1, supporting the notion that the distractor singleton captured attention. The compatibility effect obviously did not depend on the display layout or the procedure used. The effects reported depict attentional capture that did not depend on the occurrence of directed eye movements.

Overall, the presence of a distractor did slow down responding to the target singleton, $t(7) = 2.14, p < .05$. The incompatible distractor condition differed significantly from the no-distractor condition, $t(7) = 3.44$, $p < .01$. There was no difference between the no-distractor and the compatible condition.

An analysis performed on the arcsine transformed error rate indicated that none of the effects were significant, indicating that differences in response latencies were not due to a speed–accuracy trade-off.

GENERAL DISCUSSION

Both experiments clearly showed that the identity of the letter inside the irrelevant distractor singleton did have an effect on the latency of re-

Table 1

Mean Response Times (in ms) and Errors for Search Without a Distractor and Search With a Compatible or Incompatible Distractor

Measure	No distractor	Compatible	Incompatible
Mean response time	590	599	637
Errors (%)	6.2	6.6	5.8

sponding to the letter appearing inside the target singleton. These findings can be explained only by assuming that attention was captured by the irrelevant singleton, at least on a larger part of the trials. Because capturing of attention implies that focal attention was directed to the irrelevant singleton, the identity of the letter became available, thereby affecting the speed of responding to the target letter. If attention was not captured by the irrelevant singleton, then there is no plausible explanation how the identity of the letter in the irrelevant singleton could have affected responding to the target letter.

The present findings support the notion that the preattentive process calculates differences in features within dimensions (see, e.g., Theeuwes, 1994a, 1994b), resulting in a pattern of activations at different locations. For example, at the location of the red distractor singleton a large "difference" signal arises because the singleton differs from all other nontargets in color. At the location of the diamond singleton, a large "difference" signal arises because the diamond differs from all other elements in shape. Previous results (Theeuwes, 1991a, 1992) have shown that it takes less time to find a color singleton than a shape singleton, suggesting that the red color singleton produces a larger difference signal than the diamond shape singleton. Because focal attention is automatically and unintentionally shifted to the location in the display having the largest local feature difference, the color singleton is selected first. It is assumed that the source of the preattentively calculated difference signal (whether it is caused by a color singleton or a form singleton) can be recognized only after focal attention is moved to the location of the difference signal. In other words, the subject only knows whether the singleton was the target after selecting the location having the large difference signal. In the present experiment, selecting the location of the distractor singleton results in mandatory processing of the letter inside the distractor singleton. After attention is reshifted from the distractor location to the target location, the previously identified letter inside the distractor affects responding to the letter in the target singleton.

In this view, the salience of the singleton, and not its identity, its color, its shape, its brightness, and so on, will determine which element captures attention. Obviously, given this account, selection operates irrespective of the task demands. The automatic shifts of attention are considered to be the result of a relatively inflexible, hardwired mechanism that is triggered by the presence of these difference signal interrupts. In line with the work of, for example, Sagi and Julesz (1985) and Ullman (1984), it is assumed that the parallel process in singleton search performs a local-mismatch detection followed by a serial stage in which the most mismatching areas are selected for further analysis.

The present results, indicating that the identity of the letter inside the distractor does affect processing of the letter inside the target element, suggest that the capture of attention to the location of the distractor results in mandatory processing of the letter at that location. Note that one has to assume that this processing is mandatory because the distractor element (the red circle) that has putatively drawn attention to its location tells the subject that the letter inside the distractor cannot be the target. Subjects may disengage attention quickly and refocus attention to the next salient singleton, which in the present experiments is the target. It should be realized that the rapid disengagement of attention from the distractor to the target location based on the knowledge that the letter in the red circle cannot be the target does represent top-down effects. Yet, these top-down effects do not operate on selection, but on processes occurring after the distractor was selected (see e.g., Theeuwes, 1994b, for a similar explanation of the results reported by Folk et al., 1993).

The present results cannot be explained by assuming that attention to the target singleton "leaks over" to an adjacent letter, which typically is used as an explanation for the flanker compatibility effect (e.g., B. A. Eriksen & Eriksen, 1974; Yantis & Johnston, 1990). In the present experiments, only at chance level the target and distractor singleton occupied adjacent locations, and even then the minimal center-to-center distance between the letters was 2.3° of visual angle (in Experiment 2). Such a distance has generally been considered a separation sufficient to ensure no attentional spillover (e.g., B. A. Eriksen & Eriksen, 1974; Eriksen & Hoffman, 1972, 1973; but see Miller, 1991). Flanker compatibility effects tend to disappear when intervening items are placed between the relevant item and the flanker, suggesting that there is hardly any spillover of attention to nonadjacent flankers (e.g., C. W. Eriksen & St. James, 1986).

In summary, the present results confirm earlier findings that in singleton search, goal-directed attentional selection is relatively ineffective. Selection seems to be determined by the saliency of the elements in the display. The present findings indicate that attention is captured by any salient singleton, causing an attentional shift to the location of the singleton irrespective of whether the singleton is a target or a distractor.

REFERENCES

Bacon, W. F., & Egeth, H. E. (1994). Overriding stimulus-driven attentional capture. *Perception and Psychophysics, 55,* 485–496.

Bashinski, H. S., & Bacharach, V. R. (1980). Enhancement of perceptual sensitivity as the result of selectivity attending to spatial locations. *Perception and Psychophysics, 28,* 241–280.

Duncan, J. (1985). Visual search and visual attention. In M. Posner & O. Marin (Eds.), *Attention and performance, XI* (pp. 85–106). Hillsdale, NJ: Erlbaum.

Duncan, J., & Humphreys, G. W. (1989). Visual search and stimulus similarity. *Psychological Review, 96,* 433–458.

Egeth, H., Jonides, J., & Wall S., (1972). Parallel processing of multielement displays. *Cognitive Psychology, 3,* 674–698.

Eriksen, B. A., & Eriksen, C. W. (1974). Effects of noise letters upon the identification of a target letter nonsearch task. *Perception and Psychophysics, 16,* 143–149.

Eriksen, C. W., & Hoffman, J. E. (1972). Temporal and spatial characteristics of selective encoding from visual displays. *Perception and Psychophysics, 12,* 201–204.

Eriksen, C. W., & Hoffman, J. E. (1973). The extent of processing of noise elements during selective encoding from visual displays. *Perception and Psychophysics, 14,* 155–160.

Eriksen, C. W., & St. James, J. D. (1986). Visual attention within and around the field of focal attention: A zoom lens model. *Perception and Psychophysics, 40,* 225–240.

Eriksen, C. W., & Yeh, Y. Y. (1985). Allocation of attention in the visual field. *Journal of Experimental Psychology: Human Perception and Performance, 11,* 583–597.

Folk, C. L., & Remington, R. W. (1993, November). *Selectivity in attentional capture by featural singletons.* Paper presented at the 34th Annual Meeting of the Psychonomic Society, Washington, DC.

Folk, C. L., Remington, R., & Johnston, J. C. (1992). Involuntary covert orienting is contingent on attentional control settings. *Journal of Experimental Psychology: Human Perception and Performance, 18,* 1030–1044.

Folk, C. L., Remington, R., & Johnston, J. C. (1993). Attentional control setting: A reply to Yantis (1993). *Journal of Experimental Psychology: Human Perception and Performance, 19,* 682–685.

Green, M. (1991). Visual search, visual streams, and visual architectures. *Perception and Psychophysics, 50,* 388–403.

Hoffman, J. E. (1978). Search through a sequentially presented display. *Perception and Psychophysics, 23,* 1–11.

Hoffman, J. E. (1979). A two-stage model of visual search. *Perception and Psychophysics, 25,* 319–327.

Jonides, J. (1981). Voluntary vs. automatic control over the mind's eye's movement. In J. B. Long & A. D. Baddeley (Eds.), *Attention and performance, IX* (pp. 187–203). Hillsdale, NJ: Erlbaum.

Kramer, A. F., & Jacobson, A. (1991). Perceptual organization and focused attention: The role of objects and proximity in visual processing. *Perception and Psychophysics, 50,* 267–284.

Miller, J. (1991). The flanker compatibility effect as a function of visual angle, attentional locus, visual transients, and perceptual load: A search for boundary conditions. *Perception and Psychophysics, 49,* 270–288.

Pashler, H. (1988). Cross-dimensional interaction and texture segregation. *Perception and Psychophysics, 43,* 307–318.

Posner, M. (1980). Orienting of attention. *Quarterly Journal of Experimental Psychology, 32,* 3–25.

Posner, M. I., Snyder, C. R. R., & Davidson, B. J. (1980). Attention and the detection of signals. *Journal of Experimental Psychology: General, 109,* 160–174.

Sagi, D., & Julesz, B. (1985). Detection versus discrimination of visual orientation. *Perception, 14,* 619–628.

Schneider, W. (1988). Micro Experimental Laboratory: An integrated system for IBM PC compatibles. *Behavior Research Methods, Instruments, and Computers, 20,* 206–217.

Theeuwes, J. (1989). Effects of location and form cuing on the allocation of attention in visual. *Acta Psychologica, 72,* 177–192.

Theeuwes, J. (1991a). Cross-dimensional perceptual selectivity. *Perception and Psychophysics, 50,* 184–193.

Theeuwes, J. (1991b). Exogenous and endogenous control of attention: The effect of visual onsets and offsets. *Perception and Psychophysics, 49,* 83–90.

Theeuwes, J. (1992). Perceptual selectivity for color and form. *Perception and Psychophysics, 51,* 599–606.

Theeuwes, J. (1993). Visual selective attention: A theoretical analysis. *Acta Psychologica, 83,* 93–154.

Theeuwes, J. (1994a). Endogenous and exogenous control of visual selection. *Perception, 23*, 429–440.

Theeuwes, J. (1994b). Stimulus-driven capture and attentional set: Selective search for color and visual abrupt onsets. *Journal of Experimental Psychology: Human Perception and Performance, 20*, 799–806.

Theeuwes, J. (in press). Temporal and spatial characteristic of preattentive and attentive processing. *Visual Cognition.*

Todd, S., & Kramer, A. F. (1994). Attentional misguidance in visual search. *Perception and Psychophysics, 56*, 198–210.

Treisman, A. M., & Gelade, G. (1980). A feature integration theory of attention. *Cognitive Psychology, 12*, 97–136.

Treisman, A. M., & Gormican, S. (1988). Feature search in early vision: Evidence from search asymmetries. *Psychological Review, 95*, 15–48.

Treisman, A. M., Kahneman, D., & Burkell, J. (1983). Perceptual objects and the costs of filtering. *Perception and Psychophysics, 33*, 527–532.

Treisman, A. M., & Sato, S. (1990). Conjunction search revisited. *Journal of Experimental Psychology: Human Perception and Performance, 16*, 459–478.

Ullman, S. (1984). Visual routines. *Cognition, 18*, 97–159.

Van der Heijden, A. H. C., Wolters, G., Groep, J. C., & Hagenaar, R. (1987). Single-letters recognition accuracy benefits from advance cuing of location. *Perception and Psychophysics, 42*, 503–509.

Wolfe, J. M., Cave, K. R., & Franzel, S. L. (1989). Guided search: An alternative to the feature integration model for visual search. *Journal of Experimental Psychology: Human Perception and Performance, 15*, 419–433.

Yantis, S. (1993). Stimulus driven attentional capture and attentional control settings. *Journal of Experimental Psychology: Human Perception and Performance, 19*, 676–681.

Yantis, S., & Johnston, J. C. (1990). On the locus of visual selection: Evidence from focused attention tasks. *Journal of Experimental Psychology: Human Perception and Performance, 16*, 135–149.

Yantis, S., & Jonides, J. (1990). Abrupt visual onsets and selective attention: Voluntary versus automatic allocation. *Journal of Experimental Psychology: Human Perception and Performance, 16*, 121–134.

11

Novel Pop-Out, Perceptual Inhibition, and the Stability–Plasticity Dilemma

William A. Johnston, Irene S. Schwarting,
and Kevin J. Hawley

Complex organisms, such as people, display an impressive ability to become perceptually and behaviorally attuned to their familiar habitats and yet remain vigilant to deviant or unexpected intrusions. The mind appears to be biased simultaneously toward both what it most expects and what it least expects to encounter, a phenomenon that Grossberg (1987) referred to as the *stability–plasticity dilemma*.[1] The bias toward expected inputs promotes mental stability by ensuring a degree of empirical validation of the knowledge/belief system from which the expectancies arise, and the bias toward unexpected inputs promotes mental plasticity by ensuring a degree of sensitivity to disconfirmations of this same knowledge/belief system. A wealth of evidence affirms both sides of the dilemma. Mental stability is indicated by schematic perception (e.g., Biederman, Glass, & Stacy, 1973; Tulving & Gold, 1963), perceptual memory

Much of the research and thinking reflected in this chapter was supported by Grant F49620-92-J-0473 from the Air Force Office of Scientific Research. We are grateful to David Strayer and Steven Yantis, who reviewed an earlier version of this chapter and offered several helpful comments and suggestions. James Farnham contributed to some of the research summarized in Figures 1–3.

[1]We use the terms *expectancy* and *familiarity* interchangeably to refer to the passive priming of the perceptual system owing to either transitory semantic and identity priming or longer term episodic priming. We do not use these terms to refer to active search for explicit targets.

(e.g., Jacoby & Dallas, 1981), and various related phenomena such as perceptual restoration (e.g., Warren, 1970) and the word-superiority effect (e.g., Reicher, 1969). Mental plasticity is indicated by the attention-capturing power and physiological arousal potential of novel and unexpected inputs in otherwise familiar scenes or event sequences (e.g., Berlyne, 1960; Campbell, Hayne, & Richardson, 1992; Friedman, 1979; Loftus & Mackworth, 1978; Näätänen, 1992; Sokolov, 1963).

The remainder of this chapter comprises four main sections. The first section reviews the evidence for both sides of the dilemma that has been generated from a single experimental paradigm in our own laboratory. The second examines some theoretical implications of this evidence. The third summarizes a theory, called *mismatch theory*, that provides a possible account of the evidence and resolution of the dilemma. The fourth and final section reviews evidence bearing on the assumption of mismatch theory that data-driven processing for expected inputs is suppressed rather than enhanced, as is assumed by most other theories.

NOVEL POP-OUT

We have investigated the automatic capture of attention by novel objects in otherwise familiar fields (e.g., Hawley, Johnston, & Farnham, 1994; Johnston, Hawley, & Farnham, 1993; Johnston, Hawley, Plewe, Elliott, & DeWitt, 1990). In a typical study, observers receive 200-ms or briefer glimpses of backward-masked, four-object arrays. Each array is followed by a probe to localize one of the objects. The four objects in some of the arrays, called *all-familiar*, are repeated together many times across a session. The objects in other arrays, called *all-novel*, are presented one time only. Accuracy of localization is consistently higher for all-familiar arrays than for all-novel arrays. This *baseline* effect illustrates the mental bias toward expected inputs and the stability half of the stability–plasticity dilemma. In a third kind of array, called *one novel*, one of the objects from an all-familiar array is replaced by a novel object. The usual superiority of accuracy of localization for familiar over novel objects is diminished, and often reversed, in one-novel arrays. Accuracy of localization tends to rise above the all-novel baseline for the novel singletons, defining *novel pop-out*, and to fall below the all-familiar baseline for the familiar field objects, defining *familiar sink-in*. Under certain conditions, accuracy of localization is actually higher for the novel singletons than for the familiar field objects, defining *novel pop-out–familiar sink-in.* These pop-out and sink-in effects illustrate the mental bias toward unexpected inputs and the plasticity half of the stability–plasticity dilemma.

The full pattern of effects was first observed in Experiment 4 of Johnston et al. (1990). A recent replication of this experiment produced the data summarized in Figure 1. The full pattern of effects again emerged in terms of accuracy of localization (top panel) and tended to be reflected in terms of latency of localization (bottom panel). This pattern has been found to hold up under a wide range of conditions. It remains intact for durations of array exposure ranging from 33 to 200 ms (Johnston et al., 1993, Experiment 6), for both speed and accuracy emphases on responding (Johnston & Schwarting, 1995, Experiment 3), for numbers of prior repetitions of all-familiar arrays ranging from 15 to 144 (Johnston et al., 1993, Experiment 3; Farnham, 1994), and for array loads up to at least six objects. Among other things, these findings indicate that novel pop-out is not attributable to strategic processing, such as the deliberate search for novel items.

We have observed two other effects very comparable to novel pop-out. One of these, called *odd pop-out,* is that a familiar object extracted from one all-familiar array was found to pop out when it was transplanted into a different all-familiar array (Johnston et al., 1993, Experiment 5). Another effect, called *nonprimed pop-out,* is that a word, such as *CHEAT,* was found to pop out from an all-novel array when the field words were both associatively related, like *PEST, INSECT,* and *ITCHY,* and primed by a preceding word, like *FLEA* (DeWitt, 1994, Experiment 2). On the other hand, a single primed word was not observed to pop out from a field of nonprimed words (DeWitt, 1994), and a single familiar object was not observed to pop out from a field of novel objects (Johnston et al., 1990, Experiment 3). Collectively, these findings suggest that an object will tend to capture attention to the extent that it is incongruent with an associatively unitized and either episodically or semantically primed field of objects.

THEORETICAL IMPLICATIONS

We suggest that novel pop-out poses a serious challenge to the prevailing conceptual framework in the field of attention. We first outline what we regard the prevailing framework to be and then examine the challenge that novel pop-out presents to it.

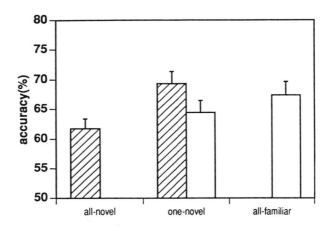

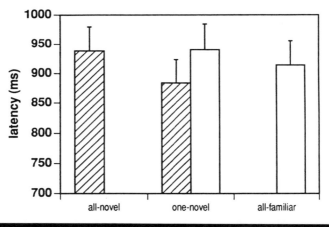

Figure 1

Mean accuracy (top panel) and latency (bottom panel) of localizations of novel and familiar words in the three array compositions (array exposure = 200 ms). Measures of novel word localization are indicated with diagonal-line fill.

Prevailing Framework

A distinction is commonly drawn between preattentive and postattentive processing of inputs (Cowan, 1988; Shiffrin & Schneider, 1977; Treisman & Gelade, 1980). Various features of inputs are analyzed in parallel during preattentive processing, and the meaningful bundles of features defining specific *attended* inputs are analyzed serially during postattentive processing. All inputs automatically undergo preattentive processing, but only attended inputs undergo postattentive processing. A special gate-keeping mechanism selects inputs for postattentive processing. This attention device, variously called *executive, attention director, central processor,* and *controlled processor,* is in charge of the limited pool of capacity or resources upon which postattentive processing depends. The executive "pays attention" to inputs by allocating a portion of its resources to them.

Within this framework, attention can be either directed to or captured by particular inputs. In the case of directed attention, the executive systematically searches external scenes and arrays for specific targets; that is, it attends to preattentively analyzed inputs one by one until it encounters a target (e.g., Shiffrin & Schneider, 1977). In the case of attention capture, the preattentively analyzed features of certain inputs automatically draw the executive's attention (e.g., Yantis, chap. 2 in this volume). Is novel pop-out a phenomenon of directed attention or one of attention capture? We argue below that novel pop-out poses an enigma to the prevailing framework regardless of how it is conceptualized.

Novel Pop-Out as a Phenomenon of Directed Attention

One directed-attention account of novel pop-out is that observers explicitly search for novel singletons. However, this account is untenable on both logical and empirical grounds. Logically, the features of novel stimuli are, by definition, not predictable and cannot be predefined targets of search. Empirically, novel pop-out has been found to survive both reductions in duration of array exposure from 200 to 33 ms (e.g., Johnston et al., 1993, Experiment 6) and, in a very recent study, increases in array load from two to six items. Indeed, the novel pop-out–familiar sink-in effect actually tended to increase with reductions in array exposure and increases in array load. If novel pop-out were a consequence of directed search for novel items, then it should decrease with reductions in array exposure and increases in array load.

Another directed-attention interpretation of novel pop-out, one that has often arisen in response to various prior presentations of some of our findings, is that it is due to the relatively fluent postattentive identification of familiar items. According to this explanation, preattentive analysis very rapidly supplies a physical representation of the object at each location, but postattentive analysis is necessary to identify it. Relatively little time and capacity are required to identify the familiar objects, allowing the executive to sequentially process more familiar objects than novel objects during the brief exposure of an array. This accounts for the baseline advantage of all-familiar arrays over all-novel arrays. Because the executive can identify familiar objects more quickly than novel objects, it is more likely to encounter the novel singleton in a one-novel array than it is to encounter any given novel item in an all-novel array. This accounts for novel pop-out. By the same token, once a novel singleton is encountered, its relatively sluggish postattentive processing consumes time and capacity that would otherwise be allocated to the remaining familiar items in the array. This accounts for familiar sink-in.

Several of our findings question this account. For example, consider the novel pop-out–familiar sink-in and odd pop-out effects. Why should familiar field items ever be *less* identifiable than novel singletons, especially at briefer array exposures and higher array loads, and why should familiar and presumably fluently identified items, pop out when they are transplanted into a different familiar field? Particularly damaging evidence against the directed-attention account was generated from a recent study in which we manipulated the perceptual fluency of the familiar items in order to directly test the prediction that novel pop-out should increase with the perceptual fluency of the field items (Johnston & Schwarting, 1995, Experiment 1). Observers viewed a long sequence of all-novel, one-novel, and both spatially predictable and spatially unpredictable all-familiar arrays. The spatial arrangement of the familiar objects remained constant in the spatially predictable arrays but varied in the spatially unpredictable arrays. Duration of array exposure was manipulated between groups at two levels (50 and 200 ms).

The data are summarized in Figure 2. As in prior studies, overall accuracy of localization increased with duration of array exposure, but the magnitude of novel pop-out was not affected. In accordance with the assumption that the executive can scan through spatially predictable familiar arrays more efficiently than spatially unpredictable ones, localization accuracy was substantially higher in the former arrays. It follows from the same assumption that a novel singleton is more likely to be encountered and identified if it is inserted into a spatially predictable field of familiar

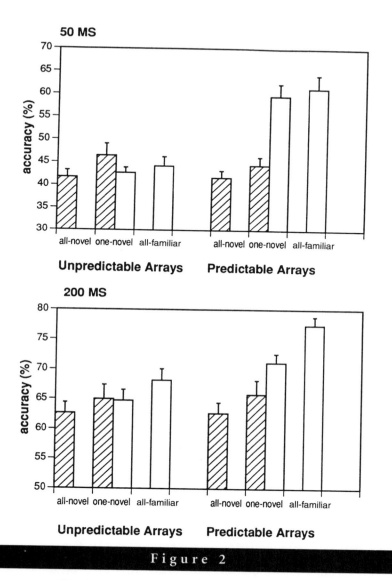

Figure 2

Mean accuracy of localizations of novel and familiar words in the three array compositions for durations of array exposure of 50 ms (upper panel) and 200 ms (lower panel) and for both predictable and unpredictable spatial configurations of the familiar words. Measures of novel word localization are indicated with diagonal-line fill.

321

objects. However, although both novel pop-out and familiar sink-in attained statistically reliable levels, they showed no inclination to be more pronounced for spatially predictable familiar fields (also see Hawley et al., 1994, Experiment 3).

Novel Pop-Out as Attention Capture

Having rejected the possibility that novel pop-out is a phenomenon of directed attention, we now consider the alternative possibility that it is a phenomenon of attention capture. Indeed, we have argued elsewhere that from the perspective of the prevailing conceptual framework, novel pop-out is best interpreted as a phenomenon of attention capture (Johnston & Schwarting, 1995). Observers cannot see all of the items in a brief array and are not encouraged to look for particular targets; they just happen to be particularly likely to see novel singletons in familiar fields. In order for novel singletons to capture attention, the deviant features by which they are defined must, by definition, be preattentively analyzed. But if the deviant features are extracted preattentively, then questions arise as to what kind of features they might be and how their deviance is detected.

The words and other objects that we use in our studies of novel pop-out are randomly assigned to serve the familiar and novel functions, and there are no apparent simple features or feature conjunctions that reliably discriminate between these words. Rather, in addition to their possible semantic properties, novel and familiar objects are likely to be distinguishable only in terms of complex bundles of physical features. This would mean that these bundles would have to be assembled, compared with expectations, and earmarked for potential attentional priority, all within a split second of preattentive analysis.

The implication that preattentive analysis is sophisticated and complex challenges theories, such as feature-integration theory (e.g., Treisman & Gelade, 1980), that delimit preattentive analysis to simple features. However, because the featural differences between our novel and familiar objects were not controlled, one might argue that novel pop-out is attributable to those novel objects that happen to bear distinctive simple features. In a recent series of studies, we tested this possibility by systematically manipulating the featural composition of novel and familiar objects. The first study tested whether simple feature analysis is sufficient to produce novel pop-out. A color-localization task was performed on arrays composed of objects that differed only in terms of the simple feature of color. All-familiar arrays always contained the same four colors, all-novel arrays contained variable combinations of other colors, and one-novel arrays contained three familiar colors and one novel color. As the left-most panel of Figure 3 shows, the full pattern of novel pop-out effects was observed. These findings attest that the analysis of simple features, at least task-relevant ones, is sufficient to produce novel pop-out.

The second study tested whether simple-feature deviancy is necessary to produce novel pop-out. A conjunction-localization task was performed on arrays composed of objects defined by unique conjunctions of five colors, five shapes, and five lengths. Five such conjunctions served as familiar objects and other conjunctions served as novel objects. The all-familiar arrays were composed of a random four of the five familiar objects. The one-novel arrays were composed of three of the five familiar objects and a reconjunction of the features defining the other two familiar objects. Specifically, the color of one these objects was conjoined with

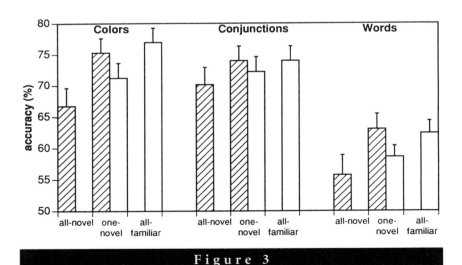

Figure 3

Mean accuracy of localizations of novel and familiar colors (left panel), feature conjunctions (middle panel), and words (right panel) in the three array compositions (array exposure = 200 ms). Measures of novel localizations are indicated with diagonal-line fill.

the shape and length of the other. Thus, all of the simple features composing a novel singleton were familiar, as was the conjunction of shape and length. Only the reconjoined color made the singleton novel. However, color was made irrelevant to the localization task by presenting the probes in a neutral color (white). Nonetheless, as the middle panel of Figure 3 shows, novel pop-out and familiar sink-in were again observed, thereby discrediting the argument that these effects are attributable exclusively to the preattentive analysis of simple features. Not only do novel conjunctions pop out, but they do so even when what is novel about them is irrelevant to the task.

The right-most panel of Figure 3 summarizes the data generated by a comparison study in which our standard word-localization task was performed on the different array types. The novel and familiar words composing these arrays were presumably distinguishable primarily in terms of complex configurations of feature conjunctions and meaning. Although the overall level of localization accuracy was lower in the word-localization study, the full pattern of novel-pop-out effects was again observed. Indeed, the pattern of effects was statistically equivalent across the three panels of Figure 3.

Critique of the Prevailing Framework

In terms of the prevailing conceptual framework, our composite findings indicate that novel pop-out is a phenomenon of attention capture. In turn, the apparent attention-capture power of novel singletons implies that preattentive processing proceeds very rapidly through several levels of physical and semantic analysis, matches the data to expectancies at each level of analysis, and earmarks for the executive any deviations from expectancies. The executive somehow immediately spots any such earmarked inputs and gives them priority entrance into postattentive processing. Indeed, the ability of preattentive processing to carry out such sophisticated computations in such a brief interval of time would seem to obviate much of the need for the executive and its postattentional resources.

In addition to these empirical constraints, Johnston and Hawley (1994) noted that interpretations of novel pop-out in terms of the prevailing framework can be criticized on theoretical grounds alone:

We submit that such ... interpretations of novel pop-out are circular and vacuous. They are circular because they essentially assert that novel objects pop out (i.e., receive more attention) because they receive more attention (i.e., pop out). They are vacuous because they do not explicate the nature of the executive and its resources. ... These "explanations" encounter the same problem of infinite regress that characterizes all appeals to intelligent processing homunculi. The mystery of the big mind is not solved by equipping it with a little mind. (p. 68)

In brief, we suggest that the phenomenon of novel pop-out drives the prevailing conceptual framework into a rather extreme and, perhaps, untenable corner. In order to preserve the idea of attention as a gatekeeping mechanism between preattentive and postattentive processing, we must allow for extremely late loci of selection, assign to preattentive processing the kinds of sophisticated computational abilities that have typically been reserved for postattentive processing, and succumb to the problem of infinite regress by granting the executive its own mysterious attention devices. We suggest that the prevailing conceptual framework has lost its usefulness and needs to be replaced by an approach that makes no appeal to attention as a special device or resource. Our own preliminary attempt to accomplish this goal, called *mismatch theory*, is summarized next.

MISMATCH THEORY
Sketch of the Theory

Mismatch theory was developed to account for the effects associated with novel pop-out and, therefore, for the stability–plasticity dilemma. More detailed descriptions of the theory are provided elsewhere (Hawley, Johnston, & Farnham, 1993; Johnston & Hawley, 1994). The perception of an array of objects is accomplished by the dynamics that unfold across two tiers of nodes: a lower, *iconic* tier and an upper, *conceptual* tier. The iconic tier encodes the physical details of external inputs, and the conceptual tier encodes their meanings. The iconic nodes are interconnected by inhibitory links, and the conceptual nodes are interconnected by excitatory links. The two tiers are interconnected by both bottom-up excitatory links and top-down inhibitory links. The onset of an array of objects launches a spreading of both inhibition and excitation throughout the system. The array-driven excitation of iconic nodes initiates both a lateral inhibition of neighboring iconic nodes and a bottom-up excitation of conceptual nodes. In turn, the excitation of conceptual nodes spreads laterally to associated conceptual nodes and ricochets a proportional volume of inhibition back down to the iconic tier. The effect of this top-down inhibition is to dampen the continued data-driven excitation of the already active conceptual nodes.

The top-down inhibition of iconic nodes is the main innovative feature of mismatch theory. This inhibition is especially pronounced in all-familiar arrays; the massive spreading of excitation across the conceptual nodes representing these arrays reflects a large volume of inhibition downward to the corresponding iconic nodes. Because conceptually driven processing suffices for the accurate perception of these arrays, it more than compensates for the suppressed data-driven processing and is responsible for the baseline advantage of all-familiar arrays. An important by-product of the suppressed data-driven processing of familiar objects is a reduction in the lateral inhibition that they would otherwise deliver to the iconic nodes representing any novel object in their midst. This disinhibition of the iconic nodes representing novel singletons accentuates both the data-driven processing of these objects, yielding novel pop-out, and the lateral inhibition that they radiate to the iconic nodes representing the familiar field objects, contributing to familiar sink-in.[2] Thus, the inhibited data-driven processing of expected objects incurs minimal costs with respect to the perception of unperturbed familiar scenes but affords an important benefit with respect to the perception of novel intrusions.

In order to assess more definitively whether mismatch theory provides a resolution to the stability–plasticity dilemma, Johnston and Hawley (1994) rendered it computationally explicit and ran it through some of our novel pop-out experiments (also see Hawley et al., 1993). Mismatch theory generated the full pattern of effects associated with novel pop-out as well as its robustness across a wide range of durations of array exposure.

In brief, the opposing mental biases are assumed to operate at different levels of perceptual analysis, the bias toward expected inputs at a con-

---

[2]Familiar sink-in is due not only to the lateral inhibition originating from novel singletons but also to the reduced spreading of excitation that results from the absence of one of the familiar items.

ceptual level and that toward unexpected inputs at a physical level. In addition, the two biases are symbiotically interdependent. The top-down inhibitory links render the conceptually driven bias toward expected inputs a precondition for the data-driven bias toward unexpected inputs. Because our familiar habitats are usually as we expect them to be, conceptually driven processing or schematic perception provides a valid and useful representation of these habitats at the same time that it prepares data-driven processing for the detection of any deviations from expectation. Thus, mismatch theory provides an elegant and adaptive solution to the stability–plasticity dilemma; it conceptualizes attention not as a mechanism or a resource but rather as an emergent by-product of ordinary perceptual processing. Attention is defined by, but is not a cause of, selective perceptual processing.

Early Versus Late Selection

In addition, mismatch theory provides a new perspective on some old issues, such as the 40-year battle between early- and late-selection theories of attention. Attention is not conceived of as a discrete transition from preattentive to postattentive processing. Indeed, no distinction is even drawn between these two levels of processing. The amount of "attention" accorded an input is defined in terms of the levels of physical and conceptual processing that it undergoes (i.e., node excitation it engenders). If physical processing is considered early and conceptual processing late, then novel singletons are selected early but familiar field items are selected late, an impossible outcome from the perspective of the prevailing framework. Moreover, the levels of physical and conceptual analyses are dynamically interdependent and highly variable from moment to moment. High levels of conceptual analysis yield low levels of physical analysis, which, in turn, attenuate conceptual analysis, and so on until the system stabilizes (which is unlikely in a normal, fluctuating world). In brief, from the perspective of mismatch theory, the question of the locus of attention is meaningless; it is everywhere and it is nowhere. As William James (1890/1950) suggested,

> Attention may have to go, like many a faculty once deemed essential, like many a verbal phantom, like many an idol of the tribe. . . .
> No need of it to drag ideas before consciousness or fix them, when we see how perfectly they drag and fix each other there. (p. 452)

Mismatch Theory Versus Interactive-Activation Theory

As the quotation above indicates, we are not the first to raise the question of whether attention is best viewed as an epiphenomenon rather than as a causal mechanism. More than 100 years ago, William James (1890/1950) noted that attention can be viewed as an *effect*, rather than *cause*, of selective perceptual processing. In particular, he suggested that attention may be a passive by-product of perceptual priming. For example, he explained how priming can account for the well-known cocktail-party problem:

> We see how we can attend to a companion's voice in the midst of noises which pass unnoticed though objectively much louder than the words we hear. Each word is *doubly* awakened; once from without by the lips of the talker, but already before that from within by the premonitory processes irradiating from the previous words, and by the dim arousal of all processes that are connected with the "topic" of the talk. (p. 450)

The essence of William James's effect theory is retained today in many variants of interactive-activation theory (e.g., McClelland & Rumelhart, 1981; Treisman, 1988; Treisman & Sato, 1990; Wolfe, chap. 8 in this volume). Like mismatch theory, this class of theory appeals to top-down links between higher and lower order nodes. However, in sharp contrast to mismatch theory, interactive-activation theory assumes that these links are excitatory for expected inputs, inhibitory for unexpected inputs, or both. Because interactive-activation theory postulates that both lower and higher levels of perceptual analysis are biased toward expected inputs, it can readily account for facilitatory effects of expectancy but has trouble with inhibitory effects. By contrast, because mismatch theory assumes that the two levels can be differentially biased toward unexpected and expected inputs, it can potentially account for both facilitatory and inhibitory effects of expectancy. Specifically, facilitatory effects can be attributed to higher level, conceptual processing and inhibitory effects to lower level, physical processing. Thus, we suggest that any observed inhibitory effects of expectancy would tend to favor mismatch theory.

EVIDENCE OF PERCEPTUAL INHIBITORY EFFECTS OF EXPECTANCY

A vast empirical literature reveals a net facilitatory effect of input repetition, familiarity, and transitory expectancies. Within the framework of mismatch theory, this net effect of expectancy is attributable to a biasing of most tasks and dependent variables toward conceptually driven processing. However, when these biases favor data-driven processing, the net effect could be one of inhibition. Johnston and Hawley (1994) reviewed a wide range of evidence for inhibitory effects of expectancy, a diagnostic sample of which is summarized below.

Primed Pop-Out

When primed (i.e., expected) and nonprimed items are intermixed in the same very brief display, which kind of item should pop out? Interactive-activation theory clearly predicts that the primed items should pop out because all levels of the perceptual system are biased toward them. Indeed, support for this prediction has recently been reported by Dark and Vochatzer (1992). On the critical trials, observers saw a prime word (e.g., *NIECE*) followed immediately by a briefly exposed two-word array containing both a nonprimed word (e.g., *COSTUME*) and a primed word (e.g., *NEPHEW*). The task was to identify the words. Accuracy of identification was higher for primed words than nonprimed words, indicating primed pop-out.

Although interactive-activation theory readily accommodates primed pop-out, it encounters a serious problem in the apparently contradictory phenomenon of novel pop-out. By contrast, mismatch theory can accommodate both phenomena and resolve the empirical ambiguity. Because conceptual processing is facilitated for expected inputs, primed pop-out is likely to be observed when the tasks and measures are biased toward conceptual processing, as may be the case in Dark and Vochatzer's (1992) item-identification task. By contrast, because data-driven processing is inhibited for expected inputs, primed sink-in is likely to be observed when the tasks and measures are biased relatively more toward data-driven processing, as may be the case in our standard item-localization task. In a recent test of this possibility, we adapted the priming procedures used by

Dark and Vochatzer to our item-localization procedures. Observers performed our standard localization task on a long series of four-word arrays. On occasion, the word that appeared as a probe for a localization response to one array was a prime for one of the words in the next array. Accuracy of localization was reliably *lower* for primed singletons (55%) than for non-primed field words (59%), indicating primed sink-in rather than pop-out (also see DeWitt, 1994). This primed sink-in effect constitutes new evidence for the inhibited data-driven processing of expected inputs and, along with novel pop-out, contradicts interactive-activation theories.

Semantic Priming

In semantic priming, the presentation of a prime word such as *DOCTOR* facilitates the response to an ensuing, individually presented, and semantically related test word such as *NURSE* (for a review, see Neely, 1991). Although semantic priming holds up across a wide range of conditions, one of several important boundary conditions appears to be the conceptual processing of the test word. For example, Besner, Smith, and MacLeod (1990) observed not only the usual facilitatory effect of semantic primes on time to make lexical decisions to test words but also an inhibitory effect on time to decide whether the prime-test pairs had letters in common. These findings support our proposal that conceptual processing (e.g., lexical-decision making) is facilitated for expected inputs but physical processing (e.g., letter matching) is inhibited.

Word-Superiority Effect

The word-superiority effect refers to the higher detectability of a letter (e.g., *D*) when it is presented in the context of a word (e.g., *WORD*) than when it is presented in the same spatial location but by itself (e.g., Reicher, 1969). However, this facilitatory effect of a word context on letter detection appears to be limited to conditions in which the words themselves are presented individually. When the words are imbedded in meaningful passages of text, the detection of their component letters tends to be inhibited (e.g., Healy & Drewnowski, 1983). When words are presented individually so that the contextual constraints between letters prevail over those between words, then the conceptually driven facilitation of letter processing may outweigh any data-driven inhibition. However, when words are presented in the context of a sentence or passage so that the contextual constraints between words prevail, then the conceptually driven processing of the word as a unit may so thoroughly inhibit data-driven processing of its physical details that perception of individual letters is hindered.

Schematic Perception

Schematic perception refers to the automatic, knowledge-aided processing of familiar scenes and meaningful passages of text. For example, explicit memory for the content of ambiguous passages is improved if people are provided in advance with a disambiguating title (Bransford & Johnson, 1972). Again, the usual facilitatory effect of active schemata on conceptual processing may obscure an underlying inhibitory effect on data-driven processing, an effect that might be revealed by a measure more sensitive to data-driven processing. In a test of this possibility, von Hippel, Jonides, Hilton, and Sowmya (1993) examined the effect of a disambiguating title on the implicit, perceptual memory for an ambiguous passage of text. Perceptual memory is known to be more sensitive than explicit memory to the data-driven processing of input information (e.g., Jacoby, 1983). In line with the assumption that schematic perception is accompanied by an inhibition of data-driven processing, a disambiguating title was found to reduce perceptual memory for words from the passage.

Summary of Evidence

In brief, the usual facilitatory effects of expectancy, as exemplified by primed pop-out, semantic priming, the word-superiority effect, and schematic perception, is attributable to the customary use of tasks and measures that are biased toward conceptually driven processing as opposed to data-driven processing. When the tasks and measures are biased more toward data-driven processing, the net effect of expectancy can be inhibitory. These findings are consistent with mismatch theory but not with interactive-activation theory.

GENERAL SUMMARY

Evolution appears to have engineered two very adaptive, but superficially contradictory, mental biases: the bias toward expected inputs and familiar environments, and the bias toward unexpected inputs and novel intrusions. These biases define the stability–plasticity dilemma and are exemplified in the typical pattern of novel pop-out effects. Mismatch theory attributes the former bias to conceptually driven processing and the latter to data-driven processing. A top-down inhibitory link between the two levels of processing renders the two biases dynamically interdependent. The facilitated conceptual processing of expected inputs dampens their physical processing, which in turn disinhibits the physical processing of any unexpected singletons in their midst. The bias toward unexpected inputs is a natural by-product of the bias toward expected inputs. Thus, mismatch theory resolves the stability–plasticity dilemma without appealing to special attention mechanisms or resources. The two horns of the dilemma are conceptualized as emergent phenomena of ordinary perceptual dynamics rather than sophisticated feats performed by an intelligent homunculus.

A diverse prior literature and various findings from our own laboratory support the assumed inhibition of the data-driven processing of expected inputs. This assumption distinguishes mismatch theory from other effect theories of attention (e.g., interactive-activation theory) and renders it uniquely capable of accommodating both facilitatory and inhibitory effects of expectancy. In addition to its theoretical implications, the assumed inhibition of the bottom-up processing of expected inputs has implications for the phenomenology of everyday perception. Because organisms typically inhabit familiar environments, their perceptual experiences of these environments should be more conceptually than data-driven. We may not see the wear marks on our living-room furniture or the signs of age on our reflections in the mirror. To underscore this idea, we close with another quote from William James (1890/1950): "Whilst part of what we perceive comes through our senses . . . another part (*and it may be the larger part*) always comes . . . out of our own head" (p. 747).[3]

REFERENCES

Berlyne, D. (1960). *Conflict, arousal and curiosity.* New York: McGraw-Hill.

Besner, D., Smith, M. C., & MacLeod, C. M. (1990). Visual word recognition: A dis-

---

[3]We are grateful to Endel Tulving for making us aware of this quotation in the context of his review of the article by Johnston and Hawley (1994).

sociation of lexical and semantic processing. *Journal of Experimental Psychology: Learning, Memory, and Cognition, 16*, 862–869.

Biederman, I., Glass, A. L., & Stacy, E. (1973). Searching for objects in real-world scenes. *Journal of Experimental Psychology, 9*, 22–27.

Bransford, J. D., & Johnson, M. K. (1972). Contextual prerequisites for understanding: Some investigations of comprehension and recall. *Journal of Learning and Verbal Behavior, 11*, 717–726.

Campbell, B. A., Hayne, H., & Richardson, R. (1992). *Attention and information processing in infants and adults: Perspectives from human and animal research.* Hillsdale, NJ: Erlbaum.

Cowan, N. (1988). Evolving conceptions of memory storage, selective attention, and their mutual constraints within the human information-processing system. *Psychological Bulletin, 104*, 163–193.

Dark, V. J., & Vochatzer, K. G. (1992, November). *Semantic priming can lead to selective attention.* Paper presented at the 33rd Annual Meeting of the Psychonomic Society, St. Louis, MO.

DeWitt, M. J. (1994). *Attention capture by primed and unprimed stimuli.* Unpublished doctoral dissertation, University of Utah, Salt Lake City.

Farnham, J. M. (1994). *Novel popout: The effect of field familiarity.* Unpublished master's thesis, University of Utah, Salt Lake City.

Friedman, A. (1979). Framing pictures: The role of knowledge in automatized encoding and memory for gist. *Journal of Experimental Psychology: General, 108*, 316–355.

Grossberg, S. (1987). Competitive learning: From interactive activation to adaptive resonance. *Cognitive Science, 11*, 23–63.

Hawley, K. J., Johnston, W. A., & Farnham, J. M. (1993, May). *Mismatch theory of novel popout: A computational model.* Paper presented at the Third West Coast Attention Conference, Eugene, OR.

Hawley, K. J., Johnston, W. A., & Farnham, J. M. (1994). Novel popout with nonsense strings: Effects of object length and spatial predictability. *Perception and Psychophysics, 55*, 261–268.

Healy, A. F., & Drewnowski, A. (1983). Investigating the boundaries of reading units: Letter detection in misspelled words. *Journal of Experimental Psychology: Human Perception and Performance, 9*, 413–426.

Jacoby, L. L. (1983). Remembering the data: Analyzing interactive process in reading. *Journal of Verbal Learning and Verbal Behavior, 22*, 485–508.

Jacoby, L. L., & Dallas, M. (1981). On the relationship between autobiographical memory and perceptual learning. *Journal of Experimental Psychology: General,* *110,* 306–338.

James, W. (1950). *The principles of psychology.* New York: Dover. (Original work published 1890)

Johnston, W. A., & Hawley, K. J. (1994). Perceptual inhibition of expected inputs: The key that opens closed minds. *Psychonomic Bulletin and Review, 1,* 56–72.

Johnston, W. A., Hawley, K. J., & Farnham, J. M. (1993). Novel popout: Empirical boundaries and tentative theory. *Journal of Experimental Psychology: Human Perception and Performance, 19,* 140–153.

Johnston, W. A., Hawley, K. J., Plewe, S. H., Elliott, J. M. G., & DeWitt, M. J. (1990). Attention capture by novel stimuli. *Journal of Experimental Psychology: General,* *119,* 397–411.

Johnston, W. A., & Schwarting, I. S. (1995). *Novel pop-out: An enigma for conventional theories of attention.* Unpublished manuscript.

Loftus, G. R., & Mackworth, N. H. (1978). Cognitive determinants of fixation location during picture viewing. *Journal of Experimental Psychology: Human Perception and Performance, 4,* 565–572.

McClelland, J. L., & Rumelhart, D. E. (1981). An interactive/activation model of context effects in letter perception: Part 1. An account of basic findings. *Psychological Review, 88,* 375–407.

Näätänen, R. (1992). *Attention and brain function.* Hillsdale, NJ: Erlbaum.

Neely, J. H. (1991). Semantic priming effects in visual word recognition: A selective review of current findings and theories. In D. Besner & G. Humphries (Eds.), *Basic processes in reading: Visual word recognition* (pp. 264–336). Hillsdale, NJ: Erlbaum.

Reicher, G. M. (1969). Perceptual recognition as a function of meaningfulness of stimulus material. *Journal of Experimental Psychology, 81,* 275–280.

Shiffrin, R. M., & Schneider, W. (1977). Controlled and automatic human information processing: II. Perceptual learning, automatic attending, and a general theory. *Psychological Review, 84,* 127–190.

Sokolov, E. N. (1963). Higher nervous functions: The orienting reflex. *Annual Review of Psychology, 25,* 545–580.

Treisman, A. M. (1988). Features and objects: The Fourteenth Bartlett Memorial Lecture. *Quarterly Journal of Experimental Psychology, 40*A, 201–237.

Treisman, A. M., & Gelade, G. (1980). A feature-integration theory of attention. *Cognitive Psychology, 12,* 97–136.

Treisman, A. M., & Sato, S. (1990). Conjunction search revisited. *Journal of Experimental Psychology: Human Perception and Performance, 16,* 459–478.

Tulving, E., & Gold, C. (1963). Stimulus information and contextual information as determinants of tachistoscopic recognition of words. *Journal of Experimental Psychology, 66,* 319–327.

von Hippel, W., Jonides, J., Hilton, J. L., & Sowmya, N. (1993). The inhibitory effect of schematic processing on perceptual encoding. *Journal of Personality and Social Psychology, 64,* 921–935.

Warren, R. (1970). Perceptual restoration of missing speech sounds. *Science, 167,* 392–393.

12

Distinguishing Between Inhibition-Based and Episodic Retrieval-Based Accounts of Negative Priming

Steven P. Tipper and Bruce Milliken

Negative priming (NP) is defined by slower responses and/or higher error rates to items that served as distractors in an immediately preceding display. One prominent account of this effect is that it reflects the existence of inhibitory mechanisms of selective attention (Neill, 1977; Tipper, 1985). The logic underlying this account is as follows: If the internal representations of a distractor object are inhibited during response to a target object, then subsequent responses to that distractor may be impaired. Figure 1 shows one way in which this has been demonstrated experimentally. Subjects are asked to identify one of two items, first in a prime display and then in a probe display. If a picture of a trumpet is ignored during a selective response to a picture of a kite in the prime display, then a subsequent response to the picture of a trumpet in the probe display will be slower (Tipper, 1985).

Effects of this sort were first documented in the Stroop task (Dalrymple-Alford & Budayr, 1966; Lowe, 1979; Neill, 1977; Neill & West-

This research was supported by a Natural Science and Engineering Research Council of Canada (NSERC) operating grant awarded to Steve Tipper and by an NSERC postdoctoral fellowship awarded to Bruce Milliken. We would like to thank Bruce Weaver, Jamie Brehaut, and Dan Meegan for their ongoing contributions to this work, and also Gordon Logan for helpful comments on an earlier version of the chapter.

Primes

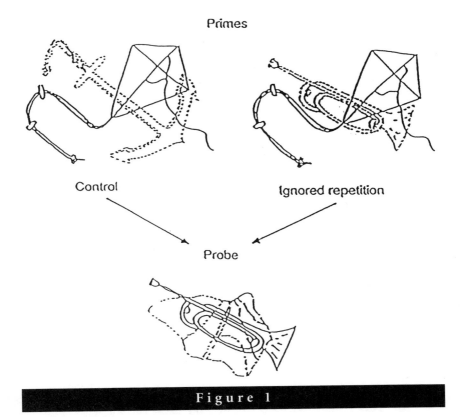

Control

Ignored repetition

Probe

Figure 1

Sample displays from a study demonstrating negative priming. Subjects were required to name the red object (solid line) while ignoring a green distractor (broken line). In the control prime display the target and distractor were unrelated to the subsequent target probe, but in the ignored repetition condition the ignored prime was the same identity as the subsequent probe. Reaction time to name the probe target was longer after the ignored repetition than after the control prime display: This constitutes the negative priming effect.

berry, 1987) but have since also been shown in tasks requiring identification of overlapping letters (Allport, Tipper, & Chmiel, 1985; Tipper & Cranston, 1985), identification of overlapping pictures (Allport et al., 1985; Tipper, 1985), same–different matching tasks (Neill, Lissner, & Beck, 1990), and spatial localization tasks (Tipper, Brehaut, & Driver, 1990), to name just a few.

The NP literature has grown steadily over the past decade, due in part to its generalizability to a wide assortment of experimental tasks, and in part to the burgeoning of research that has studied NP in clinical and developmental populations. It has been shown that children (Tipper, Bourque, Anderson, & Brehaut, 1989), elderly people (Hasher, Stoltzfus, Zacks, & Rypma, 1991; Tipper, 1991; but see Kramer, Humphrey, Larish, & Logan, 1994; Sullivan & Faust, 1993), schizophrenic patients (Beech, Powell, McWilliam, & Claridge, 1989), patients with Alzheimer's disease (Mueller & Baylis, 1994), and depressed patients (Benoit et al., 1992) are often less efficient at selecting target items (i.e., they show more interference in prime display responses) and also tend to show less NP than an appropriate control group. These differences between populations have been attributed to deficits in inhibitory mechanisms of selective attention for the clinical and aged populations.

Because theories of cognitive functioning within these populations are now being developed through the use of NP procedures, the validity of the claim that NP reflects the operation of an inhibitory mechanism is quite important. Note that the existence of NP is consistent with the notion of an inhibitory selective attention mechanism but does not imply such a mechanism. This observation suggests that it would be worthwhile to evaluate the alternatives.

AN ALTERNATIVE TO THE DISTRACTOR INHIBITION HYPOTHESIS

Recently, Neill and his colleagues (Neill & Valdes, 1992; Neill, Valdes, Terry, & Gorfein, 1992) proposed an account of NP that explicitly rejects the notion that NP reflects an inhibitory mechanism of selection. They suggested that a target stimulus in a probe display cues the retrieval of previous processing episodes involving the same stimulus in a prime display (e.g., Logan, 1988). If the retrieved stimulus was recently ignored, retrieval of that processing episode may interfere with current response selection. Neill et al. (1992) described this notion as follows:

> If processing episodes include information about ignored stimuli as well as attended stimuli, then the response to a stimulus would probably be hampered by retrieving an episode in which a similar stimulus was ignored. Interference [NP] might result from competition between the correct response and some form of non-response en-

coded in the retrieved episode. Alternatively, the lack of appropriate response information in the retrieved episode might force reliance on the slower, controlled processing algorithm. (p. 997)

One of the central claims of this model is that "if NP is caused by the retrieval of an episode in which the current target stimulus was ignored, then negative priming cannot be assumed to directly index the processing that occurred during the priming trial [prime display]" (Neill et al., 1992, p. 998).

The purpose of this chapter is to contrast episodic retrieval and inhibition-based accounts of NP. We start this process by noting a rudimentary similarity between the two models. Both inhibition- and episodic retrieval-based models posit that NP occurs because response to a probe display requires access to an internal representation of an object that is ignored in a prime display. Having noted this similarity, the differences between the two models revolve around why this access requirement leads to poor performance relative to an appropriate baseline condition. According to Neill et al.'s (1992) episodic account, NP occurs because access to an episodic representation that contains prime response information (a "do-not-respond" tag) interferes with the probe response. By such an account, NP should be large when prime display representations are highly accessible, and therefore retrievable. On the other hand, an inhibition-based account assumes that NP reflects the poorer than normal accessibility of prime display representations.

The rest of this chapter focuses on a wide body of evidence that must be considered in order to evaluate these two models. Two particular relevant areas of research deal with the time course (or persistence) of NP and with the relationship between distractor interference in the prime display and NP. These two topics are considered in some detail in the following two sections. In a third section, we consider a host of other relevant research findings. We conclude by entertaining the possibility that both episodic and inhibitory processes play a role in NP.

THE TIME COURSE OF NEGATIVE PRIMING

One of the empirical issues that most directly addresses the distinction between inhibitory and episodic accounts of NP is the nature of its decay across time. Most inhibitory models predict that NP should decay fairly quickly. Indeed, Houghton and Tipper (1994) have recently proposed a neural network model in which inhibition associated with an ignored distractor does decay over a fairly short period of time following offset of the prime stimulus. Several behavioral studies have shown this effect as well. In particular, Neill and Westberry (1987) showed that NP in the Stroop task disappears within 2 s of the response to the prime stimulus (see also Banks & Roberts, in press; Neumann & Hood, 1993).

However, a number of other observations question the generality of this relatively rapid decay. First, using both a spatial localization task and an object identification task, Tipper, Weaver, Cameron, Brehaut, and Bastedo (1991) observed NP up to 6 s following response to the prime. Furthermore, this effect did not disappear when another stimulus requiring a response was presented during the prime–probe response stimulus interval (RSI; see also Hasher et al., 1991). Even more dramatically, De-Schepper and Treisman (1991) have reported NP over periods of minutes. An important aspect of the procedure used by DeSchepper and Treisman was that subjects performed a same–different matching task with meaningless shapes they had not previously seen. These unique experimental conditions appear to have played an important role in the long-term nature of the NP that was observed, because unpublished studies in our laboratory (Wilson, 1992) consistently failed to show NP effects with lags between the prime and probe displays in excess of 7 s.

Hence, when there are not multiple representations associated with distractor items to obscure the specific nature of an episodic code, retrieval of episodic information appears to play a role in determining NP. Moreover, the NP that results from this episodic retrieval appears to survive a substantial time lag between the prime and probe displays. This observation is not consistent with a model of NP that relies on analogy to the transient effects of inhibition at the level of the neuron, and perhaps serves as an impetus to consider a model of NP that depends on the retrieval of episodic information created at the time the prime distracting item is ignored.

A second, and more intricate, property of the time course of NP has also been offered as evidence in favor of an episodic retrieval account of NP. Neill et al. (1992) demonstrated that NP is more likely to decline with increasing prime–probe RSI if RSI is manipulated within rather than between subjects. As a result, they concluded that recency of the prime display to the probe display alone does not determine the decay of NP. Following Baddeley (1976), they suggested that retrieval of an episodic memory trace, and thus NP, depends both on recency and on discriminability of that trace.

This observation led Neill et al. (1992) to vary the RSI between the prime and probe display of one trial (the current trial) independently of the RSI between the current prime display and the previous probe display (PRSI). They reasoned that if better discriminability of the prime episode leads to better retrieval of that episode, and if NP is determined by retrieval of the prime episode, then NP should be greatest under conditions in which the RSI is short and the PRSI is long. Indeed, the data of Neill et al., displayed in Table 1, suggest that this is the case. At both the 500-ms and 4,000-ms RSIs, NP was larger when the PRSI was 4,000 ms than when it was 500 ms (39 vs. 26 ms for 500-ms RSI; 20 vs. 14 ms for 4,000-ms RSI). Presumably, these effects are due to the better discriminability of the prime episode from other recent events when the PRSI is 4,000 ms. If distractor inhibition is the sole mechanism responsible for NP, then there is no reason for PRSI to have such an effect. As such, an account in which episodic retrieval plays a role in determining NP appears to handle these data more easily.

To summarize, there are two results related to the time course of NP that are consistent with an episodic retrieval account of NP but that appear difficult to reconcile with an inhibition-based account of NP. The most provocative is that of NP effects observed across periods of minutes (DeSchepper & Treisman, 1991). The other result was reported by Neill and colleagues and showed that the discriminability of the prime episode from the previous probe episode modulates NP.

RELATIONSHIP BETWEEN INTERFERENCE AND NEGATIVE PRIMING

The core argument of the episodic view is that NP does not reflect directly the processes that are engaged during selection of the prime target. The relationship between NP and processing in the prime is an indirect one because NP begins with the process of retrieval of the prime distractor. To the extent that this retrieval is successful, the do-not-respond information that is associated with the prime becomes available and interferes with the ability to respond correctly to the probe. Thus, NP is primarily dependent on the success of a process, the temporal genesis of which corresponds to the onset of the probe display. However, the success of retrieval of the prime distractor will depend on the success of encoding of that distractor. Thus, episodic retrieval models of NP appear to predict that the relationship between prime interference and NP should be positive. The more intrusive is a prime distractor, the more likely it is to be encoded and thus later retrieved.

An inhibition-based model also handles a positive relation between interference and NP quite naturally. That is, as distractors become more intrusive, more inhibition must be directed toward them so that selection remains efficient. Indeed, Houghton and Tipper (1994) have developed a connectionist model that produces a positive relation between NP and interference in the following way. The differential activation of the prime target and distractor is achieved in part by active suppression of the distractor. This inhibitory process acts as a counterbalance against the bottom-up excitatory effect attributable to the physical presence of the stimulus. Upon offset of the prime stimulus, the inhibition directed toward the distractor no longer has an excitatory counterforce. As a result, an inhibitory rebound occurs, during which the activation level of the distractor does fall below its resting level. Clearly, for more intrusive prime distractors a stronger inhibitory process is required to allow efficient selection of the prime target. A consequence of this stronger inhibitory process will be a stronger inhibitory rebound, and hence a larger NP effect.

In summary, then, both episodic and inhibition-based models of NP predict that a positive relation between prime interference and NP can occur. Indeed, a positive relationship between interference and NP has been observed in a number of studies (Fuentes & Tudela, 1992; Houghton, Tipper, Weaver, & Shore, 1995; Meegan & Tipper, 1995; Milliken, Tipper, & Weaver, 1994; Neill, Valdes, & Terry, 1995; Tipper, Lortie, & Baylis, 1992). For example, Houghton et al. (1995) observed that as they made a distractor more salient by increasing its brightness, both interference and NP increased.

However, negative relationships between interference and inhibition can also be observed. In particular, the results of a large number of studies with clinical and developmental populations (e.g., schizophrenic and elderly people) suggest that subjects who are especially inefficient selectors (as evidenced by large distractor interference effects) also tend to show smaller than normal NP effects. Several results of this nature have been observed (Fox, 1995; McDowd & Oseas-Kreger, 1991; Tipper, 1991; Tipper & Baylis, 1987; Tipper et al., 1989). Other studies have shown that more efficient subjects (fast responders) appear to show greater NP effects (Driver & Baylis, 1993; Fox, 1995; Neumann & DeSchepper, 1992). These results are consistent with the notion that an inhibitory mechanism may be responsible for efficient selection of the prime target and that when this mechanism is not working optimally, prime interference will be large and NP small.

The Houghton and Tipper (1994) model accommodates negative relationships between interference and negative priming quite naturally. With any given task requiring selection, more time is required to select the prime target without an inhibitory mechanism than with one. Thus, large interference effects are predicted when inhibitory mechanisms are disabled. However, without an inhibitory mechanism acting on the prime distractor, an inhibitory rebound will not occur. Instead, the internal representation of the prime distractor will fall back to a resting level of activity in a passive manner. Because it is the inhibitory rebound that causes a below-resting activation level for the distractor (and thus also causes NP), large interference effects and small NP effects are natural consequences of a disabled inhibitory mechanism.

An episodic retrieval model, on the other hand, would account for negative relationships between interference and NP somewhat more awkwardly. Lack of NP can mean that either the prime distractor was not tagged as an item to be ignored or that a prime distractor was appropriately encoded but was not retrieved. However, the fact that poor selectors tend to show more interference in responding to the prime display may constrain such accounts. If it follows that larger interference effects reflect increased intrusiveness of distractors, then it also follows that the likelihood of explicitly encoding the prime distractor as an item to be ignored should be higher rather than lower when interference is large. Thus, it is reasonable to assume that large prime interference effects are accompanied by a more robust representation of the to-be-ignored character of the prime distractor. This being the case, if larger than normal interference effects are accompanied by smaller than normal NP effects, then it must be argued that deficits in retrieval are so profound as to outweigh potential benefits of having better encoded the prime distractor.

Although it is not unfathomable, we view this account of a negative relation between interference and NP as more cumbersome than one based on distractor inhibition. At the same time, inhibition-based models also encounter difficulties when trying to account for all of the observed relations between interference and NP. In particular, there have been several reports of no relation between interference and NP (e.g., Allport et al., 1985, Experiments 6–8; Driver & Tipper, 1989). Together with the already described positive and negative relationships, the observation of independence between interference and NP completes a list containing all possible relationships.

Why might so much inconsistency exist in the answer to what seems a very simple question? We cannot answer this question from the standpoint of Neill et al.'s (1992) episodic retrieval account of NP, because it is not sufficiently specified. However, two possible explanations for the complex nature of the relation between interference and NP, from an inhibition point of view, are discussed below.

First, to see a strong relationship between interference and NP, one must assume that inhibition is the primary, and perhaps only, mechanism of selection. Clearly, this is unlikely. The selective attention literature was founded on the notion of an excitatory selective mechanism. Inhibitory processes are not meant to replace those of excitation but to complement them. So, from the distractor inhibition perspective, selection is achieved both by directing excitatory processing to the internal representations of target items and by directing inhibitory processing to internal representations of distractor items. Thus, efficient selection can be maintained by increasing the activity of either inhibitory or excitatory mechanisms of selection.

Although it can be argued that a dual-mechanisms model of selection is unparsimonious, there are two reasons why such a model may be essential (see also Houghton & Tipper, 1994). First, any amplifying or inhibitory mechanism functioning in biological (neural) hardware must operate within finite limits. Thus, the rate at which one signal can be boosted relative to another stable signal must have some finite upper bound. It is noteworthy, then, that a dual mechanism that can excite a target and inhibit a distractor signal in parallel can double the rate at which target and distractor can be separated. Such rapid selection is clearly vital for inter-actions with complex, and often dangerous, environments. A second rea-son for dual mechanisms of selection is that signals in a biological infor-mation-processing system must have a limited dynamic range—maximum and minimum amplitudes. Therefore, if two very intense stimuli were pres-ent, neural responses to them would be close to the maximum firing rates for those cells. Thus, selection with only an excitation mechanism would be difficult. On the other hand, two very weak stimuli close to threshold may not be easily separated by a single inhibition mechanism. Of course, two mechanisms (excitation and inhibition) working in parallel would al-ways be able to separate target and distractor signals, regardless of the neural firing rate.

Furthermore, in the model of Houghton and Tipper (1994), a clear relationship between interference and NP can be quite elusive. The model postulates that weights in both the excitation and inhibition feedback sys-tems are independent, therefore subtle changes in the neurotransmitters that control them can conceivably affect one system only. This is particu-larly important in considering that biological systems are inherently noisy, with levels-of-processing efficiency varying in a phasic fashion. Now con-sider that prime interference can be conceptualized as depending on the joint efficiency of two mechanisms: excitation and inhibition. Fluctuation in the efficiency of the excitation mechanism will make it very difficult to observe a consistent relationship between interference and a behavioral measure such as negative priming that depends only on the efficiency of the inhibitory mechanism. Indeed, in one simulation (Houghton & Tip-per, 1994) the excitation feedback weights were allowed to fluctuate. With this added noise in the selection process, systematic changes in the level of inhibition could not be observed in the model's responses. Clearly, with all other factors held constant, increased inhibition must have led to more rapid suppression of distractors, and thus also to less interference. How-ever, when excitation directed to the target was not fixed, the joint occur-rence of decreased excitation and increased inhibition often led to im-paired selection. Thus, it is not inconsistent with an excitation–inhibition model of selection that, under some conditions, prime interference may increase despite an increase in inhibition.

The second point is somewhat more complex and has previously been made by Sullivan and Faust (1993). This argument is presented in two parts for clarity. First, consider that only properties of distracting items that compete for control of overt behavior may be subject to inhibition. For example, when a person is identifying objects, it is semantic properties that control overt behavior, and it is specifically these properties of the distractor that compete for the control of action. An efficient inhibitory mechanism, therefore, would limit inhibitory processing to these goal-relevant properties (see Tipper, Weaver, & Houghton, 1994).

Support for such a view comes from a variety of laboratories. De-Schepper and Treisman (1991) demonstrated that when subjects match meaningless shapes, NP can be associated with the perceptual properties of a distractor and not with semantic or response representations (see also Neill et al., 1990). In contrast, Tipper and Driver (1988) showed that when subjects categorize objects, NP is associated with semantic properties of the distractor and not with perceptual or response properties. Finally, Tipper et al. (1992) showed that when subjects reach for objects, NP is associated with action-based rather than perceptual or semantic representations (see also Milliken et al., 1994). Tipper et al. (1994) speculated that inhibition may function in different cortical structures depending on behavioral goals: Extrastriate cortex when responding to perceptual structure, inferior temporal lobe when identifying or categorizing, and parietal-frontal regions when reaching directly for objects.

Now, consider also that the measure of interference that is compared with NP can in many cases be attributed to interference at multiple levels of representation. For example, when identifying a target, low-level perceptual processes triggered by the onset of a distractor could interfere with selection of a target over and above the interference produced by the distractor's semantic properties. Clearly, if a measure of distractor interference is determined, at least in part, by levels of representation that are unaffected by an inhibitory mechanism, then the relation between interference and NP will be less than perfect. In the extreme, these two measures may even be dissociable from one another. In a later section we describe one such dissociation (Meegan & Tipper, 1995).

A considerable portion of this chapter has been devoted to a discussion of the relationship between interference and NP. As discussed, much work has been done in this area, but the data as a whole appear quite contradictory. However, these apparent contradictions are comprehensible when the complexity of the selection process is taken into account. First, there may be both positive and negative relationships between interference and NP. Which of the two occurs in a given situation may depend on whether the task exhausts the inhibitory resources of the subject being tested. Second, both facilitatory and inhibitory mechanisms are almost certainly involved in the selection process. This complexity leaves much room for freedom in the relationship between interference and NP. Third, we believe it likely that inhibition is directed to specific internal representations, whereas interference may be produced by a variety of different levels of representation. Hence, the relationship between interference and NP may be masked by interference effects that reflect competition at a different level of representation than the one that is the target of inhibition.

EXPERIMENTAL TESTS OF THE INHIBITION AND EPISODIC ACCOUNTS

Having read to this point in the chapter, the reader may have come to the conclusion that although episodic retrieval models are not sufficiently specified to account for the wide range of relationships between interference and NP, such models suffer more from immaturity than from inaccuracy. In contrast, inhibition-based models of NP are more highly specified (i.e., Houghton & Tipper, 1994), and thereby provide concrete explanations for many of the empirical phenomena that proved troublesome for early and simpler notions of distractor inhibition. Conceivably, an episodic retrieval model can also be molded to account for the various details of the NP literature. However, the following section presents a number of experimental findings that may be difficult to accommodate in subsequent specifications of an episodic retrieval model.

Interference Without Negative Priming

In a recent study by Meegan and Tipper (1995), subjects were asked to reach for and depress target keys adjacent to red lights while ignoring distractors adjacent to yellow lights. It had been shown previously (Tipper et al., 1992) that the interference produced in this task depends on the spatial relationship between the distractors and the responding hand. Distractors nearest and ipsilateral to the responding hand produce more interference, and more NP, than distractors in other locations.

In the Meegan and Tipper (1995) study the difficulty of the reach toward one of the distractors was manipulated. In one situation, depicted in Figure 2A, action was simple and direct; in another, an occluding transparent surface was placed between the distractor and the responding hand (see Figure 2B). This made reaches to that object much more complex, and hence slower. The model developed by Meegan and Tipper proposes a race between stimuli for the control of action. Stimuli that evoke simple and quickly computed actions interfere more than those that evoke action that is complex and slowly computed. Thus, if NP reflects an inhibitory mechanism that prevents action from being directed to objects that evoke conflicting responses, then NP should be positively related to the amount of interference produced by that distractor. For example, in the case of a distractor at the occluded location, a relatively slowly developing competing response should lead to less interference, and thus also to less NP.

It is not clear what an episodic retrieval account of NP would predict for the relation between interference and NP in the occluded and unoccluded conditions. It is possible that encoding of an occluded location as a distractor would be more complete than that for an unoccluded location, given that it is an oddball relative to the other three locations. If this were the case, then one might expect more NP for occluded than unoccluded locations. We cannot rule out the possibility that an episodic retrieval model could account for other patterns of results, but, as mentioned previously, at present there is not an episodic retrieval model that is sufficiently specified that this can be done in an a priori manner.

At any rate, the results of the study demonstrated clearly that interference was reduced when the distractor appeared at an occluded location. This finding supports a race or continuous flow model, in which the complexity of an action toward a distracting item determines how intrusive that distractor is. Also, a positive relationship between interference and NP was observed. That is, where interference was high (no-occlusion condition), NP was obtained. On the other hand, when interference was reduced (occlusion condition), not only was NP not observed, but positive priming was produced.

It is not clear how an episodic retrieval model would account for such a result. Although the interference effect was reduced when the distractor was occluded, it remained significant. Therefore, there should still have been incompatible response information associated with the retrieved

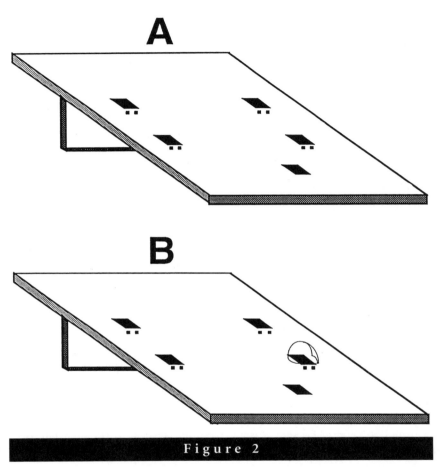

Figure 2

An example of the displays used by Meegan and Tipper (1995). The important object is in the near-right location relative to the starting position of the responding right hand. In Panel A the near-right object is not occluded. Rapid responses can be made to this object, and, as a result, it interferes substantially with response to other objects. Meegan and Tipper suggested that this action is actively inhibited, as evidenced by significant negative priming effects. Panel B represents the displays where a transparent occluder was placed over the near-right object. This occluder had the effect of making the response to depress the key at that location much more complex. Note that the hand has to detour around the obstructing surface while maintaining the availability of the crucial visual information (key and red and yellow lights). Interference by the near-right object is reduced in this occlusion condition because this distractor loses the race for the control of action. Even more striking, negative priming is no longer observed; in fact, reaches to the near-right object were faster when it was ignored on the previous trial.

prime episode, and that incompatible information should have impaired response to the subsequent probe target.

On the other hand, an inhibition-based model explains these results by reference to a point made earlier. There, it was mentioned that relationships between interference and NP may be obscured because the two effects may be determined at different levels of representation. It is possible that NP is determined by the behavioral goal of moving the hand to depress the target key. That is, inhibition may have been associated specifically with action-based representations. With that in mind, there may have been no need to inhibit an action-based representation of the distractor in the occlusion condition because the action toward the target was prohibitively more likely to win the race to gain control of the response. In fact, it appears that the distractor was encoded and remained active, thus facilitating subsequent probe display responses.

At the same time, the interference effect of the occluded distractor may have been produced by earlier perceptual processes. Thus, when the target appeared alone, rapid detection of target onset by the transient visual system may have been sufficient to initiate action. In contrast, when this transient system detected onset of stimulation in two positions, further processing was required to identify which item was the target. The sustained system, which is capable of processing color, may then have been charged with the task of distinguishing which object was red and which yellow. Thus, it is likely that responses were slower in the selection situation because of early perceptual analysis that occurred before response selection began. In this way, the occurrence of interference effects due to very early perceptual analysis is not inconsistent with the co-occurrence of facilitatory priming.

Internally Versus Externally Generated Selection

Other research approaches have also confirmed the link between selection demands and the use of inhibitory mechanisms. Experiments by Baylis and Tipper (1995) manipulated whether selection was internally or externally generated. In a typical NP study, the target may be specified for the subject on the basis of its color. For example, subjects may be asked to identify the red item and ignore the green item. This type of selection can be labeled as externally generated. However, it is possible to have subjects perform tasks that are similar but in which selection is generated internally. That is, subjects can be left free to decide which of two objects will be the target. In the Baylis and Tipper study, two letters, such as *B* and *D*, were presented. Subjects were required to report the location of either one of these letters in the first display (the prime display). However, they were also asked to note which letter they chose and to continue selectively locating that letter in subsequent displays. Thus, internally generated selection characterized their response to the prime display, and externally generated selection their response to following displays.

The data from the Baylis and Tipper (1995) experiments suggest that selection was slower and that subjects had greater awareness of the distractor's identity when selection was internally generated. Interestingly, only with external selection was NP obtained. It appears that internally generated selection was much less efficient, leading distractors to be analyzed to a much deeper level. If selection took place only after such lengthy analysis, it follows that even if inhibition were used to aid in selection, such inhibition could not overcome the facilitatory advantage afforded by attentive processing.

It is interesting to note what might be predicted by an episodic retrieval theory of NP in this case. If NP is determined by the retrieval of incompatible response information, surely that information would be more available after more lengthy, attentive encoding of the distractor. However, NP is not observed under such selection conditions. Clearly, this is a result that is difficult to reconcile with the notion that NP is determined by the retrieval of response information from the prime display.

Effects From Other Priming Conditions

Recent experiments investigating the changes in inhibitory control processes associated with aging have also questioned whether episodic models can completely replace inhibition accounts. Kane, Hasher, Stoltzfus, Zacks, and Connelly (1994) raised both theoretical and empirical objections to episodic theories. Following Logan's (1988) instance theory of automatization, they suggested that in tasks in which an object can be both a target and distractor, as is the case in many NP tasks, retrieval of individual traces should provide little useful information, and so they should be ignored, even if automatically retrieved.

Their empirical evidence arises from other priming conditions that should also produce a marked priming effect if prior episodes are retrieved. For example, trials in which a target in the prime display is presented as a distractor in the subsequent probe display should be responded to slowly relative to baseline. This slowing would be due to the mismatch between response information for a to-be-ignored probe object that retrieves a prime object to be named. In fact, the opposite pattern of results was obtained: Responses were faster in this situation rather than slower relative to baseline. Kane et al. (1994) went on to argue that if the failure to observe NP in older adults is due to failure to retrieve prior episodes, and if, somehow, episodic mechanisms produced the facilitation in the target-to-distractor condition, then elderly people should also show no effect in this latter condition. However, they produce facilitation that is equivalent to that in young adults.

Kane et al. (1994) suggested that these results, taken together, question the episodic account of NP. In particular, if episodic theory were adapted to account for both the impaired responses on distractor-to-target trials and the facilitation observed on target-to-distractor trials, it still could not account for the fact that older subjects show only one of these patterns of data. They concluded the following: "Thus, the data from older adults helps to suggest that the slowdown young adults show here (and throughout a large literature) for trials on which the new target had been the previous distractor is indeed due to an inhibitory mechanism, one which, for older adults, is clearly impaired" (Kane et al., 1994, p. 111).

Similarity Between Prime and Probe Displays

According to an episodic retrieval account, one might expect retrieval of the prime episode to depend on the similarity of the prime display to the probe display. Indeed, this argument has been used to account for the finding that, in many experimental situations, for NP effects to be observed it is necessary for selection processes to be engaged in the probe display (Lowe, 1979; Maxfield, 1992; Moore, 1994; Tipper & Cranston, 1985; Tipper et al., 1990). Neill et al. (1992) suggested that the presence or absence of a distractor could influence the contextual similarity of a probe trial to a preceding prime trial. Hence, when the probe does not contain a distractor it may be sufficiently different from the preceding

Table 1

Mean Response Times to Probe Displays in Experiment 1 of
Neill, Valdes, Terry, and Gorfein (1992)

PRSI/RSI (ms)	Related	Unrelated	Difference (priming effect)
500/500	511	485	26
500/4,000	498	484	14
4,000/500	529	490	39
4,000/4,000	501	481	20

NOTE: RSI = response–stimulus interval; PSRI = RSI between the prime display and the preceding probe display.

prime (which does contain a distractor), that it becomes a less effective retrieval cue.

In contrast, Tipper and Cranston (1985) suggested that inhibitory mechanisms leave the representation of an ignored item in an active state but block access of response systems to that active representation. By their account it is not the similarity between the prime and probe display that leads to NP, but the requirement that selection take place in the probe display. Tipper and Cranston proposed that when probe selection is required, the selection state adopted in the prime display is maintained to cope with probe display selection. A consequence of this maintained selection state is that the process blocking the ignored distractor from response mechanisms stays in place for the probe display, thus causing NP.

To the uninitiated, it may appear that there is little to distinguish between Tipper and Cranston's (1985) blocking account of NP and Neill et al.'s (1992) episodic retrieval model of NP. However, in Neill et al.'s model, NP occurs when retrieval of the prime distractor's representation is successful. Subsequent interference with prime display response information that is part of the retrieved prime display representation leads directly to the NP effect. In contrast, the blocking mechanism proposed by Tipper and Cranston was not implied to be a property of the prime representation itself. Rather, it was meant to be an active cognitive process that prevents access to a primed representation. When this process is relaxed, as might be the case when the probe display does not require selection, an underlying positively primed representation is revealed. Thus, whereas an episodic retrieval model presumes that NP occurs as a result of an accessible prime display representation that interferes with response, Tipper and Cranston's response-blocking account presumes that NP occurs because the prime distractor's representation is available but inaccessible.

Both recent and past data cast doubt on the notion that the similarity of the prime and probe display episodes determines whether NP occurs. First, Moore (1994) showed that if trials are introduced to the probe task in which a single object is presented but no response is required, then NP can be obtained for a no-selection probe item. Clearly, a model proposing that retrieval of the prior episode may not be possible when the displays are different (target and distractor vs. target alone) cannot account for such a result. On the other hand, the original interpretation of Tipper and Cranston (1985) may be able to explain such data. That is, an inhibitory block may be maintained when there are no-go trials included in the session, so that action can be prevented to lone distractor objects.

A second set of data that is awkward to account for in terms of a prime–probe similarity argument are those of Tipper and Driver (1988). They demonstrated NP when subjects ignored pictures of objects and then categorized semantically related words. These data test the limits of the notion that NP is caused by the retrieval of episodes, with the retrieval itself being triggered by the onset of the same stimulus that was ignored in the prime display. An episodic theory can be made more flexible by arguing that the probe target retrieves similar as well as identical episodes. Indeed, Logan's (1988) instance theory suggests that the retrieval of prior episodes can be based on abstract representations. However, this approach raises other problems for the episodic account of NP. That is, Logan proposed that the information that is included in instances is that which is subject to attention. However, attention is not directed at the ignored distractor in the prime display in a negative priming trial. Furthermore, ignored objects in many NP studies cannot be recalled immediately after presentation and do not appear to enter awareness (e.g., Tipper, 1985). It remains an open issue whether episodes of the type proposed by Logan can be created for unattended stimuli, and thus also whether NP can be accounted for by retrieval of such episodes.

Time Course of Negative Priming (Revisited)

As noted earlier, observation of relatively long-term NP has been suggested to support the notion that some form of episodic retrieval plays a role in determining NP. However, many models of higher level processes propose decay to be an exponential process. If the decay of inhibition is exponential, then in theory one would expect inhibition to dissipate completely only at infinity (we thank Gordon Logan for pointing this out). Therefore, long-term NP need not be incompatible with an inhibition account. More generally, as long as NP decreases monotonically with increasing lag, we lack the kind of evidence necessary to distinguish between episodic retrieval and inhibition-based models of NP.

We also reported earlier the results of a study by Neill et al. (1992) in which it is claimed that the magnitude of NP changes solely by virtue of the discriminability of the prime display episode from the previous probe display episode. We are referring here to an experiment in which the RSI between the previous probe display and the present prime display (PRSI) is manipulated independently of that between the present prime and probe display (RSI). However, careful inspection of the Neill et al. data suggests an alternative explanation. To show that the smaller NP for shorter PRSI is directly due to the PRSI manipulation, it is also necessary to show that changing the PRSI did not have any spurious effect on other aspects of prime display processing. That is, Neill et al.'s conclusion that NP is directly affected by PRSI, and therefore must reflect the success of retrieval operations, makes the assumption that processing of the prime display itself is equivalent for PRSIs of 500 and 4,000 ms. This assumption is crucial in this context to show that NP does not reflect the success of selection processes acting on the prime display, a position favored by an inhibition account of NP. Instead, if reduced NP with shorter PRSI were accompanied by less efficient prime selection, the results of Neill et al. (1992) would be quite comfortably accounted for by a model proposing inhibitory selection processes.

In fact, although NP was reduced in the short PRSI condition, it does appear that there was less efficient selection of a target following short interdisplay intervals. This difference was reflected both in longer response times (504 ms vs. 491 ms) and higher error rates (2.1% vs. 1.4%) for responses following a 500-ms RSI than for responses following a 4,000-ms

RSI.[1] Thus, it is conceivable that the relatively short interval between the previous probe display and the prime display led subjects to engage in selection at a later point in processing (because of less than optimal alertness, for example). Accordingly, the prime distractor may have been analyzed in more detail with the shorter PRSI, thus leading to less NP. Therefore, although it is interesting, unless the Neill et al. (1992) result can be observed in situations in which processing in the prime display is kept constant across two conditions, differences between those two conditions cannot be attributed solely to retrieval processes.

One final property of the time course of NP also presents a problem for Neill et al.'s (1992) episodic retrieval model. Banks and Roberts (in press) showed recently that in an auditory NP task, as the interval between prime and probe increased, NP turned into positive priming. Neill et al.'s episodic model may predict that it becomes harder to retrieve the prime episode as the interval between prime and probe increases, but it does not predict that the representation should change such that the no-response tag is lost. Together with other results reported here, this reversal in the priming effect with increasing interval between the prime and probe points out an area in which further specification of an episodic retrieval model is required.

INTEGRATING EPISODIC AND INHIBITORY MODELS?

The vast range and complexity of observations reported here makes any single-mechanism account of NP very unlikely. Long-term NP effects suggest that, under certain conditions, a stable episodic code is involved. However, other data appear better accounted for by the action of inhibitory mechanisms. In fact, Milliken et al. (1994) have shown quite clearly that within a single experimental procedure, at least two completely different processes can produce NP. One of these processes appears to be an inhibitory one, and the other a review of prior processing episodes, not un-

---

[1] In the method used by Neill et al. (1992), a single display served as both a probe for the previous display and a prime for the following display. Because of this, the only comparison that they reported that was relevant to our argument was that of the main effect of RSI. This is what is reported above. It is our understanding that these RSIs actually served both as RSIs and PRSIs, in the terminology of Neill et al.

like that proposed in the episodic theory of Neill et al. (1992; see also Park & Kanwisher, 1994).

Thus, it appears that the question as to what mechanism underlies NP does not have a simple answer. We suggest that it should not be surprising that the field of NP has become so complex. Relative to many other experimental procedures used to study attention, the requirement to respond to a prime–probe display sequence encompasses a much larger chunk of the human repertoire. Indeed, we are trying to explain not just selective behavior (attention) and not just sequential behavior (priming). Rather, we are trying to understand how selective and sequential behaviors are played out in unison. We suspect that the complexity revealed here is an unavoidable consequence of inflated ambition. In that the NP procedure is a step closer than others to measuring the kind of complex attentive behavior that characterizes human interactions with the environment, it is perhaps best to be guided at this point by ecological concerns.

Tipper et al. (1991) proposed that in some circumstances, where encoding of stimuli is predictable, long-term inhibition of irrelevant items may serve a useful behavioral function. For example, in a particular context, one stimulus may be consistently selected for action while another is always ignored. Hence, inhibition associated with the distractors within that context would facilitate selective action directed toward the target. In this view, long-term NP when the context of a prior processing episode is reinstated may not be as aberrant as it first appears.

The episodic account offered by Neill and colleagues argues for conflict between memory representations as the cause for NP effects. The ignored object in the prime display is tagged with a no-response label, which conflicts with subsequent processing of that object when a response is required. What is left unspecified in such a model, however, is how the no-response tag is associated with the internal representations of the distractor object. Clearly, some process acting on the internal representations of the distractor during selection of the target causes the no-response tag to be assigned. Perhaps this process is one of inhibition associated with the internal representations of distracting stimuli during target selection. Such inhibitory processes could conceivably have long-term effects if, for example, they altered weights in a distributed network.

Of course, such attempts to account for all of NP with a single, elegant theory may be what has led to the present state of complexity. Understanding may be better served if researchers acknowledge that two (or more) separate and independent mechanisms may be responsible for NP. Indeed, the data from time-course studies of NP suggest two such underlying processes. That is, an initial rapid decay appears to occur over the first second or so (Neill & Westberry, 1987), followed by a more stable residual effect (De-Schepper & Treisman, 1991; Hasher et al., 1991; Tipper et al., 1991). Ratcliff, Hockley, and McKoon (1985) have made a similar proposal to explain the decay function for repetition priming in lexical decision. Such data profiles have implicated two systems in research areas further afield as well. One example is that of the sensitivity of the visual system. Adaptation after exposure to bright light has a rapid initial phase over the first 5 min, followed by a slower increase in sensitivity over the next 20 min. These two components to this curve reflect initial rapid cone and subsequent slow rod adaptation processes. Perhaps the same logic applies to NP. An initial rapid decay may be due to decay of an inhibition process, whereas the smaller long-term effects may reflect episodic retrieval processes.

Although demonstrating the generality of NP to many different experimental situations has been valuable, a better understanding of the cause of NP may require that researchers complement this broadening of experimental inquiry with extremely focused examination of individual paradigms. With any luck, such an approach will lead to a sensible description of how and when inhibition and episodic retrieval mechanisms play their respective roles.

REFERENCES

Allport, D. A., Tipper, S., & Chmiel, N. (1985). Perceptual integration and post-categorical filtering. In M. I. Posner & O. S. M. Marin (Eds.), *Attention and performance, XI* (pp. 107–132). Hillsdale, NJ: Erlbaum.

Baddeley, A. (1976). *The psychology of memory.* New York: Basic Books.

Banks, W. P., & Roberts, D. (in press). Negative priming in auditory attention. *Journal of Experimental Psychology: Human Perception and Performance.*

Baylis, G. C., & Tipper, S. P. (1995). *Externally cued and internally generated selection: Differences in distractor analysis and inhibition.* Manuscript in preparation.

Beech, A. R., Powell, T. J., McWilliam, J., & Claridge, G. (1989). Evidence of reduced "cognitive inhibition" in schizophrenia. *British Journal of Clinical Psychology, 28,* 110–116.

Benoit, G., Fortin, L., Lemelin, S., LaPlante, L., Thomas, J., & Everett, J. (1992). L'attention selective dans la depression majeure: Ralentissement clinique et inhibition cognitive [Selective attention in major depression: Clinical slowing and cognitive inhibition]. *Canadian Journal of Psychology, 46*, 41–52.

Dalrymple-Alford, E. C., & Budayr, B. (1966). Examination of some aspects of the Stroop Colour-Word Test. *Perceptual and Motor Skills, 23*, 1211–1214.

DeSchepper, B., & Treisman, A. (1991, November). *Novel visual shapes in negative priming*. Paper presented at the 32nd Annual Meeting of the Psychonomic Society, San Francisco.

Driver, J., & Baylis, G. C. (1993). Cross-modal negative priming and interference in selective attention. *Bulletin of the Psychonomic Society, 31*, 45–48.

Driver, J., & Tipper, S. P. (1989). On the nonselectivity of "selective" seeing: Contrasts between interference and priming in selective attention. *Journal of Experimental Psychology: Human Perception and Performance, 15*, 304–314.

Fox, E. (1995). Precuing target location reduces interference but not negative priming from visual distractors. *Quarterly Journal of Experimental Psychology, 48A*, 26–40.

Fuentes, L. J., & Tudela, P. (1992). Semantic processing of foveally and parafoveally presented words in a lexical decision task. *Quarterly Journal of Experimental Psychology, 45A*, 299–232.

Hasher, L., Stoltzfus, E. R., Zacks, R., & Rypma, B. (1991). Age and inhibition. *Journal of Experimental Psychology: Learning, Memory, and Cognition, 17*, 163–169.

Houghton, G., & Tipper, S. P. (1994). A model of inhibitory mechanisms in selective attention. In D. Dagenbach & T. Carr (Eds.), *Inhibitory processes in attention, memory, and language* (pp. 53–112). San Diego, CA: Academic Press.

Houghton, G., Tipper, S. P., Weaver, B., & Shore, D. (1995). *The dynamics of inhibitory processes in selective attention: Some tests of a neural network model*. Manuscript in preparation.

Kane, M. J., Hasher, L., Stoltzfus, E. R., Zacks, R., & Connelly, S. L. (1994). Inhibitory attentional mechanisms and aging. *Psychology and Aging, 9*, 103–112.

Kramer, A. F., Humphrey, D. G., Larish, J. F., & Logan, G. D. (1994). Aging and inhibition: Beyond a unitary view of inhibitory processing in attention. *Psychology and Aging, 9*, 491–512.

Logan, G. D. (1988). Toward an instance theory of automatization. *Psychological Review, 95*, 492–527.

Lowe, D. G. (1979). Strategies, content, and the mechanisms of response inhibition. *Memory and Cognition, 7*, 382–389.

Maxfield, L. M. (1992). *The time course of positive and negative priming and the necessity of target selection.* Unpublished master's thesis, Syracuse University, Syracuse, NY.

McDowd, J. M., & Oseas-Kreger, D. M. (1991). Aging, inhibitory processes, and negative priming. *Journal of Gerontology: Psychology Sciences, 46,* 340–345.

Meegan, D., & Tipper, S. P. (1995). *Distractor interference in a reaching task: Evidence for a horse-race model of selective action.* Manuscript in preparation.

Moore, C. (1994). Negative priming effects depend on probe-trial conflict: Where has all the inhibition gone? *Perception and Psychophysics, 56, 133–147.*

Milliken, B., Tipper, S. P., & Weaver, B. (1994). Mechanisms underlying negative priming: Distractor inhibition and object review. *Journal of Experimental Psychology: Human Perception and Performance, 20,* 624–646.

Mueller, P. M., & Baylis, G. C. (1994). *Effects of normal aging and Alzheimer's disease on attention: 2. Inter-trial priming effects.* Manuscript submitted for publication.

Neill, W. T. (1977). Inhibition and facilitation processes in selective attention. *Journal of Experimental Psychology: Human Perception and Performance, 3,* 444–450.

Neill, W. T., Lissner, L. S., & Beck, J. L. (1990). Negative priming in same–different matching: Further evidence for a central locus of inhibition. *Perception & Psychophysics, 48,* 398–400.

Neill, W. T., & Valdes, L. A. (1992). Persistence of negative priming: Steady-state or decay? *Journal of Experimental Psychology: Learning, Memory, and Cognition, 18,* 565–576.

Neill, W. T., Valdes, L., & Terry, K. (1995). Selective attention and inhibitory control of cognition. In F. N. Dempster & C. J. Brainerd (Eds.), *New perspectives on interference and inhibition in cognition* (pp. 207–263). San Diego, CA: Academic Press.

Neill, W. T., Valdes, L. A., Terry, K. M., & Gorfein, D. S. (1992). Persistence of negative priming: II. Evidence for episodic trace retrieval. *Journal of Experimental Psychology: Learning, Memory, and Cognition, 18,* 993–1000.

Neill, W. T., & Westberry, R. L. (1987). Selective attention and the suppression of cognitive noise. *Journal of Experimental Psychology: Learning, Memory, and Cognition, 13,* 327–334.

Neumann, E., & DeSchepper, B. G. (1992). An inhibition based fan effect: Evidence for an active suppression mechanism in selective attention. *Canadian Journal of Psychology, 46,* 1–40.

Neumann, E., & Hood, K. (1993, November). *Decay of distractor inhibition in a local-global letter matching task.* Paper presented at the 34th Annual Meeting of the Psychonomic Society, Washington, DC.

Park, J., & Kanwisher, N. (1994). Negative priming for spatial locations: Identity mismatching, not distractor inhibition. *Journal of Experimental Psychology: Human Perception and Performance, 20,* 613–623.

Ratcliff, R., Hockley, W., & McKoon, G. (1985). Components of activation: Repetition and priming effects in lexical decision and recognition. *Journal of Experimental Psychology: General, 114,* 435–450.

Sullivan, M. P., & Faust, M. E. (1993). Evidence for identity inhibition during selective attention in old adults. *Psychology and Aging, 8,* 589–598.

Tipper, S. P. (1985). The negative priming effect: Inhibitory effects of ignored primes. *Quarterly Journal of Experimental Psychology, 37A,* 571–590.

Tipper, S. P. (1991). Less attentional selectivity as a result of declining inhibition in older adults. *Bulletin of the Psychonomic Society, 29,* 45–47.

Tipper, S. P., & Baylis, G. C. (1987). Individual differences in selective attention: The relation of priming and interference to cognitive failure. *Personality and Individual Differences, 8,* 667–675.

Tipper, S. P., Bourque, T., Anderson, S., & Brehaut, J. C. (1989). Mechanisms of attention: A developmental study. *Journal of Experimental Child Psychology, 48,* 353–378.

Tipper, S. P., Brehaut, J. C., & Driver, J. (1990). Selection of moving and static objects for the control of spatially directed action. *Journal of Experimental Psychology: Human Perception and Performance, 16,* 492–504.

Tipper, S. P., & Cranston, M. (1985). Selective attention and priming: Inhibitory and facilitatory effects of ignored primes. *Quarterly Journal of Experimental Psychology, 37A,* 591–611.

Tipper, S. P., & Driver, J. (1988). Negative priming between pictures and words: Evidence for semantic analysis of ignored stimuli. *Memory and Cognition, 16,* 64–70.

Tipper, S. P., Lortie, C., & Baylis, G. C. (1992). Selective reaching: Evidence for action-centered attention. *Journal of Experimental Psychology: Human Perception and Performance, 18,* 891–905.

Tipper, S. P., Weaver, B., Cameron, S., Brehaut, J. C., & Bastedo, J. (1991). Inhibitory mechanisms of attention in identification and localization tasks: Time course and disruption. *Journal of Experimental Psychology: Learning, Memory, and Cognition, 17,* 681–692.

Tipper, S. P., Weaver, B., & Houghton, G. (1994). Behavioral goals determine inhibitory mechanisms of selective attention. *Quarterly Journal of Experimental Psychology, 47A,* 809–840.

Wilson, C. (1992). *Context manipulations in a selective attention task: In search of long-term inhibitory and facilitatory effects of distracting stimuli.* Unpublished master's thesis, McMaster University, Hamilton, Ontario, Canada.

13

Competitive Mechanisms of Selection by Space and Object: A Neuropsychological Approach

Glyn W. Humphreys, Andrew Olson, Cristina Romani, and M. Jane Riddoch

Since the classic research on flanker interference in letter identification reported by Eriksen and his colleagues in the early 1970s (e.g., B. A. Eriksen & Eriksen, 1974; C. W. Eriksen & Hoffman, 1972), it has been clear that competition for selection for action in vision can be mediated by space; stimuli that are closer together compete for selection more strongly than those that are spaced farther apart. Work using this interference paradigm, along with related work using procedures such as spatial cuing (e.g., Posner, 1980), has led to a common view of selection in vision as being spatially mediated. Selection is based on selective attention to the location of target stimuli (e.g., Van der Heijden, 1992).

Strong support for such a spatial account of visual selection has come from the neuropsychological literature, and in particular from evidence of unilateral visual neglect and unilateral spatial extinction. In the syndrome of unilateral visual neglect, patients with brain injuries fail to respond to stimuli presented on the side of space contralateral to the site of their lesion. In gross cases, the patients may fail to eat food from one side of a

The work reported in this chapter was supported by grants from the Human Frontier Science Programme and from the Medical Research Council and the Joint Research Council Initiative in Cognitive Science and Human Computer Interaction, United Kingdom.

plate, to cancel the lines on one half of a page, and to draw in one half of an object they are copying (Heilman, 1979). Because the symptoms of neglect do not necessarily co-occur with visual field deficits in patients, the problem is not simply one of loss of vision to the affected side (e.g., Halligan, Marshall, & Wade, 1990). Also, cuing patients to attend to the affected side can alleviate their neglect (Posner, Walker, Friedrich, & Rafal, 1984; Riddoch & Humphreys, 1983). This last result suggests that neglect might involve a failure to direct visual attention to the contralesional side. Unilateral spatial extinction is often thought to be a milder form of neglect in which patients may be able to detect and identify a single stimulus presented on the contralesional side of space, but fail to identify or even detect the same stimulus when a competing stimulus is presented simultaneously on the ipsilesional side. This has been conceptualized either in terms of contralesional and ipsilesional stimuli competing for spatial selection, with the contralesional stimulus having less impact in the competition (Desimone & Duncan, 1995), or in terms of a difficulty in disengaging visual attention once it has been engaged on a stimulus on the ipsilesional side in order to attend to contralesional stimuli (Posner et al., 1984). Because in both neglect and extinction there is a deficit for stimuli presented on the contralesional side of space, the syndromes support the view that space acts as the medium for visual selection, with spatial selection being impaired in these patients.

Despite such evidence favoring spatial selection, there is mounting evidence that selection can also be affected by other visual properties of stimuli. For example, interference from nearest neighbors in the flanker paradigm can be overriden by interference from stimuli that are farther away but that share a common pattern of motion with a target letter (e.g., Baylis & Driver, 1992). The interference found when normal subjects report more than one visual attribute from a briefly presented, multiattribute display is a function of whether the attributes belong to the same or to different objects (Duncan, 1984). In neuropsychological studies, patients with problems in selecting multiple, simultaneously presented stimuli can have their performance improved by linking the stimuli to form a single object (Humphreys & Riddoch, 1993a; Luria, 1959). Such linking can also prevent extinction of a contralesional stimulus by the ipsilesional one (Ward, Goodrich, & Driver, 1994), and it can shift a delay in responding to stimuli on the contralesional side to one in responding to stimuli on the ipsilesional side if stimuli rotate so that the contralesional stimulus moves to the ipsilesional side (and vice versa; Behrmann & Tipper, 1994). Such evidence suggests that visual selection can be modulated by properties of objects, such as whether parts group by gestalt properties such as common movement or connectedness (cf. Palmer & Rock, 1994), or even whether parts cohere by means of activating stored representations (Ward et al., 1994).

Attempts to relate the evidence for object-based selection to that for spatial selection have been made by Farah, Wallace, and Vecera (1993) and by Humphreys and Riddoch (1993a, 1993b). These researchers have proposed that selection involves two distinct systems: a spatial attention system that serves to activate an early stage of visual processing in which representations are spatially coded, and an object recognition system, which can feed activation back to support early location-coded features but in this case according to whether the features are consistent with a given object representation. If common stages of processing are activated by the spatial attention and object recognition systems, then both spatial and object-based forms of visual selection may emerge, modulated by activation levels in early, spatially coded visual representations. Within such a general framework, competition for selection may remain solely mediated by space, based on the activity in multiple early, spatially coded visual representations. Figure 1 illustrates this general framework.

Recent neuropsychological studies in our laboratory, however, indicate that spatial and object-based effects on selection can be dissociated to reveal forms of competition that can be influenced by independent cues, including (a) whether stimuli are represented as parts of objects rather than as separate objects in their own right, and (b) whether stimuli are closed or open shapes. Such evidence suggests that rather than a single mechanism of selection in vision based on the activation of early, spatially coded visual representations (see Figure 1), there are multiple mechanisms involving separate forms of competition, which are nonspatially as well as spatially mediated. In this chapter we summarize the results leading to this proposal and demonstrate by computer simulation that the results can be captured within a model incorporating multiple competitive interactions between stimuli at various stages of processing.

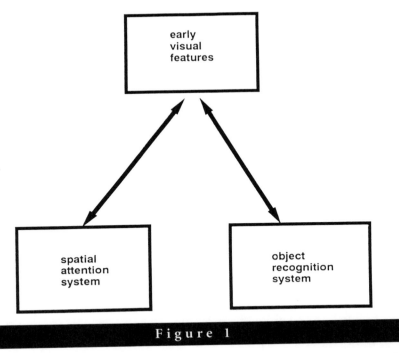

A framework for a "single locus" account of selection in vision, in which separate spatial attention and object recognition modules feedback to activate early visual representations. From *Attention and Performance XIV* (p. 147), edited by D. E. Meyer and S. Kornblum, 1993, Cambridge, MA: MIT Press. Copyright 1993 by MIT Press. Adapted with permission.

We first present evidence based on dissociations between neglect for stimuli represented as parts of objects and neglect for stimuli represented as independent perceptual objects; there are independent effects of cuing on neglect according to the form of representation mediating performance (Study 1). We then show that extinction can be nonspatial as well as spatial in nature, by means of a patient who neglects open shapes in favor of closed ones (Study 2). In a further study of extinction in the same patient we show opposite effects of similarity between stimuli according to whether the stimuli compete for selection or are linked to form a new perceptual objects (Study 3). It is this last pattern of results that we capture in a computer simulation (Study 4). After briefly presenting these results, we sketch an outline for a multiple locus account of visual selection in the brain.

STUDY 1: NEGLECT WITHIN AND BETWEEN PERCEPTUAL OBJECTS

This study was undertaken with a 56-year-old patient, JR, who had sustained lesions to the right cerebellum, the left occipitoparietal region, and the right frontoparietal region following a stroke. There were no visual field defects on perimetric testing and no clinical signs of the cerebellum lesion, and there was only relatively minor motor weakness; however, there was evidence of neglect. JR made right-side omissions when asked to cancel a set of lines on a page (Albert, 1973), and he failed to complete the right side of a drawing he was asked to copy. Interestingly, when asked to read aloud single words he made left-side errors, consistent with left-side neglect dyslexia (e.g., naming *home* as *come*). This pattern of right-side neglect apparent in some tasks, yet left-side neglect in others, was examined in a series of experiments where we varied the nature of the stimuli and the tasks (see Humphreys & Riddoch, 1995, for a full presentation of the case).

In one set of experiments, JR was presented with multiple stimuli positioned randomly on a page (words and nonwords, pictures, single lines), and he was asked either to name the stimuli (with words, nonwords, and pictures) or to mark a line bisecting the stimulus (with the lines). Individual stimuli were randomly positioned in multielement displays. The words, pictures and lines fell in roughly the same locations in the field. In the reading tests there were 12 letter strings (6 words, 6 nonwords) per page, and there were 8 pages in total (48 letter strings left and right). In the picture tests, there were 6 pages each with 11 pictures. In the line bisection test, there were 12 pages each with 21 lines (7 left, 7 center, 7 right). The pattern of results was the same across the different stimuli and tasks. JR made a number of omissions where he failed to respond to the stimuli present, and all of these were to stimuli on the right of the page. In contrast, when identifying or bisecting individual stimuli, JR made left-side errors. Left-side identification errors occurred with both words and nonwords (*trick–brick; yole–hole*), and he made naming errors to pictures, which independent observers rated as reflecting the right side of the pictures (e.g., naming an opened umbrella as a walking stick, when the handle was on the right of the picture and the canopy on the left). When he was bisecting individual lines, his responses fell consistently to the right of center (and outside the range of error expected from control subjects), indicating left neglect. The left- and right-side neglect were also affected by different variables. For example, the likelihood of a left-side error occurring on an individual letter string was higher for nonwords than for words, although equal numbers of omission errors occurred to the two string types. Also, the rate of omission errors, but not the rate of misidentification errors, was influenced by the position of the stimuli with respect to the midline of JR's body (with most errors in JR's right hemispace).

This set of results rules out certain accounts of our initial observation of left-side errors in reading and right-side errors in line-cancellation tasks. For example, it cannot be that the deficits are specific to the stimuli or the tasks (e.g., with left-side neglect dyslexia and right-side neglect of "space"; cf. Costello & Warrington, 1987; Patterson & Wilson, 1990), because the effects generalize from words to pictures and to single lines and from naming to bisection tasks. Nevertheless, several interpretations remain possible. For example, the right-side omissions may be due to a visual field defect (see Young, Newcombe, & Ellis, 1991, for evidence on the relation between field defects and omission errors), which may be independent of left spatial neglect in this patient. Further experiments suggested that this account was unlikely.

JR was asked to read aloud large words and nonwords that covered the whole width of a page. The right-side letters in these strings fell in locations where JR typically made omission errors in the studies with multiple words, pictures, and lines. Nonwords were used as well as words in order to prevent JR from guessing the identity of right-side letters from those on the left. Interestingly, the pattern of performance was the same as when he was presented with small words and nonwords; he made left-side errors. Thus, given 20 five-letter words and the same number of nonwords, JR made 8, 8, 0, 0, and 1 error at each position in the words and 12, 8, 4, 1, and 0 errors at each position in the nonwords. JR correctly read aloud the right-side letters that fell in formerly neglected parts of the field.

JR was also asked to name aloud the letters in letter strings. Now instead of making left-side errors, he made right-side omission errors. With 30 letter strings (15 words, 15 nonwords, 5 letters long) JR made 0, 0, 4, 10, and 10 errors at Positions 1, 2, 3, 4, and 5, respectively. This pattern of errors is the opposite of the one observed when JR was asked to read the whole strings aloud, even though the letters fell in the same locations in the field. A field defect cannot explain the data. Also, when reading aloud single letters JR performed no better with words than with nonwords, although his reading of whole strings was better with words than with nonwords (see Table 1), and when he was reading the letters aloud, all his errors were omissions, whereas he primarily made substitution errors when reading aloud whole strings. Such a divergence in the variables affecting his performance in the two tasks suggests that the tasks were mediated by different representations.

One account of these contrasting patterns of performance is that JR showed left-side neglect when visual stimuli were represented as single ob-

Table 1

Left- and Right-Side Neglect in Reading Aloud (Words and Nonwords),
Picture Naming, and Line Bisection by Patient JR

Task	Words	Nonwords
Reading		
Left-side misidentifications	4/44	12/43
Right-side misidentifications	0/44	0/43
Left-side omissions	0/48	0/48
Right-side omissions	4/48	5/48
Picture naming		
Left-side misidentifications	7/62	
Visual or left-side misidentifications	4/62	
Right-side misidentifications	0/62	
Left-side omissions	0/66	
Right-side omissions	4/66	
Line bisection		
Mean bisection errors		
(+ indicates right of center)	1.13 (in.)	
Left-side omissions	7/84	
Right-side omissions	21/84	

NOTE: For picture naming, errors were scored by independent judges. The visual or left-side misidentifications category indicates disagreement on whether there were left-side misidentifications or nonspatially localized errors.

jects (when reading words and nonwords as whole strings and when identifying pictures and bisecting single lines) but that he showed right-sided neglect when stimuli were represented as separate perceptual objects (e.g., when letters in words and nonwords were coded individually for single-letter identification and when multiple words, nonwords, pictures, and lines were coded on the pages). Given the bilateral lesions in his case, it may be that there are separate lesions to systems that deal with (a) the spatial relations between parts of single objects and (b) the spatial relations between separate objects. We term these, respectively, *within-object spatial relations* and *between-object spatial relations* (Humphreys & Riddoch, 1994, 1995; see also Baylis & Driver, 1993, for a similar distinction).

Even if the contrasting patterns of neglect apparent in JR reflect independent forms of spatial representation, it remains possible that there exists a single locus of selection, which holds for each form of spatial representation. For example, selection could involve attention to an early visual representation, to separate a target from background stimuli, and higher order within- and between-object spatial representations may be constructed from the selected, early target representation. If this is the case, then cuing JR to attend to one side of space may have a common effect on both within- and between-object neglect. A contrasting view to this is that selection operates independently in within- and between-object spatial representations, in which case there may be independent cuing effects.

The effects of cuing were examined in a task requiring the reading aloud of multiple letter strings (words and nonwords, positioned randomly on the page). In a string-cue condition, each letter string had a colored patch either just before the first or just after the last letter (left- and right-side cues were presented on separate pages). JR had to name each color patch and then the immediately adjoining letter string. Each page also had a colored line down either its left or right side, which JR was told to ignore. In a page-cue condition he was given the same stimuli, but this time he had to name the color of the line and to ignore the color patches alongside each word. Contrasting effects of the two cuing conditions emerged. In the string-cue condition, there was no effect of the left- and right-side cues on omission errors (out of 180 strings, 15 on each of 12 pages, he made 11 right omissions with the left-side string cues and 10 with right-side string cues). However, there was an effect of the string cue on left-side misidentification errors (9/79 left-side misidentification errors on attempted strings with a left-side cue vs. 20/80 with a right-side cue). In the page-cue condition, there was an effect of the cue on right-side omission errors (3/90 omissions with a right-side page cue vs. 12/90 with a left-side cue), but no effect on left-side misidentification errors (22/87 left-side misidentification errors on attempted strings with a left-cue vs. 17/78 with a right-side cue). The string and page cues had separate effects on the two forms of neglect that JR manifested. Cuing him to the left of individual strings reduced his (within-object) neglect of those strings but had no effect on his (between-object) omission errors; cuing him to the right side of the page reduced his (between-object) neglect but had no effect on (within-object) neglect of individual strings.

These contrasting patterns of cuing effects suggest that there are independent loci for the effects of string and page cues; this is consistent with a model in which selection operates independently in the two forms of spatial representation we have identified. That is, there are multiple loci rather than a single locus for selection in vision.

STUDY 2: NONSPATIAL EXTINCTION

Although the evidence from our study of JR suggests independent loci of selection in vision, the forms of selection involved still appeared to be spatial: There was neglect of either the left or the right of spatial representations of either single or multiple perceptual objects (within- and between-object spatial representations). As we have already noted, spatial extinction provides further strong evidence for spatial selection in vision. Evidence against the concept that space is the sole medium of selection requires that some form of nonspatial extinction be demonstrated. This possibility was examined in Study 2 in a set of experiments conducted in collaboration with John Duncan.

The experiments were carried out with a patient, GK, who had suffered bilateral parietal lesions following two strokes (a right occipito-parietal lesion and a left temporoparietal lesion). GK had several deficits in everyday life, including some word-finding problems and a marked visual disorientation (Holmes, 1918). He typically misreached to objects under visual guidance and often acted as if he was aware of only one object in the environment at a time.

In tests of extinction we contrasted his ability to identify or to detect single words and single pictures with his ability to identify or detect both a word and a picture when they were presented simultaneously. The pictures comprised either line drawings of real objects or drawings of closed nonsense shapes (taken from Kroll & Potter, 1984; see Figure 2). The stimuli were centered at fixation and presented for 2 s. His pattern of performance was striking. When asked to identify the stimuli, he scored 100% correct at identifying single real objects and nonsense shapes (here he simply said that the stimulus was a nonsense shape) and 95% correct at identifying single words. With words and pictures presented simultaneously, he named both correctly on just 20% of the trials. On 70% of the trials with a word and a drawing of a real object he identified just the drawing, and on 75% of the trials with a word and a nonsense shape he identified just the nonsense shape. He never just identified the word. When simply asked to detect the presence of pictures or words or both, performance was similar. GK was 100% correct on single item trials for each kind of stimulus, but he detected both on only 40% of the trials when both were present. On 45% of the trials with a real object and a word he detected just the real object, and on 75% of the trials with a nonsense shape and a word he detected just the nonsense shape. He never detected just the word.

These results demonstrate selective extinction for words when they competed for selection against pictures. We replicated these results on several occasions and found that pictures extinguished words even when the stimuli were spatially separated and words were centered at fixation (Humphreys, Romani, Olson, Riddoch, & Duncan, 1994). Pictures could dominate selection over words for several reasons. Pictures may access their meaning more rapidly (Potter & Faulconer, 1975), they may be darker, and only pictures are closed figures. Because we observed similar effects with nonsense shapes and with pictures of real objects, it is unlikely that access to meaning is crucial. We examined whether closure was important by having GK select figures that differed in the ease with which closure could be computed. GK was presented with square and diamond shapes formed either from the corner brackets of the shapes (bracket shapes) or from the midsections of the edges (with the brackets omitted; line shapes), as shown in Figure 3. Previous work indicates that closure can be computed more easily between than across corner brackets (Biederman, 1987). On a given trial he was presented with either a single diamond, a single square, or a square and a diamond (randomly above or

(a)

(b) **NATURE** **LAND**

Figure 2

Examples of the words and pictures used to examine nonspatial extinction in Patient GK (Study 2). In the research reported here, words were centered at fixation and spatially overlapped line drawings of either real objects or nonsense shapes (a). We have also examined performance with spatially nonoverlapping words and pictures, with words centered at fixation (b). Essentially, similar results occur with overlapping and with nonoverlapping stimuli.

below fixation). Single stimuli could be either bracket or line shapes, and when both a square and a diamond were present, one was a bracket and one a line shape. GK simply had to decide whether a square or a diamond occurred, with displays presented for 500 ms centered on a computer

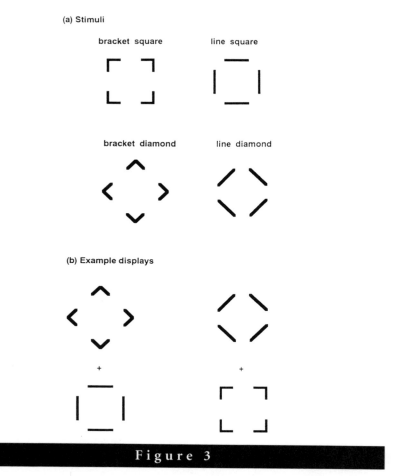

(a) Stimuli

bracket square   line square

bracket diamond   line diamond

(b) Example displays

Figure 3

Examples of closed and open shapes used with Patient GK. Closure should be easier to compute with "bracket" relative to "line" shapes, even though the shapes cover the same spatial area and have the same amount of line contour (cf. Biederman, 1987). In the experiment, diamonds as well as squares could be presented, and the task required the detection of squares.

screen. He scored 100% correct with single shapes. On two-shape trials, he always saw the square when it was the bracket shape and the diamond when it was the line shape (100% correct), and he never saw the square when it was a line shape and the diamond when it was a bracket shape (0% correct). GK failed to detect the line square pitted against the bracket shape diamond, although he was able to detect each type of shape when it was presented in isolation. In other control experiments, we went on to rule out possible effects of increased local contrast for bracket versus line shapes. Instead, we suggest that for GK, closed shapes extinguished open ones. The selective extinction of words by pictures can also be attributed to only pictures having closure.

These results demonstrate for the first time that extinction is not necessarily spatial in nature. Indeed, nonspatial selection, based on object properties such as closure, appeared to override even a strong spatial selection cue, such as identifying an item at fixation and ignoring an item presented more peripherally (see Figure 2b). Interestingly, GK was also impaired at localizing stimuli. For instance, in tests of the effects of closure on extinction, we asked him to decide whether the square, when detected, was above or below fixation; he was at chance at this task. The evidence for object-based selection along with poor spatial localization and our finding that object-based properties of stimuli could dominate a spatial cue for selection (when the task required report of the stimulus at fixation; see Figure 2b) suggests that object-based selection can operate independently of spatial selection; that is, it is consistent with there being multiple loci of selection in vision.

STUDY 3: WITHIN-OBJECT GROUPING AND BETWEEN-OBJECT COMPETITION

Although GK showed clear effects in which object properties dominated space in extinction tasks, other tests revealed that spatial location did play a role in his extinction under particular circumstances (e.g., when there was no asymmetry between stimuli in the degree of closure present and when the stimuli were presented in his left and right visual fields). In the third study, we examined the influence of object properties, such as whether parts cohered to form a single object, on GK's spatial extinction.

Recently, two studies have reported that the degree of spatial extinction found in a given patient can be moderated by similarity relationships between the extinguished and the extinguishing stimuli. Baylis, Driver, and Rafal (1993) had patients with unilateral parietal damage carry out forced-choice letter or color identification tasks to displays containing either 1 or 2 colored letters. Single letters were presented in either the ipsi- or the contralesional field, and when 2 letters were present, 1 was in the ipsi- and 1 in the contralesional field. Also, when 2 letters were present they could either have the same or different colors, or the same or a different shape. Baylis et al. found that although the patients could identify single stimuli in the contralesional field, the identification of contralesional stimuli was disrupted when an ipsilesional stimulus was presented simultaneously (i.e., there was an extinction effect). Moreover, the magnitude of this extinction effect was increased if the contra- and ipsilesional stimuli were identical in the properties on which selection was based (e.g., if they had the same color and the task was color identification; if they had the same shape and the task was shape identification). Interestingly, performance was unaffected when the contra- and ipsilesional stimuli were identical on a dimension irrelevant for the response.

Ward et al. (1994) reported an apparently contradictory result. They required patients with unilateral parietal lesions to detect the presence of 0, 1, or 2 briefly presented stimuli, where 2 stimuli, when present, occurred simultaneously in the ipsi- and contralesional sides of space. On 2-stimulus trials, the items either did or did not group (e.g., in the grouping condition, the stimuli were [and]; in the no-grouping condition, the stimuli were [and ⌐). Ward et al. found that patients were more likely to decide correctly that 2 stimuli were present if the items grouped (e.g., with [and]) than if they did not group ([and ⌐). This result is consistent with models in which grouping between object parts can determine selection, with items being selected together if they group to form a single object (e.g., Duncan & Humphreys, 1989; Humphreys & Müller, 1993). The data run counter to the idea that similar stimuli inhibit one another in order that visual attention is directed to the most salient stimulus in the field (e.g., Cave & Wolfe, 1990).

In Study 3, we assessed whether it might be possible to demonstrate both positive and negative effects of similarity on spatial extinction in the same patient, according to the particular experimental conditions. GK took part in two experiments. In the first, he had to identify a central red letter (presented at fixation), which could flanked by a green letter presented either to the right or left of the central target letter. The stimuli were presented for 200 ms. The red letter was either curved (e.g., C, G, O) or angular (e.g., A, E, T), and the green letter, when present, had either similar features (i.e., both letters were curved or both angular) or dissimilar features (i.e., the target was angular and the green distractor curved, or vice versa).

In the second experiment, GK had to decide if a central red target letter was an A or a C. The target could be presented by itself or it could be flanked by a green distractor symbol presented to the right of the target. Display durations were limited to 250 ms to set a performance level of around 85% when single targets were presented. The distractor was either a closing parenthesis ( )) or a closing parenthesis rotated 90° (⌒) form. These two distractors were chosen so that the closing parenthesis grouped with the target C and the parenthesis rotated 90° did not. Neither distractor grouped with the target A. Following Ward et al.'s (1994) result, identification of the target C might be better with the distractor) than with the distractor ⌒ , because the C and the) can be grouped by closure and symmetry to form a single object (i.e., the stimuli could be seen as an emergent oval shape). Performance with the A target was used to assess the effects of guessing the identity of the target from the distractor. For example, if GK guessed that the target was a C from the) distractor, performance for A) displays should then be consistently incorrect.

The results are presented in Figure 4. In the first experiment (see Figure 4a) GK identified about 85% of the single-target letters correctly, but had only about 75% correct when a flanking left distractor was presented and about 40% correct when a flanking right distractor occurred. There was an effect of space on his performance, because he found it harder to identify a central target that was to the left of a flanking distractor than to identify the same target when it was to the right of the distractor. There was also a negative effect of letter similarity, which was most marked when the flanker was to the right of the target (target identification dropped from more than 50% correct with a dissimilar distractor to under 30% correct with a similar distractor).

In the second experiment (see Figure 4b) GK again performed better when the target was alone relative to when it was flanked by a distractor to its right, but there was now a positive effect of target–distractor similarity. For the target C, performance was considerably better with a) distractor than with a ⌒ distractor. This was not simply due to guessing from one particular distractor, because there was no difference between the two distractor types when the target A occurred. For C) displays, GK reported

(a)

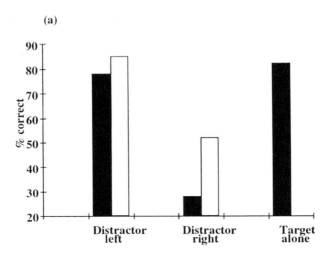

(b)

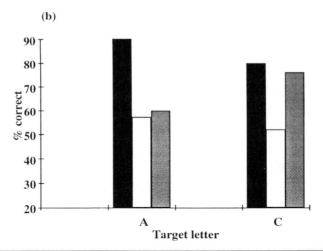

Figure 4

(a) Graph of the percentage of correct identification responses made by Patient GK as a function of whether target letters were presented alone or flanked by a similar distractor letter (represented by solid black bars) or dissimilar distractor letters (white bars); the distractor appeared in either the left or right visual field. (b) Graph of the percentage of correct forced-choice A versus C responses made by Patient GK as a function of whether a right-field distractor was vertical ( ) ; indicated by shaded bars) or horizontal (⌒ ; white bars). In all cases, the target was at fixation. Solid black bars represent measures of the target presented alone.

that he often saw an oval object and that this informed him that the target must have been a C.

Our finding that both positive and negative effects of target–distractor similarity can occur in the same patient demonstrates that previous contradictory results were not simply failures to replicate. Rather, there is something about the nature of the particular displays and tasks in the two experiments that generates the opposite effects. We suggest that the crucial factor is the strength of the representation of the distractor (in the privileged spatial location) relative to that of the emergent target–distractor "object." Grouping between the target and distractor facilitated computation of the emergent object description, benefiting target report. When grouping relations decreased (e.g., with the ⌒ distractor), the representation of the distractor dominated that of the emergent target–distractor because of GK's spatial bias, leading to poor target report. In contrast to this, in the first experiment, the representation of the distractor (as a familiar letter) may have dominated that of the emergent target–distractor object, whose parts did not cohere to form a familiar single object. In this instance, high target–distractor similarity may simply reinforce the identification of the distractor as the dominant object for selection. The opposite effects of target–distractor similarity arise essentially because of two forms of competition for selection: one for grouping parts into objects and the other between putative object representations. In Study 4, we provide a formal computer simulation incorporating these ideas. Baylis et al. (1993) put forward a rather different account, suggesting that target–distractor similarity impaired target selection because patients with parietal dysfunction are poor at distinguishing contralesional from ipsilesional tokens of the same stimulus (note that they examined performance with identical contra- and ipsilesional stimuli). However, we demonstrated negative effects of stimulus similarity between nonidentical targets and distractors (see Figure 4a), which ought not to be assigned the same token representation.

STUDY 4: A COMPUTER SIMULATION

At least two previous attempts have been made to simulate aspects of spatial neglect and extinction in explicit computational models. Cohen, Farah, Romero, and Servan-Schreiber (1994) used a simple competitive network to demonstrate that apparent problems in disengaging visual attention from the ipsilesional side of space (cf. Posner et al., 1984) could emerge from unilateral lesions that unbalance competition between systems acting to orient attention to either the left or right side. Mozer and Behrmann (1990) proposed a model incorporating separate object recognition and spatial attention components. Spatial deficits were simulated by unilateral lesions to the spatial attention system so that activation was weaker to objects on one side of space. They showed that such unilateral impairments could be mitigated if stimuli in the impaired and unimpaired fields activated a common stored object representation (the stimuli were letters and the stored object representation a word). This last pattern of results fits with the positive effects of within-object grouping we observed in Study 3. However, it is more difficult to see how negative as well as positive effects of similarity might emerge, because this might require more than one locus of competition for selection.

We examined whether the two effects of similarity could emerge in a model with multiple loci of competition and with competitive grouping mechanisms using simple principles of similarity based on the number of shared features. Humphreys and Müller (1993) proposed the SERR model of visual selection (SEarch via Recursive Rejection) in order to explain a large body of visual search results in which performance is affected by grouping relations between distractors and between targets and distractors. The architecture of the model is shown in Figure 5. This is a multicomponent model, in which stimuli composed of horizontal and vertical line edges activate a set of hierarchically organized representations. Most critically for our present purposes, units representing parts of stimuli (e.g., corner junctions) interact in a cooperative–competitive manner to group into perceptual objects. These interactions take place at the level of the "match maps" in the model and involve mutual excitation between units within a match map and mutual inhibition between units at the same location in different match maps. In addition, "template" units, corresponding to stored object representations, compete for selection (if one template is strongly activated, this will inhibit the competing templates). Thus, there are two loci for competition for selection.

Spatial deficits were simulated by selectively lesioning outputs from the match maps to the template units from one half of the model's visual

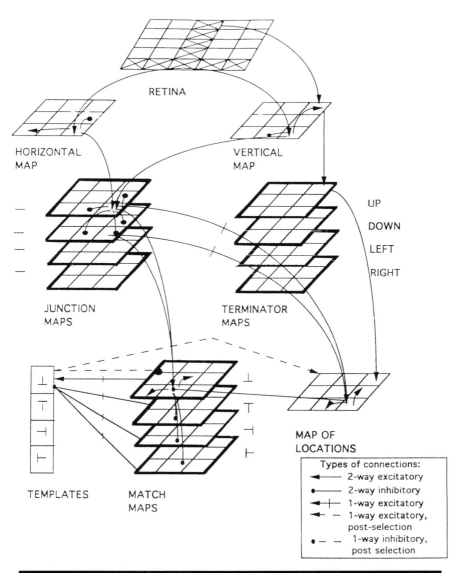

RETINA

HORIZONTAL
MAP

VERTICAL
MAP

UP

DOWN

LEFT

RIGHT

JUNCTION
MAPS

TERMINATOR
MAPS

MAP OF
LOCATIONS

TEMPLATES

MATCH
MAPS

Types of connections:
◀——— 2-way excitatory
●——— 2-way inhibitory
◀—┼— 1-way excitatory
◀— — 1-way excitatory,
      post-selection
●— — 1-way inhibitory,
      post selection

Figure 5

Functional architecture of the search via recursive rejection model of visual selective attention. From "SEarch Via Recursive Rejection (SERR): A Connectionist Model of Visual Search," by G. W. Humphreys and H. M. Müller, 1993, *Cognitive Psychology*, 25, p. 52. Copyright 1993 by Academic Press. Reprinted with permission.

field (this involved decreasing the likelihood that a template unit would be activated even if there was appropriate input from connected match-map units). Performance was examined under two conditions, which both required detection of an inverted T target presented in the "lesioned" part of the field. First, the inverted T had to be identified either alone or in the presence of either an upright T or a ⊣ distractor. The stimuli were presented for a limited number of cycles to the model, in order to fix the identification of single targets at around the 80% level. The inverted and upright Ts share a common vertical line feature in the same relative location within the shape, whereas the inverted T and the ⊣ distractor share no features in the same relative location. This means that the inverted T target partially activates the match map unit for an upright T distractor at the target's location. There is then competition for that location between the target unit and a unit corresponding to the distractor, with activation for the upright T distractor at the target location supported by the presence of the distractor in the unlesioned part of the field; there is also competition between templates, with the distractor template being further supported by activation of distractor units at the target's location. Within these competitive interactions the inverted T target tends to lose against the upright T distractor because the inverted T falls within a lesioned area of field. Consequently, the match-map unit dominant at the target location may correspond to the (similar) distractor rather than the target, thus supporting the distractor template. The result of such competition is that target selection is more difficult when the distractor is present than when the target is alone, and performance is worse with a similar than with a dissimilar distractor because competition at the match map level is fiercer in the former case (see Figure 6a). Negative effects of similarity reflect competition for selection between the separate target and distractor objects, represented in different match-maps and templates.

In the second condition, the inverted T target was paired with a distractor that was a nonobject for the model, in the sense that corresponding representations did not exist at either the match-map or template levels: a ⌐⌐ or a ⌐. Similarly to an upright T distractor, the ⌐ but not the ⌐ distractor shares features at the same relative locations as the features in the inverted T target (and also with representations of upright T distractors, which remain represented at the match-map level). The ⌐ distractor will partially activate the inverted T unit at its location, as well as

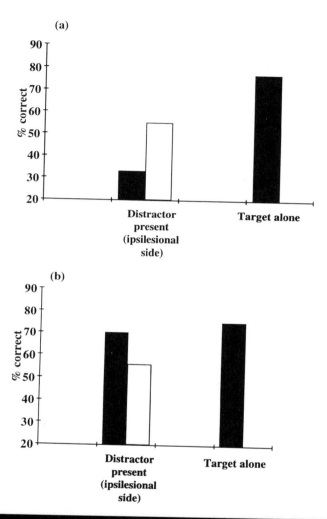

Figure 6

Graphs showing percentage of correct identifications made by search via recursive rejection to inverted T targets presented on the lesioned side of space: (a) with similar (T) or dissimilar (⊣) distractor letters; and (b) with similar (⊐) or dissimilar (⊓) distractor nonobjects. Solid black bars indicate similar letters or nonobjects, and white bars indicate dissimilar letters or nonobjects.

that of the upright T distractor. However, given also the presence of an inverted T target, activation for the inverted T units now tends to win the competition for the distractor location within the match-map units, providing extra support for the target (inverted T) template relative to when the ⊢ distractor is present. (Such a distractor provides no partial activation of target units at the match-map level while partially activating units for ⊣ and ⊢ distractors; the target unit at the distractor location does not dominate competition in this instance, with the result that templates for ⊣ and ⊢ units can enter into competition with that for the target.) The net effect is that performance is better when the target is paired by a similar nonobject distractor (sharing features with the target) than when it is paired with a dissimilar nonobject distractor (see Figure 6b), because similar nonobject distractors become bound to the target representation at the match-map level, lessening the competition to form separate perceptual objects.

These simulations show that both positive and negative effects of target–distractor similarity can emerge within a single model that incorporates more than one locus of competition for visual selection. Although such a simulation can never prove that such a model is correct, it does show that an account developed on the basis of a large body of data on a related but nevertheless different topic (in this case visual search) is consistent with the data.

We have shown positive effects of similarity when the target has stored representations and the distractor does not, and negative effects when distractors as well as targets have stored representations, and we suggest that within the framework of the model, using distractors with stored representations can shift the critical level of competition from (a) the level where stimuli are coded into perceptual objects (here it helps if the stimuli are similar and cooperate to form a single perceptual object to (b) that involving separate templates for responding (here similarity can increase competition). However, what is likely to be critical is not the presence or absence of stored representations as simulated, but the relative strength of the representations for individual targets and distractors and for target–distractor groups. If, when combined, targets and distractors form a more familiar or better object than the distractor alone, the emergent object formed by grouping the stimuli together may sometimes win the competition for selection over a distractor placed in a spatially advantaged position (e.g., in the right visual field of a patient showing left neglect). This may occur even if distractors as well as targets are in the response set for the experiment (cf. Ward et al., 1994).

GENERAL DISCUSSION

We have presented four sets of results that indicate that there can be multiple loci of competition for selection in vision and that some forms of competition are nonspatial. Space is not the sole medium for competition for selection in vision. The strongest evidence for nonspatial selection was presented in Study 2, where we reported a striking pattern of extinction for open relative to closed shapes in a single case. The other studies do not show nonspatial competition but support the argument that there are multiple loci of competition for selection, because (a) cuing effects were specific to whether stimuli were represented as parts of a single object or as separate perceptual objects (Study 1); (b) both positive and negative effects of similarity between targets and distractors occurred in the same patient (Study 3); and (c) these opposite effects were captured by competition at different levels within a model incorporating multiple loci of competition for selection (Study 4).

What will define the modules within which independent forms of competition may operate? We have distinguished competition based on spatial location and competition between object-based representations to account for the evidence both for spatial (Studies 3 and 4) and nonspatial (object-based) extinction (Study 2). This distinction can also be applied to the data from Study 1. There we argued for the existence of separate within-object and between-object spatial representations. We suggest that within-object representations involve the coding of the parts of the object in relation to some property of the object itself, such as its principal axis (cf. Marr, 1982); that is, such representations are object based in the sense that the same representation will be encoded even when the stimulus is shifted into a different spatial position. In contrast, between-object representations may be encoded relative to a coordinate scheme intrinsic to the viewer (e.g., the retina or the midline of the body), enabling these representations to be encoded even when objects are placed in arbitrary locations with respect to one another (within-object representations are nonarbitrary, because they will require either nonaccidental relations to exist between stimuli or the existence of stored representations; see Humphreys & Riddoch, 1994, for a fuller discussion). Between-object representations are space based. Thus, from the present data we do no more than specify two broad processing modules, for coding objects and for coding objects in space. The object-coding module may subserve object recognition. The spatial-coding module may represent locations for the guidance of actions. Note that the suggested space- and object-based systems fit with a broad range of data from experimental psychology (e.g., Baylis & Driver, 1993), neuropsychology (e.g., Egly, Driver, & Rafal, 1994; Humphreys & Riddoch, 1993a), neurophysiology (e.g., Ungerleider & Mishkin, 1982), and cognitive science (e.g., Jacobs & Jordan, 1992; Rueckl, Cave, & Kosslyn, 1989). We suggest that wherever possible, converging evidence should be used to help constrain our understanding of the processing modules within which there is competition for selection. Neuropsychological dissociations can provide some striking indications of such modules.

Does the distinction we have made between within- and between-object representations amount to anything other than the distinction between (respectively) local and global representations (cf. Navon, 1977)? As applied to Patient JR (Study 1), is there neglect of the left local parts of objects but neglect of the right of global representations? We think that this is probably not the case, at least if the distinction between local and global representations is couched in terms of high and low spatial frequencies or in terms of overall shape versus a part-based representation (cf. Farah, 1990). For example, JR's word and letter reading were studied using stimuli printed in uppercase, and uppercase words contain minimal overall shape information (such as the envelope, based on a low spatial frequency description of the word) that may be used for identification purposes (see Paap, Newsome, & Noel, 1984). Evidence from studies of normal readers indicates that high spatial frequency information, coded at a letter level, remains important for reading such words as well as for reading letters (see Humphreys & Bruce, 1989, for a review). Nevertheless, JR neglected on the left in a word-reading task and on the right in a letter-reading task using the same stimuli. Another way to phrase the local–global distinction is in terms of a hierarchical representation, in which the local elements are coded as parts of the global whole. This proposal is close to our view of a within-object representation. Note that the representation itself may be coded at different spatial scales.

Consider a stimulus such as a word. A within-object representation may be formed of the word as a single perceptual object in which the letters are coded as the parts; however, a within-object representation may also be formed of one of the letters as a perceptual object, and in this case the strokes of the letter will be represented as the parts (see Marr, 1982, for a discussion of hierarchical coding). What matters in each case is that the representation of the whole is affected by the nature and spatial relations between the parts (be the parts letters or strokes). In contrast to this, a between-object representation will specify just the locations but not the identities of the stimuli. For instance, it may take the form of a location-map in which the positions of the objects in the field are marked, although these objects may also be coded at different levels of spatial resolution. A coarse resolution may be used when actions are addressed to the location of the center of mass of an object, and a finer resolution may be used when actions are directed to the locations of individual parts. This distinction, between hierarchical representations in which the identities and locations of the elements matter (within-object representations) and those in which just the locations matter (between-objects representations), matches a distinction made by Pomerantz in 1983, between Type N and Type P visual representations (in Type N representations the nature of the elements is important; in Type P representations only their positions are important). Our proposal goes beyond that of Pomerantz by making it clear that each type of representation can be coded hierarchically and, furthermore, that the two types of representation may serve different purposes (e.g., object recognition and action).

The patient who showed nonspatial extinction, GK, had suffered bilateral parietal lesions. The parietal lobes are typically thought to modulate spatial processing in the brain (Ungerleider & Mishkin, 1982), and they may mediate spatial selection (Posner & Petersen, 1990; Posner et al., 1984). Bilateral parietal lesions may thus severely impair spatial selection. In terms of the distinctions we have raised, such lesions can be supposed to disrupt the coding of between-objects representations. In contrast, (ventral) occipitotemporal areas, mediating object recognition (Ungerleider & Mishkin, 1982), were relatively intact in GK. Such areas may mediate the encoding of within-object representations. Closed shapes may dominate competition for selection over open shapes within ventral visual areas specialized for processing object properties. The result may be extinction based on object properties rather than space. (Although it should also be noted that GK's performance was pathologically impaired, because selection of both stimuli is trivially easy for normal subjects under the display conditions we used. It may be that the parietal lobes are important not only for spatial selection but also for modulating switches of attention; hence, GK had difficulty switching attention once an object had been selected.) Relatively pure object-based selection may be revealed here because the lesioned spatial selection system does not modulate performance.

Our proposal is that there can be separate forms of competition for selection, some spatially mediate and some nonspatial and based on object properties and that these separate forms of competition take place in independent neural areas. Nevertheless, as indicated by the framework in Figure 1, object-based and space-based selection may normally interact so that there is coordination of the outcomes of competition within the separate neural areas coding each property. Such coordination will require the binding together of activity across separate brain regions, so that an object's shape, location, and other properties are concurrently available for the control of behavior (Desimone & Duncan, 1995). It may also require procedures to enable representations that are of the same object but coded at local and more global levels to cooperate rather than compete for selection. How the binding and the cooperative procedures might operate are major questions for future research.

REFERENCES

Albert, M. L. (1973). A simple test of visual neglect. *Neurology, 40,* 1278–1281.

Baylis, G. C., & Driver, J. (1992). Visual parsing and response competition: The effect of grouping factors. *Perception and Psychophysics, 51,* 145–162.

Baylis, G. C., & Driver, J. (1993). Visual attention and objects: Evidence for hierarchical coding of locations. *Journal of Experimental Psychology: Human Perception and Performance, 19,* 451–470.

Baylis, G. C., Driver, J., & Rafal, R. D. (1993). Visual extinction and stimulus repetition. *Journal of Cognitive Neuroscience, 5,* 453–466.

Behrmann, M., & Tipper, S. P. (1994). Object-based visual attention: Evidence from unilateral neglect. In C. Umilta & M. Moscovitch (Eds.), *Attention and performance 15* (pp. 351–375). Cambridge, MA: MIT Press.

Biederman, I. (1987). Recognition-by-components: A theory of human image understanding. *Psychological Review, 94,* 115–147.

Cave, K. R., & Wolfe, J. M. (1990). Modelling the role of parallel processing in visual search. *Cognitive Psychology, 22,* 225–271.

Cohen, J. D., Farah, M. J., Romero, R. D., & Servan-Schreiber, D. (1994). Mechanisms of spatial attention: The relation of macrostructure to microstructure in parietal attentional deficits. *Journal of Cognitive Neuroscience, 64,* 377–387.

Costello, A., & Warrington, E. K. (1987). The dissociation of visuospatial neglect and neglect dyslexia. *Journal of Neurology, Neurosurgery and Neuropsychiatry, 50,* 1110–1116.

Desimone, R., & Duncan, J. (1995). Neural mechanisms of visual selective attention. *Annual Review of Neuroscience, 18,* 193–222.

Duncan, J. (1984). Selective attention and the organization of visual information. *Journal of Experimental Psychology: General, 113,* 501–517.

Duncan, J., & Humphreys, G. W. (1989). Visual search and stimulus similarity. *Psychological Review, 96,* 433–458.

Egly, R., Driver, J., & Rafal, R. D. (1994). Shifting visual attention between objects and locations: Evidence from normal and parietal lesion subjects. *Journal of Experimental Psychology: General, 123,* 161–177.

Eriksen, B. A., & Eriksen, C. W. (1974). Effects of noise letters upon the identification of a target letter in a non-search task. *Perception and Psychophysics, 16,* 143–149.

Eriksen, C. W., & Hoffman, J. (1972). Temporal and spatial characteristics of selective encoding from visual displays. *Perception and Psychophysics, 12,* 201–204.

Farah, M. J. (1990). *Visual agnosia.* Cambridge, MA: MIT Press.

Farah, M. J., Wallace, M. A., & Vecera, S. P. (1993). "What" and "where" in visual attention: Evidence from the neglect syndrome. In I. H. Robertson & J. C. Marshall (Eds.), *Unilateral neglect: Clinical and experimental studies* (pp. 123–138). Hillsdale, NJ: Erlbaum.

Halligan, P. W., Marshall, J. C., & Wade, D. T. (1990). Do visual field defects exacerbate visuospatial neglect? *Journal of Neurology, Neurosurgery and Neuropsychiatry, 53,* 487–491.

Heilman, K. M. (1979). Neglect and related disorders. In K. M. Heilman & E. Valenstein (Eds.), *Clinical neuropsychology* (pp. 268–307). New York: Oxford University Press.

Holmes, G. (1918). Disturbances of vision by cerebral lesions. *British Journal of Ophthalmology, 2,* 353–384.

Humphreys, G. W., & Bruce, V. (1989). *Visual cognition: Computational, experimental and neuropsychological perspectives*. Hillsdale, NJ: Erlbaum.

Humphreys, G. W., & Müller, H. J. (1993). Search via recursive rejection (SERR): A connectionist model of visual search. *Cognitive Psychology, 25*, 43–110.

Humphreys, G. W., & Riddoch, M. J. (1993a). Interactions between object and space vision revealed through neuropsychology. In D. E. Meyer & S. Kornblum (Eds.), *Attention and performance, XIV* (pp. 143–162). Hillsdale, NJ: Erlbaum.

Humphreys, G. W., & Riddoch, M. J. (1993b). Interactive attentional systems and unilateral visual neglect. In I. Robertson & J. C. Marshall (Eds.), *Unilateral neglect: Clinical and experimental studies* (pp. 139–168). Hillsdale, NJ: Erlbaum.

Humphreys, G. W. & Riddoch, M. J. (1994). Attention to within-object and between-object spatial representations: Multiple loci for visual selection. *Cognitive Neuropsychology, 11*, 207–242.

Humphreys, G. W., & Riddoch, M. J. (1995). Separate coding of space within and between perceptual objects: Evidence from unilateral visual neglect. *Cognitive Neuropsychology, 12*, 283–311.

Humphreys, G. W., Romani, C., Olson, A., Riddoch, M. J., & Duncan, J. (1994). Non-spatial extinction following lesions of the parietal lobe in man. *Nature, 372*, 357–359.

Jacobs, R. A., & Jordan, M. I. (1992). Computational consequences of a bias toward short connections. *Journal of Cognitive Neuroscience, 4*, 323–336.

Kroll, J. F., & Potter, M. C. (1984). Recognizing words, pictures and concepts: A comparison of lexical, object and reality decisions. *Journal of Verbal Learning and Verbal Behavior, 23*, 39–66.

Luria, A. R. (1959). Disorders of "simultaneous perception" in a case of bilateral occipitoparietal brain injury. *Brain, 83*, 437–449.

Marr, D. (1982). *Vision*. San Francisco: Freeman.

Mozer, M. C., & Behrmann, M. (1990). On the interaction of selective attention and lexical knowledge: A connectionist account of neglect dyslexia. *Journal of Cognitive Neuroscience, 2*, 96–123.

Navon, D. (1977). Forest before trees: The precedence of global features in visual perception. *Cognitive Psychology, 9*, 353–383.

Paap, K. R., Newsome, S. L., & Noel, R. W. (1984). Word shapes in poor shape for the race to the lexicon. *Journal of Experimental Psychology: Human Perception and Performance, 10*, 413–428.

Palmer, S. E., & Rock, I. (1994). Rethinking perceptual organization: The role of uniform connectedness. *Psychonomic Bulletin and Review, 1*, 29–55.

Patterson, K. E., & Wilson, B. (1990). A ROSE is a ROSE or a NOSE: A deficit in initial letter identification. *Cognitive Neuropsychology, 7*, 447–477.

Pomerantz, J. R. (1983). Global and local precedence: Selective attention in form and motion perception. *Journal of Experimental Psychology: General, 112*, 516–540.

Posner, M. I. (1980). Orienting of attention. *Quarterly Journal of Experimental Psychology, 32*, 3–25.

Posner, M. I., & Petersen, S. E. (1990). The attention system of the human brain. *Annual Review of Neuroscience, 13*, 25–42.

Posner, M. I., Walker, J. A., Friedrich, F. J., & Rafal, R. D. (1984). Effects of parietal lobe injury on converting orienting of visual attention. *Journal of Neuroscience, 4*, 1863–1874.

Potter, M. C., & Faulconer, B. A. (1975). Time to understand pictures and words. *Nature, 253*, 437–438.

Riddoch, M. J., & Humphreys, G. W. (1983). The effect of cueing on unilateral neglect. *Neuropsychologia, 21*, 589–599.

Rueckl, J. G., Cave, K. R., & Kosslyn, S. M. (1989). Why are "what" and "where" processed by separate cortical visual systems? A computational investigation. *Journal of Cognitive Neuroscience, 1*, 171–186.

Ungerleider, L. G., & Mishkin, M. (1982). Two cortical visual systems. In J. Ingle, M. A. Goodale, & R. J. W. Mansfield (Eds.), *Analysis of visual behavior* (pp. 549–586). Cambridge, MA: MIT Press.

Van der Heijden, A. H. C. (1992). *Selective attention in vision*. New York: Routledge & Kegan Paul.

Ward, R., Goodrich, S. J., & Driver, J. (1994). Grouping reduces visual extinction: Neuropsychological evidence for weight-linkage in visual selection. *Visual Cognition, 1*, 101–130.

Young, A. W., Newcombe, F., & Ellis, A. W. (1991). Different impairments contribute to neglect dyslexia. *Cognitive Neuropsychology, 8*, 177–191.

14

Object-Based Visual Selection and the Principle of Uniform Connectedness

Arthur F. Kramer and Stephen E. Watson

I n the past 2 decades, two different classes of models, space-based and object-based models, have been proposed to account for the distribution of attention in the visual field. Space-based models have suggested that spotlights, zoom lenses, and gradients provide apt analogies for the allocation of attention. For example, models based on the notion of a spotlight argue that attention is distributed in contiguous regions of the visual field (Broadbent, 1982; Posner, Snyder, & Davidson, 1980; Shulman, Remington, & McLean, 1979; Tsal & Lavie, 1988). Stimuli that fall within the spotlight are extensively processed, whereas events that occur outside this area are ignored. The requirement to process information in non-contiguous areas of the visual field necessitates movement of the spotlight.

Evidence that has been taken to support the spotlight model has been obtained in response competition, spatial priming, and divided attention paradigms. C. W. Eriksen and colleagues (B. A. Eriksen & Eriksen, 1974; C. W. Eriksen & Hoffman, 1973) have found that response-incompatible distractors produce large performance costs when they are

This research was supported by Grant N00014-92-J-1792 from the Office of Naval Research. We thank Michael Coles, Dave Irwin, and Gordon Logan for helpful comments on a previous version of this chapter.

located within 1° of visual angle from a task-relevant target. On the other hand, distractors have little or no effect when presented at more distant locations. In spatial priming paradigms, subjects are cued to attend to a particular location in the visual field. When a stimulus occurs at the cued location, responses are fast and accurate. However, if a stimulus occurs at an uncued location performance declines (Bashinski & Bacharach, 1980; Posner, 1980; Remington & Pierce, 1984). These effects have been interpreted in terms of the spotlight model; the performance costs associated with the stimuli at the uncued locations are attributed to the requirement to reorient the spotlight. Finally, a number of divided attention studies have found enhanced performance when the stimuli are located in close spatial proximity (J. E. Hoffman, Houck, McMillian, Simons, & Oatman, 1985; J. E. Hoffman & Nelson, 1981), suggesting that attention is distributed over a restricted area of visual space.

The zoom lens and gradient approaches have been proposed to accommodate findings that suggest that, depending on subject strategies and task demands, efficient processing can occur over either a narrow or a wide area of the visual field (Jonides, 1983; LaBerge & Brown, 1989). Within the zoom lens model (C. W. Eriksen & St. James, 1986), attention can be dynamically allocated along a continuum from tightly focused to widely distributed. The resolution of the attentional system is inversely related to the width of the attentional beam. Thus, with difficult discriminations a concentrated beam of attention with high resolving power would be necessary for successful processing of the stimulus array. On the other hand, relatively easy discriminations could be made with attention distributed across the visual field (Treisman & Gormican, 1988).

In addition to the psychophysical evidence in support of space-based conceptions of visual selective attention, neuropsychological data have been obtained that are consistent with the space-based models. For example, patients with unilateral visual neglect, a syndrome associated with parietal lobe damage to a single hemisphere, have difficulty responding to stimuli presented on the side of space contralateral to their lesion. Interestingly, failure to respond to contralesional stimuli is not usually accompanied by a loss of vision on the affected side. However, cuing stimuli in the affected field has been found to reduce the unilateral neglect (Posner, Walker, Friedrich, & Rafal, 1984; Riddoch & Humphreys, 1983). This finding suggests that neglect might result in a reduced ability to direct attention to the contralesional side of space.

Although each of the space-based models proposes different mechanisms to account for the changes in processing efficiency across the visual field, the common thread in these models is the primary role of space in the control of attention. These space-based models can be contrasted with object-based models of visual attention. Instead of treating space or physical proximity as the sole factor in the control of attention, object-based models suggest that other grouping factors such as similarity, common fate, and good continuation also influence the distribution of attention. These models are descendants of earlier research and theorizing by Gestalt psychologists who argued for the role of perceptual organization in visual and auditory processing (Wertheimer, 1923).

One such object-based attentional model was proposed by Neisser (1967). In the first stage of the model the visual field is preattentively segmented into separate figural units or objects on the basis of gestalt properties such as continuity, proximity, similarity, and movement. In the second stage focal attention is used to analyze specific objects in more detail. More recently, Kahneman and colleagues (Kahneman & Henik, 1981; Kahneman & Treisman, 1984; Kahneman, Treisman, & Gibbs, 1992; Treisman, Kahneman, & Burkell, 1983) have also argued that attention operates on perceptual units or objects that are organized by preattentive processes. Focusing attention on a particular object results in the mandatory processing of all properties of that object. Thus, different properties of an object are processed in parallel and different objects are processed serially.

The theoretical assumptions of the object-based models have implications for both focused and divided attention tasks. In the case of a focused attention task, performance should improve to the degree that any conflicting information can be located on different objects from the relevant information. On the other hand, performance on divided attention tasks should be best when all of the information can be located on a single object.

Support for object-based views has been obtained in studies that have investigated the degree to which subjects' reports of several properties can be improved when these properties are located on the same object. For example, Duncan (1984) reported an important series of studies in which subjects were presented with two superimposed objects and were required to identify either two properties of a single object or one property on each of two objects. Performance was best when both of the properties were on the same object (see also Duncan, 1993; Kahneman et al., 1992). Other researchers (Baylis & Driver, 1992, 1993; Kramer & Jacobson, 1991) have found larger performance costs when an irrelevant and response-incompatible distractor was embedded in the target object or perceptual group than when the distractor was located in a different object.

Evidence in support of object-based visual selection has also been provided in a number of recent neuropsychological studies. For example, several studies have reported cases of neglect not only for the side of the visual field contralateral to the patient's lesion but also for a particular side of an object independent of the area of the visual field in which the object appeared (Behrmann & Moscovitch, 1994; Driver & Halligan, 1991). Other studies have found that extinction effects, reporting only one of two simultaneously presented objects, can be eliminated when the objects are linked (Humphreys & Riddoch, 1993; see also Humphreys, Olson, Romani, & Riddoch, chap. 13 of this volume).

SPACE- OR OBJECT-BASED SELECTION? WHAT FACTORS DETERMINE THE MODE OF SELECTION?

Although it now seems clear that both space- and object-based modes of attention play an important role in visual selection, the factors that determine the mode of selection that will be used in any particular situation are, at present, unknown. Recently, Vecera and Farah (1994) argued that selection will be object based when the task requires judgments about geometric characteristics such as shape that can be most easily computed within object-centered representations (e.g., Marr, 1982). On the other hand, space-based selection will occur in Vecera and Farah's scheme when the task involves judgments of features such as hue, saturation, and brightness that are coded in an array format by the visual cortex.

There is some support for Vecera and Farah's (1994) shape judgment hypothesis. The hypothesis is consistent with the finding of better performance with single than with dual-object judgments of the aspect ratio and gap side of the box, and the orientation of the line in Duncan's (1984) task. The hypothesis is also consistent with Yantis's (1992) finding that subjects were more successful in tracking the position of a number of moving dots when the subjects imagined the dots as corners of a rigid object that was rotating and translating in two-dimensional space. Finally, Baylis and Driver (1993) reported that judgments about the apices of two convex shapes were quicker and more accurate if these shapes were viewed as parts of a single object than if they were perceived as parts of two different objects (see also Baylis, 1994). Thus, in each of these studies, performance improved when subjects were able to reference shape judgments to a single rather than multiple objects.

However, Egly, Driver, and Rafal (1994) recently found a same-object performance benefit when subjects performed a luminance detection task. In this study a precue indicated the potential location of a luminance target at the end of one of two rectangles that were presented side-by-side. On trials in which the target appeared at an uncued (invalid) location, performance costs were larger when the uncued (invalid) location was in the uncued rectangle than when it was in the cued rectangle. Egly et al. (1994) interpreted these results as evidence that object-based selection can take place even in the absence of the judgment of geometric characteristics, because subjects were required only to detect the occurrence of a luminance increment in their study.

However, there is some reason to question Egly et al.'s (1994) interpretation. In their study the potential target location was precued by brightening the end of the rectangle, in essence emphasizing the shape of the cued object. Furthermore, the luminance increment target was presented by filling in the end of a rectangle to form a square. Thus, given the emphasis on the shape of the rectangles with the precue and luminance target it seems conceivable that subjects may have been making a judgment about the shape or size of the rectangles (e.g., respond when the height of the rectangle changes—due to the filling in of one side of the rectangle). Given the possibility of this strategy in the Egly et al. study, Vecera and Farah's (1994) shape judgment hypothesis remains viable.

Another hypothesis that was briefly discussed above is that once an object is selected, all of its properties are mandatorily processed (Kahneman & Henik, 1981; Kahneman et al., 1992). Within this framework performance benefits should be obtained whenever subjects judge two properties of a single object, as compared with situations in which one property is located on each of two objects, regardless of whether the judgments involve the shape, color, or luminance of the objects. Indeed, this mandatory processing hypothesis is consistent with the well-known Stroop effect (MacLeod, 1991), in which subjects report the color of ink in which a word is printed. Trials on which the word and ink are incongruent (e.g., the word *RED* printed in blue ink) are responded to more slowly than trials on which the ink color and word are congruent. Similar performance effects have been reported in the Eriksen paradigm in situations in which distractors are presented in the same color or embedded in the same object as the target (Baylis & Driver, 1992; Bundesen & Pedersen, 1983; Kramer & Jacobson, 1991).

Palmer and Rock (1994) have recently proposed a model of perceptual organization that may provide a third hypothesis concerning the factors that influence the mode of visual selection. In the Palmer and Rock model, early processes of edge and line detection and figure–ground segregation serve to define an entry-level unit or percept. The entry-level percept is defined on the basis of what Palmer and Rock referred to as *uniform connectedness* (UC). The principle of UC states that regions of the visual field that have relatively homogeneous surface characteristics such as lightness, color, motion, and texture tend to be perceived initially as single units, or percepts. These entry-level percepts, defined by UC, can then be combined into larger units through gestalt grouping principles such as similarity, proximity, closure, good continuation, and so forth. The entry-level units can also be divided into smaller units via parsing processes (cf. D. Hoffman & Richards, 1984; Hummel & Biederman, 1992). Thus, Palmer and Rock (1994) suggested that objects can be conceived of as being organized in a hierarchical fashion, at a number of different levels of scale, with the UC defined percept serving as the organizational primitive.

Palmer and Rock (1994) argued, on the basis of a number of demonstrations, that even after grouping or parsing, the UC regions continue to have a strongly perceived identity. Thus, in a sense the UC entry-level percepts have a special status in the organizational hierarchy of visual perception. An interesting question is whether UC regions also exert a strong influence on the mode of attentional selection. For instance, a UC hypothesis might state that object-based performance benefits will be obtained whenever a task requires the processing of multiple properties of a

UC region. On the other hand, object-based costs may be obtained when properties of several different UC regions are to be judged. In this case, attention might be directed in a serial fashion among the UC regions.

In the present study we investigated the potential determinants of object-based selection by contrasting the mandatory processing, shape judgment, and UC hypotheses. Subjects performed a conjunction judgment task in which they determined whether two predefined properties were present on each trial. The two properties could appear on one object or one property could appear on one object and one on another object.

The displays that subjects viewed along with the properties that were judged are illustrated in Figure 1. In the leftmost panel subjects judged whether the set of wrenches possessed an open-end and a bent-end. Hereafter, this will be referred to as the open-end–bent-end study. In the second panel from the left, subjects judged the orientation and color of the texture. Hereafter, this will be referred to as the texture–color study. In the third panel from the left, subjects judged the color of the patch (lower right side of the wrench on the left of the panel) and the size of the gap (bottom left of the wrench on the right side of the panel). Hereafter, this will be referred to as the color–gap study. Finally, in the rightmost panel, subjects made the same judgments as in the leftmost panel, whether the wrenches possessed a bent end and an open end. Hereafter, this will be referred to as the open-end–bent-end non-UC study.

The important question is how these different judgments map to the three hypotheses described above. Table 1 provides a summary of the map-

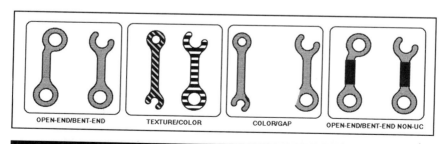

| OPEN-END/BENT-END | TEXTURE/COLOR | COLOR/GAP | OPEN-END/BENT-END NON-UC |

Figure 1

A graphic illustration of the displays presented in the four different conjunction judgment tasks. UC = uniform connectedness.

Table 1

Summary of the Predictions of the Three Hypotheses With Respect to the Occurrence of Object-Based Effects for the Four Display Panels Presented in Figure 1

Object-based selection hypotheses	Conjunction judgment			
	Open–bent	Texture–color	Color–gap	Open–bent (non-UC)
Mandatory processing	X	X	X	X
Shape judgment	X			X
Uniform connectedness	X	X		

NOTE: Predictions of object-based benefits are indicated by an X in the table. UC = uniform connectedness.

pings from hypotheses to experimental conditions. The mandatory processing hypothesis predicts that object-based benefits should be obtained for each of the judgments. This follows because once an object is selected, in the present case one of the two wrenches, all of its properties are mandatorily processed. The shape judgment hypothesis suggests that object-based benefits will only be obtained when judgments involve geometric characteristics that can be most easily computed within object-centered representations. In the present case this would include the open-end–bent-end and open-end–bent non-UC studies because in both of these cases subjects are to judge shape characteristics of the wrenches. Finally, the UC hypothesis suggests that object-based benefits will be obtained when subjects judge multiple properties of a UC region. In the present case, this would include the open-end–bent-end and texture–color studies because in these studies subjects judge two properties that occur on a uniform region defined by luminance and texture, respectively.

METHOD

Subjects

A total of 61 students (age range of 18–30 years) participated in the studies. All of the subjects possessed corrected visual acuities of at least 20/20. Subjects were paid $5 per hour for their participation in the studies. All subjects received a perfect score on the Ishihara Color Blindness Test (1989).

Apparatus and Stimuli

Stimuli were displayed by a Gateway (Sioux City, South Dakota) model 2000 486DX2 computer with an SVGA monitor and a standard QWERTY keyboard. A schematic illustration of a prototypical stimulus from each of the four studies is presented in Figure 1. In each of the four studies, subjects were presented with pairs of wrenches on each trial and were asked to make one response if a specific conjunction of properties was present and another response if only one of the properties was present. The responses were made by depressing one of two keys on the computer keyboard. The two properties could occur on the same or on different wrenches.

In the open-end–bent-end study (see Figure 1, left panel) pairs of wrenches were presented for 50 ms. The wrench display subtended 2.6° horizontally and vertically when the bent end was not present. When one end was bent, that end was moved 0.2° toward the other wrench. The wrenches were presented on either side of fixation. The target properties (bent end and open end) could occur on any of the four wrench ends. However, only trials where the target properties occurred on different ends of one wrench or on the same end of two different wrenches were subsequently analyzed. It was in these two conditions that the separation between the target properties was equivalent in the same and different object trials.

In the texture–color study (see Figure 1, second panel from the left), pairs of wrenches were presented for 50 ms. The wrench display subtended 2.0° horizontally and 2.6° vertically. The wrenches were presented on either side of fixation. The target properties could occur on one wrench or be distributed between the two wrenches. Each subject was assigned a target conjunction that included one color (red, green, or yellow) and one orientation (horizontal, clockwise, or counterclockwise).

In the color–gap study (see Figure 1, third panel from the left), pairs of wrenches were presented for 110 ms. The wrench display subtended 3.1° horizontally and 2.6° vertically. The wrenches were presented on either side of fixation. The target properties could occur on each end of one wrench or on the same end of the two wrenches. The separation between the target properties was equivalent in the same and different object conditions. Each subject was assigned a target conjunction that included one color (red or blue) and one gap size (large or small).

In the open-end–bent-end non-UC study (see Figure 1, right panel), all aspects of the stimuli were the same as in the open-end–bent-end study, with one exception. The shafts of the wrenches were colored with a blue and red checkerboard pattern. However, this property (e.g., handle pattern) did not enter into the conjunction judgment.

Procedure

Prior to the experimental trials subjects were given a cover story in which they were told that the experimenters were assessing a number of different procedures for presenting product information to quality control inspectors. The subjects were then asked to serve in the role of a quality control inspector and to sort the wrenches on the basis of experimenter-defined conjunctions of properties. Wrenches that possessed certain properties would be sold under one label and wrenches that did not possess the experimenter-defined properties would be sold under another label. For example, in the color–gap study subjects were told that one color (red or blue) was an infrared scanner indication of a tensile strength failure in the wrench and that the large gaps also indicated an inferior product. These inferior wrenches were to be sorted so that they could be sold as seconds. The cover story was provided to (a) motivate the subjects to perform the conjunction judgment task and (b) to ensure that subjects were familiar with the nature of the stimuli and their properties.

Prior to the beginning of each trial a fixation cross was presented in the center of the display. When subjects had fixated the cross they pressed the space bar, which began the trial. The pair of wrenches was then presented for either 50 or 110 ms (as described above). The wrenches were then erased and the subjects made their response.

The subject's task was to decide whether the two target properties were present in the display regardless of whether they occurred on the same or on different wrenches. If the two properties were present subjects depressed one key on the computer keyboard (either the *l* or the *d* key). If only a single target property was present subjects pressed the other key. Subjects were instructed to respond as quickly as possible while maintaining their accuracy above 85%.

Subjects performed two experimental sessions on subsequent days. In each session they performed 30 blocks of 32 trials each. Trials within each block were evenly divided between same-object and different-object trials and between conjunction-present and conjunction-absent trials. Subjects were presented with feedback on accuracy after each block of trials.

Design

Three factors were manipulated in the study. The factors included conjunction judgment condition (open-end–bent-end, texture–color, color–gap, or open-end–bent-end non-UC), response type (conjunction present or absent), and property location (same or different object). Conjunction judgment condition was a between-subjects factor and response type and property location were randomized within blocks.

RESULTS

The main question addressed in our study was whether evidence for object-based selection would be obtained (a) whenever subjects judged two properties of a single object—the mandatory processing hypothesis, (b) whenever subjects judged an aspect of the shape of an object—the shape judgment hypothesis, or (c) whenever subjects judged two properties of a uniform connected region—the UC hypothesis. Evidence in support of the mandatory processing hypothesis would be provided if object-based effects were obtained in each of the conjunction judgment conditions. Evidence in favor of the shape judgment hypothesis would be provided if object-based effects were obtained in both of the open end–bent end conditions but not in the texture–color and color–gap conditions. Finally, a finding of object-based effects for the open end–bent-end and texture–color but not for the color–gap and open-end–bent-end non-UC conditions would be consistent with the UC hypothesis.

The mean RTs and error rate data for the conjunction-present responses in each of the experimental conditions are presented in Table 2. These data were submitted to mixed-mode analyses of variance with conjunction judgment condition as a between-subjects factor and property location as a within-subjects factor. Reaction times (RTs) were faster when the two properties were located on a single object than when the properties were distributed between the two objects, $F(1, 57) = 5.4$, $p < .02$. More important, however, a significant interaction was obtained between

Table 2

Mean Reaction Times (in ms) and Error Rates for the Same and Different Object Conditions for Each of the Four Conjunction Judgments

| | Conjunction judgment | | | |
| | | | | Open–bent |
Condition	Open–bent	Texture–color	Color–gap	(non-UC)
Same object				
RT	666	697	707	614
Error	5.3	13.5	11.0	5.7
Different object				
RT	682	741	700	616
Error	6.4	20.1	10.0	5.8
Difference				
RT	16	44	−7	2
Error	1.1	6.6	−1.0	0.1

NOTE: RT = reaction time; UC = uniform connectedness.

the conjunction judgment and property location factors for both RT, $F(3, 171) = 4.2$, $p < .01$, and error rate, $F(3, 171) = 6.3$, $p < .01$. These interaction were further decomposed by examining the differences between same- and different-object location conditions for each of the four conjunction judgments. Significant RT differences were obtained for the open-end–bent-end and texture–color judgments but not for the color–gap and open-end–bent-end non-UC judgments. The texture–color judgment attained statistical significance for the error rate measure ($p < .01$).

DISCUSSION

The data obtained in our study are consistent with the UC hypothesis. RTs were faster for the two conjunction judgment conditions that involved different aspects of a single UC region, the bent-end–open-end and texture–color conditions, than the two conjunction judgments that involved two different UC regions. Neither the shape judgment nor the mandatory processing hypotheses predicts this pattern of effects. Thus, it would appear that UC percepts exert a strong influence on visual selective attention as well as on perceptual organization, as suggested by Palmer and Rock (1994).

One might suggest, however, that the mandatory processing hypothesis has been dismissed prematurely. For example, it might be argued that in the color–gap condition subjects perceived the color patch and gap to be independent of the wrenches. That is, it is conceivable that subjects parsed the color–gap displays into four separate objects: the two wrenches, the gap, and the color patch. If this were the case, the mandatory processing hypothesis would predict the absence of an object-based performance effect; attention would have to be reoriented from the color patch to the gap regardless of whether both properties appeared on one wrench or instead were distributed between the two wrenches.

Although there may be some merit to the argument that in the color–gap study the properties were perceived as being independent of the wrenches, this same argument would seem to fare poorly in the only other condition in which object-based effects were not obtained (i.e., the bent-end–open-end non-UC condition). Although it seems feasible that subjects may see a color patch and gap as being "pasted on" to a wrench, and therefore existing as separate objects from the wrench, it seems unlikely that the two ends of the wrench, which exist in everyday life as a single tangible object, would be considered in the same way.

In an effort to examine this issue we asked subjects who had not participated in our study to view the displays and indicate on a scale of 1 to 11 (1 = *not at all*, 11 = *completely*) whether each of the properties were perceived as separate objects from the wrench. Subjects were unanimous in their ratings. Each of the 16 subjects that we queried assigned a rating of 1 to the bent end and open end in the bent-end–open-end non-UC condition and to the gap in the color–gap condition. On the other hand, all of the subjects assigned a rating of 11 to the color patch in the color–gap condition.

Therefore, it does appear possible, as suggested above, that subjects might have perceived the color patch as independent of the wrenches in the color–gap condition. In such a case, the mandatory processing hypothesis would make the same prediction as the UC hypothesis: that an object-based performance effect would not be obtained. However, the subjective ratings obtained for the two properties in the open-end–bent-end non-UC condition indicated that these properties were perceived as part of the wrenches. In this situation, then, the mandatory processing hypothesis would predict that an object-based performance effect should be obtained. However, such was not the case. To summarize, although the subjective ratings suggest that both the mandatory processing and UC hypotheses correctly predict the results obtained in the color–gap study, only the UC hypotheses correctly predict the lack of an object-based effect in the open-end–bent-end non-UC study.

Although our data are consistent with the proposal that object-based selection takes place for regions defined by UC, it seems reasonable to suppose that objects or perceptual groups can be selectively processed at a variety of levels of an organizational hierarchy. In fact, such a proposal is inherent in the model of perceptual organization suggested by Palmer and Rock (1994). A schematic illustration of the Palmer and Rock model along with a selection mechanism, referred to as the *attentional pointer*, is presented in Figure 2. In the model the UC entry-level units are created as the result of early processes of edge and line detection and figure–ground

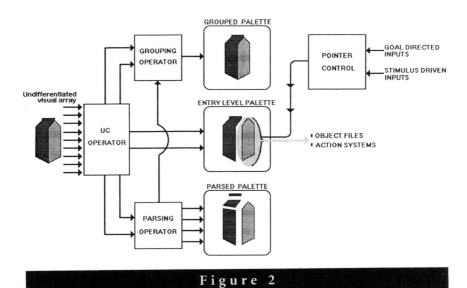

Figure 2

A graphic illustration of a model of visual selection that incorporates Palmer and Rock's (1994) uniform connectedness (UC) units.

segregation. We suggest that these UC percepts can be selectively processed or, alternatively, the attentional pointer can be directed to representations that are created through grouping or parsing operations performed on the UC regions.

Evidence in support of object-based selection at the grouped level has been provided in a number of studies. For example, Treisman et al. (1983) required subjects to report the location of a gap in a rectangular frame while reading a briefly presented word. Performance was best when the word was located inside of the frame—an object-based performance effect that does not depend on UC (see also Kahneman et al., 1992). Similarly, Yantis (1992) found that subjects were better able to track 5 randomly moving dots among a field of 10 moving dots if they imagined the target dots to be vertices of a nonrigid object. Finally, a number of researchers have found that the effects of response compatible and incompatible distractors on target processing could be magnified if the distractors were presented in the same color as the target (Baylis & Driver, 1992; Bundesen & Pedersen, 1983; Kramer & Jacobson, 1991). Thus, in each of these studies, object-based performance effects were obtained in cases in which factors other than UC were responsible for the creation of objects or perceptual groups.

An interesting question is why we did not obtain evidence of object-based processing at the grouped level in our open-end–bent-end non-UC study. That is, why did subjects not selectively process the entire wrench, resulting in faster performance on the same-object than on the different-object trials, rather than selectively processing the UC regions? Although at the present time we can only speculate on an answer, there seem to be at least two possibilities. First, it is possible that the brief presentation of the display provided insufficient time to capitalize on the grouping operations that would have been required to conjoin the multiple UC regions into a single wrench. In this case, selection might have relied on the more rapidly available UC representations. This hypothesis could be tested by systematically varying the presentation time of the display and observing whether an object-based (wrench) performance benefit was obtained at the longer durations.

An alternative possibility concerns the nature of the task. The conjunction judgment in the open-end–bent-end non-UC study could be performed without referencing the properties to the wrenches. That is, it was unnecessary to make the judgments within the context of an object-centered representation of the wrench. In such a case, the default mode of attention might be the selective processing of UC regions or object parts (e.g., from the parsed palette). If this speculation is correct, then we would expect object-based performance benefits to be obtained whenever subjects were required to judge the relations among the UC regions on a wrench. For example, this might be accomplished by informing subjects that they would occasionally be asked to determine whether a specific wrench had been presented on a previous trial. Such a judgment would require subjects to conjoin the shaft with the two ends of each of the wrenches and therefore, by definition, would require the computation of these relations within an object-centered representation.

The model presented in Figure 2 is meant to illustrate, compliments of Palmer and Rock (1994), the kinds of representations on which attentional selection might operate. However, the figure also implies a number of other characteristics of the selection process. For example, the illustration implies that attention is a unitary phenomenon (i.e., that is the attentional pointer can be focused only on a single object or perceptual group within a single representational palette at any point in time). Of course, the process of selection is actually quite flexible when one considers that a single object or perceptual group at one level in the hierarchy can be a component or part of an object at another level of the hierarchy.

However, there are limits to this flexibility in the sense that processing costs, in terms of switching time, are incurred when the pointer must be reoriented within or between palettes. This assumption appears reasonable given the many previous investigations of switching times between spatial locations (C. W. Eriksen & St. James, 1986; Krose & Julsez, 1989) as well as between local and global levels of compound stimuli (Kinchla, Solis-Macias, & Hoffman, 1983; Ward, 1982). The nature of the mechanisms that underlie the reorientation process, whether analog or discrete, remains controversial (C. W. Eriksen & Murphy, 1987; Yantis, 1988).

The illustration also implies a single selection mechanism that can be reoriented within and between palettes. In such a scheme the selection mechanism might be oriented either to a particular object or to a specific region of space within a palette. In this way a single mechanism might be used to account for both space- and object-based effects. Such proposals have been made in the past. For example, Humphreys and Riddoch (1993;

see also Farah, Wallace, & Vecera, 1993) have suggested, on the basis of human lesion studies, that image features activate both an attentional orienting system and an object recognition system and that selection occurs when a stable pattern of activation is established across both systems. We suggest a slight variant of this view. That is, that selection can take place from several different representations, some of which (e.g., UC percepts) are available before others (e.g., the grouped and parsed representations). Of course, another possibility is that separate selection mechanisms exist, with some operating on raw locations and others on objects or perceptual groups (see Humphreys, Olson, Romani, & Riddoch, chap. 13 of this volume). Additional research will be necessary to distinguish between these alternatives.

REFERENCES

Bashinski, H. S., & Bacharach, V. R. (1980). Enhancement of perceptual sensitivity as a result of selectively attending to spatial locations. *Perception and Psychophysics, 28*, 241–248.

Baylis, G. (1994). Visual attention and objects: Two-object cost with equal convexity. *Journal of Experimental Psychology: Human Perception and Performance, 20*, 208–212.

Baylis, G., & Driver, J. (1992). Visual parsing and response competition: The effect of grouping factors. *Perception and Psychophysics, 51*, 145–162.

Baylis, G., & Driver, J. (1993). Visual attention and objects: Evidence for hierarchical coding of location. *Journal of Experimental Psychology: Human Perception and Performance, 19*, 451–470.

Behrmann, M., & Moscovitch, M. (1994). Object-centered neglect in patients with unilateral neglect: Effects of left–right coordinates of objects. *Journal of Cognitive Neuroscience, 6*, 1–16.

Broadbent, D. E. (1982). Task combination and selective intake of information. *Acta Psychologica, 50*, 253–290.

Bundesen, C., & Pedersen, L. F. (1983). Color segregation and visual search. *Perception and Psychophysics, 33*, 487–493.

Driver, J., & Halligan, P. (1991). Can visual neglect operate in object-centered coordinates? *Cognitive Neuropsychology, 8*, 475–496.

Duncan, J. (1984). Selective attention and the organization of visual information. *Journal of Experimental Psychology: General, 113*, 501–517.

Duncan, J. (1993). Similarity between concurrent visual discriminations: Dimensions and objects. *Perception and Psychophysics, 54,* 425–430.

Egly, R., Driver, J., & Rafal, R. (1994). Shifting visual attention between objects and locations: Evidence from normal and parietal lesion subjects. *Journal of Experimental Psychology: General, 123,* 161–177.

Eriksen, B. A, & Eriksen, C. W. (1974). Effects of noise letters upon the identification of a target letter in a nonsearch task. *Perception and Psychophysics, 16,* 143–149.

Eriksen, C. W., & Hoffman, J. E. (1973). The extent of processing noise elements during selective encoding from visual displays. *Perception and Psychophysics, 14,* 155–160.

Eriksen, C. W., & Murphy, T. (1987). Movement of attentional focus across the visual field: A critical look at the evidence. *Perception and Psychophysics, 42,* 299–305.

Eriksen, C. W., & St. James, J. D. (1986). Visual attention within and around the field of focal attention: A zoom lens model. *Perception and Psychophysics, 40,* 225–240.

Farah, M., Wallace, M., & Vecera, S. (1993). "What" and "where" in visual attention: Evidence from the neglect syndrome. In I. Robertson & J. Marshall (Eds.), *Unilateral neglect: Clinical and experimental studies* (pp. 123–138). Hillsdale, NJ: Erlbaum.

Hoffman, D., & Richards, W. (1984). Parts of recognition. *Cognition, 18,* 65–96.

Hoffman, J. E., Houck, M. R., McMillian, F. W., Simons, R. F., & Oatman, L. C. (1985). Event related potentials elicited by automatic targets: A dual task analysis. *Journal of Experimental Psychology: Human Performance and Perception, 11,* 50–61.

Hoffman, J. E., & Nelson, B. (1981). Spatial selectivity in visual search. *Perception and Psychophysics, 30,* 283–290.

Hummel, J., & Biederman, I. (1992). Dynamic binding in a neural network for shape recognition. *Psychological Review, 99,* 480–517.

Humphreys, G., & Riddoch, M. (1993). Interactions between object and space vision revealed through neuropsychology. In D. Meyer & S. Kornblum (Eds.), *Attention and performance, XIV* (pp. 139–168). Hillsdale, NJ: Erlbaum.

Jonides, J. (1983). Further toward a model of the mind's eye movement. *Bulletin of the Psychonomic Society, 21,* 247–250.

Kahneman, D., & Henik, A. (1981). Perceptual organization and attention. In M. Kubovy & J. R. Pomerantz (Eds.), *Perceptual organization* (pp. 181–211). Hillsdale, NJ: Erlbaum.

Kahneman, D., & Treisman, A. (1984). Changing views of attention and automaticity. In R. Parasuraman & R. Davies (Eds.), *Varieties of attention* (pp. 29–62). San Diego, CA: Academic Press.

Kahneman, D., Treisman, A., & Gibbs, B. (1992). The reviewing of object files: Object-specific integration of information. *Cognitive Psychology, 24,* 175–219.

Kinchla, R., Solis-Macias, V., & Hoffman, J. (1983). Attending to different levels of structure in the visual image. *Perception and Psychophysics, 33,* 1–10.

Kramer, A. F., & Jacobson, A. (1991). Perceptual organization and focused attention: The role of objects and proximity in visual processing. *Perception and Psychophysics, 50,* 267–284.

Krose, B., & Julsez, B. (1989). The control and speed of shifts in attention. *Vision Research, 29,* 1607–1619.

LaBerge, D., & Brown, V. (1989). Theory of attentional operation in shape identification. *Psychological Review, 96,* 101–124.

MacLeod, C. (1991). Half a century on the Stroop effect: An integrative review. *Psychological Bulletin, 109,* 163–203.

Marr, D. (1982). *Vision.* San Francisco: Freeman.

Neisser, U. (1967). *Cognitive psychology.* Englewood Cliffs, NJ: Prentice Hall.

Palmer, S., & Rock, I. (1994). Rethinking perceptual organization: The role of uniform connectedness. *Psychonomic Bulletin and Review, 1,* 29–55.

Posner, M. (1980). Orienting of attention. *Quarterly Journal of Experimental Psychology, 32,* 3–25.

Posner, M. I., Snyder, C. R. R., & Davidson, B. J. (1980). Attention and the detection of signals. *Journal of Experimental Psychology: General, 109,* 160–174.

Posner, M., Walker, J., Friedrich, F., & Rafal, R. (1984). Effects of parietal lobe injury on covert orienting of visual attention. *Journal of Neuroscience, 4,* 1863–1874.

Remington, R. W., & Pierce, L. (1984). Moving attention: Evidence for time invariant shifts of visual selective attention. *Perception and Psychophysics, 35,* 393–399.

Riddoch, M., & Humphreys, G. (1983). The effect of cueing on unilateral neglect. *Neuropsychologia, 21,* 588–599.

Shulman, G. L., Remington, R. W., & McLean, J. P. (1979). Moving attention through visual space. *Journal of Experimental Psychology: Human Perception and Performance, 5,* 522–526.

Treisman, A., & Gormican, S. (1988). Feature analysis in early vision: Evidence from search asymmetries. *Psychological Review, 95,* 15–48.

Treisman, A., Kahneman, D., & Burkell, J. (1983). Perceptual objects and the cost of filtering. *Perception and Psychophysics, 33,* 527–532.

Tsal, Y., & Lavie, N. (1988). Attending to color and shape: The special role of location in selective visual processing. *Perception and Psychophysics, 44,* 15–21.

Vecera, S., & Farah, M. (1994). Does visual attention select objects or locations? *Journal of Experimental Psychology: General, 123,* 146–160.

Ward, L. (1982). Determinants of attention to local and global features of visual forms. *Journal of Experimental Psychology: Human Perception and Performance, 8,* 562–581.

Wertheimer, M. (1923). Untersuchungen zur Lehre von der Gestalt. *Psychologische Forschung, 4,* 301–350.

Yantis, S. (1988). On analog movements of visual attention. *Perception and Psychophysics, 43,* 203–206.

Yantis, S. (1992). Multielement visual tracking: Attention and perceptual organization. *Cognitive Psychology, 24,* 295–340.

15

Top-Down Control of Reference Frame Alignment in Directing Attention From Cue to Target

Gordon D. Logan

One of Charles Eriksen's greatest contributions to attention research was the development of cuing methodologies that allowed experimental control over the selective aspect of attention. Earlier researchers, such as Sperling (1960) and Averbach and Coriell (1961), used cuing methods with brief visual displays, but their focus was primarily on the persistence of information after the stimulus was turned off. Eriksen focused instead on the fact that the cue directed attention selectively to different parts of the display. He and his colleagues focused on the selective nature of cuing and used it as a way to study selective attention (see, e.g., Eriksen & Collins, 1969; Eriksen & Hoffman, 1972, 1973). Since then, their methods have become standard laboratory practice and the early spotlight theories they proposed to explain their results are still prominent in current theorizing (e.g., LaBerge & Brown, 1989; Treisman & Gormican, 1988).

The cuing method involves presenting subjects with a display of characters or simple forms and a cue that indicates which one to report. Young

This research was supported by National Science Foundation Grants BNS 88-11026 and BNS 91-09856. I thank Jane Zbrodoff for discussing the ideas, Julie Delheimer for testing the subjects and analyzing the data, and Dave Irwin and Steve Palmer for helpful comments on the chapter.

adult humans find the task easy, reporting the cued item with high accuracy, provided the display is exposed long enough. The most common dependent variable is reaction time, though some experiments with brief displays have used accuracy. The main research questions have concerned the regions of space around the cued item that influence performance (e.g., Colegate, Hoffman, & Eriksen, 1973; Eriksen & Hoffman, 1973; Juola, Bouwhuis, Cooper, & Warner, 1991; Kramer & Jacobson, 1991; LaBerge & Brown, 1989; Yantis & Johnston, 1990), the way attention moves from cue to target (Remington & Pierce, 1984; Shulman, Remington, & McLean, 1979; Tsal, 1983; but see Eriksen & Murphy, 1987; Yantis, 1988), the things that attention focuses on (objects or regions of space; Driver & Baylis, 1989; Duncan, 1984; Kahneman & Henik, 1981; Kahneman, Treisman, & Gibbs, 1992; Kramer & Jacobson, 1991), and the factors that control the direction of attention (Jonides, 1981; Jonides & Yantis, 1988; Miller, 1989; Müller & Rabbitt, 1989; Theeuwes, 1991, 1992; Yantis & Jonides, 1984, 1990).

Investigations of the control of attention have proceeded mainly by contrasting *top-down* or *goal-directed* control with *bottom-up* or *stimulus-driven* control (see, e.g., Yantis, chap. 2 of this volume). My own research on the control of attention has taken a different approach, trying to understand top-down control by itself without contrasting it with bottom-up control. My research has focused on the question How does the cue direct attention to the target? using linguistic analyses of the apprehension of spatial relations to guide experimentation (see Logan, 1995; Logan & Sadler, in press). The purpose of this chapter is to describe my approach to cuing, introducing the idea that reference frame computation is an important attentional operation, and then to describe two experiments that contrasted top-down and bottom-up control of reference frame computation.

HOW ATTENTION GETS FROM CUE TO TARGET

Recently, I proposed a theory of the apprehension of spatial relations that describes the computations necessary to direct attention from cue to target (Logan, 1994, 1995; Logan & Compton, in press; Logan & Sadler, in press). The theory involves four classes of representations and four processes that operate on them. The representations include a two- or three-dimensional *perceptual representation* of objects and surfaces arrayed in space, a *conceptual representation* consisting of two- or three-place predicates describing spatial relations between two or three objects,[1] a *reference frame* that maps the conceptual representation onto the perceptual one, and a *spatial template* representing the regions of space to which the relation applies.

The processes include *spatial indexing*, which establishes correspondence between perceptual objects or surfaces and the arguments of conceptual relations; *reference frame adjustment*, which involves aligning the reference frame with a perceptual object and setting its parameters (i.e., its origin, orientation, direction, and scale); *spatial template alignment*, which involves setting the origin, orientation, direction, and scale of the spatial template in congruence with the parameters of the reference frame; and *computation of goodness of fit*, which determines how well a given object exemplifies the relation in question with respect to the object on which the reference frame and spatial template are centered.

In a typical cuing task, in which the target is the item *next to* the cue, finding the target involves several steps. The trial begins with a conceptual representation of the predicate *next to (cue, target)*. Presentation of the cue creates an object corresponding to it in the perceptual representation, which is built by obligatory, bottom-up processes (e.g., Ullman, 1984). That object is located and set into correspondence with the symbol *cue* in the conceptual representation. Setting correspondence between a perceptual object and a symbol is the process of *spatial indexing*, which is a familiar component in most attention theories, especially object-based ones (e.g., Kahneman et al., 1992). Then, the reference frame is applied to the perceptual object corresponding to *cue* and its parameters are set. *Next to* requires setting only the origin and the scale of the reference frame; orientation and direction are largely irrelevant (Logan & Sadler, in press). Once the reference frame is centered on the cue object, the spatial template corresponding to *next to* is aligned with the reference frame, setting

---

[1]The arguments of the conceptual representation differ from each other semantically and syntactically. One is the *located object* and the other one or more objects are the *reference objects*. The relation describes the position of the located object with respect to a reference frame imposed on the reference object (Jackendoff & Landau, 1991; Talmy, 1983). The distinction between located and reference objects is important because it, together with the reference frame, defines direction in space; attention should move *from* the reference object *to* the located object. The perceptual representation does not specify direction itself. It contains information necessary to compute direction, but it does not specify it directly (Logan, 1995).

its origin to coincide with the location of the cue and its scale for the distances involved in the task. Then goodness of fit is computed for all of the objects in the perceptual representation and the one that best exemplifies the relation is chosen and set into correspondence with the symbol *target* in the conceptual representation by an act of spatial indexing. At that point, the target has been found and "further processes" can be brought to bear on it.

The steps involved in computing other relations, such as *opposite, right of*, and *above* are similar, except that different parameters of the reference frame must be specified. *Right of* and *above* require setting the origin, orientation, and direction of the reference frame but not the scale. There is some evidence that different parameters of the reference frame can be set independently (Logan, 1995, Experiment 10).

REFERENCE FRAMES AS MECHANISMS OF ATTENTION

In my theory, spatial reference frames are mechanisms of attention, just like spotlights and spatial indices in traditional theories of attention. I make this assumption because reference frame computation is a necessary step in directing attention from cues to targets (Logan, 1995). Directing attention implies apprehending the spatial relation between the cue and the target, and spatial relations are defined in terms of reference frames (Logan & Sadler, in press). I also make the assumption that reference frames are mechanisms of attention because reference frame computation has the same sort of flexibility that is associated with traditional attentional mechanisms: Reference frames can be moved around space and their parameters can be set at will. Reference frames orient attention to space, whereas spotlights and spatial indices orient attention to objects.

I assume that reference frames are more elaborate versions of the same representations and processes involved in spatial indexing. A spatial index is simply the origin of the reference frame. Spatial indexing involves setting the origin of the reference frame without setting the other parameters. A spatial index becomes a reference frame when the other parameters are set, in the sense that it can support computations based on reference frames when the other parameters are set.

TOP-DOWN CONTROL OF REFERENCE FRAME ATTENTION

Reference frame computation is interesting because it can be directed at will. It is interesting because top-down control of reference frame computation is mediated by linguistic and conceptual representations that can be controlled by an experimenter. Cuing experiments succeed because the experimenter tells the subject the relation between the cue and the target and the subject uses a representation of this relation to find the cue and direct attention to the target, which should occur in the manner described in my theory. Most cuing experiments do not manipulate the relation between the cue and the target, but it is easy to do so (see e.g., Eriksen & Collins, 1969), and that manipulation allows some insight into the top-down control of attention.

Linguistic analyses of the semantics of the different relations reveal the specific representations and processes used to direct attention. Linguistic analyses suggest the important parameters of the reference frame and the relevant spatial template. Differences in reference frame parameters and spatial templates have implications for computation—some are hard and some are easy—and those implications lead to predictions about performance in experiments.

Recently I completed a series of experiments that compared cuing with *above* and *below* with cuing with *left of* and *right of*. Cuing with *above* and *below* was 100–200 ms faster than cuing with *left* and *right* (Logan, 1995). Franklin and Tversky (1990) and Bryant, Tversky, and Franklin (1992) found similar differences in cuing objects in imagined representations rather than visible ones. The differences we found were most likely due to differences in reference frames. The spatial templates for *above* and *below* are essentially the same as those for *left* and *right* except for orientation and direction (see Logan & Sadler, in press),[2] so it is unlikely that spatial

---

[2]Spatial templates divide the space surrounding a reference object into *good, acceptable,* and *bad* regions. Located objects in good regions are good examples of the relation; objects in acceptable regions are acceptable, and so on. For *above,* the good region lies along the upper extension of the reference frame above the reference object. Acceptable regions lie on either side of the good region, above the center of the reference frame that is centered on the reference object. Bad regions lie below the good and acceptable regions, below the center of the reference object. The spatial template for *below* is the mirror image of the one for *above,* reflected about the left–right axis. The best region for below lies along the downward projection of the reference axis and acceptable regions lie on either side of it. Good and acceptable regions for above are bad for below. The spatial templates for *left of* and *right of* are rotations of the templates for *above* and *below* (see Logan & Sadler, in press, Figures 1–4).

templates produced the performance differences. However, the relations depend on different axes of the reference frame. *Above* and *below* depend on the up–down axis, which is easy to find because it is supported by gravity and bodily asymmetries (our heads are different from our feet), whereas *left* and *right* depend on the *left–right* axis, which is harder to find because it is defined with respect to the up–down and front–back axes (Clark, 1973).

I used the differences between *above–below* and *left–right* to track the movement of the reference frame around the display. The same parts of space were easy to access with *above* and *below* but hard to access with *left* and *right*. I found that the parts of the display that were easy and hard to access were not fixed in space, but rather moved around space following the cue. Whatever was above or below the cue was easy to access and whatever was left or right of it was hard. The results suggested that the origin of the reference frame could be translated across space and that the orientation of the reference frame could be rotated around space. I used the same logic in the experiments reported here.

BOTTOM-UP CONTROL OF REFERENCE FRAME ATTENTION

Palmer (1975) and Marr and Nishihara (1978) argued that bottom-up factors were important in aligning reference frames with perceptual objects. They argued that the major axis of the reference frame tends to be aligned with the axis along which an object is elongated. Thus, a blob stretched upward and downward would have a reference frame in which the up–down axis was the major axis, whereas a blob stretched sideways would have a reference frame in which the *left–right* axis was major. In Palmer's (1975) and Marr and Nishihara's (1978) schemes, reference frame alignment was an important step in object recognition (also see Biederman, 1987; Humphreys, 1983). Consequently, it was important for them to find a way to align reference frames from the results of bottom-up computations that occurred before the object was recognized, and elongation is the right sort of computation for their purposes. Palmer (1975) also argued that reference frames might be aligned with the major axis of symmetry of an object, which could also be computed by bottom-up processes.

Bottom-up processes may bias reference frame alignment, but they do not determine it completely. For one thing, subjects in my experiments aligned reference frames with asterisk cues that were not elongated in any direction and were symmetrical around six axes.[3] More generally, any object can be used as a reference object in linguistic spatial relations and linguistic instructions can override bottom-up biases. For example, deictic relations involve projecting the viewer's reference frame onto the reference object, and they impose no shape-based constraints on the things that can serve as reference objects (Jackendoff & Landau, 1991). We can say "look to the left of the ball" or "look to the right of the bat" and be easily understood. In the first case, the ball is round so there is no axis of elongation to support reference frame alignment. In the second case, the bat serves as a reference object whether or not the *left–right* axis we referred to is aligned with the intrinsic axis of elongation of the bat.

The important issue is not whether reference frame alignment is determined entirely by bottom-up processes but rather whether bottom-up processes bias top-down alignment. It could be quite difficult to overcome bottom-up biases or it could be very easy. That is an empirical question, to which the experiments reported in this chapter were addressed.

EXPERIMENT 1: ELONGATION

On each trial, subjects saw a word (*ABOVE, BELOW, LEFT,* or *RIGHT*) that told them which relation to compute between the cue and the target, and then a display containing four colored dots with a cue in the center. The cue was a cartoon drawing of a human face, presented in four different orientations (0°, 90°, 180°, and 270° from upright). Subjects were told to report the color of the dot that stood in the relation to the intrinsic axes of the face that was specified by the word that preceded it. So if the word was *ABOVE* and the face was upside down, they had to report the color of the bottom dot; if the word was *RIGHT* and the face appeared upright, they had to report the color of the dot on the left, which appeared to the right of the face. The orientation of the face was varied so that subjects could not focus attention on specific locations before the cue appeared and so that different cues could direct attention to the same parts

---

[3]The asterisks were formed from three intersecting lines, forming a figure with six points. Three axis of symmetry could be defined along the lines and three more could be defined along virtual lines that bisected the angles between points.

of space (e.g., *LEFT* presented before a face rotated 90° clockwise and *ABOVE* presented before an upright face both referred to the top dot). The parts of space that are easy and hard to access should depend on the relation, not on their absolute positions. In these respects, the experiment was similar to Logan's (1995) Experiment 10.

The new manipulation was the elongation of the face cues. For half of the subjects, the face was elongated along its up–down axis; for the other half, it was elongated along its *left–right* axis. If the contrast between *above–below* and *left–right* depends on the bottom-up assignment the major axes, then *above* and *below* should be much easier than *left* and *right* when the face was elongated up–down, and *left* and *right* should be much easier than *above* and *below* when the face was elongated left–right. If the contrast depends on top-down assignment, then the difference between *above–below* and *left–right* should be unaffected by elongating the cue. These are absolute predictions that are unlikely to be confirmed because bottom-up and top-down processes are likely to interact. Thus, the main focus of the experiment was on the relative strength of the bottom-up and top-down effects.

Another important manipulation was the color of the dot opposite the target (the *same-axis distractor*). Each display contained two red and two green dots, and the same-axis distractor was either the same color or a different color from the target. This manipulation provides a converging test of top-down influences on reference frame alignment. The hypothesis that a reference frame is an elaborated spatial index suggests that subjects have control over setting various reference frame parameters. They set only the origin when they spatially index an object; they set the origin, orientation, and direction when computing relations like *above, below, left,* and *right*. The same-axis distractor manipulation tests this hypothesis by contrasting a condition in which subjects can perform adequately by setting only the origin and the orientation (same-axis distractor same color) with a condition in which subjects must set the direction as well as the origin and the orientation. If subjects have top-down control over reference frame alignment, they should be faster when the same-axis distractor is the same color as the target. However, if the reference frame must be specified completely regardless of what the task allows, there should be no effect of the same-axis distractor. Logan (1995, Experiment 10) found that subjects were faster and the difference between *above–below* and *left–right* was attenuated when the same-axis distractor was the same color as the target. I wanted to see whether that result would replicate here.

Method

Subjects

The subjects were 48 volunteers from an introductory psychology class. Half of them served in the up–down elongation condition and half served in the left–right elongation condition. All of them were screened for red–green color blindness with the Ishihara (1987) test.

Apparatus and Stimuli

The stimuli were displayed on IBM 8513 VGA monitors controlled by IBM PS/2 Model 50 computers. There were five displays: (a) a fixation display, which was a white dot (IBM 15) presented in the center of the screen for 500 ms; (b) a word display, which consisted of the word *ABOVE, BELOW, LEFT,* or *RIGHT* presented in white at the center of the screen for 500 ms; (c) a blank screen exposed for 500 ms; (d) a cue-and-target display, which consisted of two red (IBM 12) and two green (IBM 10) dots above, below, left of, and right of the center of the screen and a head cue presented until the subject responded; and (e) a blank screen exposed for a 1,500-ms intertrial interval.

The dots in the cue-and-target display were 6.3 mm in diameter. They appeared 3.5 cm above and below and 3.3 cm left and right of the center of the screen. Each display contained two red and two green dots. In half of the displays, the dots opposite each other were the same color. In the other half, opposite dots were different colors. Each color appeared in each position equally often.

The head cues were created by drawing a front view with a special-purpose graphics program. There were two versions of the head cue, one elongated on the up–down axis and one elongated on the *left–right* axis. In both versions, the elongated axis was 1.2 cm and the short axis was 0.6 cm. The features of the face appeared in the center, in the same place in both versions. Example faces are depicted in Figure 1.

Procedure

There were four instruction words, four target positions, two target colors, two colors for the same-axis distractor, and four cue orientations.

Figure 1

Examples of face cues used in Experiment 1 (up–down and left–right elongation) and Experiment 2 (diagonal elongation).

These factors were combined factorially to produce 256 different trial types. There were two replications of the 256 different trial types, for a total of 512 trials per subject. Subjects completed all of the trials in one replication before proceeding to the next. The order of trials within each replication was randomized separately for each replication and for each subject. Subjects were allowed a brief break every 96 trials.

Subjects responded by pressing keys on the numeric keypad located beside the standard QWERTY keyboard. Half of the subjects pressed *8* if the target was red and *2* if it was green. The other half pressed *4* for red and *6* for green. Assignment to mapping condition was orthogonal to assignment to elongation condition.

Subjects were told the sequence in which the displays would appear and that their task was to report the color of one of the dots in the cue-and-target display. They were shown pictures of a typical word display and a typical cue-and-target display, and they were shown how to respond appropriately to the target display. They were told that the instruction word, the orientation of the head, and the location of the target would vary randomly from trial to trial. Then they were told about the mapping rules and they were asked to rest their index fingers lightly on the keys at all times. The trials began once they understood the instructions.

Results

Mean reaction times and accuracy scores (percentage correct) in each combination of elongation, relation (*above, below, left,* and *right*), cue orientation, and same-axis distractor condition are presented in Table 1. Accuracy was high, so the analyses focused on reaction times. The most relevant data are the interactions between relation, elongation, and same-axis distractor, which are plotted in Figure 2. The data for *above* and *below* are averaged together in the figure, as are the data for *left* and *right*.

The experiment replicated previous research by Logan (1995), Bryant et al. (1992), and Franklin and Tversky (1990) by finding a large advantage for *above–below* over *left–right* relations (Ms = 1,094 ms and 1,476 ms, respectively; difference = 382 ms). The difference appeared in both elongation conditions, though it was a little smaller with left–right elongation than with up–down elongation (*above–below* vs. *left–right* differences were 348 ms with left–right elongation vs. 417 ms with up–down elongation). Apparently, the bottom-up influence was not strong enough to reverse the usual advantage of *above–below* over *left–right*.

The elongation effects were small compared to the effects of same-axis distractor. Subjects were 271 ms faster when the same-axis distractor had the same color as the target and the effect of *above–below* versus *left–right* was much weaker (the difference was 175 ms when the same-axis distractor was the same color vs. 589 ms when the same-axis distractor was a different color). This suggests that top-down influences on reference frame alignment were much stronger than bottom-up influences.

These conclusions were supported in a 2 (group: up–down elongation vs. left–right elongation) × 4 (relation: *above, below, left,* and *right*) × 2

Table 1

Mean Reaction Times (in ms) and Percentage Correct in Experiment 1 as a Function of Elongation (Up–Down vs. Left–Right), Relation, Cue Orientation, and Same-Axis Distractor

Cue orientation	Up-down				Left–right			
	A	B	L	R	A	B	L	R
				Same-axis distractor same				
0°	994	1,023	1,204	1,238	975	1,037	1,178	1,145
	97	97	93	94	96	97	93	89
90°	1,049	1,112	1,227	1,231	1,049	1,086	1,293	1,216
	96	96	93	91	95	96	90	90
180°	1,086	1,071	1,301	1,241	1,172	1,093	1,254	1,252
	96	97	94	93	95	95	91	94
270°	1,030	1,065	1,292	1,256	1,069	1,085	1,234	1,222
	96	95	94	95	96	95	91	92
				Same-axis distractor different				
0°	1,052	1,054	1,837	1,866	1,026	1,084	1,748	1,652
	95	97	83	84	96	98	82	86
90°	1,116	1,143	1,653	1,679	1,122	1,123	1,622	1,544
	96	94	88	85	96	96	85	88
180°	1,168	1,242	1,824	1,801	1,268	1,242	1,867	1,694
	96	96	82	86	95	94	79	83
270°	1,084	1,071	1,704	1,669	1,092	1,123	1,675	1,597
	95	94	86	89	92	97	83	86

NOTE: A = above; B = below; L = left; R = right.

(same-axis distractor same or different color) × 4 (orientation: 0°, 90°, 180°, and 270°) analysis of variance on the mean reaction times. The main effects of relation, $F(3, 138) = 436.39$, $p < .01$, $MSE = 42,961.59$; same-axis distractor, $F(1, 46) = 285.02$, $p < .01$, $MSE = 98,742.97$; and orientation, $F(3, 138) = 27.72$, $p < .01$, $MSE = 25,347.25$, were significant, as were the (important) interactions between relation and elongation, $F(3, 138) = 5.08$, $p < .01$, $MSE = 42,961.59$, and between relation and same-axis distractor, $F(3, 138) = 173.38$, $p < .01$, $MSE = 31,826.17$.

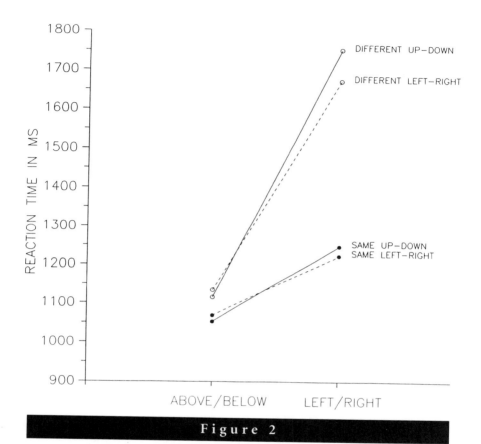

Figure 2

Mean reaction time for *above–below* and *left–right* in Experiment 1. Same-axis distractor and axis of elongation of the cue are the parameters: same = same-axis distractor same color; different = same-axis distractor opposite color; up–down = up–down axis elongated; left–right = left–right axis elongated.

Several less important interactions were significant. Orientation interacted with relation, $F(9, 414) = 6.34$, $p < .01$, $MSE = 15,415.14$, and same-axis distractor, $F(3, 183) = 21.80$, $p < .01$, $MSE = 15,890.26$, reflecting a smaller effect of orientation with *above–below* than with *left–right*, consistent with research on mental rotation (e.g., Corballis, 1988) and a smaller effect of orientation when the same-axis distractor was the same color. The interaction between orientation and elongation was significant, $F(3, 138) = 2.90$, $p < .05$, though relatively minor, as was the three-way interaction between relation, orientation, and same-axis distractor, $F(9, 414) = 6.16$, $p < .01$, $MSE = 12,241.05$.

Discussion

The results show a strong effect of cuing relation that was not mitigated much by manipulating the elongation of the *up–down* and *left–right* axes of the cue. The top-down effect of reference frame alignment was only barely influenced by bottom-up biases. By contrast, manipulating the color of the same-axis distractor had a strong effect on performance, changing the effect of cuing relation dramatically. This suggests that subjects were quite flexible when they aligned their reference frames, fixing only those parameters that were required to ensure accuracy (i.e., orientation when the same-axis distractor was the same color; orientation and direction when the same-axis distractor was a different color).

It is interesting that the effect of relation occurred in each cue orientation, even though it changed somewhat as orientation varied. This suggests that the same parts of space (i.e., the same display positions) were easy or hard to access depending on their relation to the cue, not on their absolute position in the display. The relation between the cue and the target has powerful effects on performance that cannot be ignored in theoretical accounts of cuing.

EXPERIMENT 2: SYMMETRY

Experiment 1 suggested that bottom-up processes that align the major axis of the reference frame with an object's axis of elongation do not bias the top-down processes of reference frame alignment very much. However, in Experiment 1, the axes of symmetry of the cue were always consistent with the major axis of the reference frame. Palmer (1975) argued that subjects were biased to align reference frames with an object's axes of symmetry, and the axis of symmetry could be computed by bottom-up processes (especially vertical symmetry; see Corballis & Roldan, 1975; Pashler, 1990). It is possible that the advantage of *above–below* over *left–right* was due in part to biases from bottom-up processes that align the major axis of the reference frame with the cue's axis of symmetry. Indeed, the asterisk and face cues I used in my previous experiments (Logan, 1995) were symmetrical (except for the profile view of the head cue in Experiments 10 and 11). Compatibility with axes of symmetry could account for much of the data.

Experiment 2 was conducted to determine whether the symmetry of the face cues was important in producing the advantage of *above–below* over *left–right*. The procedure was the same except that the face cues were elongated diagonally instead of up–down and left–right. Half of the faces were elongated from top right to bottom left and half were elongated from bottom right to top left. If the symmetry of the cue was important in producing the advantage of *above–below* cues over *left–right* cues, then the advantage should be reduced considerably in this experiment. However, if the top-down reference frame alignment processes are not biased much by bottom-up processes, then the advantage should be as strong as it was in the previous experiments.

Method

Subjects

The subjects were 24 volunteers from an introductory psychology class who were screened with the Ishihara (1987) test.

Apparatus and Stimuli

The apparatus and stimuli were the same as those used in Experiment 1 except for the head cue. The facial features (eyes, nose, and mouth) of the head cue remained in the same place they were in Experiment 1, but the head was elongated diagonally. Half of the head cues were elongated from top right to bottom left (tilted left) and half were elongated in the opposite orientation (tilted right). Both types of cues were 1.2 cm long and 0.6 cm wide, measured relative to their axis of symmetry. An example is presented in Figure 1.

Procedure

The procedure was the same as in the previous experiment. The two types of head cues (tilted left and tilted right) were manipulated within subjects and presented in a different random order for each subject.

Results

Mean reaction times and accuracy scores (percentage correct) in each combination of relation, same-axis distractor, and orientation conditions are presented in Table 2. Accuracy was high once again, so the analyses focused on reaction times. The most relevant datum is the interaction between relation and same-axis distractor, which is plotted in Figure 3. The data for *above* and *below* are averaged together in the figure, as are the data for *left* and *right*.

As in previous experiments, there was a large advantage for *above–below* over *left–right*. The means were 1,018 and 1,406 ms, respectively. The difference was 388 ms, very close to the 382 ms difference observed in Experiment 1 and midway between the differences for up–down and left–right elongation. Apparently, the bottom-up effect of symmetry on the reference frame alignment process was not strong enough to reverse the advantage of *above–below* over *left–right*. Same-axis distractor effects were strong. Subjects were 274 ms faster when the same-axis distractor had the same color as the target and the effect of *above–below* versus *left–right* was much weaker. The difference was 159 ms when the same-axis distractor was the same color and 617 ms when the same-axis distractor was a different color.

These conclusions were supported in a 4 (relation) × 2 (same-axis distractor) × 4 (orientation) analysis of variance on the mean reaction

Table 2

Mean Reaction Times (in ms) and Percentage Correct in Experiment 2 as a Function Relation, Cue Orientation, and Same-Axis Distractor

Cue orientation	Same				Different			
	A	B	L	R	A	B	L	R
0°	932	941	1,084	1,100	975	982	1,720	1,755
	98	95	94	95	96	96	84	84
90°	975	1,013	1,201	1,157	1,046	1,090	1,637	1,548
	97	97	93	91	96	97	89	89
180°	1,031	1,034	1,175	1,185	1,060	1,092	1,691	1,657
	98	95	91	93	97	94	85	87
270°	995	1,040	1,173	1,160	1,032	1,046	1,613	1,641
	96	97	90	95	96	98	87	90

NOTE: Same = same-axis distractor same color as target; different = same-axis distractor opposite color to target; A = above; B = below; L = left; R = right.

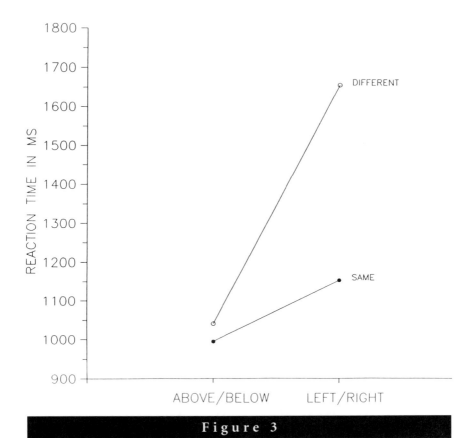

REACTION TIME IN MS

ABOVE/BELOW   LEFT/RIGHT

DIFFERENT

SAME

Figure 3

Mean reaction times for *above–below* and *left–right* in Experiment 2. Same-axis distractor is the parameter: same = same-axis distractor same color; different = same-axis distractor opposite color.

times. The main effects of relation, $F(3, 69) = 181.34$, $p < .01$, $MSE = 53,360.41$; same-axis distractor, $F(1, 23) = 223.19$, $p < .01$, $MSE = 64,817.09$; and orientation, $F(3, 138) = 4.90$, $p < .01$, $MSE = 19,564.08$, were significant, as were the interactions between relation and orientation, $F(9, 207) = 3.91$, $p < .01$, $MSE = 12,666.28$; relation and same-axis distractor, $F(3, 69) = 130.92$, $p < .01$, $MSE = 25,668.22$; orientation and same-axis distractor, $F(3, 69) = 8.15$, $p < .01$, $MSE = 13,303.83$; and relation, orientation, and same-axis distractor, $F(9, 207) = 4.05$, $p < .01$, $MSE = 13,033.50$.

Discussion

The main result of this experiment was that the advantage of *above* and *below* cues over *left* and *right* was as large as usual despite the conflict between the axis of symmetry of the cue and the main axis of the reference frame. Bottom-up processes that align the main axis of the reference frame with the axis of symmetry had little effect in this experiment. Note, however, that the features of the face (eyes, nose, and mouth) remained symmetrical when the symmetry of the outline was varied, and bottom-up processes could have detected that symmetry and aligned a reference frame with it. It is not clear how bottom-up processes would "know" that they should align the reference frame with the features of the face and not its outline. Possibly, bottom-up processes attempted to align the reference frame with the outline and with the features and suffered conflict as a result (Carlson-Radvansky & Irwin, 1993, 1994).

In other respects, this experiment replicated Experiment 1: Subjects were faster and the advantage of *above–below* over *left–right* was reduced when the same-axis distractor was the same color as the target. This suggests that subjects have some flexibility in setting the parameters of their reference frames, which is consistent with the idea that reference frame alignment is a top-down attentional process.

GENERAL DISCUSSION

The experiments showed that the process of reference frame alignment is relatively impervious to bottom-up influences. Tendencies to align the major axis of the reference frame with the axis of elongation and the axis of symmetry had little effect on the advantage of *above–below* over *left–right*. Instead, reference frame alignment was controlled by top-down processes that identified the parts of the face (top and bottom) depicted in the cue. The advantage of *above–below* over *left–right* occurred because faces have intrinsic up–down axes, whereas their left–right axes are defined with respect to up–down and front–back (Clark, 1973).

The advantage of *above* and *below* over *left* and *right* is not likely to be due to linguistic factors involved in accessing the meaning of the words. The words were presented 1 s before the display occurred, and that is plenty of time to access meaning. Evidence from semantic priming studies suggests that meanings may be activated automatically in less than 250 ms

(Neely, 1977). Evidence from studies of lexical access suggests that meanings and pronunciations are usually available in less than 1 s (Seidenberg & McClelland, 1989). In terms of my theory, it is likely that the conceptual representations of the relations and the spatial templates associated with them were retrieved before the cue-and-target display appeared. Differences between *above–below* and *left–right* were due to the processes that mapped them onto the perceptual representation of the cue and target.

My approach to top-down control of attention differs considerably from current approaches in the literature. Most researchers study top-down control by contrasting it with bottom-up, involuntary control, focusing on things like sudden onsets and feature singletons that draw attention automatically (Jonides, 1981; Jonides & Yantis, 1988; Miller, 1989; Müller & Rabbitt, 1989; Theeuwes, 1991, 1992; Yantis & Jonides, 1984, 1990). Focusing on involuntary control may be a reasonable strategy. The more we can explain in terms of involuntary processing, the less remains to be explained by voluntary processing. The homunculus problem becomes smaller and more manageable (cf. Attneave, 1960). However, this approach assumes that voluntary and involuntary processes can be neatly separated and studied independently, and that seems unlikely. There is evidence that reflexes, which are the paradigm case of involuntary processes, can be modified by attention (Anthony & Graham, 1985). We may not be able to explain involuntary behavior without first explaining volition.

Linguistic control of attention, as studied in these experiments, allows us to finesse the homunculus problem in a deeper and more interesting way than was allowed in previous approaches to attention. We can allow the experimenter's homunculus to control the subject's attention via language and thereby avoid having to explain the subject's homunculus. Although we still avoid the fundamental question, we come much closer to it by addressing the generativity and flexibility of language as it bears on the subject's attention. There are many steps between the experimenter's utterances and the subject's control of elementary mental processes that can be revealed by careful investigation.

REFERENCES

Anthony, B. J., & Graham, F. K. (1985). Blink reflex modification by selective attention: Evidence for the modulation of "automatic" processing. *Biological Psychology, 20*, 43–59.

Attneave, F. (1960). In defense of homunculi. In W. A. Rosenblith (Ed.), *Sensory communication* (pp. 777–782). Cambridge, MA: MIT Press.

Averbach, E., & Coriell, A. S. (1961). Short-term memory in vision. *Bell Systems Technical Journal, 40,* 309–328.

Biederman, I. (1987). Recognition-by-components: A theory of human image understanding. *Psychological Review, 94,* 65–96.

Bryant, D. J., Tversky, B., & Franklin, N. (1992). Internal and external spatial frameworks for representing described scenes. *Journal of Memory and Language, 31,* 74–98.

Carlson-Radvansky, L. A., & Irwin, D. E. (1993). Frames of reference in vision and language: Where is above? *Cognition, 46,* 223–244.

Carlson-Radvansky, L. A., & Irwin, D. E. (1994). Reference frame activation during spatial term assignment. *Journal of Memory and Language, 33,* 646–671.

Clark, H. H. (1973). Space, time, semantics, and the child. In T. E. Moore (Ed.), *Cognitive development and the acquisition of language* (pp. 27–63). San Diego, CA: Academic Press.

Colegate, R. L., Hoffman, J. E., & Eriksen, C. W. (1973). Selective encoding from multielement visual displays. *Perception and Psychophysics, 14,* 217–224.

Corballis, M. C. (1988). Recognition of disoriented shapes. *Psychological Review, 95,* 115–123.

Corballis, M. C., & Roldan, C. E. (1975). Detection of symmetry as a function of angular orientation. *Journal of Experimental Psychology: Human Perception and Performance, 1,* 221–230.

Driver, J., & Baylis, G. C. (1989). Movement of visual attention: The spotlight metaphor breaks down. *Journal of Experimental Psychology: Human Perception and Performance, 15,* 448–456.

Duncan, J. (1984). Selective attention and the organization of visual information. *Journal of Experimental Psychology: General, 113,* 501–517.

Eriksen, C. W., & Collins, J. F. (1969). Temporal course of selective attention. *Journal of Experimental Psychology, 80,* 254–261.

Eriksen, C. W., & Hoffman, J. E. (1972). Temporal and spatial characteristics of selective encoding from visual displays. *Perception and Psychophysics, 12,* 201–204.

Eriksen, C. W., & Hoffman, J. E. (1973). The extent of processing of noise elements during selective encoding. *Perception and Psychophysics, 14,* 115–160.

Eriksen, C. W., & Murphy, T. (1987). Movement of the attentional focus across the visual field: A critical look at the evidence. *Perception and Psychophysics, 42,* 229–305.

Franklin, N., & Tversky, B. (1990). Searching imagined environments. *Journal of Experimental Psychology: General, 119*, 63–76.

Humphreys, G. W. (1983). Reference frames and shape perception. *Cognitive Psychology, 15*, 151–196.

Ishihara, S. (1987). *Ishihara's tests for colour-blindness.* Tokyo, Japan: Kanehara.

Jackendoff, R., & Landau, B. (1991). Spatial language and spatial cognition. In D. J. Napoli & J. A. Kegl (Eds.), *Bridges between psychology and linguistics: A Swarthmore Festschrift for Lila Gleitman* (pp. 145–169). Hillsdale, NJ: Erlbaum.

Jonides, J. (1981). Voluntary vs. automatic control over the mind's eye movement. In J. Long & A. D. Baddeley (Eds.), *Attention and performance, IX* (pp. 187–203). Hillsdale, NJ: Erlbaum.

Jonides, J., & Yantis, S. (1988). Uniqueness of abrupt visual onset in capturing attention. *Perception and Psychophysics, 43*, 346–354.

Juola, J. F., Bouwhuis, D. G., Cooper, E. E., & Warner, C. B. (1991). Control of attention around the fovea. *Journal of Experimental Psychology: Human Perception and Performance, 17*, 125–141.

Kahneman, D., & Henik, A. (1981). Perceptual organization and attention. In M. Kubovy & J. R. Pomerantz (Eds.), *Perceptual organization* (pp. 181–211). Hillsdale, NJ: Erlbaum.

Kahneman, D., Treisman, A., & Gibbs, B. (1992). The reviewing of object files: Object-specific integration of information. *Cognitive Psychology, 24*, 175–219.

Kramer, A. F., & Jacobson, A. (1991). Perceptual organization and focused attention: The role of objects and proximity in visual processing. *Perception and Psychophysics, 50*, 267–284.

LaBerge, D., & Brown, V. (1989). Theory of attentional operations in shape identification. *Psychological Review, 96*, 101–124.

Logan, G. D. (1994). Spatial attention and the apprehension of spatial relations. *Journal of Experimental Psychology: Human Perception and Performance, 20*, 1015–1036.

Logan, G. D. (1995). Linguistic and conceptual control of visual spatial attention. *Cognitive Psychology, 28*, 103–174.

Logan, G. D., & Compton, B. J. (in press). Distance and distraction effects in the apprehension of spatial relations. *Journal of Experimental Psychology: Human Perception and Performance.*

Logan, G. D., & Sadler, D. D. (in press). A computational analysis of the apprehension of spatial relations. In P. Bloom, M. Peterson, L. Nadel, & M. Garritt (Eds.), *Language and space.* Cambridge, MA: MIT Press.

Marr, D., & Nishihara, H. K. (1978). Representation and recognition of the spatial organization of three-dimensional shapes. *Proceedings of the Royal Society of London, 200*, 269–294.

Miller, J. (1989). The control of attention by abrupt visual onsets and offsets. *Perception and Psychophysics, 45*, 275–291.

Müller, H. J., & Rabbitt, P. M. A. (1989). Reflexive and voluntary orienting of visual attention: Time course of activation and resistance to interruption. *Journal of Experimental Psychology: Human Perception and Performance, 15*, 315–330.

Neely, J. H. (1977). Semantic priming and retrieval from lexical memory: Roles of inhibitionless spreading activation and limited-capacity attention. *Journal of Experimental Psychology: General, 106*, 226–254.

Palmer, S. E. (1975). Visual perception and world knowledge: Notes on a model of sensory-cognitive interaction. In D. A. Norman & D. E. Rumelhart (Eds.), *Explorations in cognition* (pp. 279–307). San Francisco: Freeman.

Pashler, H. (1990). Coordinate frame for symmetry detection and object recognition. *Journal of Experimental Psychology: Human Perception and Performance, 16*, 150–163.

Remington, R., & Pierce, L. (1984). Moving attention: Evidence for time-invariant shifts of visual selective attention. *Perception and Psychophysics, 35*, 393–399.

Seidenberg, M. S., & McClelland, J. L. (1989). A distributed, developmental model of word recognition and naming. *Psychological Review, 96*, 523–568.

Shulman, G. L., Remington, R., & McLean, J. P. (1979). Moving attention through space. *Journal of Experimental Psychology: Human Perception and Performance, 5*, 522–526.

Sperling, G. (1960). The information available in brief visual presentations. *Psychological Monographs, 74*, 1–29.

Talmy, L. (1983). How language structures space. In H. L. Pick & L. P. Acredolo (Eds.), *Spatial orientation: Theory, research, and application* (pp. 225–282). New York: Plenum.

Theeuwes, J. (1991). Cross-dimensional perceptual selectivity. *Perception and Psychophysics, 50*, 184–193.

Theeuwes, J. (1992). Perceptual selectivity for color and form. *Perception and Psychophysics, 51*, 599–606.

Treisman, A., & Gormican, S. (1988). Feature analysis in early vision: Evidence from search asymmetries. *Psychological Review, 95*, 14–48.

Tsal, Y. (1983). Movements of attention across the visual field. *Journal of Experimental Psychology: Human Perception and Performance, 9*, 523–530.

Ullman, S. (1984). Visual routines. *Cognition, 18,* 97–159.

Yantis, S. (1988). On analog movements of visual attention. *Perception and Psychophysics, 43,* 203–206.

Yantis, S., & Johnston, J. C. (1990). On the locus of visual selection: Evidence from focused attention tasks. *Journal of Experimental Psychology: Human Perception and Performance, 16,* 135–149.

Yantis, S., & Jonides, J. (1984). Abrupt onsets and selective attention: Evidence from visual search. *Journal of Experimental Psychology: Human Perception and Performance, 10,* 601–621.

Yantis, S., & Jonides, J. (1990). Abrupt visual onsets and selective attention: Voluntary versus automatic allocation. *Journal of Experimental Psychology: Human Perception and Performance, 16,* 121–134.

16

Selective Attention Operates at Two Processing Loci

James C. Johnston, Robert S. McCann, and Roger W. Remington

The quest to understand the processing architecture of human cognition (see Newell, 1990) is inspiring, but it is also intimidating. It is now widely accepted (see Kosslyn & Koenig, 1992) that the human brain consists of a large number of partially autonomous processors, interacting in complex ways. In the face of such complexity, we are justifiably grateful for the existence of any phenomena that appear to reveal how information flow in the human brain is regulated. Perhaps the most striking of these is the phenomenon of selective attention: Although our senses respond to numerous stimuli simultaneously, only a few of them are allowed to gain access to higher cognitive processes where they can control overt responses, be stored in long-term memory, or both (Broadbent, 1971; Kahneman, 1973; Posner, 1980; Treisman & Gelade, 1980; Yantis & Johnston, 1990).

Much has been learned about selective attention over the last several decades, but there is little consensus about how it works. One of the first questions is surely whether selective attention is really an "it" rather than a "they." Is attentional filtering accomplished by one unitary process or by several processes? Several decades ago, attention was routinely treated as a unitary phenomenon (e.g., Broadbent, 1958; Deutsch & Deutsch, 1963).

We thank William Bacon, Charles Folk, Gordon Logan, and Lex van der Heijden for their helpful comments on earlier versions of this chapter.

An influential review by Treisman (1969) laid out numerous alternative attentional strategies, but was explicitly agnostic about whether multiple processes were involved.[1] In recent years, as attention research has mushroomed, it has become increasingly common for reviewers (e.g., Johnston & Dark, 1986) to complain about the apparent heterogeneity of methods and findings and to challenge unitary attention theories.[2] There remains, however, a scarcity of direct evidence. Recently, researchers have provided some physiological (cf. Posner & Petersen, 1990) and behavioral (Duncan, 1980; Pashler, 1989, 1991) evidence consistent with the operation of different types of attention. The case is not yet overwhelming, however, and single-process accounts of attention are still prominent (e.g., Bundesen, 1990). We review here a new line of converging behavioral evidence supporting the claim that there are two types of attention operating at different processing stages. We believe that this new line of evidence constitutes a forbidding hurdle to any theorist wishing to maintain a single-process theory of attention.

Our general approach has been to apply chronometric methods to determine the processing stage at which attention operates in two of the most widely studied attention paradigms. The two paradigms are the spatial cuing paradigm (e.g., Eriksen & Hoffman, 1972; McCann, Folk, & Johnston, 1992; Posner, Nissen, & Ogden, 1978; Posner, Snyder, & Davidson, 1980) and the psychological refractory period (PRP) paradigm (e.g., McCann & Johnston, 1992; Pashler & Johnston, 1989; Smith, 1967a, 1967b; Welford, 1952).

In the spatial cuing paradigm, a cue is used to shift attention to a particular location in space. Target stimuli are presented at either the cued location (validly cued trials) or other locations (invalidly cued trials). Valid spatial cuing has been found in many studies to facilitate performance, improving the accuracy (e.g., Bashinski & Bacharach, 1980; Downing, 1988) and speed (e.g., Posner, 1980; Posner et al., 1978) of responses to targets. Many researchers have used evidence from the spatial cuing paradigm to support claims that selective attention operates at a relatively early stage of processing. This has been particularly true of recent behavioral studies us-

---

[1] In terms of the distinction we make below, all four strategies actually appear to be different ways to configure input attention.

[2] Another important antecedent to our work is multiple resource theory (e.g., Navon & Gopher, 1979; Wickens, 1984), which contends that human performance is constrained by a number of separate pools of processing resources.

ing chronometric methods (e.g., Hawkins, Shafto, & Richardson, 1988; McCann et al., 1992; Posner, 1980; Yantis & Johnston, 1990) and of electrophysiological studies (e.g., Luck et al., 1994).

In the PRP paradigm, two successive stimuli are presented, to which subjects must make two different speeded-response judgments. In effect, subjects must perform two completely different response-time tasks. For instance, people might have to judge the pitch of a tone stimulus in one task and decide on the identity of a letter stimulus in the other task. The interval between stimuli for the two tasks is systematically varied. When the interval is long, the two tasks overlap little, and responding is rapid on both tasks. When the interval is short, the processing demands of the two tasks overlap substantially, and responses on the second task are typically delayed. The delay is usually hypothesized to occur because performance of the first task delayed the availability of attention to the second task. Research with the PRP paradigm has often been interpreted as evidence that attention operates at a relatively late stage in processing, perhaps when identified stimuli are mapped onto their appropriate responses (McCann & Johnston, 1992; Pashler & Johnston, 1989; Smith, 1967b; Welford, 1952).

Although both the spatial cuing paradigm and the PRP paradigm have been intensively investigated, research with each has proceeded along remarkably independent lines.[3] There have been few attempts to explore the architectural question of whether these two paradigms involve the same type of attention or different types (but see Pashler, 1989, 1991). Because we have been involved in both lines of research, we were naturally led to juxtapose the conclusions reached in each. Our studies, like a number of others (especially those using chronometric methods), supported the conclusion that attention operated at an early processing locus in the spatial cuing paradigm (e.g., McCann et al., 1992) but at a late processing locus in the PRP paradigm (e.g., McCann & Johnston, 1992; Pashler & Johnston, 1989). These conclusions bear a sensible relation to a functional

---

[3]So little consideration has been given to the hypothesis of separate attentional limits that many studies in each domain have confounded problems in the other domain. For instance, a study using the psychological refractory period paradigm by Smith (1967b) is commonly supposed to bear on what we call below a central attentional bottleneck. However, her tasks both used visual stimuli in separate locations in the visual field, so subjects almost certainly also encountered what we call below input attention problems. The converse problem occurs with a study by Downing (1988) that used the spatial cuing paradigm, in which subjects had to encode and report information about four stimuli per trial. This procedure is likely to have contaminated a study of input attention with substantial information losses at a more central processing locus.

analysis of the two paradigms. The spatial cuing paradigm involves only one task, and the spatial cue serves, on the face of it, to misdirect stimulus processing away from the location where the target will occur. On the other hand, the PRP paradigm involves two entirely different tasks, each with different stimulus–response (S-R) mapping requirements. It is certainly plausible, on the face of it, that response delays occur in this paradigm because the two S-R mapping operations cannot be carried out in parallel. This would indicate a more central locus for interference.

We believe that the tentative conclusions reached in each paradigm are reasonable and also intuitively plausible. The two conclusions can be reconciled if the two paradigms are not studying the same thing. We propose that the two paradigms tap two different types of attention that operate at different processing stages. We call the type that is tapped by the spatial cuing paradigm *input attention* and the type that is tapped by the PRP paradigm *central attention.*

Before accepting a proposal that will strike many as unparsimonious, we should make sure the empirical case for different processing loci is relatively tight. Two kinds of escape hatches remain open to skeptics. First, researchers using the two paradigms have made different choices of tasks and stimuli; these choices, and not some more fundamental difference between the paradigms, might account for the different results. To remedy this problem, we attempt here to carry out matching experiments in both paradigms using the same task, with identical stimuli. Second, previous chronometric studies using the two paradigms have not actually manipulated the same processing stage. To remedy this problem, we propose to manipulate the same reference stage in both paradigms. We have a very specific goal in mind: showing that this reference stage operates *after* input attention in the spatial cuing paradigm, but *before* central attention in the PRP paradigm. If this can be done, it will make it virtually impossible to avoid the conclusion that attention operates at two different stages of processing in the two paradigms.

DETERMINING THE ORDER OF PROCESSING STAGES

Sternberg's (1969) famous additive-factor method provides a way to obtain information about how many separate processing stages are present in a task, but it provides no information about the order of processing stages. For this purpose, we use the locus-of-slack method (Keele & Neill, 1978; McCann & Johnston, 1992; Pashler & Johnston, 1989; Schweickert, 1980). This method can be understood through the analogy of a building project that proceeds sequentially. Let us assume that the contractor responsible for erecting the steelwork is delayed on another job, producing slack in the schedule. What happens if the duration of another construction stage changes, increasing by time k? If this stage occurs after steelwork erection, total project time also increases by k. But if the lengthened stage occurs before steelwork erection, the increased time is absorbed (either fully or partially) into slack. If slack is greater than k, complete absorption occurs, and total project time is unchanged. Note that by measuring whether added time on one stage affects total project time, we can infer whether that stage operates before or after the slack.

Similar logic can be used to determine the order of mental processing stages (see Figure 1). To delay the onset of the processing stage at which attention operates,[4] we use either the spatial cuing paradigm (for input attention) or the PRP paradigm (for central attention). We also manipulate the duration of the critical reference stage (particulars are discussed below). If the reference stage occurs before attention is required, the stage-time increase will be absorbed into slack and total task time will be unaffected. If the reference stage occurs after attention is required, no absorption into slack will occur, and total task time will increase by exactly the amount that the individual stage time increased.

In order to make the case for multiple attention types, we needed to find a reference stage that occurred late enough to be after the stage at which input attention operates, but early enough to be before the stage at which central attention operates. The candidate we picked was the stage at which letter identification occurs. If early selection theories of input attention are correct, letter identification should be after input attention. Also, if response selection (stimulus–response mapping) is the locus of central attention, then letter identification, as part of high level stimulus classification, should still occur early enough to be before central attention. In order to manipulate the duration of letter identification, we needed

---

[4]Note that this method is neutral as to whether attention *is* a stage of processing, or is just *required by* a particular stage of processing. The method will work in either case.

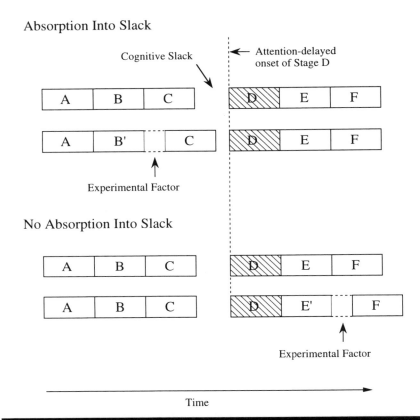

Absorption Into Slack

Cognitive Slack

Attention-delayed onset of Stage D

| A | B | C | | D | E | F |

| A | B' | C | | D | E | F |

Experimental Factor

No Absorption Into Slack

| A | B | C | | D | E | F |

| A | B | C | | D | E' | F |

Experimental Factor

Time

Figure 1

Timing diagram showing for the locus-of-slack method. All processing stages begin on completion of the preceding stage, except for D. Stage D can begin only at the time when attention becomes available (shown as the dotted vertical line). Cognitive slack (empty space on the time line) occurs between Stages C and D. The first two time lines show one set of hypothetical results of an experiment manipulating the duration of Processing Stage B. In the second time line the length of Stage B has been increased (B'). The time increase is absorbed into cognitive slack, so that the finishing time for the entire task (end of Stage F) is unaffected. The last two time lines show the hypothetical results of a different experiment manipulating the duration of Stage E. In the fourth time line the length of Stage E has been increased (E'). Now the entire increase in Stage E time shows up as an increase in the time to finish the task (end of Stage F).

to develop a new way to distort letter stimuli. Traditional degradation methods such as intensity reduction or adding stray dots are known to slow down processing, but the slowdown could be *during* feature processing. It is plausible that these forms of distortion can be cleaned up by general preprocessing perceptual algorithms, so that the letter identification process itself always receives an undegraded input. What we decided to do was alter the arrangement of strokes in the characters while leaving the strokes the same width and intensity (see Figure 2). The present distorted forms should survive any general image clean-up processes, providing the identification stage itself with an inferior (but still readily recognizable) input.

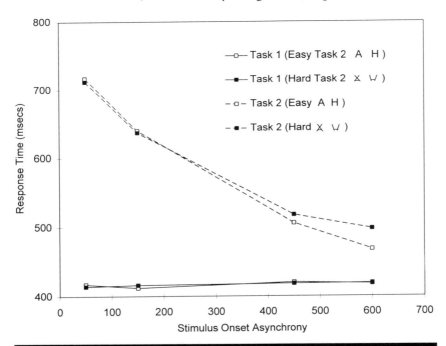

Figure 2

Data from Experiment 1, using the psychological refractory period paradigm. First task response time (RT1) was rapid and unaffected by the stimulus onset asynchrony (SOA) for the two tasks, confirming that subjects gave priority to Task 1. Second task RT (RT2) was relatively short at long SOAs, but increased strikingly at shorter SOAs, when, by hypothesis, there is a delay in the availability of central attention to Task 2. Task 2 letter difficulty affected RT2 at long SOAs, but not short SOAs. This evidence for absorption into slack indicates that letter identification occurs prior to the processing stage requiring central attention.

EXPERIMENT 1

Experiment 1 applied the locus-of-slack method to the PRP paradigm to determine whether the reference stage of processing occurs before or after the stage that requires central attention.

Method

The experiments were carried out on an IBM-compatible microcomputer. On each trial stimuli from two separate tasks were presented in rapid succession, each requiring a separate judgment and speeded response. Task 1 stimuli were a 300-Hz and a 900-Hz tone; responses were the spoken words *low* and *high* (spoken responses were self-scored by the subjects for accuracy after each trial was over). Task 2 stimuli were the letters *A* and *H*, presented at fixation on a CRT display; responses were indicated by pressing one of two adjacent keyboard keys. The stimulus onset asynchrony (SOA) between Task 1 and Task 2 stimuli varied unpredictably within trial blocks (50, 150, 450, or 600 ms). To ensure that central attention was allocated initially to Task 1, instructions emphasized responding rapidly and accurately on this task, and response-time (RT) feedback after blocks was provided only for Task 1.

To manipulate the duration of the letter-identification stage in Task 2, letters were presented either normally or distorted (see Figure 2). The form of distortion used was designed to lengthen the duration of the processing stage in which the identity of a character is determined (letter identification). Each subject experienced all combinations of SOA and letter distortion, randomized within trial blocks. Twenty-four subjects were tested for one session of 384 trials, following 128 trials of practice.

Results and Discussion

Error rates were low on both Task 1 (.015) and Task 2 (.048; normal: .043, distorted: .053). Trials with an error on either task and trials with outer response times on either trial (RT1 > 1,500 ms or RT2 > 2,000 ms; 0.5% of trials) were excluded from RT analyses. Separate analyses of variance were performed on the RT data from Task 1 and Task 2.

RTs for the tone judgment task (RT1) were fast and virtually identical across SOAs, $F(3, 60) < 1$. SOA had a strong effect on response time in the *A–H* letter discrimination task (RT2), $F(3, 69) = 199$, $p < .001$. As

SOA decreased, RT2 increased strikingly (244 ms slower at SOA 50 than at SOA 600), as is consistent with a central attentional bottleneck. Letter identification difficulty had a significant effect on RT2, $F(1, 23) = 4.7, p < .05$; and letter difficulty and SOA interacted significantly, $F(3, 69) = 3.93$, $p < .02$. At SOA 600, where task interference was minimal, letter distortion slowed RT2 by 27 ms. The slowdown was reduced to 15 ms at SOA 450 and disappeared entirely at the two shorter SOAs (-2 ms and -5 ms). These data support the conclusion that the letter-difficulty effect was completely absorbed into slack at short SOAs. By locus-of-slack logic, we conclude that letter identification occurs before the stage delayed by tying up central attention on Task 1.[5] Hence, the processing stage at which letter identification is carried out lies before the stage at which central attention operates.

EXPERIMENT 2

As far as we know, total absorption of a Task 2 difficulty effect into slack has previously been reported only with the factor of stimulus degradation (Pashler & Johnston, 1989), which presumably has its effects early in processing. Because total absorption into slack was found in Experiment 1 for a manipulation of letter identification difficulty, the new results confirm that the phenomenon can occur further into the processing system.

With our confidence in the locus-of-slack method thus enhanced, we were now ready to apply it to the spatial cuing paradigm. On most trials (valid condition) a visual cue is presented, followed by a target stimulus at the same location. On other trials (invalid condition) the cue directs attention to one location, but the target is presented in another location. RTs are known to be delayed on invalid trials compared with valid trials. There is considerable evidence that on invalid trials a time delay in processing occurs while subjects reshift input attention to the target (McCann et al., 1992). In Experiment 2, we used the locus-of-slack method to gain information about when this hypothesized delay occurs. We used the same manipulation of the duration of the same reference stage (letter identification) as in

---

[5]These results have subsequently been confirmed by finding complete absorption into slack using a different manipulation of letter identification difficulty (compressing letters vertically or horizontally).

Experiment 1. As before, we expected to get an underadditive interaction of letter difficulty and attentional delay (now manipulated by valid vs. invalid cuing) if letter identification occurs prior to the stage at which input attention operates, and additive effects of these factors if letter identification occurs after input attention.

Method

Experiment 2 used the same *A–H* letter discrimination task as Experiment 1 (without the tones task); the duration of the letter-identification stage was varied by the same manipulation of normal versus distorted characters. Each trial began with the subject looking at a central fixation cross on a CRT screen. The cross blinked off for 100 ms and then returned to alert the subject before each trial. Then, 500 ms later, a spatial cue (a small filled rectangle) was presented for 50 ms 2.7 cm (2.1° of visual angle) above or below the fixation cross. After another 50 ms, a target character 1.7 cm in height appeared, centered 1.8 cm (1.3°) above or below fixation, and remained on for 100 ms. On 80% of the trials, the spatial cue validly predicted the location of the target, which appeared just concentric to the preceding cue. On 20% of the trials the spatial cue was an invalid predictor; the target appeared in the corresponding position on the opposite side of fixation from the cue. When the target appeared, subjects classified it as an *A* or *H*, pressing a key with either the left or right index finger. On half of trials the normal version of *A* or *H* occurred; on the other half of trials the distorted version appeared.

Twenty-two subjects each completed one session of 360 experimental trials (preceded by 40 trials of practice). All subjects experienced all combinations of cuing validity and letter distortion, varying randomly within blocks.

Results and Discussion

Error rates were low overall; they were significantly lower for normal letters (.022) than for distorted letters (.042), $F(1, 21) = 7.3, p < .02$. RT data are reported only for correct trials, excluding outliers above 1,500 ms (only 0.1% of trials).

Responses were 30 ms faster with valid than with invalid cues, $F(1, 21) = 51, p < .001$, as is consistent with a need to shift input attention

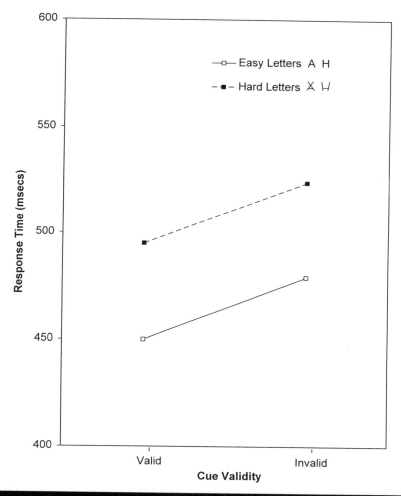

Easy Letters A H
Hard Letters X H

Figure 3

Data from Experiment 2, using the spatial cuing paradigm. Responses were 30 ms faster with valid spatial cues than invalid spatial cues. The effect of letter difficulty was 44 ms for both valid and invalid trials; the effects of letter difficulty and cue validity were almost exactly additive. These data support the hypothesis that in the spatial cuing paradigm, the stage of letter identification occurs after the processing stage requiring input attention.

from the cue to the target location on invalid trials. Letter distortion slowed responding by 44 ms, $F(1, 21) = 52$, $p < .001$.[6] Most importantly, spatial cuing and letter distortion had almost exactly additive effects; distortion slowed responding by the same length of time both with valid and with invalid cuing. Applying the locus-of-slack method, this additive result indicates that letter identification occurs after cognitive slack in the task. Because the spatial cuing paradigm is hypothesized to delay availability of input attention (creating cognitive slack on invalid trials), we conclude that letter identification occurs after the stage at which input attention operates. This conclusion is the opposite of the conclusion reached for central attention in Experiment 1.

GENERAL DISCUSSION

Attentional Bottlenecks at Multiple Loci

It is a relatively simple matter to combine our two findings into a composite stage model (see Figure 4). The stage of letter-identification occurs after the stage at which input attention operates but prior to the stage at which central attention operates. Time added to the letter-identification stage is not absorbed into slack produced by input attention, because letter identification occurs after the stage at which input attention operates.[7] Time added to the letter-identification stage is absorbed into slack produced by delayed availability of central attention, because the letter-identification precedes the central attention bottleneck.

---

[6]The effect of letter distortion in Experiment 2, 44 ms, was noticeably larger than the 27-ms effect obtained for second task reaction time for the long stimulus onset asynchrony condition of Experiment 1. Because the stimuli and tasks were virtually the same, the difference may appear puzzling. However, the difference is readily explainable by the presentation of the stimuli directly at fixation in Experiment 1 versus well off fixation in Experiment 2.

[7]Actually, our results are compatible with the hypothesis that letter identification influences precisely the stage whose onset is delayed by a lack of input attention, but other evidence suggests that input attention operates even earlier. Hawkins, Shafto and Richardson (1988) found that visual degradation interacts with spatial cuing; by additive-factors logic this finding indicates that input attention occurs at the same stage as early visual analysis (see also Prinzmetal, Presti, & Posner, 1986). Remington, Johnston, Folk, and McCann (1991) have reviewed other experiments indicating additive effects of spatial cuing and a variety of perceptual judgment factors. Shulman (1991) has recently reported evidence that spatial cuing can actually modify the extent of a motion illusion; this finding also suggests a locus within perceptual processing. The classic contrast of early versus late selection emphasized the question of whether attention operated before or after character (or, more generally, object) identification. An early locus need not be after all perceptual processing. Perception is complex and occurs in various layers or stages; input attention may operate well before the final stages of perceptual analysis. For converging electrophysiological data, see Luck and Hillyard (1994).

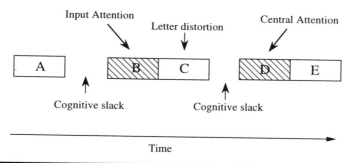

Figure 4

Stages-of-processing diagram for a dual-locus model of attention. Input attention is required for Stage B to begin; central attention is required for Stage D to begin. Letter identification is carried out in Stage C, which occurs after the stage at which input attention operates, but before the stage at which central attention operates. (Additional stages of processing not critical to the current experiments are omitted.)

Alternative Hypotheses

Our two component conclusions differ in their susceptibility to alternative accounts. It is not easy to dispute the implications of Experiment 1 using the PRP paradigm. The underadditive interaction of letter distortion and task overlap is virtually a signature for absorption into slack. Underadditive results are difficult to explain otherwise because they are extremely counterintuitive. It is surprising when an experimental task-difficulty manipulation that is known to make a task take longer when the task is done alone fails to make the task take longer when done along with another task. Surely the sensible expectation is that the effect of the difficulty manipulation would be exaggerated when the task must be done along with another task.

On the other hand, our conclusion about input attention is open to several alternative interpretations. If the spatial cuing paradigm slows responses because of a processing bottleneck that produces slack, then there is no alternative but for any factor with an additive effect to occur after the bottleneck. However, our results provide no direct evidence that cuing input attention actually produces cognitive slack. Our model could be challenged by two different types of alternative models in which spatial cuing does not produce slack. All that is required is that letter identification and spatial cuing occur in separate processing stages; in that case additive-factors logic by itself is sufficient to explain the additive results found in Experiment 2.

The first alternative model holds that spatial cuing does not stop processing at unattended locations; it only modulates the rate of stimulus processing, so that it is faster at cued than uncued locations (e.g., Shulman, Wilson, & Sheehy, 1985). This would occur according to theories positing a gradient of processing rates around the attended location (LaBerge & Brown, 1989). This hypothesis can readily explain the additivity in Experiment 2, provided that the stage influenced by input attention occurs very early in perception and terminates prior to letter identification. Note that although this model differs from ours, it hypothesizes an order of stages consistent with Figure 4, supporting our conclusion that input attention and central attention operate at different processing loci.

The second alternative model would follow the classic late-selection position that selective attention operates after letter identification to fetch completed results (Deutsch & Deutsch, 1963; Duncan, 1980; Shiffrin & Schneider, 1977). This late-selection model, like our model, hypothesizes that on invalid trials input attention first shifts to the cue location and then shifts to the target location. Unlike our model, the late-selection model assumes that the second shift does not happen until after letter identification is completed. This assumption is critical because otherwise the two factor effects would not be additive. Although this model may appear attractive (especially to those still hoping to defend late-selection in a variety of other paradigms), the assumptions required for the current paradigm are curious, to say the least. On invalid trials, the initial shift of attention to the cue location must surely be based only on its physical properties (e.g., the initial transient), because the cue has no letter identity. Yet the model must assume that subjects on the very same trials are then unable to shift attention to the target stimulus using *its* physical properties—subjects have to wait even to initiate the shift until a letter identity is available. Neither horn of this dilemma appears easy to avoid. It would probably be most in keeping with the flavor of late-selection theory to deny that it is affected by cues without task-relevant high-level object identities, but that would provide no account of the main effect of spatial cuing. The other way out of the dilemma is to argue that although attention operates to fetch object identities, its allocation is still triggered by physical properties (of both cue and target). It might be thought that this could explain the data, as long as there was a sufficient delay before the shift was executed, as that the shift always occurred after letter identification. It is not enough, however, that the shift occur just sometime after letter identification is over. To explain additivity the shift must occur contingent on when letter identification ends; otherwise, underadditivity would be found.[8]

No matter how late selection is formulated, it must still somehow explain the discrepancy in results with the two paradigms. Attention delays caused by spatial cuing in Experiment 2 must occur after letter identification has been completed to explain the additive data pattern. But attention delays caused by the PRP paradigm in Experiment 1 cannot occur after letter identification has been completed, or else additive effects of letter identification and attention delays would have been found in that experiment too; letter identification must be carried out concurrently with the PRP attention delay. It is not obvious how a unitary late selection process can operate so as to absorb the effect of letter identification in one paradigm but not the other.

Multiple Types of Attention

Even if our conclusion that attention operates at several different processing loci is granted, it is a further step to conclude that different types of attentional processes are being tapped. The former greatly strengthens the case for the latter, but there is no direct implication. In principle, it is conceivable that the same process could be operating but at different stages (Kahneman, 1973, attempted a synthesis along these lines). To make this idea concrete, consider turnstiles. Turnstiles can gate customers both as they enter a store and as they leave; there are two temporal loci, but both processes can be essentially identical. Note that in that example, the gating mechanism has the same properties in both loci. In our case it appears that manipulations of input attention hold up letter identification but that manipulations of central attention do not.

---

[8]On its face, the possibility that attention shifting would be delayed by enough time for letter identification to be over seems strained. The problem is made worse by the need to extend the account for McCann, Folk, and Johnston's (1992) related finding of additive effects of spatial cuing and word identification difficulty. The execution of spatial attention shifts would have to be delayed by several hundred milliseconds for them to occur only after word identification was complete.

Beyond this, we would appeal, appropriately in this book, to the principle of converging evidence. We have already noted that functionally the two paradigms seem to be imposing different obstacles. In the spatial cuing paradigm, only one task is present, and the only obstacle appears to be the need to handle multiple inputs. In the PRP paradigm, at least in its modern variants, care is taken to minimize competition for stimulus processing resources and delays appear to be due to the presence of multiple tasks. It may also be relevant that PRP delays are typically several hundred ms, whereas invalid spatial cuing delays responses by 30 ms or so. This would make sense if, as frequently supposed, central cognitive operations take longer than elementary stimulus-processing operations. There are also other behavioral data arguing that spatial attention cuing can be shifted while the PRP delay is actually occurring (Pashler, 1991) and that interference between two streams of stimulus processing is qualitatively different from PRP interference (Pashler, 1989). Finally, we note recent physiological data arguing that attentional manipulations related to stimulus processing have a posterior anatomical locus in the occipital cortex (Luck & Hillyard, 1994), the parietal cortex (Posner & Petersen, 1990), and the pulvinar (LaBerge & Buchsbaum, 1990), whereas attentional manipulations related to multiple tasks have a more anterior location in the cingulate cortex (Posner & Petersen, 1990).

Having made our case that there are two different types of attention operating at two different processing loci, it is hard to resist speculating about whether there may be additional types of selective attention waiting to be discriminated. We believe that this is likely to be true. One of us has previously speculated (Yantis & Johnston, 1990) that even though people use an early selection locus in focused attention tasks (as in our Experiment 2), they may be able to use a late-selection locus in divided attention tasks. That is, in divided attention tasks, people can allow a large number of stimuli into their banks of identification detectors and exercise selection by controlling what they fetch out of those detector banks. It does not seem likely that this late-selection, stimulus-processing locus is the same as the locus for the PRP bottleneck. So there is at least one more clear candidate type of selective attention waiting in the wings.

There is a more general possibility that is tantalizing to consider. Suppose the brain consists of numerous relatively autonomous processing modules, each of which can only perform one job at a time. With ingenuity, we can eventually contrive a situation in which virtually any arbitrary processing module is needed for one task when it is tied up by another. Any module that responds to this conflict by delaying processing of the later-arriving task can constitute a bottleneck. Hence, virtually every processor could be performing the function of selection. From this perspective, in a network of distributed processors, selection is a natural candidate to be a highly distributed property.

Note that this would bring the concept of attention to about the same status as the concept of memory. It is becoming increasingly accepted that the current state of every processor serves as a form of very short-term memory (because biological systems do not turn off instantly). Similarly, every process whose input–output function is tuned by experience becomes another processing locus where long-term memory resides. Perhaps in a system of multiple, semiautonomous processing modules, both memory and selection will eventually be seen as properties that a typical processor should exhibit.

Whether, as this speculation suggests, there will turn out to be a very large number of types of selective attention operating at a multitude of different processing loci is an empirical question and one that deserves to be pursued aggressively. The research method used here appears to be capable of repeated application to help decide the matter.

REFERENCES

Bashinski, H. S., & Bacharach, V. R. (1980). Enhancement of perceptual sensitivity as the result of selectively attending to spatial locations. *Perception and Psychophysics, 28,* 241–248.

Broadbent, D. E. (1958). *Perception and communication.* Elmsford, NY: Pergamon Press.

Broadbent, D. E. (1971). *Decision and stress.* San Diego, CA: Academic Press.

Bundesen, C. (1990). A theory of visual attention. *Psychological Review, 97,* 523–547.

Deutsch, J. A., & Deutsch, D. (1963). Attention: Some theoretical considerations. *Psychological Review, 70,* 80–90.

Downing, C. J. (1988). Expectancy and visual–spatial attention: Effects on perceptual quality. *Journal of Experimental Psychology: Human Perception and Performance, 14,* 188–202.

Duncan, J. (1980). The locus of interference in the perception of simultaneous stimuli. *Psychological Review, 87,* 272–300.

Eriksen, C. W., & Hoffman, J. E. (1972). Temporal and spatial characteristics of selective encoding from visual displays. *Perception and Psychophysics, 16,* 201–204.

Hawkins, H. L., Shafto, M. G., & Richardson, K. (1988). Effects of target luminance and cue validity on the latency of visual detection. *Perception and Psychophysics, 44,* 484–492.

Johnston, W. A., & Dark, V. J. (1986). Selective attention. *Annual Review of Psychology, 37,* 43–75.

Kahneman, D. (1973). *Attention and effort.* Englewood Cliffs, NJ: Prentice Hall.

Keele, S., & Neill, W. T. (1978). Mechanisms of attention. In E. C. Carterette & M. P. Friedman (Eds.), *Handbook of perception* (Vol. 9, pp. 3–47). San Diego, CA: Academic Press.

Kosslyn, S. M., & Koenig, O. (1992). *Wet mind: The new cognitive neuroscience.* New York: Free Press.

LaBerge, D., & Brown, V. (1989). Theory of attentional operations in shape identification. *Psychological Review, 96,* 101–124.

LaBerge, D., & Buchsbaum, M. S. (1990). Positron emission tomographic measurements of pulvinar activity during an attention task. *Journal of Neuroscience, 10,* 613–619.

Luck, S. J., & Hillyard, S. A. (1994). Spatial filtering during visual search: Evidence from human electrophysiology. *Journal of Experimental Psychology: Human Perception and Performance, 20,* 1000–1014.

Luck, S. J., Hillyard, S. A., Mouloua, M., Woldorff, M. G., Clark, V. P., & Hawkins, H. L. (1994). Effects of spatial cuing on luminance detectability: Psychophysical and electrophysiological evidence for early selection. *Journal of Experimental Psychology: Human Perception and Performance, 20,* 887–904.

McCann, R. S., Folk, C. L., & Johnston, J. C. (1992). The role of attention in visual word processing. *Journal of Experimental Psychology: Human Perception and Performance, 18,* 1015–1029.

McCann, R. S., & Johnston, J. C. (1992). Locus of the single-channel bottleneck in dual-task interference. *Journal of Experimental Psychology: Human Perception and Performance, 18,* 471–484.

Navon, D., & Gopher, D. (1979). On the economy of the human information-processing system. *Psychological Review, 86,* 214–255.

Newell, A. (1990). *Unified theories of cognition.* Cambridge, MA: Harvard University Press.

Pashler, H. (1989). Dissociations and dependencies between speed and accuracy: Evidence for a two-component theory of divided attention in simple tasks. *Cognitive Psychology, 21,* 469–514.

Pashler, H. (1991). Shifting visual attention and selecting motor responses: Distinct attentional mechanisms. *Journal of Experimental Psychology: Human Perception and Performance, 17,* 1023–1040.

Pashler, H., & Johnston, J. C. (1989). Chronometric evidence for central postponement in temporally overlapping tasks. *Quarterly Journal of Psychology, 41A,* 19–45.

Posner, M. (1980). Orienting of attention. *Quarterly Journal of Psychology, 32,* 3–25.

Posner, M., Nissen, M. J., & Ogden, W. C. (1978). Attended and unattended processing modes: The role of set for spatial location. In N. H. L. Pick & I. J. Saltzman (Eds.), *Modes of perceiving and processing information* (pp. 137–157). Hillsdale, NJ: Erlbaum.

Posner, M. I., & Petersen, S. E. (1990). The attention system of the human brain. *Annual Review of Neuroscience, 13,* 25.

Posner, M., Snyder, C. R. R., & Davidson, B. J. (1980). Attention and the detection of signals. *Journal of Experimental Psychology: General, 109,* 160–174.

Prinzmetal, W., Presti, D., & Posner, M. I. (1986). Does attention affect visual feature integration? *Journal of Experimental Psychology: Human Perception and Performance, 12,* 361–369.

Remington, R. W., Johnston, J. C., Folk, C. L., & McCann, R. S. (1991, June). *The locus of spatial attention in stimulus processing.* Paper presented at the Second Annual Conference on Recent Advances in the Analysis Of Attention, Davis, CA.

Schweickert, R. (1980). Critical-path scheduling of mental processes in a dual task. *Science, 209,* 704–706.

Shiffrin, R. M., & Schneider, W. (1977). Controlled and automatic human information processing: II. Perceptual learning, automatic attending, and a general theory. *Psychological Review, 87,* 127–190.

Shulman, G. L. (1991). Attentional modulation of mechanisms that analyze rotation in depth. *Journal of Experimental Psychology: Human Perception and Performance, 17,* 726–737.

Shulman, G. L., Wilson, J., & Sheehy, J. B. (1985). Spatial determinants of the distribution of attention. *Perception and Psychophysics, 37,* 59–65.

Smith, M. C. (1967a). Reaction time to a second stimulus as a function of intensity of the first stimulus. *Quarterly Journal of Psychology, 19,* 125–131.

Smith, M. C. (1967b). Theories of the psychological refractory period. *Psychological Bulletin, 67,* 202–213.

Sternberg, S. (1969). The discovery of processing stages: Extensions of Donders' method. In W. G. Koster (Ed.), *Attention and performance, II* (pp. 276–315). Amsterdam: North Holland.

Treisman, A. M. (1969). Strategies and models of selective attention. *Psychological Review, 76,* 282–299.

Treisman, A. M., & Gelade, G. (1980). A feature integration theory of attention. *Cognitive Psychology, 12,* 97.

Welford, A. T. (1952). The "psychological refractory period" and the timing of high-speed performance: A review and a theory. *British Journal of Psychology, 43,* 2–19.

Wickens, C. D. (1984). Processing resources in attention. In R. Parasuraman, J. Beatty, & R. Davies (Eds.), *Varieties of attention* (pp. 63–101). New York: Wiley.

Yantis, S., & Johnston, J. C. (1990). On the locus of visual selection: Evidence from focused attention tasks. *Journal of Experimental Psychology: Human Perception and Performance, 16,* 135–149.

17

Selective Attention as a Computational Function

A. H. C. van der Heijden

I n 1949, when behaviorism still reigned, Donald Hebb wrote

> Almost without exception psychologists have recognized the exis-
> tence of the selective central factor that reinforces now one response,
> now another. The problem is to carry out to its logical conclusion
> an incomplete line of thought that starts out preoccupied by stim-
> ulus or stimulus configuration as the source and control of action,
> eventually runs into the facts of attention . . . , and then simply
> agrees that attention is an important fact, without recognizing that
> this is inconsistent with one's earlier assumptions. To complete this
> process, we must go back and make a change in the basis of the the-
> ory. (Hebb, 1949, pp. 4–5)

It is worthwhile to notice two different complaints in Hebb's remark. The
first is that the theoretical construct *attention* was lacking in the then prevailing theories. That problem was soon taken care of. Broadbent (1958)
introduced "the selective central factor" in auditory information processing and Sperling (1960) used "attention" as an explanatory construct for
visual information processing (see Van der Heijden, in press, for a brief
overview of this history). Now, no decent information-processing theory

works without one or another concept of attention—it is a central factor that performs a lot of theoretical work (see, e.g., Van der Heijden, 1992, for an overview). It sometimes even seems as if from 1960 on, everyone doing research in perception conspired in order to effect the "change in the basis of the theory" Hebb (1949) asked for.

The second complaint is that theorists can so easily live with theoretical inconsistencies. Even when they are well aware of one or another theoretically important fact, they are capable of suppressing that knowledge and of advocating assumptions that are incompatible with that state of affairs. There is not very much reason to assume that that problem has also been taken care of. Because I hate to be critical with regard to the theoretical status of my kind of psychology, I quote Scheerer (1990), who courageously remarked,

> What is the information-processing approach about? Van der Heijden and Stebbins (1990) begin their paper . . . with a gloomy series of negations. The information-processing approach . . . employs a chaotic and unprincipled variety of theoretical languages; it does not rely on one clearly defined level of explanation; its central concepts, such as "information," "processing," or "code," are poorly defined or positively misleading. (p. 89)

Of course, as researchers in the field of information processing, we have to answer both Hebb's (1949) complaints appropriately. As stated, attention has been taken care of. So, let us have a look at theorizing and, because many problems encountered by theories are the result of getting off on the wrong foot, let us first look at its two feet: the "limited capacity" foot and the "cognitive psychology" foot.

THE ASSUMPTION OF LIMITED CAPACITY

In his now classic work on auditory information processing, Broadbent (1958, p. 5) surmised that "perhaps the point of permanent value which will remain in psychology if the fashion for communication theory wanes, will be the emphasis on problems of capacity." He was right. It was not the empirical research topic "problems of capacity" that was emphasized, however. What was emphasized as an unquestioned theoretical assumption was that the human information processor faces serious central capacity problems. (In Broadbent's, 1971, subject index, for example, the entry for capacity reads "Capacity, see limited capacity.") The following quotation serves to illustrate this, virtually omnipresent basic conviction:

> The human organism exists in an environment containing many different sources of information. It is patently impossible for the organism to process all these sources, since it has a limited information capacity, and the amount of information available for processing is always much greater than the limited capacity. (Garner, 1974, pp. 23–24)

Similar expressions are easily found (see, e.g., Broadbent, 1958, 1971, 1982; Bundesen, 1990; Kahneman, 1973; Kahneman & Treisman, 1984; Neisser, 1967; Treisman, 1988).

This basic assumption immediately indicates what empirical researchers have to look for:

> Large though the brain is, any conceivable mechanism which could cope simultaneously with all possible states of the eye, the ear and other receptors, would probably be even larger. The workings of the nervous system then are likely to incorporate a good many devices aimed at economizing on the mechanism necessary. (Broadbent, 1971, p. 9)

Two of those devices—or better, two components with different modes of operation—come readily to mind: (a) a first component that processes all the information available, but only partly, and (b) a second component that processes only part of the information available, but that part completely.

Starting with Broadbent's (1958) auditory theory, most major auditory and visual information-processing theories incorporated these two devices. For vision the nearly generally accepted point of view became that in information processing, two functionally independent sequential stages have to be distinguished. In the first, "preattentive," stage all information receives a preliminary, superficial evaluation. In the second, "attentive," stage only a part of that preprocessed information is subjected to a definitive, complete interrogation (see, e.g., Broadbent, 1958, 1971, 1982; Bundesen, 1990; Kahneman, 1973; Neisser, 1967; Sperling, 1963; Treisman, 1964, 1988).

Subsequent research led to a more complete characterization of both processing stages (see, e.g., Folk & Egeth, 1989, p. 97). The preattentive processes of the first stage were generally regarded to be (a) "automatic," that is, triggered by and under the control of external stimulation; (b) spatially parallel, that is, operating simultaneously on all locations of the visual field; and (c) unlimited in capacity, that is, capable of performing their limited repertoire of tricks when and where required.

The attentive processes of the second stage were generally regarded to be (a) "controlled," that is, guided and directed by the information processor's goals and intentions; (b) spatially restricted, that is, operating on only a small, circumscribed, "region" of the visual field; and (c) limited in capacity, that is, only capable of showing their sophisticated information-processing capacities once per unit of time.

THE MOVE FROM BEHAVIORISM TO COGNITIVE PSYCHOLOGY

In the 1950s and the early 1960s, experimental psychology still perfectly understood the main lesson taught by behaviorism. Behavioral data, collected in well-controlled experiments, were the data in need of an explanation. There were different kinds of explanations, but, basically, all theoretical effort was directed at elaborating and elucidating the "processing" in the sequence: stimulation → processing → behavior (see, e.g., Broadbent, 1958; Hebb, 1949; Miller, 1956).

Cognitive psychology, as introduced by Neisser (1967), however, had different ambitions. Its aim was to learn about "the processes by which a perceived, remembered, and thought-about world is brought into being from as unpromising a beginning as the retinal patterns" and about the "transformation of the fluctuating pressure-pattern at the ear into the sounds and the speech and music that we hear" (Neisser, 1967, p. 4). So, basically, the theoretical effort was directed at elaborating and elucidating the "processing" in the sequence: stimulation → processing → perception (see also Neisser, 1976, and Gibson, 1979, p. 252).

In the 1970s this cognitive psychology intruded into, and merged with, mainstream experimental psychology. The result was a two-headed science. One head had the ambition to explain observed behavior and the other was concerned with the explanation of perception as a subjective experience. Some leading experimental psychologists are very explicit about this double ambition. For Massaro (1986), this is simply what psychology is about:

> Psychology investigates empirically not only the behavioral and mental worlds, but the relation between the two. If the science succeeds, one outcome will be a solution to the mind–body problem. (p. 73)

Most experimental psychologists, however, simply demonstrate this double ambition in their actual theoretical practice. Please notice the see–report, experience–respond, and perceive–select pairs in the following quotations:

> Theories of visual attention are concerned with the limit on our ability to see (and later report) several things at once. (Duncan, 1984, p. 501)

> My claim is that locations in the feature maps are made available to control responses and conscious experience only through their links to those locations in the master-map that are currently selected by the attentional "spotlight." (Treisman, 1988, p. 203)

> The filtering mechanism increases the likelihood that elements belonging to a target category are perceived (selected) without biasing perception in favor of perceiving the elements as belonging to any particular category. (Bundesen, 1990, p. 525)

ATTEMPTS TO EXPLAIN BOTH MIND AND BEHAVIOR

Given the two-headed nature of psychology discussed above, the scientific program of most of contemporary information-processing psychology becomes clear. Its theoretical aim is to explain both mind (perceive, experience, see) and behavior (respond, report, select) in terms of "preattentive" and "attentive" processing.[1] Obviously, such an enterprise

---

[1] Alan Allport tried to answer the question of why the limited-central-capacity assumption is so immensely popular. In his view, "the identification of a postulated central 'limited-capacity system' with certain ideas of consciousness may be responsible at least in part of the extraordinary widespread, intuitive appeal of the concept of limited capacity" (Allport, 1989, pp. 633–634). The two-stage processing models are simply a further elaboration of the concept of limited central capacity. Therefore, it is reasonable to assume that the possiblities that two-stage models seem to offer for an explanation of *perception* and *conscious perception* may be responsible at least in part for the extraordinary widespread, intuitive appeal of these two-stage models. Sensation–perception again?

faces a real danger. That danger involves the temptation to add an insufficient and inadequate explanation of mind and an insufficient and inadequate explanation of behavior and to accept the outcome of that summation as a sufficient and adequate explanation of something of fundamental importance.

To see whether the information-processing approach really manages to escape from this danger, it is necessary to evaluate independently the quality of its explanations of perception as a subjective experience and the adequacy of its explanations of aspects of observed behavior. In my view such an independent evaluation leads inevitably to the conclusion that just as the general concept of limited central capacity does not explain much of observed behavior (see, e.g., Allport, 1987, 1989; Neumann, 1987) and does not clarify much of the mysteries of mind (see, e.g., Allport, 1988, 1989), the more specific two-stage models of contemporary information-processing psychology do not clarify much about mind and are not really effective in explaining observed behavior.

With regard to mind, in *Consciousness Explained*, Dan Dennett (1991) made clear why the type of explanation advanced by two-stage theorists can better be rejected. He exposed forcefully the inconsistencies and incoherences introduced by the "persistently seductive bad idea of the Cartesian Theatre, where a sound-and-light show is presented to a solitary but powerful audience" (Dennett, 1991, p. 227). The two-stage visual information-processing and selective attention theories are all Cartesian Theatre theories. The theatre has two "stages," a "preattentive" stage and an "attentive" stage, and a powerful audience. In the first act on the first stage the audience in the theatre sees only a vague visual world. For the second act on the second stage the help of the audience is required. (There is a "consistent appeal to some intelligent force or agent in explanations of attentional phenomena"; Johnston & Dark, 1986, p. 43). The spectators have to direct their spotlight(!) of attention at regions or objects on the first stage and then, surprise, surprise, the pale blobs so pointed at jump out as glorious, bright, detailed, and colored visual objects in front of them on the second stage.

With regard to the explanation of observed behavior, it is important to know that directors differ in opinion about how much of the world should be shown on the first stage. After Broadbent (1958), some prefer to display only a rather chaotic state of affairs (see, e.g., Treisman, 1988), but after Neisser (1967), others prefer to present much more structure (see, e.g., Bundesen, 1990). Theorists are confronted with a real dilemma here. For adequate performance, the spectators have to direct their spotlight of attention at the relevant region or object. When only a little bit is revealed on the first stage, how is the audience capable of directing their spotlight appropriately? When much more is revealed on the first stage, why is the directing of attention and a second stage required? It is exactly the solution of this dilemma that has led to inconsistent and incoherent theories.

COMPUTATIONAL REALIZABILITY

One way of avoiding inconsistencies in theories is by writing computer programs that simulate the alleged psychological processes in humans. Such a simulation presupposes a formal model and therefore forces the theorist to be more rigorous and explicit than he or she possibly otherwise would have been. Moreover, "actually running such programs on computers has the further advantage of making sure that the alleged processes are, in fact, computationally realizable" (Flanagan, 1991, p. 243). Recently, Van der Velde (1993) emphasized the fundamental importance of the computational realizability of a theory. Van der Velde, who has completed studies in physics, philosophy, and psychology and therefore has some right to speak, pointed out the following.

■ Contemporary empirical and theoretical physics could only reach its current level of sophistication because of its happy marriage with mathematics. Theory building in empirical physics can be regarded as the search, among all possible alternatives invented by mathematics, for the one and unique state of affairs that is actually realized in this universe. The empirical evidence reduces the set of viable alternatives; for example, from among all possible geometries of space, the empirical evidence strongly indicates that the one suggested by Einstein's general relativity theory is the one we have to live with.

■ There is a branch of mathematics that can perform a similar job for psychology, especially for the kind of psychology concerned with perception, memory, attention, and so on. That branch of mathematics goes under the name of "recursion theory" and is concerned with "effective procedures" or "computational functions." It is the mathematics of Turing and Church that defines "computational" in terms of the "set of recursive functions."

■ This branch of mathematics becomes available on the basis of the hypothesis that the psychological processes that this kind of psychology is concerned with are "computational processes." This hypothesis consists of two parts. The first part is the assumption that the psychological processes are produced by neural networks in the brain. The second part is the assumption that these processes are computational functions in the mathematical sense.

■ To demonstrate that a hypothesized cognitive process is a computational function, one can use the abstract mathematics of basic functions and operations introduced by Gödel and Kleene, but one need not take that route. Just because a computer simulation of the process is a decomposition of that process in terms of basic functions and operations, it is a proof that the process is a computational function in the mathematical sense. Each network that is adequately simulated on a computer is a computational function or an effective procedure—an element of the set specified by recursion theory.

■ To find, from among all computational functions that could have been realized, the one that is actually realized in the brains of human beings, one needs constraining empirical information. That empirical evidence has to reduce the set of viable alternatives provided by recursion theory. In fact, for the topic we are concerned with, there are two, nonindependent sets of relevant empirical evidence. First, there is the external, behavioral evidence obtained in standard information-processing and cognitive psychology experiments, that is, the latencies and the percentages correct. Second, there is the alien, internal evidence provided by neurophysiology and neuroanatomy, about structure and function of the brain—that is, the neurons, the networks, and their activities.

■ Taken together, simulation of a neural network on a computer is not just another game that can be played. Such a simulation basically involves the proper use of formal, mathematical methods in the empirical science that psychology is. I now turn to the search for one such computational function in the field of selective attention in vision.

SLAM: A COMPUTATIONAL FUNCTION

SLAM, developed by Phaf (1986; see also Phaf, Van der Heijden, & Hudson, 1990; Van der Heijden, 1992), stands for SeLective Attention Model. It is a connectionistic model for attention in visual selection tasks, inspired by the McClelland and Rumelhart (1981) model for word recognition. SLAM essentially consists of a structured set of interconnected nodes through which activation passes. Implemented as a computer program, SLAM is able to simulate the performance of a typical subject in a number of selective attention tasks.

SLAM was initially designed to perform a simple filtering task in a simple color, shape, position world. In the simulations there were six attributes—red, blue, disc, square, left, right—and two objects per stimulus. A typical stimulus in the task, for instance, consisted of a red disc on the left and a blue square on the right (see Figure 1). SLAM had to name one attribute (the response attribute) of an object specified by another at-

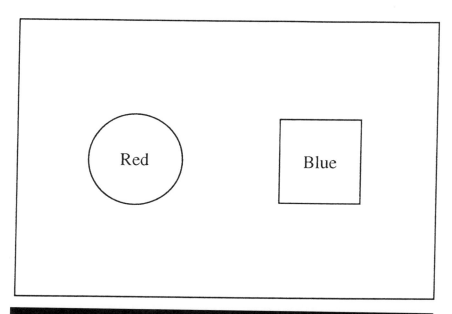

Figure 1

The SeLective Attention Model's world in the filtering task: a stimulus with a red disk at the left and a blue square at the right.

tribute (the criterion attribute). For instance, "name the color of the left one" is an appropriate instruction.

The best way to think about the inner structure of SLAM is as completely symmetric with regard to color, form, and position. This is illustrated in Figure 2, which shows a part of SLAM's processing network. There are three levels: (a) a mapping level with three modules containing nodes for all combinations of features in two dimensions (a Color × Position module, a Color × Form module, and a Form × Position module); (b) a feature level with three modules containing nodes representing single features (a color module, a form module, and a position module); and (c) a motor program level with nodes representing the six possible answers (*red, blue, left, right, disc,* and *square).* There are two groups of connections via which activation passes: between-levels connections and within-level connections. There are both bottom-up and top-down between-levels connections. The nature and strength of these connections is determined by the compatibility of the representations of the nodes. The within-level connections are all within-module inhibitory connections.

Presenting SLAM with only the stimulus, that is, activating all nodes at the lowest level that correspond with the stimulus, results in a symmetric state of activation and a random responding; all six responses are equally probable. Providing one of the two objects at the lowest level, for example the object at the left, with extra activation breaks the symmetry in favor of that object, and the three responses activated by that object will be produced with about equal frequency (*red, disc,* and *left* are equally probable). Providing all nodes in one feature module, for example the color module, with extra activation breaks the symmetry in favor of that dimension, and the two responses from that dimension will be produced with about equal frequency (*red* and *blue* are equally probable). Only when both the object at the lowest level and the feature module at the intermediate level are provided with extra activation is the required selective behavior obtained. In this example the response *red* is almost always produced (a few errors are made, but erring is human).

The fact that SLAM successfully simulates human performance proves that the theoretical view with regard to selection in vision implemented in its tiny network is an effective procedure or a computational function in the mathematical sense. That SLAM can perform its tricks only when two different selective operations cooperate and intersect strongly suggests

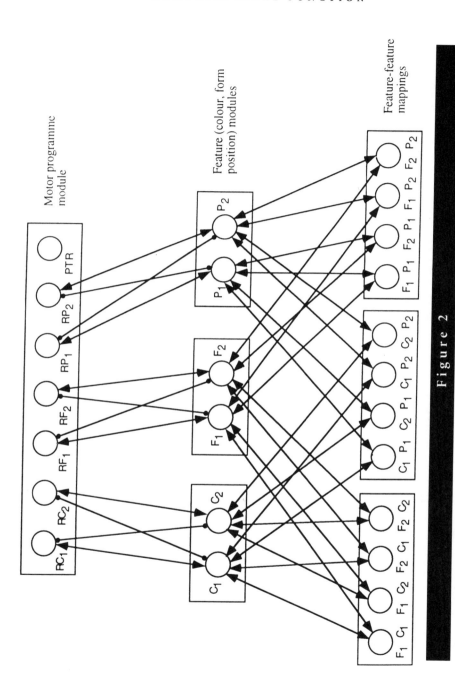

Figure 2

Part of the Selective Attention Model for performing filtering tasks. Note that only a subset of the nodes and connections is depicted.

469

that in vision two forms of attention have to be distinguished; one concerned with the selection of the relevant object and one concerned with the selection of the relevant dimension ("attention" and "intention"; see Van der Heijden, 1992). The fact that exactly the same two selective operations, termed "filtering" and "pigeonholing" (Broadbent, 1971), appear to be essential in Bundesen's (1990) mathematical theory of visual attention shows that it is not so much "connectionism," but much more "computation" that leads to complete and consistent theories (see Van der Velde, 1993).

Unfortunately, the fact that we now have a complete and consistent theory in no way guarantees that we now have also arrived at a theory that correctly accounts for a subject's internal and external affairs. What we have is a computational function, not necessarily the correct computational function. With regard to this "correctness," two related features of the theory are worth noticing. First, SLAM, and also Bundesen's (1990) theory, is completely symmetric with regard to color, form, and position. This feature makes for simple and elegant theories. Nature, however, is not concerned with simplicity and elegance, but with survival. So, what we as theorists have to look for is what sort of internal structure nature really came up with to reach its goals. On the basis of empirical constraints, we have to move from a possible computational function in the direction of the real computational function (see Van der Velde, 1993). Second, in SLAM, and also in Bundesen's theory, attention, concerned with object selection, is still largely undefined. In SLAM, it is extra activation, but where that activation comes from and who is in charge of guiding it still remain pretty vague. Also, in Bundesen's theory, "No attempt is made to discard the notion that attentional selection is controlled by an intelligent agent" (Bundesen, 1990, p. 523), and what attention exactly is remains opaque. So, there is still quite some theoretical work to do. I first deal with the symmetry and then look what can be done with attention.

INTERNAL EVIDENCE

There is quite a bit of neurological evidence that indicates that the visual information-processing system of higher animals and humans is not symmetrical with regard to color, form, and position and that spatial position has a special status. Most of this evidence stems from neurophysiological and neuroanatomical research with animals (for overviews see, e.g., DeYoe & Van Essen, 1988; Felleman & Van Essen, 1991; Livingstone & Hubel, 1988; Zeki, 1992; Zeki & Shipp, 1988). In a recent article I briefly described this evidence (see Van der Heijden, 1995). Here I summarize only the most relevant finding.

Following Ungerleider and Mishkin (1982) and Mishkin, Ungerleider, and Macko (1983), a number of neuroscientists now distinguish two parallel and diverging but strongly interacting information-processing channels. I prefer to call them the *magno channel* and the *parvo channel* (see Felleman & Van Essen, 1991, for a detailed account). The magno channel, or dorsal route, which leads to the posterior parietal cortex, carries information about movement and position and possibly global form. The idea is that it is mainly concerned with object localization and spatial organization, or with the "where."[2] The parvo stream, or ventral route, which further subdivides, leads to the inferotemporal cortex and handles color and detailed form. The idea is that this stream is primarily concerned with object recognition and identity information, or with the "what." Vaina (1990) made it clear that this distinction between parallel "what" and "where" channels equally applies to the human visual information-processing system (see also Bridgeman, 1992; Jeannerod, 1994; Livingstone & Hubel, 1988, p. 740; see also, however, Green, 1991).

Within visual information processing and selective attention psychology this information is not often really used. The reason for this neglect of relevant information is not too difficult to find. As stated earlier, the limited capacity view has led to another theoretical distinction: the distinction between a first, parallel stage of superficial information processing and a second, serial stage of thorough information processing. This distinction, which can be regarded as the unifying theoretical core around which nearly all contemporary information-processing theories are built, prevents the eager acceptance of the important information provided by the neurosciences.

In my view, the theoretical work of Treisman (1988; Treisman & Gormican, 1988) clearly demonstrates the problems subscription to the

---

[2]"Where" is possibly too narrow a characterization of the function of the dorsal, magno system. Evidence is accumulating that this channel mediates "motor interaction": navigation, reaching, grasping, and so forth (see, e.g., Jeannerod, 1994; Livingstone & Hubel, 1988; see also Van der Heijden, 1995).

orthodox two-stage theory causes for the acceptance of the more recent two-channel information. In Treisman's model, at the preattentive level a "master map of locations" precedes a number of modules concerned with the extraction of features such as color and orientation. Treisman (1990, p. 460) stated that the "model separates the functional access to 'what' and to 'where' at a preattentive level of processing, paralleling the apparent separation of physiological pathways for spatial information and for object identification described by Mishkin, Ungerleider, and Macke (1983) and others." But Mishkin et al. meant parallel pathways, not "where" and "what" in series. Moreover, exactly the "preattentive level of processing" seduced Treisman and Gormican (1988, p. 45) to consider the possibility that "the master map could perhaps correspond to area V1 where many units appear to code several properties at once." Neuroscience, however, has provided abundant evidence that not the cortical entrance module V1, but the parietal cortex, much farther down in the stream of information processing, plays the pivotal role in spatial localization (see also the comments of Green, 1991, p. 399).

At present, it is far from clear how the two distinctions, the what–where distinction and the preattentive–attentive distinction can be reconciled and combined. At first sight, such a reconciliation and combination does not seem very difficult. Just because the two distinctions are close to orthogonal, a peaceful coexistence in one ecumenical model seems to be an adequate solution. Problems, however, arise with the functional interpretation of such a compound model. The prime reason for these problems is that the multiplication of two sequential stages with two parallel channels leads to an explosion in explanatory power that is in no way required by the data that have to be explained. So, one of the distinctions is not really needed. It seems that the time has come to have a critical look at the two-stage distinction as derived from the limited capacity assumption.

EXTERNAL EVIDENCE

There is also quite a bit of behavioral evidence that indicates that the visual information-processing system is not symmetrical with regard to color, form, and position and that spatial position plays a special role. Most of this evidence stems from experiments that strongly suggest that attentional selection is always ultimately accomplished via a representation that (also) portrays visual space. The currently so popular spotlight, gradient, and zoom lens metaphors already hint at this special role for spatial position (see, e.g., Eriksen, 1990; Eriksen & Hoffman, 1974; Eriksen & Rohrbaugh, 1970; LaBerge & Brown, 1989; see also Van der Heijden, 1992, for an overview). There is, however, more evidence. I have recently reviewed that evidence elsewhere (see Van der Heijden, 1993), so here I list only what I regard as the important paradigms.

Evidence that position is special has been produced with experimental paradigms with kinds of errors and with correct responses as the important data. In the first category belong the data obtained in the rapid-serial-visual-presentation task (see Broadbent & Broadbent, 1986) and the one-response partial-report task (see Fryklund, 1975; Snyder, 1972). The errors found in these tasks strongly suggest that also in selection on the basis of color a representation of visual space is involved. In the second category belong the data obtained in a two-response partial-report task (see Nissen, 1985) and a combined partial-report and whole-report task (see Tsal & Lavie, 1988). The correct responses in these tasks strongly suggest that with selection on the basis of color, a representation of visual space is an unavoidable intermediate. Mainstream theorists in visual information-processing and selective-attention psychology find these position-special results rather difficult to accept. The reason is again not too difficult to find. The all-attributes-are-equal point of view was one of the major features of Broadbent's (1958) theory of auditory information processing: "Physical features identified as able to act as a basis for . . . selection include the intensity, pitch, and spatial localization of sounds" (p. 297). All initial limited-capacity, two-stage information-processing theories copied this assumption. The initial visual information-processing theories were therefore also symmetric with regard to color, form, and position (see, e.g., Broadbent, 1971; Kahneman, 1973; Neisser, 1967). As a result, the position-special data easily force theorists into an at first sight unattractive, because it is unorthodox, position.

In my view, the theoretical work of Bundesen (1990, 1991) clearly demonstrates how tempting it is to prefer maintaining an orthodox symmetric theory over something like scientific parsimony. Bundesen (1990) presented a detailed mathematical theory of selective attention based on Kahneman's (1973) theory. There are four primitive theoretical entities in this theory: element, color, form, and position. Unfortunately for Bundesen's theory, Nissen (1985) showed that for explaining the results obtained in her two-response partial-report task, only three primitive theoretical entities were required: color, form, and position. All functions performed by the "element" in Bundesen's theory could be performed by position in her account. Bundesen (1991) agreed, but instead of trying to reduce his four-term theory into a three-term theory, he maintained his theory and proved the obvious, namely, that Nissen's three-term data could also be explained in terms of his four-term theory. Of course, such theorizing in the wrong direction cannot be regarded as an overenthusiastic application of Ockam's razor (see Van der Velde & Van der Heijden, 1993, for a more principled discussion).

In general, models that are symmetric with regard to color, form, and position need tricks to remain consistent with the data because of ensuing tensions between theoretical statements and empirical statements (see Van der Heijden, 1993). There are two obvious and often used tricks. First, these models can add theoretical statements, that is, introduce additional ad hoc assumptions that postulate special properties of the representation of visual space (e.g., the assumption that there are differences in cue discriminability between color and position; see, e.g., Bundesen, 1990, 1991; Duncan, 1980, 1981). Second, these models can delete empirical statements, that is, discard or neglect sets of relevant data that exhibit special properties of the representation of visual space (e.g., the error data; see, e.g., Bundesen, 1990; Tsal & Lavie, 1988).

Of course, it is far from clear what purpose these tricks serve, except to maintain a beloved traditional theory. Additional assumptions are prone to make a theory incoherent and inconsistent, and neglected (error) data must nevertheless be explained (see Van der Heijden, 1993, for further details). So, from a scientific point of view the tricks cannot really be recommended. The time has come to have a critical look at the all-attributes-are-equal point of view of the orthodox two-stage theories as derived from the limited-capacity assumption.

INFERRING THE BEST EXPLANATION

The purpose of the previous two sections was to highlight constraining empirical information that allows us to move from SLAM as a possible computational function in the direction of the real computational function. As suggested, two related sets of relevant information are on the table now: the information from the neurosciences that in the visual system there is a channel that is primarily devoted to spatial position and the information from experimental psychology that in selection in vision spatial position plays a crucial role. Of course, this information does not directly point to the real computational function. One subjective step is still required: an inference to the best explanation. On the basis of the constraining empirical information, and with the set of theoretical and empirical background assumptions implemented in SLAM as given, we have to draw the inference about the internal structure of the visual information-processing system that best explains the total set of our commitments.

From my previous work it will be clear what I think such an inference to the best explanation has to come up with (see, e.g., Van der Heijden, 1992, 1993, 1995, in press). That outcome is sketched in Figure 3. In the model summarized in this figure the neurophysiological evidence about two information-processing channels is implemented as two parallel information streams; a magno stream from an input map (IN) to a location map (LO), and a parvo stream from the input map (IN) to an identity domain (ID). The psychological evidence that in selection in vision spatial position is essential is implemented as a system of feedback connections or reentry lines from LO to IN. This system of feedback lines is the attentional circuit. The assumption is that attentional selection is always ultimately accomplished via this set of feedback lines, even when relevant and irrelevant objects are defined in nonspatial terms such as color or shape (see Van der Heijden, 1992, 1993, for further details).

The reason for the conviction that this model is indeed a step from SLAM in the direction of the real computational function can, of course, not be based on one or another successful connectionistic or mathematical simulation (see De Bruijn, 1990, for a number of such connectionistic simulations). SLAM and Bundesen's (1990) theory are also successful in this respect. That reason can, however, be based on the fact that this model can provide an adequate solution for the second set of problems connected with SLAM and Bundesen's mathematical theory: the problem of the definition of attention and the problem of the control of attention.

The problem of the definition of attention is not difficult to solve. In

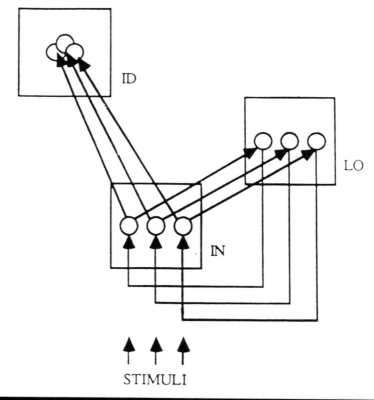

STIMULI

Figure 3

Identity and location-processing model with attentional circuit. Position information, fed back from the location map (LO) to the input map (IN), is the attention. ID = identity domain.

the model sketched in Figure 3, the system of feedback lines is an attentional circuit and therefore the activation passing along these lines is the attention. This definition immediately leads to an adequate definition of the important theoretical concepts *divided attention* and *focused attention*. There is divided attention when everywhere in LO, and consequently in the system of feedback lines, the activity level is about the same, and there is focused attention when somewhere in LO, and therefore in some subset of the feedback lines, the level of activation is relatively enhanced. The divided attention mode can be regarded as the omnipresent background mode of operation of the system (see Eriksen, 1990, for a related suggestion). A state of focused attention is superimposed on this background level of divided attention (see also Van der Heijden, 1993, p. 54).

Given these definitions, the problem of the control of attention is also easy to solve, because that problem now reduces to the problem of what determines the activation pattern in LO, and therefore also in the system of feedback lines. With regard to this problem a classic distinction is essential: the distinction between automatic attention and voluntary attention. With automatic attention the perceptual analysis of the visual scene in IN, in LO, or in both creates one or more regions of enhanced activation in LO. The mere analysis of the visual world itself selects the region that is attended. With voluntary attention, modules not included in the sketch of Figure 3 have to create one or more regions of enhanced activation in LO. Activation originating in these "higher centers" is transported, either directly or indirectly, to the relevant position in LO and selects the region that is attended (see Van der Heijden, 1992, 1993, for further details).

CONCLUSION

Orthodox visual information-processing and selective-attention theory try to explain mind and behavior in terms of limited-capacity, two-stage processing. The theory just briefly sketched is completely at variance with this program. At its basis is the assumption of unlimited capacity. That assumption entails that under normal exposure conditions and within the limits set by retinal acuity, there is full-blown automatic visual information processing without clearly discernible temporal substages (see also Van der Heijden, 1981, 1992). So, what about the explanation of mind and what about the explanation of behavior?

With regard to the explanation of mind, the important point is that the theory is fully compatible with contemporary theorizing in the philosophy of mind. As an alternative to the traditional Cartesian Theatre, Dennett (1991) introduced the multiple drafts theory, which postulates that "all varieties of perception . . . are accomplished in the brain by parallel, multitrack processes of interpretation and elaboration of sensory input" (Dennett, 1991, p. 111) and by "multiple channels in which specialist circuits try, in parallel pandemoniums, to do their various things" (Dennett, 1991, p. 254). The theory summarized in Figure 3 is a multiple drafts model of sorts, with parallel information processing in specialized maps and modules (see also Van der Heijden, 1992, 1995). This compatibility means that I can safely leave the explanation of mind to the Dennetts.

With regard to the explanation of behavior, the important point is that we did not lose some indisputable strong theoretical virtues of some of the two-stage models. For instance, there is no reason to abandon the important idea, stemming from Neisser (1967) and Kahneman (1973), that there are information-processing mechanisms that partition the visual information into objects or object regions against a ground on the basis of gestalt properties such as spatial proximity, continuity of contour, and so forth. Livingstone and Hubel (1988) were impressed by the similarity between the functions they had ascribed to the magno system and the Gestalt psychologists' list of features used to discriminate objects from each other and from the background and concluded therefore that

> the magno system may have a . . . global function of interpreting spatial organization. Magno functions may include deciding which visual elements . . . belong to and define individual objects in the scene, as well as determining the overall three-dimensional organization of the scene and the positions of objects in space and movements of objects. (pp. 747–748)

However, the fact that nothing of importance has been lost does not mean that I can safely leave the explanation of behavior to information-processing psychology. In my view, that psychology "must go back and make a change in the basis of the theory" (Hebb, 1949, p. 5). For adequate behavior an animal needs no selection for perception as postulated by two-stage models. It needs perception for selection, selection for action, and action for perception (see Gibson, 1979; see also Allport, 1987; Neumann, 1987; Van der Heijden, 1992).

REFERENCES

Allport, D. A. (1987). Selection for action: Some behavioral and neurophysiological considerations of attention and action. In H. Heuer & A. F. Sanders (Eds.), *Perspectives on perception and action* (pp. 395–419). Hillsdale, NJ: Erlbaum.

Allport, D. A. (1988). What concept of consciousness? In A. J. Marcel & E. Bisiach

(Eds.), *Consciousness in contemporary science* (pp. 159–182). Oxford, England: Clarendon Press.

Allport, D. A. (1989). Visual attention. In M. I. Posner (Ed.), *Foundations of cognitive science* (pp. 631–682). Cambridge, MA: MIT Press.

Bridgeman, B. (1992). Conscious vs. unconscious processes: The case for vision. *Theory and Psychology, 2*, 73–88.

Broadbent, D. E. (1958). *Perception and communication.* Elmsford, NY: Pergamon Press.

Broadbent, D. E. (1971). *Decision and stress.* San Diego, CA: Academic Press.

Broadbent, D. E. (1982). Task combination and selective intake of information. *Acta Psychologica, 50*, 253–290.

Broadbent, D. E., & Broadbent, M. H. P. (1986). Encoding speed of visual features and the occurrence of illusory conjunctions. *Perception, 15*, 515–524.

Bundesen, C. (1990). A theory of visual attention. *Psychological Review, 97*, 523–547.

Bundesen, C. (1991). Visual selection of features and objects: Is location special? A reinterpretation of Nissen's (1985) findings. *Perception and Psychophysics, 50*, 87–89.

De Bruijn, O. (1990). *Two visual streams: An asymmetry in the processing of colour, form and position.* Unpublished master's thesis, University of Leiden, Leiden, The Netherlands.

Dennett, D. C. (1991). *Consciousness explained.* New York: Penguin Books.

DeYoe, E. A., & Van Essen, D. C. (1988). Concurrent processing streams in monkey visual cortex. *Trends in Neurosciences, 11*, 219–226.

Duncan, J. (1980). The demonstration of capacity limitation. *Cognitive Psychology, 12*, 75–96.

Duncan, J. (1981). Directing attention in the visual field. *Perception and Psychophysics, 30*, 90–93.

Duncan, J. (1984). Selective attention and the organization of visual information. *Journal of Experimental Psychology: General, 113*, 501–517.

Eriksen, C. W. (1990). Attentional search of the visual field. In D. Brogan (Ed.), *Visual search* (pp. 3–19). Washington, DC: Taylor & Francis.

Eriksen, C. W., & Hoffman, J. E. (1974). Selective attention: Noise suppression or signal enhancement? *Bulletin of the Psychonomic Society, 4*, 587–589.

Eriksen, C. W., & Rohrbaugh, J. W. (1970). Some factors determining efficiency of selective attention. *American Journal of Psychology, 83*, 330–343.

Felleman, D. J., & Van Essen D. C. (1991). Distributed hierarchical processing in the primate cerebral cortex. *Cerebral Cortex, 1*, 1–47.

Flanagan, O. (1991). *The science of the mind* (2nd ed.). Cambridge, MA: MIT Press.

Folk, C. L., & Egeth, H. (1989). Does the identification of simple features require serial processing? *Journal of Experimental Psychology: Human Perception and Performance, 15,* 97–110.

Fryklund, I. (1975). Effects of cued-set spatial arrangement and target–background similarity in the partial-report paradigm. *Perception and Psychophysics, 17,* 375–386.

Garner, W. R. (1974). Attention: The processing of multiple sources of information. In E. C. Carterette & M. P. Friedman (Eds.), *Handbook of perception* (Vol. 2, pp. 23–59). San Diego, CA: Academic Press.

Gibson, J. J. (1979). *The ecological approach to visual perception.* Boston: Houghton Mifflin.

Green, M. (1991). Visual search, visual streams, and visual architectures. *Perception and Psychophysics, 50,* 388–403.

Hebb, D. O. (1949). *The organization of behavior.* New York: Wiley.

Jeannerod, M. (1994). The representing brain: Neural correlates of motor intention and imagery. *Behavioral and Brain Sciences, 17,* 187–202.

Johnston, W. A., & Dark, V. J. (1986). Selective attention. *Annual Review of Psychology, 37,* 43–75.

Kahneman, D. (1973). *Attention and effort.* Englewood Cliffs, NJ: Prentice Hall.

Kahneman, D., & Treisman, A. (1984). Changing views of attention and automaticity. In R. Parasuraman & P. R. Davies (Eds.), *Varieties of attention* (pp. 28–61). San Diego, CA: Academic Press.

LaBerge, D., & Brown, V. (1989). Theory of attentional operations in shape identification. *Psychological Review, 96,* 101–124.

Livingstone, M., & Hubel, D. (1988). Segregation of form, color, movement, and depth: Anatomy, physiology, and perception. *Science, 240,* 740–749.

Massaro, D. W. (1986). The computer as a metaphor for psychological inquiry: Considerations and recommendations. *Behavior, Research Methods, Instruments and Computers, 18,* 73–92.

McClelland, J. L., & Rumelhart, D. E. (1981). An interactive/activation model of context effects in letter perception: I. An account of basic findings. *Psychological Review, 88,* 375–407.

Miller, G. A. (1956). The magical number seven, plus or minus two: Some limits on our capacity for processing information. *Psychological Review, 63,* 81–97.

Mishkin, M., Ungerleider, L. G., & Macko, K. A. (1983). Object vision and spatial vision: Two cortical pathways? *Trends in Neurosciences, 6,* 414–417.

Neisser, U. (1967). *Cognitive psychology.* New York: Appleton-Century-Crofts.

Neisser, U. (1976). *Cognition and reality.* San Francisco: Freeman.

Neumann, O. (1987). Beyond capacity: A functional view of attention. In H. Heuer & A. F. Sanders (Eds.), *Perspectives on perception and action* (pp. 361–394). Hillsdale, NJ: Erlbaum.

Nissen, M. J. (1985). Accessing features and objects: Is location special? In M. I. Posner & O. S. M. Marin (Eds.), *Attention and performance, XI* (pp. 205–219). Hillsdale, NJ: Erlbaum.

Phaf, H. (1986). *A connectionist model for attention, restricting parallel processing through modularity.* Unpublished master's thesis, University of Leiden, Leiden, The Netherlands.

Phaf, R. H., Van der Heijden, A. H. C., & Hudson, P. T. W. (1990). SLAM: A connectionist mode for attention in visual selection tasks. *Cognitive Psychology, 22,* 273–341.

Scheerer, E. (1990). Domains of mental functioning: An introduction. *Psychological Research, 52,* 88–97.

Snyder, C. R. R. (1972). Selection, inspection and naming in visual search. *Journal of Experimental Psychology, 92,* 428–431.

Sperling, G. (1960). The information available in brief visual presentations. *Psychological Monographs, 74*(11, Whole No. 498).

Sperling, G. (1963). A model for visual memory tasks. *Human Factors, 5,* 19–31.

Treisman, A. M. (1964). Verbal cues, language, and meaning in selective attention. *American Journal of Psychology, 77,* 206–219.

Treisman, A. M. (1988). Features and objects: The Fourteenth Bartlett Memorial Lecture. *Quarterly Journal of Experimental Psychology, 40A,* 201–237.

Treisman, A. M. (1990). Variations on the theme of feature integration: Reply to Navon (1990). *Psychological Review, 97,* 460–463.

Treisman, A. M., & Gormican, S. (1988). Feature analysis in early vision: Evidence from search asymmetries. *Psychological Review, 95,* 15–48.

Tsal, Y., & Lavie, N. (1988). Attending to color and shape: The special role of location in selective visual processing. *Perception and Psychophysics, 44,* 15–21.

Ungerleider, L. G., & Mishkin, M. (1982). Two cortical visual systems. In D. J. Ingle, M. A. Goodale, & R. W. J. Mansfield (Eds.), *Analysis of visual behavior* (pp. 549–586). Cambridge, MA: MIT Press.

Vaina, L. M. (1990). "What" and "where" in the human visual system: Two hierarchies of visual modules. *Synthese, 83,* 49–91.

Van der Heijden, A. H. C. (1981). *Short-term visual information forgetting*. London: Routledge & Kegan Paul.

Van der Heijden, A. H. C. (1992). *Selective attention in vision*. London: Routledge & Kegan Paul.

Van der Heijden, A. H. C. (1993). The role of position in object selection in vision. *Psychological Research, 56,* 44–58.

Van der Heijden, A. H. C. (1995). Modularity and attention. *Visual Cognition, 2,* 269–302.

Van der Heijden, A. H. C. (in press). Visual attention. In O. Neumann & A. F. Sanders (Eds.), *Handbook of perception and action: Vol. 3. Attention.* San Diego, CA: Harcourt Brace Jovanovich.

Van der Heijden, A. H. C., & Stebbins, S. (1990). The information processing approach. *Psychological Research, 52,* 197–206.

Van der Velde, F. (1993). De Theoretische ontwikkeling van de cognitieve psychologie [The theoretical development of cognitive psychology]. *Nederlands Tijdschrift voor de Psychologie, 48,* 246–257.

Van der Velde, F., & Van der Heijden, A. H. C. (1993). An element in the visual field is just a conjunction of attributes: A critique of Bundesen (1991). *Perception and Psychophysics, 53,* 345–349.

Zeki, S. (1992). The visual image in mind and brain. *Scientific American, 267,* 43–50.

Zeki, S., & Shipp, S. (1988). The functional logic of cortical connections. *Nature, 355,* 311–317.

18

Selective Attention and Internal Constraints: There Is More to the Flanker Effect Than Biased Contingencies

J. Toby Mordkoff

I n both natural and laboratory settings, people are often required to focus their attention on a single stimulus or spatial location and ignore everything else that is simultaneously in view. The experimental evidence suggests, however, that when attempting to focus their attention, people can seldom completely succeed. For example, when subjects are asked to view three-item displays, restricting their attention to the center stimulus (hereafter, the *target*), the identity of the task-irrelevant left and right stimuli (the *flankers*) have consistent effects on performance. In particular, if subjects are required to press the left response key when the target letter is an *A* and the right key when the target is a *Z*, then left-key responses are faster (and more accurate) to displays of *AAA* than to *ZAZ* (e.g., B. A. Eriksen & Eriksen, 1974). Similarly, under this particular target-to-response mapping, right-key responses are faster to *ZZZ* than to *AZA*. In summary, selective-attention tasks of this sort have shown that performance depends not only on the task-relevant target, but also on the task-

This research was supported by Grant T32-MH14268 from the National Institute of Mental Health to the University of California, San Diego. I thank Charles W. Eriksen, Juan Botella, Art Kramer, Jeff Miller, and Cathleen Moore for their advice and comments and Dana Feinberg, Rima Kliore, and Danielle Picher for their help in conducting the experiments.

irrelevant flankers. This pattern of results, which demonstrates a failure of selective attention, is typically referred to as the *flanker effect*, and much of what is known about this phenomenon may be directly traced to the work of Charles W. Eriksen (e.g., B. A. Eriksen & Eriksen, 1974; see C. W. Eriksen & Schultz, 1979, for a review).

The flanker effect has not only been of interest in and of itself, but has also been used as a tool in studies of other attentional mechanisms. By manipulating the separation between the flankers and the center (target) letter, for example, investigators have used the flanker effect as a measure of the size of the attentional spotlight (e.g., C. W. Eriksen & Hoffman, 1972, 1973; C. W. Eriksen & St. James, 1986; C. W. Eriksen & Yeh, 1985). More recently, the flankers task has been used in a series of studies examining the psychophyisiological correlates of selective attention (e.g., Coles, Gratton, Bashore, Eriksen, & Donchin, 1985; Gratton, Coles, Sirevaag, Eriksen, & Donchin, 1988).

A more basic question, however, concerns why the task-irrelevant flankers—when they actually are processed—have any effect on performance. In other words, that the flankers are identified does not explain why their identities have an effect on response time. After all, subjects are instructed to ignore the flankers, and the identity of the flankers is usually uncorrelated with the identity of the target and correct response, so why do the flankers produce the effects that they do?

Previous answers to this question have usually invoked the concepts of response priming and response competition. C. W. Eriksen and Schultz (1979), for example, have argued that

> information about stimuli accumulates gradually in the visual system, and as it accumulates, responses are concurrently primed or partially activated. We conceive of several processes or levels comprising the events from stimulation to response activation. With the onset of stimulation, input channels begin to feed a continuous output to feature detectors which, in turn, continuously feed to form units. The output from the form units is a priming or activation flow to the response system. The output from each process becomes increasingly more detailed or exact over time as energy is integrated in the visual sense organ. The effect at the response level, with this continuous flow, is an initial priming of a wide range of responses.

But as the processing at the lower levels proceeds in time, the priming flow becomes increasingly restricted to fewer and fewer responses, namely, those that are still viable alternatives in terms of the increasingly more exact or complete output of the lower processes. (p. 252)

An implicit argument within C. W. Eriksen and Schultz's explanation of the flanker effect is that once a flanking letter has been fully identified—including recognition that the letter is in a task-irrelevant position—it will not be allowed further access to response processes. On this assumption it makes sense to argue in favor of continuous processing, because if no output to response processes were to be made available until all perceptual processing had finished, then there would be no reason for the flankers to have any effect.

However, this view makes an assumption that might not be warranted. In particular, this analysis appears to assume that once fully processed by perceptual mechanisms, information concerning the letters in task-irrelevant locations is represented in a way that makes its exclusion from response processes possible. This may not be correct. Furthermore, on an alternative view, the effects of the identity of task-irrelevant letters may be seen not as a failure of selective attention, but as a success by mechanisms responsible for extracting and using other forms of information that may be present within an experimental design.

INTERNAL CONSTRAINTS

In some recent analyses of the human ability to divide visual attention (Mordkoff & Egeth, 1994; Mordkoff & Yantis, 1991), the discussion highlighted how performance can be affected by certain subtle contingencies, also known as *internal constraints* (see Garner, 1962). This work has shown, for example, that when the presence of a specific letter in one display location is correlated with the presence of a target in another location, this correlation can significantly affect response time. In particular, if the correlation is positive, then responses are made faster; if the correlation is negative, responses are slowed. These contingencies had been left as uncontrolled variables in previous work concerning divided attention; however, only a model that was sensitive to these contingencies was found to provide a complete account of the data (see Mordkoff & Yantis, 1991, for a review of contingency analysis; see Garner, 1962, for a complete introduction to internal constraints). One issue to be examined regarding failures of selective attention, therefore, concerns the possibility that contingencies have been present in the designs of these experiments as well.

Definition of Terms

In this section, before continuing with a discussion of the experiments, I introduce the nomenclature, starting with the labels for the various conditions in flankers-task experiments. Throughout this chapter, it is assumed that all letters from the start of the alphabet are targets assigned to the left-hand response. Letters from the end of the alphabet are right-hand targets, and letters from the middle are neutral and assigned to neither response.

Trials on which the flankers are identical to the target (e.g., *AAA*) or are letters assigned to the same response as the target (e.g., *BAB*) are *compatible*. Trials with flankers that are assigned to the opposite response from the target (e.g., *ZAZ*) are *incompatible*. The flanker effect is defined as the difference in mean reaction time (RT) between compatible and incompatible trials. Finally, trials with flankers that are assigned to neither response (e.g., *NAN*) are *neutral*.

Next, for the equations describing the various contingencies, superscripts always specify spatial location. For example, A^C denotes the letter *A* in the center (target) location, whereas Z^F indicates that the flankers are *Z*s. Thus, the display *ZAZ* is completely described by A^C & Z^F. A superscript @ (an *at* sign) denotes the presence of at least one exemplar of a given stimulus anywhere within a display; for example, $A^@$ & $Z^@$ partially describes both *AZA* and *ZAZ*, because both displays include at least one *A* and at least one *Z*.

In contrast, subscripts always denote the correct response. Thus, R_L indicates that a left-key response is correct, and R_R indicates that a right-key response is correct. R_L partially describes both *AAA* and *ZAZ*.

To be explicit about the relevant contingencies, the following discussion refers to the experimental design shown in Table 1. This design is typical of flankers-task experiments that include only compatible and incompatible trials. The first set of contingencies to be examined are those referred to as *interstimulus contingencies* (Mordkoff & Yantis, 1991). These contingencies involve correlations between specific letters in specific lo-

Table 1

Trials per Block by Display Type for the Low-Correlation Condition in Experiment 1

Target letter	Correct response	Flanking letters				
		A	Z	B	Y	N
A	R_L	5	5	0	0	0
Z	R_R	5	5	0	0	0

NOTE: R_L = left-key response; R_R = right-key response.

cations, regardless of response relevance. In the case of the design shown in Table 1, the identity of the flanking letters gives no information about the identity of the target letter because

$$P(A^C \mid A^F) = P(Z^C \mid A^F), \tag{1a}$$

and

$$P(Z^C \mid Z^F) = P(A^C \mid Z^F), \tag{1b}$$

where $P(A^C \mid A^F)$, for example, is the probability of an A appearing in the center location given that the flanking letters are also As.[1] Whenever equalities analogous to Equations 1a and 1b are upheld, the design can be said to include no flanker–target interstimulus contingencies. Except for a few exceptions (Logan & Zbrodoff, 1979; Miller, 1987; Paquet & Lortie, 1990), experiments concerning selective attention have not included any flanker–target interstimulus contingencies.

Furthermore, because the identity of the target letter determines which response is correct, there is no response information carried by the flankers, either, because

$$P(R_L \mid A^F) = P(R_R \mid A^F), \tag{2a}$$

---

[1]It is important to note that Equations 1a and 1b assume that the two target letters appear equally often in the center location; that is, $P(A^C) = P(Z^C)$. Under more complicated designs, one must compare each conditional probability with the appropriate baseline. Thus, for example, the complete equations to verify that no flanker-target interstimulus contingencies exist within the design shown in Table 1 are $P(A^C \mid A^F) = P(A^C \mid Z^F) = P(A^C)$ and $P(Z^C \mid A^F) = P(Z^C \mid Z^F) = P(Z^C)$.

and

$$P(R_R \mid Z^F) = P(R_L \mid Z^F), \qquad (2b)$$

where $P(R_L \mid A^F)$, for example, is the probability that a left-key response is correct given that the flanking letters are As.[2] Thus, we can say that the design shown in Table 1 includes no flanker-response contingencies, either (cf. *nontarget-response contingencies*, Mordkoff & Yantis, 1991). That these values are also equal is not unusual. In summary, then, the source of the flanker effect is clearly not in the operation of mechanisms sensitive to either interstimulus or flanker-response contingencies, at least in the way that these contingencies have been defined.

A NEW TYPE OF CONTINGENCY

To this point I have considered only contingencies that rely on location-specific conditional probabilities. In other words, all of the conditional probabilities reviewed above have concerned letters in specific locations as the potential sources of useful information. This may not be sufficient. There may be other contingency-sensitive mechanisms that rely on different forms of information. For example, Miller (1987) has argued that

> in the paradigm used by C. W. Eriksen and his associates (e.g., Eriksen & Schultz, 1979), the presence of a particular letter in the display, *ignoring location*, has been a valid cue as to the correct response. Although the response was independent of the identity of the letter in the flanking positions, the presence of a certain target identity anywhere in the display was still correlated with the response, because of the many trials on which that target appeared in the relevant center position. Overall, when that particular target letter was present somewhere in the display, the response associated with that target was correct more often than not. Perhaps, then, a target cues a response not only because it is a target, but also because the presence of its identity is correlated with that response. (p. 431)

---

[2]Equations 2a and 2b have also been simplified by the assumption that $P(R_L) = P(R_R)$.

In effect, Miller has argued that there may be a new form of contingency operating under selective-attention tasks—one that does not rely on location-specific information, but only on the presence of certain letters anywhere within a display. Because the psychological device that represents a letter regardless of location has previously been called a *typenode* (e.g., Kanwisher, 1987, 1991; Mozer, 1989; cf. *logogen*, Morton, 1969; *feature map*, Treisman, 1988), these correlations are termed here *typenode-response contingencies*.

The two panels of Figure 1 illustrate how this sort of representational device operates. The upper panel depicts the state of the system when it has been presented with three *A*s in a row, as on a compatible flankers-task trial. Each letter is represented by a link between a typenode and a location token. Because at least one *A* is being represented, the *A* typenode is active. In contrast, the *Z* typenode is inactive, because no *Z*s have been presented.

The lower panel shows how the stimuli on an incompatible trial (including both an *A* and some *Z*s) would be represented. In this case, both typenodes are active. To be clear: A typenode is assumed to become active whenever the stimulus for which it codes has been perceived from any location within the visual display. For present purposes it is also assumed that all typenodes must be in one of two states, *active* or *inactive*, and that the number of exemplars (more than one) of the represented stimulus has no effect on typenode activity.

Typenode-Response Contingency Bias

Using the terminology introduced earlier, with a superscript @ denoting the presence of a letter anywhere within a display, the typenode-response contingency (TRC) between the letter *A* and response R_L can be defined as follows:

$$TRC(A \rightarrow R_L) = P(R_L \mid A^{@}). \qquad (3)$$

For the design shown in Table 1, the value of $TRC(A \rightarrow R_L)$ is 0.67, because 10 of the 15 trials that contain at least one *A* in the display require a left-key response. Similarly, the value of $TRC(Z \rightarrow R_R)$ is also 0.67, because the design is symmetrical. In contrast, the values of $TRC(A \rightarrow R_R)$ and $TRC(Z \rightarrow R_L)$ are both 0.33 (5 out of 15 each).

Type–node Representation of AAA

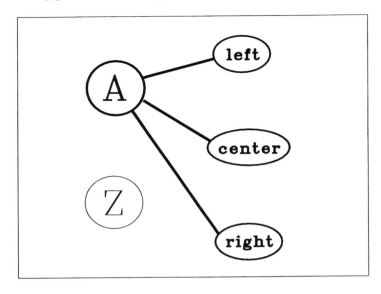

Type–node Representation of ZAZ

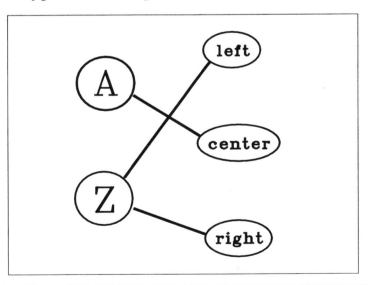

Figure 1

Schematic of part of a typenode network of visual short-term memory. The upper panel shows the network when representing a row of three As. Note that the Z typenode is inactive (thin circle). The lower panel shows the network representing the stimulus string ZAZ. In this case, both typenodes are active (thick circles).

The potential effect on performance that could result from the use of contingency information based on typenode activity—here labeled *typenode-response contingency bias* (TRCB)—is found by subtracting the baseline probability of a given response from the conditional. For example,

$$\text{TRCB}(A \to R_L) = \text{TRC}(A \to R_L) - P(R_L)$$

$$= P(R_L \mid A^{@}) - P(R_L). \qquad (4)$$

For the design shown in Table 1, the values of TRCB are $+0.17$ for both $A \to R_L$ and $Z \to R_R$. The value is -0.17 for both $A \to R_R$ and $Z \to R_L$.

This brings us to a possible source of the flanker effect. Note first that compatible displays that require R_L contain only As, whereas incompatible displays that require R_L contain both at least one A and at least one Z. Thus, given that the correct response is R_L (i.e., the target is an A), there is an extra set of contingencies operating on incompatible trials as compared with compatible trials. In particular, although both types of trial will enjoy the $+0.17$ contingency between the typenode for A and R_L (which would speed responding), the incompatible trials will also have the -0.17 contingency between the typenode for Z and R_L (which would slow responding). In summary, then, the value of TRCB for incompatible letter-response pairs gives a measure of the typenode-response contingency bias against incompatible trials; in this case, TRCB is 0.17. Because all experiments using this sort of flankers-task design have included such a bias against incompatible trials, the possibility that typenode-response contingencies are responsible for the observed flanker effect is viable.

Manipulating TRCB

In order to test this contingency-based explanation of the flanker effect, a method of manipulating TRCB is required. Fortunately, a straightforward technique is available; it involves the use of neutral trials; that is, those trials on which the flankers are letters not assigned to either response. Consider the experimental design shown in Table 2. In this case, many trials involve the neutral flanker N. By Equation 3, the value of $\text{TRC}(B \to R_L)$ is $+0.83$, because 10 of the 12 displays that include at least one B require a left-key response. Similarly, the value of $\text{TRC}(Y \to R_L)$ is -0.83. Thus, under the design shown in Table 2, TRCB is 0.33, which is twice the value obtained using the design shown in Table 1. In general, increasing the proportion of *neutral* trials within a given design will increase the value of TRCB. More specifically, increasing the proportion of trials on which a given target is surrounded by neutral flankers will increase the contingency between that letter and its associated response.

EXPERIMENT 1

The first experiment was conducted as an initial test of a contingency-based explanation of the flanker effect. This was done by combining the designs shown in Tables 1 and 2. Two letters were assigned to each response; one for the design shown in Table 1 and another for the design shown in Table 2. There was only one neutral (flanker) letter, because only the second design includes any neutral trials. In general, Experiment 1 included a within-subjects, within-blocks manipulation of TRCB. Note, however, that the letters included in the trials with nonzero frequencies in Table 1 do not appear in the trials in Table 2. This allowed for separate calculations of TRCB for the two main conditions.

Method

Subjects

Twenty-four undergraduates from the University of California, San Diego, participated for partial course credit. All reported normal or corrected-to-normal visual acuity. Each subject participated in an individual 50-min session.

Table 2

Trials per Block by Display Type for the High-Correlation Condition in Experiment 1

Target letter	Correct response	Flanking letters				
		A	*Z*	*B*	*Y*	*N*
B	R_L	0	0	2	2	6
Y	R_R	0	0	2	2	6

NOTE: R_L = left-key response; R_R = right-key response.

Apparatus, Experimental Design, and Stimuli

The stimuli were presented on NEC Multisync monitors (Tokyo, Japan) controlled by IBM-compatible microcomputers using EGA cards. The subjects responded by pressing buttons on a custom-made response box using their left and right index fingers.

The experiment included two main conditions (within-subjects), as defined by two sets of targets. One condition involved a low-strength correlation between typenode activity and the correct response (i.e., a relatively low value of TRCB); this was achieved by never having the low-correlation targets surrounded by neutral flankers (see Table 1). The other condition involved a high-strength correlation; these targets were often surrounded by neutral flankers (see Table 2). As described above, the value of TRCB for the low-correlation condition was 0.17. For the high-correlation condition, it was 0.33.

Each subject was given a different mapping of the letters A, O, T, V, and X. Two of the letters were assigned to the left-button response (one as the low-correlation target, the other as the high-correlation target), two others were assigned to the right-button response, and the fifth letter was the neutral flanker and only appeared in the nontarget locations.

Each display contained three letters: the central target and two identical flankers to the left and the right. Each letter was 0.90 cm tall and 0.64 cm wide, and the centers of the flankers were 1.10 cm from fixation. From a viewing distance of 45 cm, each letter subtended $1.15° \times 0.82°$ of visual angle, and the flanker locations were 1.40° (center-to-center) from fixation. The fixation cross was 0.30 cm $\times$ 0.30 cm ($0.38° \times 0.38°$).

Procedure

Each trial began with the presentation of the fixation cross for 1,000 ms. After a 500-ms blank interval, the trial display appeared and remained visible until a response was made or 1,500 ms had elapsed. The intertrial interval was 1,000 ms.

There were 13 blocks of trials in a session. The first block included only 20 trials and was labeled practice. After each trial in the practice block, subjects were given RT feedback if correct and were reminded of the letters-to-responses mapping if incorrect. The purpose of this block was to teach subjects their mapping. The data from this block were not recorded.

The remaining 12 blocks were each approximately 50 trials long, depending on the number of errors made by the subject. The design calls for 40-trial blocks, but a randomly selected recovery trial followed each error. There were also five warm-up trials at the start of each block. The data from the warm-up and recovery trials were not included in any analysis. RTs less than 150 ms or more than 1,200 ms were also discarded.

After each block of trials, subjects were given mean-RT and accuracy feedback during an enforced 7-s break. If their error rate was above 5%, they were also told to be "more careful." Subjects were given a 5-min break after the sixth full block. The order of trials was randomized prior to each block.

Data Analysis

The magnitude of the flanker effects (i.e., mean incompatible RT less mean compatible RT) was analyzed in a 2 × 3 analysis of variance (ANOVA) with correlation strength and session part as within-subject factors. The data were analyzed in terms of the flanker effects, rather than mean RT, to avoid having to interpret a three-way interaction. (The flanker effect, itself, is the interaction between target identity and flanker identity.) The data were divided into three parts because previous experiments have suggested that contingencies require some time to learn. Session Part 1 included Blocks 1–4; Session Part 2, Blocks 5–8; and Session Part 3, Blocks 9–12. Planned comparisons were also conducted testing for an effect of correlation strength within each session part. A similar set of analyses concerned the flanker effect in mean error rates.

Results

The mean flanker effects from Experiment 1 are shown in Figure 2. There was no significant effect of session part on the overall flanker effect, $F(2, 46) = 1.98$, nor was the main effect of correlation strength reliable, $F(1, 23) < 1$. The interaction between these two variables was significant, $F(2, 46) = 4.13$, $p < .025$. The planned comparisons showed that during Session Part 1 there was an unreliably larger flanker effect in the low-correlation condition, $t(23) = 1.09$. During Part 2 there was an insignificantly larger flanker effect in the high-correlation condition, $t(23) = 1.55$. However, during Part 3 there was a significant effect of correlation strength, with a larger flanker effect in the high-correlation condition, $t(23) = 1.86$, $p < .05$.

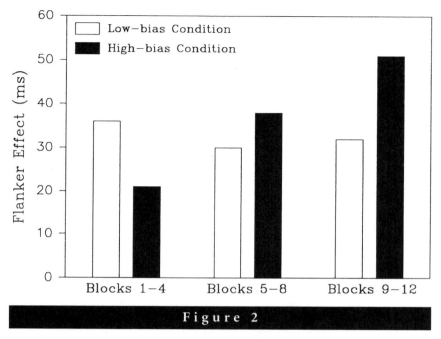

Figure 2

Mean flanker effects by session part and correlation strength; Experiment 1.

Error rates averaged about 5%. An analysis of the errors provided no evidence of a speed–accuracy trade-off; conditions with large mean RTs also had high error rates. No effect in an analogous ANOVA to that concerning RT approached significance.

Discussion

The most important finding from this experiment was that increasing the contingency between the presence of a letter anywhere within the display and the correct response increases the observed flanker effect (but only after some experience with the task). Put another way: The magnitude of the flanker effect was found to covary with the value of typenode-response contingency bias (TRCB; Equation 4). This verifies the prediction of a contingency-based model of the flanker effect.

The finding that contingencies play an important role in determining selective-attention performance extends previous work demonstrating similar effects under divided attention (Mordkoff & Egeth, 1994; Mordkoff & Yantis, 1991). In fact, if one were to reanalyze the previous studies, one could easily show that non-target-response contingencies are functionally identical to typenode-response contingencies. This suggests that the contingency-sensitive mechanisms that are operative under divided- and selective-attention conditions are one and the same.

STROOP COLOR AND WORD TEST AND VARIANTS

The present form of contingency analysis can also be applied to other tasks requiring selective attention. For example, when subjects are asked to name the color of the ink in which a word is written, the semantic value of the word itself has a strong effect on how much time is required to produce the color-naming response. In particular, the time required to say "red" to a display of the word GREEN written in red ink is much greater than that required to say "red" to a display containing either the word RED in red ink or the letter-string xxxx in red ink. This phenomenon is known as the *Stroop effect* (after Stroop, 1935).

The Stroop effect is open to an analysis in terms of typenode-response contingencies. Consider the experimental design given in Table 3, which is typical of Stroop color-naming tasks. Under the assumption that there exists a typenode for the concept *red*, which is activated by either red ink or the word RED, one may refer to trials with matching ink color and word value as *compatible* in the same sense that was used for flankers-task trials with flankers that match the target. Similarly, trials with nonmatching ink color and word value are *incompatible* (e.g., the word GREEN in red

Table 3

Trials per Block by Display Type for the Typical Stroop Color and Word Test

Ink color	Correct response	Stimulus word			
		RED	*GREEN*	*BLUE*	*YELLOW*
Red	"Red"	3	1	1	1
Green	"Green"	1	3	1	1
Blue	"Blue"	1	1	3	1
Yellow	"Yellow"	1	1	1	3

ink). As for the flankers task, we may now calculate values of TRCB for the Stroop-task design given in Table 3:

$$TRCB = P(R_{\text{"red"}} \mid red^@) - P(R_{\text{"red"}})$$

$$= P(R_{\text{"green"}} \mid green^@) - P(R_{\text{"green"}})$$

$$= P(R_{\text{"blue"}} \mid blue^@) - P(R_{\text{"blue"}})$$

$$= P(R_{\text{"yellow"}} \mid yellow^@) - P(R_{\text{"yellow"}})$$

$$= 0.67 - 0.25 = 0.42 \tag{5}$$

where $P(R_{\text{"red"}} \mid red^@)$, for example, is the probability that "red" is the correct response given that red ink or the word RED (or both) are present in the display. The 0.67 results, for example, from the correct response being "red" for 6 out of the 9 trials (per block) that include either red ink or the word RED (or both). The 0.25 is the baseline probability that "red" is the correct response. The same holds for green, blue, and yellow. Thus, the value of TRCB for this Stroop task is 0.42.[3]

In summary, the design given in Table 3, which is quite typical of published Stroop-task designs, includes a typenode-response contingency bias favoring compatible trials. Evidence of the effects of contingencies in a Stroop task has recently been obtained by Tzelgov, Henik, and Berger (1992), who manipulated the proportion of neutral trials in a manner very similar to the present Experiment 1. (The one difference is that these researchers manipulated the number of neutral trials between subjects.) An analysis of their designs and data revealed the predicted relationship between the proportion of neutral trials (and therefore the value of TRCB) and the observed magnitude of the Stroop effect (see Figure 3). Similar explanations in terms of typenode-response contingencies can also be advanced for the results of Stroop-task variants, such as the above–below task used by Logan and Zbrodoff (1979). Thus, the role that is played by

---

[3]It should be noted that the design shown in Table 3 also includes the equivalent of a flanker-target contingency bias in favor of compatible trials. In particular, the conditional probability that the color attribute is red is higher when the word is RED than when it is not. This bias also exists in most Stroop-task designs, but does not alter the present conclusion because it is not affected by manipulations of the number of neutral trials.

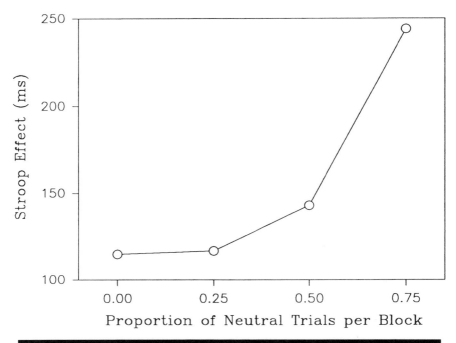

Figure 3

Mean magnitude of the Stroop effect plotted against the proportion of trials in the neutral condition. Data are from "Controlling Stroop Effects by Manipulating Expectations for Color Words," by J. Tzelgov, A. Henik, & J. Berger, 1992, *Memory and Cognition.* Copyright 1992 by the Psychonomic Society. Adapted with permission.

contingencies in determining selective-attention performance may have wide generality.

EXPERIMENT 2

The preceding discussion raises the possibility that the flanker effect is *entirely* due to the operation of typenode-response contingencies. Such a conclusion would be very important because it would raise questions about the continuous flow of partial activations (C. W. Eriksen & Schultz, 1979). This holds because the effects of typenode-response contingencies could occur after all perceptual processes have finished.

To test the idea that biased contingencies are completely responsible for the flanker effect, an experiment with zero TRCB is required. This, however, is not so simple a matter. As has been shown, adding neutral trials to an experimental design increases the contingency between typenode activation and the correct response. A design that includes no neutral trials has the lowest value of TRCB, but it is not zero. Therefore, in order to bring the value of TRCB to zero, an unbalanced design was used for Experiment 2.

Method

Experiment 2 was the same as Experiment 1 with two exceptions. First, the design was changed so that one set of targets (*A* and *Z* in Table 4) involved a zero value of TRCB. In particular, under this design,

$$P(R_L \mid A^@) = P(R_L \mid Z^@) = P(R_L) \qquad (6a)$$

and

$$P(R_R \mid A^@) = P(R_R \mid Z^@) = P(R_L), \qquad (6b)$$

so that the activation state of the *A* and *Z* typenodes provides no information concerning which response should be made. Only the data from the trials involving no TRCB were analyzed; these trials are marked with a superscript *a* in Table 4. Note that these trials also include a small flanker-response bias *against* compatible trials; this was unavoidable, but, as will

Table 4

Trials per Block by Display Type in Experiment 2

Target letter	Correct response	Flanking letters				
		A	*Z*	*B*	*Y*	*N*
A	R_L	6[a]	6[a]	0	0	0
Z	R_R	6[a]	6[a]	0	0	0
B	R_L	0	6	3	3	0
Y	R_R	6	0	3	3	0

NOTE: R_L = left-key response; R_R = right-key response.
[a]Only these trials were analyzed.

be seen, does not affect the conclusions. Second, in light of the results from Experiment 1, only the data from the final four blocks were analyzed. Twenty-four new subjects participated.

Results and Discussion

The condition without any biased typenode-response contingencies produced a small but reliable flanker effect of 26 ms, $t(23) = 2.11$, $p < .025$. Error rates again mirrored the RT data. Thus, it cannot be said that typenode-response contingencies are the sole cause of the flanker effect. That a significant flanker effect was observed when flanker-response contingencies were biased against compatible trials only increases the argument against a contingency-based explanation of the flanker effect.

As it turns out, there are several other problems with a contingency-based model of the flanker effect. Three examples of this are (a) unreported experiments have shown that the effect of contingencies in letter-detection tasks is case specific (see also Miller & Hardzinski, 1981), which contradicts any links between the present analysis and typenode systems (see Kanwisher, 1987); (b) other designs that include differing levels of TRCB (but unequal target frequencies) do not always reveal different-size flanker effects; and (c) the model predicts an advantage for compatible trials with same-response flankers (e.g., *BAB*) over those with identical flankers (e.g., *AAA*), which does not obtain (see, e.g., B. A. Eriksen & Eriksen, 1974). However, the effects observed in Experiment 1 have been replicated several times using various designs, so the influence of contingencies on selective attention must still be considered. If nothing else, it serves as an alternative interpretation of the effects of increasing the number of neutral trials (Tzelgov et al., 1992) or varying the proportion of compatible trials (Logan & Zbrodoff, 1979).

SUMMARY

This study examined selective-attention performance from the perspective of someone who is particularly fond of internal constraints (Garner, 1962). It was first shown that biased contingencies have been included in nearly all published demonstrations of the flanker effect (e.g., B. A. Eriksen & Eriksen, 1974). The results from Experiment 1 then showed that when these contingencies are manipulated, the magnitude of the flanker effect is altered as well. Similar manipulations of the contingencies in other selective-attention tasks have revealed the same pattern (e.g., Tzelgov et al., 1992). Thus, preliminary results suggest that the flanker effect of selective attention—like certain effects of divided attention (see Mordkoff & Yantis, 1991)—may be entirely due to internal constraints.

This argument was then tested in a second experiment. Here it was found that when the crucial contingency is set to zero (and other contingencies are zero or biased *against* the effect), a significant flanker effect is still observed. Thus, although it has here been shown again that internal constraints can alter performance, there is more to the flanker effect than biased contingencies.

REFERENCES

Coles, M. G. H., Gratton, G., Bashore, T. R., Eriksen, C. W., & Donchin, E. (1985). A psychophysiological investigation of the continuous flow model of human information processing. *Journal of Experimental Psychology: Human Perception and Performance, 11,* 529–553.

Eriksen, B. A., & Eriksen, C. W. (1974). Effects of noise letters upon the identification of a target letter in a nonsearch task. *Perception and Psychophysics, 16,* 143–149.

Eriksen, C. W., & Hoffman, J. E. (1972). Temporal and spatial characteristics of selective attention. *Perception and Psychophysics, 12,* 201–204

Eriksen, C. W., & Hoffman, J. E. (1973). The extent of processing of noise elements during selective encoding from visual displays. *Perception and Psychophysics, 14,* 155–160.

Eriksen, C. W., & Schultz, D. W. (1979). Information processing in visual search: A continuous flow conception and experimental results. *Perception and Psychophysics, 25,* 249–263.

Eriksen, C. W., & St. James, J. D. (1986). Visual attention within and around the field of focal attention: A zoom lens model. *Perception and Psychophysics, 40,* 225–240.

Eriksen, C. W., & Yeh, Y.-Y. (1985). Allocation of attention in the visual field. *Journal of Experimental Psychology: Human Perception and Performance, 11,* 583–597.

Garner, W. R. (1962). *Uncertainty and structure as psychological concepts.* New York: Wiley.

Gratton, G., Coles, M. G. H., Sirevaag, E. J., Eriksen, C. W., & Donchin, E. (1988). Pre- and post-stimulus activation of response channels: A psychophysiological analysis. *Journal of Experimental Psychology: Human Perception and Performance, 14*, 331–344.

Kanwisher, N. G. (1987). Repetition blindness: Type recognition without token individuation. *Cognition, 27*, 117–143.

Kanwisher, N. G. (1991). Repetition blindness and illusory conjunctions: Errors in binding visual types with visual tokens. *Journal of Experimental Psychology: Human Perception and Performance, 17*, 404–421.

Logan, G. D., & Zbrodoff, N. J. (1979). When it helps to be misled: Facilitative effects of increasing the frequency of conflicting stimuli in a Stroop-like task. *Memory and Cognition, 7*, 166–174.

Miller, J. (1987). Priming is not necessary for selective-attention failures: Semantic effects of unattended, unprimed letters. *Perception and Psychophysics, 41*, 419–434.

Miller, J., & Hardzinski, M. (1981). Case specificity of the stimulus probability effect. *Memory and Cognition, 9*, 205–216.

Mordkoff, J. T., & Egeth, H. E. (1994). Response time and accuracy revisited: Converging support for the interactive race model. *Journal of Experimental Psychology: Human Perception and Performance, 19*, 981–991.

Mordkoff, J. T., & Yantis, S. (1991). An interactive race model of divided attention. *Journal of Experimental Psychology: Human Perception and Performance, 17*, 520–538.

Morton, J. (1969). Interaction of information in word recognition. *Psychological Review, 76*, 165–178.

Mozer, M. C. (1989). Types and tokens in visual letter perception. *Journal of Experimental Psychology: Human Perception and Performance, 15*, 287–303.

Paquet, L., & Lortie, C. (1990). Evidence for early selection: Precuing target location reduces interference from same-category distractors. *Perception and Psychophysics, 48*, 382–388

Stroop, J. (1935). Studies of interference in serial verbal reaction. *Journal of Experimental Psychology, 18*, 643–662.

Treisman, A. M. (1988). Features and objects: The Fourteenth Bartlett Memorial Lecture. *Quarterly Journal of Experimental Psychology, 40A*, 201–237.

Tzelgov, J., Henik, A., & Berger, J. (1992). Controlling Stroop effects by manipulating expectations for color words. *Memory and Cognition, 20*, 727–735.

19

Decision Competition and Response Competition: Two Main Factors in the Flanker Compatibility Effect

Juan Botella

I n this chapter, I discuss the nature of the effects of distractors in the processing of an imperative stimulus. Although those effects have been sometimes interpreted in terms of peripheral competition of responses, I propose and test a more generalized concept of competition—one that exerts its influence along the continuous flow of information processing. I also propose a more empirical approach to the concept of compatibility between the imperative stimuli and the distractors.

The concept of response competition has been used to account for the costs observed in the flankers compatibility paradigm. In this paradigm, an imperative stimulus for a choice reaction time (RT) task, normally with two choices, is presented. The imperative stimulus is flanked by distractors that in the experimental task (a) have the same response assignment as the imperative stimulus (flankers compatible); (b) have a different response assignment (flankers incompatible); or (c) have no defined response (flankers neutral). Mean RT in the flankers-compatible condition

---

This research was partially supported by the Direccion General de Investigacion Cientifica y Tecnica (DGICYT) of Spain, Project PS93-0029. I wish to thank Lisa Fournier and Toby Mordkoff for their helpful comments and suggestions, which greatly improved the structure and language of the preliminary version of the chapter.

is shorter than in the flankers-incompatible condition, and the flankers-neutral condition produces an intermediate mean RT (B. A. Eriksen & Eriksen, 1974; C. W. Eriksen & Eriksen, 1979; C. W. Eriksen & Schultz, 1979). This is known as the *flanker compatibility effect.*

Some of the research related to costs in the flankers-incompatible condition has focused on searching for empirical evidence that supports the response competition hypothesis. Within the framework of continuous flow conceptions of information processing, it is proposed that responses compete with each other due to a reciprocal inhibition mechanism. It is assumed that in flankers-incompatible conditions, the imperative stimulus and the flankers preactivate their associated responses via the transmission of partial outputs during the decision stage. When the decision criterion level for the correct response is reached, the alternative incorrect response also has some degree of preactivation that must be balanced by means of reciprocal inhibition. Thus, the key factor in accounting for the observed costs and benefits in the flankers-incompatible and flankers-compatible conditions, respectively, is the differential presence of preactivation of the correct and the incorrect response systems (C. W. Eriksen & Schultz, 1979). Preactivation is adaptive, because it leads to anticipatory preparation of a response, which can lead to a quicker execution. However, this mechanism also can lead to costs when conflicting information is present—the same mechanism that produces fast responses can also generate interference, producing slow responses.

The interpretation of the interference in terms of reciprocal inhibition has been supported by the evidence from recordings of differential psychophysiological activity under compatible and incompatible conditions (Coles, Gratton, Bashore, Eriksen, & Donchin, 1985; C. W. Eriksen, Coles, Morris, & O'Hara, 1985; Gratton, Coles, Sirevaag, Eriksen, & Donchin, 1988; Smid, Mulder, & Mulder, 1990). In all of these studies, two-choice RT tasks have been used (subjects had to make their responses with a different hand for each alternative). In Smid et al.'s experiment, a flankers-neutral condition was also included. The results for overt responses were the same as those typically found, that is, shorter RTs and fewer errors in the flankers-compatible condition relative to the flankers-incompatible condition, and intermediate values in the flankers-neutral condition. However, the most interesting data generated in these experiments concern the psychophysiological measures of response activation associated with the correct and incorrect response channels.

In addition to the expected preresponse electromyographic (EMG) activity in the arm corresponding to the correct response, all of these experiments have found this and other forms of partial response sometimes associated with the incorrect response as well. Moreover, these responses are more frequently observed in the flankers-incompatible condition than in the flankers-compatible condition (Coles et al., 1985; C. W. Eriksen et al., 1985; Gratton et al., 1988; Smid et al., 1990; furthermore, in the Smid et al. experiment, an intermediate frequency was found in the flankers-neutral condition). Coles et al. (1985) found that the interval between EMG activity onset and the overt response in the correct arm was longer on incompatible than on compatible trials even on those trials in which no incorrect EMG activation was observed. This finding suggests that response competition can also occur at a more central level.

In some experiments the lateralized readiness potential (LRP) has also been recorded over the midline of the scalp (Gratton et al., 1988; Smid et al., 1990). The potential appears to become lateralized when a choice is made about the responding hand (Kutas & Donchin, 1980). Thus, its latency can be considered as reflecting response activation at a central level. Gratton et al. (1988) found signs of differential lateralization in the flankers-incompatible and flankers-compatible conditions. Smid et al. (1990) found a longer average latency of LRP in the flankers-incompatible condition than in the flankers-compatible condition, and the flankers-neutral condition showed an average latency intermediate between the other two conditions.

In short, it seems safe to say that when the array contains information associated with a different response from that associated with the imperative stimulus, one is more likely to find signs of activity associated with the incorrect response, either at central or at peripheral levels. Furthermore, this activity correlates negatively with performance. Thus, Coles et al. (1985) found the shortest mean latency in those trials for which no EMG activity was detected in the incorrect response channel, a little longer if some peripheral EMG activity was observed, and still longer if there was also observed some incipient incorrect activity in the response device (a dynamometer).

However, the results of some of these experiments suggest that response competition does not completely account for the flanker-compat-ibility effect; rather, part of the effect could be due to factors that influ-ence the information flow before response-related processes. For clarity, the processes will be separated into two groups: those processes occurring before a decision about the response is made, including stimulus evalua-tion, and those processes related to the preparation and execution of the response (the fact that these two groups of processes can overlap in time is not relevant here). For the rest of this chapter, the two groups of processes are designated *prerresponse processes* and *response processes*, re-spectively.

In a model based on multilevel competition, competition arises and produces interference at different time points during information flow. If the pre-response processes take longer in the flankers-incompatible con-dition, then the flanker compatibility effect could be due, at least in part, to that delay. Suppose that both the imperative stimulus and the flankers contribute to the gradual accumulation of evidence in the system re-sponsible for both the evaluation of stimuli and the decision process about the choices defined in the task. Compared with the neutral flankers, the compatible and incompatible flankers would decrease or increase, respec-tively, the time needed to reach a decision. Because the rate of evidence accumulation favoring the correct perceptual hypothesis is slower with in-compatible flankers and faster with compatible flankers, the decision is reached earlier on the average in the flankers-compatible condition than in the flankers-incompatible condition.

Some experimental results support this multistage competition view. The peak latency of the P300 component (of the event-related brain po-tential) has been proposed by some to be invoked after stimulus evalua-tion is completed (Kutas, McCarthy, & Donchin, 1977; McCarthy & Donchin, 1981; see also Coles et al., 1985, footnote on page 533), so it should reflect any lengthening of evaluation processes due to the flanker type. Smid et al. (1990) found a shorter mean latency for P300 in the flankers-compatible condition, an intermediate latency in the flankers-neutral condition, and a longer mean latency in the flankers-incompati-ble condition. Similarly, Coles et al. (1985) found longer latency P300s on incompatible than on compatible trials. There is also some indirect evi-dence that preresponse processes can contribute to the flanker compati-bility effect. C. W. Eriksen et al. (1985) found shorter RTs in the flankers-compatible condition even when the comparison was limited to trials of the flankers-incompatible condition without EMG activity in the channel of the incorrect response. They attributed this difference to activations too subtle to be detected by the EMG activity. However, it is possible that in some trials, the response is delayed because of some preresponse competition not reflected by a peripheral activation of the channel associated with the incorrect response. Coles et al. (1985) also found longer RTs even when the analysis was limited to trials without peripheral EMG activity on the incorrect side. They suggested that there must be some competition at a more central level.

Several authors have proposed that both groups of factors, those related to preresponse processes and those related to response processes, participate in the flanker compatibility effect. Thus, Coles et al. (1985) pointed out that response factors do not completely account for the flanker compatibility effect and that it is also partly due to a slowing of the evaluation process. Smid et al. (1990) pointed out that there must also be some competition in recognition processes. This idea supports the view that (a) pre-response processes take longer in the flankers-incompatible than in the flankers-compatible condition and (b) during preresponse processes the systems for the preparation and execution of the responses are preactivated by partial outputs.

However, the evidence reviewed above is basically correlational, and an attempt to separate the two groups of factors experimentally by Grice, Canham, and Schafer (1982) yielded negative results. They tried to separate preresponse and response competition effects by comparing the interference of flankers in a choice RT task with the interference in a go/no-go task, using compatible, neutral, and incompatible flankers. When compared with the neutral flankers condition, the compatible flankers produced a benefit of 19 ms and the incompatible flankers a cost of 20 ms in the choice RT task. However, in the go/no-go task, compatible flankers produced a statistically significant benefit of 9 ms and the incompatible flankers a nonsignificant cost of 5 ms. They concluded that an active competing response is needed for the effect to be noticeable, a conclusion incompatible with a multistage competition view. A problem with the design of that experiment was that the data analysis did not take into account the fact that flanker compatibility is not an all-or-nothing phenomenon (C. W. Eriksen & Eriksen, 1979; Yeh & Eriksen, 1984). It is possible that the letters selected for flankers in the no-go condition had a larger amount of featural overlap with one of the stimuli included in the choice RT task than with the other.

Even if a given stimulus has no overt response assignment, that stimulus may accumulate more evidence for one of the perceptual hypotheses due to a higher similarity to one of the target stimuli. Although this idea has been discussed by several investigators (C. W. Eriksen et al., 1985; Smid et al., 1990; Van der Heijden, Schreuder, Maris, & Neerincx, 1984), it is possible that these effects have been neglected in some experiments. This is reflected in the terms still used to designate the flankers for which a response is not defined. Sometimes the term *neutral* is used, implying that the flankers do activate the alternatives to the same degree. Sometimes the term *irrelevant* is used, implying that the flankers do not activate either of the alternatives. We prefer the term *nondefined* (ND). This is a purely descriptive term that indicates that the stimulus has no explicit associations within the context of the experimental task.

It is an empirical, rather than logical, issue as to whether a flanker not assigned an experimental response is really neutral or irrelevant. It is possible that "neutral" flankers in some experiments are in fact not neutral and that they produce costs and benefits that do not match expectations; de facto nonneutrality could be the explanation for some mismatches. It has been mentioned above that Grice et al. (1982) found balanced costs and benefits (20 and 19 ms) in a choice RT task, whereas Smid et al. (1990) found a cost more than twice the size of benefit in a comparable task (42 and 18 ms, respectively). Perhaps in the first case, the ND flankers were more neutral than in the second case. In a later article, Grice and Canham (1990) correctly pointed out that all stimuli included in the array (including those intended as neutral) can produce some degree of competition.

Experiments using psychophysiological measures also provide data supporting this view. For example, there have been recordings of incipient activities of the incorrect response system even in flankers-compatible conditions (Coles et al., 1985). Incipient activities of the incorrect response have also been found in the flankers-neutral condition, with a frequency intermediate between the observed frequencies in the flankers-compatible and flankers-incompatible conditions (Smid et al., 1990). Paradoxically, in the arrays used in the compatible and neutral conditions there are no stimuli experimentally associated with the incorrect response. C. W. Eriksen et al. (1985) pointed out that the presence of flankers-compatible trials with EMG activity in the incorrect side indicates that there must be some factors that are not stimulus driven in nature, calling on more central factors, such as response biases, to explain those trials. However, within this framework, those results can also be explained using only stimulus-driven factors, such as the confusability between the stimuli in the array and the perceptual hypothesis defined in the task.

The present experiment was designed to separate the contribution of two groups of factors, those related to stimulus evaluation and decision making and those related to preparation and execution of the response. These factors are separated by associating different response requirements with the flankers. The degree of neutrality of the letters used as flankers was also controlled. Neutrality was controlled by using exactly the same stimuli for the comparisons.

The difference (D1) in the average RT for letter arrays *SAS* and *TAT* in a task in which both flankers, *S* and *T*, were nondefined was compared with the same difference (D2) in another task where the letter *S* required a no-go response and *T* remained nondefined. The degree of confusability of flankers with the imperative stimulus, the letter *A*, was the same in both cases, the only difference being that in the second task the letter *S* was defined as one of the alternatives, and thus the processes related to stimulus evaluation and decision making should have suffered some extra delay.

Another comparison involved the difference (D3) between the RTs to arrays *UAU* and *SAS* in a task in which both *U* and *S* were flankers with an overt and incompatible response associated, and the same difference (D4) in another task in which the letter *U* was defined as before while the letter *S* required a no-go response. The degree of confusability with the letter *A* was controlled, leaving the only difference the requirement of an overt response for flanker *S*.

If the flanker compatibility effect was due only to the overt response requirements of the flankers, then it was predicted that D1 would equal D2 and that D3 would be less than D4. If it was due only to the interference produced during stimulus evaluation and decision making, then it was predicted that D1 would be less than D2 and that D3 would equal D4.

However, if the interference arose from both groups of processes, then it was predicted that D1 would be less than D2 and that D3 would be less than D4.

METHOD

Subjects

Eighteen undergraduate students of the University Autonoma of Madrid participated in the experiment. They were 18 to 22 years of age and had normal or corrected-to-normal vision.

Apparatus and Stimuli

The stimuli were presented and responses latencies were recorded with an IBM-PC compatible computer. The stimuli were capital letters *A, S, U,* and *T,* which appeared at the designated target position of the screen, previously marked with the fixation point, and at both sides of that position. The letters subtended 0.58° and 0.29° of visual angle in height and width. The fixation point was a cross that subtended 0.2° of visual angle in height and width. The eccentricity between the central letter and the flankers was 0.4° of visual angle, center to center.

Procedure

After fixating the cross in the center of the screen, the subject initiated a trial by pressing the space bar of the keyboard with the left hand. After 500 ms the cross was replaced for 50 ms by a letter (imperative stimulus) flanked by two different letters that were identical to each other (distractors). The subject identified the target letter by pressing designated keys on the keyboard with the dominant hand.

The subjects participated in four different tasks that were completed on three nonconsecutive days. Tasks 1 and 2 were completed in one session, and Tasks 3 and 4 were run in separate sessions. This was done in order to equate as much as possible the duration of the sessions (about 40 min). The order of the sessions was balanced following a Latin square design, and within the session for Tasks 1 and 2, the order of the tasks was counterbalanced across subjects. In all tasks, an imperative stimulus and two identical flankers were presented on each trial. Three consecutive keys of the keyboard were used for responses, where the index, middle, and ring fingers rested; those keys were designated R1, R2, and R3, respectively. The layouts of each task were as follows (see Table 1):

1. Task 1: The target stimuli were *A* (R1) and *S* (no go), and the flankers were the letters *A*, *S*, and *T*.
2. Task 2: The imperative stimuli were *A* (R1) and *U* (R2), and the flankers were the letters *A*, *U*, *T*, and *S*.
3. Task 3: The imperative stimuli were *A* (R1), *U* (R2), and *S* (no go), and the flankers were the letters *A*, *U*, *S*, and *T*.
4. Task 4: The imperative stimuli were *A* (R1), *U* (R2) and *S* (R3), and the flankers were the letters *A*, *U*, *S*, and *T*.

Each possible imperative stimulus was equiprobably combined with all the possible flankers of the appropriate task, yielding a total of 32 trials for each combination to be represented. Trials were grouped into four blocks

Table 1

Stimuli and Responses of Each Task, and Flankers Combined With Each Imperative Stimulus

| Task | Imperative stimulus | Required response | Flankers condition | | | |
| | | | | | Incompatible | |
			Compatible	Nondefined	No go	Go
1	A	R1	*A*	*T*	*S*	
	S	No go	*S*	*T*		*A*
2	A	R1	*A*	*T,S*		*U*
	U	R2	*U*	*T,S*		*A*
3	A	R1	*A*	*T*	*S*	*U*
	U	R2	*U*	*T*	*S*	*A*
	S	No go	*S*	*T*		*A,U*
4	A	R1	*A*	*T*		*U,S*
	U	R2	*U*	*T*		*A,S*
	S	R3	*S*	*T*		*A,U*

of eight trials of each target–flanker combination. Trials with an error were run again after the corresponding block in order to allow the calculation of the mean RTs over the same number of trials. After every two blocks, a short rest was allowed. The first block of each task was considered practice and the data from this block were excluded from data analysis. All statistical analyses were based only on those trials for which the imperative stimulus was the letter *A*, and thus the correct response was pressing R1 with the index finger. There were two reasons for doing this. First, this type of trial was the only one that was common to all tasks and conditions. Second, several factors that could possibly confound the interpretation of the results were equated (they share the same imperative stimulus, letter *A*, and the same response, key R1).

RESULTS

The average RT in each condition for each task was calculated for each subject (see Table 2). The differences observed could not be attributed to speed–accuracy trade-offs, because the error rates, always small, were larger for the conditions with larger mean RT.

Separate analyses of variance were calculated for each task, with flanker type as the independent variable: compatible (C), nondefined (ND), in-

Table 2

Mean Reaction Times (ms) for the Conditions of Each Task

		Flankers condition				
					Incompatible	
		Nondefined			Go	
Task	Compatible (*A*)	*T*	*S*	No go (*S*)	*S*	*U*
1	363	371		378		
2	407	425	418			462
3	418	430		439		461
4	481	495			502	510

compatible (I), or no go (NG). Tukey tests were used for post hoc paired comparisons.

In Task 1 the analysis of variance showed a significant effect of flanker type, $F(2, 34) = 6.88$, $p < .01$; the only paired comparison that reached statistical significance was between compatible and incompatible flankers ($p < .01$). This is not exactly the same pattern of results found by Grice et al. (1982) in their go/no-go task. Recall that they found a significant benefit but no cost. Although the difference between the flankers-incompatible and flankers-compatible conditions in Task 1 is similar to their difference (14 ms in their experiment and 15 in this one), the ND flanker condition was associated with a more intermediate value, probably because these neutral flankers are more "neutral" than the flankers in their comparable condition. In fact, here the paired comparisons show that the only statistically significant effect was the sum of the cost plus benefit.

In Task 2, the means for both letters used as nondefined flankers were averaged for each subject. There was a significant effect of flanker type, $F(2, 34) = 70.75$, $p < .001$, and all post hoc paired comparisons were significant ($p < .05$ for C-ND and $p < .01$ for C-I and ND-I). The same pattern of results was obtained for the nondefined condition when only data for the flanker T were included. This means that the flanker effect cannot be due to the fact that the letter S, a nondefined flanker in this task, was used in other tasks as a no-go or even as a go alternative.

In Task 3 there was again a significant effect of flanker type, $F(3, 51) = 27.17$, $p < .001$. The post hoc paired differences between the incompatible and the other three conditions and between compatible and no-go conditions were significant ($p < .01$).

In Task 4, data for the two letters used as incompatible flankers were averaged. Again, a significant effect of flanker type was found, $F(2, 34) = 10.18$, $p < .001$. The differences between the compatible and the other two conditions were significant ($p < .05$ for nondefined and $p < .01$ for incompatible). The same pattern appears for the incompatible condition when only data from the flanker U are included (see the argument for Task 2).

The major purpose of this experiment was to separate out the specific effects of the flankers when an overt response was associated with them while at the same time controlling the degree of neutrality of the nondefined flankers (see Table 3). To achieve this, the differences between the mean RTs in each of the conditions shown in Table 3 were computed for each subject separately. Table 3 shows the average of these differences in mean RTs between conditions in which the degree of neutrality of the ND flankers was controlled.

The values shown in Table 3 represent estimates of the difference in the degree of interference that is produced by two types of flankers that were not identical to the imperative stimulus. Thus, D1 reflects the difference in the degree of interference produced by two flankers, neither of which was associated with any defined overt response. If a defined (although no-go) response was associated with a flanker and this flanker produced some specific interference, due to preresponse factors, then the difference D2 should be larger than the difference D1. The t test revealed a statistically significant difference between the mean values of D1 and D2, $t(17) = 2.95$, $p < .01$, with D2 being larger than D1. Notice that D2 was calculated with data from Task 3 because Tasks 2 and 3 share the same number of go alternatives, a point that was thought a priori to be essential for an appropriate comparison; however, when D2 was computed on the basis of Task 1 data, the result was about the same (9 ms in Task 3 versus 7 ms in Task 1).

Following the same logic, if an overt response was associated with the flankers and the flankers produced some specific interference, due to response competition, then D4 must be larger than D3. A t test showed that the difference between the mean values of D4 and D3 was also statistically significant, $t(17) = 2.61$, $p < .02$, with D4 being larger than in D3.

Table 3

Differences Between Conditions Involved in Critical Comparisons
(Parentheses Contain the Letters Used as Distractors)

Name	Conditions involved	Task	Value
D1	Nondefined (S)—Nondefined (T)	2	−7
D2	No go (S)—Nondefined (T)	3	9
D3	Incompatible (U)—Incompatible (S)	4	8
D4	Incompatible (U)—No go (S)	3	22

DISCUSSION

The main conclusion from the results described above is that flankers that are associated with a choice produce interference even if they do not have a motor response associated with them (i.e., the flankers are associated with a no-go response). However, this interference is increased significantly if flankers also have a motor response associated with them (i.e., the flankers are associated with a go response). This finding supports the importance of the motor aspect of the response for the effect, but it also makes clear that response competition cannot account for the whole phenomenon. The results of the present experiment converge with the view that preresponse factors (stimulus evaluation and decision making) and response factors contribute separately to the flanker compatibility effect, a position already pointed out by other authors (Coles et al., 1985; Gratton et al., 1988; Smid et al., 1990).

However, there are some alternative explanations of these results that must be mentioned. First, it is possible that the use of the same letter (S) for different mappings could contaminate the degree of competition observed for each particular task, especially in the session in which Tasks 1 and 2 were completed. However, when data were selected for subjects who performed Tasks 1 and 2 in their first session, there was no evidence of any effect of order (i.e., no differences between subjects who performed Task 1 first vs. those who performed Task 2). Similarly, when subjects who first performed Task 4 (where the letter S was a go alternative) and then performed Tasks 1 and 2 were compared with subjects who first performed Tasks 1 and 2, and then performed Task 4, there was again no evidence of any order effect.

Another possible explanation for the results is that a no-go response still represents a choice (to respond or not to respond), and it may still compete with go choice responses. In this experiment, the separation between response competition (in the sense of overt response) and other factors was intended. The no-go option was still an alternative, but the possible interference produced by the no-go action was separated from factors related to overt response requirements. Furthermore, the fact that the no-go flankers interfered more than the nondefined flankers but less than the go flankers is consistent with the view that these no-go flankers interfered with processes related to stimulus evaluation and decision mak-

515

ing (as much as nondefined flankers). In addition, the no-go flankers interfered less than incompatible flankers, which interfered with the processes of response preparation and execution.

The term *response competition* is equivocal, because it encourages a too simplistic and peripheral view of the competition generated by conflicting stimuli. In choice RT tasks a response is always required. Thus, all of the interference will finally show up as a delay of the overt response, even though this delay may be due to the interference produced and accumulated at different points of the information flow. The fact that flankers that were associated with a nonmotor experimental choice significantly increased interference suggests that there is multilevel or multistage competition. During the evaluation and decision-making stage, the conflicting information delays the decision. During this stage, partial outputs are sent to the operations of preparation and execution of the response. When the response is to be executed, these partial outputs cause the channels of the correct and the incorrect responses to have different levels of activation. But to demonstrate this, it is important to acknowledge that the neutrality or irrelevance of flankers is an empirical issue, not a logical one. It must be statistically controlled for in data analysis.

The present results also point to the presence of decision and response competition in classic choice RT tasks, as has been previously pointed out (Grice & Canham, 1990; Van der Heijden et al., 1984). In Task 2 there are two motor alternatives, in Task 3 there are two motor and one no-go alternative, and in Task 4 there are three motor alternatives. If the absolute magnitude of average RTs in these tasks is compared, Task 3 appears more similar to Task 2 than to Task 4, even though three choices are involved. However, it shares with Task 2 the number of motor choices. Perhaps part of the effect of the number of response alternatives in classic choice RT tasks (Luce, 1986) is due to the response competition produced by the presence of "active" motor alternatives. Another result that points to the same conclusion is that the cost of incompatibility is smaller in Task 4 than in Task 2. There may be less preactivation in the correct channel, and the preactivation that is not accumulated in the correct channel is distributed between two incorrect channels instead of one, so that there is less interference even though it takes longer to make a response decision; this post hoc interpretation must, of course, be tested.

The concept of response competition has also been applied to account for some other phenomena, such as the fast-same effect (C. W. Eriksen, O'Hara, & Eriksen, 1982) and some paradoxical results found when subjects must discriminate between multidimensional stimuli (C. W. Eriksen, 1993). Thus, the competition concept appears to be very useful in the analysis of a variety of tasks. However, the results from these tasks could also be interpreted in terms of decision competition. In particular, the results of the present experiment suggest that both kinds of factors probably contribute to the delay of the responses in choice RT tasks, and thus both could also be present in other situations.

REFERENCES

Coles, M. G. H., Gratton, G., Bashore, T. R., Eriksen, C. W., & Donchin, E. (1985). A psychophysiological investigation of the continuous flow model of human information processing. *Journal of Experimental Psychology: Human Perception and Performance, 11,* 529–553.

Eriksen, B. A., & Eriksen, C. W. (1974). Effects of noise letters upon the identification of target letter in a non-search task. *Perception and Psychophysics, 16,* 143–149.

Eriksen, C. W. (1993, September). *The flankers task and response competition paradigm: A useful tool for investigating a variety of cognitive problems.* Paper presented at the sixth conference of the European Society for Cognitive Psychology, Elsinore, Denmark.

Eriksen, C. W., Coles, M. G. H., Morris, L. R., & O'Hara, W. P. (1985). An electromyographic examination of response competition. *Bulletin of the Psychonomic Society, 23,* 165–168.

Eriksen, C. W., & Eriksen, B. A. (1979). Target redundancy in visual search: Do repetitions of the target within the display impair processing? *Perception and Psychophysics, 26,* 195–205.

Eriksen, C. W., O'Hara, W. P., & Eriksen, B. A. (1982). Response competition effects in same–different judgments. *Perception and Psychophysics, 32,* 261–270.

Eriksen, C. W., & Schultz, D. W. (1979). Information processing in visual search: A continuous flow conception and experimental results. *Perception and Psychophysics, 25,* 249–263.

Gratton, G., Coles, M. G. H., Sirevaag, E. J., Eriksen, C. W., & Donchin, E. (1988). Pre- and post-stimulus activation of response channels: A psychophysiological analysis. *Journal of Experimental Psychology: Human Perception and Performance, 14,* 331–344.

Grice, G. R., & Canham, L. (1990). Redundancy phenomena are affected by response requirements. *Perception and Psychophysics, 48,* 209–213.

Grice, G. R., Canham, L., & Schafer, C. (1982). Role of the response in associative interference. *Bulletin of the Psychonomic Society, 20,* 214–216.

Kutas, M., & Donchin, E. (1980). Preparation to respond as manifested by movement-related brain potential. *Brain Research, 202,* 95–115.

Kutas, M., McCarthy, G., & Donchin, E. (1977). Augmenting mental chronometry: The P300 as a measure of stimulus evaluation time. *Science, 197,* 792–795.

Luce, R. D. (1986). *Response times.* New York: Oxford University Press.

McCarthy, G., & Donchin, E. (1981). A metric for thought: A comparison of P300 latency and reaction time. *Science, 211,* 77–80.

Smid, H. G. O. M., Mulder, G., & Mulder, L. J. M. (1990). Selective response activation can begin before stimulus recognition is complete: A psychophysiological and error analysis of continuous flow. *Acta Psychologica, 74,* 169–201.

Van der Heijden, A. H. C., Schreuder, R., Maris, L., & Neerincx, M. (1984). Some evidence for correlated separate activation in a simple letter-detection task. *Perception and Psychophysics, 36,* 577–585.

Yeh, Y. Y., & Eriksen, C. W. (1984). Name codes and features in the discrimination of letter forms. *Perception and Psychophysics, 36,* 225–233.

Author Index

Numbers in italics refer to listings in the reference sections.

Subject Index

About the Editors

Arthur F. Kramer is Professor of Psychology and Industrial Engineering at the University of Illinois at Urbana–Champaign. He received his PhD from the University of Illinois in 1984. He is currently Associate Editor of *Perception and Psychophysics* and serves on the editorial board of several other major journals. Kramer has published numerous articles and chapters on basic and applied issues in the domains of selective and divided attention, skill acquisition and automaticity, cognition and aging, and human factors.

Michael G. H. Coles is Professor of Psychology at the University of Illinois at Urbana–Champaign. He received his PhD in psychology from the University of Exeter, England, in 1971. He has been President of the Society for Psychophysiological Research and Editor-in-Chief of *Psychophysiology*. He has written numerous articles on cognitive psychophysiology and has coedited of several books, including *Handbook of Cognitive Psychophysiology* (1991) and *Electrophysiology of Mind* (1995).

Gordon D. Logan is Professor of Psychology at the University of Illinois at Urbana–Champaign. He received his PhD from McGill University in 1975. He serves on the editorial board of several major journals. He has published theoretical and empirical articles on attention and automaticity that address basic and applied issues, including the nature of the attention deficit in attention deficit/hyperactivity disorder.